W9-BVX-969

MEANING *and* ACTION
A Critical History of Pragmatism

H. S. THAYER

The City College of the City University of New York

Theodore Lownik Library
Illinois Benedictine College
Lisle, Illinois 60532

MEANING
and
ACTION

A Critical History of Pragmatism

HACKETT PUBLISHING COMPANY
Indianapolis · Cambridge

144.309
T 37/m
1981

First edition published in 1968 by
The Bobbs-Merrill Company, Inc.

Copyright © 1981 by H. Standish Thayer

All rights reserved

Printed in the United States of America

Second edition, first printing

Paperback cover design by Laszlo J. Balogh
For further information, please address
Hackett Publishing Company, Box 55573
Indianapolis, Indiana 46205

Library of Congress Cataloging in Publication Data

Thayer, Horace Standish, 1923–
    Meaning and action.

    Bibliography: p.
    Includes index.
    1.   Pragmatism.   I.   Title.
B832.T48   1980   144'.3'09   80–20890
ISBN 0–915144–73–5
ISBN 0–915144–74–3 (pbk.)

To my father and mother
V. T. *and* FLORENCE THAYER

πατρὸς σωφροσύνη μέγιστον
τέκνοις παράγγελμα

Democritus

Contents

Preface to the Second Edition   xiii

Preface to the First Edition   xv

Introduction   3

1. Subject and Intentions   3
2. About Pragmatism   4
3. Pragmatism and 'Pragmatism': An Appeal to Etymology   7

Part One

THE PHILOSOPHIC BACKGROUND: 1650–1850
The Emerging Problem of Modern Philosophy

INTRODUCTION   10

CHAPTER ONE   *The Shaping of the Problem*

4. The Cartesian Revolution   13
5. The Seventeenth-Century Dilemma of a Philosophy of Science   19
6. Locke's Problem   22
7. The Enlightenment   24

CHAPTER TWO   *Responses to the Problem*

8. Transcendental and Critical Philosophy   27
9. Eighteenth-Century Enlightenment   29
10. Kant   35
11. Kant's Critical Synthesis of Science and Values   36
12. Transcendental Idealism: The Regulative Function of Ideas   40
13. Experience, Interpretations, Symbols: Romanticism   43

CHAPTER THREE   *The Modern Idealisms*

14. Romanticism   46
15. The Romantic Protest and New Idealism   50
16. Fichte and Unstiffening Kantian Theory   53

17. The Nineteenth Century   58
18. Conclusion   64

Part Two

AMERICAN PRAGMATISM

INTRODUCTION   68

CHAPTER ONE   *Charles Sanders Peirce*

19. The Main Lines of Development   79
20. Peirce's Theory of Inquiry   83
21. Peirce and Pragmatism   86
22. Peirce's Empiricism: The Theory of Knowledge and
    Probability   101
23. Meaning and Truth   120
24. Critical Issues in Peirce's Definition of Truth   125

CHAPTER TWO   *William James*

25. James and Pragmatism   133
26. James's Bifocal Vision   135
27. Empiricism and Pragmatism   136
28. Mind as Teleological   141
29. James and Language: A Word About the Use of Words   145
30. A Note on Bypassing Meaning   146
31. The Moral Basis of Truth   147
32. Trouble over Truth   148
33. James's Wager: The Right to Believe and Right Beliefs   153
34. James's Legacy: The Inheritance of Uncompleted Theory   159

CHAPTER THREE   *John Dewey*

35. Dewey and Pragmatism   165
36. Instrumentalism   169
37. Continuity: Growth and the Theory of Education   174
38. Sensation and Response: Reflex Arc and Circuit   183
39. The Pattern of Inquiry   190
40. Truth   192
41. Inquiry as Evaluation   199
42. Some Problems in Pragmatism   201

CHAPTER FOUR   *C.I. Lewis*

43. Conceptualistic Pragmatism   205
44. Logic and Order   207
45. Mind and World Order   212
46. Valuation as Empirical Judgment   221
47. Meaning and Mind   225

CHAPTER FIVE   *George Herbert Mead*

48. The Social Point of View   232
49. A Problem of Materials   234
50. Social Behaviorism   236
51. Genetic Psychology and Social Theory   237
52. Social Gesture and Language   241
53. The Significant Symbol   244
54. Language as Gesture   246
55. A Schematization of Gestures and Significant Symbols   248
56. An Actor Prepares   250
57. The Discovery of the Self   252
58. Play, Games, Roles, and the Generalized Other   255
59. The Self as "I" and "Me"   258
60. Social Objects: The Pragma of Things   261
61. Social Pragmatism: Conclusion   264

Part Three

PRAGMATISM IN EUROPE: ALLIANCES AND MISALLIANCES

INTRODUCTION   270

CHAPTER ONE   *England: F.C.S. Schiller*

62. Schiller and Pragmatism   273
63. The Critical Orientation   276
64. Humanism, Butt-End-Foremost   283
65. The Private Thinker and the Postulated World   285
66. Psychology and Logic   292
67. The Critique of Logic   294
68. Making Truth and Reality   297
69. Final Reflections   301

CHAPTER TWO *England: F. P. Ramsey and Ludwig Wittgenstein*

    70. Some Missing Links   304
    71. F. P. Ramsey   309
    72. Ludwig Wittgenstein   311

CHAPTER THREE *France*

    73. Pragmatism and *Pragmatisme*   314
    74. Georges Sorel   320
    75. Sorel and Mussolini   321

CHAPTER FOUR *Italy*

    76. Papini, Prezzolini, Vailati, and Calderoni   324
    77. Summary   345

Part Four

SOME PRAGMATIC CONSEQUENCES OF PRAGMATISM

INTRODUCTION   348

CHAPTER ONE *The Methodological Spirit*

    78. Fallibilism   349
    79. Pragmatic Contextualism   352
    80. The Given, A Priori, and Logic   358

CHAPTER TWO *The Instrumentalist Interpretation of the Structure of Knowledge*

    81. Logic and the Structure of Science   364
    82. Some Historical Factors   366
    83. Interpretations of the Theoretical Structure of Science   369
    84. The Instrumentalist Point of View   371
    85. Leading Principles   376
    86. Some Critical Issues and Conclusion   380

CHAPTER THREE *The Construction of Good*

    87. Constructing the Good   383

88. The Problem of Ethical Judgment   384
89. Ought and Is   385
90. A Modified Naturalistic Ethic   389
91. Situation, Value, and Valuation   390
92. The Biological Basis of Desire: The Origins of Valuation   393
93. The Rational Element in Desire: Valuation-Propositions   395
94. Intelligent Desiring: Ends-Means   398
95. Propositions and the Criterion of Valuation   400
96. Desire and the Desirable   402
97. Some Last Observations and Questions   409
98. Conclusion   412

Part Five

SPECULATIONS

INTRODUCTION   416

CHAPTER ONE   *The Meaning of Pragmatism*

99. The Moral Basis of Pragmatism   419
100. Knowledge as Valuation   423
101. What Pragmatism Is   424

CHAPTER TWO   *Pragmatism and American Life*

102. The Import of Some Ideas   432
103. The Dilemma of American Philosophy   433
104. Pragmatism: Wit and Philosophy in America   435
105. Our Two-Part Culture: Angelic Impulses and
     Predatory Lusts   437
106. Conclusion   446

CHAPTER THREE   *Conclusion*

107. The Revolutionary Point of View   448
108. The New Organon: A Theory of Meaning and Action   454

Appendixes

1. Dewey: Continuity—Hegel and Darwin   460
   A. Continuity   460

   B. The Background of Continuity: Hegel   461
   C. G. S. Morris and T. H. Green   466
   D. Nineteenth-Century Philosophizing and the Concepts of
       Continuity, Possibility, and Identity   486

2. The Background of Peirce's Pragmatism   488
   A. The First Statement of Pragmatism   488
   B. Peirce and Chauncey Wright   490

3. Peirce on Pragmatism   493
   A. Peirce's Statement   493
   B. Peirce's Description of Pragmatism   494

4. Peirce on Truth and Some References to Boole   496

5. Berkeley and Some Anticipations of Pragmatism   499

6. Analytic and Synthetic   508
   A. Analyticity   508
   B. The Import of the Distinction   509
   C. The Analytic, Pragmatism, Dewey on Propositions, Lewis
       on Meaning   511
   D. Pragmatism and Formalism   519

7. Pragmatism and the Category of Possibility   522
   A. The Importance of the Notion of Physical Possibility   522
   B. The Problem of Clarifying the Concept of Possibility   524

8. William James's Theory of Truth   527
   A. Philosophic Background of the Controversy   530
   B. The Meaning of Truth   537
   C. Conclusion   550
   D. Three Notes   551

Epilogue   557
   I   1968: A Reflection on the Philosophic Scene   557
   II   Some Recent Literature   566

Bibliographical References   571

Index   591

Preface to the Second Edition

This edition of *Meaning and Action* is a revised and slightly enlarged version of the original which first appeared in 1968. Many of the revisions are of a minor kind—correcting inaccuracies and mistakes in the bibliographical references and in printer's errors which had escaped detection in earlier proofreading. These repairs have affected some forty pages. A few of the revisions are more substantial. Several paragraphs have been rewritten and supplemented with new material (as in the account of Dewey's theory of inquiry, §§ 39–40). This major additions are two: an Epilogue surveys some matters pertaining to the present edition and the literature on pragmatism that has appeared in the last twelve years; a reconsideration and further discussion of James's theory of truth (of §§ 31–32) was developed, which thus issued in a new appendix chapter (Appendix Eight).

As I am all too keenly aware, a volume with eight appendixes is in danger of imbalance; the proliferation of appendixes threatens to encroach upon the main text, to dominate or distract, or even to become another book. However, I have been advised by friendly readers that the earlier appendixes were worth retaining and that the new material was worth adding. To have forced this treatment of the theory of truth into the chapter on James would have created another kind of imbalance. Thus, it was not a complete neglect of esthetic scruples or sense of proportion that directed these pages to their presently destined place.

I should add a word of explanation about certain changes that have *not* been made in this printing; for the reader might otherwise well wonder why I have been remiss. The changes in question are principally two.

First, in the years since the publication of *Meaning and Action,* there has appeared an extensive literature on pragmatism and on the work of the major philosophers of pragmatism. There are also new critical editions of the works of James and of Dewey and one (forthcoming) of Peirce's writings. They will be the standard texts and sources of reference for all future scholarship on these philosophers. In the absence of such critically established texts, my practice was, where possible, to cite first printings and revised printings when it mattered (and for Peirce, the *Collected Papers* or the periodical and manuscript source for material not included in those volumes). To revise now and redirect all these references in pages, footnotes, and the bibliography to the new editions would be prohibitively expensive in printer's costs. And to make proper acknowledgment and give due consideration to the recent literature on pragmatism would have required overhauling and rewriting of much of the book. To make some amends, however, and to assist the reader who might wish to know about it, the Epilogue provides a selected survey of the recent literature.

Second, there is the story of the Introduction to Part Two, about Peirce and his attic study, accessible only by ladder, to which he was able to escape his creditors and engage in undistracted philosophizing. The story, I am assured by Peirce scholars, is false. A visit to Peirce's house, Arisbe*, in Milford, Pennsylvania, confirms as much. The story is apocryphal. But it is one of those vivid fictions that ought to be true. So I have let it remain with this admission and warning to those whose predilection is for things literal.

Palisades, New York   H. S. T.
January, 1980

---

* Now being made into a Peirce memorial museum as a property of the National Park Service.

Preface to the First Edition

I

Prospective readers of this book should not be misled by the main title. In these pages I do not attempt a theory of *meaning* nor issue a call to *action*. Hence the subtitle is added to convey more of my purpose.

The words "Meaning and Action," however, are descriptive of philosophically basic and centrally developing aspects of pragmatism. A more accurate but recondite heading for this book might have been: "Meaning, Truth, Value, Inquiry, Knowledge, and Action"—thus a straining to encompass the dominant concerns in the pragmatism of Peirce, James, Dewey, Mead, and Lewis. Against this inelegance, my title abbreviates matters that can be spelled out more fully in the rest of the book. This title, incidentally, is not my own invention. It is borrowed from C. I. Lewis' way of summing up the content of Dewey's Logic. It capsulizes, if three words can, the intellectual substance of pragmatism and thus two major topics, along with the others just mentioned, of this book.

The subtitle, *A Critical History of Pragmatism*, expresses an attempt to combine two objectives, one of which is mainly critical while the other is historical. The history of philosophic ideas, by virtue of being both historical and philosophic, invites this combining of approaches. The result is that instead of a purely narrative interest in the historical development of the philosophy in question, or instead of exclusive concern with critical evaluations of what is suggestive, or true, or can be learned from it—we get something of both. Instead of history *or* philosophy, the net product aimed for is history *and* philosophy.

It should be evident that by the word 'critical' here, and its use in the title, I do not intend *criticism* in a narrow sense of severe faultfinding with intent to condemn. I use 'critical' in reference to the endeavor to formulate the cardinal ideas of pragmatism, to take note of certain difficulties and problems that are logically relevant (or that have been thought so) in examining these ideas and in assessing their merits and consequences.

Of the two objectives just observed, that of the critical discussion of pragmatism occupies the larger part of this book. Matters of history are not dealt with at great length and are often presented as augmenting and clarifying the critical task. Still, because of an inevitable and deliberate converging of both approaches to our subject, and because of certain historical topics deemed worthy of attention and interest, history has not been ignored.

As to the history of pragmatism, I think it is fair to say that there exists no thorough and comprehensive treatment. Special studies of special philosophical aspects and historical moments are plentiful. Some of these are excellent, and among them should be mentioned the sketch by Dewey,[1] Philip Wiener's investigation of the genesis and early background,[2] and Herbert Schneider's book,[3] in the last part of which the development of pragmatism within the history of American philosophy is exhibited. However, a detailed and complete presentation of the pragmatist movement in all of its phases and periods and changes from the 1870's to the present day remains to be undertaken. Though the general picture of the history of American pragmatism is by now familiar, the rich and significant details concerning the climate of the times and the development of ideas, the influences and interests operative in American and European philosophy and contemporary intellectual life that affected the various representatives of pragmatism have never been portrayed. Nor could this be accomplished until the chronology of events has been established, biographies and the critical editions of the works of these philosophers have become available.[4] The full history, therefore, remains for the future, and consequently mine is not and makes no claim to be a definitive history of pragmatism. Furthermore, instead of restating the findings of the historical literature that now exists, I have sometimes preferred to direct the interested reader to that literature itself and to proceed to less familiar matters.

One gain of this strategy is the space it affords for closer attention to the more philosophical side of pragmatism. In addition, I am also thereby able to assume a wider scope than other studies of pragmatism have hitherto. This has resulted in the inclusion of two important figures in American pragmatism, usually neglected in expositions of the subject, George Herbert Mead and C. I. Lewis, as well as the survey of European pragmatism in Part Three and the philosophizing about pragmatism in Parts Four and Five.

I should add that there is one figure who may appear strangely neglected in this history: Oliver Wendell Holmes, Jr., a member of the club in which pragmatism was born (see § 19 below). However, it is debatable that Holmes's "prediction theory of the law" was ever seriously influenced by the pragmatism of Peirce or James; and judging by some of the comments he made in correspondence later in life, it is debatable whether Holmes understood Peirce's pragmatism (of §§ 20–21) or the full philosophic import of the doctrine (as surveyed in §§ 100–101 below) at all.[5]

[1] "The Development of American Pragmatism." Hereafter, throughout this book, references to literature will be given briefly by author or title or both. The complete reference will be found in the Bibliography.
[2] *Evolution and the Founders of Pragmatism.*
[3] *A History of American Philosophy.* See also Blau, Parts 5, 7, and 9.
[4] A critical edition of Dewey's works is in the process of publication by the Southern Illinois University Press. Nothing of this kind has been done for the other pragmatists, however. The invaluable eight-volume *Collected Papers* of Peirce is by no means a critical or definitive edition.
[5] The most persuasive argument for regarding Holmes's prediction theory as part of the genesis of pragmatism is set forth by Max H. Fisch in his paper on Holmes in 1942. See however, his later reflection, "Was There a Metaphysical Club?" p. 23. For more general affinities between Holmes's thought and pragmatism, see Wiener, ch. 8. Philosophically, Holmes later found more interest in and sympathy for Dewey's outlook (as developed in *Experience and Nature*, 1925) than in that of James or Peirce. On this, see his letters to Wu, in Wiener, pp. 186–187.

One last remark about history needs to be made. The intellectual origins of pragmatism are a part of the history of modern philosophy. In what sense this is meant, in what sense it is so, will be dealt with in the pages immediately to follow. As a consequence, however, of this point of view shortly to be enlarged upon, I have thought it relevant and important to include a discussion of certain recurring problems and themes in the history of modern philosophy which have profoundly affected the emergence of the ideas taken up in later chapters. This is the purpose of Part One, something of an experiment, as the Introduction to that Part explains.

The history *and* philosophy of pragmatism, to preserve the distinction made above, are best understood, I contend, when viewed broadly and fundamentally as an attempt to develop in one inclusive framework a reliable interpretation of scientific knowledge and ethical judgment. This object, as later pages will show, was conceived in somewhat different ways and, hence, as encouraging differences in perspective and conceptual efforts in its behalf; and this is natural among thinkers, especially those inclined to eschew orthodoxies, however allied they might be in their overall aim and outlook. There is diversity in this common history and among its proponents, as is noted in the Introduction that follows (and also in the Introduction to Part Two). Reservations, qualifications, and finer analytical delineations are in order, too, concerning what, in the development of pragmatism, is comprised by the floating terms "scientific knowledge" and "ethical judgment." This also is part of the story of later chapters. But generally, and for the moment, it may be said that the pragmatists advanced a theory of inquiry and judgment for which the logical characteristics and operations that issue in knowledge and in moral valuation and decision are integrally related. As I see it, and have tried to trace it in this book, basic to this theory is the conception of knowing and valuing as forms of action in environments consisting of centers of resistance, conflict, and conditions of manipulation—environments requiring continual examination and readaptation of the conceptual and linguistic techniques of human action. This, basically and in brief, was a theory of meaning and action.

Pragmatism so viewed, as an attempt to develop an integration of knowledge and values, reflects certain historical antecedents, for example, Kant, Spinoza, Descartes, or St. Thomas, although in the past the problem had usually been felt to be one of drawing a boundary between Reason and Faith. Clearly the current interest in the problem of "two cultures," one scientific and the other humanistic, is about as old as the hills, or at least as old as the history of philosophy since the Middle Ages. Pragmatism, while benefitting from a more adequate conception of science and human behavior than anything to be found in the past, a result mainly of the development of modern science itself, still carries the inheritance of that classic endeavor of philosophy: the assimilation of science, technology, and moral ideals in one coherent interpretive outlook, rather than the alternative rejection of reason, or of the world, or of human faith.

To some, it may seem surprising, in these days when pragmatism is unfashionable, to put it in the company of the great philosophies of the past. But in mat-

xviii *Preface*

ters of intelligence and art, fashions are less to be trusted than feared. Few virtues and many vices may be fashionable. One difference between good and bad philosophic thought is that the former has a way of enduring in pertinence and effect despite fashions, while the latter, if not fashionable, is nothing. Pragmatism, I think, has achieved permanence and has a future, though as a suggestive body of ideas rather than as a school of thought. While I have not tried to win converts or any one case in this book, a reader has a right to know an author's stand. And this, along with such preliminary declarations of intent as have been made, it befits a preface to explain. Even at the risk then of incurring the disappointment of some readers, I will affirm here what I have tried more accurately to illustrate in chapters to come: it is my belief that pragmatism has been the most ambitious and important effort in our time to accomplish the objective described above as a critical synthesizing of knowledge and the methods of science with the moral heritage and aspirations that shape human conduct. In one form or another this has long been conceived as the chief function of philosophy; and when it is exercised in ways at once most responsible and most liberal, this vocation of philosophy is the fulfillment of a rational life.

II

In engaging in the view of the historical background and the central theme of Part One I have been influenced no doubt by the writings of Dewey and of Mead. But I wish in particular to acknowledge an intellectual debt to John Herman Randall, Jr., from whom, over the past dozen years of friendship and professional association, I have profited immensely. I hasten to add, however, that it is doubtful that many of the things said, and my way of saying them, would have Mr. Randall's approval. He is certainly not to be held responsible for anything in this Part or in this book.

There are other acknowledgments I am happy to record. My thanks to Paul Edwards for encouraging the expansion into a book of my chapter in D. J. O'Connor's *Critical History of Western Philosophy*. Some scattered remnants of that piece are embedded in the present work. To Mr. John K. Jordan, I am grateful for several important criticisms of a draft of the book; and to Mrs. Jordan, for invaluable help in typing part of the manuscript, and to John Jordan, Jr., for his aid in this connection. I appreciate the criticisms of the publisher's readers; the moving of material originally intended for Appendixes into § 22 and § 70, as presently constituted, was only one beneficial result of their reading. Professor Rose Cascio of the Casa Italiana, Columbia University, kindly helped me with translations of some passages from Papini. Mr. Joseph Papaleo of Sarah Lawrence College, an authority on contemporary American and European literature, gave me characteristically expert advice on portions of the manuscript, particularly § 76.

Unless otherwise indicated by translations cited in the Bibliography, I am responsible for the renditions here from Greek, Latin, German, French, and Italian.

I have kept my translations as literal as possible, and in the case of disputable or difficult passages, I have supplied the original text in footnote.

It is a pleasure to acknowledge the intellectual benefits derived from discussion with Ernest Nagel and the late James R. Newman. I am similarly indebted to my colleagues and students at City College, where I arrived from Columbia University in 1961 to find much philosophic stimulation from the friendship and encouragement of able and dedicated colleagues, nonetheless friendly for the diversity of philosophic points of view among us.

To the City College General Faculty Committee on Research, 1964–1965, I am grateful for a grant-in-aid to meet the cost of typing the manuscript.

To my wife Beth I am indebted most of all. Whatever is good here was made better with her help.

H. S. T.

Palisades, New York
August 1, 1966

Acknowledgments

In all essentials, the writing of this book was completed in 1964, but unavoidable circumstances delayed the preparation for publication. As a result, in some instances I have been able to make note of additions to the literature bearing upon my subject that have appeared since 1964. At the same time I have been uncomfortably conscious of coming under Seneca's indictment: *Ut ominium rerum sic litterarrum queque intemperantia laboramus,* "As in everything, so in literature, we suffer from an excess."

For permission to quote copyrighted material, I make grateful acknowledgment to the following:

Atlantic-Little, Brown and Co., for Ralph Barton Perry, *The Thought and Character of William James* (Boston, 1936). Copyright 1935 by Henry James.

Beacon Press, for John Dewey, *Reconstruction in Philosophy.* Copyright © 1948 (enlarged edition) by Beacon Press.

The Belknap Press of Harvard University Press (Cambridge, Mass.), for Charles Hartshorne, Paul Weiss, Arthur W. Burks (eds.), *The Collected Papers of Charles Sanders Peirce.* Copyright by the President and Fellows of Harvard College: Vol. I, 1931, 1959. Vol. II, 1932, 1960. Vol. III, 1933, 1961. Vol. IV, 1933, 1961. Vol. V, 1934, 1962. Vol. VI, 1935, 1963. Vol. VII, 1958. Vol. VIII, 1958.

Roberta L. Dewey, for John Dewey, "The Naturalization of Intelligence" and "The Construction of Good" in *The Quest for Certainty;* "The Development of American Pragmatism" in *Philosophy and Civilization; Democracy and Education;* and *Logic: The Theory of Inquiry.*

Dover Publications, Inc., for C. I. Lewis, *Mind and the World Order* (New York, 1956).

Harvard University Press (Cambridge, Mass.), for much of the material in my essay "William James's Theory of Truth," most of which is drawn from my Introduction to *The Meaning of Truth: A Sequel to Pragmatism,* by William James, edited by Frederick Burkhardt, Fredson Bowers and Ignas K. Skrupskelis. Copyright 1975 by the President and Fellows of Harvard College.

Holt, Rinehart and Winston, Inc., for John Dewey, *Logic: The Theory of Inquiry* (New York, 1938). Copyright 1938 by Holt, Rinehart and Winston, Inc. Copyright © 1966 by Roberta L. Dewey.

David McKay Company, Inc., for William James, *Collected Essays and Reviews* (New York and London, 1920).

The Macmillan Company, for John Dewey, *Democracy and Education.* Copyright 1916 by The Macmillan Company, renewed 1944 by John Dewey.

The Open Court Publishing Company, for C. I. Lewis, *An Analysis of Knowledge and Valuation* (La Salle, Illinois, 1946).

Paul R. Reynolds, Inc., for *The Letters of William James.*

The University of Chicago Press, for John Dewey, *Theory of Valuation.* Copyright 1939 by the University of Chicago. All rights reserved. Published July 1939. And for George Herbert Mead, *Mind, Self and Society.* Copyright 1934 by the University of Chicago. All rights reserved. Published December 1934.

The Viking Press, Inc., and the author, for Morton White, *Social Thought in America* (New York, 1949).

H. S. T.

1967

MEANING *and* ACTION
A Critical History of Pragmatism

Introduction

§ 1. Subject and Intentions

The central purpose of this book is to trace and examine the historical development and major intellectual contributions of American pragmatism.

Pragmatism was the most influential philosophy in America during the first quarter of the twentieth century. Viewed against other idealisms and intellectual currents that have characterized American life, it stands out as a movement that not only had an impact upon academic philosophy but profoundly influenced students of the law, education, political and social theory, religion, and the arts. It is as a movement—both critical of much of traditional philosophy and concerned to establish certain positive aims—that pragmatism is best understood. It is in this respect, rather than by any exclusive doctrine, that pragmatism became the major contribution of America to the world of philosophy.

It so happens that the individual thinkers who contributed most to the formation and articulation of pragmatism, Peirce, James, and Dewey, were the three greatest philosophers America has yet produced.[1] Did these philosophers achieve greatness because of their pragmatism, or pragmatism achieve significance because of their greatness? The rhetorical query comes by a straining of artificial distinctions; but it is opportune, for it prompts the following word of caution.

While Peirce, James, and Dewey gave decisive form and direction to the development of pragmatism, each of them, in addition, worked out in a rather distinct way a comprehensive philosophy of his own. Peirce constructed a version of objective idealism, an architectonic cosmogony inspired in important respects by Kant and Schelling.[2] James, who had taken to pragmatism after his work in psychology, went on to set forth his philosophy of radical empiricism and pluralism.[3] Dewey's pragmatism was an evolving if central strand in a thoroughly elaborated philosophic naturalism.[4] It is not my intention in this book to describe these three different positions in general or in detail—nor those of C. I. Lewis and George Herbert Mead, whose work is important to us and will be dealt with in later chapters—but to concern myself primarily with a select group of ideas, with their origins, the problems and insights that inspired them, what consequences

[1] I exclude Santayana in this judgment, but only because he often insisted (though perhaps did protest too much) that he was not an American by birth or temperament.
[2] For the growth and structure of Peirce's philosophy, see Buchler, Gallie, Goudge, Thomson, Murphey.
[3] For the development of James's thought, the two-volume work of Perry is the best.
[4] A comprehensive presentation of the growth and content of Dewey's philosophy remains to be written. See, however, Geiger, Hook.

3

they have had, and what conclusions we may draw from them. Two principles of selection have been used: what is important historically in accounting for the evolution and emergence of pragmatism, and what appears of intrinsic analytic interest and value to philosophic thought of the present day. Happily these dual procedures have not conflicted, and in some cases have combined in working to the same end.

The plan of the present work is as follows.

Part One is a descriptive account of the growth of a select group of conspicuous and importunate problems in the course of philosophic thought since the dawn of modern science. Broadly, the problems have to do with discovering some integral relation between the nature of scientific knowledge and the status of moral values.

The focus is on how these problems evolved and, thereafter, on their reception and the intellectual consequences distinctive of the history of pragmatism. The reader will discover that often in subsequent parts of the book, references to this historical background will help to illuminate the discussion under way. Such is the intended function of Part One.

Part Two deals with the chief contributions of the leading pragmatists—Peirce, James, Dewey, Lewis, and Mead—to the working out of the pragmatic interpretation of intelligence and action, of meaning and truth, of knowledge and valuation. Accompanying this is an analysis of certain problems and critical philosophic issues affecting the development of pragmatic philosophizing.

Part Three is a critical survey of pragmatism (or alleged versions of the same) and the pragmatisms more or less directly influenced by the American doctrines in England, France, and Italy.

Part Four is an attempt to state clearly some of the significant consequences of pragmatism and to analyze and assess them in some detail. This is a more philosophic endeavor concerned with three fundamental contributions of pragmatism: a philosophic contextualism, an instrumental interpretation of scientific knowledge, and a theory of value and valuation. These, in general, are the distinctive responses to the problems described in Part One and approaches discussed in Part Two.

Part Five is a concluding reflection on the meaning of pragmatism and a discussion of the larger effects and place of pragmatism in American culture.

A group of Appendixes provide substantiation, historical information, detailed observations, and some inevitable philosophizing on issues occurring in the text but best set aside for this special treatment.

§ 2. *About Pragmatism*

The origins of pragmatism are clear in broad outline and obscure in fine detail. The more conspicuous features lend themselves to easy and by now familiar reportage. Thus, in a word: pragmatism is a method of philosophizing often identified as a theory of meaning first stated by Charles Peirce in the 1870's[5]; revived primarily as a theory of truth in 1898 by William James; and further developed, expanded, and disseminated by John Dewey and F. C. S. Schiller.

The broad outline is helpful: as a guide it directs us to where to start looking if we want to find out about pragmatism. That there should be considerable uncertainty about some of the more specific formative conditions is another matter —perplexing in proportion to one's curiosity about them. Much of the obscurity over these details of history derives from one or both of two influential factors.

First, it is odd that the founders of pragmatism were neither very clear nor consistent in the accounts they gave concerning the historical origins of their doctrine.[6] As a partial explanation of this fact, they were not entirely in agreement on what pragmatism stood for, as a philosophic position or as a nucleus of ideas. Peirce and James took a catholic view of the historical ancestry: Socrates, Aristotle, even Spinoza, Locke, Berkeley, Hume, Kant, and Mill, and an assorted variety of scientists, were all credited with a philosophic conduct becoming to pragmatism, and above the call of special doctrines. Dewey saw Francis Bacon as "the prophet of a pragmatic conception of knowledge."[7] With a genial hospitality for the past, James referred to pragmatism as "a new name for some old ways of thinking,"[8] thus sounding a note of gracious deference and generosity. Schiller however, might have dashed all hopes of there ever being a history of pragmatism: When Professor Lovejoy, in a welcome effort to clarify what pragmatism purported to be, distinguished thirteen versions of the doctrine (in 1908), Schiller replied in a spirit of pluralism well nigh intoxicating that theoretically there were as many pragmatisms as there were pragmatists.[9] A strange appeal to an extensional definition of the word 'pragmatism'—as if one were to discover what it meant by counting heads.

The second factor beclouding the historical development of pragmatism is a firmly established inaccurate generalization: pragmatism is a doctrine holding that the meaning and truth of thought is determined (somehow) by criteria of practical *usefulness*. Some of the colloquial and uncritical language of the lead-

[5] In a later reflection upon pragmatism, Peirce wrote to James (1904): "pragmatism solves no real problem. It only shows that supposed problems are not real problems." *CP* 8.25.
Hereafter references to Peirce's writings, following the practice of the editors of *The Collected Papers of Charles Sanders Peirce*, will take this form: *CP* refers to this standard edition; the numbers indicate volume and paragraph. Thus, 8.25 is volume 8, paragraph 25.
[6] In 1900, when Peirce was preparing his articles for Baldwin's *Dictionary of Philosophy and Psychology* (1902), he wrote James: "Who originated the term *pragmatism*, I or you? Where did it first appear in print? What do you understand by it?" James replied: "You invented 'pragmatism' for which I gave you full credit in a lecture entitled 'Philosophical conceptions and practical results' of which I sent you 2 (unacknowledged) copies a couple of years ago." *CP* 8.253.
[7] *Reconstruction in Philosophy*, p. 38.
[8] The subtitle of *Pragmatism*—a new name that was ugly, to boot, as James acknowledged on p. vii of that book.
[9] A. O. Lovejoy, "The Thirteen Pragmatisms"; F. C. S. Schiller, "William James and the Making of Pragmatism," p. 92.

ing pragmatists would seem to support this generalization, for the founders of pragmatism grossly overestimated the extent to which the language they used was free from divers interpretations. Still, this way of characterizing pragmatism is a mistake. What is especially at fault lies not so much in a misrepresentation of the essential, as in an essential irrelevance.

The conception of human thought and knowledge as subject to a norm of practical results, where a standard of usefulness is also a test of significance in matters rational, is by far a more ancient and venerated doctrine than anything yet to be found in pragmatism. It is as old as the human race: it has its origins in primitive magic and religion; it received ample and various dramatic and philosophic expressions in classical Greek literature; in the dissillusioned and despairing Hellenistic world it became a dominant thesis in the several competing philosophies (or "schools") of salvation; through Augustinian Christianity it continued to be reiterated by any number of Franciscan schoolmen throughout the Middle Ages; it found its way into the pronouncements of the early champions of modern science and the "new knowledge."[10] The contexts are different, but the upshot of the deliverance was much the same: knowledge is power, the value of thought lies in its practical uses. The dictum holds for any interpretation of practical uses, sacred or profane, whether it be taken as recommending the subservience of all things to a moral aim or to material gain. For the theologically minded, what is more practical than the salvation of one's soul? How else is intelligence to be justified but as an auxiliary and derivative instrument to this end?

To identify pragmatism as a philosophic rationalization of the spirit of modern industry and big business because of an alleged emphasis upon the practical and useful in thinking, or as a philosophy of power, is to forget history. Ironically, the theologians who have most severely indicted pragmatism as a crass version of modern utilitarianism show a surprisingly short memory in this respect. For, on its own premises, there is no more recalcitrant form of utilitarianism to be found than in Western theology.

While pragmatists do make considerable *use* of the notions of useful and practical results in judging certain kinds of human activities, these are not exclusive preoccupations. To be committed to a preference for useful over useless pursuits in the business of living is not a pertinent criterion of pragmatism nor its manifestation. It is less than informative to single out pragmatism as a philosophy of the useful. On the whole the characterization is useless.

Where this misidentification of the main ideas of pragmatism becomes taxingly irrelevant is in its all too inclusive historical sweep. In the American colonies, many a puritan divine and itinerant preacher, teaching men what is "useful for

[10] Thus, when Francis Bacon announced that "knowledge is power," he was echoing an unbroken tradition of thought stretching back to his namesake, Roger Bacon, in the thirteenth century, and deeper into the early Middle Ages. Both Bacons were prophets of a new experimental science, but both cast their prophetic vision in the language of Franciscan schoolmen.

them to know," qualify, accordingly, as pragmatists. And an incipient pragmatism will be easily discovered threading the whole fabric of American social experience: the founding of schools in the Colonies, the opening of the West and the demand for teachers and preachers, the origins of public education—each for the imparting of useful knowledge. In the theoretically complicated and loose practical connection between the Protestant ethic and capitalistic free enterprise in America, "useful knowledge" meant the means to both piety and prosperity. As Franklin put it, there is "nothing so likely to make a man's fortune as virtue." And one might attribute a nascent "pragmatism" to Franklin's rejection of a metaphysical treatise he had written and published: "I began to suspect that this Doctrine tho' it might be true, was not very useful." James pointed to a similar emphasis upon practical results as a test of religious belief in Jonathan Edwards.[11]

No doubt various forms of idealism and practices in American social experience have a bearing upon the growth of its most distinctive philosophic movement. It was not an accident that James found in pragmatism a solution to an otherwise unbearable and deadening separation of vital moral and metaphysical problems and daily conduct and experience (§ 25). Nor was it by mere chance that Dewey should have devoted so much of his attention to the educational implications of the "pragmatic conception of knowledge."[12] These are reflective concerns, responsive to deeply felt demands and conflicting interests lodged in the American tradition. The shaping of pragmatism does have a history, and part of that history is undoubtedly a result of the intellectual climate and social environment in which it was born. These are matters of detail worth historical investigation, being potentially informative where irrelevant generalizations are not. But it is over such details, as we have been observing, that obscurity sets in.

§ *3.   Pragmatism and 'Pragmatism':
      An Appeal to Etymology*

'Pragmatism,' said William James, was a new name for some old ways of thinking. But there is reason for doubting the propriety of James's comment. In some of its senses—senses to be distinguished shortly—*pragmatism* might with equal justice have been said to be an old name for a new way of thinking.

Etymology supports this cavil. *Pragma* is the Greek for *things, facts, deeds, affairs,* or, as James himself notes, "meaning action, from which our words 'practice' and 'practical' come."[13] The word is often so used by Plato and Aristotle; but it has had another sort of career and made other appearances as well. The eighteenth-century Holy Roman Emperor Charles VI early in his reign took steps

---

[11] See Anderson and Fisch, pp. 125, 144, for these and other examples of "latent pragmatism"; also James, *The Varieties of Religious Experience,* p. 21.
[12] In his most important book on education, significantly called *Democracy and Education,* Dewey defined philosophy as "the general theory of education." See below, § 37.
[13] *Pragmatism,* p. 42.

to insure that his dominions could be inherited by female heirs in lieu of males. Hence the Pragmatic Sanction, in this case a partly new name for a Hapsburg way of thinking, proving very convenient to Charles's daughter, Maria Theresa. In Germany, one expression for a practical-minded person is *ein pragmatischer Kopf*. And in Germany, too, in the nineteenth century, there was developed what was called the "pragmatic method in history" concerned with the practical consequences and uses of the study of history.[14] But the notion goes far back to the Greek historian Polybius (204–122 B.C.), who liked to regard his *Histories* as instructive and useful to the living and, accordingly, often referred to his work as *pragmatike historia*.[15]

Now this casual undefinitive etymology of 'pragmatism' is germane to what pragmatism, as philosophic doctrine, is not. Some of James's more popular and carefree pronouncements on the "practical" character of pragmatism do court associations with the root Greek word. But Peirce, who was credited with originally formulating pragmatism, was not thinking in Greek; he was evidently guided by ideas to be found in Kant (see § 27).

An apt symbol of the propensity in the history of pragmatism to multiply into pragmatisms is found in its baptismal beginnings. While Peirce in America had in the 1870's begun to use 'pragmatism' to designate some of his theories, the French thinker, Maurice Blondel, was seeking a label for his own philosophy. In 1888 he first thought of calling his views "pragmatism," but later chose the title of *Action*.[16] It was James who made the name *pragmatism* famous in a lecture of 1898. Yet what James meant by 'pragmatism' was not quite what Peirce had meant by it, nor Blondel. Thus the history of pragmatism commences with a variety of proposed *practical* and *active* philosophic doctrines, severally claiming the reference, and by dint of much stretching and gerrymandering, all entitled to be called "pragmatism." The parceling out of 'pragmatism' to cover a medley of pragmatisms helped to confuse pragmatists and non-pragmatists alike, as we shall see.

It is Peirce's early formulation of pragmatism; James's widening of the scope of the initial pronouncements and intentions of Peirce; Dewey's attempt to provide a carefully reformulated statement of the leading ideas, his instrumentalism; C. I. Lewis' revival and reinterpretation of certain leading ideas in Peirce and James in the light of modern logic, which became his conceptualistic pragmatism; Mead's bio-social theory of human action, mind, and language—these constitute the substance of the history of pragmatism. Etymology not proving very helpful, we are better advised to turn to this history itself.

---

[14] See Ernst Bernheim, *Lehrbuch der historischen Methode*, for a discussion of the method; or Conrad Herrmann, *Geschichte der Philosophie in pragmatischer Behandlung* (1867). In the Introduction to the *Philosophy of History*, Hegel describes "pragmatic history" as the second kind of reflective history.

[15] E.g., *Histories* I. 2. For a survey of instances of pragmatism in the philosophical past, see Waiblel.

[16] Cf. André Lalande, pp. 122–123*n*. For Blondel, see § 73 below.

THE PHILOSOPHIC

BACKGROUND:

1650–1850

The Emerging Problem of Modern Philosophy

Part One

Pragmatism, as a distinct and consciously conceived way of philosophizing, made its appearance at the end of the nineteenth century. As we have already noticed and shall see more clearly later, any number of anticipations and semblances of what was to be called "the pragmatic way of thinking" can be found in the episodic course of philosophy—indeed, not only in the professional record of philosophy but in the evolution and history of human thought as a biological and social development. It was this common and recurring way of dealing with problems, in otherwise diversified contexts of philosophy and science and in the habitual intellectual practices of the race, that led James to call pragmatism "a new name for some old ways of thinking."

As a doctrine and the core of a contemporary philosophic movement, however, pragmatism has definite if tangled roots in the preceding two centuries of philosophy. It is the purpose of the present chapters to take a closer look— albeit a broad one—at the movements of thought from which pragmatism emerged. Since this background happens to be the setting for all (with very little exception) of the various currents of contemporary philosophy, it presents rather obvious difficulties of characterization and assessment. In richness of thought and temper, in the contrasts of social experience and historical directions, these preceding centuries—say, 1650–1850—are surely no less complex nor more susceptible to easy descriptive formulations than our own. It also would appear, judging by the problems and dominant interests of current philosophy, that we are in many respects closer to that earlier period of Enlightenment and the Romantic revolt bred within it than to its later post-Hegelian apotheosis. Curiously, the kinds of problems and the respective efforts made to deal with them in Rousseau and Kant, Fichte and Hegel, Locke, Berkeley, and Hume seem much more vital to us than the philosophies of evolution and idealism that dominated the later nineteenth century. The history of philosophy is not a chronicle and ought never to be so treated; what comes last is not always best or most alive. We are able to take a faintly detached view of the philosophies of Comte, Mill and Spencer, Green and Bradley. That is because intellectually, though not chronologically, they are more remote from us than the Enlightenment. For this reason, too, by proximity of temperament, accurate appraisals of the earlier period come less easily to us and must be taken as tentative at best.

To see why these difficulties of historical perspective are difficulties is to see beyond them into the background. For the present our concern is to focus upon certain selective tendencies of the past leading to the development of pragmatism. The view thus taken will help to distinguish and explain the somewhat uneven and divergent developments in America and in Europe.

To avoid possible misunderstanding of what this first Part attempts, I should explain here that these pages are devoted to illustrating and reflecting upon the evolution of one main problem (or string of problems) in modern philosophy. The history of pragmatism is very much a critical response to this problem. Our view of it in the three chapters to follow is historical, but, due to limitation of space, for the most part this is an impressionistic sketch. A sketch can be broad, even inclusive in its way, yet it is also extremely selective. I have availed myself of convenient symbols, appropriate to sketching, such as *science* to mean physics and astronomy (excluding, here, other disciplines, e.g., biology, chemistry, medicine); or a division between *heart* and *head* to characterize the eighteenth-century Enlightenment. My discussion of the problem—the emerging problem of *knowledge*, the conflict between a scientific conception of reality and a slowly changing pattern of moral values—owes much to the critical historical writings of Dewey.[1] But I am not here arguing a historical thesis or for a point of view. I am sketching with a point of view, in the hope of illuminating and gauging more effectively other matters to come later.

[1] Also to Mead's writings on the cultural impact of science and the transformations that have resulted from the incorporation of science into Western society. This historical view has received careful and impressive elaboration in Randall's *The Career of Modern Philosophy*.

CHAPTER ONE

The Shaping of the Problem

§ 4. The Cartesian Revolution

Descartes is often said to be the father of modern philosophy. This is not without good reason, even though the ascriptions of *paternity* and *modernity* are not without some suspicion.

Descartes is fond of giving the impression that he created his philosophy *ex nihilo*. But no philosophy and no era of thought occur this way; they happen, but not by single acts of invention or through discovery by single minds. Descartes was a genius living in a century of genius, an age which very much shaped, if it did not create, the modern mind. The occasion of being a father requires the existence of a mother; for all of his disavowels and the rather contemptuous manner with which Descartes concealed his dependence on the intellectual past, this was his partner, *das Ewig-Weibliche*. Platonism; Augustinian Christianity; the brilliant tradition in mathematical philosophy of a long line of Franciscan thinkers; the rediscovery of Alexandrian mathematics in the early Renaissance; the emerging mathematical science of nature in Copernicus, Kepler, and Galileo; and his own Jesuit schooling were but some of the accomplishments and lore of the *femme fatale* with whom Descartes brought forth modern philosophy.

Then, too, modernity is not an absolute appropriation. Every philosophical generation beginning with the Greeks has thought of itself as modern. And, when troubling to look backward, each generation has lauded as modern some semblance of its own current preoccupations. In the nineteenth century the pre-Socratic philosophers were modern because they had discovered atomism and evolution. These days they are accredited modern for their use of religious and psychiatric symbols, their existentialism, and their foreseeing a universal holocaust. In the early fourteenth century, some three hundred years before Descartes, a modern and old way of philosophizing had been distinguished; perhaps with some justice modern philosophy is to be regarded as having its inception with the falling out

13

of that garrulous company of philosophers, the *via moderna* and *via antiqua*. Rarely will any philosopher renounce all claims to being modern—and the greatest of philosophers are always modern. All of this proves, then, that there is nothing quite so old-fashioned as the claim to being modern.

In spite of these solemn doubts over the details, Descartes is rightly regarded as the founder of modern philosophy. If the modern mind has a paternal ancestor, it is surely he; if there are intellectual revolutions, the "Cartesian revolution" of the seventeenth century was surely the matrix of all subsequent revolutions in thought, for it brought into relief with great clarity the moral, scientific, and religious facets of major problems that have invited divers responses and attitudes in all later philosophizing. Cartesianism is deceptively deep-rooted, a thick tree of many tendrils and branches, an evolution of revolutions.

There are three pronounced and characteristically "modern" features of Descartes's philosophy: its intellectual independence from the authority of the Church and from the moral aims of medieval philosophy; its receptivity to modern science; its spirit of revolt from the past. These are related tendencies in Descartes and with them others combine to make up the specific philosophic outlook which —he liked to assure his readers—took nothing for granted. It was to be almost all new and absolutely true.

Of these characteristic features, the most important historically and that of most significance in later philosophy was the influence of science on Descartes. While the seventeenth century did not divorce natural science and philosophy, as we do now, Descartes stands out conspicuously from many physicists, mathematicians, astronomers, and philosophers of nature of his own age and earlier as the first thinker to try to assimilate the existence of modern science into the available patterns of European thought. And he is the first great thinker to undertake a major philosophic explanation and defense of the new science. He thus makes abundantly clear the fact that scientific knowledge posed a number of problems—problems of adjustment and synthesis with other human interests, the inherited values and ideals of European culture vigorously and variously challenged, reasserted, revived, in the peculiarly imaginative and skeptical temper of the Renaissance and in the religious conflicts of the sixteenth century. He also makes it clear that scientific knowledge itself, as an existing fact, was a "problem" urgently demanding clarification and understanding—one subsequently pursued and described as "the problem of knowledge." For *how* the natural world could be known by man was not at all evident from what the new science of the seventeenth century said that natural world was like. This last problem, so recurrent and disturbing in the development of modern philosophy (and the history of pragmatism) deserves closer study, and we will return to it shortly.

Outwardly, and in its most general form, there was nothing very new about this philosophic response to science in the seventeenth century. For the history of philosophy exhibits several momentous periods in which the growth of science

precipitated an intellectual challenge to long-established patterns for interpreting human experience and threatened the accustomed modes of evaluating it.

Generally, such being the tried and worldly wit of the race, the procedure has
been to preserve most at least cost. Common-sense utilities and scientific refinements of them, even innovations in knowledge, are too valuable to be denied
outright or utterly condemned by a reigning idealism because of incompatibili-
ties or conceptual friction. The winning strategy has always been conceptual tolerance—a relaxing of ideological rigidity and literalness; the once hard dogmas
of untutored and lay minds undergo transformation into ideal symbols of an
educated elite. Ancient and cherished truths retain their function in allegorical symbols, and the new literal truths are received among them easily or alloted an un-
obtrusive domain of their own. The strategy is that of a marriage of new knowledge and traditional values and conceptions of knowledge. Where marriage is not
wholly possible, a conciliatory spirit is: the spirit of rendering unto science that
which is science's and unto faith that which is faith's. For Plato and Aristotle in
the ancient world, for St. Thomas in the thirteenth century, and again for men
in the fourteenth and fifteenth centuries, this practice of the strategy, this quest
for an adequate interpretation of science, for a conceptual framework in which
human ideals and natural knowledge were integrally related was the first and
highest office of philosophy. With Descartes this quest was renewed, and continued subsequently by Locke, Leibniz, and Kant. Systematic effort thus at length
arrives at the conserving of the old and the new—in the peace that possesseth
understanding.

Despite the great differences among them, in every one of these impressive
philosophic endeavors to understand and incorporate the institution of science
into a larger conceptual framework there is rooted one inevitable and instructive
historical fact. To engage in scientific inquiry and contribute to scientific knowledge, and to reflect upon what science is or how scientific knowledge is acquired
are not identical activities. No more so than are the act of knowing an object and
the act of philosophizing about how that object is known; these are separate kinds
of activities and distinguishable accordingly. Thus science evolves as one of several social activities displaying an unrivaled efficacy in the coherence and reliability of its explanations and predictions of events. Still, the hypotheses, the
critical procedures, and the over-all development of the conceptual structure of
science have exhibited an essentially autonomous character—once it freed itself
from its ancient origins in myth, magic, and religion. Guided by its own developing structure and rational techniques, scientific activity consists in the mus-
tering of intellectual energies to an ever increasing understanding of the world.
It little matters how or from what quarters the necessary energy is derived or
from what sources ideas may be inspired. Usually it is from a gestation of complexities within science that great scientific advancements are hatched. Sometimes
the initial revelatory idea comes from without. What does matter is the process of
disseminating the original insight—determining its consequences and utility

within the established structure, reckoning its use and adaptability to the end in view.

Faced with this phenomenon of the growth of science, men have been given to wonder. For many reasons, some of them noted above, an explanation of the meaning of science was wanted. Now logically (as John Dewey was to urge) explanations of the nature of scientific knowledge might best have been constructed under the auspices and according to the intellectual practices of science. This would be an empirical science of the natural sciences and of scientific judgment. But the history of thought is often a truant to logical schooling. And the historical fact has been that when men shift from philosophizing in science to philosophizing about it, they have invariably had to make use of earlier philosophical ideas and to draw upon one of several traditional conceptions of knowledge, knowing, and the known—traditions first established by Plato, Democritus, Aristotle, and subsequently elaborated with such prunings and graftings and under so many accidental and fortuitous changes of climate as to be generically recognizable only to specialists. Nonetheless, the accumulated stock of interpretive materials was there, and it provided philosophers with the only instruments—by way of concepts, distinctions, and explanatory principles—available for comprehending science in the interest of a synthesis of knowledge and values, readjusting the new to the old heritages. This is why, incidentally, brilliant and inventive scientists have often come forth with rather prosaic and sometimes naive philosophic accounts of science. It is why, less incidentally, Descartes's explanation of philosophy of science and knowledge derived its leading ideas, as well as its strength and plausibility, from an established and tried tradition: ancient and medieval Platonism with some well chosen supplementations from St. Thomas.

One distinction of Descartes's attempt to articulate the meaning of science, which set it off from earlier enterprises and introduced another "modern" note, was characteristic of seventeenth-century science: it was a mathematical science of nature. Indeed, Descartes played an important role in helping to give the new science this direction; he was a mathematical physicist convinced that the essence of scientific knowledge lay in its use of mathematical reasoning.

The other great philosophic systems of the seventeenth century, those of Spinoza, Hobbes, and Leibniz, were likewise profoundly affected by the advent of physics and astronomy. In each of these great rational visions two immensely valuable and fascinating components of the science Galileo had helped to found and which later was called "experimental philosophy" were appreciatively seized upon. The new science was revealing to man, far more successfully than any earlier philosophies of nature, the kind of universe in which he lived. It revealed as well how the world was to be known. Science had not only clarified the object of knowledge—what there *is*—it had also developed a method of knowing. On the whole, for Galileo and Descartes, the world was viewed as a system of bodies subject to universal mathematical laws. Nature was a single mechanical structure of particles in motion; and the way to know and formulate truths about this structure was, as Descartes put it, through the cultivation of "universal mathematics." Behind the pronouncements on the nature of scientific knowledge made by these two eminent knowers, one can see the coming together of two ancient traditions: the scientific world was a Democritean system of atomic particles obeying rigid laws; the scientific method of knowing was that of the mathematical principles, intuitions and forms of Platonism. To each and all of the subsequent advocates, interpreters, and philosophers of this conception of nature and knowledge, science was not only the way to explain the world, it was also immensely useful as a power for controlling nature. It was intellectually beautiful and true, yes, but also a vital good. This knowledge was power—and (with the partial exception of Spinoza) since *power* meant mechanical force, scientific knowledge was seen as an active force transforming man's social and physical existence.

Descartes died in 1650. But the Cartesian revolution remained very much alive. The triumph of Reason was established in France and Holland. Scientific preeminence was transferred from Italy to the north. Descartes was the symbol of reason and science until the end of the century, when the crown was captured by Newton.

Briefly, what did Descartes do? What did the Cartesian revolution mean to the age that first inherited it and felt it most?

First, the Cartesian philosophy had brought about a unified scientific cosmology. The labors of many physicists and mathematicians and Descartes's own mathematical and optical studies now bore fruit in a daring theory of the origin and development of the universe: the mechanical system. "Give me extension and motion," said Descartes, "and I will construct the universe." And he sought to do just that. Archimedes had stated the simple condition required to move the world. But Descartes was stating how the world was made and how explained— as a geometer explains a figure by showing what set of assumptions and operations are necessary to derive it. So Descartes set forth the simple and ultimate notions from which all phenomena could be explained. The universe is a vast machine of simple and compound parts; and knowledge advances by analysis, by resolution of complexes into their simplest parts. Logical method and mechanical subject matters follow the same pattern for Descartes. The vision of the universe as a huge mechanism, in spite of certain difficulties it presented, gave science a comprehensive theoretical framework within which new ideas and critical advances could be incorporated or suggested.

The mechanical system appeared to leave the medieval conception of a hierarchy of Being—a tidy and ordered universe with ranks of perfections and purposes—only a pious and imaginative memory. All movement in this system was interpreted as mechanical contacts among bodies; all qualities were analyzed as due to the size, shape, and motion of material particles.

Second, the Cartesian philosophy heralded a new intellectual method—the method of mathematical intuition, logical certainties, clear and distinct conceptions. Reason was supposed to illuminate and relate logically the meanings of ideas. What was conceived clearly and distinctly was known with certainty to be true.

Third, the scientific world system and the method of Reason each seemed to provide a place for God and religion. Indeed, the philosophy of Descartes absolutely required God for the following reasons and in the following ways.

In Descartes's mechanical system of nature there is no empty space. The universe is a material *plenum*. There are degrees of matter; there are huge chunks and stretches of a "virtually perfect fluid" of minute particles, later called "the ether." But there are no empty holes in the universe. There were many and oft debated reasons for this concept of a material continuum: how could action, changes, and forces operate where there was nothing; how could connections among things occur through intervals (of space or time) of nothing? The logic of Parmenides, the Aristotelian objections to a vacuum, some empirical evidence, and Descartes's geometrical methods—all worked against the notion of empty spaces. The material world is thus construed as complete: matter is not created or destroyed; the distribution of material complexes is always changing, but the quantity is constant. So motion, for Descartes, remains constant. Something is always going on everywhere in the system, but motion is simply the continuous distribution and redistribution of material parts of the material whole. Change is a fact, but nothing radically novel, no undetermined evolution can take place; and the world is thus scientifically closed—capable even, ideally, of a complete explanation.

According to these dictates of his physics, it seemed to follow readily for Descartes that there must be a cause of matter and motion. That cause, like all physical causation, must have been an efficient cause, a force. A machine does not begin to run of itself. God thus imparted motion to the universal matter; he introduced power into extension—the cosmos began as a great vortex of matter and from that rotation and its inner sweepings and centrifugal gatherings of parts the world took shape.

Similar arguments hold for the mind and its contents. It is a self-evident certainty that the thinking being exists; that "I exist" is necessarily true, argues Descartes. But my idea of myself or my existence cannot come from nothing. Thus its efficient and logical cause is the idea of God and (as a result of further argumentation) the idea of God in us was caused by God himself.

Finally, the method of clear and distinct conceptions required validation. How can we be certain that what we do conceive as mathematically or logically clear and distinct is true? God, Descartes answers, being known to exist and to be good, guarantees that "whatever is clearly and distinctly conceived is true."[1]

Thus the existence of God seems to answer a scientific and philosophic need. While forms, purposes, functions are banished from the world of nature, the will of God is not. God made the machine and set it going and, as Scotists and Cal-

[1] See the conclusions of the Fourth and Fifth Meditations.

vinists had also said, nature and nature's laws express the will of God. Physics has this pious office in revealing the work and ways and intentions of the Creator. Of enormous interest and influence in the century after Descartes's death was the idea that a scientific theology had been created and was assured of being saved by Reason. Hence, expounding his own version of scientific theology to explain the fundamental assumptions of physics, Newton concluded in his famous General Scholium that to discourse of God "from the appearances of things does certainly belong to natural philosophy."[2] But Malebranche best symbolizes this last achievement of Cartesian Reason. He found a perfect harmony and beauty of reason between Descartes's view of a universal mathematics of nature and Augustinian Christianity.

We have been looking at the general position and background of Descartes's philosophic reception and organization of the new science. We must now inspect more closely a peculiar problem—or complex of problems—inherent in the attempts to interpret the nature of scientific knowledge. The problem results from certain assumptions—not of science, but authorized by many practicing scientists; and the assumptions are such that the problem they generate admits of no solution at all, or of such elaborate circumlocutions and dialectical maneuvers as result in a waste of ingenuity, in an excess of *ad hoc* artificiality. With respect to this problem the systems of Descartes, Hobbes, and Locke come to grief. Spinoza and Berkeley carefully avoid the dangerous assumptions. Hume accepts the assumptions provisionally and is accordingly led to skeptical doubts about what can be known at all.

The pattern of inquiry exhibits four stages—or five, if we count as a first stage the antecedent troubled and indeterminate situation within and from which inquiry is generated. But strictly speaking, the initial conditions prompting inquiry are not a first stage *of* inquiry; they are rather the conditions that form the situation *for* inquiry.

It is important to recognize that the larger issue of a philosophic defense of scientific knowledge is dependent upon this problem and its outcome. For while philosophers could and did argue for the place of scientific reason in a system of values and set forth to work out syntheses of scientific knowledge and cultural, intellectual, and religious ideas, it was a source of acute embarrassment and critical weakness that Reason could make little or no sense of how scientific knowing was possible. This was the "critical problem" of modern philosophy.

§ 5. *The Seventeenth-Century Dilemma of a Philosophy of Science*

The problem in question received what has become a classic statement of it by Galileo. Freely translated it is:

[2] *Principia*, Book III.

I say that whenever I conceive of any material or corporeal substance, I immediately feel myself necessitated to conceive of it as bounded and as having this or that shape, as large or small in relation to other things, and in this or that place, in this or that time, as being at motion or at rest, as touching or not touching some other body, as being one, few, or many; nor can I separate it from these conditions by any stretch of the imagination. But that it must be white or red, bitter or sweet, noisy or silent, of pleasant or unpleasant odor—I do not find my mind compelled to apprehend it as necessarily accompanied by such further conditions. If the senses had not been our guide, perhaps reason or imagination would never have arrived at these [conditions] by themselves. Hence, I think that these tastes, odors, colors, etc., as far as the object in which they appear to reside is concerned, are nothing but mere names, and they reside only in the sensitive body [*nel corpo sensitivo*]; so that if the living creature were removed, all these qualities would be removed and annihilated. But since we have given special names to these qualities, different from those of the other primary and real properties [*primi e reali accidenti*], we are tempted to believe that they also really and truly exist.

. . . I do not believe there is in external bodies anything to excite in us our tastes, odors, and sounds, except shape, numbers, and motions, slow or rapid. And I judge that if the ears, tongue, and nose were taken away, the shape, number, and motions of bodies would remain, but not their tastes, sounds, and odors. The latter, when separated from the living creature are, I believe, nothing but mere names; just as tickling and titillation are nothing but names if the armpit and nasal membrane were removed.[3]

It should be clear that as far as Galileo was concerned there is no problem here at all. He was simply stating what sort of objects science is concerned to investigate. As a clarification of the subject matter of natural science (psychology aside) and as a statement of intentions, the pronouncement has some justification. It stands as an injunction to treat what can be treated mathematically and mechanically and renounce all else. Such is the harsh and thrifty puritanism of the practicing physical scientist. It works, and that is all he asks for. The barbed thicket of metaphysical and epistemological difficulties that encloses these comments is of no professional concern to him. He sees a workable theory of reality trimmed down to the shapes, motions, and mathematically measurable properties of bodies. This is nature, *physis,* as Democritus put it, and the sensible qualities we attribute to bodies are sheer conventions, *nomos.* The thicket of difficulties are scientific irrelevancies to be bypassed or passed on to the philosopher.

Philosophically, this doctrine of the "primary and real properties" of bodies and secondary subjective and illusory sense qualities was to be a notoriously persistent source of perplexities. With some differences in formulation it received continual expression in the seventeenth century, in Descartes, Hobbes, Newton, and Locke, and has been restated any number of times since—recently and vigorously by Russell and Eddington (§ 79). The general problem is this: if the

---

[3] Galileo, *Il Saggiatore*, pp. 333–336.

"objective" world of bodies and the "subjective" realm of mind and ideas are of a radically different character, how does the knowing mind, or how do ideas, ever give us reliable information about bodies?

Once again, it was Descartes who first stated the problem (and the attempted solution) with admirable clarity. In the *Meditations* the two crucial questions are asked. Describing *ideas* as pictures or images in the mind, Descartes inquires whether (a) some of these pictures are caused by objects outside the mind; (b) whether, if there are such causes, our ideas resemble their causes. The inquiry is thus twofold: (a) are there external real things; (b) if there are, can we know anything about them? The whole of natural science, if taken seriously and not relegated to illusion or unreality, depends upon a Yes answer to both questions. But in order to prove the validity of the Yes answer, Descartes fell back upon Augustinian Platonism. He revives each of the major insights carefully elaborated by Augustine and medieval Franciscans. The mind, conscious and indubitably certain of its own existence and the existence of God, is shown to be illuminated by the "light of nature," an intuitive source of principles and axiomatic truths. In the very act of thinking the thinker uncovers certain necessarily true propositions and ideas. The illuminated mind in turn illuminates and interprets sensations and bodily images. Perception, argues Descartes in Augustinian fashion, is really an act of "the understanding alone"—an intellectual interpretation of sense data—not mere sensation. The mind understands the natural world, the scene of bodies, according to this inner *nous* and higher *logos*. Each created object possesses an intelligible structure or rational character (*ratio*). Things and relations, *ratios*, are expressible by numbers—as Augustine and Scripture declared. The language of natural science is thus mathematics.

Descartes's Yes answer to the questions just raised comes through confidently, but the answer is made possible by his theory of knowledge and proofs of the existence of God. However, this answer, as Descartes developed it, raised other questions. The notion of mind illuminated by God to first truths and universal principles, working upon individual sense data and bodily images of a mechanical world, left the character of the individuality of the soul, the individual activity of knowing, and of human freedom in doubt. Descartes seemed to be doughtily reviving the central theses of Averroism against which St. Thomas had conducted a sustained attack in the thirteenth century. The church and the Jesuits were rightly suspicious of this marriage of modern science and medieval theology. Sniffing heresy behind these adroit maneuvers and wise to the ways of the world, they viewed with alarm the prospective issue of this Cartesian wedding. The result was the birth of rational theology which, like the proverbial minister's son, schooled in parental piety, took the first opportunity to go to the devil. Hume was this devil's advocate.

Others, with a Protestant distrust of scholasticism in religion or rationalism in science—or both—objected to Descarte's excessive indictment of immediate experience. There is much obscurity concerning just what immediate experience consists of, but in principle (if not in some of his specific scientific investigations) Descartes's outlook is decidedly unempirical. So much is this true of later Cartesianism that even a rationalistic mind like that of Leibniz could comment, "I prefer a Leeuwenhoek who tells me what he sees to a Cartesian who tells me what he thinks."[4] Descartes's many warnings about sense experience, the quality of felt events, and all reveries and emotional reverberations of the same are of both a scientific and moral persuasion. Like Galileo, he discounts sensation as unnecessary and illusory to the knowledge of bodies. Knowledge comes through reason and clear and distinct conceptions, not sense data. At first inspired by the ideal of a mathematical science, Descartes was to deny that sensation is a significant element in knowledge. Later he sought to reduce sense experience to mechanical explanations, thus amicably allowing the senses and feelings a modicum of reality and importance. But it was also consonant with his intellectual vision of truth—what reality is and how it is known—that the bodily senses and attendant passions individuate men, often to misguiding and setting brother against brother. Understanding, Reason, is universal, and man was made to reason. Reason, the intuitive light of nature, divests experience of its deceptive individual sensory clothing; the naked truth shines in clear and distinct conceptions.

§ 6.   Locke's Problem

The great spokesman for empiricism and common sense in science, religion, and morals at the end of the seventeenth century was Locke. In many respects he represents the opposite of Descartes's rather intricate and abstruse dialectical philosophizing over the foundations of knowledge. Locke disdains the lofty flights of logic and a priori launchings. He professed and stoutly tried to keep his feet firmly planted on—if not the ground—experience. Always impatient of dialectical subtleties, Locke's philosophy resembles a patchwork quilt in comparison to the elegant systems of continual thought in the seventeenth century. In fact, however, as any reader of Locke's great *Essay Concerning Human Understanding* soon discovers, this new analysis of knowledge is far from being destitute of complexities and paradoxes.

The source of most of the confusion in Locke's theory of knowledge is the very same that makes it so difficult to characterize his position and the "empiricism" of which he is the outstanding advocate. The welcome emphasis upon common sense, solid facts, observation, and experimentation; the rejection of innate principles—these are sustained and guided by many of the controlling assumptions and principles of Cartesian rationalism. Having inherited incom-

---

[4] In a letter to Huygens, Feb. 1690. See Gerhardt, p. 641.

patible conceptual orientations and procedures of analysis, Locke puts them to use and reaps the paradoxical results. He defines knowledge as "the perception of the agreement or disagreement of two ideas."[5] But surely knowledge, for an empiricist, is not perception *of ideas*, but of the world. The definition suits a rationalist who may construe 'ideas' as Platonic forms or Aristotelian principles. Locke had to append another, very different, definition of knowledge of "real existence."[6] While Descartes had difficulties, Locke had desperate troubles in giving the basic units of his theorizing a fixed and coherent meaning: 'idea,' 'object,' 'substance,' 'knowledge,' are imbued with a flux of meanings. Finally, the Cartesian dualisms of knower and known, mind and nature are vigorously perpetuated by Locke.

The problem of knowledge, glossed by Galileo, presents as serious a difficulty for Locke as it had for Descartes. There was never any doubt that we do have scientific knowledge of the world. Descartes pretends to doubt this, but his famous methodic skepticism is purely didactic: he wants to explain and illustrate and convince his readers of the value of his *method* of knowledge. Locke deals with the problem as a preliminary step in his investigation of the operation of the Understanding. Guided by and reiterating the traditional scientific assumptions of Galileo, Boyle, and Newton, Locke distinguished the "primary and real qualities" of physical objects—whose existence and character are not dependent upon the perceiving creature—and secondary qualities, which are "nothing in the objects themselves but powers to produce various sensations" or ideas in the perceiver.[7] Thus, "real" are the shape, weight, and bulk of the lump of sugar; "secondary," as effects in us, are the qualities of white and sweet. The mind is furnished with simple *ideas* of primary and of secondary qualities. Science, therefore, works with ideas of primary qualities, and the ideas of secondary qualities are left outside of science and confined to a less respectable, largely unintelligible level of relative, subjective, fluctuating animal sentience.

Of the many paradoxes in Locke's account of how the physical world is known, the most famous occurs at this point. For while ideas of primary qualities *resemble* those qualities of objects, our ideas of secondary qualities do not. Descartes, we have seen, dealt at length with this assumption of a resemblance of some ideas to objects. Curiously and revealingly, Locke ignores the issue. Ideas of primary qualities *do* resemble their causes in bodies, he insists. But he is unable to prove this contention, although the whole edifice of scientific knowledge logically depends upon it. The existence of what Locke called "real knowledge," knowledge of material objects, thus is left without any reasoned foundation.

The *Essay* commences with the assumptions of seventeenth-century science and a tribute to the "incomparable Mr. Newton." But proceeding from those

[5] *Essay Concerning Human Understanding,* Book IV, ch. 1, sec. 2.
[6] *Ibid.*, Book IV, ch. 1, sec. 7 and ch. 3, secs. 21 ff.
[7] *Ibid.*, Book II, ch. 8, sec. 10.

assumptions, Locke is led evenutally to conclude that we can have no "scientifical" (i.e., certain) knowledge of bodies. It is a curious tendency of empiricism to start with the premisses of scientific knowledge and to eventuate in doubt about their validity or reasonableness. But it is too easy to criticize Locke as alone responsible for the inconsistencies and confusions in his procedure. Many of the glaring problems in the *Essay* result from this fidelity to inimical features and confusions in seventeenth-century philosophizing about science. It is to Locke's credit that having inherited these problems, he was too honest to cover them up or smooth them over with philosophic frosting.

As to the above question, however, concerning empirical, or "real knowledge," and Locke's inability to make sense of it in his own theory, it remained for Berkeley in one way, Hume in another, to draw the devastating conclusions. Failing to explain how we could *know* that some of our ideas do resemble "external" objects, we are left, on Locke's theory, with the uninvited conclusion that all we do know or can know is our own ideas. The Understanding remains closed in its own private room and cut off from the world. Generally, if the seventeenth-century world picture was true, it could not possibly be *known* to be true.

Such was the critical problem of knowledge as Locke bequeathed it to his successors. As the *Essay* happened to find favor and acclaim from a powerful commercial middle class, whose interests had received articulate expression in Locke's liberal political and moral philosophy, it was an immediate and immense success. This expression of "science," "reason," and "experience" as the original of intellectual and moral truth, in contrast to established tradition or divine rights, was enormously influential on philosophers and politicians alike.

§ 7. The Enlightenment

The two most effective thinkers who ushered in the eighteenth-century Enlightenment are Newton and Locke. They are the bright lights of the age of brilliance, the fixed symbols of order and reasonableness in all things. Newton had unlocked the secrets of nature; Locke had used the same key to disclose the workings of human nature. Reason had uncovered an impeccable if difficult mathematical system of nature and had joined this with a tolerantly sagacious, an unruffled and pithy utilitarian humility concerning the sources, practical operations, and the limits of human knowledge. Reason brought natural and moral philosophy together into a working harmony—not as a single harmonious whole, for that Reason could not do. Rather, to the admiring lay mind, through the interstices of an austere theorizing concerning the heavens, bodies, and understanding, came mortal accents, a deft and shrewd moralizing on the social uses and aims of reason, of other-worldly hopes and worldly passions, and of human happiness. Still the problem we have been reviewing, Locke's problem which he shared with Newton, remained unresolved. Both Locke and Newton (in his epistemological moments) are left affirming the existence of a world and of knowing minds but with no intelligible connection discoverable between them. The inconsistencies and paradoxes in Locke's theory of knowledge, resulting from his uncritical commitments to the divisive currents of continental rationalism and experimental empiricism of the Royal Society, are next to kin to those in Newton's philosophizing. Thus Newton argues that the fundamental principles of his science have their origin in sense experience—they are "deduced from phenomena,"[8] and thence given a mathematical form. Yet the most basic of his concepts, mass-particles, absolute time, space, and motion, are not such as could be experienced or derived from sensory observation. They were, of course, rationally justifiable as necessary to Newtonian science; but they were not empirical facts. Kant drew this conclusion: these were necessary postulates of physical experience. It is interesting to see both Newton and Locke turn the very coinage of empiricism into possible counterfeit by declaring, in almost identical phrasing, that we can never know the nature of substance or what things "really" are. At best we can but know things by their properties and effects.[9] Substances remain inaccessible, objective unknowns. It is attributes and experienced effects that constitute the ephemeral stuff of our tantalized reckonings with and probings into nature.

Given, then, this entrenchment of the problem of knowledge, and, by virtue of its centrality in the outlook and procedures of these two great English philosophers, its authoritative and influential sponsorship, one of two possible ways out of the thorny Galilean thicket (to reminisce on the metaphor of § 5) occurred to the eighteenth-century philosophers. The first was to undertake a new look at and radical analysis of the problem, in the course of which the indefensible metaphysical roots and prehensile presuppositions of the problem are brought to light. This way issued a critical revision and clarification of the concepts of 'substance,' 'mind,' and 'idea.' This was to effect a reconstruction of philosophic theories of experience and knowledge. This was the way of Berkeley and later of Kant.

The other way out was to make the 'scientific' and Lockean position consistent and draw the absurd or skeptical conclusions. This was the way of Hume. Hume's way was not taken in order to lead to a new conception of experience and knowledge, nor to a new theory of empirical science; that it could was incidental to Hume. (While Berkeley and Kant were called by Truth to solve Locke's problem, Hume followed literary fame and fortune.) Hume's way was to discover a method of critical analysis of beliefs and ideas (and meanings, see below, § 27). He forged a blade so light and sharp that with one clean sweep common sense, science, and systematic philosophy alike were severed from their foundations. In effect these towering growths stood as before in undiminished luxuriance, but

[8] From the famous General Scholium, *Principia*, Book III. See also Book III, Rule 3, Rules of Reasoning in Philosophy.

[9] For a note on this, see H. S. Thayer, *Newton's Philosophy of Nature*, p. 187.

now by sheer gravity. Such, as Hume saw well, was the inertia of belief to defy the laws of bodies, and of custom to unfailingly fail the dictates of logic. Like trees neatly sliced at the trunk, these ideational superstructures could still stand, supported precariously at the very point of disconnection by the old earth, and sustained from above, perhaps, by a renewed faith in heaven graced with windless skies.

Hume's relentless methodology ironically proved to be the instrument that destroyed the older rationalism only to make way for a new faith and possible irrationalisms. By conclusively demonstrating that there are no rational grounds for belief in miracles and no knowledge of fact beyond observed sequences of events, Hume affirmed the miraculous propensity of man to believe and his need to trade upon ideas about the world apparently unwarranted by or unconfined to rules of evidence. Hume concluded his famous analysis of miracles with the reasonable recognition of beliefs going beyond reason: "Our most holy religion is founded on faith, not on reason."[10] The reasoners of the Enlightenment recognized, thanks especially to Hume, that man is a creature of sentiment as well as of logic. It was as important to *feel* things as to know them. The appropriate example is captured in an incident in which Hume, undone by feelings of friendship for Rousseau, wept copiously.[11] The man of Reason was supported through this outburst in the arms of Rousseau, the man of Feeling, the dry-eyed philosopher of the heart.

Hume's critical method, and, more so, Berkeley's procedural rule for determining the meaning, language, or notions (i.e., of signs and reasoning) through establishing their empirical reference, so that the meaning of an expression is its reference to immediately observed or predictable sense experience, were formative influences upon pragmatism.[12] But so, too, was the great Kantian attempt to interpret and rescue science from Humean skepticism—to solve Locke's problem anew—and to determine by an analysis of reason itself the scope and conditions of scientific, moral, and metaphysical experience. No sooner had the Kantian analysis and answers to these intellectual demands and problems of philosophy been set forth, in outline, than it underwent modifications at the hands of post-Kantian idealists, and was subject to all of the varied currents of romanticism, rationalism and empiricism, in criticism, revision, supplementation, and dismemberment—the culmination of those diverging tendencies which had collectively initiated and been carried within Kant's "revolution." All of this is relevant and vital to the view we have been taking; some of it—short of a voluminous study of the whole—calls for a closer, albeit selective pursual in the next pages.

---

[10] *Inquiry Concerning Human Understanding,* sec. 10.
[11] The incident is described by Morley, Vol. II, p. 129.
[12] For this subject, see Appendix 5 below.

CHAPTER TWO

Responses to the Problem

§ 8. Transcendental and Critical Philosophy

The banal observation that Descartes cast modern philosophy in a thoroughly subjective mold with his *cogito* and emphasis on Mind is as unfounded as it is inaccurate. For there is nothing individual, or genuinely private, or "subjective" (in most senses of that abused word) in either the operation or the content of *knowledge* for Descartes. Cartesian understanding, as we noticed earlier, is universal; sense experience is individually unique. Then, too, according to Descartes, the first and clearest of ideas in the human mind is not of oneself—not *cogito ergo sum*—but of God, the intelligible being which makes all thinking possible.[1] Indeed, it makes little sense to speak of the "subjectivity" of knowing or mind here, since, unlike bodies, mind is spaceless. There is no geometry of souls; knowing literally does not occur in any place. The subjectivity characteristic of modern philosophy derived its impetus from an intolerant Galilean cosmology (as in the above § 5), which drove mind and knowing out of nature, and from Locke's problem, which unintentionally left the knowing mind with nothing but itself for a subject matter.

Less banal and more accurate is the observation that Descartes initiated the transcendental method in modern philosophy, the view that *knowing* imposes, or mind determines certain conditions and effects in the objects known. The method is an attempt to discover what Mind (i.e., prior conceptualization, habits, will—or sheer metaphysical insight) contributes to our sensations of objects in order to produce the net result of knowledge.

The light of nature and source of certain innate and intuitively self-certified "ideas" performed the transcendental function for Descartes: Mind, illuminated

---

[1] The Third Meditation brings this out: "the notion of God is prior to that of myself. . . ." The idea of God is "the truest, the clearest, and most distinct of all the ideas which I have in my mind."

to the necessary axioms and truths, infallibly discerned the order of nature and character of reality. Locke, more intimidated by natural science, relying upon mechanical analogies in his depiction of mental operations and the Understanding passively reacting to nature, found no possibility of asserting the doctrine of transcendental ideas.[2] In this, Locke's concern to stay scientifically up-to-date was less lasting than Descartes's revival of the Augustinian philosophy of knowledge—a philosophy which had been elaborated in the thirteenth century to absorb and account for experimental and mathematical science, notably by Roger Bacon and Robert Grosseteste, and which had received an elegant formulation by St. Bonaventure. (The latter's influence in theology and his "a priorism" and conception of "synthetic a priori knowledge" significantly continued to thrive in Germany.) This transcendentalism conceives knowledge of nature as the discovery and application of logically necessary principles to sense experience; all sensation is threaded with logical fibers; sense data are signs (or bearers) of rational principles; facts are instances or fragments of conceptual structures. The world as we experience it becomes knowable to us because diversified objects and sensations are alike sewn with rational principles of order. That order is derived from a higher *logos* and is reflected in the a priori structure of nature and in the rational illuminations of mind. Descartes's signal contribution was in adapting this philosophy of knowledge to the new seventeenth-century mechanical and mathematical conception of nature. Cartesian philosophy stands to Cartesian and Galilean mechanics as something like the grafting of Platonism onto Democritean physics.

The transcendental philosophy of knowledge thrived on the continent, undergoing varied and complex modifications. It also found vigorous and imaginative spokesmen in England, in the Cambridge Platonists, there receiving a religious and moral expression.[3] In due course, during the eighteenth century in England, a major critical controversy over the origin and analysis of moral ideas called forth new and ingenious adaptations of the transcendental method. As Intellect imparted order to experience, rendering natural facts intelligible, so Intellect, or Will (especially for Protestant theologians), or even Feeling—so the positions were taken—operated as the prerequisites for the stability and meaningful character of moral facts and experience.

This sketch necessarily overlooks the diversity of positions in which the tran-

---

[2] Though he did assert as intuitively certain the existence of the self and the demonstrative certainty of God. See Locke's *Essay*, Book 4, ch. 3, sec. 21.

[3] For Ralph Cudworth (1617–1688), the founder of this School, knowledge is an act of intellectual anticipation, *prolepsis*, by which sense phantasms are given significance, rather than being copied by or imitated in the mind. "Sensible things themselves (as for example light and colours) are not known or understood . . . but by intelligible ideas exerted from the mind itself, that is by something native and domestic to it." *The True Intellectual System of the Universe* (1678), Vol. III, p. 62. This Platonism, derived from Ficino but with the Augustinian theory of knowing behind it, and behind it, too, the influence of Descartes in England, is a good statement of what we have been describing as transcendental philosophy.

scendental philosophy has received expression. In some cases it is mind which, illumined by a higher *logos* or Ideas, actively derives moral truths and applies principles or categories to sense experience. In other cases, mind, nature, and sense experience are alike vested with logical principles or structures; knowing is the assimilation of these structures in an act of similitude, convergence, or adequation. The transcendental method derives from Plato: from his myths (or, to some, his doctrine) of knowledge as remembering, *anamnēsis*, in which the soul is described as in possession of the principles—the vision of Forms—necessary to (and really the content of) all knowing. There are also occasional arguments in which Plato says, for example, "Knowledge does not consist in the impressions, but in reasoning [*syllogismō*] about them. It is in that, and not in impressions, that it is possible to grasp being [*ousia*] and truth."[4]

In all these various developments of the transcendental method in the eighteenth century, the seeds of Kantian synthesizing and the succor of romanticism were nourished and prepared.

§ 9. *Eighteenth-Century Enlightenment*

The idea that human history is a series of successive phases and therefore exhibits fairly distinct and describable stages is largely the invention of historians. Moved partly by expository necessities of plot, selection, and organization, partly by theory or academic duties, the historian reads order into otherwise errant and chaotic events; and, by virtue of a confounding of facts with discourse about them, the past basks in the limpid sentences and cadenced punctuation of the historian's prose.

An impulse to poetry, for the first historians were poets, has also prompted historians to capture the past in snatches of description or in labels, to characterize epochs, ages, periods. And while to be dead is to be futureless, nothing could come as more astonishing to the once-living dead than the summations and pronouncements of future historians practicing that come-lately and backward-looking art. The Greeks would be stunned to learn that they were "ancients," the denizens of the "Middle Ages" utterly bewildered. To all this the eighteenth-century Enlightenment is an exception. For it succeeded, were the thing but possible, in all but inventing itself: pondering itself in rapt fascination, engaged in quizzical self-scrutiny, it called itself the "age of enlightenment," asked what this meant, gave its own answers, and proceeded to write its own history.

To the eighteenth century, the philosophers of the seventeenth century had been addicted to the *esprit de système*. In contradistinction it liked to regard

---

[4] *Theaetetus*, 186d. In addition to Platonism, one would have to recognize the influence of ancient Stoics and Epicureans on the history of transcendental philosophy. For the Epicurean *prolepsis*, see *Diogenes Laërtius* X. 33, and Cicero, *De Natura Deorum* I. 16–17.

itself as "the age of criticism." "Our age is, in especial degree, the age of criticism [*Kritik*] and to criticism everything must submit,"⁵ said Kant. And indeed, it was that, subjecting the great systems of reasoning of Descartes, Hobbes, Spinoza, and Leibniz, as well as of Newton and Locke, to a continuous evaluation of doctrines and acute analyses of methods and assumptions.

Both of these were centuries of Reason—given some latitude for vicissitudes in the conception of Reason, its uses, and rightful domain. Reason that had earlier found its vocation in the spirit of systems gave way in the eighteenth century to the spirit of systematic reasonableness. Systems can be confining, suffocating—even worse, provincial. And there is nothing enlightenment likes less than to be left stranded in the provinces.

But while first to acknowledge itself as a critical age, the Enlightenment had an additional view to append to its autobiography. D'Alembert, one of its most representative and influential spokesmen, said, "Our century is called . . . the century of philosophy *par excellence*."⁶ He describes the revolutionary advances in natural science, and he emphasizes the beneficial results that the application of the new method of scientific reasonableness has produced in taste, music, morals, theology, economics, and politics. Truly a remarkable century of philosophic reason: wit and wisdom in letters, elegance in manners, enlightened self-interest in politics and economics, and progress in all things. So the eighteenth-century Enlightenment has recommended, portrayed, and successfully established itself as the bright image in the mirror of history and, if a little flashy, still quite in fashion.

This self-portrait of the Enlightenment, which has served as a model for later reproductions and investigations, while not a fake, is far from the whole truth. There is something missing from the picture drawn for us by these men of letters, the witty and sapient *philosophes*, and missing, too, from later copies. What this is may be found just below the surface impression of order, reasonableness, and the spread of rational progress in the arts, sciences, and politics. In literary style, in its cleverest versification, in the *bon mots* of eminent wits, the Enlightenment mind regularly uses and reveals itself in disparate conjunctions, unexpected joinings of dissimilar trains of ideas and opposed sentiments, epigrammatical and paradoxical turns of thought. It is this, never quite said but accompanying most of what was said, that exposes a fundamental trait of the Enlightenment: a felt duality and expressed polarity of intellectual interests, aims, and feelings, pervading all aspects of human experience—a perpetual soliciting of divided loyalties to the heart and to the head.

Keen and concerned men had already foreseen the growing conflict, for these discordant tendencies had older roots: the previous century had been nourishing what was to become the *esprit* of the Enlightenment and its ripening season.

⁵ Kant, *Critique of Pure Reason*. Preface to the First Edition, A xiⁿ. See also Kant's *Beantwortung der Frage: Was heist Aufklärung?* (1784. *Reply to the Question: What is Enlightenment?*)
⁶ From *Elements of Philosophy*, in Cassirer, p. 3.

Pascal (1623–1662) for one, with disarming acumen, had pointed out that while Cartesian science, Reason triumphant, answered many urgent questions, it did not answer them all. Reason was right, but not enough. There was, he was led to urge, that other source of truth, *le coeur*; and there was faith.[7] Man is a creature of heart and soul as well as intellect. And man needs religion; he calls for God from the depths of the heart. Christianity answers to this need; it completes and resolves and illumines the mystery of man's soul, as science explains the world. This is Pascal's foreshadowing of romantic and modern defenses of religion and the will to believe.

Pascal's famous wager in behalf of religious belief sheds light upon this emerging problem of religion as well as upon his own critical intentions. The wager is an appeal to intellect from the heart, an address to Reason to trust in a way and a wisdom it cannot fathom and was never fashioned to comprehend. As an argument for religion, the wager may seem lacking in logic and piety. But as a way of interpreting the function of religious belief, as part of an apologia and religious philosophy, the critical motive was sound. For the wager is a prophetic warning against the dissolution of religion by science. The defense of religion cannot come from science, certainly not Cartesian science. That defense is successful only at the cost of religion. No defense of religion (including, by the way, Pascal's) can escape this paradox: the sacred is made contingent upon the profane, religious belief loses its primacy by becoming a consequent of other and more ultimate convictions. But Pascal was right, as the eighteenth century was to discover. Cartesian and Newtonian rational theology was the sacrifice of religion on the altar of a scientific deity. God was a scientific abstraction, a mechanical force or a geometer. His glory, His chief justification for existing was put succinctly by Pope: He

Let Newton be, and all was light.[8]

Hume had little trouble and took delight in puncturing the superficial defenses erected for religion by scientific reason. Hume killed rational theology, but Laplace wrote the epitaph.

Laplace had with great elegance and beauty set forth the Newtonian science of nature and explained how the solar system originated from the cooling and condensation of nebulae. When it occurred to Napoleon to ask where God fitted into this system, Laplace answered, so the story goes, "Sire, I have no need of that hypothesis." The unintended but more devastating effect of that reply no doubt escaped Laplace but would have been recognized by Pascal. It is not so much that there is no place for God in the scientific world-view that assails the religious sensibility, for this is an old idea, a familiar, almost comfortable, heresy. It is rather that God is counted as one more hypothesis for the mighty mind of

---

[7] For, as God says to Job (38:36): *Who hath put wisdom in the inward parts? or who hath given understanding to the heart?* (King James version.)
[8] Pope, *Intended Epitaph for Sir Isaac Newton*.

man to weigh, ponder, and destine finally to oblivion or acceptance. But for anything like a truly religious temperament and faith, the Lord God Jehovah is not a hypothesis.

It was the head that found the idea of God to be a scientifically useless hypothesis. Hence, for the Enlightenment, if the head could not contain religion, men would have to look elsewhere, to the heart, or to Will. For, with the empiricism that the Enlightenment derived from Newtonian science, one could not remain forever blind to facts, and religious belief was a fact, and so, too, was the general moral and scientific interest in the phenomena and institutions of religion.

In their respective ways heart and head struggled with these facts of religious experience as they strained for a critical understanding of one another, seeking a *rapprochment* and clarification of the intellectual, social, and aesthetic future of man, man enlightened from servitude to the cultural past.

This tension between heart and head in charting the future of man, subject to a simultaneous skeptical rending and optimistic reweaving of the lines of communication, caused both the vitality and paradoxical character of the eighteenth-century Enlightenment. This was an age of Reason in which men took great pains to develop their faculties of feeling and taste; in which sentiment was encouraged to be as reasonable as possible, and in which Reason was increasingly concerned to uncover its own limitations; and one in which philosophy, by being consistent, often succeeded in being unbelievable. It prided itself on knowledge about all things, yet was markedly skeptical about what could be known; it thought that nearly everything of value and importance could be explained by Science, yet found almost everything of interest and concern to man lying outside of science. It was an age which condemned civil society as a source of human misery and proclaimed social life as the salvation and fulfillment of man. It stated and championed the inalienable rights of individuals while formulating the ideals of collective social existence. It announced the dignity of the common man while its economy thrived on agricultural and industrial slavery. The intellectual elite, drawn to the sophisticated circles in large cities, spoke of the virtues of a simple country life. Those who could afford to eat cake wittily reflected that man does not live by bread alone.

This paradoxical and divisive mind of the Enlightenment, breeding and encouraging schisms, quite naturally abetted two divergent intellectual tendencies: intolerant scientific rationalism on the one hand, a protesting and vigorous romanticism on the other.

'Enlightenment' is one word but not one state of mind. In England, in France, and in Germany, Enlightenment, *éclaircissement, Aufklärung,* referred to quite different forms and directions of cultural expression. *Aufklärung* came more slowly to Germany.

Unlike Italy, France, and England, Germany had not gone through that intellectual liberation, a cultural and artistic quickening described as the Renaissance of the fifteenth and sixteenth centuries. Germany had a Reformation, but Renaissance was to come later. It came as a part of the eighteenth-century Enlightenment, first manifesting itself as the romantic *Sturm und Drang* movement. This Renaissance had its origin and continued resources in an emerging interest in classical culture beginning with Greek sculpture. The Renaissance and romantic movement in Germany is associated with Winkelmann (1717–1768), Lessing, Schiller, and Friedrich Hölderlin. In Schiller's *The Gods of Greece* (1788) the romantic protest, the pattern to be followed by Wordsworth, Keats, and later romanticism, is clear: science has destroyed the once divine and imaginative world of nature—a world of Greek gods—and has killed something in the soul of man as well. This is echoed in Wordsworth's cry,

> Great God! I'd rather be
> A pagan suckled in a creed outworn,

and in Keats's complaint that the Newtonian

> Philosophy will clip an Angel's wings

and had destroyed the rainbow, unweaving it by scientific explanation.[9]

Kant described the Enlightenment as man's freeing himself from intellectual servitude; man's daring to know what can be known. While the critical force of enlightened thought in France was anti-clerical, addressed in the name of Reason and Science against a political and social order glutted with corruption in which the Church had become immersed, this was not so in Germany. Critical French radicalism and revolutionary doctrines, urbane British constitutionalism, political theorizing and skeptical empiricism were felt in Germany, but always as imports from the outside—something not truly German.

Aufklärung was felt as a rising of winds upon the waters where the German soul brooded—a change, an undoubted transformation of surface levels and directions, compelling, tossing the soul of man to a new intellectual adventure and intellectual self-discovery. But the waters have their native deeps and hushed ancestral floor, so that all surface changes are partially conditioned by the medium of things below.

Two cultural conditions affected the spread of the Enlightenment in Germany, giving it a distinctive shape and coloring different from that in England and France. First, there was a medieval heritage which had not been destroyed or rendered otiose by the mathematical-scientific world view. Germany was never captured by the Newtonian philosophy of nature, as England and France were; she was not lured into neglecting the philosophizing of the past, or ignoring the possibilities of alternative views of the world. Leibniz among others had seen to that. The new science could not explain everything, nor could it explain very much of itself. It exhibited considerable knowledge, but little wisdom. And wisdom, mellow, antique, loving to hide in secret formulas and recondite doctrines, calling for magical keys and ponderous intellectual labors, was stored in the

[9] Wordsworth, sonnet, "The World is too much with us." Keats, *Lamia*, II, 229–237.

systems of the past. Moral, mystical, and unabashedly imaginative interpretations of nature and life continued to thrive in Germany, being the tributaries of the scholasticism that lived on in German academic philosophy.

Coupled with this first condition was another in shaping the mind and future of the German Enlightenment. This was the Protestant heritage; and it, too, was viewed as a precious and vital link with the past, reaching back in spirit and values into the early Middle Ages.

Luther, the greatest of the reformers, scorning theology and all other institutions that purported to serve religion while furthering the separation between man and God, drew upon what was the earliest of medieval philosophic traditions, Augustinianism, or one strand of Augustinianism: the view of man's naturally sinful condition and moral weakness, and the conception of personal grace and the mystical relation of the individual soul to God. In faith, and in immediate experience, come unsullied deliverances of religious truth. As it happened, the Protestant theologians found *experience* as the "original" of faith (to transplant the language of Locke) and rendered *experience* as something personal, immediate, full of moral and mystical lights, the subjective source of revelation and action. They had, thereby, unintentionally anticipated the view of experience as an internal drama and passage of intuitions and ideas that seventeenth-century science was to force in upon modern philosophy. Locke's problem of knowledge is indeed an unLockian premiss of the Protestant theology of a century earlier. And when the critical empiricist was driven by the assumptions of Newton and Locke to the skeptical conclusion that all we can know is our own minds, Protestant theology could respond with a wealth of moral and religious philosophizing and luminous insights quite compatible—if only coincidental—with that bankrupt epistemology.

It is a curious fact that the anti-scientific spirit of the reformers, with their distrust of "Natural Reason" and natural science, should issue in a moral conception of experience so perfectly prepared to receive and support the conclusions of philosophers of science. But this was not the first time that a thoroughly subjective version of experience, rendered as a private play of will and ideation, served to combine mysticism in morals and skepticism in knowledge.

The philosophy of the Reformation was thought to be, by those who believed it, a new assertion of ancient truths, emphasizing the moral importance of the individual and the personal nature of the religious life—the experiment perilous of the individual soul seeking and sometimes saved by universal Divine Will. To a considerable extent, modern German philosophy from Kant through Hegel was a rationalizing of the suggestions and a technical defense of the controlling ideas of Protestant theology. At any rate, the German *Aufklärung* was never neutral to religion nor anti-clerical in spirit. In this Enlightenment it was never seriously supposed that religion might gradually be replaced by a utilitarian social idealism or a collectivistic reform of society.

Thus it was in Germany in the eighteenth century that the first impressive critical reaction to science took place. There, in a culture both proud of and fascinated with its moral and religious linkage to the medieval past, never overwhelmed by science, it was science and not religion which had to be critically examined, reappraised, and subordinated to other values and alternative kinds of experience. Accordingly, the limits of science began to be expounded by German rationalism.

The important figure instigating this rationalism in Germany was Leibniz. But it was Christian Wolff (d. 1754) who developed a dry yet popular expression of the soul of rationalism, deriving the metaphysical ideas from Leibniz while ignoring the latter's scientific thought. Wolff sought to absorb mechanical science into a larger metaphysical and religious outlook, a unity established by Reason. He maintained that Reason could demonstrate matters of fact (a view resolutely criticized by Hume)[10] and that the truths of natural science could be shown to follow logically from the principles of logic or "laws of thought" alone. Against this rationalism, which dominated the German universities, came a scientifically oriented empiricism in which it was argued that reason in itself cannot arrive a priori at knowledge of matters of fact. Not concerned to develop the extremes of Humean skepticism, however, the German scientific empiricists set themselves the task of exploring what are the assumptions of reason and observation that are implied and presupposed by the laws of mechanical science. The Swiss mathematician and scientist Euler (d. 1783), for example, held that time and space are the basic rational assumptions of mechanics. The conclusions of mechanics are true, but they are implied by the assumptions of mechanics, and these assumptions are not themselves based upon experience or observation. The assumptions are "ideal," the rational postulates necessary to confer order upon a system of scientific experience which Euler was convinced was itself true. Euler's critical empirical analysis of mechanics was a precursor of the Kantian philosophy of science.

§ *10. Kant*

Once again we come back to the main theme of these pages: the intellectual challenge brought to modern thinking by the cumulative changes in Western culture; but more especially and pertinently, the disruptive conflict of science and values; of new knowledge against older cultural patterns and ethical ideals.

These conflicts occurred differently and were treated in differing terms and ways by the men who felt them most in successive periods. But each was a crisis in human affairs. The challenge provoking philosophic thought to interpret and reinterpret man's moral experience and to clarify the meaning and scope of science, of knowledge, thus exhibits one dominant concern: to achieve an intelligent integration, a working equilibrium of moral aims and scientific truth.

[10] See Appendix 6 below on Hume's argument, and Part IV, ch. 2.

It cannot be said that the history of Western philosophy is marked with many successes in this central undertaking. Exempting the Greeks and our own contemporaries from this momentarily critical long glance, the West can boast of three great expositions and theoretical syntheses of knowledge and values, of human experience taken synoptically as a whole, the subject matter of articulate science and at the same time the source of moral possibilites and aims and aesthetic satisfactions. Of these three great intellectual syntheses and interpretations of experience, the first came from St. Thomas in the thirteenth century, the second from Spinoza in the seventeenth century, and the third from Kant at the close of the eighteenth century.[11] To this last we now must turn.

§ 11. Kant's Critical Synthesis of Science and Values

An allusion was made some pages back to Kant's attempt to "save" science from the skeptical and critical consequences of Hume's analysis of knowledge. Kant's was not, however, an attempt to salvage scientific knowledge from philosophic skepticism. For scientific achievements won by arduous intellectual effort or sometimes by gambling with good ideas have never been seriously jeopardized by philosophic doubts. Science combines motives of utility with the sheer rational impulse to know things as they are, thus yielding the twin benefits of prediction and explanation. Scientific activity so motivated is unlikely to become inhibited by questions, however plausible, as to the possibility of its terminating in illusions. Therefore the philosophers' questions about the reliability of the senses, or the existence of the world, do little to discomfit the scientist in recording what he sees and in investigating the world. Kant's labors, then, were directed to saving the philosophy of science from a skepticism that left the fact of science unintelligible. His purpose was to make the existence of scientific knowledge philosophically, rationally, understandable.

The science that Kant was explaining, the science that he saw Humean skepticism and dogmatic rationalism alike unable to account for, was Newtonian. A major part of Kant's great Critique of Pure Reason is describable as a philosophic investigation into the assumptions and rational foundations of Newtonian mechanics.

But this was only one of Kant's aims. In addition to stating and clarifying those conditions and presuppositions which accounted for the possibility of science, Kant sought to disclose the basic assumptions that made man's moral and aesthetic experience possible (i.e., intelligible). Kant's spirit here is conservative. He was concerned to preserve and justify each of these aspects of experience— that is, each of these kinds of experience is vital, no one of them is to be excluded

---

[11] Perhaps, less dogmatically and with more justice, one should add the figure of Duns Scotus alongside that of Thomas, and of Leibniz to that of Spinoza.

from philosophic investigation and explanation. These, in Kant's outlook, constitute the comprehensive setting of human nature and experience.

Kant's analysis of science thus exhibits a twofold purpose: to make the fact of science understandable, but, in so doing, also to show how and why the scientific assimilation of experience does not conflict with these other equally significant areas of human experience.

To do this Kant's thought moves within both of the philosophic traditions of his time. Rationalism, he held, was right in insisting upon the formal character of knowledge, upon the use of concepts and logical principles, but wrong and "dogmatic" in supposing that matters of fact (whether experienced or not) could be deduced from an antecedent metaphysical structure. On this last point Kant sides with Locke's emphasis: sense experience supplies the origin and content of our knowledge of nature. But while they were right in stressing the importance of experience, the empiricists were mistaken in their explanation of experience and knowing, for they, on the other hand, failed to appreciate the necessary role of concepts and purely rational principles in knowledge. They assumed that sensations and ideas—the basic units of knowledge—represented or served as images of natural objects. This, too, was a piece of dogmatism, argued Kant, for the empiricists were assuming that something outside of experience, something lying beyond experienced images, could be known through experience.

Kant thus attempted to bring into his analysis of knowledge these otherwise competing and disparate points of view: the notion of *ideas* as perceptions grounded in sense experience, the view of Berkeley and Hume; and *ideas* as intelligible forms, and acts of judgment, argued by Henry More, Leibniz, and the Cartesians. For the empiricists, knowledge results from the fact of individual perceptions; priority is assigned to *sense*. For the rationalists, knowledge results from the fact of unified rational principles; priority is assigned to *reason*. For Locke and Hume, scientific knowledge consists of the probable inferences drawn from our perceptual experience; for Descartes and Spinoza, it consists of the necessary logical relations among ideas. Put crudely, the empiricists and rationalists were divided over whether feeling or thinking has the fundamental part in our knowledge of nature.

Kant developed an alternative position which integrated the two views. Basic to his theory was his "revolutionary" discovery that the mind is active rather than passive in knowing and brings to experience the principles necessary for interpreting and ordering sense data. It happens that this discovery had been made before.[12] But Kant was developing this insight within a critical examination of Hume's "scientific" empiricism. To some he appeared then to be destroying the narrow philosophies of scientific rationalism and empiricism and proving the essentially moral and creative possibilities of the mind. Wordsworth caught the spirit of this discovery in his Preface to the *Excursion*:

[12] By Henry More (see § 8 above) and Berkeley, among others; see Appendix 5.

How exquisitely the individual Mind
. . . to the external World
Is fitted:—and how exquisitely, too—
Theme this but little heard of among men—
The external World is fitted to the Mind;
And the Creation (by no lower name
Can it be called) which they with blended might
Accomplish.[13]

This "discovery" was in fact a careful elaboration of the transcendental method which, as we have seen (§ 8 above), had been advanced earlier by Descartes. The method provided Kant with an explanation of how and what purely rational conditions are invested in sense experience to make knowledge possible. Kant described the purpose of his "transcendental philosophy" as concerned "not so much with objects as with the manner of our cognition of objects, in so far as it is possible *a priori.*"[14]

Hume had shown that we do not and cannot derive logically necessary principles from perceptual experience. His famous analysis of the causal relation among events[15] was a lucid illustration of his thesis that logically necessary relations are found among our ideas and not (as far as we can know) among matters of fact. Thus, in nature, causal connections are observed constant conjunctions of events about which we reason inductively and draw probable but not necessary conclusions. The stone once thrown will fall to the earth; but there is nothing logically *necessary* in these events such that to deny that the stone once thrown will fall is absurd or contradictory. Still, Hume pointed out, there may be a propensity in the mind *always* to associate the *idea* of one event (the "cause") with the idea of another (the "effect"). That propensity or habit is the source of necessity. But then, Hume concluded, necessity "exists in the mind, not in objects."[16]

Kant agreed, or seemed to, or did so in a qualified sense that has called forth more than a fair share of casuistry and comparing of texts. In a sense, *necessity* is in the mind, with a suitable enlarging of the "mind" to "the Understanding," granting, too, that necessity and a priori principles are not derived from experience. However, for Kant (and for Newton also) the propositions of science do not assert constant conjunctions among events; the laws of nature are not stated as empirical generalizations; they are assertions to the effect that it is *always* the case that certain kinds of events are related to other kinds of events. How, then,

---

[13] The lines that Wordsworth quotes in the Preface, 1814 edn., are from his *The Recluse*, end of Book I. Wordsworth's friend Coleridge was urging the same idea in a critical philosophic manner: "If the mind be not *passive*, if it be indeed made in God's Image, and that, too, in the sublimest sense, the *Image of the Creator*, there is ground for suspicion that any system built on the passiveness of the mind must be false, as a system." *Letters*, I, 352. See B. Willey, p. 14.
[14] *Critique of Pure Reason*, Introduction, A11-12—B25.
[15] *Treatise*, Book I, Part III, sec. 14. See also Appendix 6 below.
[16] *Treatise*, Book I, Part III, sec. 14.

is this step beyond generalization to universally necessary propositions to be explained?[17]

The overall function of reason is organizing, relating, and synthesizing sense experience. Reason is an interpreting of experience. The fact that experience is ordered and exhibits a structure is, Kant maintained, unintelligible according to Hume's atomistic psychology of ideas and impressions; but though Hume had shown that principles of organization, like that of causality, were not derived from sense data, yet these logically valid universal principles are imperative for any view of experience as a connected and related whole. Indeed, the very idea of *experience* as an ordered whole follows from and depends upon these principles. They are, then, necessary conditions of experience as organized. And since they are not derived or generalized from experience—for they are the universal conditions of the possibility of experience and of things as possible objects of experience—their source must be a priori, originating in the understanding. Thus Kant states his fundamental conclusion: "The Understanding does not derive its laws (a priori) from, but prescribes them to, nature."[18]

As an essential part of his analysis of knowledge Kant was led to insist that all theoretical knowledge is confined to objects of possible experience. That is, *knowledge* results from applying concepts to percepts in certain ways. That which cannot be perceived, or lies outside of experience, may be thought but cannot be known. To paraphrase Kant, concepts and percepts cooperate: concepts without percepts are empty (or meaningless) and percepts without concepts are blind. Two very important conclusions followed from this affirmation of experience, or perception, as a necessary condition of knowledge. First, sense experience is analyzable into sensations (Kant calls it intuition, *Anschauung*) each of which is a representation (*Vorstellung*) of some object, a thing-in-itself, as its cause. Groups and orders of sense-representations constitute *phenomena*. It is to phenomena that the understanding applies categories and principles. Thus, scientific knowledge is an interpretation of phenomena, of things as they are experienced according to the structure of their appearing and the operations of our minds. But science tells us nothing about the thing-in-itself, the world and those objects that cause, but lie beyond, phenomena. What the *real* world is, or what objects are *really* like, is beyond the province of knowledge and the limitations of our interpretative instruments for analyzing experience.

The second conclusion drawn from this theory of knowledge is that all unperceived but thinkable or conceivable objects, or beings of thought, *noumena*, remain unknown. Thus the usual objects of alleged metaphysical knowledge, the world (taken as a whole); the soul (or mind of knowing beings), and God, remain inaccessible to human knowledge. Here Kant is the critic of rational theology and traditional metaphysics. The philosopher of the transcendental as

---

[17] A fuller and more careful discussion of this and related issues is found below in Part IV, ch. 2.

[18] *Prolegomena*, Part II, sec. 37.

the very basis of experience thus eschewed a transcendant form of knowledge. The critical position was deep and impressive enough for Mendelssohn and Heine alike to call Kant the "all-destroyer." But Kant had not destroyed these objects. Their function in human experience as matters of vital concern was neither altered nor obliterated by this conceptual re-allocation. For Kant had set forth the limits of reason in order to make room for faith. As he said concerning God, Freedom, and Immortality: "I have therefore found it necessary to deny *knowledge*, in order to make room for faith."[19]

Kant went on to examine this other kind of experience, the subject matter of faith, in which man is led beyond mechanics and the scientific interpretation of the world. Thus reason is not wholly confined to its theoretical uses. Besides the objects of thought, there are those of *will* and feeling. These are matters of Practical Reason, having to do with the fact of man's moral experience. And in the logic of Practical Reason, God, Freedom, and Immortality function as necessary postulates of moral impulses and endeavors. The postulates explain and illuminate these facts and are necessary for rendering the facts intelligible and "possible" even though the assumptions cannot be proved by theoretical reason.

This means that, for Kant, there are kinds of experience that cannot be forced into or subsumed under the interpretive scheme of science. At the same time, these kinds of experience—those of moral obligation, the apprehension of beauty and religious aspirations—are too patently real, recalcitrant, rich, and efficacious to be dismissed as illusions. There is more in heaven and earth (and especially in the insistent demands of human nature) than is dreamt of in the mechanical philosophy of nature.

§ 12.   Transcendental Idealism: The Regulative Function of Ideas

Kant's "discovery" that the mind is an active agent in ordering and interpreting sense data was not merely stated. He ventured in a great complexity of argument, often unbearably diffuse, to account for the specific ways in which that activity is expressed and made possible. The technical core of his discovery, the details of which we shall avoid here, was his doctrine of the "synthetic a priori" judgment. These are judgments in which a *conceptual* and perceptual component are logically related. Whereas philosophic tradition in the eighteenth century had distinguished logically necessary (a priori) truths of reason and empirically contingent (synthetic) truths of fact,[20] Kant argued that some judgments had the property of being logically prior to all experience, i.e., necessarily true and not derived from experience (a priori) yet applying to experience (synthetic). In these judgments, logical necessity laces empirical fact. Kant's critical philosophy is an

---

[19] *Critique of Pure Reason,* Preface to Second Edition, B xxx.
[20] For a further word on this, see Appendix 6, sec. A below.

elaborate investigation of all theoretical and moral knowledge in order to exhibit
and justify these judgments.

The various logical forms that objective empirical judgments take constitute
Categories, and synthetic a priori judgments are applications of Categories to
the data of sense given in space and time. All theoretical knowledge consists in
the organization, by means of Categories, of the materials of sense perception
occurring in space and time. Without the Categories no meaningful judgments
of nature would be possible.

But in addition to Categories, so necessary to scientific judgment and to knowledge, Kant held that reason can form Ideas which, it happens, are reflections of
reason upon itself[21] and which serve to strengthen and further the employment
of reason in the acquisition of knowledge. The Ideas are products of pure reason,
not experience. Kant cites the ideas of the self (or 'I' viewed as "thinking nature
or soul"),[22] the world in general, and the idea of God. While we cannot have
knowledge of these objects, we can nonetheless *think* (conceive) what these
mean and what they imply in our understanding of human experience. So we can
form these Ideas; we have a compelling natural disposition to do so, and reason
—for the sake of reason—requires them for its guidance and unification. We
form an Idea, a purely rational and consistent concept of these objects in general,
although the Ideas have no *known* object corresponding to them in experience.[23]
For Ideas are products of pure reason and are concepts transcending sense experience.[24] We must not look for an experimental reference or empirical content to
them; we must not attempt to derive *knowledge* from them on pain of contradiction or antinomies. This is the mistake and consequent dilemma of traditional
metaphysics, which cannot, therefore, be considered a source of knowledge. The
Ideas, Kant argues, do not have a *constitutive* role, they do not determine or inform us of objects; they have a *regulative* function in reason. They function as
maxims[25] or ideals: namely, "that of directing the understanding towards a certain goal"[26] "marking out the path towards systematic unity."[27] The value and use
of Ideas consists in the unification, order, and systematic purpose they contribute
to the understanding and to the exercise of reason in its reference to nature.

In short, an Idea functions not as referring to real objects, but as "a schema
constructed in accordance with the conditions of the greatest possible unity of
reason."[28] The Ideas buttress and supplement empirical knowledge within its
limits, supplying a direction, breadth, and depth to the rational analysis of ex-

[21] *Critique of Pure Reason*, A680-B708: "Pure reason is in fact occupied with nothing
but itself."
[22] *Ibid.*, A682-B710.
[23] *Ibid.*, "The Transcendental Ideas," A327-B383: "I understand by idea a necessary
concept of reason to which no corresponding object can be given in sense experience."
[24] *Ibid.*, see A320-B377.
[25] *Ibid.*, A666-B694.
[26] *Ibid.*, A644-B672.
[27] *Ibid.*, A668-B696. Also, *Prolegomena*, Part III, sec. 56. The Ideas "bring our use of
the understanding into thorough agreement, completeness, and synthetical unity."
[28] *Ibid.*, A670-B698.

perience. Thus, in their regulative capacity, the Ideas serve as necessary conditions of completeness of our interpretive schematizing of experience. Accordingly, Kant says the Ideas take a postulational and schematic form: in psychology appearances and actions are given unification when we think of the mind *as if* it were a simple substance; in cosmology we think of the series of appearances *as if* endless, or we proceed in the analysis of nature *as if* we are dealing with a series of conditions whose totality is infinite; in theology we view all things *as if* they formed a unity and *as if* they originated from a single creative reason.[29] These *as if* assumptions, or ideas, fill in our conceptual efforts by extending and completing them, not as objects, but as schemata, or ideals—"regulative" principles of "the systematic unity of all knowledge of nature."[30]

For all of his sensitivity to and energetic critical study of the kinds of assumptions men make in reasoning about the world, Kant's philosophy of knowledge is developed from several assumptions which the "all-destroyer" left substantially unquestioned. Kant supposed, and never seriously doubted, that the state of mathematics at the time (especially geometry), Newtonian physics, and Aristotelian logic were each completed disciplines, or so nearly finished that the analysis of them through his critical philosophy would disclose all of the important synthetic a priori judgments in our system of knowledge. The structure of knowledge was thus theoretically complete. The introduction of non-Euclidian geometry, a new mathematical logic, and revelations in modern physics have thus presented a serious challenge to the Kantian philosophy of science and necessitated major reinterpretations of the Kantian assumptions.

The same drastic revisions which these unforeseen developments demand of Kant's theory of science drive an opening wedge into his account of the Transcendental Regulative Ideas. For a necessary and imperative condition of the Ideas is that while their objects are *noumenal*—not given empirically—and their function is regulative—not *constitutive* as principles for extending knowledge beyond experience—they must never contradict or run counter to empirical knowledge. But with the major changes since Kant in our knowledge of facts and our conceptualization, such as those just noted, the critical criterion of Ideas is alike subject to alterations and liberalization. A variety of possible Ideas and their formulation as regulative principles accordingly suggest themselves alongside, or even in place of, those set forth by Kant.

This in fact is what happened. Kant's doctrine of the "Regulative Employment of Ideas" was influential in the pragmatism of Peirce and Dewey and in that species of "pragmatism" found in Vaihinger. In Peirce and in Dewey, for example, the idea of continuity as a regulative principle of inquiry (see § 37 below) is very clearly in the spirit of Kant. So, too, is Peirce's conception of truth (§ 23) which, through Dewey, acquired the reputation of "the pragmatic definition of truth" along with Dewey's own view of truth as "warranted assertion" (see § 40).

29 *Ibid.*, A672-B700.
30 *Ibid.*, A673-4—B701-2.

Both of these versions of pragmatic truth are more than usually misunderstood if one overlooks the doctrine of regulative ideas with which they are associated. In later history, the Ideas themselves were subject to critical changes and sometimes disappeared; but Kant's theory of the function of Ideas continued to have a significant application in the late nineteenth-century philosophies of absolute, evolutionary, and naturalistic idealisms.

We observed earlier that Kant draws a boundary between scientific and moral experience. The metaphysics of morals is concerned with the a priori conditions of what *ought to be*. In their bearing upon man's rational interpretation of moral experience, the Ideas of God, Freedom, and Immortality function as regulative principles and also as postulates of faith. Man as a creature of sense, a phenomenal or empirical being, is a part of the deterministic causal order of mechanical nature. But on this level, responsibility, will, and obligation have no meaning. Ultimately, according to Kant, man's nature is *noumenal*. He is a rational being, and here the Idea of freedom which is *thought* but not *known* (i.e., *conceived* but is not *knowledge*) illuminates and unifies the sense of duty that prompts us to act according to what we recognize *ought* to be done. The Ideas of God and immortal soul have a similar function. They are justified as the assumptions we must make if the moral and religious impulses we do inevitably experience are to have any meaning at all. Since these assumptions and this kind of experience lie outside of science, since science itself is unable to tell us what the world in itself is really like, since we must make choices of right or wrong *as if* we were free to choose, and *as if* universal moral law guided our choosing, and *as if* a God were to judge and reward our endeavor, and *as if* the perfecting of moral behavior was an eternal quest for complete rationality (hence, requiring immortality of the soul), we must act on these assumptions and are justified in supposing them to be true. There is no reason to think them untrue, and we need them and are compelled to accept them in moral conduct. This is Kant's rational defense of faith, an elaborate pragmatic and rational extension of the kind of reflections that had found simple expression in Pascal, and which was to be revived from a psychological point of view by William James.

§ *13.*   *Experience, Interpretations, Symbols:*
       Romanticism

Kant's formidable rational clarification of science and moral experience carried in it all of the most forceful impulses of Enlightenment thought, touched upon earlier. Hume, who had aroused Kant from the dogmatic slumber in the comfortable bed of rationalism, had been "answered"—a philosophy of scientific knowledge had been saved, or won. Rousseau, whom Kant read avidly and regularly, supplied the faith—faith in man's freedom and equality under the moral law, and in the will that achieves the good by willing it universally. The head and the heart, Understanding and Will, were thus reconciled in the metaphysics of experience. That one human castle, critical philosophy, could open its gates amid rejoicing to send forth its two knights-errant, Pure and Practical Reason, into the unknown world, theirs the adventure to the glory of the kingdom.

Kant's critical philosophy made its appearance in the latter part of the eighteenth century. For a time it was ignored, then severely attacked, and very shortly thereafter its influence was felt—though not always accurately disseminated—as the triumph of the century. Kant was received as having delivered a compelling and final answer, not to Hume—for Kant's most eager followers were not interested in science and mostly ignorant of Hume—but to the shortcomings of the earlier Enlightenment in France. One could sympathize with the critical radicalism of the *philosophes*, their scathing refutations of shallow and pretentious orthodoxy in religion, their condemnation of social corruption. But as the French Revolution seemed to demonstrate, the scientific optimism of these rationalists was too shallow, too indefinite, too narrow to provide positive guidance and working ideals through the large and urgent problems these very radicals had helped to expose. Voltaire, for example, the master of effective ridicule and rapier criticism could deftly expose the diseases in the anatomy of the body social. His surgery is inspired, but not his healing efforts. His appeal to a wraith-like reasonableness, to a vague right of equality, to friendship, work, and hope are mild medicines indeed. After an incredibly panoramic experience in this topsy-turvy wicked world, Candide's final deliverance of apostolic wisdom—bidding us "cultivate our garden"—is hardly inspiring. One might have expected that piece of moral philosophy from the Candide with whom the story began; the wisdom of Candide requires hardly any experience at all. This, of course, is Voltaire's point—to ridicule an optimism about living that can never learn a lesson from life. Voltaire, unlike Candide, knew that the world was wicked and knew that something ought and possibly could be done about it. But what and how? Voltaire's answers come no more forcibly nor are they less remote and vapid than Candide's. Blake saw this:

> Mock on, Mock on, Voltaire, Rousseau;
> Mock on, Mock on; 'tis all in vain!
> You throw the sand against the wind,
> And the wind blows it back again.[31]

Kant's philosophy, however, was taken as a great demonstration of the rational justification of faith, that is, of enlightened and creative belief, offering what was ultimately a profound moral vision of knowledge and action. For Kant had seemed conclusively to demonstrate that knowledge, science, was *one* way of interpreting experience. Science works with its assumptions and conceptual principles, its "ideals," but Kant had shown that these principles constitute *how* we view the world. They are not, as far as we can tell, of the world itself—for what

31 William Blake, *Verses and Fragments*, 2nd series (1800–1810).

the world *is* in itself, we cannot know. But then science is a human creation. As one way of viewing and judging experience, science is like art, or religion, or like life itself. All of these are *interpretations*, differing in the kinds of principles or ideals and symbols used and in their organization. But basically, so Kant was assumed to have taught, all human thought is symbolic: poetry, art, and science are each ways in which symbols reveal and express the truths of experience.

This response to Kant's philosophy came from romanticism, a consolidation and vigorous assertion of tendencies that had long been at work alongside the scientific rationalism of the Enlightenment.

Kant, too, had felt the sweep and attraction of this romantic idealism. Rationalism and romanticism in the eighteenth-century Enlightenment had this in common: both were assertions of individuality against older systems of governmental repression. Both Locke and Rousseau, otherwise so different in temper, spoke for this demand of reason and of heart (and, as it happens, for the commercial middle classes): unrestrained individualism as far as possible in the business economy, in ideas, in religion, and in taste. Life and experience being after all a collection of private and individual episodes, the conditions of life, liberty, and happiness are to be freely chosen and worked out by men according to the dictates of conscience and reason. This is the common good, and its jeopardy is the only justified restraint over the actions of one or more individuals. The common enemy is social, intellectual, and moral tyranny. To the coldly reasoned new scientific criticism and rejection of past dogmas, the romanticists added fire and imagination, zealously if not consistently announcing the new faith in the sacred right of the individual personality to free and creative self-expression and self-realization. Such were the varied and impassioned suggestions to come from Rousseau in France, Goethe and Schiller in Germany, the younger Coleridge and Wordsworth in England—and Shelley and Byron—and the New England transcendentalists, Emerson and Thoreau.

CHAPTER THREE

The Modern Idealisms

§ 14. Romanticism

'Romanticism,' like the subject matter it attempts to designate, is a general and not very precise term referring to all of the just mentioned tendencies exhibited during the middle of the eighteenth century, and breaking forth impulsively, sometimes riotously, in the dawn of the nineteenth century.[1]

In philosophy, *romanticism* is characterized by those extensions of what were germinal possibilities in one part of Kant's philosophy: systems of thought are assertions and acts of faith in which man, essentially a creature of will, of impulses, feelings, and imagination, attempts to work out an inspiring interpretation of nature and human life. Nature, the self, and life, indeed all objects, are *ideas*, and the transcendental philosophy, romanticized, gives up talking about objects altogether. The thing-in-itself, unutterable, unknowable, vanished in a new dialectic of ideals. In this dialectic our idea of ourself, the ego, evolves its ideals and myths from its own mysterious resources and sends them forth, not only as symbols of

[1] In these pages 'romanticism,' 'idealism,' and 'romantic idealism' are each being used in a very broad descriptive sense as an attempt to indicate—not define—rather general movements of thought especially vigorous in Germany in the later eighteenth and in the nineteenth centuries. Of these appellations, 'romantic' is the subject of widespread definitional disagreement. (See Lovejoy, ch. 12, "On the Discrimination of Romanticisms," and also chs. 10 and 11.) German historians place much more restricted use upon this term than do Anglo-American writers. It would apply to Schelling (perhaps), Schlegel, Novalis, Solgar, G. H. Schubert; but not to Kant, Fichte, or Hegel. However, the more flexible use of this term and of 'romantic idealism' serves the purpose of the present study, which is not an attempt to portray the history of German thought. Were it relevant and space afforded it, we should have to take note of the contribution of Schelling and especially Schiller in developing an influential *aesthetic* philosophy of reason, partly a critical evaluation of Kant's *Critique of Judgment,* partly developed before his coming to Kant (see, e.g., his famous poem, "Die Künstler"). The mechanical and moral aspects of man's life, ordinarily in conflict, become resolved and completed in the ideal of *schöne Seele*—the realization of full manhood. The model of Man, the ideal of this romantic philosophy, is the moral genius, an aesthetic aristocrat, foreshadowing Nietzsche's superman; in person, a Goethe or a Byron.

reality, but *as the reality*, there to delight and engage its interest and invite action. That action is self-realization. The ideal becomes the real in this enactment. We are dramatists, all, from moment to moment; transcendental reason sets forth the play and the respective parts which we then proceed to act out. The important injunction is to make the play as rich and imaginative and satisfying as possible. We need the play, but we want one that will guide us best in life, that is, one that promises the values we seek and crave. But great variety and pluralism is quite possible here, not only because each of us may change the play at times, but also because many plays are available for many persons, among them, science, art, religion, politics.

Such is the spirit of romanticism and romantic idealism, not so much a philosophy as a loosely associated gathering of philosophical attitudes, exhibited most fully and outspokenly by poets and artists rather than the philosophers. Nietzsche alone was able to speak both tongues, or to give an expression to this philosophizing in a medium consistent with its content.

The romantic philosopher's emphasis on faith, imagination, and action is supported by a hypostatizing of egotism in morals and of experience in metaphysics. Self-realization, though it may be depicted as an unrealistic ideal, an eternal striving, is the moral concern of man. But self-realization and all striving is felt and recognized in experience. So the drama and ultimate conditions of life occur by experience, for experience, and in experience, and the self floats like a sponge in this watery world seeking to soak up what it can—not aimlessly but according to the varieties in the fluids that attract it, and according to its own interior transcendental mechanism for selective absorbings and evacuations. Then, too, the waters are never really external to the sponge; they are "posited" there as an ideal medium for the purpose of being absorbed or rejected in interesting, curious, and novel ways.

Romantic idealism, in its preoccupation with the self and experience, very deliberately refused to recognize Kant's fundamental distinction of Pure and Practical Reason. What *is* and what *ought* to be the postulates and system of knowledge and the postulated system of action, understanding, and willing are but different ways in which the self seeks to interpret experience. Kant had asked how we interpret the meaning of experience. Fichte asked what *is* the meaning of experience. Kant never explained why reason or science works, and why men construct systematic accounts of experience. Fichte asked these questions and concluded that all reason is practical; all knowledge and all thinking contributes to our striving. The world exists to be conquered, and this is the meaning of life and of the world. We are free in striving, in impulses and thrusts (*anstösse*) of self-consciousness, awareness, and action. We are free in the world of nature and causality and sense (which Kant had denied) because the natural world is "my world"; I make it and fix it. Thus, it is man who gives meaning and value to experience; and he does this by and through his striving. "I create God every day," said Fichte. And he would have argued that subatomic particles were not "real" before the twentieth century; they are "real" because of the theories and efforts of contemporary physicists.

When the wall between Pure and Practical Reason, so earnestly and carefully set up by Kant, is obliterated, the consequences are rather novel and surprising. Kant built the wall to protect moral experience from a confusion, from mixing with natural science, for it should then have to compete as an illusion with scientific facts. The romantic idealists, equally concerned with the reality of values and moral experience, saw no need for this separation. In addition, they felt that Kant's own ethic, with its universal rational law, and the stern corollaries or commands of duty derived from it, was itself a kind of Newtonianism imposed upon the will of man. However, even one chink in the wall, as in the story of Pyramus and Thisbe, promised trouble. In these circumstances one could leave well enough alone, or forsake Kant entirely, or bring the wall down and begin rebuilding the system from the inside.

This last alternative was taken by the idealists. They continued to find profoundly true Kant's claim that the understanding does not derive its laws from, but prescribes them to, nature. But understanding is not scientific reason (it is not *mere* "understanding" as Jacobi, we shall notice below, dubbed scientific thought); it is Reason which includes in it faith, will, vital impulses, and intuitive truths expressed in symbols and ideals. As for Kant's argument that attempts to derive knowledge of matters of fact from thought alone result in antinomies and contradictions, this was radically reinterpreted and given a new meaning. The idealists, Fichte and Schelling, projected these antinomies of thought into the very fabric of experience and facts. Life, the world, and all existence, they held, are driven through with paradoxes and contradictions. Experience, the material for striving, is a field of clashing forces of oppositions and polarities. This romantic translation of Kant's doctrine of antinomies into a description of reality was absorbed into a new kind of rationalism under Hegel. There the paradoxical character of experience receives restatement as the dialectical pattern of historical and developmental processes.

After 1806, the German defeat at Jena, *striving* took a new direction for Fichte and romanticism. Instead of striving for the sake of striving, the new ideal became the German Nation. Nationalism began to stimulate and offer a mysterious floating ideal to romantic cravings. The Nation and the State recommended themselves as powerful ideals to a philosophy that felt called by the future and was bent on explaining not just German professors, but Man. Very easily the idea of an immediate and empirical *self* was demarcated from the idea of the realized "true" Self. The former was the individual person, moving in time and subject to the peculiar local conditions of historical experience; but the latter was the ideal, the universal Self, namely, the State, which is the goal toward which all individual selves strive as they seek to converge into one Humanity.

Fichte's doctrine of striving has a parallel enunciation in the greatest poem of romanticism, Goethe's *Faust*. Faust at first yearns for the all-important apple of the romanticists' eye, *experience*—all experience. Knowledge he has, but it brings no comfort. He has studied everything only to learn nothing, or rather, he is brought to recognize the vanity and vacuity of sheer learning and of science. He is wiser than other pedagogues only in this painful discovery of what that Faustian figure of the Renaissance, Nicholas Cusanus, called "learned ignorance"—a discovery, as it happens, not remarkably original. It is a recurrent theme in Hellenistic thought, in the skepticism of medieval theologians, and in the humanism of the Renaissance, where it finds utterance in Petrarch, Erasmus, and Montaigne, and even, if for a moment, in Descartes. Faust's conclusion that "we know nothing finally" is the prelude to Descartes's *Meditations*, although that prelude leads to an un-Faustian quest of intellectual certainty and the source of scientific knowledge.

Knowledge, however, is far too meager sustenance for Goethe's hero. His yearning spirit has already felt the truth of the Devil's wisdom that "grey is all theory, and green the golden tree of life."[2] That insight has dawned on Faust when, at the beginning of the drama, he, like a scholarly Luther, has decided to translate the Bible. After several starts, he renders the first line of Genesis according to John as: "In the beginning was the Deed!"[3] *Logos*, the Word, or for the Greeks, articulate reason, is for the romantic temperament, *action*! Faust's quest for experience, aided by magic and under a lasting symbol of beauty, leads him through the world of violence and love and through the classical world as well. Eventually he learns that it is not just experience—certainly not experience swallowed compulsively and without discrimination, or taken in passively as one might play with a kaleidoscope—that answers to his restless soul. It is not the content of experience but the striving for it that counts, and this is the controlled acquisition of experience under the imposition of some ideal. Existence then becomes a deed. Man, aspiring for some ideal, is bound to err, but in erring is led to the one true way, says the Lord.[4] Faust discovers that "He only deserves freedom and life, who must daily win them anew."[5]

Faust's long life and dramatic encounter with experience teaches him two hard-won lessons—each the turbulent *Sturm und Drang* confirmation in life of a less lively lecture from Kant: thought without experience is empty and vain—this led Faust into the world. On the other hand, experience without thought (that is, without rational ideals and faith) is blind and purposeless. It is this that romanticism had trouble learning. Faust's final heroic efforts, ending with his deliverance into the higher atmosphere of romantic salvation, do exhibit something approaching an ideal aim: the aim of a creative artist prompted to leave some image of himself in nature, some personal signature of will and intuition impressed upon

---

[2] *Faust*, Part I, scene iv, lines 2038–39.
[3] Part I, scene iii, line 1237.
[4] Prologue in Heaven.
[5] Part II, Act V, scene v, lines 11575–76. But also V.vii. 11936–37, Angels:
> "Wer immer strebend sich bemüht
> Den Können wir erlösen."

"Who ever aspiring, strives on, him we can redeem." Goethe put these lines in quotation marks to emphasize their importance. He said to Eckermann (June 6, 1831) that in these lines lay the key to Faust's salvation.

things and so transforming them. Faust's artistic impulse is characteristically directed to what the Greeks regarded as the master art, statecraft, the organization and administration of a nation. Aristotle called it the architectonic art. Faust's efforts in establishing a new community, namely, Holland, are not marked with success. But, again, it is the effort, striving, the errant but ever assertive ambassador of unsatisfied will, that really matters and is man's salvation.

Perhaps the best way to recapitulate and capture the mutable character of romantic idealism is to remember Locke's theory of property. Locke's conception of property is highly individualistic and almost unintelligible in an industrialized society of factories, absentee ownership, capital investments and goods, banks, and the division of labor. But his disdain for these developments is shared by later romanticism. In addition to one's person, says Locke, the labor of one's body and work of one's hands are properly ours; and "whatsoever then he removes out of the state that nature has provided and left it in, he has mixed his labor with, and joined it to something that is his own, and thereby makes it his property."[6] Man creates property by mixing his labor with the things of nature and joining these to himself. Property is a kind of extension of one's self into nature through labor. Now romantic idealism is a translation of this theory to the workings of reason and imagination. Through its exercise of symbols and ideals, the self mixes its labor with the world, joins experience to ideals, and thereby makes of the world its own property. Thus the transcendental ego, or the will, with its ideals, creates and infuses value into the world of possible experience to produce some image of itself.

But how is the Self guided in this artistic creation to achieve noble works of property? By faith, feeling, an immediate deliverance of intuition, subjective but far more "certain" than logical reasoning. Jacobi (1743–1819), an influential spokesman for this view, called this wellspring of intuitive truth "Faith" (Glaube) but later spoke of it as "Reason" (Vernunft), much to the confusion of his followers, and contrasted the latter "Reason" with scientific reasoning, which he called "Understanding" (Verstand)—usually, mere Understanding. This view that Reason (or Faith) is to be set off from mere Understanding as the source of profound rational inspirations is followed by Coleridge, Carlyle, and Emerson, as well as by Schelling and Hegel and, later, by Bergson.

§ 15.   The Romantic Protest and New Idealism

Kant's critical reaction to the early eighteenth-century ideal of Science as Reason (the sweep of Cartesian and Newtonian science), coupled with his equally critical assessment of German rationalism and British empiricism, led him to a

---

[6] The Second Treatise of Government, ch. 5, sec. 27. And in this connection, see Holmes's account of the views of Kant and Hegel on property in The Common Law, pp. 163–164: "Possession is to be protected because a man by taking possession of an object has brought it within the sphere of his will. He has extended his personality into or over that object. As Hegel would have said, possession is the objective realization of free will."

new comprehensive interpretation of reason and experience. Romanticism was a protest against the early Enlightenment's exclusive preoccupation with the ideal of scientific reason and the obvious inability of that ideal to account for all human experience and all the vicissitudes of human intelligence. This romantic reaction to Reason, or Science, took a wide variety of forms. In some quarters it was thoroughly anti-scientific, lamenting the very existence of science and championing a higher and truer wisdom of intuition and feeling. In others, it was not anti-scientific but simply disinterested in the uses, problems, and results of scientific thought. In general, either as an outright protest against science or a renewal of interest in non-scientific matters, or as both, romanticism exhibited a marked departure from excessive philosophic rationalism and from science, and a revival of moral, literary, aesthetic, and religious pursuits.

The romantic reaction to the early eighteenth century resembles that of Socrates to Greek natural philosophy or of Hellenism to earlier Greek thought, or the reaction of the Renaissance to the medieval tradition. Kant's thought was influenced by this romantic protest, and his philosophy was, in turn, the matrix of most of the later developments of romanticism. For he not only served to articulate the romantic attitudes, clarifying and organizing them; within the province of pure reason, he provided the chief intellectual justification of the romantic outlook. By providing the rational ground, he liberated, encouraged, and directed what before had been *felt* in romanticism. Reason made faith rational; ethics, art, religion were subject matters not of scientific knowledge but regulative ideas of reason—resulting, nonetheless, in transcendental rather than constitutive "truth."

Romantic idealism, we have had occasion to see, is a philosophy that prizes diversity. It speaks for many kinds of experience and exhorts us to many kinds of action in willing the future. It can be portrayed as an essentially youthful philosophy: wonderfully vital if sometimes painfully awkward, sensitive and attentive to the nuances of existence while courageously bent upon finding new worlds to conquer. Its conception of those eternal philosophic idols, the True, Good, and Beautiful, would have Faust's will working upon Kant's Understanding in the person and life of a Byron or Napoleon. It is a philosophy that easily lends itself to ridicule when it attempts to be, at one and the same time, revolutionary in the sphere of action and profoundly sagacious in contemplation. Such was the case when its doctrines, so utterly out of place and alien in spirit to the circumstances, were propounded by professors of philosophy in German lecture halls.

This pejorative portraiture will not do, however, for two reasons. It leaves us unable to explain how such a philosophic outlook could ever have been seriously entertained and believed. Furthermore, in treating this philosophy in the spirit of William James's maxim, that to study the abnormal is the best way of understanding the normal, as if one were patiently and clinically translating the witless discourse and gestures of a madman, is to be blinded to what is sober, eminently sane, and lasting in romantic idealism.

Let us rather take note of the fact that this critical reaction to the eighteenth-century ideal of Reason as Science, this view of the plural character of experience and interpretive ideals, this affirmation of the practical function of thought in which ideas are invitations to will and action—all led to a new emphasis upon experimentalism in reason and action, upon a certain open-mindedness in intellectual matters, and upon the notions of growth and development of subject matters in time, and the conviction that no set of facts is completely known or exhaustively analyzed. The *ideal* (the regulative idea) of complete knowledge, of "the last analysis," remains only an efficacious principle of practice. There is always the possibility of something more, something not yet understood in our philosophizing over experience. In short, the injunctions and frame of mind which we now think of as typically scientific in spirit and procedure were ushered into modern thought by romanticism. Almost by accident these unscientific thinkers helped to shape some of the most fundamental and characteristic ideas in contemporary attempts to think about modern science.

Kant, we saw earlier, (§ 11) began his great critical philosophy of knowledge with the question of how to make the fact of scientific knowledge intelligible. He asked how this fact was to be explained and understood, not whether we in fact do possess such knowledge. This he took for granted. Raising this question is to ask, in the Kantian philosophy, how it is that men are able to apply concepts to experience and attain knowledge. Or, how does it happen that man's conceptualization when brought to the data of his sensory fare with the world results in knowledge? Idealist philosophers influenced by studies of biological evolution in the nineteenth century—studies readily assimilable into the idealistic dialectic of historical and social change (organic and evolutionary theories going back to Leibniz, Lessing, and Herder)—began to suggest answers. The pattern of Reason, the conceptual structure that man brings to experience, is an evolving organization of habits and adjustments relating to experience over a long period of trials and errors through a process of biological adaptation. The nineteenth century also had a social answer to the question: the conceptual scheme of reason and science constitutes the way—and the agreed upon method—by which a community of men talk about and deal with experience. The scientific system for understanding things is a communal adaptation which has proved itself successful in furthering the wants and satisfactions of the community in the world. This is a Hegelian view of the system of reason, one aspect of *Vernunft*, partly revealed in nature, but more clearly manifested in human history.

In either case, these accounts of how man learns and succeeds in knowing do not separate Pure and Practical Reason as Kant had done. The emphasis here is upon Reason as a technique of human survival and a means to anticipated experiences in the future. As Fichte put it: "We act not because we know, but we know because we are called upon to act: the practical reason is the root of all reason."[7]

[7] *The Vocation of Man*, "Faith," pp. 98–99.

§ *16.*   *Fichte and Unstiffening Kantian Theory*

The Kantian philosophy of science, worked out not as a fixed structure of reason given once for all but in the light of biological evolution, leads into the pragmatism of James. The laws which the understanding prescribes to nature become "unstiffened," to use James's expression;[8] these are the deposits, the accumulations of the tried experience of the race; a priori principles and propositions are not the transcendental products of reason reflecting upon itself, they are proposals, fairly regular and successful ways of ticketing and organizing experienced data and serving as cues for future actions and continued organization. James says: "Our fundamental ways of thinking about things are discoveries of exceedingly remote ancestors, which have been able to preserve themselves throughout the experience of all subsequent time. . . . All our theories are *instrumental*, are mental modes of *adaptation* to reality."[9]

The Hegelian view of science and the activity of knowing as a social institution was the basis for Peirce's theory of the communal nature of scientific inquiry and of Dewey's instrumentalism.

In important respects these anticipations of pragmatism derive as much from Fichte (1762–1814) as they do initially from Kant. For Fichte directed attention to the idea of thought, or reason, as a function of the self, the ego; and ways in which thought represented the world and experience were ultimately derived from the needs of the ego to express itself and to render consciousness—or conscious experience—stable, coherent, and ideally satisfying to the self. (The satisfactory interpretation of experience must remain an "ideal" only, for actual satisfactions can occasion a suspension of striving, and this is the great sin in Fichte's philosophy.)

In the thought of every philosopher we can find something to praise and something to condemn—relative, of course, to our own critical demands and predilections. Fichte's philosophizing runs to extremes: what is bad gets very, very bad, and what is good gets lost. What is "bad" in this case is the intrepid and rashly self-preoccupied and demanding egotism; and egotism commencing in a state of self-discovery, as it posits itself. This is a kind of public solipsism, which would be a contradiction in terms but for Fichte's announced use of *the* Self (or Ego) to mean all selves.[10] From this initial posit, by soliloquizing thrusts

---

[8] For the context, see the early pages of § 76.

[9] *Pragmatism*, p. 194.

[10] Fichte often seems to be a solipsist, but his commitment to the self, at the start of his philosophizing, does not mean *him*self. Thus, see the last paragraph of his Foreword to *The Vocation of Man*. The propensity in German philosophy to hypostatize nouns, e.g., to speak not of egos, states, wills, and ideals, but rather of the Ego, the State, the Will, and the Ideal, is one that has bred some nefarious and fantastic speculations purporting to be transcriptions of literal facts. But in this instance the same propensity saves Fichte from an otherwise ridiculous and helpless solipsism. Without it his philosophy would be no more

of consciousness, the ego "posits" or creates the world, the Non-ego. Then begins the succession of further thrusts in which the ego wrestles with Non-ego, culminating in an arrogant and fanatical nationalism in which the ego is German and its goal is to establish a German nation—the created God—in which individuality, free will, and foreign influences will be annihilated. This is the Fichte of the *Addresses to the German Nation*, whose totalitarian enthusiasms have repelled many non-German readers, some Germans, and the victims of that nightmare reality that took the place of the philosopher's dream.

There is another side to Fichte's thought, not detachable in every detail from the former—for he was not two independent philosophers—but capable of extensions that do not embody this reckless and repellent idealism and disastrous social theory. This is the Fichte who argues that knowledge begins in an act of immediate perception, an awareness, or consciousness of oneself as a passing of sensations and feelings. These immediate impressions are the raw data of philosophic analysis; and Fichte's analysis proceeds to distinguish the occurring data and the consciousness of the data. For the data to occur one must be conscious; but then, one's being conscious *and* the data of consciousness are theoretically distinguishable. Fichte puts this in various ways, for he seems to have had trouble with it, and as the first step in the conscious construction of self, knowledge, and the world, it is important. Roughly, the first step consists in delineating these two items of immediate awareness: (1) being aware that one (or something, or "oneself") is aware; (2) being aware of some data.[11] Here the first posits are made. From (1) we posit the ego, and from (2) we are led to posit the data of consciousness—the field of "immediate knowledge"—and from thence to posit things—the field of "mediate knowledge," the supposed objects our immediate data represent. Still the world and particular objects in it are extensions of our consciousness, posits that follow from posits in successive emanations from the self.[12]

Thus Fichte attempts to explain how our notions of self and the world evolve from a state of "pure experience" where *experience* is taken to be immediate consciousness, a substratum, it should be noticed, from which all other "objects" (self, data, and the world of things) are derived as constructions or posits. These are the interpretations we put upon the material of consciousness, tagging, sift-

---

than a record of private injunctions or entertainments, like the reminders we leave for ourselves on scraps of paper commencing with "Do tomorrow," or as if a man were to occupy himself sending out self-addressed postcards saying, "Having a fair time, but hope to improve things here—trust that you are striving to do the same—let's get together soon —I am always, Yours." By *the* Ego Fichte did not mean Johann Gottlieb Fichte, born 1762, deceased 1814. Otherwise, see Russell's brief and devastating critique in *Power*, p. 259.

11 "The immediate consciousness of yourself, and of your own determinations, is therefore the imperative condition of all other consciousness; and you know a thing only in so far as you know that you know it. . . ." *The Vocation of Man*, p. 37.

12 "Strictly speaking, you have no *consciousness of things*, but only a *consciousness* (produced by a passage from your actual consciousness by means of the principle of causality) *of a consciousness of things*. . . ." *Ibid.*, p. 51.

ing, and apportioning out of this raw presentational flux how and what we will into assertions of "red" or "sweet," "real" or "illusory," "subjective" or "objective," and the like. But this flux, this *given*, does not come ordered or classified for us. The given becomes ordered in our act of taking it; and knowledge is an interpretive *taking* of the given. No structure, no Kantian thing-in-itself (albeit unknown) lies in or behind the given to affect or assist our interpretive efforts. The thing-in-itself is either thought, in which case it is a thing of ourself, or unthought, in which case it is not anything at all.[13]

But what ruling considerations work to effect, shape, and determine our posits and conceptual interpretations of pure experience? Why are certain constructions and assertions to be preferred over other possible ones? How, of many variant ways available to us, are we to take the given? Fichte's answer to these questions about what would ordinarily be said to be the "truth" of our interpretations of experience is twofold.

In the first place, the idea of an independent order of reality external to our conceptualizing—or consciousness—is itself only an idea. We cannot go outside of our interpretative scheme, our categories and posits, to see if indeed it does truly represent reality. For Fichte, this is impossible; it would require our going outside of consciousness, or, really, going out of our minds. We are, then, doomed to remain within the framework of our own making in taking and dealing with the given (the framework of our thinking about our thinking about things). Metaphysically, and this is Fichte's subjectivism, there is no outside reality anyway. For logically, and this is his appeal to a pragmatic rationale, the notion of reality outside of all consciousness can have no practical or verifiable consequences whatever. But though doomed to remain within the framework of his thinking, man is nonetheless free to order, revise, and expand his interpretive activity, seeking to illuminate, enrich, and even discover and anticipate increasingly more of consciousness, the flux of pure experience. Our categories and posits, our methods of representing experience—including the procedure of science—will be subject to criteria exercised critically over any of the parts and over all of the whole; namely, of the serviceability of thought to satisfy what we want and need and care about.

Viewing the standards of thought as judged by their capacity to serve our needs introduces the second part of Fichte's answer to the question of truth. Knowledge, he holds, is no isolated deployment of human energy and resources. Rather, in its very function and structure, it is organically a part of the central directive of the self. It is through and through a means, an auxiliary, of a more serious calling—that of impulse, sensibility, and will, and, of course, of action. "Your vocation is not *to know*, but to *act* according to your knowledge," writes Fichte.

[13] "All attempts to conceive of an absolute connection between things *in themselves* and the *I in itself*, are but attempts to ignore our own thought—a strange forgetfulness of the undeniable fact that we can have no thought without having thought it." *Ibid.*, p. 74. The thing *in itself*, Fichte adds, is a thought, namely, the great thought which no man has yet thought.

"Your action, and your action alone, determines your worth."[14] It is the human self, the whole responsive organism as a moving and driven network of felt deficiencies and judged inadequacies, but also of a Will to completion and a higher unification of the self with other selves, that gives a purpose and practical moral direction to all of our activities. Momentary states of consciousness, the given itself, all reflexes and assertions fall into place as subsidiary phases in this single, orchestrated address of the self to its own chosen obligation—the free and complete merging of two orders, the spiritual which is willed, and the sensuous in which deeds are acted.[15] From thence, man enters into the eternal life of infinite reason,[16] and into the mystery and glory of the ideal of ultimate self-realization in God.

Into those esoteric and inspired climes of what Fichte calls *Faith* we here cannot, and need not, try to enter. It is enough to have taken note of the thoroughly voluntaristic, practical, and purposive character of thought and imagination, as Fichte views it, in behalf of the self, half-immersed in the vicissitudes of experience, half-captured with an ideal of eternal union and oneness,[17] and both halves converging in the activity of life.

Fichte's doctrine of pure experience (or consciousness of presented data), and the controlling motives and norms that function in our interpretations of experience have a detectable route into a number of modern philosophies of experience and knowledge. Two lessons drawn from Kant provide the material of a vigorous transformation at the center of Fichte's new philosophy of man. First, the given, pure sense experience as it occurs and is noted, is not knowledge. It is, we might say, the stuff of knowledge, but it becomes knowledge only when the self has acted to give it form. In this interpretive activity sense presentations become informed; the act is literally the condition under which *stuff* becomes *information*.

The view that pure experience, prior to conceptualization, is accordingly neutral to all distinctions—is neither subjective nor objective, real nor unreal— and that physical and mental attributions of experience are composed or constructed *from* this given, rather than being given, was developed in different ways by J. F. Herbart (1776–1841), Avenarius (1843–1896), Renouvier (1815–1903), Mach (1838–1916); the pragmatists, Peirce and James (§ 27); and to some extent by Vaihinger. It should be added that, historically, Berkeley had very carefully stated an earlier version of this doctrine. For Berkeley immediate sense qualities (i.e., *ideas*) do not constitute knowledge until the mind discovers the ways in which single qualities are regular signs of other qualities. Knowledge is of the order of experience, of how given data imply other data and how what is perceived signifies something else to be perceived.[18]

[14] *Ibid.*, pp. 83–88, in Book III, "Faith."
[15] See *ibid.*, Book III, sec. 3, pp. 124 ff.
[16] See *ibid.*, Book III, sec. 3, pp. 124–127.
[17] *Ibid.*, Book III, sec. 4, p. 135.
[18] See Appendix 5 below.

But, to return to Fichte, if we should happen to will and require scientific knowledge, then the transcendental expression of this demand might well appear in the utilitarian strategy of conceptual conveniences and "shorthand" devices for ordering and condensing our otherwise truant and disorderly experience, all in the spirit of Mach.[19] On the other hand, what might be demanded is some sense of the moral diversity and richness of experience, something in which we can believe, and faith that satisfies and fulfills the dreaming, desiring, animate man. Then the transcendental method will be bent on producing a consistent and forceful idealized version of reality, one that "works" by awakening our hopeful aspirations, and leads us to act as if it were true, which, in the sphere of action, justifies and confirms its truth, quite in the tenor of Renouvier and William James.

The other Kantian lesson, absorbed and accordingly transformed by Fichte, is that of the transcendental method (§ 8 and § 11 above). In Fichte's bold renovation, that method is no longer conceived of as an inviolate intellectual process by which the understanding, furnished with purely rational and universally necessary principles, draws its grid over experience and grinds out order. The intellectual machinery assigned by Kant to this task is austere, recondite: the very essence of a determined and laboring Reason.

Kant's style calls up the image of a Prussian academician, the scholar who gives his orders to the "facts" and commands his subject matter like a field marshal. We see the figure bent over the battle map of experience, veined and flushed with cerebral straining to deliver the transcendental strategy for the invasion of the world of sense. In content, quite apart from the style, what Kant says in his analysis of transcendental reason is often tentative in spirit, lacks the air of finality, and reveals the experimental character of the conclusions he has drawn.

Fichte, with more romantic and revolutionary zest, abjures the transcendental apparatus of Reason, as we have seen earlier, and with it he rejects Kant's style. His idiom is direct, even brash, when he is most effective; it is least so and nearly unintelligible when he tries to engage in technical dialectics over the ego and the law of identity. But it is a part of this very directness, as the untechnical and moralizing idealist who converts the logical mechanism of Reason into a vital expression of the self as a function of moral interests, Will, and the struggle for self-expression and "freedom" in power and action, that Fichte's influence has been felt in modern philosophy. One can find it disseminated, directly or indirectly, in Schopenhauer, Nietzsche, Bergson, Renouvier (and through him) William James, and in several current versions of existentialism.

What may be taken as sound and of lasting value in the philosophy of Fichte has, we observed before, been obscured by the conspicuously less admirable

[19] It was Karl Pearson who described science as a conceptual "shorthand" for rendering our otherwise long-winded soliloquizing over sensible experience. But the best statement of the notion as a ruling ideal of conceptual economy is by Mach.

popular form to which he was given to philosophizing for the German nation. That his influence has been recognized, if not carefully studied, is evident enough from some of the more severe denunciations of pragmatism as a Fichtean revival of irresponsible egotism, fanatical will, and social power. What gives the denunciation an apparent plausibility is its grain of truth. For some currents of what passed as "pragmatism" in Europe[20] and some of the conceptions of William James's pragmatism expounded by his disciples (again, mostly outside of America), which James tolerantly and too flexibly welcomed "into the fold," were indeed Fichtean revivals. Furthermore, there is, we saw, a connection between Fichte's critical reaction to Kant, his doctrine of pure experience, the role of conceptualization as a manipulation of experience and a guide to action, the activity of will and interest in the function and forms taken by thought, and the pragmatism of Peirce, James, Dewey, Mead, and C. I. Lewis. This historical connection, however, while significant, does not warrant the scorn and deplorable consequences visited upon pragmatism for its associations with Fichte.

What is bad in Fichte and what is thoroughly misunderstood about pragmatism seem to have been destined for one another. But this misalliance, or the erroneous impressions it has encouraged of what pragmatism is and is meant to be, will become clearer in the chapters that follow. Perhaps, as we become clearer about what pragmatism is, some of the more ill-conceived impressions of it may be dispelled.

§ 17.   The Nineteenth Century[21]

Intellectually, the nineteenth century exhibited a greater complexity of scope and resources than preceding centuries had. There are several reasons for this. For one, it came handsomely endowed with what the energetic eighteenth-century thinkers had created. The nineteenth drew upon this inheritance—but it also proceeded to uncover further riches. The art and practice of history which the Enlightenment had stimulated and the romantic movement in Germany eagerly extended into an imaginative rediscovery of classical Greek culture became a powerful scholarly industry in the nineteenth century with its center in Germany. The dominant philosophy of the century, Hegelian idealism, is the very enactment of this historical spirit.

A new sense of the importance of time, which carried the nineteenth-century mind back into history to look for the present and future and to discover how thought and culture "progress," was only one factor in this complex intellectual age. There was also an expansion in space; new nations and cultures—America, Russia, the oriental East—made contributions to European thought. And, of

---

[20] For which, see Part III below.
[21] This sketch of some aspects of nineteenth-century thought is resumed in later pages; cf. particularly § 63 and Appendix 1.

course, the great European nations began to engage in exporting to their colonies European habits in exchange for material goods—a process called "civilizing the native," who received bullets, missionaries, and European clothes in return for markets, his labor, and the resources of his homeland. Still, on top of the "white man's burden" there was some exchange of ideas in the imperialistic expansion of the later nineteenth century.

We must also recall the agricultural and industrial revolutions of the nineteenth century spreading outward from England. Mechanized production meant far more than a new realization of man's power over nature. In England it was not only expressed in the factory system with its division of labor and techniques of mass production, but also reflected in the rapid growth of "social sciences" such as history, economics, and sociology, all thoroughly indebted to that most useful and spreading branch of learning: statistics. British utilitarianism was a very clear attempt to work out a mechanical philosophy of human happiness and a statistically grounded version of the Good in an industrial society. It was in England, too, that mechanical models in scientific theorizing were most championed and that technological skills, industrial invention, and scientific theory converged, far more so than in the eighteenth century, to produce new combinations. Thus the scientific theory of electricity brought forth an industry; and the industrial use of steam machinery helped create the science of thermodynamics.[22]

The historical and social facts of expanding industrial economics, the growth of imperial powers, and progress in scientific knowledge during the nineteenth century accompany the popularity of the categories of *expansion, growth,* and *progress* in the thought of most intellectuals of the period.

The fundamental idea in the mind of most men, and seemingly the philosophic core of these other categories, was *continuity.* The nineteenth century saw, or thought it saw, continuity everywhere and in all things, in mathematics and physics, in biological evolution, in culture, and in history. And here, too, statistics proved handy, for statistical methods and probabilities seemed to provide ways in which apparently discontinuous and discrete subject matters could be dealt with as "really" continuous. Hegel, and the philosophers most influenced by him, proceeded to enunciate and champion—not always very clearly—the continuity, even amid conflicts, of reality and thought in all of their manifestations. Darwinian evolution, when it came, despite the protests of theological proponents of discrete and special creations, was heralded as one more inevitable confirmation of continuity, this time in the growth and development of living creatures in changing environments.

The Darwinian "revolution," as it is sometimes called, dates from the publication of the *Origin of Species* in 1859. But in both piety to the author of that epochal work and the interest of accuracy, it should rather be called the Dar-

[22] The illustration is drawn from Pledge, p. 149. For some reflections on this theme in pragmatism see § 22 and Appendix 1 below.

winian evolution. For while the impact of Darwin's book had the rest of the century talking the language of development and survival, and while that impact marks a truly revolutionary change in man's understanding and analysis of himself and nature, Darwin did not create this revolution by himself and suddenly in 1859. The leading ideas of evolution had been suggested, speculated upon, and gaining acceptance for about a century. Darwin selectively and systematically reformulated the speculative notion into a scientific theory and supported it with a great mass of evidence. The concepts of the struggle for existence and the survival of the fittest make up a second part of the theory and serve as explanatory hypotheses (or "laws") to account for the course and variations of forms in the evolution of life from a common ancestry. But here, too, Darwin made use of a number of existing ideas, in particular, Malthus' theory of population;[23] and his exposition of the conditions under which species compete for survival is in many striking respects like the laissez-faire doctrines of English and French economists, and like seventeenth-century philosophizing over the origins of society from a freely competitive state of nature. The immediate and almost universal acceptance that Darwin's theory had on its appearance is in large part understandable for just these reasons: by the middle of the nineteenth century, most intellectuals were already predisposed to its main themes.

Like all major scientific achievements, Darwin's work was the subject of many popularizations. And like Newton's *Principia* in the seventeenth century or Einstein's theory of relativity in our own, Darwin's book was thought to supply scientific answers to any number of pressing philosophic questions. The lay reader has an easier time with Darwin than with either Newton or Einstein. But inventively interpreted and explained, as was the case late in the century and still today, Darwin's views can be made to yield quite a variety of answers. A veritable plethora of philosophic speculations of utterly incompatible content have claimed an origin and verification in Darwinism.

This is the other reason for the popular reception of Darwin's theory: it was made to mean many different things to many differing interests. It could be brought to the defense of various tendencies of romanticism in which life is depicted as a struggle and experience as a process of development; Goethe's interests in biology had already given prestige to the language of growth and organic unity. The romantic interest in heroic individuals could be viewed as anticipating the mechanism of evolution working in a species to produce the

---

[23] As Darwin puts it: "As more individuals are produced than can possibly survive, there must in every case be a struggle for existence, either one individual with another of the same species, or with the individuals of distinct species, or with the physical conditions of life. It is the doctrine of Malthus applied with manifold force to the whole animal and vegetable Kingdoms." *Origin of Species*, ch. 4, first paragraph of the section, "Geometrical Rate of Increase." Cf. also the concluding pages of his Introduction.

It is worth noting, incidentally, that Charles Peirce had detected the connection between Malthus' and Darwin's theories before Darwin made this acknowledgment. See *CP* 5.364, note 1.

most "fit" individuals in the future.[24] The philosophies of Fichte and Hegel were easily read into Darwin's theory; for example, as a young man in his thirties, John Dewey had developed (in 1893) a thoroughly Hegelian version of Darwinian evolution and the hypothesis of the survival of the fittest.[25]

Primarily as a result of Darwin's success, the notions of organic growth and biological organisms and processes began to be taken as fundamental to the scientific analysis of natural contexts and the conditions of change.[26] This outlook, and something like a reversion to Leibniz, eventually found its way into theoretical physics to replace the more mechanical and atomistic viewpoint of the eighteenth century. At the same time Darwinian concepts of struggle and survival were applied in political history to analyze the clashes of national powers and the "organic evolution" of large states.

One respect in which speculation was stimulated by the doctrine of evolution is reminiscent of the view of Fichte concerning the practical character of human thought. By a somewhat tenuous but possible extension of Darwin, it occurred to some men that human thought and man's conceptual organization of experience is subject to conditions of biological economy and survival of the fittest. Ideas and conceptualization that proved valuable by increasing the chances of man to adapt to and control his environment were to be favored over those that proved useless in the long struggle of human evolution. Thus a kind of Darwinism and vaguely suggestive foreshadowing of pragmatism was applied to the evolution of human thought to explain how and why certain systems of philosophy and scientific theories continued to be "meaningful" or useful while some were discarded as relics of antiquity.

Here, too, there are presentiments of some of James's views concerning the function and evaluation of thought. For when thinking and the organization and "advancement of the brain"[27] is regarded in light of the mechanism of evolution by which man has succeeded in the struggle for survival, standards of *truth* and *good* are determined by conditions of organic utility and evolutionary *uses*. Truth and good are made, or evolve, in the specific struggles of men to establish satisfactory relations with their surroundings (see §§ 26, 31). Such, speculatively, is the Jamesian coloring of Darwinian theory.

To men with different religious interests and convictions Darwinism was made to yield different answers. For some, evolution was regarded as evidence for

[24] Attitudes of hero-worship, or of certain races as "higher types," and some pessimism concerning life in general and man in particular were alike stimulated by Darwin's now often forgotten subtitle to *On the Origin of Species*, viz., *The Preservation of Favoured Races in the Struggle for Life.*

[25] See Appendix 1 below.

[26] Thus Charles Peirce's comment about the great questions that occupied the nineteenth century: "*the* question that everybody is now asking, in metaphysics, in the theory of reasoning, in psychology, in general history, in philology, in sociology, in astronomy, perhaps even in molecular physics, is the question *How things grow.*" *CP* 7.267n., and below, Appendix 1, last paragraph.

[27] The phrase is Darwin's, *Origin of Species*, ch. 5, the second paragraph of the section, "On the Degree to which Organization Tends to Advance."

belief in a purpose and goal for the universe. Evolution thus exhibited God's way of ordering life. To some, evolution was God. To others, Darwin had shown there was no God, evolution had taken his place. To still others, the acceptance of evolution was thought an occasion of stoic or romantic despair. Human life was shown to be but a momentary and accidental product of vast and aimless powers. The wages of life is death; man who has ruthlessly advanced to his place in the scale of evolution will just as ruthlessly be eliminated by a more vigorous species.

Darwin himself ended on a very optimistic note, although he may have been partly attempting to gain favor for the theory by offering a reassuring message to his readers:

> We may look with some confidence to a secure future of great length. And as natural selection works solely by and for the good of each being, all corporeal and mental endowments will tend to progress toward perfection.[28]

Evolution thus appeared to provide a long-sought answer to the question we have seen taking various historical forms in the course of European philosophic thought: science at last seemed to disclose as well as authenticate the source of human values; enveloped in the natural basis of life was a working and ideal good; change carried implications of perfection. Hume, who had argued so effectively that *ought* cannot be deduced from *is*, and Pope, who had declared that whatever is, is right, were both refuted: evolution "proved" that what will be ought to be, that what is to come is right.

Aside from the pessimistic interpretation and from some exclamations against the brutality of the working of evolution as offensive and shocking to persons of refined sentiments, the Darwinisms did seem to provide many intellectuals with a new faith. Moreover, not since the systems of Descartes and Newton had men been so assured that faith was scientifically grounded, that the facts of evolution confirmed certain moral principles and values. This "scientific faith" was in growth, progress, and an operative perfection in the universe. The new faith, so rosy and robust in the first flush of youth, was destined to be short-lived. European history, culminating in World War I, made the popular appeal of ever-increasing perfection suspect; among the victims of the war was the nineteenth-century belief in progress. But this faith was doomed anyway, not only because of certain theoretical difficulties in Darwinian theory or even more serious philosophical difficulties in the supposition that moral principles and values are "confirmed" by science or by "facts" of nature.[29] The main shortcoming of this faith was the

---

[28] *Ibid.*, the next to final paragraph of the Conclusion.

Russell's comment in *Unpopular Essays*, p. 78: "Bernard Bosanquet, until his death one of the recognized leaders of British philosophy, maintained in his *Logic*, ostensibly on logical grounds, that 'it would be hard to believe, for example, in the likelihood of a catastrophe which should overwhelm a progressive civilization like that of modern Europe and its colonies.' "

[29] The philosophic refutation of this "faith" and the exposure of its chief theoretical error came brilliantly and effectively from G. E. Moore in 1903 in *Principia Ethica*. The error is what Moore called "the naturalistic fallacy." See *Principia Ethica*, ch. 1, and on evolution, especially secs. 30 ff. But for another variation on this theme, see § 90 below.

ease with which it became vitiated and hollow by the very inclusiveness, the indecisive and polyglot uses of the language it so championed: "growth," "progress," "perfection" could be made to mean almost anything. Any one of an indefinite number of fortuitous happenings were classifiable, accordingly, as instances of progress. By meaning anything and finding confirmation in everything, the terms signified nothing. The new scientific faith was a breeder of irrationalism.

Philosophy in the nineteenth century, after Hegel, tended to go two increasingly separate ways. On one side there was a traditional and scholarly pursuit of technical ideas in the universities. Kant and Hegel dominated German thought and gradually that domination spread to France and, in spite of the empiricism of Mill, captured the universities in England as well. Hegel had been the spokesman for the universe; his academic followers were spokesmen for Hegel in the universities. Aside from the empirical and utilitarian philosophy of Mill (1808–1873), the notable leaders of idealism were Lotze (1817–1881), Green, Bradley, and Bosanquet.[30] The influence and position of Lotze is interesting and curious. He is no longer read at all; but in America early in the present century, he was carefully studied. Santayana wrote his doctoral thesis on Lotze, and Dewey made a detailed study of his doctrines. Russell treated his doctrines carefully in *Principles of Mathematics*.

On the other side, distinct from the universities, philosophy was far from inactive. Utilitarianism and, more so, the left-wing Hegelianism of Marx and Engels found a direct and active role in the unacademic problems and social conflicts of an increasingly industrialized and mass society that still aspired to the eighteenth-century ideals of individual freedom, equality, and liberty.

The tendency of academic philosophizing to lose touch with urgent political and social problems and scientific developments of the age meant, of course, that more interesting and important kinds of thinking were taking place outside of philosophy proper than inside. For most intellectuals, forceful, attractive, and sometimes dangerous ideologies proved more inviting than the abstract refinements made by philosophers in the dialectic of idealism and the language of the Absolute. Early in the present century academic philosophy and the reigning idealism went through a severe critical re-evaluation from the inside. The instruments that idealism had helped to develop, logic and a theory of meaning (or a method of analyzing ideas and experience) saw radical changes and new possibilities as a result of developments in mathematics and the natural sciences, especially physics and psychology. And when directed against the philosophy that had once prized them most, these new techniques proved ruinous to the finely spun arguments and supposed proofs upon which that philosophy rested. Moore and Russell conducted the attack upon Bradley in England. In Germany, this critical reaction to idealism was headed by Husserl in *Logische Untersuchungen* (1900) and the work of Meinong. In America, pragmatists and realists joined in a critical effort that not even the ingenious and energetic Royce could

---

[30] For some further comments on these men and the period, see § 63 and Appendix 1 below; on Green in particular, Appendix 1, sec. C.

meet, although Dewey's instrumentalism was never wholly antithetical to idealism, and important conceptual links between the positions of Peirce, Royce, James, and Dewey were obscured but not severed during this critical period. However, for the time being, the great systems of idealism are now but memories of proud and noble works of the past.

§ 18. Conclusion

We have been looking at some of the philosophically more important episodes in the history of a problem, that, broadly stated, of the continuous impacts and reactions generated in European intellectual life by the growth of scientific knowledge since the seventeenth century.

If the culture of Europe since the twelfth century exhibits any one summary fact it is that of change: change in almost every dimension of the scope, resources, and direction of economic activities, and correspondingly rapid changes in the institutional arrangements and organization of society and in social experience. Cultural change is itself the matrix and occasion, the cause and effect of all kinds and varieties of problems: new demands, new experience, new knowledge work against the old to foster the conflicts and alliances, the protests and readjustments that make up the course of philosophic thought.

The problem with which we have been concerned is thus only one out of a multitude presenting themselves in Western philosophy. Yet this problem—the conflict between new knowledge and new kinds of experience and the old, the cultural inheritances, the values and attitudes and modes of interpretation borne from the past—is by its breadth and relevance pertinent to all other more specific intellectual problems that characterize the philosophical outlooks of our changing European civilization.

The object of the present three chapters has been to take note of this problem, its changing character, and the several major kinds of philosophic reactions and developments that have occurred as they have bearing upon philosophy in our own time. This should aid us toward increased understanding of much of our contemporary philosophic thought. For as every previous century, so ours has inherited attitudes and patterns of interpretation by which we respond to the intellectual challenges of our rapidly changing culture and new kinds of experience.

We have the advantage every new generation enjoys over its predecessors: we can, if we are reasonable, profit from the errors and the successes of the past; we have more to go by and more to select from in organizing our intellectual equipment for dealing with our problems. But we suffer from one disadvantage unprecedented in history. The problems we face, and in particular the central issue we have been reflecting upon here and whose emergence we have studied above—the problem of understanding science and developing a responsible and coherent synthesis of science, technology, and human values—is more acute and ominously urgent than ever before. Thus far, having hardly succeeded in this undertaking, we find ourselves in the worst of all possible and most dangerous positions: we improve the instruments and powers of social change and neglect to plan for their uses. The danger is typified very realistically in our awareness of having entered into the "atomic age." Immense effort and scientific thought has been devoted to the technical development of atomic energy, but little or no scientific thought has gone into considering the consequences of this vast enterprise. Meantime, we continue to build atom bombs and some day, presumably, will start to think about the problem of what to do with them.

These somber thoughts are not entirely irrelevant here. As these chapters have been devoted to the history of one main problem in modern philosophy, the chapters to follow are concerned with the history of pragmatism as one modern philosophical movement. It is of some significance that the most important leaders of this movement, Peirce, James, and Dewey, were very much concerned with the problem of the relation of science and ethical values. Peirce's lifelong attempts to construct an architectonic philosophic system were primarily guided by this ideal of a comprehensive theory that would include, as a fundamental part, "normative science" along with natural science and metaphysics.[31] The dream was evidently inspired by the two great and comprehensive philosophic outlooks that Peirce most admired, those of Aristotle and Kant.

Over his long and productive philosophic lifetime, Dewey continued to insist that the conflict between scientific knowledge and morals "is one of the most pressing of contemporary problems" (see § 35).

The seventeenth-century problem of knowledge, with which we started, and these brief references to current questions of human power and its uses, with which we conclude, are not unrelated. They are the differently situated patterns woven into the same historical and intellectual cloth. The threads have led us from one pattern of problems to terminate in others. And throughout, as we have seen, the recurring and unifying theme has been successive demands for a philosophy capable of articulating the historically changing forms of significance in man's cultural, moral, and scientific experience. So viewed, as a continuously felt, if changing, cultural demand, philosophy is an attempt to formulate an organized critical expression of the meanings in human experience—clarifying the existent and possible forms of human action—in past experience, in that passing, and in experience to come.

Meaning, action, and *experience* are the crucial terms in which the task of modern philosophy has been conceived and its enterprise carried on. The terms are both crucial and treacherous. In the chapters that follow, we will see how and in what ways these terms initiated a new effort aimed at their analysis and eventuating in the formation of pragmatism as a philosophy of meaning and action.

[31] See Murphey, esp. ch. 17.

AMERICAN
PRAGMATISM

Part Two

We come now to the development of American pragmatism, and will consider in some detail the distinctive efforts of Peirce, James, Dewey, Mead, and Lewis.

These five expressions of pragmatism are in basic agreement on the interpretation of knowledge and on accounting for its function in experience. But there are also differences and important variations in theorizing over the nature of thought and the means or cooperative forms that intelligence supposedly takes in realizing the aims of rational life. These liberal spokesmen for the rational community of men, for intelligence as a social art and good, happened also to be rather solid individualists. There is much that is unique and even radically incommensurable in how these five philosophers viewed their vocation and aims. When the impulses and aspirations of philosophizing become serious, Aristotle's advice is sound: friends and truth are dear, but piety requires us to honor truth above our friends.

If pragmatism acquired its mind and intellectual apprenticeship in European philosophy—and such has been insinuated in Part One and is the contention of later pages—its body and voice were born in New England. For as the biographies that follow show, pragmatism came to light in three Massachusetts men, one Vermonter, and one who, while born in New York City, centered his active life around Harvard. Before turning to the philosophic thought of these men, it may be of interest to survey briefly the *Dramatis Personae*.

CHARLES SANDERS PEIRCE was born in Cambridge, Massachusetts, in 1839.[1] He was the second son of Benjamin Peirce, an eminent astronomer and mathematician and professor of these subjects at Harvard. Of his father Peirce accurately commented: "My father was universally acknowledged to be by far the strongest mathematician in the country. . . ."[2] Charles was a precocious child, showing great interest in puzzles, mathematical games, card tricks, and codes. Among the children he was the favorite, and in turn idolized his father. Benjamin Peirce undertook to educate the children himself in novel and rigorous ways. For example, to teach Charles to concentrate, they played "rapid games of double dummy together from ten in the evening until sunrise, the father sharply criticizing every error."

Pierce entered Harvard College in 1855 and was graduated in 1859, one of the youngest with one of the poorest records in his class. His father looked forward to the boy's pursual of a scientific career, though Peirce had been reading deeply in Kant and in Schiller's *Aesthetische Briefe* as well as in science. After his graduation from college, Peirce spent the next year

---

[1] For much of this account of Peirce's life I follow Paul Weiss, "Charles Sanders Peirce."
[2] For the full passage and sources, see Lieb, p. 37; also Murphey, pp. 12–13.

surveying in Louisiana.[3] In 1861 he became a paid assistant of the United
States Coast Survey, a service in which, while intermittently engaged
in other activities, he remained for thirty years.

In 1862, Peirce married Harriet Melusina Fay, a woman much respected
in Cambridge circles who later became known as a writer and feminist organizer.
And about the same time, Peirce first met William James.

Peirce received his M.A. in 1862 and in 1863 took the Sc.B. degree in
chemistry, *summa cum laude*, the first man to do so in Harvard's history.
In 1864–1865 Pierce lectured on the philosophy of science at Harvard,
although, as he wrote F. E. Abbot (March 17, 1865), "My lectures fell through
for want of an audience." In 1866–1867 he was honored by giving the
Lowell Institute Lectures in Boston, and in 1869–1870 gave a series of
fifteen University Lectures in philosophy.[4] This was a special distinction,
for such luminaries as Bowen, Emerson, and John Fiske were also offering
lectures in this program. In 1871 Peirce founded the Metaphysical Club
(see § 19 below).

These were the years of brilliant promise in Peirce's life. Still in his twenties,
his exceptional gifts had been recognized by Harvard, and no one in
Cambridge doubted that he was headed for acclaim and the highest intellectual
achievements. His father believed that his son would surpass him by becoming
a greater mathematician. In addition to giving occasional lectures on logic,
Peirce was appointed an Assistant at the Harvard Observatory in 1869 and
there made the observations that are contained in his *Photometric
Researches* (1878), the only book of his published during his lifetime.

The year 1875 was an especially bright one in Pierce's life. He sailed
to Liverpool and remained in Europe for almost a year and a half.
On the voyage to Liverpool one of the passengers, W. H. Appleton, offered
to pay well for articles Peirce might contribute to the *Popular Science Monthly*.
Peirce's series, "Illustrations of the Logic of Science," was the eventual response.
The first paper in the series of six, "The Fixation of Belief," appeared
in 1877 (for which, see §§ 20 and 22 below). Pragmatism, although the
name was not used, was launched in this series. In April of the same year Peirce

---

[3] See *CP* 5.64.
[4] In 1867 Peirce read a paper to the American Academy of Arts and Sciences, "On an
Improvement in Boole's Calculus of Logic," *CP* 3.1-19. This was the first of a series of
writings that established him, with Frege, as the greatest logician of his time. As Weiss
summarizes Peirce's accomplishments:
> He radically modified, extended and transformed the Boolean algebra, making it appli-
> cable to propositions, relations, probability and arithmetic. Practically single-handed,
> following De Morgan, Peirce laid the foundations of the logic of relations, the instrument
> for the logical analysis of mathematics. He invented the copula of inclusion, the most
> important symbol in the logic of classes, two new logical algebras, two new systems of
> logical graphs, discovered the link between the logic of classes and the logic of proposi-
> tions, was the first to give the fundamental principle for the logical development of
> mathematics, and made exceedingly important contributions to probability theory, in-
> duction, and the logic of scientific methodology.

Weiss, p. 400. For Peirce's scientific work in astronomy, see the valuable study by Lenzen.

visited Cambridge University and was escorted by James Clerk Maxwell through his new laboratory. Peirce discussed certain ideas about pendulums with Maxwell and found Maxwell in agreement. A month later Peirce received an invitation to attend the Royal Society meetings. He visited with W. K. Clifford and also saw Herbert Spencer. Clifford was supposed to have said later that he thought Peirce was the greatest living logician, the second man (the other being Boole) since Aristotle to add significantly to the subject.[5]

These years of promise never brought a season of achievement, however. Peirce's genius, his superb talents never weakened or deserted him. But an incapacity or disinclination to direct his thought into a permanent form, the published result, seems to have become fixed. The permanent result depends in part on negotiations and dealings with other persons. This was something about which Peirce was both careless and aloof, and he often seems not really to have cared about putting the results of his efforts before an audience. It was enough that *he* knew what he was about and what he could do. In short, the young Peirce had been overassured and overprotected concerning the future outcome of his undoubted abilities. His wife made an acute observation on the factor that was to work tragedy in Peirce's life. In a letter of 1875 she said: "All his life from boyhood it seems as though everything conspired to spoil him with indulgence."[6] As the years passed the promise faded in complications, and young Peirce was to be referred to later as "poor Peirce."

From 1879–1884 Peirce taught at Johns Hopkins. There he seems to have been a popular teacher, with such students as Christine Ladd, Oscar Mitchell, Josiah Royce, John Dewey, Thorstein Veblen, Joseph Jastrow, and Lester Ward. But, for reasons never explained, Peirce was dismissed from Johns Hopkins in 1884. He never again secured an academic position—this despite his obvious abilities and influential friends. However, he gave occasional lectures, among them those at the Lowell Institute in 1892 and 1903.

In these same years Peirce was active in a number of important scientific projects. He was the American delegate to the International Geodetic Conference (1875) and in charge of weights and measures for the United States Coast and Measure Survey (1884–1885). But in 1891 Peirce's active scientific work and career with the government was suddenly brought to a close. Apparently he quarrelled with his superiors in the Coast Survey. He had, by this time, become recognized as a difficult person to work with. His wife left him in 1876, and he divorced her in 1883. Soon after he was remarried to a lady of French descent, Juliette Froissy, Mme. Pourtalai.

In 1887, having inherited a small amount of money, Peirce, then aged forty-eight, retired to Milford, Pennsylvania. He collected a valuable library of scientific and philosophical books. In isolation he wrote upon a philosophical system he called "synechism." But over the years Peirce's financial position worsened. He

[5] See Fisch, "A Chronicle of Pragmaticism," p. 461, for the source.
[6] See Murphey, p. 17, for the source and a discussion of this.

attempted to make up some of the loss by writing reviews for the *Nation*. He also wrote pieces for the *Century Dictionary* and Baldwin's *Dictionary of Philosophy and Psychology*. The loyal William James arranged for him to give occasional lectures. In 1914, in poverty, and suffering from cancer for which he took morphine to allay the pain, Peirce died, "a frustrated, isolated man, still working on his logic, without a publisher, with scarcely a disciple, unknown to the public at large."[7]

Peirce was "a queer being," commented William James. He inspired dislike in some men of high position (such as Eliot, President of Harvard). He became known for an inability to get along with others, for a bad temper, pride, and for being easily affronted. He was also said to have been careless and erratic about hours, social responsibilities, and dress.

There are men who have been ruined by being kept within universities. Pierce was not ruined by being kept out, but he was harmed. For the university was the one place where he could have found active interest and encouragement in his work, and the stimulus of colleagues and of keeping informed of advances in scholarship.[8]

Peirce once made a revealing and moving appraisal of himself and William James: "Who, for example, could be of a nature so different from his as I? He is so concrete, so living; I a mere table of contents, so abstract, a very snarl of twine."[9]

At his death Peirce left a huge collection of manuscripts in more or less fragmentary condition. These were given to Harvard and have been selectively organized and edited in eight volumes as *The Collected Papers of Charles Sanders Peirce*. In attempting to get at Peirce's philosophic thought in these volumes of ambitious but incomplete writings, one is often in a position not unlike Peirce's creditors who came to the Milford house to collect on their bills. Peirce had an attic study accessible only by ladder, and there he retreated to uninterrupted philosophizing by drawing up the ladder behind him.

WILLIAM JAMES was born in New York City in 1842.[10] One of his younger brothers was Henry James (1843–1916), the writer. It once was fashionable to say that Henry wrote novels like a philosopher while his elder brother wrote philosophy like a novelist.

The James's children, in much the same way as the Peirces', were subject to a father's theories concerning the proper course of their formal education. The family moved to Europe, to Albany, New York, and to New York City in the course of a few years, and the children attended a variety of schools. Henry, Sr. regarded the frequent trips to Europe taken by the family as a part of the educational curriculum. Henry, Jr. later described this period as "incorrigible vagueness of current in our educational drift." The family lived, during intervals,

[7] Weiss, p. 403.
[8] This point is well brought out by Gallie, p. 39, and also Murphey, p. 293.
[9] *CP* 6.184.
[10] The source for James's biography is Perry, Vols. I and II, and his "William James."

in Geneva, London, Paris, and Belgium. This educational experiment produced results, not the least of them being William James's complete familiarity with European thought, languages, and literature. For a time William studied to be a painter, attending the atelier of Léon Coigniet in Paris.

In 1861 William James's long connection with Harvard commenced as he entered the Lawrence Scientific School. There he studied chemistry (under Charles W. Eliot), comparative anatomy, and physiology. In 1864 James entered Harvard Medical School, but his studies were interrupted in 1865 when he joined Louis Agassiz' zoological expedition in the Amazon. Through this experience he learned the procedure of making acute firsthand observations, a technique he continued to exercise throughout his life. He also learned that the profession of a field naturalist was not for him. He resumed his studies in medical school but in 1867 went to Europe to recover from ill health and depression, living in Paris, Dresden, and Berlin. This was a period of brooding, of reading in German literature and philosophy, and of "a great efflorescence of his aesthetic interests, stimulated both by galleries and by his general reading."[11]

James returned to Cambridge and received his medical degree in 1868. But during the next year he again suffered from ill health and, especially, depression. In the year 1870 he went through a spiritual crisis: "The spiritual crisis was the ebbing of the will to live, for lack of a philosophy to live by—a paralysis of action occasioned by a sense of moral impotence."[12] The crisis and the first steps of recovery are vividly described by James himself (see below, § 25). He attributed his recovery to reading Renouvier's *Traité de psychologie* (1859), but restoration to full health also came through the start of his teaching career in 1872 and his marriage in 1878.

James was appointed Instructor of Physiology at Harvard in 1872. He taught comparative anatomy, comparative physiology, and hygiene for some ten years. During this time he was responding to new developments in physiology, for he had studied the work of Helmholtz and Wundt earlier when in Germany in 1868. In 1875 he introduced a new graduate course, "Relations Between Physiology and Psychology," which, from 1877 to 1880, was transferred to the department of philosophy. A year later a similar course was introduced for undergraduates, and at the same time he developed a laboratory of psychology. (G. Stanley Hall was a student of James's in 1876–1878 and was later to establish his famous laboratory at Johns Hopkins.) Physiology was exerting a considerable influence upon psychology and so, too, was the thought of Spencer and the general implications of biological evolution, of which James was fully aware. These movements of thought initiated his new course "Philosophy of Evolution," started in 1879.[13]

[11] Perry, I, 237.
[12] Perry, I, 322.
[13] In 1878 James had written a very important paper in determining much of his future thought, "Remarks on Spencer's Definition of Mind as Correspondence." See § 28 below for a discussion of this.

At this time James became increasingly known to European readers through his articles in *Critique Philosophique* and *Mind.* James was in correspondence with many European scholars; his trips abroad and his ingratiating ways made it possible for him to establish warm personal contacts. In 1880 he visited Renouvier in Avignon; in 1882 he saw Mach in Prague and Carl Stumpf. In England he had personal contact with Shadworth Hodgson, George Croom Robertson (editor of *Mind*), Leslie Stephen, Frederick Pollock, Edmund Gurney, and Henry Sidgwick.

In 1890 James's great *Principles of Psychology* was published, central parts of which had been developed earlier in articles. His "Remarks on Spencer's Definition of the Mind" (1878, discussed in § 28 below) is a key to his thought. The articles "Are We Automata?" (1878), "The Spatial Quale" (1879), "The Feeling of Effort" (1880), and "What is an Emotion?" (1884) are important anticipations of James's later philosophic outlook. The last-mentioned paper, his analysis of emotion as our feeling of the organic activities of its expression—we feel sad because we cry, feel happy because we laugh[14]—was also advanced independently in the same year by the Danish psychologist, Lange. The position has since become known as the James-Lange theory of emotions.

James was afflicted with heart trouble and ill health in 1899. His growing reputation took its toll, for he was famous the world over and in constant demand as a lecturer. In 1905 he attended the International Congress of Psychology in Rome. There he met Papini (see below, § 76) and began to realize how famous he had become. James unsuccessfully struggled against fame and its attendant distractions in devoting his last years to a more rigorous and technical exposition of his pragmatic philosophy, a work left unfinished at his death. In 1907 he retired from Harvard, and three years later died in his country home at Chocorua, New Hampshire.

JOHN DEWEY was born in Burlington, Vermont, in 1859. His father was a merchant whose ancestry was traceable back to 1640; his mother was the daughter of a prosperous Vermont farmer. Dewey studied in common schools, attended the University of Vermont, and was graduated from there in 1879.

For the next few years Dewey taught school in Pennsylvania and in general county schools in Vermont. In Burlington he took walks with Professor H. A. P. Torrey, formerly his philosophy teacher in college.[15] Torrey supervised his reading of classics in the history of philosophy, and at this time, Dewey became hopeful of teaching philosophy. While still in college he had been

---

[14] The 1884 paper is reprinted in *Collected Essays and Reviews.* There, p. 247, as well as in his *Psychology*, II, 449, James states his thesis: "that *the bodily changes follow directly* the PERCEPTION *of the exciting fact, and that our feeling of the same changes as they occur* IS *the emotion.* Common sense says, we lose our fortunte, are sorry and weep; we meet a bear, are frightened and run. . . . The hypothesis here to be defended says that this order of sequence is incorrect . . . that the more *rational statement is that we feel sorry because we cry . . . afraid because we tremble. . . .*"

[15] For a further mention of Torrey, see § 63, n. 17 below.

influenced by German philosophy through the writings of Coleridge, the thought of T. H. Green, and the transcendentalism of Emerson—an influence which continued. In 1882 he wrote an essay and sent it to W. T. Harris who, while superintendent of schools in St. Louis, was leader of a Hegelian circle there. Harris was also the editor of the *Journal of Speculative Philosophy*, then the one fully philosophical journal in the United States. In great trepidation Dewey sent his paper to Dr. Harris and asked whether he should go into philosophy as a profession. Harris' response was an important factor in John Dewey's becoming a philosopher, for Harris wrote him that the essay showed a high philosophic mind. The paper appeared in the 1882 issue of the *Journal* as "The Metaphysical Assumptions of Materialism," and subsequently the *Journal* printed two other of Dewey's articles. Thus encouraged, he borrowed five hundred dollars from his aunt and in 1882 entered Johns Hopkins University as a graduate student. He received his Ph.D. in 1884, writing his dissertation on "The Psychology of Kant."

While at Johns Hopkins, Dewey was a student in two courses taught by Peirce, but it was not until some years later that the importance of Peirce had its effect (see § 35 below). The most important philosophic influence came from another of his teachers, G. S. Morris, a Hegelian who also found a place for Aristotle in his outlook. Morris was altogether a stimulating intellect, an excellent teacher. He liked to develop a contrast between the "real" logic (of Hegel and Aristotle) and formal logic; the latter he deplored.[16] Dewey's later development of an instrumental, logical theory into which formal and "real" aspects of the process of acquiring knowledge were included had its start in his association with Morris. The other significant influence on Dewey came from his work in psychology: the lectures of G. Stanley Hall, and his friendship with James McKeen Cattell, the psychologist who later went to Columbia. Dewey's lasting conviction of the intimate connection between psychology and philosophy, exhibited in his early work in ethics, was fixed at that time (see § 38 below). James's *Psychology*, appearing some six years later, reconfirmed and redirected the nature of this conviction in Dewey's thinking.

From 1884 to 1888 Dewey was an instructor in philosophy at the University of Michigan, an appointment initially arranged by G. S. Morris, who was then teaching there. The publication of his first book, *Psychology*, was in 1887. For a year he taught at the University of Minnesota, returning to Michigan in 1889 as professor and head of the department of philosophy. It was in the Michigan department that he established his lasting friendships, first with James H. Tufts, and shortly afterward with George H. Mead and Arthur H. Lloyd.

In 1894 Dewey moved from Michigan to Chicago. A reason for this change was the inclusion by the University of Chicago of a course in pedagogy in its department of philosophy and psychology. In Chicago Dewey started what was later called the "Laboratory School," and, more popularly, the "Dewey School."

[16] For a further note on Morris, see § 63, n. 15, and Appendix 1, sec. C.

His *School and Society*, originated from talks given to raise money for the elementary school, presents his theory and aims for it. Dewey's active role in reshaping American elementary education commenced at this time. Also during this period he became close friends with Ella Flagg Young and Jane Addams of Hull House.

His closest philosophical associates at Chicago were Tufts and Mead. But there was also James R. Angell, the most active promoter of "functional psychology" (for which, see the first pages of § 38 and § 49 below). Another important figure then in Dewey's life was Addison Moore, the most aggressive and articulate of the pragmatist group in Chicago. (This Chicago group is well represented in the collective volume *Creative Intelligence*, 1917).

Dewey's book *Human Nature and Conduct* (1922) is the later distillation of one of his main courses at Chicago, "Psychological Ethics." In 1903, *Studies in Logical Theory*, a volume of essays by graduate students with several chapters by Dewey, was published. In the same year there appeared his important and long-ignored monograph, *Logical Conditions of a Scientific Treatment of Morality*.

In 1904 as a result of difficulties with the president of the university over the Laboratory School, Dewey resigned from Chicago and moved to Columbia University, where the rest of his career was centered. He produced a long series of important articles and books over the years at Columbia, among them *Ethics* (1908, with James Tufts), *The Influence of Darwin on Philosophy* (1910), *Democracy and Education* (1916), *Reconstruction in Philosophy* (1920), *Experience and Nature* (1925), and *The Quest for Certainty* (1929). Contact with F. J. E. Woodbridge and W. P. Montague at Columbia and with distinguished philosophers in nearby universities brought about a transition and consolidation of Dewey's thought from earlier psychologcal idealism to a more realistic and empirical naturalism.

Friendship with Dr. Albert Barnes of Pennsylvania, beginning in 1915, encouraged the development of Dewey's views on art. The result was the volume *Art as Experience* (1934). This, accompanied by *Democracy and Education*, is probably the best introduction to Dewey's philosophy. In New York he became an active proponent of teachers' rights and of liberal causes generally. He lectured in Japan at Tokyo Imperial University in 1918, and also at the Universities of Peking and Nanking, where he met many of his former students. In 1924 he went to Turkey to report on the new government schools.

In 1928, at the invitation of the Soviet government, Dewey visited Russia. He was impressed with the experiments in education there and wrote articles about it which earned him the labels of "Bolshevik" and "red" in the press. Later, in 1937, he was chairman of the commission of inquiry into the charges against Leon Trotsky at the Moscow trial. Part of the hearings occurred in Trotsky's home in Mexico. The findings of the commission favored Trotsky and were published as *Not Guilty*, which caused left-wing circles then to regard Dewey as a reactionary or Trotskyite.

From 1930 to 1939 Dewey was Professor Emeritus of Philosophy in Residence at Columbia. He published several important books at this time, including *Freedom and Culture* (1939), *Theory of Valuation* (1939, for a discussion of which see §§ 87–98), and *Logic: The Theory of Inquiry* (see § 39). Dewey, who had married in 1886 and whose wife died in 1927, remarried at the age of eighty-seven in 1946.

His life took him a long way from the rocky soil of his native Vermont. But in his shrewd common sense and touches of humor, in the quiet but sustaining energy and hard internal resources, he remained a Vermonter nonetheless. He died in 1952.

GEORGE HERBERT MEAD was born in South Hadley, Massachusetts, in 1863. His ancestors had long been farmers and clergymen; his father, Hiram, was pastor of the local congregation. When Mead was seven, the family moved to Oberlin, Ohio, where Hiram Mead became professor of homiletics in Oberlin Theological Seminary.

Mead entered Oberlin College in 1879 and was graduated in 1883. It was the program in classics that seems to have been most meaningful to him; in later life he continued to read the classics in the Greek and Latin. After his graduation, the next four years were spent teaching school, tutoring, and working as a surveyor for the Wisconsin Central Railroad.

In 1887 Mead entered Harvard and was graduated with the class of 1888. Here he seems to have found his lifelong interest in psychology and philosophy. He studied primarily under Royce and James, and was the tutor of the James children during the year and summer that followed. After leaving Harvard he spent the following three years studying philosophy and psychology at the universities of Berlin and Leipzig. He was married in Berlin to Helen Castle, a longtime friend.

When Mead returned to the United States he started teaching at the University of Michigan. In his career there, from 1891 to 1894, he was a close friend of Dewey, and with Dewey moved to Chicago in 1894 to teach at the University of Chicago. In 1931 he accepted an appointment to Columbia, but died in the spring of that year.

Mead was a great teacher and a great mind. His ability to develop his thought seems to have come most easily in conversation and lecture—in *logos* as the classic tradition knew it—rather than in writing. The wealth of suggestive and luminous ideas contained in his literary remains and published writings attest to philosophic genius. There is proportionate tragedy in his death at sixty-two, when he had finally come to developing his thought with increasing ease and clarity in written form.

Dewey, who knew Mead well, described him as "a seminal mind of the very first order."[17] He also said of him that he was "the most original mind in

[17] Page xi in Mead, *The Philosophy of the Present.*

philosophy in America of the last generation" and added, "I dislike to think of what my own thinking might have been were it not for the seminal ideas which I derived from him."[18]

CLARENCE IRVING LEWIS was born in Stoneham, Massachusetts, in 1883. He attended Harvard College and was graduated in 1906. At Harvard he studied logic with Royce, which was the basis for his own later distinguished work. He received his doctorate in philosophy in 1910.

Lewis started his academic career as a high school teacher in Quincy, Massachusetts, in 1906. He taught at the universities of Colorado and California. In 1920 he returned to Harvard, becoming a full professor there in 1930. He developed a course on Kant's "Critique of Pure Reason" which became famous for generations of Harvard students. Lewis was Edgar Peirce Professor of Philosophy at Harvard until his retirement in 1953.

His early work was devoted to symbolic logic and modal logic, in which he was a pioneer. His *Survey of Symbolic Logic* (1918) was an important historical and analytical study of logical systems. This was much supplemented later by *Symbolic Logic* (1932), written in collaboration with C. H. Langford. Lewis' theory of knowledge, called "conceptualistic pragmatism," was set forth in *Mind and the World Order* (1929). The same position, developed more fully and including an analysis of value, appeared in *An Analysis of Knowledge and Valuation* (1947). Lewis' later works on value theory and ethics are *The Ground and Nature of Right* (1955) and *Our Social Inheritance* (1957). At the close of life Lewis was developing his position on ethics as distinct from his theory of value. His papers on this subject are being organized and edited for future publication.

In 1950 Lewis was the recipient of the Butler Medal of Columbia University for "outstanding contributions to modern formal logic." The citation described him as "a creative systematizer of the pragmatic theory of logic, a distinguished and influential teacher of philosophy." He died in 1964.

As is evident from these last pages, Lewis was younger than Mead by twenty years. However, in the fourth and fifth chapters of this Part, for the sake of preserving a certain continuity and development of themes with earlier chapters, I have violated chronology by placing the study of Lewis before that of Mead. Those who might prefer to have the chronological order retained may easily be satisfied by reading Chapter Five before turning to Four.

---

18 "George Herbert Mead," pp. 310–311.

CHAPTER ONE

Charles Sanders Peirce

§ 19. The Main Lines of Development

Pragmatism, it was remarked at the outset of § 2, was conceived as a *method* of philosophizing subject to certain qualifications. The method pragmatism is regarded to have introduced into philosophy is a procedure for deciding and ruling upon the meaning of beliefs, ideas, and uses of language. Roughly, the method to be followed is to ascertain and formulate the distinct empirical consequences that result from using, experimenting with, or acting upon a given idea in given circumstances. The resulting consequences, if any, are then to be interpreted as indicative of the meaning, if any, of the idea under consideration. The *formulation* of those consequences is understood as a schema or translation, in part or in whole, of the meaning of the idea, its "pragmatic significance."

Peirce described the method as characteristic of the experimentalist's procedure in the laboratory:

> Whatever assertion you may make to him, he will either understand as meaning that if a given prescription for an experiment ever can be and ever is carried out in act, an experience of a given description will result, else he will see no sense at all in what you say.

And generally:

> if one can define accurately all the conceivable experimental phenomena which the affirmation or denial of a concept could imply, one will have therein a complete definition of the concept.[1]

Peirce thought of the method as applying primarily to the use of language and as a way of clarification and analysis of assertions and concepts.[2] But when James

[1] *CP* 5.411–412.
[2] There is much in common in the motives that led Peirce to ennunciate his maxim of pragmatism (§ 21), and led Wittgenstein to the well-known injunction to ask not for the

took up the method, pragmatism was not confined to these limits, nor was the method itself quite the same. Peirce's recommendation to study the logical consequences of concepts, under certain prescribed conditions, became converted into an evaluation of the moral, psychological, and social effects of ideas. The analysis of meaning shaded off into an appraisal of the value and truth of ideas. Peirce's "maxim" (§ 21 below), as he called his method of analysis, became James's universal "mission."[3] In looking away from first principles, a priori or metaphysical antecedents in which to ground meaning and truth, the pragmatic method of analyzing experimental implications was to issue in a philosophy of experience, of thought, and of action.

Peirce's laboratory, then, was rebuilt into a hotel by James: pragmatism was the corridor, and "innumerable chambers open out of it."[4] But it was not very clear whether the corridor really led to the chambers, or whether most of the odd inhabitants of the chambers ever used the corridor at all. Schiller, one of the proprietors of the establishment, noting that hotels are man-made and that man is the measure of all things, instigated a continuous rebuilding program according to which each and all of the residents, beginning from their own chambers, would proceed to remake the hotel, each according to his own measurements and in his own way. Presumably all kinds of possible rooms were to be added, requiring all kinds of possible corridors. The future of the hotel was to be novel, expanding, wide open. But Dewey, with more sober forethought, reasoned that wide-open hotels are not hotels at all; and seeing the danger of a general collapse of the whole structure, or its degeneration into a slum for recluses, he began to tear down the flimsy beehive compartments and to expand the corridor. Since one socializes best in corridors, private chambers were abolished; rooms were to have windows but no doors. But the corridor was the essential thing. It was restored with some of its Peircian furnishings of the laboratory and called "inquiry." If Dewey could have had his way, the hotel and the corridor would have become a single unit.

Leaving this picturesque mythologizing, let us return to take a less fanciful and more incisive look at the formation of pragmatism. Peirce has left a valuable record of the events that led to the first conscious expression of it. His account suggests that pragmatism was not regarded as a surprisingly novel doctrine at its inception and that it came and was fashioned out of cooperative deliberation. Thus the mention of Bain and the presence of Chauncey Wright are clues to important influences upon the early history of pragmatism.[5]

---

meaning of a sign—as if the meaning was an object coexistent with the sign—but for the *use* of the sign; in many cases, "the meaning of a word is its use in the language." Wittgenstein, *Philosophical Investigations*, p. 43; *The Blue and Brown Books*, p. 4.

[3] *Pragmatism*, p. vii.

[4] *Ibid.*, p. 54.

[5] Cf. Fisch, "Alexander Bain and the Genealogy of Pragmatism"; on Wright, cf. Cohen, Preface to *Chance, Love and Logic*, Kennedy, and the two works of Madden. See, too, Appendix 2 below. Another source for Peirce's pragmatism was Venn's *The Logic of Chance*, see § 22, note 101 below.

It was in the earliest seventies that a knot of us young men in Old Cambridge, calling ourselves, half-ironically, half-defiantly, "The Metaphysical Club,"—for agnosticism was then riding its high horse, and was frowning superbly upon all metaphysics—used to meet, sometimes in my study, sometimes in that of William James.

The membership in the "Club" included Oliver Wendell Holmes, Jr. (the future Justice) and Nicholas St. John Green, a lawyer and disciple of Jeremy Bentham, who, in particular,

often urged the importance of applying Bain's definition of belief, as "that upon which a man is prepared to act." From this definition, pragmatism is scarce more than a corollary; so that I am disposed to think of him as the grandfather of pragmatism. Chauncey Wright, something of a philosophical celebrity in those days, was never absent from our meetings. . . . Wright, James, and I were men of science, rather scrutinizing the doctrines of the metaphysicians on their scientific side than regarding them as very momentous spiritually. The type of our thought was decidedly British. I, alone of our number, had come through the doorway of Kant, and even my ideas were acquiring the English accent.

Our metaphysical proceedings had all been in winged words . . . until at length, lest the club should be dissolved, without leaving any material *souvenir* behind, I drew up a little paper expressing some of the opinions that I had been urging all along under the name of pragmatism. This paper was received with such unlooked-for kindness, that I was encouraged, some half dozen years later . . . to insert it, somewhat expanded, in the *Popular Science Monthly* for November, 1877 and January, 1878. . . .[6]

It is of some interest to compare this description with the one in which Locke recounts the occasion that prompted his writing of the great *Essay*, and tells of the group of friends that met in the early sixteen-seventies, just two hundred years before the "Metaphysical Club" was born.[7] Locke's "Club" was discussing the principles of morality and religion, but soon found their conversations hedged about with difficulties. What was needed, as Locke goes on to explain, and as the *Essay* attempts to accomplish, was a clarification, linguistic and conceptual, of the Understanding—of how and with what sort of "objects" it works and is "fitted to deal with." The popular reception of the *Essay* made it one of the most influential sources of the kind of problems that have since dominated modern philosophy: critical in spirit (aimed at removing "the rubbish blocking knowledge"), conscious of the uses and intellectual abuses of language,[8] concerned with the nature of knowledge. Peirce had come to philosophy through Kant (§ 27); but in point of this critical philosophizing about the limits and certainty of knowledge, Locke

---

[6] *CP* 5.12–13. For more on Peirce's account of the Club and its members, see Appendix 2 below; also the recent definitive article on the subject by Fisch, "Was There a Metaphysical Club in Cambridge?"

[7] The third paragraph of Epistle to the Reader in *An Essay Concerning Human Understanding*.

[8] For Locke, clarity of thought and discourse depends on "determined" ideas—ideas constantly correlated to signs, "to a name or articulate sound." Cf. Epistle to the Reader.

and Kant are kin.[9] Peirce's modest start, his now famous paper, "How to Make Our Ideas Clear," is the spiritual heir of this same critical quest.

The 'critical problem,' or so-called 'problem of knowledge,' that has so preoccupied modern philosophy since Descartes and Locke is in fact a nest of many problems. We have seen something of its evolution in Part One. The ancients had debated the question of what is knowledge; what kind of activity related in what ways to what kind of objects constitutes *knowing*? Aristotle, whose name, like the word 'philosophy,' connoted *science* in the Middle Ages, had said that scientific knowledge *(epistēmē)* is of the universal, sensation is of particulars.[10] The problem that then went through the fine screen of scholastic analysis had to do with what and where the universal is and whether or not the human mind is able to know external objects. This problem was raised with another in the same prickly nest: namely, how and in what ways concepts of things were related to things signified, and whether some illuminative power or Intelligence distinct from human faculties was necessary whereby the signifying of things by concepts could be achieved. These questions involved others, and required a general examination of the nature of *concepts*, or signs, and *signification*. The possibility of what Locke later called knowledge of "real existence,"[11] our knowledge of existing things, was a thesis whose clarification and defense was thought dependent on the outcome of these technical excursions into signs and their uses. Duns Scotus, one of Peirce's favorites, explored the question of the correspondence between objects and "real concepts" (i.e., concepts of externally existing things, *res extra animam*).[12] He asked the key question: "What in the thing corresponds to those concepts?" (*Quid istis conceptibus correspondeat in re*).[13]

The question, and the way Duns Scotus states it, would have interested Peirce. His pragmatic maxim, designed as a general answer to such inquiries from the point of view of medieval *realism*, was to serve also as a general way to arrive at a specific clarification of concepts in specific cases. It is his early statement of pragmatism that has had the most influence historically; and it is this initial formation of the idea with which we shall be primarily concerned below. But it should be observed that for Peirce himself these first expressions were only suggestions whose fuller development enlists the insights of medieval logic. The later pragmatism of Peirce is to be found in his work on an extensive theory of signs.

---

[9] Thus Pringle-Pattison's introduction to Locke's *Essay*, p. xiv: "Locke has sometimes been enrolled as the first critical philosopher. There is, indeed, a striking similarity between the language in which Locke describes the motives and occasion of his inquiry and the description afterwards given by Kant, in the *Critique of Pure Reason* and in the *Prolegomena*, of his own investigation . . . and the similarity extends even to the metaphors in which they clothe their thesis." See also Kant's reference to Locke in his Preface to the *Critique of Pure Reason*.

[10] *De anima* II, 5, 417b22.

[11] *Essay Concerning Human Understanding*, Book IV, ch. 1, secs. 2, 7, ch. 3, secs. 21 ff.

[12] For example, St. Thomas had said: "The idea signified by the name is the conception in the intellect of the thing signified by the name" (*Ratio enim quam significat nomen, est conceptio intellectus de re significata per nomen*). *Summa Theologiae* I, q. 13, a. 4.

[13] *Metaphysicorum Aristotelis*, Book 7, q. 19, n. 4; VII, 465b. Scotus' answer is developed in his theory of the *formal distinction*.

What has come to be known as Peirce's pragmatism derives chiefly from his study of the phenomenology of human thought and the uses of language. For Peirce, the investigation of thought and language, and therefore the way into specific analyses of all kinds of claims, assertions, beliefs, and ideas, depends upon our understanding of signs. One of Peirce's lasting ideals, resolutely pursued but never completely achieved, was to work out a general theory of signs: that is, a classification and analysis of the types of signs and sign relations and significations that, in the broadest sense, make communication possible. A sign is anything that stands for something else. While this ancient way of putting it admits of a trivial construction (signs are things that *stand for*—are *signs of*—things, i.e., signs are signs), what is important for Peirce is that signs are socially standardized ways in which one thing (a thought, word, gesture, or object as *sign*) refers *us* (a community) to something else (the interpretant, the significant effect or translation of the sign, being itself another sign). Thus signs presuppose minds in communication with other minds, which in turn presupposes a community (of interpreters) and a system of communication.

It is time, however, to turn to Peirce's pragmatism itself.

§ 20.   *Peirce's Theory of Inquiry*

Peirce's account of the function of thought—roughly, what we do and why we do it when we can be said to think—is remarkable on several counts. The novelty of the construction alone, though not of exclusive importance, is of great interest.

Much of the outward form of the theory has affinities with an older idealism: that thought is a means to establishing an equilibrium with our momentarily severed connections with "reality"; that every thought (or belief) is but a partial half-truth falling short of the totality of Truth; that the goal of thought is the cessation of thought in one's becoming one with the Whole. But beneath the guise of these familiar and once engagingly respectable influences Peirce effects a radical recasting of our interpretation of the function of thought. Most noteworthy in this respect is the attempt to construe thought within a more inclusive theory of organic behavior.

The resulting hypothesis, and the core of the theory, is that thought is one intervening phase of a single behavioral process, mediate between a phase of sensory stimulation and a phase of purposeful resolution. As a process whose occurrence, span, and termination will differ under differing stimulus conditions plus our differing humanly inherited equipment for response, the sequence of phases will exhibit variations in manifestation and in their grading off from one to another. Nonetheless, specific and describable operations occur within the phase of thought and afford classification and analysis of the "fixation of belief" and of logic in a broad sense.[14]

[14] I.e., as a general theory of signs, semiotic, the "philosophy of representation." *CP* 1.539.

In brief and in general, for Peirce, *doubt* is an irritating condition usually originating externally from surprise.[15] Doubt is a state of uneasiness and hesitancy; habits of action—and thereby in some cases action itself—have come up against an interfering obstacle. The resolution of doubt, the removal of an obstacle, is attained by *belief.* Thus doubt occasions a struggle to attain a state of belief. This struggle Peirce calls "inquiry." Inquiry, or thought, "is excited by the irritatation of doubt, and ceases when belief is attained: so that the production of belief is the sole function of thought."[16] Belief not only brings doubt to an end but also contains a reference to action. This is not to say that belief is action, nor that belief always produces action. Belief, says Peirce, is the establishment of a habit—that is, a rule of action. Belief has these three features: it is an item of awareness (i.e., we are conscious of our beliefs[17]); it destroys the irritation of doubt; it produces a habit.

It should be clear that on this view doubt is not a condition we can will into existence. Doubt and belief are like physical pain in this respect; they occur or not regardless of what we will. Thus, when philosophers ask us to entertain doubts as to the existence of the world, for example, they are asking what is in fact impossible, if 'doubt' is taken in Peirce's sense. He calls this the "Cartesian error." Descartes' skeptical doubts were not genuine (i.e., Peircian) cases of doubt at all. At best, most so-called philosophical doubts possess a heuristic value indicating what might be learned if we were to examine in a detached spirit some of our most ingrained and sluggish convictions. But Peircian doubt has little in common with such sophisticated reflectiveness, and were a man to have such doubts as to the existence of the world, or of his mind, the pathological results would be beyond philosophic repair by Cartesian "proofs."

Thought, the modulator of activity by which disconcerting stimuli eventuate, under interpretation (or "transformation"), as regimented conditions falling under a general rule or formula of action, has just this instrumental function and no other, Peirce argues. "Thought in action" (i.e., inquiry) "has for its only possible motive the attainment of thought at rest" (i.e., belief). Belief then arrests and is the stopping-place of any one phase of thought; but "since belief is a rule for action, the application of which involves further doubt and further thought, at the same time that it is a stopping-place, it is also a new starting-place for thought."[18] From birth to death, intelligent life is a continuous activity of these starts and stops strung together more or less coherently as the case may be, and, as the case must be, exercised within an environment whose objects are variously the occasions of doubt and belief.

What has come to be regarded as a characteristically *pragmatic* consideration is introduced by Peirce into his theory of inquiry as follows. Since belief produces a habit, beliefs are to be distinguished by the habits resulting from them. Belief is,

---

[15] *CP* 5.443.
[16] *CP* 5.394.
[17] There are passages in which Peirce insists on this condition, others in which he waives it.
[18] *CP* 5.397.

or contains, a resolve to act in a specified way under certain conditions.[19] Habits, or rules of action, thus provide the criterion for two sorts of determinations concerning belief: (*a*) beliefs will differ or not depending on whether the rules of action they provide will differ or not; (*b*) the significance of a belief is determined by the rule of action it prescribes. An analogue of (*a*) is Peirce's doctrine that differences among signs will consist in the differences among the logical interpretants of signs; and an analogue of (*b*) is his doctrine that the "ultimate" logical interpretant of a sign, concept, or proposition ("the real meaning") is a habit.[20]

The rationale behind both (*a*) and (*b*) need not be confined merely to beliefs and habits: Indeed, (*a*) and (*b*) are special applications of two historical precursors; (*a*) is an instance of the venerable principle that Leibniz called the "identity of indiscernibles," here used by Peirce to maintain that beliefs differ only if some of their properties, or practical or experimental consequences differ; and (*b*) is an instance of the injunction, "By their fruits shall ye know them" which, Peirce notes, is part of the ancestral history of pragmatism.

As habits provide the criterion by which we can distinguish different beliefs, or avoid making false (or merely verbal) distinctions, a similar procedure applies to habits. Habits are to be distinguished and their significance understood by action.

. . . The whole function of thought is to produce habits of action. . . . To develop its meaning, we have, therefore, simply to determine what habit it produces, for what a thing means is simply what habits it involves. . . . What the habit is depends on *when* and *how* it causes us to act. As for the *when*, every stimulus to action is derived from perception; as for the *how*, every purpose of action is to produce some sensible result. Thus we come down to what is tangible and conceiv-

---

[19] There is much room for clarification and analysis of Peirce's views on *belief* and *habit*, and the sense in which a habit is "a rule of action." Note the ambiguity above in saying belief *is* or *contains* a habit. This reproduces Peirce's own apparent indecision; for he will say that belief is a habit, and also say that belief establishes or produces a habit (a point noted by Buchler, p. 55). Thus the relation of belief to action, or belief to habit to action, remains somewhat confused in Peirce's discussion. Peirce's use of 'habit,' like much of his terminology, has a classical and medieval lineage. Aristotle includes habit in the category of Quality (*Categories* 8, 8b25): "habits [*hexeis*] differ from dispositions in being more stable and of longer duration." That is, Aristotle adds, habits are changed only if "some great upheaval comes about" (which is the sort of shock Peirce regards as essential to genuine doubt). Dispositions are easily changed. Yet habits are dispositions, "for those who possess a habit have also, in virtue of this, a disposition" and are thus disposed in some way (9a10). In Peirce's language, "belief contains a reference to action."

The Aristotelian classificant of *habit* as a quality allows one to speak of habits (and dispositions) of all sorts of natural objects. This usage is familiar in medieval philosophy (see, e.g., St. Thomas' discussion of the two senses of 'to have,' *habere*, in *Summa Theologiae* I–II, q. 49, a. 1). It is retained by Peirce in his speaking of habits and general ideas of action prevailing in the universe, and even in mundane objects, such as a die; see e.g., note 67 and § 22 below.

As to what is meant by 'belief' and 'habit' we have these further attempts at clarification from Peirce: "belief consists mainly in being deliberately prepared to adopt the formula believed in as a guide to action," *CP* 5.27. And on belief and habit: "A genuine belief, or opinion, is something on which a man is prepared to act, and is, therefore, in a general sense a habit," *CP* 2.148.

[20] *CP* 5.491.

ably practical, as the root of every real distinction of thought, no matter how subtle it may be; and there is no distinction of meaning so fine as to consist in anything but a possible difference of practice.[21]

Peirce illustrates these remarks, or "the principle" they are aimed at eliciting, with an aperçu of medieval disputation on the doctrine of transubstantiation. Can we rightly suppose that the objects in this case are "really" flesh and blood while possessing the sensible qualities of cakes and wine? We mean by *wine* that which has certain sensible effects, and to talk of something having just the sensible properties of wine, yet really being blood, "is senseless jargon." This is not to argue as did an eleventh-century dialectician, Berengarius of Tours, that the accidents of bread or wine cannot continue to exist while their substances are entirely changed. For Peirce is not speaking about substances underlying accidents but rather about situations in which language is used correctly or senselessly. We fall into jargon when, given a certain set of stimuli which (without any noticeable or specifiable deviation from past situations) have correctly occasioned the use of 'wine,' we exchange that use for another, namely, 'blood,' without any evident reason or justification for departing from the uniformity of word usage.[22]

While there is room for demurring over details of the illustration and of Peirce's rather free assignment of meanings and meaningfulness alike to objects (e.g., wine), words (e.g., 'wine'), concepts, and ideas, still the general intention is clear. Clarity of thought and our use of language is a function of certain kinds of habits of behavior, in certain kinds of situations leading to certain kinds of sensible results. A cryptic and oft-quoted comment of Peirce's is "our idea of anything is our idea of its sensible effects."[23] And from this Berkeleyan-sounding phrase it is but a short step to Peirce's maxim of pragmatism.

§ 21.   Peirce and Pragmatism

Consider what effects, that might conceivably have practical bearings, we conceive the object of our conception to have. Then our conception of these effects is the whole of our conception of the object.[24]

[21] *CP* 5.400. The word 'conceivably' in the above passage about the tangible and conceivably practical as the root of real distinctions of thought, is a later addition by Peirce. It is a significant qualification to be commented on shortly.

[22] The retort readily to be expected from the defender of the events and description of the Eucharist is that a miracle is an evident (if not an empirical) reason for declaring the use of 'wine' incorrect under the circumstances. He might also reply, in more empirical fashion, that the stimulus conditions ordinarily prompting the correct use of 'wine' have in fact been altered.

[23] *CP* 5.401.

[24] *CP* 5.402. "How to Make Our Ideas Clear." Buchler, p. 94*n.*, expresses reasonable doubts as to the wisdom of making this passage the core and *locus classicus* of an interpretation of Peirce's pragmatism. With a view to understanding Peirce's philosophy, this doubt, often unheeded by writers on Peirce, is probably sound. The present discussion, however, is not directed to a clarification of Peirce's intentions, but to what became a central theme, despite misunderstandings of origins, in the development of pragmatism. There is, in my opinion, a much better general statement by Peirce of what pragmatism is—to be found below in Appendix 3, sec. B.

Ironically, this most famous and often repeated of Peirce's statements on pragmatism is probably the unclearest recommendation for how to make our ideas clear in the history of philosophy. Peirce himself takes note of his use "five times over of derivatives of *concipere*,"[25] explaining that recrudescence as an emphatic attempt to indicate that he was concerned here with "intellectual purport." Concepts are to be explained by concepts, not by images, not by actions.[26] While this may not excuse the inelegance of his formulation, it is a noteworthy addendum.[27] Access to the meanings of concepts is gained only through traffic with concepts.

"Clarity of apprehension," to use Peirce's expression, or, in effect, *meaning*, is had by a replacing (or translation) of concepts with concepts. A replacing, one might add, of unclear concepts with clear ones. But the addition is trivial counsel pending agreement upon some criterion of clarity (or meaning). One approach to a criterion is hinted at in the above maxim: replace our initial conception of an object with a conception of the conceivable practical bearings or effects of that object. But this advice, to be effective, must await elucidation of 'concept,' 'conceivable practical effects,' and 'conception of conceivable practical effects.' Alas, however, the wanted elucidations are not to be found in Peirce's writings. There are scattered comments bearing upon these matters, but they are often recondite and apparently at variance with one another. Putting the pieces together would be a difficult task but laudable for what it might contribute to our understanding of Peirce.

Some observations concerning the maxim of pragmatism are worth registering.

1)   Peirce's pragmatism, often said to be a "theory of meaning," was regarded by Peirce himself as a maxim, rule, and method for ascertaining the meaning of signs.[28] But pragmatism is not concerned with the meanings of all signs; it is concerned "merely to lay down a method of determining the meanings of intellectual concepts, that is, of those upon which reasonings may turn."[29] Exactly what the limits are upon this class of concepts is not clear. Peirce bars "names of feelings," like 'red' and 'blue,' apparently because feelings are subjective, indeterminate, and the practical effects of feelings effect nothing more than other feelings: "those qualities have no intrinsic significations beyond themselves."[30] The point is obscure. Peirce evidently confuses the determination of the *meaning* of names 'red' and 'blue' with the *fact* that red and blue are "subjective feelings." But that subjective feelings do not yield to an analysis of meaning in no way excludes the *names* of feelings from an analysis of meaning. Other terms, such as

---

[25] *CP* 5.403.

[26] Just as, for Peirce, signs and propositions take other signs and propositions as their logical interpretants. "The meaning of a sign is the sign it has to be translated into," *CP* 4.132. And "all thought whatsoever is a sign. . . ," *CP* 5.421.

[27] James, on the contrary, was to speak of the pragmatic meaning of images, and regarded actions as giving the meaning of "ideas."

[28] Or of some signs: "I understand pragmatism to be a method of ascertaining the meanings, not of all ideas, but . . . intellectual concepts, that is to say, of those upon the structure of which, arguments concerning objective fact may hinge," *CP* 5.467.

[29] *CP* 5.8.

[30] *CP* 5.467.

those designating individual objects, are also to be excluded from pragmatic analysis,[31] and non-descriptive logical components of sentences, such as 'and,' 'or,' 'if-then,' and the like.

Despite much uncertainty as to if and how pragmatic analysis of meaning applies to a considerable portion of discourse, two things are clear. Pragmatic meaning is not ubiquitous nor is the application of the pragmatic rule to hold for all kinds of communication. Peirce inclines to a view of kinds of meaning among which the pragmatic is but one. Second, pragmatic determination of meaning does not apply to words or word usage in general, but more directly to *concepts*, or what Peirce calls "the intellectual purport" of words. For Peirce, the broadest category of instruments of communication is that of *signs*. Words, concepts, and certain standardized forms of overt behavior are each kinds of signs. In a broad description, then, pragmatism is a theory, or set of procedural rules, for clarifying (or determining) the meaning of certain classes of signs.[32]

Apparently Peirce regarded linguistic clarity, explicit and unambiguous discourse, as a dependent offshoot of conceptual clarity. A *conception* is, to cite a further definition, "the rational purport of a word or other expression."[33] Still discourse and conceptualization, by virtue of the relation between what purports and what is purported, work together; their connection can engender cross fertilizations of confusion or clarity. Thus while the pragmatic maxim is aimed at an overall clarification of "ideas," its most immediate application and assessable results may be found in the province of language and linguistic usage.

2)   In saying that our conception of an object turns upon conceiving its "practical bearings" or "effects," Peirce did not intend to be taken as expounding a doctrine of crass utilitarianism. Some of the more uncautious statements of James lend themselves to that interpretation so that one might say the "meaning" of a concept, or of an object, is its practical use for some individual. Nor was it Peirce's intention to suggest that all thought (or conceiving) issues in action; nor that the "purport" or "interpretation" of concepts lies in acts. Thought, says Peirce, may ultimately apply to action, but it will be "to *conceived* action."[34] Peirce repeatedly emphasized that pragmatism was not a philosophy of action nor one in which, somehow, meaning is wedded to action. His attempts to disassociate his view from such misunderstandings and from some of the developments James and others were giving to what they called "pragmatism" eventually led him to rebaptize his own position as "pragmaticism."[35]

---

[31] *CP* 5.429. On proper names Peirce wavers, seeming to rule them out of pragmatic translation of meaning, yet insofar as proper names figure in *types* of assertions (or "*the like* of it, being common to all assertions . . .") they may have "pragmatic import." As to what these "designations of an individual object are, as names, and concerning obvious differences among kinds of terms that name, or purport to name, Peirce leaves us in the dark. For an effective critical survey of these matters, see Buchler, p. 99.

[32] Just what classes of signs fall under a pragmatic critique is, as noted above, not altogether clear. Some but not all words, some concepts, some acts of expression, some kinds of diagrams, some mathematical signs are subject to pragmatic meaning. For aspects of his work in logic and probability theory, Peirce also invokes his pragmatism.

[33] *CP* 5.412.

[34] *CP* 5.403*n*.

[35] A word ugly enough, he commented, to be safe from kidnappers.

3)   Pragmatism is a method for achieving clarity of our ideas, for "deter-mining the meanings of intellectual concepts." But what are meanings? We get no very clear-cut answer from Peirce. But then, for all his erratic brilliance, this is not to be wondered at; for we get no completely satisfactory answer from philosophy at all, the clearest of traditional answers proving clearly inadequate. But we can, if a little lamely, give Peirce credit for having anticipated much of what seems to be sound in recent critical advances upon the fringes of a theory of meaning.

So firmly rooted in the philosophic past are several dominant ways of thinking and talking about *meaning* that we tend to acquiesce to them, almost as second nature, while we are still cutting our philosophic teeth and know no better. Prominent among these and ancestor of them all is the Aristotelian treatment of meanings as stated essences,[36] which, despite many vicissitudes of theorizing over the long interval, reappears (e.g.) in Locke's view of meanings as ideas.[37] In each case, as an essence stated or as an idea named, a meaning is easily construed as an entity or object of some sort. It is then but an easy step to regard the meaning of a term as the object named by the term (be the object an essence or idea). But this step invites confusion, as Plato first pointed out with the term 'non-being'—for 'non-being' names nothing, yet is meaningful—and as Frege and Russell along somewhat different paths have made clear.[38] If much of con-temporary discussion of meaning has taken a negative turn, pointing out where not to look and how not to talk when considering questions of the meaning of 'meaning,' the effect has been salutary in disenthralling us with some of the more stubborn misconceptions of the past.

For Peirce, meanings are not objects, essential or otherwise; nor are they ideas,

---

[36] Thus Aristotle, in *Metaphysics* 1029b ff, says that the essence (*ousia*) is stated in a formula (*logos*) or definition (*horismos*) and what is meant is the what-it-is-to-be (*to ti ēn einai*) that thing. Or: clearly "definition [*horismos*] states (or is the formula [*logos*] what-it-is-to-be" something (1031a12).

[37] Thus Locke: Meanings are ideas of which words are sensible marks, *Essay*, Book III, ch. 2, sec. 3. Or: definition is the explaining of words "so that the meaning or idea it stands for may be certainly known," Book III, ch. 10.

Locke, however, locates ideas *in* the mind (or sometimes as mediate between mind and external objects). Meanings therefore become attributes of mental particles, simple and compound, in the realm of the Understanding. The meaning of an idea is an idea of an idea. Locke thus departs from the Aristotelian objectification of essences; that departure attends the notorious difficulties he has over the meaning of 'idea,' whereas, for example, the *idea* of a thing as its intelligible form is retained by Spinoza.

Historically, it is of interest to notice how Locke's view here (though it is the result of an earlier tradition) becomes standardized in lexicography. Thus in Samuel Johnson's Preface to the *English Dictionary* (1755): "words are the daughters of earth, and . . . things are the sons of heaven. Language is only the instrument of science, and words are but the signs of ideas: I wish, however, that the instrument might be less apt to decay, and that signs might be permanent like the things they denote." Observe how this last sentence represents a rupture with those previous; earlier a word was a sign of an *idea*, now it is said to be a sign (alas, impermanent) which denotes a *thing*. Locke's trouble in keeping *ideas* and *things* distinct has become well established.

[38] Thus note the troublesome cases of alleged names like 'nihil' or 'ignorance' for Locke. Since they do not name ideas, "negative words" as he calls them "relate to positive ideas and signify their absence." Essay, Book III, ch. 1, sec. 4. The negative term 'nonbeing' re-lates to the positive idea of *being* and, somehow, "signifies" the absence of that idea. For recent discussion of the confusion of meaning with naming, see Quine, *From A Logical Point of View*, and references therein.

representational or otherwise. In spite of an ample number of very different descriptions Peirce gave from time to time of what he initially intended by the "pragmatic rule," one professed motive stands out: the pragmatic rule is a proposed procedure for the analysis and definition of some of the signs[39] (or terms) necessary for the communication of knowledge and the attainment of true belief.[40]

Peirce applies this rule to our ideas of *hardness, weight, force,* and *reality.* Thus we mean by the sign 'hard thing' a thing that will not be scratched by many other substances. "The whole conception of this quality, as of every other, lies in its conceived effects."[41] We mean by 'force' "what is completely involved in its effects" or "if we know what the effects of force are, we are acquainted with every fact which is implied in saying that a force exists, and there is nothing more to know."[42] The principle behind these uses, however, invites closer scrutiny.

The sign 'hard,' says Peirce, means "will not be scratched by many other substances." Peirce does not mistake meaning and naming; the meaning of the word 'hard' is not its extension nor the class of things that will not be scratched by many substances. The "will not be scratched" refers to a certain operation—namely, a scratch test—and to certain results of the test always to be observed or expected.[43] To speak of some object O as hard is to say "if a certain operation under certain circumstances is performed on O, then such and such results will occur," where, of course, the operation, circumstances, and results are specified. This is to provide a conditional explication of 'hard'; and of explications of "intellectual concepts," Peirce writes that he found them taking this form:

> Proceed according to such and such a general rule. Then if such and such a concept is applicable to such and such an object, the operation will have such and such a general result; and conversely.[44]

Note that the operation (e.g., scratch-testing) is a general procedure or "rule" and the result will be general and capable of "a definite general description."

[39] Here the word 'sign' is intended to cover the fluctuation already noted in earlier pages between Peirce's speaking of the meaning of *concepts, ideas,* and *words.* Henceforth, to save multiplying locutions, we will often let 'sign' stand for *concept, idea, belief, word,* in discussing Peirce. This follows Peirce's own view that the inclusive category of vehicles of communication is that of *signs.*

[40] It is not clear whether Peirce intended pragmatism to be limited to scientific terms only, or to any form of communication and settling of belief in which truth and falsehood is recognized. He speaks of the scientific (or experiential) method of settling opinion as the only one in which truth and falsehood is recognized (*CP* 5.406). 'Science' is evidently to be taken in a large sense. Pragmatism is to apply to concepts and words in science, philosophy, metaphysics, and any genre in which truth-claims have significance.

[41] *CP* 5.403.

[42] *CP* 4.404.

[43] It also refers to a certain universal "general" trait existing in things, Peirce's "realism." Peirce's "scholastic realism" which often crops up in his writings and to which references continue to be made in the discussion below holds that "*some* general objects are real" (*CP* 5.430) and that there is experimental evidence for this position. A familiar pronouncement is: "General principles are really operative in nature. That is the doctrine of scholastic realism," *CP* 5.101. For a discussion of this position see Bronstein, pp. 47 ff; McKeon; and in the discussion that follows, see notes 47, 54, 57, 67, and 165 below.

[44] *CP* 5.483. Also in the same: "to predicate any . . . concept of a real or imaginary object is equivalent to declaring that a certain operation, if performed upon that object would . . . be followed by a result of a definite general description."

Obviously, any single operation if carried out will be subject to any number of individual and local conditions ("this metal at this time, place and temperature, scratched with this substance. . . ," etc.). These peculiar, contingent, individual conditions making specific operations possible, however, are just what do not count in the explication of *hard* or other concepts. What is wanted is the "definite general description." That description, too, is what Peirce elsewhere seems to mean by our "conception of the effects" or " practical bearings," or our idea of the "sensible effects" of any object. These sensible effects are not to be taken as private and varying from observer to observer; they are the publicly shared effects. Just so the common denominators of operations, of results, and of results described (or forecast) figure in the pragmatic determination of concepts.

In sum, Peirce's rule turns out to be an injunction, hence, a maxim, to translate and explicate a sign[45] by providing a conditional statement of an experimental situation[46] in which a definite operation will produce a definite result. Thus let T be such a term, $ExpS$ the experimental situation, O some operation and R, the result. The method of learning or "gaining a perceptual acquaintance with the object of the word" or illustrating the meaning of T is actually to instigate $ExpS$, and O producing R. The analysis and explication of T consists in showing that $T_1 = T_2$ and 'T_2' refers to the conditional statement "If $ExpS$ and O then R." Call this last statement S. Then for Peirce, the "whole meaning" of T is expressed by T_2, and T_2 is equivalent in meaning to S. Thus in the case of the predicate 'hard' the pragmatic method of determining meaning is, roughly:

T_1 ('hard') $= T_2$ and $T_2 = S$ where S is the conditional statement of the form "If such and such $ExpS$ and if O (i.e., scratch test) then R (i.e., will not be scratched)."

The same procedure is in principle extendable from predicates to statements containing one or more predicates.[47]

Peirce refers to this pragmatic method of conditional explication of signs as a "prescription" or "precept." The conditionals are recipes informing us of what we are to do if we wish to find out the kind of conditions to which the sign applies. That the method is the very substance of what has come to be known as "operationalism" is by now a familiar observation. But it is ironical that this

[45] Again, as lately noticed, not all signs or terms.

[46] Specifying the experimental situation for explications of signs is, on this theory, a matter of some importance. The specification will introduce a number of boundary conditions upon the use of signs. One wants to avoid the anomaly of inferring water is hard, resulting from defining 'hard' as "will not be scratched."

[47] Thus the statement 'X is hard' $= S$ (namely, 'If $ExpS$ and X and O, then X will exhibit R—i.e., 'X will not be scratched'). Peirce sometimes adds the significant provision that 'X is hard' will mean that *in every case*, in every experimental trial, S remains true. This carries a future tense into the 'will' of 'will not be scratched.' 'Will not be scratched' refers to an indefinitely large number of conceivable tests. Accordingly, says Peirce, meaning has a futurative and predictive component; the meaning of a concept or sign "lies in the future." Peirce was also led to think of 'will be' as possessing an objective reference in its role within the explication of predicates. This is a part of his "scholastic realism." That a stone *will not be* scratched, whenever tested, that putty *will be*, are objectively existent facts, just as real as stones and putty. See his letter to Woods on "would be," *CP* 8.380. See also further related comments in the discussion (§ 23) that follows below.

particular aspect of Peirce's work should merit attention by way of its appealing resemblance to operationalism; for operationalism, at its inception, as a theory of defining the meanings of concepts in physics, was far less rigorous in its formulation and considerably muddier in obscuring essential details than its Peircian forebear.[48] A more suggestive connection of ideas, and one deserving of study, is the striking resemblance of Peirce's method of determining the meaning of concepts with the "method of determination of terms by reduction statements" devised more recently (1936) by Carnap.[49] It should be added, however that Peirce would have objected to the "nominalistic" spirit of Carnap's earlier writings and to the hope that the meaning of an "intellectual concept" could be expressed in reports of individual sense data. For Peirce, particular sensations are destitute of cognitive significance; it is the definite *general* description which conveys the meaning of concepts. But Carnap's aim at a systematic explication of terms by means of logical constructions is anticipated in Peirce.

4) The procedure just outlined, of clarifying concepts by and through conditional recipes, leads into a number of problems of logic and language which, so far, have stoutly resisted most attempts at effective penetration. The problems have to do with interpreting disposition terms and contrary-to-fact conditional statements. The chief problem is one of arriving at more than a piecemeal understanding of these uses of language, and whether or not an adequate theoretical analysis of them can be made to cover more than certain select and fragmentary portions of language. Not only are dispositional terms (like 'hard') prominent among those in Peirce's discussions of the pragmatic clarification of concepts, the conditional statements by which clarification is to be effected are contrary-to-fact conditionals. Peirce recognized this, saying:

> Pragmaticism makes the ultimate intellectual purport of what you please to consist in conceived conditional resolutions . . .; the conditional propositions, with their hypothetical antecedents, in which such resolutions consist, being of the ultimate nature of meaning, must be capable of being true.[50]

[48] This is not to deny the valuable role played by "operationalism" and by Bridgman's book, *The Logic of Modern Physics*, from whence it comes, in initiating a new look at the language of science, in uncovering important problems and attempting a pragmatic resolution of them, and in effective encouraging of a more critical empiricism for keeping pace with developments within modern physics. However, Bridgman's initial thesis stated in general that "we mean by any concept nothing more than a set of operations; *the concept is synonymous with the corresponding set of operations*," p. 5. But what sort of things are to be included, what excluded as irrelevant to an *operation* is left obscure, since a criterion of operations is nowhere supplied. What the sense of 'synonymous' is in which *concepts* and *operations* can be said to have the same meaning, is also in doubt, as is the notion of *correspondence* between concepts and operations. The synonymy issue in Peirce rests between conceptions and concepts *of* an operation and its consequences. In this respect, operationalism is closer to Jamesian than to Peircian pragmatism.

[49] For an elementary sketch see Carnap's paper in the *Encyclopedia of Unified Science*, Vol. I, no. 1, p. 50. For the fuller statement, "Testability and Meaning." For recent changes in the position, "The Methodological Character of Theoretical Concepts." For an illuminating study of issues relating to, but passed over in the last comments in the above paragraph, see Bernstein.

[50] CP 5.453. Peirce also described the "pregnant principle" of the "kernel of pragmatism" this way: "the *whole* meaning of an intellectual predicate is that certain kinds of events

The fact that there are many unresolved and puzzling difficulties concerning counterfactual statements[51] does not of itself threaten the value of Peirce's recommended procedure of analysis of terms via conditional statements. The procedure does indeed depend upon our making sense of counterfactual statements apart from the fact that we can and often do make sense with them. But since we do in fact often use counterfactual statements in communicating significant information, there is no reason to think, on this score, that there is any special difficulty in Peirce's method of using these statements for rendering the meanings of terms. It is only when we have occasion to reflect upon the method itself and in general that general issues concerning the nature of counterfactual statements are relevant, and where our understanding of these latter may have critical bearing upon the former. As matters stand, however, it is to Peirce's credit that he was sensitive to the importance of counterfactual statements in ordinary and scientific discourse as well as to their role in the systematic clarification of scientific language.

5)   An awkward problem arises in Peirce's original formulation of the pragmatic meaning of signs which made him later change some of his views. Briefly, the problem is as follows. If the meaning of a sign refers to certain conditional operations, as discussed some pages back, can we meaningfully use a sign in cases where no equivalent operations have or could be performed? Peirce writes:

> let us ask what we mean by calling a thing *hard*. Evidently that it will not be scratched by many other substances. The whole conception of this quality, as of every other, lies in its conceived effects.

But in the next sentence he adds:

> There is absolutely no difference between a hard thing and a soft thing so long as they are not brought to the test.[52]

Now the problem is that we do often make a difference between a hard thing and a soft thing *without* bringing either to the scratch test. But it is not clear that this is counter to what Peirce is saying, because it is not altogether clear what he intended to say here.

Peirce goes on to maintain that if a diamond happened to be crystallized on a cushion and remained there without ever being scratch-tested until it finally was burned up, it would not be false to say that the diamond was soft. But he

---

would happen, once in so often, in the course of experience, under certain kinds of existential conditions—provided it can be proved to be true," *CP* 5.468. The word 'would' in this passage should be read according to Peirce's special doctrine of *would* be, noted earlier, note 47, and below, §§ 22, 23. Peirce's definition of a hypothetical proposition is relevant in considering the conditional statements of meanings of predicates. "The peculiarity of the hypothetical proposition is that it goes out beyond the actual state of things and declares what *would* happen were things other than they are or may be. The utility of this is that it puts us in possession of a rule, say that 'if A is true, B is true,'" *CP* 3.374.

[51] For recent discussions see Chisholm, Goodman. It has been argued more recently, see Ayers, p. 347, "that there is no special problem about verification or analysis of counterfactual . . . statements."

[52] *CP* 5.403.

adds that this would "involve a modification of our present usage of speech." If we argued that every hard substance remains soft until the moment of scratch-testing at which its resistance to being scratched suddenly increases, this would not be *false*. We should have changed some uses of the terms 'hard' and 'soft'— or better, there would be some conditions under which what we *ordinarily* would call hard we would call soft. But the meanings of the terms remain the same, "For they represent no fact to be different from what it is; only they involve arrangements of facts which would be exceedingly maladroit."[53]

One point that Peirce seems to want to establish here is that where no experimental operations or evidence can be instituted for establishing the quality of a thing (e.g., its hardness or softness) or possible differences of character, there is no "meaning" in assigning it one quality rather than another. But Peirce also seems to argue that where no experimental operation is decisive, different possible hypothetical representations of facts—even maladroit arrangements— are none of them false. Yet since we are supposing *different* possible interpretations in this case, if they are none of them false, they are not true either. What is suggested here is some doctrine of the identification of truth with verification. Where verification or empirical operations upon hypotheses are not decisive, the truth values of the hypotheses do not exist.

But there are difficulties in what Peirce says, or seems to say. There are substances that will not be scratched by many other substances, yet no one would wish to call them *hard*—liquids and cotton, for example. Further, to say that a diamond is *hard* means it will not be scratched *can* be translated to mean that: only after a test is performed is it true to say 'the diamond is hard.' But this in turn implies that *before* the diamond is scratch-tested (*a*) it is meaningless to say the diamond is hard; (*b*) it makes no difference to say the diamond is hard or soft. But clearly we often do and want to say that something is hard, although we have not tested it. And we certainly do want often to speak of hard diamonds and soft cotton even though we have not had them "brought to the test."

The main problem in interpreting Peirce in the foregoing passages lies in his use of the words 'will not be scratched.' For this can be construed in such a way as to permit the above constructions. It can be taken to mean: until the diamond is scratch-tested it is not hard; or it is meaningless to call it hard; or it is not false to call it soft. Peirce later changed the dispositional terms; instead of '*will*-be' (or 'will not be') he used '*would*-be' (or 'would not be') and this avoids some of the difficulties noted. But Peirce also later decided that his argument about the diamond as possibly becoming hard only when scratch-tested was not wholly dependent upon a mere matter modifying "our present usage of speech." The step to be taken, rather, was toward a more extreme realism.[54] Thus, twenty-five years later he wrote of the untested diamond that crystallized and then perished:

> The question is, was that diamond *really* hard? It is certain that no discernible *actual* fact determined it to be so. But is its hardness not, nevertheless, a *real* fact?

[53] CP 5.403.
[54] A realism of *would-be's* and "real Necessity and real Possibility," CP 5.457.

To say, as the article of January 1878 seems to intend, that it is just as an arbitrary "usage of speech" chooses to arrange its thoughts, is as much as to decide against the reality of the property, since the real is that which is such as it is regardless of how it is, at any time, thought to be. Remember that this diamond's condition is not an isolated fact. There is no such thing; and an isolated fact could hardly be real.[55]

Peirce goes on to say that the quality of *hardness* of the diamond, though not tested for its presence, is known to be associated with other qualities that are, in this case, observed to be present. Hardness is not an isolated fact. Thus a certain "perversion of the word and concept *real*" occurs in saying that the absence of a scratch test prevented the hardness of a diamond "from having the reality which it otherwise" would have had.[56]

Peirce concludes that the hardness of the diamond consists, not in occult states, but in the truth of a general conditional proposition:

> if a substance of a certain kind should be exposed to an agency of a certain kind, a certain kind of sensible result *would* ensue, according to our experiences hitherto. . . . nothing else than this can be so much as *meant* by saying that an object possesses a character.

But then, Peirce adds, this means that one is

> obliged to subscribe to the doctrines of real Modality, including real Necessity and real Possibility.[57]

Finally, then, to say of a substance that by calling it hard we mean it *would not* be scratched is a different position from that in which it is maintained, as Peirce first did, that there is "no difference between a hard thing and a soft thing so long as they are not brought to the test."

6) Conditional statements, we saw, in which a definite operation is prescribed and a definite general result predicted serve to explicate and to give the pragmatic meaning of signs. Signs that do not admit of translation by some conditional statement of this sort are thus pragmatically meaningless. But it is worth recognizing Peirce's liberal expansion of meaningfulness to include *conceivable* operations and results, conceivable practical effects, and even assertions concerning imaginary objects.

Thus the notions of an *experimental situation*, of a *definite operation*, and of a *practical result* are each subject to equally liberal strictures. The meanings of mathematical statements, for example, take the same conditional form in which

---

[55] *CP* 5.457.
[56] *CP* 5.457.
[57] *CP* 5.457. For a discussion of related problems and the above passages from Peirce, see Bronstein. See also Peirce's letter to Calderoni, *CP* 8.205–213, in which he discusses this same issue and says, *CP* 8.208: "I myself went too far in the direction of nominalism when I said that it was a mere question of the convenience of speech whether we say that a diamond is hard when it is not pressed upon, or whether we say that it is soft until it is pressed upon. I *now* say that experiment will prove that the diamond is hard, as a positive fact. That is, it is a real fact that it *would* resist pressure, which amounts to extreme scholastic realism."

conceivable practical effects are expressed. Pragmatic meaning includes "any flight of imagination, provided this imagination ultimately alights upon a possible practical effect."[58] The "possible effect" of a belief concerning the incommensurability of the diagonal "relates to what is expectable for a person dealing with fractions."[59]

While the qualifications to be met by signs endowed with pragmatic meaning are substantially enlarged to allow mathematical, imaginary, and perhaps even mythical expressions a place alongside straightforward statements of fact, a corresponding tightening of restrictions upon meaningfulness is suggested by Peirce's use of "possible" or "conceivable" effects or consequences as a necessary condition for statement meaning. The precise sense of 'possible' or 'conceivable' remains obscure. But Peirce evidently did not intend to argue that to have pragmatic meaning a statement need only possess *logically possible* (or logically conceivable) consequences, else any statement would qualify as meaningful. Some of those vain disputes of philosophers "which no observation of facts could settle" and for which pragmatism was initially designed as a method of critical demolition would thereby be restored to a respectable status. That an expression merely have logically possible consequences to be meaningful is obviously too weak a criterion of meaning. Under it even near hits at nonsense are admissible as meaningful (thus, 'Ink always dreams dolefully' and thus, 'Some of the spots on this page are dolefully dreaming').

7)   That we should happen to find the notions of the *conceivable* or *possible* consequences or "practical bearings" of concepts obscure is a pretty serious matter. It is worth our attention for a moment to reexamine more closely what Peirce says on the matter. For, clearly, these notions are basic to his formulation of pragmatic meaning to the maxim and to its uses as a principle of analysis. Then, too, James followed Peirce in confidently assigning the meaning of ideas to "their conceivable practical consequences" (see below, § 27 and Appendix 3). So our doubts about these notions, if reasonable, are of some relevance to the history we have thus far been studying.

Peirce's statement of the maxim informs us that our *conception* of the *conceivable* practical bearings (or sensible effects) of an object is "the whole" of our conception of the object.[60] The question is, just what is meant by the word 'con-

58 *CP* 5.196.
59 *CP* 5.541.
60 After stating the maxim, Peirce uses the words "sensible effects" rather than "practical bearings" in his subsequent discussion and illustrations of its significance. But he was not maintaining that the sensible effects of an object constitute its meaning. He was saying that our *conception* of the object is our *conception* of its sensible effects. He says that our conception of those effects is "the whole" of our conception of the object. Sometimes he appeared to deny that, in saying one concept is "the whole" of another, he was arguing that one concept is the *meaning* of another, or that he was talking about meaning at all. Thus, in a letter to James, Perry II, 432–433: "I do not think I have often spoken of the 'meaning of a concept' whether 'serious' or not. I have said that the concept itself 'is' *nothing more* than the concept, not of any concrete difference that *will* be made to someone, but is nothing more than the concept of the *conceivable* practical applications of it." This statement (of 1904) makes hash of many uncritical interpretations

ceivable' in this context. Now Peirce evidently did not mean by 'conceivable' what we are *able* to conceive; else the meanings of concepts will vary according to the wit, ingenuity, and I.Q. of those of us who happen to—in Peirce's words— "consider" the effects that "might" conceivably be practical bearings of the object of our conception. But how, then, are we to understand what the conceivable practical bearings of the conceived object *might* be?

It is generally thought that Peirce was implicitly making use of some notion of *possibility* here.[61] The conceivable practical bearings or effects of "the object of our conception" are its *possible* practical (or sensible) effects. We conceive of an object as having a range of possible practical effects and our conception of the object *is* (or means) the concept of those possible effects.

It is Descartes who made this distinction a conspicuous addition to the modern philosopher's equipment in epistemology and analysis. He distinguished *conceiving* from *sensation* and *imagination* on the grounds that the former, unlike the latter, is not confined to fact or experience for its occurrence; nor for its share of meaning and truth. One can imagine and conceive of triangles; but one cannot imagine (i.e., picture to oneself) a thousand-sided figure, though the same is easily conceived.[62] Conceiving, Descartes pointed out, is a matter of apprehending definitions (and what is signified by concepts).[63] While sense and imagination are tied to our experience of "bodies," what limits our conceptual power? What defines conceivability? Presumably the laws of logic for Descartes. Thus X is conceivable if X is logically possible; the inconceivable is the logically contradictory (or all cases of logical impossibility).

This Cartesian distinction has had considerable influence upon modern philosophy; its presence is observable in much of the categorizing of knowledge into sense experience and rational (or "purely" logical) laws, a posteriori and a priori, synthetic and analytic;[64] it dominates most philosophizing on the nature of logic and mathematics. It is tempting to cling to old categories in the absence of any-

---

of Peirce's maxim as a "theory" of meaning. However, one must also note that in later years Peirce indulged in a profuse variety of pronouncements on what he meant by 'pragmatism.' It is clear that he was searching, and that his pragmatism was never one finished doctrine but a series of ephemeral and evolving phases of several related lines of inquiry. His interest in "the analysis of concepts," as he liked to call it, and the papers in which the pragmatic maxim is stated, do exhibit a concern with *meaning* and the clarification of concepts. Thus, writing about pragmatism in 1905, he speaks of pragmatism as supplying the "wanted" "method for ascertaining the real meaning of any concept, doctrine, proposition, word, or other sign," *CP* 5.6.

61 See, e.g., Gallie, pp. 126–131, who, discussing Peirce's view of signs and interpretants, often uses 'possible' in pointing out that "every sign allows a number of alternative possible interpretants. . . through a succession of further possible signs . . . ," p. 127; or Barnes, p. 57, "the word *conceivably* has nothing to do with conceiving but means merely possibly." And Peirce himself occasionally substitutes 'possible' for 'conceivable.' For some general problems concerning pragmatism and *possibility*, see Appendix 7 below.

62 See the beginning of the Sixth Meditation. The distinction goes back—as all things philosophical do—to Plato, e.g., the latter part of *Theaetetus*; or see Aristotle, *De anima* III, 3, 428a ff.

63 Rule XIV, *Rules for the Direction of the Mind*. See also the first paragraphs of the Sixth Meditation.

64 See Appendix 6.

thing better. Thus, when faced with the question of how to make sense of the notions of *conceivable effects* or consequences, as we are just now, it is tempting to resort to the expeditious notion of *possibility,* as we did just a moment ago. But the light from Descartes does not illuminate our problem. Troubled by what might understandably be said to be the conceivable sensible effects of some object X of our conception, we are advised that these are the possible sensible effects. Do we mean by the 'possible effects' those that are not logically impossible, or are not physically impossible? Will a concept of the possible sensible effects of an object be one which is not *necessarily* false? Use of the terms 'necessity' and 'possibility' as physical modalities stands in as much need of clarification in this case as did 'conceivable.' Furthermore, our troubles are multiplied when we reflect that to conceive of the possible sensible effects of X is something like being asked to conceive of everything possibly true of X (in either a physical or logical sense of 'possibility'). This is a vast undertaking; the chances of ever finding out what the *concept* of X means, if we had to follow this procedure, are slight indeed.

These, and related difficulties not set forth above but not hard to uncover, are engendered by some uncertainty over how we are to interpret the word 'conceivable' in Peirce's statement of the pragmatic maxim. As is the case with most words ending with 'able,' to ask about their meaning is to raise questions of modalities, of possibility, and of necessity.[65] Peirce evidently came to believe that his pragmatic maxim of meaning rested upon a doctrine of possibility: it amounted "to saying that possibility is sometimes of a real kind."[66] Although his arguments and the doctrine do not make easy reading, Peirce does make clear that he thought "a doctrine of a real Modality" was entailed by his analysis of meaning and was required for the truth of the conditional statements (and the counter-factual conditional statements noticed above) in which the meaning of "intellectual predicates" gets stated.[67]

But the doctrine of real modality does not seem to help us with our initial perplexity concerning 'conceivable.' One can still ask, in actual instances where the clarification of a concept is the aim, what are the *relevant* conceivable sensible effects of an object that are to count as parts of "the whole" of our conception of it. There are hints from Peirce that our concept of the conceivable effects of an object can be made manageable and need not require our entertaining all

---

[65] For more on this topic, see Appendix 7.

[66] *CP* 5.453.

[67] This, again, is a feature of Peirce's "scholastic realism," cf. *CP* 5.453.

In this connection see Peirce's "The Doctrine of Chances" in which the scholastic realism and real modalities are strongly affirmed, thus the tendency of a die to behave as it does when thrown is like a human *habit, CP* 2.664:

> I am, then, to define the meanings of the statement that the *probability,* that if a die be thrown from a dice box it will turn up a number divisible by three, is one-third. The statement means that the die has a certain "would-be"; and to say that a die has a "would-be" is to say that it has a property, quite analogous to any *habit* that a man might have.

For a further discussion of this passage, see the latter part of § 22.

of the "possible" sensible effects. For he does maintain that considerations of use, the particular contexts and purposes we have in mind, will have the beneficial effect of imposing some conditions of relevance and irrelevance upon our thinking about what *the* "practical bearings" (or sensible effects) of an object are. Thus it is not every *conceivable* sensible effect which *might* be possible that compels our attention in developing meaningful concepts of objects.[68]

8) Whatever the sense of 'conceivable' or 'possible' in Peirce's talk of conceivable and possible effects, which concepts and statements must have if pragmatically meaningful, the primary motivation is clear: since statements have consequences, it is a class of stated, confirmable, experimental consequences that statements *mean*. The translation of any term or statement into the conditional form discussed earlier is a translation resulting in an assertion that, on experiment, a certain operation if performed will lead to certain confirmable results. From such considerations it follows that to have meaning a statement must be confirmable, i.e., in principle or "conceivably" capable of experimental verification. A further but less certain conclusion suggests itself and seems occasionally to come from Peirce himself: namely, the (pragmatic) meaning of any statement is the procedure of its verification.[69]

This last thought about meaning, if indeed it is to be found urged by Peirce, has become familiar in the literature of modern empiricism. It is simply one way of asserting the "verification theory of meaning," a theory emphatically and effectively used, and all but stated by Berkeley.[70] Much of the more recent discussion of this theory need not concern us for the moment. But one point does matter. Proponents of the theory, in giving their different versions, have occa-

[68] For example, despite the appearance of 'conceivable,' note the qualifications in parentheses in the following statement (*CP* 5.467), that pragmatism asserts
> that the *total* meaning of a predication of an intellectual concept is contained in an affirmation that, under all conceivable circumstances of a given kind (or under this or that more or less indefinite part of the cases of their fulfillment, should the predication be modal) the subject of the predication would behave in a certain general way—that is, it would be true under given experiential circumstances (or under a more or less definitely stated proportion of them, *taken as they would occur*, that is in the same order of succession, *in experience*).

A further discussion of this passage is to be found in the latter part of § 22 below.

In these pages I have been questioning Peirce's use of "conceivable effects" or "consequences" as part of the pragmatic maxim. I am aware that Peirce knew of the medieval doctrine of *consequentia* (*CP* 4.45, 4.51). As he says, *CP* 4.43*n.*: "In the language of logic 'consequence' does not mean that which follows, which is called the *consequent,* but means the fact that a consequent follows from an antecedent." But this distinction, important as it is in other contexts of Peirce's writings, does not resolve the difficulties raised above.

[69] *CP* 1.615: "Take any general term whatever. I say of a stone that it is *hard*. That means that so long as the stone remains hard, every essay to scratch it by the moderate pressure of a knife will surely fail. To call the stone hard is to predict that no matter how often you try the experiment, it will fail every time. That innumerable series of conditional predications is involved in the meaning of this lowly adjective."

[70] Cf. his famous pronouncement on the meaning of the term *exist*, which, incidentally, also takes the conditional form in which Peirce casts pragmatic meaning. "The table I write on, I say, exists, that is I see and feel it; and if I were out of my study I should say it existed, meaning thereby that if I was in my study I might perceive it, or that some other spirit actually does perceive it." Berkeley, *Principles*, I. 3. See also Appendix 5 below.

sionally spoken as if the meaning of a statement and a class of overt actions or events—namely, the verifications of the statement—can somehow be equated. The statement 'there are more than 100 persons in New York City' might be said to mean "if anyone in New York City starts counting persons, the count will exceed 100." Since the statement is verifiable, i.e., confirmable or disconfirmable, it may be said by some to be meaningful. But if it is also said that the meaning of the statement *is* its verification (or the method of testing it[71]), then presumably the act of going to New York City and counting persons becomes a *meaning*. Just so, a red book on the table and our looking at it will be said to be the meaning of "there is a red book on the table." But it is not at all evident that the physical objects (red book and table) and optical activity (our looking) are *meanings* at all; pending, of course, some understanding of *meaning*—but that is just the troublesome point.

A more cautious rendering of the theory might include distinctions between a statement ("here is a red book on the table"), the occasion and method of its verification (our looking for red book and table), and the statement of the method and results of its verification ("a red book on the table is now being observed").[72] The occasion of verifying a statement is then not regarded or obscured as a *synonym* of that statement; but the statement or statements describing its verification could be considered as giving its meaning. Meaning and sameness of meaning is then held to statements and relations between statements, rather than directed to statements and physical events. Such seems to be Peirce's intention when he is being careful in discussing pragmatic meaning. The pragmatic meaning of a concept, word, or statement is not its practical bearings, or testable and sensible effects, but a description (a conditional statement) of its conceivable consequences. Pragmatic meaning is not verification; the meaning of signs is not identified with the operations and conditions to which signs refer. The meaning of signs is identified with other signs, namely, with conditional statements after the manner already discussed earlier.

Finally, it is a characteristic of Peirce, and of his meaning theory, to maintain

---

[71] Cf. Carnap in "Testability and Meaning," Introduction, sec. 1, p. 420: "Thus the meaning of a sentence is in a certain sense identical with the way we determine its truth or falsehood."

That the meaning of a sentence is the method of its verification is a thesis that once seemed to receive impressive support from procedures in modern physics, e.g., Einstein in 1916 discussing the "sense of the statement" that two flashes of lightning occurred simultaneously. Of 'simultaneous,' Einstein writes, p. 22: "The concept does not exist for the physicist until he has the possibility of discovering whether or not it is fulfilled in an actual case. We thus require a definition of simultaneity such that this definition supplies us with the method by means of which, in the present case, he can decide by experiment whether or not both the lightning strokes occurred simultaneously. As long as this requirement is not satisfied, I allow myself to be deceived . . . when I imagine that I am able to attach a meaning to the statement of simultaneity."

[72] Such is the spirit of Hempel's description of one of the earlier forms of the theory, in "Problems and Changes in the Empiricist Criterion of Meaning," p. 44; Linsky, p. 166: "A sentence S has empirical meaning if and only if it is possible to indicate a finite set of observation sentences, O_1, O_2 . . . . O_n, such that if these are true, then S is necessarily true, too." The difficulties in this and other improved attempts to state the theory are cogently dealt with by Hempel in this article.

that the meaning of a sign has reference to an indefinite number of confirmable consequences. To say "X is hard" means, according to Peirce, "to predict that no matter how often you try the experiment" of scratching X, "it will fail every time." The limited number of experiments upon X which we may care to try in a day or a lifetime are each singly or as a finite whole degrees of confirmation of the statement "X is hard." A limited number of such tests may make the meaning of the statement *clear* to those of us who cannot reckon in any other way. But what the meaning is and how it is prompted or taught differ in this respect: the records of actual confirming instances are ordinarily but a sub-class of the meaning of the sign or term. For the statement asserts, or means, that it is *always* the case, *whenever* you try, that X *will* not be scratched. Thus, understanding the meaning of a sign, we will know how to supply a confirming instance of the sign. But knowing how to confirm and knowing the meaning of a sign are not the same. Knowing the meaning involves understanding an assertion about an "innumerable series" of confirming instances.

§ 22.   Peirce's Empiricism: The Theory of Knowledge and Probability

Before proceeding to consider several vexed issues in Peirce's views on truth, something should be said about another of his contributions to pragmatism and to modern philosophy.

I refer to Peirce's conception of the nature of empirical knowledge. For while he has no treatise on this subject, his writings are rich with critical insights concerning the acquisition and character of empirical knowledge. A number of Peirce's discussions of the interpretation of probability statements, of the justification of beliefs, and of the inductive methods used to attain knowledge have proved themselves very fruitful for further inquiry. Doubtless one reason for this is that Peirce had a thorough training in the sciences he was writing and thinking about. Thus, his suggestions for how the procedures and organization of empirical science are to be interpreted and explained have an authentic connection with actual practices in the sciences. That connection, for Peirce, is the key to the only adequate theory or explanation of knowledge.

Four of these suggestions merit our consideration here, for each has become a cardinal thesis of contemporary empiricism. Three of these are of a general philosophical nature; the best arrangement will be to discuss them first before turning to the other, the subject of probability, which demands a more extended analysis and which will concern us in the latter and longer half of this section.

1)   As a part of his analysis of the actual causal conditions of doubt and of inquiry (§ 20 above), Peirce was led to argue that theoretical explanations of the existence of knowledge do not require the imputation of indubitable or absolutely certain basic beliefs and propositions. Philosophic tradition has all too

often assured us otherwise. That is, it has been reasoned that a system of knowledge is only as true and acceptable as the premises and beliefs upon which it rests. This reasoning Peirce does not deny; the conclusions of a carefully constructed argument are good or bad depending on the premises employed. But Peirce's objection is to the further line of reasoning that this little lesson in logic is alleged to support. For the further reasoning comes to something like this: if the system of scientific knowledge can be accounted for at all, there must be some basic truths, some ultimate propositions or premises that determine the truth of the system (of the other beliefs and propositions) supported by and depending upon them. Aristotle held that the premises of the conceptual system of science cannot stretch back *ad infinitum*. For if the sources and causes of demonstration have themselves to be demonstrated, we are lost in an infinite regress and should never be able to produce a finished demonstration. Thus he develops the argument for some "primary" and "immediate" basic truths of demonstration;[73] these are indemonstrable and are known by *nous*, rational intuition.[74] In a quite similar vein (we saw in Part One, § 5), Descartes argued for clear and distinct conceptions.

Here, as so often in the study of philosophic argument, it is illuminating to watch the use of metaphors and similes. For these serve not only as means of stating arguments; they sometimes operate, if unconsciously, to guide and help sustain the argument in question. Thus the argument for basic truths, or indubitable premises, takes as its model geometry, and also the architecture and mechanics of buildings. A system of geometry does commence with a set of basic concepts—definitions, axioms, and postulates—and the truth of theorems is dependent upon the truth of these premises. A sense of the logical structure of geometry encourages metaphors of physical structure. Thus the system of knowledge is "firm" if its "foundations" are "solid"; or, if the "edifice" does not rest on "bedrock" truth, then the "building collapses."[75]

We saw briefly in § 20 that according to Peirce's theory of inquiry, thought *in fact* does not spring from wholesale doubting of beliefs, nor does it seek or result in indubitable beliefs. Thought begins with "a real and living doubt,"[76] and issues in a state of belief. "Doubt is an uneasy and dissatisfied state from which

---

[73] *Posterior Analytics* I. 2-3 (esp. 72b20).

[74] The famous account, *ibid.* II. 19. For a related discussion of this point, see § 22 below, and further, § 82.

[75] Historically a famous and important instance of this model (though not the first or last) is found in the second paragraph of Descartes's First Meditation:

> since the destruction of the foundation necessarily involves the collapse of all the rest of the edifice, I shall first attack the principles upon which all my former opinions were founded.

The skeptical argument—against the senses as sources of knowledge—that then follows readies the reader for the needed remedy: clear and distinct, absolutely certain and necessarily true beliefs for a new foundation.

On these metaphors and their roles as "representations" of reasoning, Vailati (§ 76 below) has an interesting study, "On Material Representations of Deductive Processes.

[76] *CP* 5.376.

we struggle to free ourselves and pass into the state of belief."[77] Peirce's objection to the theory of indubitable truths as the foundation of knowledge is that it misrepresents the actual character of and the procedures for attaining empirical knowledge. He thus writes:

> It is a very common idea that a demonstration must rest on some ultimate and absolutely indubitable propositions. . . . But, in point of fact, an inquiry, to have that completely satisfactory result called demonstration, has only to start with propositions perfectly free from all actual doubt. If the premises are not in fact doubted at all, they cannot be more satisfactory than they are.[78]

This, notice, is intended as an empirical objection to theories that do "in point of fact" mistake the nature of thought and the operation of inquiry.

Coupled with this objection is Peirce's view that the test conditions and warranting of a system of beliefs or propositions lie not in a search for basic truths or indubitability, but rather consist in determining the logical and probable *consequences* of our beliefs.

Finally, Peirce argues with much effect that the "basic" features in the system of empirical knowledge are not to be identified as ultimate, indubitable propositions but rather as the *methods* that are employed, the formulated "leading principles," the "habits" of inference, the "inferential procedure" according to which conclusions and consequences of beliefs are attained.[79] The guiding principles of reasoning count most in determining the success and progress of a system of knowledge.

Peirce's theory of inquiry, it should be observed, is an ambitious and carefully developed alternative to the Cartesian transcendental philosophy of clear and distinct indubitable concepts (see Part One, especially §§ 4–5) as the "foundation" of scientific knowledge.

2)   A second important suggestion found in Peirce's discussions of empirical knowledge comes with his recognition that the analysis of the meanings of concepts is a contextual procedure. That is, the way meanings are explicated is partly determined by the kinds of interests and conditions, the controlling aims and circumstances in which analysis of meaning occurs and is thought to be needed. Peirce is not a champion of a method for finding *the* meaning of a concept. His emphasis is less on the meaning than upon the recognizable ways of *using* certain kinds of terms in certain kinds of situations. We have seen (in § 21) how Peirce proposed that the explication of meanings of signs is achieved through the analysis of and conscious control over certain operations or uses of signs. But this is also to emphasize that the pragmatic meaning of signs, for Peirce, is not a separate or adjunct event of language. Pragmatic meaning is not to be sought

[77] *CP* 5.372.
[78] *CP* 5.376.
[79] See *CP* 5.366; also 5.280. For a discussion of this idea, the reader is referred to § 85 below.

inside or attached to signs, as if meanings are events linked somehow to signs. Furthermore, for Peirce, meaning is not to be sought in single signs or in isolation from a whole system of signs, from the rules governing the uses of signs, and from those habits of behavior and kinds of conduct that are also constituent parts of a system of signs.

3) The third way in which Peirce has helped enlighten us as to the nature of empirical knowledge is in his view of the process of the verification of truth claims, or beliefs and assertions. The single point I wish to note here concerning Peirce's accounts of the process of verification—for he has many things to say about this—is his view of the thoroughly social or communal form that it assumed for him. The act of verification is far from consisting in the matching of a claim against a fact or the confrontation of some belief with some fact or indubitable idea. Peirce saw the process of verification (like the explication of meaning) as occurring within and mediated by a system of established procedures and a related body of claims and beliefs. Verification occurs within an elaborate socially inherited system of knowledge (as is further remarked below in § 22). The techniques of verification, the supporting conditions of an act of testing a claim, the working standards of procedure and control are all, for Peirce, the creation and possession of the scientific community as a whole. And that community is active in and through the activities of its individual members inquiring into facts, or analyzing meanings, or testing claims and beliefs.

But this matter of verification brings us to the last of the four basic ideas in Peirce's empiricism that we set out to consider. This is the idea of *probability*.

4) Judging from his writings on the subject, Peirce's theory of probability is the unifying and most important part of his interpretation of empirical knowledge. This is one reason for now coming to that theory; but there is another reason as well. In Peirce's pragmatism there is an especially significant linking of the maxim of pragmatism with the theory of probability. This is of particular interest to us in the present pages. Accordingly, the discussion that follows is directed to an explanation of each of these matters.

Peirce was impressed with the success of the "statistical method" in the history of science in the nineteenth century. The Darwinian controversy was then raging, and the figure of Darwin is often the focus in Peirce's view of the development and widespread applications of statistical procedures in nineteenth-century science.[80]

The Darwinian controversy is, in large part, a question of logic. Mr. Darwin proposed to apply the statistical method to biology. The same thing had been done in a widely different branch of science, the theory of gases. Though unable to say what the movements of any particular molecule of gas would be on a certain hypothesis regarding the constitution of this class of bodies, Clausius and Maxwell were yet able, eight years before the publication of Darwin's immortal work, by

[80] For the background and reaction to Darwinian evolution in the history of pragmatism, see Wiener's *Evolution and the Founders of Pragmatism*.

the application of the doctrine of probabilities, to predict that in the long run such a proportion of the molecules would, under given circumstances, acquire such and such velocities . . . and from these propositions were able to deduce certain properties of gases. . . . In like manner, Darwin, while unable to say what the operation of variation and natural selection in any individual case will be, demonstrates that in the long run they will [or would][81] adapt animals to their circumstances.[82]

For Peirce, the theory of probabilities is the logic of modern science.[83] With his view of the history of nineteenth-century science, in the spirit of Quetelet, the Belgian astronomer, "the Faradays, the Helmholtzes, and the Mendeléefs,"[84] Peirce championed a thoroughly *statistical* version of probability. "The word probability, taken in the sense in which the insurance business uses it, means a well-founded statistical generalization."[85]

There is another reason why Peirce was led to emphasize the importance of statistical methods in science. It should not be forgotten that Peirce was thoroughly trained in chemistry, surveying, and astronomy.[86] His philosophical thought is often guided by his scientific background. (For instance, the illustrations of *weight* and *force* in his discussion of the pragmatic method of clarifying ideas in his famous paper, "How to Make Our Ideas Clear," are related to work he had been conducting on pendulums.[87])

The firsthand experience in astronomy and surveying in particular furnished Peirce with a sound understanding of the techniques of mathematical probability in the systematizing and correcting of measurements and observations. As he frequently observed, the "theory of errors" and "the method of least squares" played major roles in the subsequent history of measurement, probability theory, and statistics.[88] In these mathematical techniques one can find many ideas that

[81] The word 'would' is not in the original, the editors note; see *CP* 5.364. As we shall see below, 'would' is a very important term (and "in the long run" an important phrase) in Peirce's theory of probability.
[82] *CP* 5.364.
[83] *CP* 7.177. Also: "The theory of probabilities is simply the science of logic quantitatively treated. . . . Thus the problem of probabilities is simply the general problem of logic," *CP* 2.647.
[84] *CP* 7.177.
[85] *CP* 7.177.
[86] See the review of Peirce's early studies and work in the Introduction to this Part. Fisch in his "Chronicle of Pragmaticism," p. 465, rightly cites as one of the factors in the genesis of pragmatism "Peirce's observational and theoretical work as a scientist in the period 1860–1878, and particularly in chemistry, spectroscopy, stellar photometry, metrology and geodesy."
It should perhaps be added here that Peirce's early work (in 1867) in improving Boole's calculus was motivated by the idea that the calculus provided a precise way of dealing with problems of probability: "The principle use of Boole's Calculus of Logic lies in its application to problems concerning probability," *CP* 3.1.
[87] Lenzen, pp. 33–34, notes this.
[88] Peirce remarks, *CP* 7.22, that according to the method of least squares, "the multiplication of observations will indefinitely reduce the error of their mean." For examples, see *CP* 7.13, 7.23.
Peirce wrote a paper "On the Theory of Errors of Observation" (1873) "with the design of showing what the limitations to the applicability of the method of least squares are, and what course is to be pursued when that method fails," p. 200. In this memoir, which well

become of philosophic importance in Peirce's writings: for example, the distinction between estimated and approximate measures, and optimal or true values. The convergence to truth or a limit of probable and statistical methods "if persistently applied"[89] and "in the long run" are characteristic features of Peirce's philosophical view of inquiry and knowledge. Some of this we have come upon earlier and some remains to be elicited in the pages to follow.[90]

An example of one such mathematical technique may help to make some of these anticipations of philosophic ideas clear. It is often important in scientific work that the measurements or observations of subject matter be as accurate as possible. It is also often evident that actual measurements that can be made exhibit certain discrepancies and variations. The method of least squares had its first applications in just such circumstances. Thus let U be some unknown quantity which we want to determine with our instruments of measurement. We make n number of readings, $r_1, r_2, r \ldots r_n$, which have varying results, and this we attribute to errors in our measuring procedures. The question is: What is the most reliable "true" or "optimal" value of U? Traditionally, one answer was that of determining the arithmetical mean, m:

$$m = \frac{r_1 + r_2 + \ldots + r_n}{n}$$

To justify this last step takes us directly into the subject of probability theory. But it is to be noticed that we could select any value for U. Then the differences $U - r_1, U - r_2 \ldots U - r_n$ would be the varied deviations from U of the different readings. Now it is reasonable to suppose that the optimal value for U will be one whose total deviation is the smallest possible. (Although why this is reasonable again takes us directly into probability theory.) However, following Gauss, we can conveniently arrange to take the squares of the devient readings of U,

$$(U - r_1)^2, (U - r_2)^2 \ldots (U - r_n)^2$$

as our measures of inaccuracy. We can then establish as the optimal value for U, among all of the possible values, one whose sum of the squares of deviations

---

deserves republication and which Lenzen (pp. 41–42) comments on, is found a lucid application of Peirce's logic of relations to probability (for which see also the first papers in *CP* 3 and the second paragraph of note 86 above). Working with a traditional distinction of "absolute" and "relative" terms, Peirce introduces a symbolism for easily expressing—in effect—the *quantification* of statements about *all* or *some* members of classes to which may be assigned in *all* cases or in a relative number, or average number of cases, a certain property. These relative (or average) numbers are important; for they are probabilities. "The importance of average numbers arises from the fact that all our knowledge really consists of nothing but average numbers; for all our knowledge is derived from induction, and its analogue, hypothesis," p. 201. The general nature of induction, Peirce continues, is everywhere the same, viz., reasoning from samples of classes, or relative numbers of cases, to an approximate general ratio. In this process, if my conclusion is in error, "it is an error which the repetition of the same process must tend to rectify," p. 201. He points out that "the law of least squares recognizes the possibility of any error positive or negative, however great, though the probability of indefinitely great errors will be indefinitely small," p. 207.

[89] *CP* 2.776.
[90] See § 23, also § 78.

$$(U - r_1)^2 + (U - r_2)^2 + \ldots + (U - r_n)^2$$

will be as small as possible. It can be easily shown that the optimal value for U is the arithmetic mean *m*, and this is the initial step in the development of Gauss's method of least squares.[91]

A statistical approximation to truth, if persisted in, is clear in the employment of the method of least squares, ignoring here the limitations of that method. "Probability," writes Peirce, "is a statistical ratio" and this "must be of the nature of a *real fact* and not a *state of mind.*"[92] In another of his accounts of the development of nineteenth-century science in using the "statistical method" Peirce says:

> The *Origin of Species* was published toward the end of the year 1859. The preceding years since 1846 had been one of the most productive . . . in the entire history of science. . . . The idea that chance begets order, which is one of the corner-stones of modern physics . . . was at that time put into its clearest light. Quetelet had opened the discussion by his *Letters on the Application of Probabilities to the Moral and Political Sciences*,[93] a work which deeply impressed the best minds of the day. . . . Meanwhile the "statistical method" had, under that very name, been applied with brilliant success to molecular physics. Dr. John Herapath, an English chemist, had outlined the kinetical theory of gases . . . and the interest the theory excited had been refreshed . . . by Clausius and Krönig. In the very summer preceding Darwin's publication, Maxwell had read before the British Association the first and most important of his researches on this subject."[94]

"Chance begets order," writes Peirce. He reflects something of the enthusiasm that Quetelet, and before him Poisson (many of whose ideas Quetelet popularized) had for the idea that in disorder and the apparently fortuitous course of events was the working of order, systematic regularities, and law.[95] The basic idea here is that a certain discoverable regularity in groups of events increases in degree as the number of occurring instances of events increases. Behind this idea is what has generally been regarded as the cornerstone (to recall Peirce's language in the above quotation) of statistical probability, namely, Bernoulli's theorem.

Daniel Bernoulli employed the probability calculus in laying the foundations of the kinetic theory of gases. With his brother, Jacob, he saw how the calculus of probability could be made to establish regularities and uniformities in the *mean* values of classes of events, rather than for the single event.

Jacob Bernoulli's theorem, contained in the fourth part of his *Ars conjectandi* (1713), may be very roughly outlined as follows. Consider the tossing of a coin. Assuming the coin is not "biased" there is an equal possibility of its turning up heads or tails. The number of heads, H, to the number of tails, T, is $\frac{H}{T}$; and

[91] See Courant and Robbins, pp. 265–266, for this example.
[92] *CP* 5.21.
[93] Bruxelles, 1846. But Quetelet had shortly after 1823 commenced his long series of papers on the application of probability to social statistics. See Keynes, p. 334.
[94] *CP* 6.297.
[95] See Keynes, pp. 334–335.

the probability of a head is $\dfrac{H}{H+T}$. It was Laplace who stated the classical definition of probability as the quotient of the number of favorable cases over the
number of all possible cases. Here, in the example of the coin, the probability
of a favorable case is found in the relative *frequency* of heads turning up among
all of the tosses (i.e., in $H + T$), but with this addition: "when a large number
of tosses are made." The notion of a relative frequency of an event, in "a large
number of cases," takes us to Bernoulli's theorem (or, since Poisson's description, often referred to as "the law of large numbers").

Let p be the probability of the occurrence of some event E in a single trial
(such as a coin landing heads when tossed). Now in a series of trials Tr,[96] in
which E may or may not occur, the most probable proportion, or frequency of
occurrences of E to the total number of Tr (i.e., $\dfrac{E}{E+Tr}$), is p. Moreover, the
probability of the frequency of E's deviating from p will be less than any small
positive number ϵ, no matter how small ϵ may be, provided that the number of
trials Tr is large. As the number of Tr is increased, the probability of the frequency of E deviating from p by less than ϵ increases.

Since in our illustration of the coin, p is $\frac{1}{2}$ (on the assumption that the turn-
ing-up of heads or tails is equally possible), then as the number of tosses (i.e.,
Tr) increases (and Tr must be large), the proportion of heads (i.e., E's) turning
up will not deviate from p (i.e., $\frac{1}{2}$) by more than ϵ, however small ϵ may be.

A result of the theorem is sometimes stated this way: if the sequence of tosses
Tr is "long enough," it becomes increasingly likely (or certain) that the number
of heads (i.e., E's) will deviate by less than 0.1 per cent from half of Tr.[97]

The frequency interpretation of probability adopted by Peirce is found in
Aristotle,[98] Bolzano, and Cournot. It was further developed by Ellis[99] and
Venn.[100] Peirce's own statements of the position depart only slightly from Venn,
to whom he acknowledges indebtedness.[101] The most original contribution by

[96] It might be noted that in these paragraphs the phrases "large number of cases," or
"large number of trials" (or Kneale's "a sufficiently large set" of the next footnote) are not
so easily made more precise in answer to the natural question, How large is a large number?

[97] Thus, von Mises, p. 175. Kneale, p. 139, states the theorem this way: "In a sufficiently
large set of a things it is almost certain that the relative frequency of β things will approximate to the probability of an a thing's being β within any degree of approximation
which may be desired. Here the phrase 'almost certain' is to be understood as a convenient
way of saying that there is a probability as near as we like to 1."

[98] Interpreting *Rhetoric* I. 2, 1357a35: "A probability is a thing that for the most part
happens."

[99] Ellis, "On the Foundations of the Theory of Probabilities" (1849).

[100] Venn, *The Logic of Chance* (1866).

[101] See CP 2.651, note 1. In addition to Venn's discussion of probability, Peirce may
well have responded to some of Venn's philosophical arguments even though critical of his
empiricism. In the chapter on "Gradations of Belief" in *The Logic of Chance*, Venn says
about *belief*, p. 82:

it will probably be admitted that a readiness to act upon the proposition believed in
is an inseparable accompaniment of that state of mind. There can be no alteration in
the belief without a possible alteration in the conduct, nor anything in the conduct
which is not connected with something in the belief.

This is close to Peirce's own analysis of belief and to the view of Bain of which, said
Peirce, pragmatism is "scarce more than a corollary" (see above, § 19). See also Fisch,
"A Chronicle of Pragmaticism," p. 446.

Peirce was to show how the frequency interpretation applied to classes of inferences or modes of argument, and thus to his conception of leading principles and
his theory of meaning and truth.[102]

The relative frequency interpretation of probability takes as its point of departure the idea that if a certain event E occurs in m cases out of n, m is
the "frequency" of the occurrence of E, and the ratio $\frac{m}{n}$ is the "relative frequency" of E. Two important conditions are necessary to the relative frequency
view of Venn and Peirce. First, probability statements make no references to
individual entities or events; they refer only to some specified characteristic or
property of elements or events of a non-empty class (or series, or group).[103]
Probability statements are about some designated property or characteristic of the
class, occurring with a certain relative frequency. Second, a rudimentary notion
in the frequency interpretation is that *probability* is a relative frequency of E,
when cases or classes m and n are "large." The relative frequency of E refers to
the occurrence of E "in the long run," that is, the reference is to a *limit* of a relative frequency.

Suppose that the class of events or elements is the throwing of a die. The turning up of one side is the characteristic or property. Then, as the die has six
sides, all of which turn up with equal frequency (in "the long run," a phrase to
be looked at more closely later on), the relative frequency of one characteristic
occurring, say, a six, in any one toss is $\frac{1}{6}$. This Peirce described as a material or
factual conception of probability: "the proportion of times in which an occurrence of one kind is accompanied by an occurrence of another kind.[104]

We want to distinguish this interpretation of probability from others according
to which probability is a measure of belief,[105] or is construed as a special logical
relation between propositions.[106] It should also be kept in mind that there is a
fundamental distinction between the calculus of probability, which is a branch
of pure mathematics, and *applications* of the calculus, via theories and interpretative rules, to empirical subject matters. There is an important difference in
interpreting the statement "the chance of throwing heads with an unbiased penny
is $\frac{1}{2}$." This may be treated as an empirical statistical statement that a coin satisfying certain physical conditions (i.e., "unbiased" referring to material, composition, and shape) will actually exhibit the stated relative frequence in a series
of tosses. Or the statement might be taken in a sense in which an "unbiased" coin
is defined as one that satisfies the calculus of probability. In this case the statement
tells us no more than that, for any two equally probable events, the probability of
one of them occurring is $\frac{1}{2}$. But this is an arithmetical truth; it tells us nothing
about the world and is no more informative than to say that one-half of one is
one-half.[107]

---

[102] This will be pointed out in pages below; also see § 85.
[103] E.g., Venn, p. 4, for whom the fundamental concept is that of *series*.
[104] *CP* 2.673.
[105] See, e.g., *CP* 2.673.
[106] See Nagel, *Principles of the Theory of Probability*, pp. 44–51.
[107] This point and several illuminating comments on problems in the relation of a
priori probability to empirical subject matters are to be found in Ayer, "Chance."

While probability as described earlier refers to certain ratios of occurrences of properties of classes of elements, Peirce himself was most interested in applying the idea of probability to *inferences* and arguments.

There is a difference between speaking of the probability of *events* occurring or not occurring and of *propositions, arguments,* and classes of *inferences* being true, or leading to true conclusions. Peirce does not always keep the difference clear and in some cases the difference is unimportant; for whether we speak of a die coming up a six as an *event* or as the *proposition* " 'the die has come up a six' is true" is often only a matter of verbal convenience. But the difference is important when Peirce proceeds to employ the idea of relative frequency as the cardinal principle in his novel and important interpretations of the nature of probable inference, induction, and the justification of induction.

Peirce often quotes Locke's statement in the *Essay*, that assent to a probable argument is due to "the proof being such as for the most part carries truth with it."[108] In accord with the description of the frequency view of probability given above, we can say that, for Peirce, a probable inference (or argument) is to be treated as a member of a class of inferences (or arguments) "all constructed in the same way,"[109] and in which the frequency of the conclusions being true or successful is a ratio of the premises being true. As Peirce puts it:

> To find the probability that from a given class of premises A, a given class of conclusions, B, follows, it is simply necessary to ascertain what proportion of the times in which premises of that class are true, the appropriate conclusions are also true. In other words, it is the number of cases of the occurrence of both events A and B, divided by the total number of cases of the occurrence of the event A.[110]

It is to be noticed that, for Peirce, a class or mode of inferences being the "method" or "habit or rule active in us" by which we pass from a set of premises A to conclusions B is called a *leading principle.* The "habit" (see above, § 20) or leading principle "is logically good provided it would never (or in the case of probable inference, seldom) lead from true premises to a false conclusion; otherwise, it is logically bad."[111] (For more on the subject of leading principles, see Part Four, Chapter Three, below.)

Peirce regards inductive reasoning as a form of probable inference.[112] It therefore is also analyzable in terms of relative frequencies of true conclusions drawn from true premises according to some rule of inference. Induction is a generalization about a class of things based upon a sampling of a portion of that class.

---

[108] In Locke's *Essay,* Book IV, ch. 15, sec. 1. For Peirce on this passage, CP 2.649, 2.696; and note Peirce's emphasis: "the probable argument is '*such as* for the most part carries truth with it,' " i.e., a probable argument is a *type* or of a class. See also *CP* 8.2 for an important early statement.
[109] *CP* 2.649.
[110] *CP* 2.658. Also, *CP* 2.650: "We may, therefore, define the probability of a mode of argument as the proportion of cases in which it carries truth with it."
[111] *CP* 3.164. This passage and the idea of leading principles are discussed more fully in §§ 84–85 below.
[112] See *CP* 2.783, as well as references cited below.

"Induction is reasoning from a sample taken at random to the whole lot sampled."[113] Certain conditions of independence and randomness of sampling enter into the determination of the reasonableness and success of inductions.[114] Generally, in "the long run" each sample is to be drawn with the same relative frequency. When these conditions do pertain, then

> judging of the statistical composition of a whole from a sample if judging by a method which will be right on the average in the long run, and, by the reasoning of the doctrine of chances, will be nearly right oftener than it will be far from right.[115]

Inductions are of two basic kinds.[116] First, there are inductions "where we judge what approximate proportion of the members of a collection have a predesignate character by a sample drawn." Second, there is a kind of induction comprising "those cases in which the inductive method if persisted in will certainly in time correct any error that it may have led us into."[117] The fact that induction is self-corrective as a method is its most important feature for Peirce, and this is the fundamental consideration when questions about the justification of induction are deliberated.[118]

Three important aspects of Peirce's interpretation of probability must be noted here.

First, probability statements are of an empirical statistical nature,[119] based, or purporting to be based upon some course of experience and upon regularities of

[113] *CP* 1.93.
[114] *CP* 1.93. E.g., in general, "an induction from more instances is, other things being equal, stronger than an induction from fewer instances," *CP* 2.780. For other stated conditions, see *CP* 7.208 ff. The notion of *random* sampling is extremely difficult to make precise, and is still the subject of controversy. Peirce's definition, *CP* 2.726, is as follows: "the sample should be drawn at random and independently from the whole lot sampled. That is to say, the sample must be taken according to a precept or method which, being applied over and over again indefinitely, would result in the drawing of any one set of instances as often as any other set of the same number."
[115] *CP* 1.93.
[116] There is a third kind discussed in *CP* 7.216.
[117] *CP* 7.208. Peirce goes on to discuss three conditions necessary to the process of fair sampling.
[118] Thus, *CP* 2.769:
> The true guarantee of the validity of induction is that it is a method of reaching conclusions which, if it is persisted in long enough, will assuredly correct any error concerning future experience into which it may temporarily lead us.

Also, *CP* 2.729:
> Nor must we lose sight of the constant tendency of the inductive process to correct itself. This is its essence. This is the marvel of it. The probability of its conclusion only consists in the fact that if the true value of the ratio sought has not been reached, an extension of the inductive process will lead to a closer approximation.

For more on this topic see § 71 and §§ 85–86 below. There are difficulties in Peirce's arguments about the self-corrective character of induction and his views of the justification of induction. Since I have not attempted to discuss them in these pages, the reader may be referred to the papers by Madden, Burks, and Lenz contained in the volume of Moore and Robin. See also Braithwaite, pp. 255–292; Nagel, *Principles of the Theory of Probability*, p. 77.
[119] *CP* 2.677: "Probability to have any value at all must express a fact. It is therefore a thing to be inferred upon evidence."

characteristics among elements of classes.[120] This is to underscore the terms 'course' and 'experience' in such statements by Peirce as: "An objective probability is the ratio of frequency of a specific to a generic event *in the ordinary course of experience*."[121]

Second, since probability statements refer to relative frequences of occurrences of characteristics in classes of elements (or refer to *types* of inferences, i.e., classes of leading principles), the probability of a unique characteristic or single event (or single inference) can have no precise meaning. Long-favored theological arguments, such as Bishop Butler's, based upon the "probability" of a designer or creator of this universe (or the "improbability" of this world not having a cause) have no merit by this interpretation of probability. Peirce remarks that "the relative probability of this or that arrangement of Nature is something we should have a right to talk about if universes were as plenty as blackberries."[122] Where significant assertions of probability *seem* to be assigning a probability to a single event (such as, "it will probably rain today"), these are to be treated as expediently condensed and implicit ways of asserting the likelihood of the occurrence of an event (a rainfall) as a member of a class of events (rainfalls) which occur with a certain relative frequency when certain *other* kinds of events (changes in the season, in the weather and temperature, etc.) also occur.[123]

Third, the relative-frequency interpretation of probability entails the general notion of "a long run" and the more precise mathematical idea of a *limit* of the relative frequency of the occurrence of a characteristic of a class of elements.[124] Thus, when it is said that the probability of a coin falling heads is $\frac{1}{2}$, this means that as the number of tosses increases indefinitely, the ratio between the number of heads and the total number of tosses will come to be very near $\frac{1}{2}$; in fact, the proportion of heads will come to differ from $\frac{1}{2}$ by less than any fraction, however small the fraction may be. If we let H be the number of heads, T the number of tails, then in general, the probability of a head turning up when the coin is tossed is $\frac{H}{H+T}$. This is a proper fraction having values between 0 and 1. Given the equal probability of heads and tails, the conclusion thus far of the probability of $\frac{1}{2}$ can be taken as an a priori probability, as we saw earlier. For Peirce, the equal probability of heads or tails is that the frequency of occurrence of H and T are equal "in an indefinitely long series of occurrences." But the essen-

---

[120] See *CP* 2.741–743.

[121] *CP* 2.777. See, too, *CP* 2.692.

[122] *CP* 2.684. He further comments that even if universes were plentiful, to make samples from them and calculate ratios of occurring characteristics among them would require one "containing" universe—and for this universe, the concept of probability has no application.

[123] See *CP* 3.19, where Peirce discusses the statement "it is possible that it will rain" as a "reference to certain indications of rain" and "a certain kind of argument that it will rain—and means to say that there is an argument that it will rain, which is of a kind of which but a small proportion fail."

[124] Probability, writes Peirce, "refers to a *long run*, that is, to an indefinitely long series of occurrences taken together in the order of their occurrence in possible experience," *CP* 5.22.

tial feature here, at the moment, is this idea of "indefinitely long" or a "long run."

Now what is meant by "the long run"? The phrase is only used in saying that the ratio of frequency of an event has such and such a value in the long run. The meaning is that if the occasion referred to upon which the event might happen were to recur indefinitely, and if tallies were to be kept of the occurrences and the non-occurrences, then [the] ratio of the one number to the other, as the occasions went on, would indefinitely converge toward a definite limit.[125]

In earlier pages (i.e., § 21) we recognized how Peirce's thought moved from an initially somewhat nominalistic way of construing the conditional explications and meanings of concepts to a later realism. There is a corresponding change in his conception of probability. This hinges on the interpretation of "long run." In later comments on his earlier views Peirce invokes the notion of *would be* (just as he does in his later realistic method of analyzing predicates generally, so that *hardness*, for example, is not to mean 'will resist scratching by many substances when put to the test', but 'would resist being scratched by most substances, whether tested or no').[126] Thus he remarks in 1910 about "The Doctrine of Chances" (of 1878)[127] that he had erred in defining probability as, in effect, the number of times in which the occurrence of an event of one kind in a specified class is accompanied by the occurrence of an event of another kind in that class. "For probability relates to the future," and how do we know how often a coin will be tossed?[128] Probability "is the ratio that there *would be* in the long run."[129] Peirce goes on to argue that the statement of the *probability* that if a die is thrown it will turn up a three or a six is ⅓.

means that the die has a certain "would-be" and to say that a die has a "would-be" is to say that it has a property, quite analogous to any habit a man might have.[130]

Probability thus becomes interpreted as "a certain disposition of behavior."[131]

---

[125] *CP* 7.210. For other explanations of "in the long run," e.g., as "the probability-limit of an endless succession of fractional values," see *CP* 2.758. Also, *CP* 2.650: "in the long run, there is a real fact which corresponds to the idea of probability, and it is that a given mode of inference sometimes proves successful and sometimes not, and that in a ratio ultimately fixed. As we go on drawing inference after inference of the given kind, during the first ten or hundred cases the ratio of successes may be expected to show considerable fluctuations; but when we come into the thousands and millions, these fluctuations become less and less; and if we continue long enough, the ratio will approximate toward a fixed limit.

[126] This difference was discussed above in § 21.

[127] This being the third of the series "Illustrations of the Logic of Science." See *CP* 2.645–660, and for the later comment of 1910, *CP* 2.661–668.

[128] *CP* 2.661.

[129] *CP* 2.661.

[130] *CP* 2.664.

[131] *CP* 8.225. For a valuable discussion of these two versions of probability, and problems arising in the latter interpretation, see Burks's "Peirce's Two Theories of Probability." Following a point made there (p. 149), we can illustrate the difference between the earlier and later interpretation of probability by the statements below concerning the chance of throwing heads with a coin. The more nominalistic language of the first statement makes way for the realist-dispositional expression in the second. Using the scheme developed in the previous section (i.e., § 21, p. 91) let 'ExpS' stand for the experimental situation in which the coin is determined unbiased and prepared for testing, and let 'O'

Moreover, Peirce maintains:

> what *would* be, can, it is true, only be learned through observation of what happens to be; but nevertheless no collection of happenings can constitute one trillionth of one *per cent* of what might be and what would be under supposable conditions.[132]

And

> the will *be's*, the actually *is's*, and the *have beens* are not the sum of the reals. They only cover actuality. There are besides *would be's* and *can be's* that are real.[133]

The foregoing sketch of Peirce's views on probability enables us to deal with some important issues concerning the maxim of pragmatism of § 21 not adequately discussed earlier. There is one fundamental question to which we must address ourselves here: What is the connection between the pragmatic technique for clarifying the meanings of signs and Peirce's theory of probability? The question has two separate parts: first, how does the maxim of pragmatism lead to or suggest Peirce's frequency theory of probability; second, how does Peirce's idea of probability operate (if at all) in actual analyses of the pragmatic meaning of signs? I will discuss these *seriatim*.

1)   In "How to Make Our Ideas Clear," Peirce illustrated the application of the pragmatic maxim (although he did not use the word 'pragmatism') to the signs of *hardness, weight, force,* and *reality* (examined in § 21 above). But in further papers of the series Peirce stated his interest in getting "a clear idea of what we mean by probability."[134] There is no doubt that Peirce saw, and often affirmed a connection between his pragmatic technique for clarifying signs and the meaning of probability. But the connection is only suggested in his writings, it is never made fully explicit.

Peirce initiates his investigation of probability in a manner quite in accord with his earlier accounts and illustrations of the use of the pragmatic maxim. Thus in seeking "a clear idea of probability" he says,

---

represent the operation of tossing, 'R' represent the general result of O in ExpS, namely, the result of tossing a head or tail.

1) The probability of throwing heads is $\frac{1}{2}$ = if in ExpS, O is performed, then R:
i.e., the ratio of the occurrence of heads to the number of tosses (i.e., $\frac{H}{H+T}$) will be (or approximates) $\frac{1}{2}$.

2) The probability of heads is $\frac{1}{2}$ = if an ExpS were to be realized with a coin that remains in the same physical condition (i.e., does not dissolve, CP 2.661) and O performed "forever," the relative frequency of heads *would-be* $\frac{1}{2}$.

A stronger variant of (2) is suggested by other remarks by Peirce, in CP 2.664–665, which are quoted within the following:

The possibility that the coin will land tails is $\frac{1}{2}$ = the coin has a would-be whose "full expression" (in ExpS) is $\frac{1}{2}$, if it "should undergo an endless series of throws."

[132] CP 6.327.

[133] CP 8.216.

[134] CP 2.649. This is "The Doctrine of Chances," the third paper in the series of six "Illustrations of the Logic of Science." "How to Make Our Ideas Clear" was second in the series.

we have to consider what real and sensible difference there is between one degree of probability and another.[135]

Emphasizing that probability has primarily to do with inferences, as we have seen earlier, Peirce goes on to develop his relative-frequency interpretation.

But how does the relative-frequency view follow as a logical analysis of the meaning of 'probability'? The answer is to be found in Peirce's pragmatic clarification and interpretation of *reality* and *truth*. In the earliest rounded statement of his theory of probability,[136] Peirce already indicated this much, saying:

> Truth being, then, the agreement of a representation with its object, and there being nothing *in re* answering to a degree of credence, a modification of a judgment in that respect cannot make it more true, although it may indicate the proportion of *such* judgments which are true *in the long run*. That is, indeed, the precise and only use or significance of these fractions termed probabilities: they give security in the long run.[137]

In "The Fixation of Belief"[138] Peirce reasoned that of the four methods of forming and maintaining belief (which he distinguishes as tenacity, authority, a priori and the scientific), the scientific method has one important advantage over the others. It is the only one that allows us to arrive at conclusions (i.e., beliefs) which we have any reason to think are true. In practicing the other methods one's beliefs are the result of mere persistant willing and fancy; or the influence of authorities; or a preference, as in matters of taste, for what seems "agreeable to reason."[139] These are respectively the methods of tenacity, authority, and a priori. It is, of course, logically possible that in employing one of these methods a man might arrive at a true belief. But since there are no objective controls over their practice, and no objective criterion for assessing the truth of the beliefs thus produced (and indeed, no critical interest in the validity of belief), there is no *reason* for thinking that the beliefs thus arrived at are true. This is one criticism of these methods, if truth matters at all.

However, truth does matter, and Peirce's explanation of why this is so is the most novel and important part of his argument.

We seek belief in order to satisfy the irritation of doubt (as we noticed in his theory of inquiry, § 20). Now the trouble with the above methods of fixing belief is that they tend, "in the long run," to be unsatisfactory. Peirce does not state the objection with deliberate appeal to inductive probability,[140] but we may put it thus: the more the above methods are practiced (that is, by more persons more

---

[135] *CP* 2.649.

[136] Found in his 1867 review of Venn's *The Logic of Chance*, *CP* 8.1–6. This was eleven years before the publication of "The Doctrine of Chances" cited above.

[137] *CP* 8.3. This is from the review of Venn's *The Logic of Chance*.

[138] The first paper, 1877, in the series "Illustrations of the Logic of Science."

[139] *CP* 5.382. Peirce adds: "it does not mean that which agrees with experience, but that which we find ourselves inclined to believe."

[140] Peirce *suggests* the inductive criterion, here speculatively developed, when in completing his review of the last of the other methods he heralds the account of the scientific method, thus: "and so we are driven in Lord Bacon's phrase, to true induction," *CP* 5.383.

frequently), the larger the proportion of experienced real doubts over the opinions arrived at through the employment of the methods, and hence, eventually, an increase of doubts about the methods themselves. Why should this be so? Because, says Peirce, nothing shakes and unsettles one's own beliefs so much as the discovery that other persons may hold beliefs differing from ours on the same subject. The social impulse works against these other methods. One cannot, or can only rarely and temporarily compel all men to hold the same beliefs on all subjects. But then, Peirce points out:

> The feeling that gives rise to any method of fixing belief is dissatisfaction at two repugnant propositions. But here already is a vague concession that there is some *one* thing which a proposition should represent.[141]

It is thus natively, intuitively, rationally that we are led to a conception of reality, to "some *one* thing which a proposition should represent." And the notion of *truth* is also forthcoming as the ultimate conclusion of every man who practices a method which takes as its "fundamental hypothesis" the idea of reality as "external permanency," the controlling and validating condition of belief. Here, also, "the social impulse" has its satisfaction, for the method is communal and those who practice it are participants in a community of inquirers, cooperatively engaged in seeking the *one* thing that propositions should represent. For all who practice this method of settling belief with this hypothesis "will be led to the one True conclusion."[142]

So Peirce argues.

> To satisfy our doubts, therefore it is necessary that a method should be found by which our beliefs may be determined [originally, "caused"] by nothing human, but by some external permanency—by something upon which our thinking has no effect. . . . It must be something which affects or might affect, every man. And, though these affections are necessarily as various as are individual conditions, yet the method must be such that the ultimate conclusion of every man shall be the same. Such is the method of science.[143]

This is what Peirce called his "new conception"[144] of reality. We may defer to later pages (i.e., §§ 23, 24) a discussion of this concept and its role in Peirce's philosophy and theory of truth. For the present we are concerned with its relation to his interpretation of probability.

This relation begins to be evident as Peirce proceeds to argue that the method of science "is the only one of the four methods that presents any distinction of a right and a wrong way."[145] I may investigate a problem, but the rules I follow "may not be such as investigation would approve." But the test of whether I am or am not following the method "is not an immediate appeal to my feelings or pur-

---

141 *CP* 5.384.
142 The full meaning of this apparently debatable statement is explored in §§ 23, 24 below.
143 *CP* 5.384.
144 *CP* 5.384.
145 *CP* 5.385.

poses."[146] Presumably this *is* the test in using the other methods. Here "on the contrary" the test "itself involves the application of the method."[147] The scientific method then is self-applicable and self-corrective in exactly the way that probable and inductive methods are, as we saw earlier.

In the next paper of the series,[148] Peirce refers to the comments just noted above, saying:

> as we have seen in the former paper, the ideas of truth and falsehood, in their full development, appertain exclusively to the experiential [originally, "scientific"] method of settling opinion.[149]

This method, we observed Peirce to say, is such "that the ultimate conclusion of every man shall be the same." Some twenty-six years later he added to this sentence: "or would be the same if inquiry were sufficiently persisted in."[150] This later qualification is in harmony with the description, set forth in the second paper, of the process of scientific method, working with the new conception of reality and of truth. The words "would-be" in this qualification are, as we have seen in other contexts several times (most recently, some pages back, in explication of "a long run"), items in the nomenclature of Peirce's realism. Probability is the ratio of the occurrence of some characteristic of an event to the occurrence of the characteristics in a class of those events, and "it is the ratio that there *would be* in the long run."[151] "This long run can be nothing but an endlessly long run."[152] The later qualification and the key concepts in his theory of probability are also fundamental in the description, in the second paper, of the process of scientific method.

> . . . All the followers of science are animated by a cheerful hope [originally, "are fully persuaded"] that the processes of investigation, if only pushed far enough, will give one certain solution to each [originally, "every"] question to which they apply it. . . . They may at first obtain different results, but, as each perfects his method and his processes, the results are found to move [originally, "will move"] steadily together toward a destined centre.

Now this great hope that animates scientific investigation

is embodied in the conception of truth and reality.

He explains those conceptions in a statement that has become famous (discussed in §§ 23, 24 below):

> The opinion which is fated to be ultimately agreed to by all who investigate, is what we mean by the truth, and the object represented in this opinion is the real.[153]

[146] *CP* 5.385.
[147] *CP* 5.385.
[148] I.e., "How to Make Our Ideas Clear," the second (1878) of the series "Illustrations of the Logic of Science."
[149] *CP* 5.406.
[150] *CP* 5.384, note 1.
[151] *CP* 2.661.
[152] *CP* 2.661.
[153] *CP* 5.407.

The probability of an inference, or of an inductive argument is thus included in this definition of truth; for the probability is the limit of the relative frequency of a mode of inference, or type of argument, leading to truth; leading, that is, to conclusions "fated to be ultimately agreed to." Thus, we may say that a true opinion is the limit of a relative frequency of what would be affirmed by all who investigate.[154]

How the idea of probability is incorporated in Peirce's view of reality and truth, and how the pragmatic maxim clarifies the meaning of probability can be witnessed in one last quotation.

> . . . That real and sensible difference between one degree of probability and another, in which the meaning of the distinction lies, is that in the frequent employment of two different modes of inference, one will carry truth with it oftener than the other. It is evident that this is the only difference there is in the existing fact. Having certain premises, a man draws a certain conclusion, and as far as this inference alone is concerned the only possible practical question is whether that conclusion is true or not, and between existence and non-existence there is no middle term. "Being only is and nothing is altogether not," said Parmenides; and this is in strict accordance with the analysis of the conception of reality given in the last paper ["How to Make Our Ideas Clear"]. For we found that the distinction of reality and fiction depends on the supposition that sufficient investigation would cause one opinion to be universally received and all others rejected. . . . But in the long run, there is a real fact which corresponds to the idea of probability, and it is that a given mode of inference sometimes proves successful and sometimes not, and that in a ratio ultimately fixed. . . . If we continue long enough, the ratio will approximate toward a fixed limit. We may, therefore define the probability of a mode of argument as the proportion of cases in which it carries truth with it.[155]

2)   The other question still to be answered was: How does Peirce's conception of probability apply in the pragmatic explication of the meanings of general concepts? Part of the answer to this question has been anticipated in our earlier discussions in which we noticed that Peirce's conditional form for determining the meaning of a sign entails reference to an "innumerable series" of confirmable instances of the sign (§ 21, especially the last paragraph). Understanding the meaning of 'hard,' then, entails a reference to an indefinite number of confirmable consequences, that is, entails: 'always resists scratching by all (or most) substances.' In some late reflections on this aspect of his pragmatic analysis of meaning (and one writing in particular, in 1906), Peirce says he intends the word 'hard' "in its strict mineralogical sense, 'would resist a knife-edge.'"[156] The 'would,' once again, is an important word in the vocabulary of Peirce's realism. For realism (or "scholastic realism") is thought by Peirce to be implied by and to be the only

---

[154] See Lenz, p. 154. We can enlarge upon this last statement: a true opinion O is one for which in the case of the ratio $\dfrac{\text{assentors to } O}{\text{dissentors from } O}$ the number of assentors approaches 1, while that of dissenters approaches O. Or: the number of assentors to O and investigators of O becomes the same, "in the long run."
[155] CP 2.650.
[156] CP 5.467.

intelligible way of explaining the meaning of disposition terms such as 'would' (or 'would-be,' 'can-be,' and the like).

Intellectual concepts, Peirce writes,

> essentially carry some implication concerning the general behavior either of some conscious being or of some inanimate object, and so convey more, not merely than any feeling, but more, too, than any existential fact, namely, the "would-acts," "would-dos" of habitual behavior; and no conglomeration of actual happenings can ever completely fill up the meaning of a "would-be."[157]

But then the evident conclusion is that the *meaning* of intellectual concepts (or *signs*, as we agreed to use for a blanket term earlier[158]) is made accessible and clear to us by means of those conceptual instruments of the theory of probability that we studied earlier. That is, the concepts of an ordered class of events, with a certain proportion of occurring characteristics taken in the long run as approximating toward a fixed limit, are operative in determining the *meaning* of a concept. We can say, then, that the concept of *hardness* has reference to a *would-be*, a mode of general behavior, in this case, 'would resist a knife-edge.' The *would-be* is a real fact approximated, in the long run, by an innumerable (but necessarily finite) number of tests.[159] It is nonsensical to say that *hardness* has a certain probability, or that probability attaches to some single hard object. The suggestion I wish to offer here is that, for Peirce, the meaning of 'hardness,' and of all "intellectual concepts" for which pragmatism serves as a technique of clarification, has a reference to some statistical fact. The reference, in each case of general predicates, is to proportions of things that do and do not exhibit a *would-be*, or mode of behavior, under certain experienced conditions. This, I take it, is at least part of what Peirce had in mind when he wrote that pragmatism asserts

> that the *total* meaning of the predication of an intellectual concept is contained in the affirmation that under all conceivable circumstances of a given kind (or under this or that more or less indefinite part of the cases of their fulfillment, should the predication be modal) the subject of the predication would behave in a certain general way—that is, it would be true under given experiential circumstances (or under a more or less definitely stated proportion of them, *taken as they would occur*, that is in the same order of succession, *in experience.*[160]

To say of something X that it is hard is to predict that X would behave in a certain general way under given experiential circumstances. This thesis we have scrutinized earlier (in § 21). My suggestion at the moment is that, for Peirce, an analysis of the meaning of the sign 'hard' in sentences like 'X is hard' requires the introduction and subsequent use of ideas drawn from the frequency theory of probability. These ideas serve as instruments in pragmatic analyses of meaning.

---

[157] *CP* 5.467.

[158] Above in § 21, note 39.

[159] The *would-be* of an object's hardness, i.e., its resistance to scratching, is actualized in a given test. But it must be recalled that no actual happening can "fill up the meaning of a would-be." For 'would-be' (like all general concepts) contains a reference to the future and to possibility.

[160] *CP* 5.467.

Roughly: a predicate (e.g., 'hard') *means* (that is, is clarified by the concept of) the limit of a relative frequency of occurrences of a mode of behavior (i.e., resisting a knife edge) under all conceivable circumstances of a given kind (i.e., tests of scratching, pressures, etc.) of some class—or proportion of a class—of things (i.e., physical objects).

In this sense, *meaning* is reference to *action*, to would-be, to the frequency of certain kinds of specified occurrences under certain kinds of conditions.

This is Peirce's "pregnant principle" and "kernal of pragmatism,"[161]

that the *whole* meaning of an intellectual predicate is that certain kinds of events would happen, once so often, in the course of experience, under certain kinds of existential conditions.[162]

To sum up. We have seen that the pragmatism of Peirce contains two important doctrines: (1) the frequency interpretation of probability is implied as a result of the pragmatic analysis of the meaning of 'probability'; (2) in the pragmatic analysis of concepts, certain notions of the frequency theory of probability play central roles in the analysis of the very meaning of the concepts in question.

All this is an important part of Peirce's profoundly suggestive philosophy of empirical knowledge. The notions of verification, probability, and analysis of meanings that concerned us above lead naturally to considerations of meaning and truth.

§ 23. Meaning and Truth

We have so far surveyed Peirce's theory of *inquiry* and of the pragmatic (or as he often called it, the "scientific," "experiential," "experimental") method of attaining the meaning of signs and beliefs. Viewed through this theory, the restless and babbling human race exhibits among its most fundamental traits—paradoxically—an energetic drive to achieve inertia. Ideally all action, thought, inquiry is aimed at the suspension of action (and dissipation of doubt). Belief, when achieved, is such a state of inaction, though containing a fixed reference to action; belief is the undisturbed and conclusive decision to act always in such and such a situation, in such and such a way with respect to such and such objects. Just when we will and do act and how we act in specific situations is the function of habit. For habits are the more specific vehicles through which beliefs pass into conceived action.

A pattern of analogous distinctions, or repeated series of similarly related functions, runs through Peirce's analysis of inquiry and meaning. As the pragmatic meaning or interpretant of a sign is related to a conditional statement, or as the meaning of a term consists of a stated prescription for a certain experimental

---

[161] See *CP* 5.468.
[162] *CP* 5.468.

operation which will produce certain stated results, so belief is related to habit—the meaning of a belief being the habit or rule of action it prescribes. And so, too, habit is related to action. The over-all pattern is the same; the "meaning" of any one sign is expressed or interpreted by another sign and each sign in the series has a twofold function: it expresses (or means) the "conceivable practical" consequences prescribed by an antecedent sign, and, in addition, it prescribes certain consequences expressed by some further sign.

There are a number of passages in which Peirce develops this idea, of signs as the logical interpretants of signs, where the relation of one sign to another is evidently more than a logical relation. If the pragmatic meaning of a belief lies in the habit that the belief prescribes, the habit is more than just a logical consequent of the belief; it is also, in some sense, a causal consequent. While Peirce is by no means as clear on this as one could wish, the idea is of interest and importance to his pragmatism. The relations between signs—between a concept and its meaning (or conditional explication, § 21 above), between belief, habit, and action, between sign and its sign-interpretant—is one both of a logical character and of causal efficacy.

Teleological considerations, called by Peirce "the purposive bearing" nature of words, propositions, and concepts, are involved in this idea of meanings and general terms as efficacious and productive causes of their consequences. Sometimes Peirce speaks of "general ideas of action" prevailing throughout the universe, and since our minds are products of the universe, by "logical necessity" these laws are incorporated into the being of man's mind.[163] Dewey once offered the following explanation of Peirce's view of concepts (or meanings) as causally efficacious: "The meanings 'the air is stuffy' and 'stuffy air is unwholesome' may determine, for example, the opening of a window."[164] But how seriously this is to be taken as an explanation, or how accurately it explains Peirce, is an open question. For one wonders about this sense of 'determines' and to what length one can go in attributing physical causation to meanings. In Dewey's example, if the "meanings" had not operated as they had, one might imagine the surprising notice in next day's newspaper:

> John Smith was found dead in his room this morning. Death was evidently caused by two meanings, 'the gas jet is on' and 'gas is asphyxiating.' The meanings are still at large.

Whatever the precise intent and metaphysical bearings of this aspect of his thought, that habits and meanings are *general, real, purposive,* and can be defined

---

[163] CP 5.603.
[164] The Peirce commemorative issue of *Journal of Philosophy, Psychology and Scientific Methods*, p. 711. For the passage in question see CP 5.431, beginning "Not only may generals be real, but they may also be *physically efficient,*" in the sense in which "human purposes are *physically efficient.*" Peirce speaks of "generals" (i.e., general facts, Forms, general truths) and thoughts, and not directly of *meanings.* But he does conclude with a comment on the "great fact," that "the ideas 'justice' and 'truth' are, notwithstanding the iniquity of the world, the mightiest of forces that move it."

and communicated, it is frequently expounded by Peirce under what he called his "scholastic realism." And these convictions play a part in his view of *truth*. For while meaning and verification of general ideas or beliefs are not identical, as argued some pages back, and while, in general, determining the *meaning* of a belief is not a test of its truth, the scientific method or pragmatic determination of *meanings* does evidently carry with it a test of the validity of beliefs. That is, the procedure by which the *meaning* of a term is explicated is also the method to be employed in *confirming* (or infirming) the term. The experimental situation, the operation prescribed, and the definite experimental results predicted which constitute the meaning of 'hard' or 'this stone is hard' are also tests of the truth of these terms with respect to what each asserts to be the case and how they are applied at various times by various persons in various situations.[165]

For Peirce, as mentioned earlier, the meaning of a term as expressed by a conditional statement (§ 21) contains an assertion of an innumerable series of confirming instances of the term. This, as was noted in passing (end of § 21) is related to the doctrine that the "rational meaning of every proposition lies in the future."[166] An infinite series of confirmations is thus involved in both the pragmatic meaning and truth of any term. A part of this same teaching is Peirce's "fallibilism," which is but the moral to be drawn from these prior considerations: namely, if pragmatic (or "scientific") meaning and truth are so conceived, it follows that at any one time no single belief (or term) can be regarded as wholly true. Or, conversely, an ingredient of error and obscurity infects each and every one of the terms (beliefs, ideas, statements) and judgments of each and every one of us. Truth and meaningfulness are had with the progressive elimination of

[165] That we can test and *verify* single predicates (e.g., 'hard' or 'force,' etc.) appears, on the surface, a little odd. For we might imagine someone saying "hard," "force," and whatever such utterances might mean, they seem altogether devoid of truth values. Such would be the objection from those of us oriented to think of truth (or falsehood) as having to do with statements, or utterances of statements, or beliefs (if beliefs be taken as other than "subvocal" uttered sentences). Peirce's counter to the objection would seem to be that determination of the meaning or the truth of all such "general" predicates consists in treating them as components of statements, thus: 'this stone is hard,' or even, 'hard exists.' The meaning and truth of the predicate then becomes evident by a systematic embedding of these statements into larger conditional statements, thus: 'if this stone is hard' (or 'if there is something hard') then . . . ,' where the blank is filled by a further conditional statement of the sort discussed above, § 21.
It happens, however, that Peirce's "realism" commits him to more than saying, e.g., some hard things exist, '(∃ x) (x is hard).' He also holds that *hardness* and other generals exist in their own right. The hard thing comprises at least two objects: there is the individual hard thing x, but there is also *hardness* operative upon x and all hard things, although, for Peirce, not existing separately from particular hard things. In the idiom of logical theory we are thus encouraged to quantify over predicate as well as individual variables (or predicates become an order of "objects" in addition to individuals sharing them). Such is the way of scholastic realism. In his review of the works of Berkeley, *CP* 8.7–38, Peirce wrote, 8.14: "a thing in the general is as real as in the concrete. It is perfectly true that all white things have whiteness in them, for that is only saying, in another form of words, that all white things are white; but since it is true that real things possess whiteness, whiteness is real." That was in 1871. Later, in 1909, Peirce described a *realist* as a man who believes that "the property, the character, the predicate, *hardness* . . . is really and truly in the hard things and is one in them all, as a description of habit, disposition, or behavior," *CP* 1.27n.
[166] *CP* 5.427.

this ingredient of error and opacity. But it should be emphasized that this gradual process of elimination does not proceed in private or as a redeeming effort of individual consciousness. It is operative in the publicly shared beliefs and system of communication of common sense and science. Indeed, the transition from common sense to scientific knowledge is an instance of this evolving process.

While thought or inquiry has as its sole purpose the production of belief, there are several characteristic methods by which belief can be attained. Only one of these methods, that of science, takes into consideration a right and wrong way of fixing beliefs; it is employed by those who wish not only to believe (since all of us do), but to have their beliefs "coincide with fact." Now Peirce regarded it as a psychological fact that to hold some belief B and to think *B is true* are the same mental acts.[167] Thus for us all, the sum of our beliefs and an enumeration of what we think to be true come to one and the same order of thoughts. But which of any of our beliefs are in fact true or false is a matter to be determined on grounds other than the act of believing or the satisfaction thus incurred. For while a belief may in fact be false, as soon "as a firm belief is reached we are entirely satisfied."

Truth, then, is not identified with belief, nor is the subjective satisfaction accompanying believing a test of truth at all. The key to the pragmatic definition of truth is the concept of reality. Pragmatic meaning and truth overlap and coalesce with the idea of the Real.

Pragmatically defined, i.e., via its "sensible effects," the *real* is that which causes belief.[168] In one of his earliest papers,[169] one most revealing of the direction his thought was to take, Peirce sets forth as a new "conception of reality" these points:

1) The real is that which, unaffected by what we may think about it, influences our sensations, which in turn cause thinking.

2) All human thought or opinion is subject to certain accidental limitations and contains an element of inaccuracy.

3) To every question there is a true answer, a final conclusion to which the opinion of every man is constantly gravitating.

4) This final opinion is independent of how anyone, or any number of men think.

5) Everything which will be thought to exist in the final opinion is real.

The idea of a continuous gravitation to a final conclusion is essential for Peirce. "There is a general *drift* in the history of human thought which will lead to one general agreement, one catholic consent."[170] The real is what the community of

---

[167] *CP* 5.375: "We think each one of our beliefs to be true, and, indeed, it is mere tautology to say so." This point has sometimes been disputed as paradoxical. But it is a built-in feature of Peirce's theory of doubt and belief that to say 'I believe B' and 'B is true' are the same; to say "I wonder if my belief B is true" is no longer to believe B and to "create a doubt in place of that belief."

[168] *CP* 5.406.

[169] I.e., his review of Fraser's edition of the works of Berkeley, *The North American Review* (1871), *CP* 8.7–38, esp. 12–17.

[170] *CP* 8.12.

thought construes it to be; consensus, common confession, is our one reliable interpretation of reality. And since we have no access to the Real except by means of conceptual interpretation, pragmatically the real *is* what, in the final opinion, thought represents it to be. Notice that even under this ideal of a "final opinion" there is room for the possibility of error. If the last arbiter of truth is scientific method, and its final pronouncement should issue an unimprovable scientific theory (the final conclusion about that which is real—point 5), there is still the possibility that the whole product from start to finish is the labor of a delusion, the moonshine of a midsummer night's dream, or the wiles of a Cartesian demon. However, in the absence of any check upon our conceptual interpretation of the reality we experience (point 1) other than conceptualization and experience, and assuming ideally a "final conclusion" once-achieved, the possibility of a gross error upon which that conclusion rests, in whole or in part, remains an engaging thought without the slightest consequences for Peirce's argument. Such is the fate of Descartes's demon bent on falsifying every one of our beliefs. He is one of those curios of possibility banishèd from the domain of pragmatic significance and working concerns, when working concerns count most.

In large part this "new conception of reality" was initiated as an alternative to older versions of Realism striving to maintain a claim to philosophic veracity by appealing to clear and distinct (thus necessarily true) conceptions, or to a theory of truth as the correspondence of idea and object. The latter doctrine in particular begins to give way under examination of its three components: its psychology of ideas as images; its obscure sense of 'correspondence'; its mechanical physiology of how objects "cause" ideas. Even waiving these misgivings, were 'truth' somehow adequately defined as the *correspondence* of an idea (or belief or proposition) and an object, little or no allowance is made for our ever knowing a truth or verifying an idea. For the latter to be possible we should have to perform a feat of self-transcendence by which we could become observers of two objects, our idea and some alleged object as its cause, and scrutinize the degree of correspondence between them. We are being asked to vacate our minds, or conceptual scheme, to judge this "correspondence" with reality. In general, the pragmatic objection to the correspondence theory of truth is that, short of the impossible feat of self-transcendence, it provides no place for verification, and thus, by misprescribing its use, renders useless the otherwise useful term 'truth.' Advocates of a more sophisticated correspondence theory, on the other hand, have been equally disturbed over difficulties in the pragmatic theory. But more of this later.

As was mentioned three paragraphs earlier, the fundamental idea in Peirce's theory of truth is the *real*—not reality as the sum and substance of all that *is*, be it noted, but the *concept* of the real. We *conceive* the real to be the cause of thought and belief. Truth is accordingly *conceived* as a characteristic of the belief we would possess if it were affected by nothing but the real and if the real were the only object represented in these beliefs.[171] Such a belief will be "final"; unlike

171 *CP* 5.384.

ordinary opinion it will be free of the accidental, human, subjective elements of error (cf. point 2). For Peirce, then, a true belief—a belief that represents a real object—and what is thought to exist in the final opinion are pragmatically equivalent. To distinguish a true conception of a thing and the thing as *real* is simply to "regard one and the same thing from two different points of view; for the immediate object of thought in a true judgment *is* the reality."[172]

The "final opinion" is simply part of what Peirce took as an ideal of the endless application of scientific method to belief. Hence his well-known definition of 'truth':

> The opinion which is fated to be ultimately agreed upon by all who investigate is what we mean by truth, and the object represented by this opinion is real.[173]

The definition reflects Peirce's metaphysical view of an ultimate purpose of thought; the evolution of all thought, especially the history of science, exhibits purpose. But what that ultimate purpose is we do not know.[174] The conception of truth is vested with this metaphysics of a gravitation of thought toward a "final conclusion" (point 3) in which reality or the universe cooperates.

§ 24. Critical Issues in Peirce's Definition of Truth

The above definitions of truth have achieved a prominence in more recent discussions of pragmatism considerably out of proportion to the importance Peirce himself attached to them. For he scarcely discusses them, and, apparently, never took an interest in developing a comprehensive explanation or theory of truth. But Peirce's two definitions have an important place in the history of pragmatism for, James's view of truth aside, they are revived by Dewey and incorporated into his conception of truth as "warranted assertibility" (cf. § 40). There are, by the way, any number of scattered comments by Peirce on the meaning of truth which would find approval from philosophers who happen to be particularly critical of those cited above.

Peirce's two definitions of truth have been variously criticized. To speak of "the opinion which is fated to be ultimately agreed upon by all who investigate" as "what we mean by truth" sounds odd; the word 'fated' is discomforting, and seems to attribute an occult power to true opinions and a mysterious efficacy to truth. But Peirce explained that he meant nothing superstitious by 'fate,' merely that which is sure to happen, e.g., "we are all fated to die."[175] The opinion which

---

[172] *CP* 8.16. Cf. also 5.432.
[173] *CP* 5.407. Also: "Truth is that concordance of an abstract statement with the ideal limit towards which endless investigation would tend to bring scientific belief, which concordance the abstract statement may possess by virtue of the confession of its inaccuracy and one-sidedness, and this confession is an essential ingredient of truth," *CP* 5.565.
[174] *CP* 5.403.
[175] *CP* 5.407, note 1.

is fated to be agreed upon is one which "ultimately" *will* command agreement "and can nohow be avoided."[176] If a man were to say, "there exists a certain opinion which we are fated to believe, nor can we avoid it," this, indeed, would sound mysterious. But if he said, "there is a certain question and our investigating it will in due course inevitably lead to an agreed upon answer," we would hardly accuse him of being a mystic. The statement might be false, but that is beside the point here. This latter way of putting it is substantially what Peirce had intended.[177] He was describing what we *mean* by calling an opinion true, not speculating about the *existence* of opinions fated to be and be agreed upon.

Peirce thought that truth could be defined by using the mathematical notion of a *limit* and the philosophic notion of a *community* of interpreters, inquirers, and confirmers. The two notions are easily traced in such phrases as the "ultimately agreed upon" belief, the "ideal limit towards which endless scientific investigation would tend to bring scientific belief." As the meaning of every proposition contains a reference to the future and is prescriptive of an infinite number of confirming instances (end of § 21), so also the ideas of its truth. We are to think of the mathematical sense of an "ideal limit" of "endless investigation" as including a chronological sense as well; we are to think of that "concordance" of a statement with the limit toward which *endless* investigation would *tend* to bring belief.[178] Notice that Peirce speaks of the concordance of an *abstract* statement with the ideal limit toward which investigation brings scientific belief. He seems to have meant by 'abstract statement' one that is general, containing hypothetical but undetermined references to (purportedly) real things and an ingredient of inaccuracy.

The notion of a community of investigators and confirmers is found in Pierce's account of *reality* as well as of truth. "The conception of reality . . . essentially involves the notion of a COMMUNITY."[179] For Peirce, we have no way of understanding reality except through our representations: we have no access to *what* a real thing is other than our experience and conceptual representations of its sensible effects. Reality in itself, or in its uninterpreted nakedness, is a pragmatically meaningless notion, for it is a notion (thus an attempted conception) of the unknowable (thus the "incognizable" or unconceived).[180] Hence, "reality consists in the agreement that the whole community would eventually come to."[181] This does not mean that reality is a matter of arbitrary decisions on the part of the scientific community; nor is what is real established by sheer con-

---

[176] *CP* 5.407, note 1.

[177] Thus: "it is unphilosophical to suppose that, with regard to any given question (which has any clear meaning), investigation would not bring forth a solution of it, if it were carried far enough," *CP* 5.409.

[178] For some thought about this idea see Appendix 4.

[179] *CP* 5.311.

[180] *CP* 5.310: "The meaning of a word is the conception it conveys, the absolutely incognizable has no meaning because no conception attaches to it. It is therefore a meaningless word. . . ."

[181] *CP* 5.331.

vention. But what is conceived to be real does establish itself as the unanimous and "irresistible effect of inquiry,"[182] that is, in the confirmed beliefs of the scientific community. These confirmed beliefs tend to approximate truth, i.e., the opinion "ultimately agreed upon by all who investigate."

Peirce bids us think of truth, then, in these ways: a true opinion represents a real object; a true belief is one that would *tend* to result from an endless scientific investigation.

Peirce's definition of truth has had its critics, not the least of them Russell, who found that 'truth' so defined is of no philosophical importance.[183] Russell argues that the idea of an opinion "ultimately agreed upon by all who investigate," if taken in a chronological sense of 'ultimately,' would "make 'truth' depend upon the opinions of the last man left alone as the earth becomes too cold to support life."[184] But this dismal prospect of man's sorry state, which atom-bomb warfare may prevent us from anticipating, fails to be relevant to Peirce's definition. For the definition does not assert that the meaning of 'truth' entails the existence of a final opinion of living men. Peirce's definition does not commit him to believing that there will in fact ever be a final opinion at all. Nor does it follow from the definition, as it does from Russell's reading of it, that no one will ever know what 'truth' means except the final investigator in the final moment of his enjoying his final opinion.

It does follow from Peirce's definition that no single belief can be known with certainty to be true. But this is hardly a novel thesis. Where novelty is evident is in Peirce's suggestion that this same thesis—or some specific expression of it within and relevant to the contexts of statements—adds to the truth of statements. This is an application of Peirce's *fallibilism*. He goes further than maintaining that all human opinion (and, presumably, any statement of fact) is subject to an element of inaccuracy and error. He thinks that a "confession of inaccuracy and one-sidedness" incorporated within a belief (or statement) is "an essential ingredient of truth."[185] If this confessional element is not included, since every belief (and statement) *does* contain a degree of error, there is an increase of error. This confessional element is to be construed as a reference to that ideal limit toward which endless investigation would bring belief. Thus by appending a statement of approximateness to, or into, statements that are approximate, we increase their truth. There may be some trouble in envisioning the syntax of those statements when we try to construct them as Peirce would have us do, with fallibilism embodied in their content.[186] Maybe in practice we can achieve the same end by using familiar qualifying devices and occasional dodges of the cautionary sort that make for drab conversation, but for good gambling with

---

[182] *CP* 5.494.
[183] "Dewey's New Logic," in Schilpp, *Philosophy of John Dewey*, p. 144.
[184] *Ibid.*, p. 145.
[185] See the second definition above, note 173.
[186] For the confession of its inaccuracy construed as a part of a statement seems to require inclusion of statements about the statement among the components of one and the same statement. And statements containing self-referential components can be troublesome.

statements of fact: seeing it raining we can say, "I think it is raining, but I might be mistaken."[187]

There was another reason for Peirce's inclusion of the principle of fallibilism in his definition of truth. A belief for which no admission of fallibility is provided puts an end to inquiry. It satisfies doubt (as all belief does, § 20), but its truth is then no longer a matter of concern and its settlement no longer calls for the continued use of scientific method. The element of confessed fallibility in our beliefs works as a permanent stimulus to further inquiry. Even were belief to approach that ideal limit toward which endless investigation tends, the element of confessed inaccuracy is to be retained. Peirce once commented that the only infallible statement is that all statements are fallible.[188]

Peirce, and Dewey following him, took this idea of confessed inaccuracy very seriously. They saw it, in principle, not only as a condition of the truth of assertions but also as an essential characteristic of scientific method. Fallibilism is a reflection upon the so-called self-corrective tendency of scientific method.[189]

There are other ways in which Peirce's definitions of truth have been found objectionable—his use of the mathematical notion of a limit, for instance, which works nicely for numbers, but is not very clear when statements of beliefs are in some analogous way to be thought of as approaching a limit. This particular analogy, and the idea of an infinitely prolonged analysis tending to a limit, is found in Leibniz;[190] and Peirce's own statement of the idea is clearly anticipated in Boole.[191] In addition to some doubts concerning the legitimacy of the analogy, however, there is a further question of whether an endless application of scientific method to belief would necessarily eventuate in one unique conclusion—the

[187] But this phrasing does not really get around the problem mentioned in the previous footnote. For what is being said here is something like: " 'It is raining' is, I think, likely to be true." The confessional element comes through as a statement in its own right—a statement *about* a statement—and not merely as a component of the same statement.

[188] CP 2.75. The statement has an air of paradox about it and encourages the quizzical mood. Thus one wonders, how fallible is the belief in fallibilism? Peirce once explained that in affirming the proposition "no proposition is infallible," or, in saying that a true proposition is one which the community of inquirers would ultimately come to accept (as we saw in § 23, and especially note 154n of § 22), we are not inadvertently committed to believing there is one infallible proposition (viz., "All propositions are fallible") or that it is infallibly true that inquiry will arrive at truth. He pointed out that the doctrine of fallibilism is not a proposition, or belief, but a way of describing knowledge and a defining condition of propositions. In a letter of 1908 to Lady Welby in her *Other Dimensions*, p. 301, or Leib, p. 26, he commented: "But you will say, I am setting up this very proposition as infallible truth. Not at all; it is a mere definition. I do not say that it is infallibly true that there is any belief to which a person would come if he were to carry his inquiries far enough. I only say that that alone is what I call Truth. I cannot infallibly know that there *is* any truth."

[189] Thus Peirce says, "certain methods of mathematical computation tend to correct themselves. . . ." It is "one of the most wonderful features of reasoning and one of the most important philosophemes in the doctrine of science . . . that reasoning tends to correct itself," CP 5.574–575. This point is related to Peirce's view of the "justification" of induction and the self-corrective tendency of scientific method discussed in § 22.

[190] On this idea in Leibniz, see Couturat, *La Logique*, p. 213.

[191] In *The Laws of Thought*, p. 406. For the passage and a speculation about Boole and Peirce's view of truth, see Appendix 4 below.

ideal result, *the* fated opinion.[192] There is, for example, Poincaré's famous proof that where one mechanical model is used to explain a subject matter, an infinity of others is possible. And similarly motivated deliberations upon the developments of beliefs and theories in the actual course of scientific inquiries may make us skeptical concerning the possibility of "endless" investigations ever tending to one opinion to the exclusion of any others.

One begins to wonder, then, impressed with the apparent reasonableness of these last objections, how Peirce failed to foresee this much. What led him to stumble and Dewey behind him to fall into this treacherous doctrine with its unedifying consequences? The answer is fairly simple and worth stating if we are not to perpetuate the fundamental misunderstanding from whence most of these objections issue.

In defining truth as he does, Peirce was no doubt guided by some of his own characteristic philosophical and metaphysical convictions, and some of these (at least the five listed earlier in § 23) are easily recognizable in the two definitions we have been considering. Thus, as a matter of historical fact, Peirce was evidently convinced that certain beliefs were indeed "fated" to find acceptance in the community of inquiry and that continuous investigation would tend to a "final conclusion." Presumably the effect of inquiry upon beliefs and abstract statements would be to increase the degree to which each represents a real object while decreasing its degree of inaccuracy, or vice versa. Thus "ultimately" the sheep and the goats get separated. There is a ratio of truth to error in each of our beliefs and in the state of our knowledge as a whole. The drift of thought, sped by inquiry, will lead to the concentration of truth and the dispersion of error. So at least Peirce thought.

These, and like ideas, are the *convictions* registered in Peirce's definitions of truth. And over such matters of conviction, or belief, we may object; we may be persuaded otherwise, or we may be less than confident about the evidence for Peirce's views. The philosophic doubts just considered, as to the adequacy or significance of Peirce's definitions, seem to take this line. There is little or no reason to think, so it is argued in sum, that there is (or will be) "the opinion which is fated to be ultimately agreed upon by all who investigate."

Now suppose this much were to be granted, that the convictions reflected in Peirce's definitions of truth are at least open to doubt. This would be quite in accord with Pierce's own view that all our beliefs are fallible. His convictions happen to entail a number of beliefs about what in fact will happen in the future—that continuous inquiry *will* tend to a "final opinion." Peirce recog-

[192] Quine, in *Word and Object*, p. 23, has questioned Peirce's use of the analogy and also his "imputation of uniqueness ('*the* ideal result')." Whereas Peirce is talking about beliefs or statements, Quine interprets the definition of truth as asserting that an ideal *theory* will emerge from the endless application of scientific method "on continuing experience." And Quine rightly suspects the assumption that applied scientific method will in fact result in one theory "scientifically simpler or better than all possible others." But, as is pointed out below, there is a serious question as to whether Peirce's definition makes or rests upon this assumption at all.

nized that these beliefs were also hopes; the convictions were not certain; but there was, he thought, evidence for them, especially in the history of scientific thought. But the main purpose of the definitions of truth was not that of expressing these *convictions*. The definitions were proposed as a *clarification* of the concept of truth. So viewed, the questions as to whether there ever will in fact be a final opinion to which endless investigation *would tend*, are misdirected. The definitions were intended to provide us with an account of what is meant by truth by stating the conditions under which an opinion or statement is *true* and an object *real*. It is our *conception* of these conditions as satisfied that yields the *meaning* of truth for Peirce. The definitions of truth are not statements purporting to be true, to the effect that a certain belief *will* occur in a certain way in the future and this occurrence is what 'truth' means. Peirce was not arguing that, in order to state what we mean by 'truth,' we must subscribe to the following:

> There exists some (at least one) opinion *O*, and if *O* is subjected to endless scientific investigation, there will be a time when every investigator of *O* will agree that *O* represents a real object.

Even if this statement is doubtful or flatly false, still the definition of 'truth' is not rendered useless nor are we at a loss as to what 'truth' means for Peirce. He himself makes this much clear, as we noticed previously (note 188), when he says:

> I do not say that it is infallibly true that there is any belief to which a person would come if he were to carry his inquiries far enough. I only say that that alone is what I call Truth. I cannot infallibly know that there *is* any truth.

In seeking to clarify the idea of truth Peirce evidently followed his pragmatic method for treating general terms. To discover what is meant by the concept of a true belief (or true opinion) is to provide a description of the kind of conditions to which the concept applies. These descriptions, we have seen above, are conditional statements in which operations of a certain kind, performed upon an object of a certain kind, are said to produce a general result of a specified kind. Thus in wondering what is meant by truth, or a true opinion, or by '*O* is true,' Peirce's advice would seem to be: first consider the kind of operations and objects that are involved in our use of the concept 'true.' The objects here are *representations*, beliefs, and statements asserting something to *be* the case, i.e., representations of reality.[193] The operation in this case is one of investigation and experimental verification. The general result might consist of a predictive statement concerning the confirmation of the belief in question. Let us try, in a rough outline, to restate the substance of Peirce's definitions in the following ways:

[193] See *CP* 5.553 and 5.554: "Truth is the conformity of a representamen to its object, *its* object. . . ."

We mean by the *truth* of any opinion (or statement) *O*: If *O* is investigated experimentally, *O* will be confirmed.

Here the meaning of truth is simply subsumed under the not so simple ideas of verification or confirmation. But the definitions also say something more, namely: '*O* is true' means 'everyone who investigates *O*, and on every investigation, agrees that the object of *O* is real.'

If we choose as an example of *O*, say, 'iron expands when heated,' Peirce's account of truth might be said to go this way. We *mean* by the truth of *O* that, for any piece of iron *X*, and for any test case *T* in which *X* is heated, and for all scientific investigators *SI*, it is *always* the case:

1) if *T*, then *X* expands,
2) *SI* agree upon the opinion expressed by (1),
3) the belief '*X* expands when heated' represents a real object,
4) the belief stated in (3) contains a degree of inaccuracy . . .[194]

This sketch can only be of value in helping to emphasize the one point that matters. The question of the meaning of 'truth' was thought, by Peirce, to be capable of a meaningful answer by describing those conditions that serve as a kind of model for interpreting the term. Ideally, the conditions described are just those that are implied by our use of the term, and its "practical bearings" and the scope of its relation to "conceived action."

In stating his view of what truth is, Peirce not only made use of the analogy of beliefs, like a series of numbers, tending to a limit, but also employed the idea, familiar in the analysis of scientific concepts, of *ideal conditions*. Thus, to take a famous example, in Euclid's *Elements*, a *point* is defined as "that which has no part." If we wanted to use Euclidian geometry in making measurements upon a field, we would look in vain for those objects which could rightly serve as points according to that definition. We might find scatterings of birdshot and several boulders on the field, but no points. In a metaphysical mood we might conclude that points do not exist. But, in our concern to measure the field, this stratagem occurs to us: we could construe Euclid's points as objects of a certain minimum volume, say, bird shot. In a semantical mood we could even define 'part' as at least twice the volume of one piece of bird shot. Thus semantics defies metaphysics, and points are restored to existence.

But this last triumph of strategy aside, we could proceed with our measure-

---

[194] Perhaps this "confession of inaccuracy" by which (4) is made one of the supplementary conditions of the meaning of truth, comes to this: the opinion expressed in (1) is (somehow) "onesided" and capable of being made more precise; the possibility of (1) being disconfirmed tends with "endless investigation" to become continuously less likely. But this suggests that a true opinion is one which cannot (or should we say, will not) possibly be disconfirmed; and this in turn suggests, vaguely, some notion of a true opinion enjoying the status of a necessary truth. Or, to speculate, perhaps the truth of a true opinion is to be conceived of as what would be the case if the opinion were universally confirmed. But the notion of *universal confirmation*, like that of a *degree of confirmation*, is far too complicated and teasing to be ventured into here.

ments, having points of a sort to work with, while denying in candid strictness that points "really" exist. The most interesting feature of the bird shot is their approximation to points; they, more than boulders, come closer to being points by some standard of minimum volume applied equally to bird shot and boulders. To deny that points exist as ideal Euclidean objects is not to protest that statements (or concepts) of these, or of any other ideal objects, are without use or significance. This would be a ruthless empiricism under which empirical science would never have started. As in the above illustration, statements of ideal conditions can be supplemented with others more directly geared to existing objects, through which the informative value and regulative function of ideally stated conditions is kept intact. The benefits of this procedure for actual investigations of facts can be invaluable—ideal conditions come through pragmatically as standards of relevance in assessing what aspects of what subject matters most concern the inquiry at hand, and in conferring upon it such divers utilities as simplifying certain calculations and suggesting certain theoretical goals and pursuits.

Peirce's concept of truth is to be understood in a similar spirit as referring to those ideal conditions wherein opinion (or statement) stands in a certain relation to real objects as a result of inquiry. And existing opinions (or statements) are, by the same view, regarded as more or less approximating these ideal conditions. The concept of truth for Peirce has exactly the function that Kant ascribed to "regulative ideas" (see above, § 12).

The meaning of truth in general, as Peirce defines it, or that meaning narrowed down to particular working cases of the sort outlined above (page 131), has a twofold purpose. In general the idea of truth represents an ideal of scientific progress. Truth is our conception of what our beliefs would be if they represented (or were effected by) nothing but reality. This is the ideal of finished scientific knowledge. In its application to any of our beliefs at any one time, however, the idea of truth is to serve as a working standard of criticism, a norm for appraising the reliability of beliefs, and a constant reminder that no claim to the discovery of truth can be honored without its submission to impartial experimental investigation and no belief is in principle exempt from the community of inquiry and the pressure of continual testing.

We have looked this long at Peirce's definition of truth because it and the topic of truth comes up repeatedly in later discussions of pragmatism. But this is to have strayed beyond the limits Peirce set for pragmatism as a method of settling disputable meanings or avoiding meaningless disputes.

Such, in substance and in retrospect, was Peirce's contribution to the founding of pragmatism: a biologically oriented theory of inquiry issuing in an analytically empirical and experimental criterion of meaning. And such in substance were the ideas that lay unnoticed for twenty years until James gave them a new reception with results unforeseen, and mostly unintended, by Peirce.

CHAPTER TWO

William James

§ 25. *James and Pragmatism*

It was in a lecture of 1898 that James first invoked pragmatism, crediting the idea to Peirce. For James as for Peirce, pragmatism was but one of many philosophic themes pursued over a lifetime.

In the background of James's pragmatism was his scientific training in medicine, his teaching of physiology and later of psychology, and his great *Principles of Psychology* (1890). Further back was his early ambition to become a painter, an articulate observer of color and shape and of expressive details[1]—a versatility James never lost as a writer. Anticipations of his pragmatism can be found in the *Psychology*, in several early articles, and in *The Will to Believe* (1897); and no sharp line divides the pragmatism from later ventures into radical empiricism (though James notes that pragmatism and radical empiricism can be taken as logically independent doctrines).[2]

Pragmatism and its forerunner, the will to believe, had their philosophic initiation in a moment of trial and personal crisis for James when in his late twenties. From his medical studies and readings in science, the idea began to force itself upon James that man is a mechanism doomed from the start to action in a mechanically closed universe. From the idea, like the universe it represented, there seemed no escape. The prospects of suicide or madness apparently hung

---

[1] This is said with no knowledge of James's painting, his use of colors, or whether his paintings still exist. But his sketches, some of which have been reproduced, show just that knack for catching significant individual details which he commanded with words. In both instances, stylistically, James represents the antithesis of impersonal "classical" idioms given to conveying the "universal" traits of things. His nominalism, accompanying his respect for novelty and uniqueness of experienced objects, his distrust of the rationalists' predilection for abstract objects, of the reality claimed for "common natures," came to James before his philosophy and its post-philosophic justifications. The philosopher's doctrine, that *relations* are particular items of direct experience on a par with *objects* related —the empirical core of *radical empiricism*—has its picturesque pre-philosophic exemplification in the youthful painter's sketchbook.
[2] The Preface to *Pragmatism*, p. ix.

133

equally in balance for James. Other fears accompanied this insufferable conviction, or followed from it, such as that of horror and dread described in *The Varieties of Religious Experience*.[3]

An entry James made in his diary in 1870 is most revealing of the crisis and the healing that came by way of a decisive philosophic commitment. It is an illuminating instance of James's personally tried and personally "proven" view of the function of philosophic thought and belief.

> I think that yesterday was a crisis in my life. I finished the first part of Renouvier's second "Essais" and see no reason why his definition of Free Will—"the sustaining of a thought *because I choose to* when I might have other thoughts"—need be the definition of an illusion. At any rate, I will assume for the present—until next year—that it is no illusion. My first act of free will shall be to believe in free will. For the remainder of the year, I will abstain from the mere speculation and contemplative *Grüblei* in which my nature takes most delight, and voluntarily cultivate the feeling of moral freedom, by reading books favorable to it, as well as by acting. . . . For the present then remember: care little for speculation; much for the *form* of my action; recollect that only when habits of order are formed can we advance to really interesting fields of action—and consequently accumulate grain on grain of willful choice like a very miser . . . *Principiis obsta* —Today has furnished the exceptionally passionate initiative which Bain posits as needful for the acquisition of habits. I will see to the sequel. Not in maxims, not in *Anschauungen*, but in accumulated *acts* of thought lies salvation. . . . I will go a step further with my will, not only act with it, but believe as well; believe in my individual reality and creative power. My belief, to be sure, *can't* be optimistic—but I will posit life (the real, the good) in the self-governing *resistance* of the ego to the world. Life shall be built in doing and suffering and creating.[4]

The affirmation of free will, of action, of creative life, buttressed by reading in Renouvier and Darwin and by his own incipient pragmatism saved James.

This early and private record of James's thought is impressive as a disclosure of central motives and circumstances in the making of his pragmatism. But it would be a mistake to treat the passage just quoted as in any way relevant to assaying the truth or adequacy of his later published views—a mistake illustrative of the so-called genetic fallacy and not uncommon among sociologically and psychoanalytically minded historians of ideas. The passage helps explain James's pragmatism, not explain it away. It throws much light on how pragmatism, as James conceived the doctrine, could function as an invaluable guide to the acquisition of "creative" and "satisfactory" acts of thought and belief. It also helps to explain the shift in content and direction that James brought upon Peirce's original formulation of pragmatism: fundamentally a shift from the analysis of meanings of ideas to an analysis of their value or moral uses, a matter to be commented upon below.

For James, accordingly, pragmatism was more than a critical maxim for achiev-

---

[3] In the chapter on the "Sick Soul," disguised as the report of a "French correspondent."
[4] *The Letters of William James*, Vol. I, pp. 147–148.

ing clarity of meaning. It provided a method for resolving moral, religious, and metaphysical problems;[5] hence, freeing us "from abstraction and insufficiency, from fixed principles, closed systems, and pretended absolutes and origins." It directs us to "concreteness and adequacy, towards facts, towards action and towards power."[6]

§ 26.   James's Bifocal Vision

James makes it clear that he regards pragmatism as both a *method* for analyzing philosophic problems and a *theory of truth*—one pair of conceptual glasses for taking a short- or long-distance philosophic view of things.

Peirce, we have noticed, incidentally, favored keeping questions of *meaning* and of *truth* distinct: pragmatism was a method of explicating meanings, not a theory of truth. Nonetheless, as we have seen, despite these avowals, questions of truth can arise when the method is applied to ekeing out the meaning of terms. Moreover, since the method enjoins us to look for the meaning of terms by considering their application to objects in experimental situations with (conceivable) experimental consequences, some notion of truth and verification is foreshadowed in the method itself. Finally, there is evidently no reason why the term 'truth' is not a fit subject for pragmatic analysis of meaning. But a pragmatic definition of truth, if possible, is surely just that incursion of pragmatism into truth theory that Peirce renounced as unpragmatic.

In thus extending the scope by doubling the focus of pragmatism, James has often been accused of an errant exploitation of Peirce's pragmatic maxim. There is little question that James and Peirce differed in their interpretations of what pragmatism stood for. But whether James is justly accused of misunderstanding and misapplying Pierce's ideas is a fine point of interpretation. We can regard James's pragmatism as a secondhand article or, because of its disparities with the original, as largely his own invention. For James was not lacking in inventive power, though it was characteristic of him to give credit to others in direct proportion to what was best and most original in his own work. Recent tradition, tending to favor Peirce over James in their philosophizing about meaning and truth, has represented the Jamesian doctrines as debased currency. The tendency has sometimes been encouraged by an ill-disguised if understandable attempt to "save" pragmatism. However, the weight of tradition, as Peirce was fond of remarking, is no worthy arbiter of philosophic ideas.

While James argued for pragmatism as a method, drawing upon, supplementing, and revising what he found in Peirce, and continued to illustrate its use,

---

[5] According to one of James's descriptions, "the pragmatic method is primarily a method of settling metaphysical disputes that otherwise might be interminable," *Pragmatism*, p. 45. Note the ambiguity of 'settling' here, which can mean *clarifying the meaning* of questions under dispute, or *resolving* the disputes by providing a satisfactory *answer*.

[6] *Pragmatism*, p. 51.

it was the other half of his vision—the theory of truth—which occupied more of his attention. The pragmatic theory of truth incorporated two related functions: because theories are instruments according to James, pragmatism is a device enabling us in specific instances to discover and attain true beliefs; pragmatism is also a means for explaining the meaning of truth generally.

We shall be helped to a better critical understanding of these ideas by an interim reflection upon some points of historical (§ 27) and linguistic (§§ 29, 30) interest in their evolution.

§ 27. Empiricism and Pragmatism

A notably favorite thesis of empiricism is that all ideas are derived from experience. Different accounts of this derivation, from the most simple to the most complicated, are but variations wrung from essentially the same empirical theory. In Locke and Hume the thesis receives more than usual emphasis by way of being, in addition to a statement of principle, a practice of critical philosophical analysis.

Historically, the notion of *derivation* was flexible enough to suggest the complementing of one piece of theory with another: from thinking of ideas as causally derived from experience, to thinking of the meaning of ideas as reducible (or translatable) to events (or terms) of immediate experience. Contemporary versions of reductionism are linguistically based, envisaging a reduction by means of logical constructions of the descriptive terms of science to terms referring to immediate sense data. This term-for-term reduction has its parallel in the psychology of eighteenth-century empiricists with its reduction of ideas to simple sensations.

But reductionism,[7] of old or of late, has proved capable of turning its otherwise innocent pursuit of explanation into a scouting party of criticism—from explaining how ideas are derived from sensations (of old) or how theoretical terms are constructed from sense-data reports (of late), to critical raids upon such of those ideas or terms as fail to stand up under reductive explanation. To fail of reductive explanation, be it an idea (of old) or a unit of language

---

[7] To avoid a possible misunderstanding, it should be added that the above comments on *reductionism* have nothing to do with the idea, dating from Aristotle, of certain portions of a science being reducible to others—in which fundamental definitions and laws of one science (e.g., biology) are shown to be logically derivable from another science (e.g., physics). Rather, the thesis here alluded to (and one that James supported and advocated in rough outline) is that of providing terms or descriptive reports of immediately experienced data as translations of the abstract, general, and theoretical concepts of a science or system of knowledge. So translated, the latter often complex notions are *reducible* to the former, and can in principle be dispensed with in favor of a language of simple empirical observations. As a program, reductionism in this sense has achieved only fragmentary success; the model of effort and ingenuity in sketching the program for physics and psychology is Carnap's *Logische Aufbau* (1928).

Further comments on this topic are resumed below, in §§ 27, 79, and Part IV, ch. 2, esp. § 83.

(of late), is to fail to show any traceable lineal descent from sense experience; the penalty is an implication of bastardy, in this case, "meaningless." Thus are the plowshares of reductive explanation converted into swords of criticism. Santayana, seeing as much behind the psychologizing tendency of British empiricists, labeled it a "malicious psychology."

Hume's reductive approach is clear. Beginning with an account of the origins of ideas as "derived" from impressions, the explanation is subtly worked over into a critical test of the meaningfulness of those ideas or beliefs purporting to be about matters of fact. Examining the idea or belief in the *self*, or in *causality*, Hume asks from what impressions are these derived? Finding none, he treats the alleged ideas to be meaningless or the belief false (note the encroachment of truth under the criterion of meaning). On the other hand, a "justified" belief in the self or in causality, namely, Hume's, as against unjustified rationalism, fits the reductive bill. Thus Hume has been read, perhaps not correctly,[8] as maintaining that a reductive uncovering of the experiential causes of ideas and beliefs about the world is a test of meaning and validity.

Both Peirce and James took an alternative course in giving priority to the *consequences* of ideas and beliefs when questions of truth or meaning were under consideration. This was not an alternative to empiricism, but rather a fundamental shift and a resulting revision within the theory and practices of empiricism. One could continue to affirm sense experience as the original of ideas and immediate experience as the cause of thought and stimulus to inquiry. But ideas and beliefs were no longer to be regarded as somehow reflections or products of presumably simple and inspectable impressions. Nor were ideas to be construed as images, usually said to be the less "vivid" semblances of antecedent sensations. Imagining, believing, thinking, having ideas—each and all do have causes and are, perhaps, "derived from experience." For the pragmatist, however, the experiential causes of ideas and beliefs may be necessary conditions of their *occurrence*, but not a sufficient condition in the analysis of what they *are*, viz., what (in any case) they mean, or whether they are or are not true.

For Peirce, James, and Dewey, the weakest and most troublesome points in traditional empirical theory were three: its interpretation of sensation (or sense data); its interpretation of ideas (thinking and mind); its persistent attempt at a reductive analysis of mental phenomena. In short, empiricism, to the pragmatic eye, was suffering from a faulty philosophical physiology, psychology, and method of analysis.

There are important differences between Peirce, James, and Dewey concerning how the positive steps of revision were to proceed. Peirce, we have seen (§ 21),

---

[8] For a different interpretation, see Randall, *Career*, pp. 635–649. In suggesting that Hume is a reductivist critic of ideas, I ought to be more precise. Strictly speaking, *ideas* are never meaningless for Hume. It is *terms*, beliefs, assertions, allegations purporting to derive from or express ideas that are suspect and subject to a "meaning analysis" for Hume —his criterion of meaningfulness for these being: (*a*) a term fails to be meaningful if its purported relation to an idea cannot be specified; (*b*) an alleged idea fails to be "real" or clear (or an idea) if reduction to impressions (thus, origins) cannot be carried out.

appealed to a criterion of the conceivable consequences, i.e., the class of confirming instances, under standard test conditions, as the one right way of determining the meaning of signs (i.e., ideas, beliefs, predicates, statements). And the "justification" or truth of signs, as "confirming instances" suggest, is undertaken in an analogous, though not identical way (§§ 21, 23). The appeal is never to a particular test case, never to a single operation, a single result, and a single sense experience, as giving the meaning of a term. Meaning (as well as verification) is not had that way; particular tests, or particular sense experiences are at best but intimations, or signs of meaning. Meaning is found in the "generals" only; it is found in a kind or form of operation and result (expressed by conditional statements; see the first half of § 21). Meanings are present in formulas; not in specific actions or events, but in rules of action. Peirce's pragmatic empiricism, his "critical common sensism," comes from Kant (but also Berkeley) rather than from the British empiricism of Locke, Hume, and Mill.[9] While he rejects the *Ding-an-sich* and, evidently, the synthetic a priori, which normally would stand as a rejection of Kant altogether, he writes that he was led to the maxim of pragmatism (see the beginning paragraph of § 21) from reflection upon Kant's *Critique of Pure Reason*.[10] The view of meanings as general, as expressed in formulas prescribing *kinds* of operations and results, as found in forms and rules of action, is directly linked to Kant. The word 'pragmatism' as a name for this outlook, Peirce says, was a translation of Kant's *pragmatisch*. It does not mean 'practical,' but empirical or experimental. For Kant, practical laws are "given through reason completely *a priori*"; pragmatic laws are "empirically conditioned," based on and applying to experience.[11]

In an article of 1905 Peirce explained more fully the Kantian origin of the name invented for his new doctrine. Here it is interesting to notice Peirce's emphasis on the recognition of the purposive nature of cognition as the salient feature of his pragmatism. Of his invention he writes:

> Some of his friends wished him to call it *practicism* or *practicalism*. . . . But for one who had learned philosophy out of Kant, as the writer, along with nineteen out of every twenty experimentalists who have turned to philosophy, had done, and who still thought in Kantian terms most readily, *praktisch* and *pragmatisch* were as far apart as the two poles, the former belonging in a region of thought where no mind of the experimentalist type can ever make sure of solid ground under his feet, the latter expressing relation to some definite human purpose. Now quite the most striking feature of the new theory was its recognition of an inseparable

---

[9] Though also from the Scottish "Philosophy of Common Sense," *CP* 5.439. Peirce also comments, *CP* 5.452: "The present writer was a pure Kantist until he was forced by successive steps into Pragmaticism." As noted at the outset of Appendix 5 below, Peirce cites Berkeley as the founder of pragmatism.

[10] *CP* 5.3.

[11] Cf. *Critique of Pure Reason*, A800-B828. The same fundamental distinction is made in *The Metaphysics of Morals*.

connection between rational cognition and rational purpose; and that consideration
it was which determined the preference for the name *pragmatism*.[12]

A neat point of comparative difference between Peirce and James is found
in a comment by James on the meaning of 'pragmatic.' James neglects the strict
allegiance to Kantian use which Peirce intended for 'pragmatism.' Altogether
contrary to Peirce's efforts to rid pragmatism of associations with the practical,
or with actions, James remarks that the history of the idea shows what pragmatism means, "the term is derived from the same Greek word πράγμα, meaning
action, from which our words 'practice' and 'practical' come."[13]

James, remaining closer to British empiricism than either Peirce or Dewey,
gave the principle of consequences a thoroughly nominalistic application. This,
too, is a divergence from Peirce. Indeed, reading Peirce, one is struck by the
frequency of his incursions upon nominalism, usually brief, acrid, and none too
clear. But Peirce's basic philosophical dissent from James's accounts of pragmatism is clear. It is an objection Peirce often made, and one of considerable
theoretical importance. James interpreted the principle of *conceivable effects* in
Peirce's enunciation of the pragmatic maxim (see beginning of § 21 above)
as a procedure for determining the meaning of a concept by references to *sensations* and to particular, practical forms of sense experience. For Peirce, the pragmatic meaning of concepts cannot be reduced to experience in this sense. In a

---

[12] "What Pragmatism Is" (1905), *CP* 5.412. In the *Critique of Pure Reason* (II, ch. 2,
sec. 3) Kant discusses the nature of *belief*, as distinct from opinion and knowledge, in practical judgments. The "practical point of view is either in reference to *skill* or in reference
to *morality*, the former being concerned with optional and contingent ends, the latter with
ends that are absolutely necessary," A823–B851. A contingent belief is one that we will
entertain with more or less (i.e., degrees) of confidence. "Such contingent belief, which
yet forms the ground for the actual employment of means to certain actions, I entitle
pragmatic belief," A824-B852.
    It is of interest to note that in these passages Kant singles out *betting* as the usual way
of testing the conviction and degree of confidence of a man's assertions and beliefs. Kant's
text here suggests the source of Peirce's appreciation of Bain's definition of belief, about
which Peirce remarked that pragmatism was "scarce more than a corollary" (§ 19 and
note 6) and of Venn's analysis of belief as "readiness to act" (§ 22, note 101).
    In the *Fundamental Principles of the Metaphysic of Morals* (Second Section, pp. 32–34)
Kant defines the *pragmatic* imperative, in contrast to the categorical imperative, as one kind
of hypothetical imperative in which an action is prescribed as good "only as a means *to
something else*" and accordingly "good for some purpose, *possible* or *actual*." He connects
this kind of imperative with those of *skill*, not skill relating to *any* purpose, but only to
achieving happiness. "Skill in the choice of means to one's own greatest well-being may be
called prudence." Counsels of prudence may then be called "*pragmatic* (belonging to wel-
fare)." These obligate the will, desire, and purposeful thought with respect to attaining
happiness.
    In "The Sentiment of Rationality" (1879) James had emphasized the instrumental and
purposeful nature of conception: "What now is a *conception*? It is a *teleological instrument*. It is a partial aspect of a thing which *for our purpose* we regard as its essential aspect,
as the representative of the entire thing," *Collected Essays and Reviews*, pp. 86–87. In
his *Psychology*, II, 335, he quoted this passage in a note, and argued for the view that
conceptions (and presumably meanings) were the products of interest and purpose: "The
essence of a thing is that one of its properties which is so *important for my interests* that
. . . I may neglect the rest."
[13] *Pragmatism*, p. 46.

letter he once put the difference between his pragmatism and James's in a forcible way, thus:

> Although James calls himself a pragmatist, and no doubt derived his ideas on the subject from me,[14] yet there is a most essential difference between his pragmatism and mine. My point is that the meaning of a *concept* . . . lies in the manner in which it could *conceivably* modify purposive action, and *in this alone*. James, on the contrary, whose natural turn of mind is away from generals, and who is besides so soaked in ultra-sensationalist psychology that like most modern psychologists he has almost lost the power of regarding matters from the logical point of view, in defining pragmatism, speaks of it as referring ideas to *experiences*, meaning evidently the sensational side of experience, while I regard *concepts* as affairs of habit or disposition, and of how we should react.[15]

While Peirce dissented from James's *Will to Believe* and his account of truth, the underlying discord is realism vs. nominalism. It divides James's pragmatism from Peirce's pragmaticism. What counted as the "consequences" of thought or belief for James was just that level of experience which excluded generality, and thus meanings, for Peirce, *viz.*, practical effects, sensations, conduct, actions.[16] To James it is this level of live differences of choice, chance, and resolutions that is most "meaningful." It is there that the value of philosophic concepts is found and tested. In a phrase that permanently shocked some of his British critics, James spoke of the "cash value" of ideas, referring to both meaning and truth.

Now since the level of live differences finds men differently situated, with differences of needs, wants, and satisfactions, the "value"—the meaning and truth —of ideas is subject to the same range of local and relative differences. That this must be the case follows, for James, from the psychological observation that the primary function of thought and of ideas is that of bringing us to and keeping

---

[14] There is doubt about this.

[15] In a letter to Christine Ladd-Franklin quoted in her article in the Peirce commemorative issue of the *Journal of Philosophy*, p. 718.

The value of single observations, or sensations, either as a source or termination of theoretical knowledge is minimum for Peirce. This has not been sufficiently noticed in expositions of his theory of knowledge. A single observation, like the single case of a characteristic event in the frequency theory of probability, does not *as such* (i.e., as "absolutely dumb" and "individual," see CP 7.622, 625) admit of judgment at all. For the theory of perceptual judgment, see Bernstein's study. There is an analogue between the status of a single characteristic event in a class of events, and the single sensation or observation in the determination of the character of some object. The value of the single sensation or observation consists in its role as a *function* or statistical quantity. What counts in the evolution of knowledge and operation of judgment is not single sensations but a series of the same, for which as a series a certain average (probable) value of accuracy can be established. See "On the Theory of Errors of Observation," and § 22 above, esp. note 88.

[16] James also allows for an interpretation of *consequences* of a more general scope, thus speaking of clearness "in our thoughts of an object" as a consideration of "what conceivable effects of a practical kind the object may involve—what sensations we are to expect from it, and what reactions we must prepare. Our conception of these effects, whether immediate or remote, is then for us the whole of our conception of the object," *Pragmatism*, pp. 46–47. But here, as elsewhere, James fluctuates; "conceivable effects" is qualified by the addition "of a practical kind." And little if any suggestion is forthcoming as to the limits of remoteness; i.e., to what length of being "remote" can our conception of the practical effects of an object go, before being excluded from "our conception of the object"?

us in satisfactory relations with the world of persons and things in which we live and move and have our being. The observation stems from James's functional psychology. His "functional method" consists in the analysis of mental phenomena as processes or activities (rather than as objects or entities) to be distinguished and so described by the difference their presence makes in relation to other processes or exhibits in experience. The approach is seen in James's general description of the *mental*, or the presence of mind in phenomena, at the beginning of the *Psychology*:

> *the pursuance of future ends and the choice of means for their attainment are thus the mark and criterion of the presence of mentality* in a phenomenon.[17]

And the thoroughly purposive nature of thought, for James, is evident here as well.

Basically, and in the most dramatic exemplifications of its function, thought is an instrument of survival. But in any case, the circumstances in which survival of a man, or men, or a society is a major concern are amply variegated. Furthermore, as sages have been wont to remind us, survival is but one among many human interests and does not invariably take first place. So it is that thought is called upon as assisting in the satisfaction of many kinds of interests. And so, too, according to James, the value of thought—or the specific products of thought, ideas, beliefs—is to be judged on each of numerous occasions by a standard of effectiveness and efficiency as means. But means to what? Means, says James, "that will carry us prosperously from any one part of our experience to any other part, linking things satisfactorily, working securely, simplifying, saving labor."[18]

§ 28. Mind as Teleological

In several early papers James developed an interpretation of mind and mental behavior that became the fundamental and controlling idea in his psychology, his theory of knowledge, and his analysis of religious belief.

James argued from the first that the thinking process is not only or primarily a response to external conditions; for this notion of its function really explains nothing about thought or external conditions as they are related to or affect mental behavior. Rather, James maintained, thinking operates exclusively for the sake of purposes and ends that have their origin in immediately felt emotional and practical wants and concerns. These "subjective interests,"[19] as he referred to them, direct the thinking process; and, as against the "correspondence" theory,

---

[17] I, 8.

[18] *Pragmatism*, p. 58. Cf. " 'knowing' . . . may . . . be *only one way of getting into fruitful relations with reality*," "Humanism and Truth," in *The Meaning of Truth*, pp. 80–81.

[19] It was one of Dewey's critical aims in reworking some of James's ideas to elaborate quite carefully the sense in which wants, feelings, and concerns are not *subjective* in the sense of "private," "inner mental states," "hidden motives," etc. For some of this, see § 38 and Part IV, ch. 3.

this analysis of thought recognizes that external conditions are themselves *conditional*—that is, colored and selectively interpreted according to our operative practical and passional concerns. Moreover, some "external" conditions, such as ideal aims and not (or not *yet*) existing objects (*"shall's"* and *"should-be"* conditions), are understandable objectives of thoughtful behavior for James's theory, whereas they are not for the theory of mind as simply mirroring or responding to and reckoning with external phenomena.

The theory of mind as a mode of adjustment to and correspondence with outer conditions, the theory James criticizes, was set forth by Herbert Spencer. The theory is not original with Spencer—indeed little was—and it has a long history in philosophy. Spencer added an evolutionary dimension to the older construction. In what became a famous formula, Spencer defined 'life' as "adjustment of inner to outer relations," and this definition also subsumed under it "the entire process of mental evolution." In a paper of 1878[20] James shows that the apparent solidity of Spencer's elaborate and detailed description of mental evolution—depicted as extensions of this evolutionary process of adjustment, or "correspondence"—disappears on the slightest scrutiny.

> The ascertainment of outward fact constitutes only one species of mental activity. The genus contains, in addition to purely cognitive judgments, or judgments of the actual—judgments that things do, as a matter of fact, exist so or so—an immense number of emotional judgments: judgments of the ideal, judgments that things *should* exist thus and not so. How much of our mental life is occupied with this matter of a better or a worse?[21]

In most of our thinking moments, James pointed out, we are occupied with a rich medley of topics and interests having nothing to do directly with "cognizing the actual." Rather, we are engaged much of the time in selecting from "alternative possible actuals" some one of these and cognizing that as the ideal.[22]

Spencer's notion of mental activity as *"mere* correspondence with the outer world," James concludes, is one on which "it is wholly impossible to base a definition of mental action."[23]

In assigning the primary role to "subjective interests" in our cognitive activity, James makes the interesting suggestion that these interests are the *a priori* element in cognition.[24] He means by this that the function of such interests, their

---

[20] "Remarks on Spencer's Definition of Mind as Correspondence." Another early and equally important paper was "The Function of Cognition," published in *Mind*, 1885.
[21] "Remarks on Spencer's Definition of Mind," p. 2; in *Collected Essays and Reviews*, p. 45. References in the following eight notes are to the original publication but, for convenience, references to the reprinted paper in *Collected Essays and Reviews* are also given.
[22] *Ibid.*, p. 3; *Collected Essays and Reviews*, p. 46. The notion, here stressed by James, of "possible actuals" and selective purposive behavior with respect to possibles is fundamental in the pragmatist's conception of mind, thought, and action. Some reflections upon the core of this doctrine—i.e., the concept of *physical possibility*—might be expected here and in later pages where the idea is recurrent. In order not to interrupt the course of discussion, however, this topic is reserved for Appendix 7 below.
[23] *Ibid.*, p. 6; *Collected Essays and Reviews*, p. 50.
[24] See *ibid.*, p. 6, *n.* 1; *Collected Essays and Reviews*, p. 50*n.*

effect upon what sorts of things we tend to think of, or the sorts of objects we take special notice of, is determined by these prior and ruling interests. Conscience, he argues, not only serves a given purpose, it also *brings* final purposes, posits, and declares them.[25] To many things in the environment we may have registered "inward correlatives," says James. But suppose some of these inner correlatives are accented with pleasure and some with pain. These are additions and supplements to our mere cognizing of external things, and they present cognitive occurrences which have "no outward correlative." But these occurring facts which create or affect definite relations of cognition to environing conditions and correspondences are ordered in this way:

> the pleasant or interesting items are signaled out, dwelt upon, developed into farther connections, whilst the unpleasant or insipid ones are ignored or suppressed. The future of the Mind's development is thus mapped out in advance by the way in which the lines of pleasure and pain run. The interests precede the outer relations noticed.[26]

In cases where there is an absence of response to given environmental relations —e.g., in an uninquisitive person or animal—the inertia to respond to any of the enormous range and complexity of existing external conditions, James says, can be altered only

> after you *previously awaken an interest*—i.e., produce a susceptibility to intellectual pleasure in certain modes of cognitive exercise.[27]

The acknowledgment of the function of *interests*, then, is crucial to psychology —and also, it is readily seen, to education. Certainly no philosophic theory of mind is adequate in which these motivating and guiding contributaries to intellectual activity are ignored.

We may have serious reservations (as did Dewey) about the merits of the apparatus of "inner" and "external" terms and relations with "correlatives" as the connecting links between thought and objects. That apparatus, initially no doubt projected to facilitate our talking about and understanding mental behavior, defeats its purpose by raising many more problems than it was designed to solve. But aside from this, James's main critical argument is important. From his recognition of the significance of *interests*[28] in the processes of thought, James is led to some general philosophical conclusions that were to emerge as characteristic and cardinal doctrines in his later writings.

---

[25] On this teleological activity of thought, James writes, *ibid.*, p. 15, *Collected Essays and Reviews*, p. 64: "It not only *serves* a final purpose, but *brings* a final purpose—posits, declares it. This purpose is not a mere hypothesis—"*if* survival is to occur, then the brain must so perform," etc., but an imperative decree: "Survival *shall* occur, and, therefore, brain *must* so perform!"

[26] *Ibid.*, p. 6, *n.* 1; *Collected Essays and Reviews*, p. 50n. Here he also says: "These interests are the real a priori element in cognition."

[27] *Ibid.*, p. 6, *n.* 1; *Collected Essays and Reviews*, p. 50n.

[28] I.e., "the luxuriant foliage of ideal interests—aesthetic, philosophic, theologic, and the rest—which co-exist along with that of survival . . . ," *ibid.*, p. 9; *Collected Essays and Reviews*, p. 54.

I, for my part, cannot escape the consideration, forced upon me at every turn, that the knower is not simply a mirror floating with no foot-hold anywhere, and passively reflecting an order that he comes upon and finds simply existing. The knower is an actor, and coefficient of the truth which he helps to create. Mental interests, hypotheses, postulates, so far as they are bases for human action—action which to a great extent transforms the world—help to *make* the truth which they declare. In other words, there belongs to mind, from its birth upward, a spontaneity, a vote. It is in the game, and not a mere looker-on; and its judgments of the should-be, its ideals, cannot be peeled off from the body of the *cogitandum* as if they were excrescences, or meant, at most, survival. We know so little about the ultimate nature of things, or of ourselves, that it would be sheer folly dogmatically to say that an ideal rational order may not be real. The only objective criterion of reality is coerciveness, in the long run, over thought. Objective facts, Spencer's outward relations, are real only because they coerce sensation. Any interest which should be coercive on the same massive scale would be *eodem jure* real. By its very essence, the reality of a thought is proportionate to the way it grasps us. Its intensity, its seriousness—its interest, in a word—taking these qualities, not at any given instant, but as shown by the total upshot of experience. If judgments of the *should-be* are fated to grasp us in this way, they are what "correspond."[29]

In this single statement we can easily detect the seeds of James's pragmatism, the clear anticipations of the argument of the will to believe and the making of truth. In the *Will to Believe* James referred to this earlier essay, and one of the seeds comes to flower: the mind, he says, is

an essentially teleological mechanism. I mean by this that the conceiving or theorizing faculty—the mind's middle department—functions *exclusively for the sake of ends* that do not exist at all in the world of impressions we receive by way of our senses, but are set by our emotional and practical subjectivity altogether. It is a transformer of the world of our impressions into a totally different world,—the world of our conception; and the transformation is effected in the interests of our volitional nature, and for no other purpose.[30]

James's theory of mind as teleological was the matrix for his own pragmatism, and from it much of the philosophizing of later pragmatists was derived.[31]

But it should also be noticed in passing that James's language in the previous quotation and his way of locating the only "objective criterion of reality" in "coerciveness, in the long run, over thought" and of thought "fated" to be affected in certain ways, exhibit a striking resemblance to Peirce's views expressed in "How to Make Our Ideas Clear" (see above, §§ 23, 24). James's paper appeared in the same month and same year, 1878, of the publication of Peirce's article. The history of pragmatism can be thought to have its beginning jointly in

[29] *Ibid.*, pp. 17–18; *Collected Essays and Reviews*, pp. 67–68.
[30] *The Will to Believe*, "Reflex Action and Theism," p. 117.
[31] James also influenced Peirce and Royce with this doctrine of the purposive nature of thought. His theory as quoted in the passages above may be said, too, to have supplied the core of Schiller's pragmatism—see § 62, below.

these two works by James and Peirce. But this is not the received view, nor the
one James made popular by giving the credit for invention to Peirce.

§ 29. James and Language:
A Word About the Use of Words

It is not surprising, taking James's interpretation of thought thus outlined in
§ 27 and § 28, that certain ways of speaking about thought, about ideas and
beliefs, and about the standard governing such judgments as we pronounce upon
our thinking, should be adopted as more readily expressive and expedient than
others for purposes of communication. And since much of philosophic theory-
making and all theory-stating goes on in language, the linguistic medium itself,
taken as an object of study, often repays scrutiny by bringing us closer to the
fuller gist of intended meaning. This is to switch attention momentarily from
what a theory states to how it is stated. A retrospective analysis of the terms in
which a theory is stated can often help disclose what the theory and inventor
of theory is about. It encourages a retracing of the moves that went into the
construction of theory, thus affording a glimpse into some of the deliberations
that guided its articulation.[32] Then, too, the selection of certain words over others,
the use of certain illustrations, analogies, and metaphors in the phrasing of theory
can be revealing. For phrasings, while ordinarily passing for clues to the meaning
of theory, are in fact usually contrived according to antecedent promptings of
theory itself and are embodiments of it. The articulations of unburdening thought,
e.g., a metaphor, while said to be "expressive of" thought—on subsequent examination as to how and why just *that* metaphor was chosen as expressive—may tell
us more than its prosaic counterpart or literal transcription.

Thus, watchwords and earmarks of theory-stating, even clichés and parrotings
of doctrine, are not always to be dismissed by the judicious historian, sensitive to
the interplay between what philosophers say and how their philosophy is said.

It was James more than anyone who gave pragmatism its mother tongue, its
characteristic vocabulary, its identifying phrases and stock of illustrative materials. This explains why, especially outside of America, when pragmatism is under
consideration—be it Peirce's or Dewey's or Schiller's—the *modus operandi* of
discussion and understanding has its base in the writings of James. To do this,
James did not, like Peirce, resort to inventing new terms. He made colorful and
crisp use of the ordinary language of the man on the street, with a knack for
transplanting work-a-day functional expressions into philosophy and imbuing
the available fund of philosophic terms with new significance. There was a
genius for apt characterization, the very opposite of pedantry, by which James

---

[32] In art criticism, analogously, there is a view that perception of the materials and their
organization in a work of art is a "re-living" of the creative effort and process of its production—and this is basic to an appreciation and "understanding" of art. Thus, Dewey, *Art
as Experience*, pp. 108 ff.

warmed and delighted his audience. Who but James would have thought of praising Bergson's lucid style as resulting from "a flexibility of verbal resource that follows the thought without a crease or wrinkle, as elastic silk underclothing follows the movement of one's body."[33]

§ 30.   A Note on Bypassing Meaning

We have several times taken a passing but fragmentary notice of James's conception of *meaning*, of pragmatic *method* as distinct from pragmatic *truth*. But a redoubling of effort to gain a more coherent view of a doctrine of meaning is obstructed by the fact that James himself apparently had little interest in enunciating such a theory. His discussions of meaning are confined to suggesting a few general principles and to many illustrations of their practical value and uses.[34] Whereas Peirce labored long and carefully to develop a full-sized theory of meaning, no such esoteric interest moved James. While Peirce set out to understand meaning and how it is that terms mean, James sought a workable rule by which various sorts of expressions or ideas could be shown to have certain specific practical consequences. To show the consequences was to test whether or not an expression possessed meaning and a clarification of that meaning. Peirce undertook to explicate the idea of meaning; James was concerned to explicate the meanings of ideas.

Further obstacles to finding a theory of meaning in or behind James's pragmatic method are encountered where questions of the meaning of ideas shade off into questions of *value* and *truth*. Thus (speaking of the "pragmatic test"):

> The serious meaning of a concept, says Mr. Peirce, lies in the concrete difference to some one which its being true will make. . . if it can make no practical difference which of two statements be true, then they are really one statement in two verbal forms; if it can make no practical difference whether a given statement be true or false, then the statement has no real meaning.[35]

Here, if anywhere, the charge that James's pragmatism was a step backward from Peirce might find justification. The fact is that James used 'meaning' in much the same unsophisticated and vague way as it figures in ordinary speech, when we say, for example, that a life or occupation is "meaningful," or discuss the "meaning" of our foreign policy. In any event, we are acquitted from looking for a Jamesian theory of meaning where none was intended or is to be found. Truth, however, is quite a different matter.

---

[33] *Radical Empiricism and a Pluralistic Universe*, p. 227.
[34] James was like Wittgenstein in this respect; both men confined their efforts at philosophical clarification of meanings to examples, drawing back at the prospect of generalizing into a theory the principles used and illustrated in these practices. See Wittgenstein's critical remarks about the "craving for generality," *The Blue and Brown Books*, pp. 17 ff.
[35] "Humanism and Truth," in *The Meaning of Truth*, pp. 51–52.

§ 31. The Moral Basis of Truth

Among the most notable of catchwords and phrases in pragmatic theory were James's characterization of ideas and beliefs as "plans of action," and of thought, concepts, and theories as "instruments" or "modes of adaptation to reality"; his appeal to a standard (calling it the "pragmatic method") of "practical consequences," "practical differences," of the "useful" and "workable"; his rendition of "experience" as the foreground of stimulation, attention, and effort—the diversified flux of individual events and sense data, which, by occasionally "boiling over," forces upon us a continual readaptation of our conceptual schemes to reality. Experience includes experiencers, and James emphasized the role of the willing, believing, acting human agent who participates in "making reality" what it is, even making ideas true or false (by real-izing their plans).

A reason for these idioms, impelling and reflected in them, is not far to seek. The philosopher in James, as distinct from the scientist, was through and through a moralist. Moral interests dominate his popular writings and motivate even the most technical excursions of radical empiricism. Moral objectives guide his account of philosophy:

> The whole function of philosophy ought to be to find out what definite difference it will make to you and me, at definite instants of our life, if this world-formula or that world-formula be the true one.[36]

Two concepts are indispensable in the use of moral language: *good* and *value*: and language aside, without them we would be rendered artless in the business of making moral decisions, and the professional moralists would be utterly disarmed. One would expect, therefore, if the remarks made immediately above are well taken, to find these two concepts regularly employed by James. And so one will, if one wishes, with only the effort of browsing.[37] These concepts appear with particular frequency in *Pragmatism* and *The Meaning of Truth*, pairing off with two others: *right* and *useful*. As for the latter members of the two pairs, *value* and *useful*, the words 'expedient,' 'workable,' and 'successful' often figure as substitutes.

It is in this medium of moral interests facilitated by the terminology of value that James's definition of truth was formulated. Lifted from that context, this version of truth looks absurdly and patently wrong. So lifted, it became the *bête noire* of critical reactions to pragmatism.

That *truth* is anchored in a theory of *good* and *value* is clear enough from such centrally located pronouncements of James as:

[36] *Pragmatism*, p. 50.
[37] By a rough count, the word 'value' appears more often than any other term in the centrally located contexts of Pragmatism when *meaning, truth, thought,* and *action* are under discussion.

truth is one species of good, and not . . . a category distinct from good, and co-ordinate with it. *The true is the name of whatever proves itself to be good in the way of belief.* . . .[38]

The idea continues to be reiterated in each of the locutions mentioned above. The 'true' is that which is valuable, useful, expedient, workable, successful, profitable, etc. While each of these terms is applicable to a wide range of referential conditions, the extremities in outline are evident; at the one end reference is directed to conditions of adaptation and survival, at the other to any improvement in "life's practical struggles" or any yield of "vital benefits." The notion of truth is thus a part of James's view of the practical function of thought. That thought (which includes believing and willing and even talking) is a means to the satisfactory organization of experience, we noticed earlier. 'True,' then, refers to such of those means as *work efficiently* and *satisfactorily*, and 'false' to those that do not. Moreover, 'true' (and 'false') like 'good' and 'value' (or 'not good' and 'valueless') will admit of no absolute and universal application, since their reference to means is relative to those circumstances in which our differences of needs determine differences of satisfactions—differences, accordingly, in what means we regard as useful or useless.[39]

The venerable thesis of ethical relativity, while shunned by many, has rarely (since Herodotus) been looked on as an anomaly. But James's casting of truth in a like mould seemed to strike most contemporary philosophers as queer. James was alert to this, saying, "I am well aware how odd it must seem to some of you to hear me say an idea is 'true' so long as to believe it is profitable to our lives. That it is *good*, for as much as it profits, you will gladly admit."[40] But this was not the only novelty occasioning misunderstanding nor the one most basic. In point of fact, James seems to have been unaware of how far he had departed from customary nomenclature and traditional doctrine in issuing his new version of truth.

§ 32. Trouble over Truth

A spaniel at the heels of the new doctrine and always a nuisance was James's disinclination to give his ideas a rigorous and explicit formulation, to free what he meant from the ambiguities and unguarded language of his more popular accounts of truth, even overcoming his own indecision on what was to count as an admissible object of reference for the word 'truth' and what was not.[41] The conciliatory spirit of the man worked against the precise settling of his

---

[38] *Pragmatism*, p. 76.
[39] *Pragmatism*, p. 61: "to a certain degree . . . everything here is plastic."
[40] *Pragmatism*, p. 75.
[41] See, e.g., the important "suggestion"—really a letter of warning—from Dewey in which he urges James not to let truth be extended from "statement, idea or belief" to reality or facts as well, a concession James was prepared to make to the idealisms of Bradley and Royce (Perry, II, 530). For James's confession of uncertainty and perplexity over the meaning of truth, see Perry, II, 502–512.

thought. The meaning of truth was kept malleable while James tried to adapt his views to what he felt was sound in Bradley, Royce, and Peirce on one side, Dewey, the Chicago School, and Schiller on the other.[42] To fail at this was to fail at the impossible. James eventually gave up trying and turned to other philosophical pursuits, leaving pragmatic truth for Dewey to work out as best he could.

As matters stood, the meaning of truth as good, with some reshuffling of James's exposition, came to this: the truth of an "idea (opinion, belief, statement, or what not)"[43] is (1) its agreement with reality: (2) its workableness, or that concrete difference which its being true makes in anyone's actual life;[44] (3) the process of verification.

The senses in which an idea can be said to "agree with reality," and thus admit of truth, are several. Ideas are true when they (in some sense) correspond to facts, or when they (in some sense) partake of logically necessary relations. With a paraphrasing of Locke and Hume, James distinguishes the two orders of "reality"—the sensible order of facts, the ideal order of relations among ideas. Our ideas must "agree" with each of these orders "under penalty of endless inconsistency and frustration."[45] A third sense of truth as agreement follows the other two: any new idea, to be true, must be compatible with "the whole body of other truths already in our possession."[46]

What have traditionally been distinguished as *correspondence* and *coherence* theories of truth are thus brought together by James as the two parts of one general theory. Yet while in theory these parts are of equal importance, in his discussions of truth James betrays his radical empirical bias (and reductive interests, see § 27). Cases of direct confrontation of beliefs or ideas with experienced facts are assigned a privileged status as the "originals and prototypes of the truth-process." Truth systematically articulated, like truth systematically pursued, is rooted in truths of immediate experience. The primacy of what James calls "direct face-to-face verifications" tends to obscure his account of the role of logical truths and "relations among ideas." The structure of knowledge is viewed primarily along lines of its empirical depth rather than its logical breadth.

Still "agreement with reality" as a formula of truth remains vague at best, for to distinguish the different sorts of objects with which ideas will or will not "agree" throws no light on what 'agreement' might mean. James attempted to supply a remedy for what is missing by offering a functional description of the conditions under which agreement occurs. This, he argues, is the pragmatic meaning of the notion:

To 'agree' in the widest sense with a reality *can only mean to be guided either straight up to it or into its surroundings, or to be put into such working touch with it as to handle either it or something connected with it better than if we disagreed.*

[42] See Schneider, pp. 530–534.
[43] *The Meaning of Truth*, Preface, p. v.
[44] *Ibid.*, p. v.
[45] *Pragmatism*, p. 211.
[46] *Pragmatism*, p. 212.

Better either intellectually or practically! And often agreement will only mean the negative fact that nothing contradictory from the quarter of that reality comes to interfere with the way in which our ideas guide us elsewhere. To copy a reality is, indeed, one very important way of agreeing with it, but it is far from being essential. The essential thing is the process of being guided. Any idea that helps us *deal*, whether practically or intellectually, with either the reality or its belongings, that doesn't entangle our progress in frustrations, that *fits*, in fact, and adapts our life to the reality's whole setting, will agree sufficiently to meet the requirement. It will hold true of that reality.[47]

The description helps as an apt picture of intellectual practice, uncovering the circumstances and motives that might usually prompt our assent to an idea, to our calling it "valuable" for a given purpose, even to calling it "true." But the description is something less than revealing of what the word 'true' might mean, beyond being a vague adjective of approval for the serviceability of an idea. To say that ideas agree with reality when they help us deal with it is not to explain, beyond a hint or two, what the *agreement* consists of or how it occurs. And there is always this teaser: is it because they help us deal with reality that ideas are true, or is it because they are true that ideas help us deal with reality?

Had James been more painstaking in developing the pragmatic meaning of *agreement*, he might have avoided some of the harsher rejections of his doctrine and some of the confusion it engendered. He remarks, for example, of an idea or belief that is useful to us in our dealings with the world, that we can say: " 'it is useful because it is true' or that 'it is true because it is useful.' Both phrases mean exactly the same thing."[48] Perhaps with a certain interpretation and restriction upon 'useful,' a case can be made for the equation.[49] But 'useful' in its ordinary ill-defined plenitude of uses makes the equation startling. It was rejected by many readers for the simple reason that, while most true beliefs may be useful, it is by no means evident that because a belief is useful it is true. Similar statements from James that truth is what "works" or "pays" among our ideas and beliefs were also vehemently condemned.

The year that *Pragmatism* was published (1907), James attended a philosophy convention and attempted to specify more fully the sense in which he meant to define 'truth' as 'agreement with reality.'[50] In a statement reminiscent of Peirce, James first points out that in his "realistic" account of truth, the

---

[47] *Pragmatism*, pp. 212–213. Notice that James speaks of realities in the plural here. This is to allow *agreement* of ideas to apply equally to sensible objects of experience, to "mental objects" and relations, and the two orders of these "realities," concrete and abstract, sensible and ideal, respectively.

[48] *Pragmatism*, p. 204.

[49] Such, to speculate for a moment, as is found in Spinoza's equating of *good* and *useful*, in *Ethics*, Part IV, Def. 1. But Spinoza does not say simply that the good is useful; rather he qualifies, saying: "By good [*bonum*] I understand that which we certainly know is useful [*utile*] to us."

[50] Remarks delivered at a meeting of the American Philosophical Association, Cornell University, 1907. The remarks are reprinted as ch. 9, "The Meaning of the Word Truth," in *The Meaning of Truth*.

notion of a reality independent of either of us, taken from ordinary social experience, lies at the base of the pragmatist definition of truth. With some such reality any statement, in order to be counted true, must agree.[51]

But as he proceeds to explain what he means by "some such reality," it becomes clear that James is speaking of certain modes of *behavior* having reference both to a statement purporting to be true and to certain existential conditions as stated. The mode of behavior, it would seem for James, is an interpretation of the *meaning* of the statement, and also determines the statement's *verification*. Thus James continues:

> Pragmatism defines 'agreeing' to mean certain ways of 'working,' be they actual or potential. Thus, for my statement 'the desk exists' to be true of a desk recognized as real by you, it must be able to lead me to shake your desk . . . to make a drawing that is like the desk you see, etc. . . . Reference then to something determinate, and some sort of adaptation to it worthy of the name of agreement, are thus constituent elements in the definition of any statement of mine as 'true.'[52]

The suggestion is interesting. Truth as *agreement* means here not a correspondence of statement with facts, but corroboration, a *working agreement*, with respect to certain ways of behaving among persons responding to the statement "in *that* reality."[53] The "agreement" is a socially organized response, or group of responses on the part of those persons reacting to the statement in question, in a commonly established situation ("in *that* reality"). The "agreement" has to do with a social, or interpersonal way of adaptation to the common situation as a consequence of the statement made and the character of the conditions it asserts. The important ideas in this version of truth as *agreement* are those of *adaptation* and *workings*. But while James recognized this, the needed clarification of these ideas was unfortunately not undertaken.[54]

The many critical rejections of James's version of truth turned for the most part on one underlying objection, one forcibly put by Russell.[55] James seemed to have yielded to subjectivity and irrationality, and seemed to justify sheer irresponsible expediency in so conceiving—or misconceiving—the criterion of truth. Like the alarmed Plato combating Thrasymachus in the *Republic*, Russell proceeded to "examine" pragmatism, by analysis and by caricature.

Indeed, Russell's caricatures of the pragmatic doctrine of truth eventually reached a wider audience than the literature being parodied. One, or something like it, went: imagine a group of philosophers to be pondering the truth or falsehood of such recondite and vexing beliefs as that Caesar crossed the Rubicon, that

[51] *Ibid.*, pp. 217–218.
[52] *Ibid.*, p. 218.
[53] *Ibid.*, p. 218.
[54] He does say about the truth of statements: "You cannot get at either the reference or the adaptation without using the notion of the workings," *ibid.*, p. 218; and p. 220, "You *cannot define what you mean* by calling them true without referring to their functional possibilities."
[55] *Philosophical Essays*, ch. 5.

the earth is round, that the moon is made of green cheese. Each of the philosophers prudently attempts to survey the evidence upon which his beliefs concerning these troublesome matters is founded. Each, that is, except for the pragmatist, who happens also to be present. Instead, he asks himself what, in each case, will be profitable or useful to believe. He calls what pays, "true," and what doesn't, "false." If, for example, he should happen to own a share in a firm doing business in cheeses—thus deriving an income allowing him to philosophize at leisure—he may find it profitable to believe that nature's sublime satellite of the earth is made of cheese. The proverbial child who cries for the moon, our pragmatist might cleverly explain, is really crying for cheese. While other philosophers look to the world, or to those portions of it that are relevant for the confirmation of belief, the pragmatist looks at himself and confirms beliefs according to his needs and purposes. Hence, the subjectivity of pragmatic truth. Hence, too, the irrationality of it all. For if truth is merely what we want, or think we want to believe, the once eternal separation of truth and falsehood becomes as fluid, confused, and ephemeral as the conditions that generate belief and just as fanciful as wishing.

Furthermore, as Russell has pointed out, while it may be good, or profitable, for students taking an examination to believe that the earth is round, it may be profitable for the teacher who must grade the examination papers if most of the students believe that the earth is flat. The result is a chaotic conflict of profit interests and conceptions of truth.

The caricature (as well as the moralizing it prompts) is unjust, however, and essentially so since its critical motivation is mistaken. James was cognizant of the need for objective and socially shared controls over what to count as truth and what as falsehood, among those ideas that can take such a count at all. Controls are thought of as present in each and all of the senses of *agreement with reality*, which, we lately noticed, is a condition of truth according to James. The chief shortcoming in James's account of truth—aside from its confinement to a level of introductory generalizing—is not in its denial of objective conditions under which ideas are determined true or false, but in the assumption that the conspicuous nature of the controls in question required little or no supplementary buttressing with explanations.

But that ideas do or do not agree with reality and that agreement—and thus truth—is not a matter of private desires or sheer willing it so is evident from James's warning:

> Our experience . . . is all shot through with regularities. One bit of it can warn us to get ready for another bit, can 'intend' or be 'significant of' that remoter object. . . . Truth . . . is manifestly incompatible with waywardness on our part. Woe to him whose beliefs play fast and loose with the order which realities follow in his experience; they will lead him nowhere or else make false connections.[56]

[56] *Pragmatism*, p. 205. See the even clearer note of caution in James's discussion of religious belief, *The Varieties of Religious Experience*, ch. 1, esp. p. 17: "what immediately feels most 'good' is not always most 'true' when measured by the verdict of the rest of experience."

James, then, was not espousing a subjective doctrine of truth nor on the whole unconsciously lapsing into one. Truth as a species of good, as "whatever proves itself to be good in the way of belief," is in fact subject to objective conditions of occurrence, and in principle subject to objective procedures of verification, as the word 'proves' was no doubt supposed to suggest.

§ 33. James's Wager:
The Right to Believe and Right Beliefs

James's pragmatic interpretation of 'agreement with reality,' in defining truth, coincides with the second of the three ways mentioned above (at the beginning of § 32) in which he expounded the meaning of truth. 'Agreement,' pragmatically understood in this case, means truth as the workableness of ideas. Thus James says, "the truth of an idea will mean then only its workings." Or in a more famous statement: *'the true' . . . is only the expedient in the way of our thinking, just as 'the right' is only the expedient in the way of our behaving.*"[57] Expedient "in the long run and on the whole," James adds, evidently in an allusion to the order of experienced realities and the existing body of accumulated knowledge as alike constituting the regulative controls over ideas and over calculable prospects of expediency. Still the allusion is only an allusion. One can continue to be troubled about what these qualifying phrases qualify—how long is a long run, how whole is on the whole?[58] This, beyond merely quibbling over words, is to question how James's recognizable allusions to the critical limits and standards of truth as expediency can be given a rigorous formulation and thereby be made more effective in their capacity as regulative controls over beliefs.

The need to be explicit and rigorous occurs most where the standards for assessing truth-claims begin to go slack. A constant threat of slack comes from the fact that while our beliefs tend to be prolific, the rational grounds for them tend to remain disproportionately sparse. And while this all too human phenomenon is not of necessity a troublemaker, it becomes so when it is unacknowledged and left unchecked.

Some projecting of beliefs beyond the limits of rational defenses for them is natural to us, perhaps a necessity for psychological stability and an escape from the claustrophobia of sheer rationality; at any rate, no cause for alarm. Somewhat more serious and disturbing are the occasional attempts of philosophers and theologians to "justify" certain beliefs as true where none of the usual canons of logic and empirical evidence are known to be applicable. A currently fashionable school of thought has argued that our most vital beliefs become invested in symbols, and that various "systems" of symbolization—such as art, science, religion,

[57] *Pragmatism*, p. 222.
[58] The phrase "in the long run" does have a technical sense for Peirce. See § 22, point 3, above.

and politics—are but variant mythologies, each in its own way being an expression of some ultimate Truth, and each embodying man's eternal quest of the same. Whatever the merits of this new syncretism, its appeal depends upon keeping the notions of *symbol, myth,* and especially *truth* sufficiently vague to insure its overall unity against breakage by incidental distinctions. The slack sets in accordingly over the meaning of truth. It was against this recurrent tendency of philosophers to indulge in a relaxing or obscuring of truth standards, in order to continue to entertain certain beliefs and weave them into systems, that the logical positivists initiated their critical and sweeping reform of truth and meaning.

James, too, appeared to be one of those philosophers willing to engage in a specious justification of religious beliefs. So, at least, his *Will to Believe* was judged by its critics. For James was thought to have argued that where the evidence is equally indecisive for each of two contradictory opinions (e.g., God exists or God does not exist), we have a right to adopt the religious attitude. Furthermore, the "vital good" that is supposedly gained from believing is lost to the disbeliever, and lost as well to the skeptic who, by suspending belief, is also in fact taking a decisive position.

It is curious that, in spite of James's repeated and emphatic statements of them, several important points are usually ignored when the argument has been paraphrased and examined for its flaws. James insists that the argument holds only in those cases and for those persons where the beliefs in question are "live," i.e., involve a willingness to act upon them, and where the option or decision between two incompatible and live beliefs is also live, forced, and momentous. To some, the beliefs that there is a god, or no god, are alike neither alive, urgent, nor important. In general, James's argument was limited to those situations in which someone feels compelled to decide between two important beliefs, where the evidence for either admits of no arguable settlement one way or the other. Situations of this kind occur infrequently, James maintains. Usually, on most questions, we do not feel forced to choose between complete belief or disbelief in an idea, excluding all shades of doubt. It is therefore a mistake to suppose, as some have, that James's argument fails by not accounting for cases where we accept or reject a belief tentatively. For such cases are excluded at the outset from the province of his argument.[59]

James goes on to develop a theoretical justification of choice of belief using a criterion of the *effects* of belief for the person believing. Roughly, beliefs which are of the forced, living, momentous kind, those whose effects are of "vital benefit" to the life of the person choosing them, justify the choice. A more novel and

[59] Thus Russell's objection: "Suppose, for instance, I am looking for a book in my shelves. I think, 'It *may* be in this shelf,' and I proceed to look; but I do not think, 'It *is* in this shelf' until I see it. We habitually act upon hypotheses, but not precisely as we act upon certainties," *History of Western Philosophy*, p. 815. The trouble with the example is that it is not what James called a *"genuine option."* The hypotheses "the book is in this shelf" or "it is not in this shelf" are not *forced, living,* and *momentous.* The will to believe, therefore, does not apply here at all.

surprising feature of James's argument was his contention that belief about some fact may itself be a condition for the occurrence of the fact. Thus, the act of believing may contribute to the truth of a belief.

The tennis player, for example, who believes he will win, other things being equal, may have increased his chances of winning; or his belief that he will lose may contribute to his losing. James himself, we saw earlier, thought that by believing he was free, he could act as though he were. Since the practical (and, for James, pragmatic) meaning of a belief is the action it leads to, to believe oneself free is to act as if one is free—but this, pragmatically, is what it means to be free.

Nonetheless, we may object that James overlooks a fine but important difference between the consequences of the fact *that* a belief occurs, and *what* the belief expresses. Thus, the fact that the tennis player believes he will win might be one among many causal conditions, e.g., his baffling serve, to be included in an explanation of why he won. We can say *that* the belief occurred was one of the causes of his winning, and so also the fact that he can baffle his opponents with his serve. But the actual occurrence of that belief, like the actual performance of the baffling serve, is not endowed with truth or with falsehood. Rather, truth or falsehood pertain to what the belief may be said to express or assert—in this case, "I will (or can) win the game." And while the state of believing may be one of the causes contributing to the player's winning, it by no means follows that the truth of the belief as expressed is in any way a causal condition of winning or productive of that outcome. In sum, to believe that a fact will occur may be one of the causal conditions contributing to the actual occurrence of the fact; but the truth or falsehood of the belief, its truth values, are not causal agents. Beliefs (or, strictly speaking, occasions of believing) may be causes of certain facts, helping to create them, as James says; but it is a confusion to attribute a similar causal efficacy to the truth or falsehood of what the beliefs happen to express.

The argument of *The Will to Believe* with some modification reappears in James's *Pragmatism.* James continued to maintain that certain ideas might be justified or "true" on grounds other than direct confrontation with facts or the accustomed procedures of empirical reasoning. Seen in connection with his view of truth as *workableness,* James reasoned that since the "work," or function, of ideas and beliefs is to help us establish satisfactory relations with our environment, those who needed to believe in the Absolute, God, Freedom, or Design had a right to do so, provided only that the need was real and the working of belief beneficial. The belief was then to count as pragmatically true. Both Peirce and Dewey were, among others, critical of James's strong, but not wholly clear affirmation of this "right" to belief.[60] James could say, "On pragmatistic principles, if

[60] Peirce called *The Will to Believe* "a very exaggerated utterance such as injures a serious man very much" and alluded to it as "suicidal," Perry II, 438. For Dewey's critical observations, see "What Pragmatism Means by Practical," a review of James's *Pragmatism,* ch. 12 of *Essays in Experimental Logic.*

the hypothesis of God works satisfactorily in the widest sense of the word, it is true."[61]

James later regretted the license which this loosely stated condition of *workableness* seemed to permit. For almost any belief could be passed off as true; one had only to *believe* that the results of believing were beneficial. An obvious weak link in the argument was how "real needs" and "beneficial working" were to be determined and how they were to be distinguished from those mistaken or feigned. But this is precisely the question of truth standards—or the threat of their slackening—just remarked on.

In partial defense of our right, under the appropriate conditions, to believe that "the Absolute exists," James said:

> of two competing views of the universe which in all other respects are equal, but of which the first denies some vital human need while the second satisfies it, the second will be favored by sane men for the simple reason that it makes the world seem more rational.[62]

There are several interesting points in this thought that, while open to criticism, will help us to get a clearer view of an otherwise hidden and important feature of James's theorizing about truth.

1) In the first place, there is the standing difficulty, as observed some pages back (and see § 27), of confusing the cause of a belief with its truth. This is a difficulty which Peirce, James, and Dewey usually take pains to avoid by making the *consequences*, rather than the origins of a belief the test of its truth. James, however, was less consistent, so it would appear, than Peirce or Dewey in this respect. The appeal to a "vital human need" as somehow justifying belief in the Absolute, or God, looks suspiciously like an appeal to the origins of the belief, *how* it arose, as conferring truth upon it. Vital needs, we should reply, may explain *why* we believe what we do, but they in no way determine the truth or falsehood of *what* we believe. And even if truth is taken as the *workableness* of a belief, a vital need is of itself no guarantee of the workableness of a belief. Following James, one might hold, very roughly, that a belief "works" when it satisfies some need. A need, once felt, may prompt a belief; but the fact that a need is felt, provides no basis whatever for determining how it is best, or most workably, satisfied. This is a problem for inquiry, as Dewey has emphasized, and one of the tasks for inquiry is an accurate interpretation of the nature of the need, as it occurs, as well as how the need, once understood, is to be satisfied. Truth or falsehood thus characterizes the *inquiry* into needs and their satisfaction (the inquiry produces a satisfactory result, i.e., one that is "true," or it does not, i.e., one that is "false"), but truth is neither a property of a need nor of the satisfaction that results from a belief.

---

[61] *Pragmatism*, p. 299. We have had doubts about the phrases "long run" and "on the whole" earlier; here, in the same way, we should have to enter a caveat over "the widest sense" of a word.
[62] Preface to *The Meaning of Truth*, p. ix.

2)   Suppose, as James asks us to imagine, there were two theoretical views of the universe, θ_1 and θ_2, in all other respects equal, except that θ_1 denies the vital human need to believe "the Absolute exists," while θ_2 affirms this belief. James says that we shall favor θ_2, because it makes the world seem more rational. But furthermore, as a hypothesis that works (is needed and is beneficial), the belief in the Absolute is "true."

There is something amiss in this matter of a choice between θ_1 and θ_2, namely, the artificiality of the conditions laid out for our choosing. Let B stand for the belief "the Absolute exists." The question then is, what distinguishes θ_1 from θ_2 except that B is denied by the former and affirmed by the latter? If, but for this one exception, θ_1 and θ_2 are, as James says, "in all other respects equal," then nothing distinguishes them and they collapse to one theory, θ. The choice then comes down to this: Shall I choose θ and not B, or shall I choose both θ and B? Since in either of the imagined cases I *am* choosing θ, we can eliminate this much from the question of choice. But the choice to be decided then reduces further to: Shall I affirm or shall I deny B?

But perhaps James intended something else. Perhaps he did not mean that the theories were *equal* in the sense of being identical, aside from B. He might have meant something else by the word 'equal': for example, that the two theories were of equal explanatory power, yet not identical as constructions, nor one reducible to the other.[63] But if he meant something like this, then the point of his example is vitiated. For if θ_1 and θ_2 differ in any other way, in addition to differing over accommodating or failing to accommodate B, then our choice of one over the other will be guided by any number of more immediate rational considerations as well.

Whatever James really meant by the example of two competing theories being in all respects "equal" but for B, the point just considered comes closest to representing what is actually involved in a choice between theories. It is to be seriously doubted that, at least outside of philosophy, a choice between theories ever rests upon the acceptance or rejection of a single isolated statement. James's example pictures θ_1 in which B is denied and θ_2 in which B is affirmed. But to deny or affirm B is to deny or affirm any one or all of numerous interrelated and logically connected statements linked to the statements 'B is false' and 'B is true,' respectively. The decision to be made in choosing θ_1 or θ_2 will then involve more than a decision to accept or reject B, since the affirmation or denial of other related statements coming under other theoretical deliberations are all equally at stake.

The reason for thinking a belief such as "the Absolute exists" is justified or workable (or for thinking it unjustified) is therefore far less simple than James's argument would suggest.

3)   Ordinarily, beliefs of the metaphysical and religious kind that James was

[63] 'Reducible' is the sense briefly noted at the beginning of § 27 and discussed in § 79 and § 83.

considering—"the Absolute exists," "God exists," etc.—are understood to be assertions of the existence of certain kinds of objects. The beliefs entail statements of existence:

$$S_1: \text{'}(\exists x) \ (x = \text{the Absolute}),\text{' or } S_2: \text{'}(\exists x) \ (x = \text{God})\text{'}$$

saying there *is* something and it is the Absolute, or it is God.[64] Either of the statements S_1 or S_2 is true if in fact the object said to exist does exist, and false otherwise. Mankind has long been divided between those who think these statements (especially S_2) true, and those who think them false. The division is due to two related questions: What kind of object is it which is alleged to exist? And, does it exist? (Or: What is it that the words 'Absolute' and 'God' purport to name, and do they name?). Obviously no intelligible answer to the second question could be given until the first has been settled. We must agree on what S_1 and S_2 say there is (or what kind of object each asserts to exist), before we can attempt to arrive at a verdict concerning their truth or falsehood. And, depending on how the first question is answered, we may or may not arrive at an answer to the second.

James's approach to these questions differs in a novel way from the above. His interest throughout is not upon the question of the existence of objects, or kinds of objects, but upon the *belief* in the objects and how beliefs function. In the development of his analysis of religious belief, James's empirical outlook, his pragmatic method, and his acumen and learning in psychology work together. Regarding the question of the existence of the Absolute, or of God, as speculative, and confined largely to the discussions of philosophers and theologians, James turned instead to facts. The facts, in this case, are instances of human belief; James's functional analysis (see the end of § 27) is directed to exploring and discerning what difference the presence of belief makes in the experience of men. This is to ask, pragmatically, "what conceivable effects of a practical kind the object [i.e., the belief] may involve." James did not cease to argue that certain metaphysical and religious beliefs could be "justified" by their effects in organizing, stimulating, and adding a sense of value to human life and experience. But that argument, whatever we may think of it, and the concern with justification, does not detract from the fruitfulness of James's method of analysis, nor should doubts about the former blind us to the value of the latter. James's method continues to recommend itself as a way of clarifying the nature of religious belief and the function of religious language.

The pragmatic analysis of the meaning of metaphysical and religious beliefs and assertions effects a major recasting of their stated content. The older expressive forms, preserved in S_1 and S_2, come out under the new translation thus:

'The Absolute exists' = 'some justification of a feeling of security in the presence of the universe exists.'

[64] Or, in the usual form deriving from Russell: '$(\exists y) \ (x) \ (x = y \equiv \text{God } x)$' and roughly paraphrased: "There is something y, such that for any x, x is identical with y if and only if x is God."

The concepts 'God,' 'freedom,' and 'design' all mean "the presence of promise in the world."[65] S_2, 'God exists,' comes out to be something close to 'there is something and it promises better things in the future.'[66] Not only does the traditionally religious language undergo a change in meaning, but the other components of traditional statements like S_1 and S_2 are also affected, particularly the word 'exists.' For in the context of religious beliefs, to say "God exists," "design exists," etc., is to say "there is a justification for such and such a feeling (or belief)." In this context, 'x exists' is translated 'belief in x is justified' (where 'x' is 'promise in the world'). And it was because he construed the *justification* of a belief as consisting in the effects of believing upon the life of the believer that James's doctrine seems at first so startling. For it follows that belief in God may be true (or justified) for some persons and not for others. And, further, as we have seen, in judging the truth of the statement 'God exists,' the question of whether there is in fact an existing God is not of paramount importance. But these conclusions are startling and perplexing just to the extent that we fail to note James's departure from other more traditional modes of discussing religious beliefs and religious language. And James's analysis of belief becomes additionally confusing if we overlook his replacement of the notion of truth as the correspondence of a belief to fact by his own view of truth as the workableness of belief.

§ 34. James's Legacy:
The Inheritance of Uncompleted Theory

James's pragmatic theory of truth was left in a rough and unfinished state. While he turned his attention to other matters, the theory was taken up by Dewey, who effected a patient and thorough reformulation. James's statement of the theory had brought down a torrent of criticism at its inception (1907), and, under the spreading influence of pragmatism at the time, truth became the hotly contested issue between James and his critics. Historically, it was this aspect of pragmatism, rather than its conception of method (and of meaning), that came in for most punishment, turning into a *cause célèbre* and *experimentum crucis* of the movement under James's leadership. The movement slowed down, indeed bogged down under the ensuing critical controversy.

Looking back on it now, we see that the debate over truth was clouded in crosspurposes. Pragmatists and their antagonists alike failed to appreciate the extent of essential differences between the conceptual positions from which their discussions of truth issued. That the positions taken and the uses of language reflected in them were often widely disparate may have been unavoidable; but failure to recognize this fact was not. What was needed, but not forthcoming, was an attempt to arrive at some agreement concerning the nature of the basic disagreements, and an ac-

---

[65] Preface to *The Meaning of Truth*, p. x. Also see *Pragmatism*, pp. 109, 115.

[66] "This vague confidence in the future is the sole pragmatic meaning at present discernible in the terms design and designer," *Pragmatism*, p. 115.

ceptable way of talking about them in common. To make sense in common about fundamental divisions of opinion is not to resolve them, but to make them understandable to the parties concerned. But philosophers are not always addicted to common sense.

Two pieces of stated but unfinished business in James's account of truth were to prove both troublesome and of considerable importance in the subsequent development of Dewey's pragmatism. These call for a final word, though controversial details are best deferred to the later discussion of Dewey's theory.

1) One of the innovations of James's theory of truth, we noticed some pages back (the conclusion of § 31), is its relativistic doctrine of truth judgments. The much abused word 'relativity' brings forth unwarranted associations with that which is subjective and of indeterminate character. These unwanted associations should not be foisted upon James's theory. To call something relative is not to describe or prejudge its condition beyond indicating that it bears a relation to something else.

The "dictionary" definition of truth, as James calls it, is that ideas are true by virtue of their agreement with reality; failing to agree with reality, ideas are false. We have been seeing how James gave a pragmatic interpretation of this notion of *agreement*. The relative character of truth and falsity in James's theory comes by way of identifying truth with the usefulness of ideas (or the "value" of ideas in "leading" us to other looked-for ideas and experiences). Relativity is encountered here, with usefulness and because of it; for things are or are not useful relative to certain purposes, in certain situations, for certain persons, etc. Ideas, like instruments or plans, are or are not of help to us subject to a similar range of provisions in any particular case. Let us follow Dewey in calling this complex of conditions, in which ideas (or beliefs) are put to work and their usefulness is tested, a *situation*. Situations, of course, will always include human agents and one or more of various human interests and purposes, along with any number of other conditions. We can then say that for James and Dewey, the truth of ideas and beliefs is relative to the situations in which ideas and beliefs occur. In any one situation, the truth or falsehood of an idea exists not as some property peculiar to the idea itself, nor in a relation between an idea and some fact; rather, *Truth*, for the pragmatist, is a characteristic of the performance of an idea in a situation. But even this way of putting the matter can be misleading; for if we are to gain a clear view of what is most distinct and original in the pragmatic theory, what needs to be especially stressed is the part about *performance*. Truth or falsehood is not a trait that ideas, beliefs, even statements, display in isolation from any or all situations. Traits of a situation do not necessarily inhere in its parts, nor do the characteristics of a situation survive among some of its isolated fragments—and ideas, beliefs, or statements, each taken on its own, like single facts and purposes, are fragments of situations. Truth and falsehood are located, then, not in ideas, beliefs, or statements, but in and amongst situations. It is how ideas perform, how beliefs function, how statements are used in situations that occasions their truth or falsehood.

This emphasis upon the performance or workableness of ideas constituting their truth is an application of James's *functional* method of analysis (see the concluding paragraphs of § 27). The principle to be followed is that of discovering what practical and accountable differences the presence of a given idea makes within a given situation. Such, for James, is the way to get at the *meaning* of ideas. In the case of *truth*, we are directed accordingly to consider how ideas affect the situation in which they occur with respect to the purposes and interests involved. But this is to observe and talk about performances, or operations *of* ideas in relation to all the other constituent conditions of a situation. Fundamentally, truth or falsehood (just as usefulness or uselessness) pertain to *operations* rather than to the things operating.[67] Specifically, where our choices and purposes are clear, ideas, beliefs, or statements that operate effectively relative to those purposes are "true"; if ineffective or obstructive in operating to the same end, they are "false."

From this it follows that judgments of truth and falsehood are relative; in this case relative to situations and to what proves effective, what ineffective, in the operative conceptualization taking place. We may differ of course in what we adjudge to be cases of truth or falsehood; sizing up situations differently, we shall be led to differences over what to commend as the pragmatically effective rational conditions and operations thus exhibited, and what not. Even where no such disparity of interpretations exists, we may still find that the effectiveness of the ideas, beliefs, and statements under judgment remains a debatable matter. But such prevailing relativity is not to be thought of as yielding to subjectivity and giving up definite judgments altogether. How we size up situations is subject to those critical canons of evidence and inference that govern our talk generally about the world.

Describing a *situation* is an empirical affair of recording and interpreting observed data, even making predictions. The resulting description allows, we have seen, judgments of the truth or falsity of certain conceptual features of the situation thus described. The value and accuracy of such judgments depends in part upon the description. But descriptive appraisals of situations are themselves subject to similar critical considerations of effectiveness and relative usefulness according to a further order of purposes and interests. To render a description of a situation is itself the occurrence of a situation.

The orientation of judgment remains in all outward respects the same; the focus always is upon how ideas operate or perform in given contexts, relative to some working purpose and point of view. The contexts, indeed, may differ, as we have seen, being different under different interpretations, or different depending upon whether what we are considering is a situation, a judgment of a situation, a judgment of a previously judged situation, etc. But, once granting this relativity of contexts and of rulings upon useful and useless conceptualizations, and granting, too, the various working purposes to which pragmatic judgments of

[67] It is the operation of *leading* that is all-important in James's conception of the *truth* of ideas. "The truth of a state of mind means this function of *a leading that is worth while*," *Pragmatism*, p. 205.

truth and falsehood are perforce confined, we can still affirm that the resulting judgments of truth are just as absolute and objective as any that could be desired.

2) The second of the two ideas left in a state of nascency by James has already found its way into the foregoing discussion of relativity. This is the contention that truth and falsehood, while generally attributed to ideas, beliefs, and statements, are more accurately thought of as applying to the uses or operations of ideas, beliefs, and statements in given situations. Strictly speaking, if one hazards a strict interpretation of James on this matter, it is not ideas, beliefs, or statements that are true or false, but the occurrence or assertion of these in relation to other circumstances within situations. Truth or falsehood characterize a certain manner of operating peculiar to ideas, beliefs, or statements—namely, their use or uselessness in a context; but this is to characterize a complex of occurring and related events, rather than any one single piece of the complex. In a word, the words 'truth' and 'falsehood' are employed to describe or comment upon certain selected features of situations—it is the occurrences and uses of ideas, beliefs, and statements that are selected; and their effects and usefulness in the situation as a whole are the object of comment. James says:

> The truth of an idea is not a stagnant property inherent in it. Truth *happens* to an idea. It *becomes* true, is *made* true by events. Its verity *is* in fact an event, a process, the process namely of its verifying itself, its veri-*fication*. Its validity is the process of its valid-*ation*.[68]

The relevance of this statement to our present reflections is clear. To call an idea 'true' is, relative to a given purpose, to approve of the manner in which an idea performs and the consequences of its use in a given context.

James, however, was led somewhat astray in his concern to emphasize that truth is a characteristic of certain *functions*, or operations of ideas. He allowed himself to confuse this thesis with another according to which truth is not defined as a certain characteristic kind of function of ideas, but becomes identified with that function itself. This results in equating the truth of an idea with its verification, and the last two sentences of the above quotation do just this. Whether James really intended to make this last assertion or not is difficult to ascertain. But there is no question that he *seemed* to be wishing to assert this and did in fact assert it several times. What was being asserted was something more than simply saying that we mean by a true idea one that is certified or confirmed. This is a different thesis, one whose advocates have argued that the less clear notions of *truth* and

---

[68] *Pragmatism*, p. 201. What we have here been attempting to locate and clarify as the "functional" character of James's theory of truth—where truth or falsehood attach to performances or operations of ideas in context—is illustrated by the following forthright statement (p. 218) in which James likens truth "processes" to other workable and profitable living "functions": "Our account of truth is an account of truths in the plural, of processes of leading, realized *in rebus*, and having only this quality in common, that they *pay*. . . . Truth for us is simply a collective name for verification-processes, just as health, wealth, strength are names for other processes connected with life, and also pursued because it pays to pursue them. Truth is *made*, just as health, wealth, and strength are made, in the course of experience."

falsehood can be replaced by the clearer notion of *verification* (or confirmation and disconfirmation).[69] But James was asserting that the truth of an idea is an event, or process, namely, the actual process of verification. This, while it leads to an odd attribution of truth to things, events, or processes, also results in an obliteration of an important and useful distinction between the meaning of 'truth' and how in fact particular ideas happen to become verified. It was rightly objected that James had confused what the word 'true' means with the events that verify ideas or statements, as well as with the way we proceed to discover and to decide the verification of an idea. In general, knowing what is meant by calling an idea or statement 'true,' and knowing whether an idea or statement *is* true, is a difference well worth distinguishing.

As we have thus far been reviewing it, James's contribution to the history of pragmatism was twofold. He shaped and expanded the insights of Peirce into the leading ideas of a coherent, if loosely woven, moral interpretation of thought and experience—the hypothesis that we rely upon when we take experience "radically" as it comes to us in living and acting. James also brought to a head the main problems of pragmatism: the contestable grounds and the defensible positions began to be clear. Pragmatism, which had been born as a principle of analysis and a criticism of certain uses of language, now began a critical development of its own.

James's departure from Peirce's conception of pragmatism, his endowing pragmatism with some of its central problems, has often been attributed to his distrust of systems and his disdain of systematic reasoning generally in dealing with philosophical matters. But these characteristics are noticeably lacking in the many technical philosophic papers he published during his lifetime. He did often express his distrust of logically neat and tightly fitted interpretations of the world. But that distrust was consistent with his view of experience as shot through with discontinuity along with continuity, disorder along with order, novelties and spontaneities along with humdrum regularities. Experience, he said, "has ways of boiling over and making us correct our present formulas."[70] In all this, right or wrong, James was reflecting his own conception of philosophy as a partly spontaneous, risky and tentative, never finished, always changeable vision:

> . . . the habit of always seeking an alternative, of not taking the usual for granted, of making conventionalities fluid again, of imagining foreign states of mind. . . . it means the possession of mental perspective.
>
> . . . Its educational essence lies in the quickening of the spirit to its *problems*.[71]

What appears as an unsystematic and analytically careless spirit in James's writ-

---

[69] It is to be seriously doubted, however, that *verification* is the clearer notion. A thoroughgoing explication of 'verification' is among the most needed tasks in modern philosophy and philosophy of science, considering the important role this notion plays in current philosophical literature.

It can be shown, incidentally, that some of the major objections to the identification of *meaning* with *verification* (see the concluding pages of § 21) apply in a like way to many of the attempts to identify *truth* with *verification*.

[70] *Pragmatism*, p. 222.

[71] From a letter to the *Nation*, Sept. 21, 1876, reprinted in Kallen, pp. 57–59.

ings is, more often than not, a misleading manifestation of genuine puzzlement, and an uncertainty over drawing final conclusions where interesting alternatives and genuine differences are felt. The spirit is one of systematically refusing to be led into systematic falsifications of experience.

James was a great philosopher but an even greater man. It is rarely the case in the literature of philosophy that the spirit of the man illuminates and quickens what he writes or that one senses that living presence even in the most attenuated stretches of argument. Rarer still is the perfect coincidence of the spirit of the man in the body of his arguments. James's words breathe the man—utterly frank and inveterately human. No one reading the philosopher could fail to love the man.

Once, in stating his credo—willingness to live and let live—William James wrote: "no outward changes of condition in life can keep the nightingale of its eternal meaning from singing in all sorts of different men's hearts."[72] That bird sang sweetly and easily in James's age, an age that closed with World War I. And perhaps in no other man did it sing more keenly or with such discerning notes.

[72] From "What Makes a Life Significant," in *Talks to Teachers on Psychology*, p. 301.

CHAPTER THREE

John Dewey

§ 35. *Dewey and Pragmatism*

We have been considering the development of pragmatism as occupied with certain fundamental questions of meaning and truth and with formulating a theoretical method for analyzing and resolving those questions.

In turning to Dewey we witness the coalescence of the critical and scientific motives of Peirce's pragmatism with the moral implications and ideals of James. But those outlooks are not only combined in Dewey; they are intensified through a long lifetime devoted to exploration and analysis of their respective consequences in a variety of philosophic contexts, and to their continuous expansion under inquiry responsive to new currents of thought.

This is not meant to convey the impression that Dewey started out in philosophy as a disciple of Peirce and James, and spent the rest of his days in weaving a synthesis of their teachings. Dewey's philosophic career began under the influence of Hegelian idealism and neo-Kantism. His early interests appear to have been primarily in epistemology, at that time a mixture of doctrines and questions of psychology and logic concerning the nature of thinking and judgment.

Dewey's ninety-three years spanned three major revolutions. Born in the year which saw the publication of Darwin's *Origin of Species* (1859), a witness to the effects of relativity theory in physics, Dewey died in 1952, when men throughout the world were desperately struggling to realize the fact that a new atomic age had suddenly and ominously arrived. These revolutions furnish a cardinal insight into Dewey's thought. For the revolutions had their origins within science, but their most violent impact and disturbing effects continued in the regions of social and moral experience. Despite several major intellectual changes, one singularly acute and fixed concern threaded the seventy years of Dewey's productive philosophic activity: the relation of science and human values.

The problem of restoring integration and co-operation between man's beliefs about the world in which he lives and his beliefs about values and purposes that should direct his conduct is the deepest problem of any philosophy that is not isolated from life.

And an unisolated philosophy must reckon with this central problem.

Its central problem is the relation that exists between the beliefs about the nature of things *due to natural science* to beliefs about *values*—using that word to designate whatever is taken to have rightful authority in the direction of conduct.[1]

As a young man in his thirties, Dewey was already pointing out that this was "one of the most pressing of contemporary problems."[2] In his sixties, the same problem was forcibly advanced as the central theme of *Reconstruction in Philosophy*[3]— carefully formulated by a man who, over the long years, had gained a penetrating understanding of the nature of human problems and had evolved a theory for inquiring into them. Again, when he was eighty-six, looking back on this earlier work, Dewey restated his conviction that the reconstructive task of philosophy lies in bridging the separation (in establishing continuity)[4] between morals and science.

Dewey's own recommended reconstruction of this problem, as we shall see, was worked out within what he called "instrumentalism," indeed, formed the very core of instrumentalism itself. For Dewey, the separation of science and ethics into distinct kinds of experience and intellectual attitudes is the greatest misfortune and most serious intellectual error of the present century. In place of this cleavage, he continued to advocate a marriage via the theory of inquiry (§ 39) and inquiry as evaluation (§ 41; cf. Part Four, Chapter Three).

It is noteworthy that as a graduate student at Johns Hopkins (1882) Dewey was not at all influenced by Peirce, who was then teaching there.[5] He began to

[1] *The Quest for Certainty*, pp. 255–256. This book appeared in 1929. But, significantly, in 1939 Dewey emphatically quoted these passages (and in italics) in again stressing the same problem. Thus, see Schilpp, p. 523.

[2] At this early stage, the "problem" was conceived in a limited and naive way as a need for the reconciliation of science and religion. Thus, in a review, Dewey greeted a book by Caird as showing that "the categories of physical science can be reconciled with the principles of the moral and religious life," *Andover Review*, 1890. For more on this, see Appendix 1, sec. C below.

[3] See pp. 173–174: "When the consciousness of science is fully impregnated with the consciousness of human value, the greatest dualism which now weighs humanity down, the split between the material, the mechanical, the scientific and the moral ideal will be destroyed. . . . At the same time that morals are made to focus intelligence, things intellectual are moralized. The vexatious and wasteful conflict between naturalism and humanism is terminated."

[4] From the fifth paragraph of the Introduction, "Reconstruction As Seen Twenty-Five Years Later": "The reconstruction to be undertaken is . . . to carry over into any inquiry into human and moral subjects the kind of method (the method of observation, theory as hypothesis, and experimental test) by which understanding of physical nature has been brought to its present pitch." On continuity, see § 37 and Appendix 1 below.

[5] Dewey took courses in advanced logic and philosophical terminology under Peirce in 1883–1884. See Wiener and Young, pp. 369–370.

recognize the importance of Peirce some twenty years later after gradually and with difficulty beginning to free himself from Hegelianism. The later interest in Peirce, who had made the notion of *inquiry* "the primary and ultimate source of logical subject-matter,"[6] was a factor in Dewey's break with idealism.

But that breaking away had started to occur earlier. Roughly, from 1890 to 1900 Dewey's Hegelianism went through a conversion under Darwinian evolution, and Dewey was responding to the thought of Alfred Lloyd and George Herbert Mead, his colleagues at Michigan, and to the *Psychology* of James. The idealism, with its categories of the organic whole, and development viewed as a passage from "contradictions" to "syntheses," gave way to the evolutionary and biologically conceived notions of growth as a process of "conflicts" and "resolutions." The outward forms of the idealist tradition began to disappear with what Dewey called his "experimental idealism." The remaining substance of the Hegelian inheritance became the leaven in the emergence of instrumentalism.

Dewey, in describing his view of the positions from which Peirce and James shaped the history of pragmatism, refers to Peirce's attempt to give an "experimental, not an *a priori* explanation of Kant," and to James's pragmatism as inspired by British empiricism. But he also points to this difference: "Peirce wrote as a logician and James as a humanist."[7] Now in fact it is not difficult to find significant strains of humanism in Peirce's writings, and James's analyses of thought and belief, the instrumental character of ideas, concepts, and theories, of experimental verification and truth were major contributions to the logic of pragmatism.

Nonetheless, there was, as Dewey says, and as we have seen several times illustrated in earlier sections, a notable difference of emphasis in how Peirce and James each envisioned the philosophic import of pragmatism, which allows us to distinguish its two simultaneously evolving aspects: a *theory of logic*, and a *guiding principle for ethical analysis*. The distinction neither repudiates nor overlooks the metaphysical, social, and esthetic commitments that go with each or both of these theoretical developments; nor does it ignore the divers subject matters from which they emerged as general procedures capable of a conceptual treatment and investigation on their own.

Dewey's lifelong interest in education and his many writings on the subject serve appropriately to evoke the sense of the distinction just made. The studies in education commence in earnest after Dewey had already worked out a conception of "logic" (as a philosophic psychology of the function of thought) and ethical

6 *Logic: The Theory of Inquiry*, p. 9n.
7 "The Development of American Pragmatism," p. 21. The point is of more than passing interest, for see Dewey's further comment, p. 19: "Peirce was above all a logician; whereas James was an educator and wished to force the general public to realize that certain problems, certain philosophical debates have a real importance for mankind, because the beliefs which they bring into play lead to very different modes of conduct. If this important distinction is not grasped, it is impossible to understand the majority of the ambiguities and errors which belong to the later period in the pragmatic movement."

theory.[8] Elementary education served initially as the subject matter for these ideas; the Laboratory School (more popularly called the "Dewey School") at the University of Chicago provided the experimental situation. In due time, however, the experience in education effected important modifications of the logical and ethical ideas Dewey had originally brought to pedagogy. From reflections upon this modification, the theory of instrumentalism began to emerge.

The two final chapters of Dewey's most influential book on education[9] are symbolic of the distinction made above: the pragmatic approach to "Theories of Knowledge" is followed by the chapter "Theories of Morals." Characteristically, the chapter on the method of knowing begins by pointing out how moral interests and social conditions affect the construction of theories of knowledge. The chapter on moral theory begins with a comment upon how theories of knowing reflect themselves in theories of morals. But to recognize reciprocal influences and points in common among theories is still to preserve a distinction between them.

Here, in viewing pragmatism as a theory of logic and a principle of ethical analysis, we are taking note as well of two sides of Dewey's philosophic interest. On the one side was his concern with a number of detailed and technical philosophic problems calling for equally technical solutions. On the other side was his concern with the larger social problems confronting modern democratic society undergoing an industrial and technological revolution.

Dewey's writings—or those most expressive of his pragmatism—can be roughly divided in this way: those of a technical and logical nature, which fall under the heading of *Instrumentalism,* "a theory of the general forms of conception and reasoning"[10] (a theory which does not exclude moral judgments, or set them off as of a radically different kind from judgments of fact); those in which Dewey is concerned with questions of value in human conduct and experience and in which the general pragmatic principle of *consequences* (§ 27) is developed as a method of social criticism and evaluation. It is in this second group that the nature of the various consequences, in and for human life, of institutions, customs, social arrangements, and ideas occupy Dewey's attention and provoke his critical suggestions. One of the primary and always necessary critical functions of philosophy, as Dewey viewed it, was the task of critically evaluating experience as a part of the "continuous reconstruction of experience." This was a task he also regarded as the "articulation and revelation of the meanings of the current course

[8] Logic, says Dewey, in the *Studies in Logical Theory* (1903), is concerned with "the natural history of thinking as a life process," and thus viewed, logical theory can "come to terms with psychology," p. 13.

In 1891 the third edition of Dewey's *Psychology* appeared and also the *Outlines of a Critical Theory of Ethics.* In 1895–1897 the flow of articles on education, well started in 1894, became voluminous.

[9] *Democracy and Education.* It has been observed that *School and Society* is Dewey's most influential book (see Schilpp, p. 28). The influence of a book is mostly conjecture, and, conjecturing, one can suppose *Democracy and Education* at least ties for first place, and supplied as well one of the best general introductions to Dewey's philosophy.

[10] "The Development of American Pragmatism," p. 26.

of events."[11] Indeed, in this expanded form as a principle of ethical analysis, Dewey's pragmatism gave him a way of evaluating philosophy itself:

> There is . . . a first rate test of the value of any philosophy which is offered us: Does it end in conclusions which, when they are referred back to ordinary life-experience and their predicaments, render them more significant, more luminous to us, and make our dealings with them more fruitful?[12]

The history of pragmatism begins with Peirce, who wrote as a logician, and James, who wrote as a humanist and educator. Its Hegelian synthesis was achieved in the disenchanted Hegelian Dewey, who was both logician and humanist.

§ *36. Instrumentalism*

"Instrumentalism" is the name Dewey gave to what are in fact several interrelated and carefully elaborated theses concerning the function of thought in situations. That is, if the earlier comment on situations is recalled (§ 34), "instrumentalism" is Dewey's theory of those conditions in which reasoning occurs and of the forms, or controlling operations, that are characteristic of thought in attaining and establishing future consequences.

James had regarded ideas, concepts, and theories as instruments, whose function and value lay in their capacity to lead us to future facts and experiences. Dewey's instrumentalism was initiated as an attempt to provide a complete description and systematic analysis of this instrumental interpretation of reasoning.

> Instrumentalism is an attempt to constitute a precise logical theory of concepts, of judgments and inferences in their various forms, by considering primarily how thought functions in the experimental determinations of future consequences. . . . it attempts to establish universally recognized distinctions and rules of logic by deriving them from the reconstructive or mediative function ascribed to reason. It aims to constitute a theory of the general forms of conception and reasoning, and not of this or that particular judgment or concept related to its own content, or to its particular implications.[13]

The theory was developed over many years and in many writings:[14] into it went the products of Dewey's reflections on logic and the nature of thought, his own contributions to psychology, the influence of the biological and functional

[11] *Reconstruction in Philosophy*, p. 213.
[12] *Experience and Nature*, p. 7.
[13] "The Development of American Pragmatism," p. 26.
[14] The main works in the forging of instrumentalism are Dewey's contributions to *Studies in Logical Theory* (1903), *How We Think* (1910), *Essays in Experimental Logic* (1916), *Human Nature and Conduct* (1922).
    Two contributions to psychology deserve special mention: "The Reflext Arc Concept in Psychology" (1896), for which see § 37 below, and "Conduct and Experience" (1930).

aspects of James's *Psychology*,[15] and the influence of Peirce. The definitive statement came in 1938 with the publication of *Logic: The Theory of Inquiry*.

Instrumentalism, as embodied in the theory of inquiry, comprises two objectives, although in Dewey's exposition there is an imperceptible grading off of the boundary between them. There is first the objective of setting out an accurate description of the phenomena of thinking, of how thought is said to manifest itself as a distinctive trait of human behavior and of "how thought functions." This is primarily a matter of working out a descriptive interpretation of thinking as one among other "life processes,"[16] of writing the "natural history of thinking" just as faithfully as the empirical facts will permit. On this score, the pragmatists thought they had succeeded where other logical theories failed,[17] by providing a place for the actual occurrence of thinking and showing how the natural growth of knowledge is relevant to the formal machinery traditionally distinguished as the subject matter of logic. This was, in short, to argue that logic has an empirical subject matter in the generalized forms of reasoning, and to show how intelligence "works" in situations. So conceived, social, biological, psychological, and physiological information would be relevant to the development and articulation of a general theory of logical forms.

The other objective of the instrumental theory of logic derives from and is a generalization of the first. It attempts to make explicit and to account for the assumptions and implications that are involved in the achievement of the first objective. This second objective differs from the first in being of a more "theoretical" and explanatory character. The "mediative function" of thought in situations, its instrumental role in establishing consequences, when recognized, calls for a further explanation of the kind of conditions that initiate the function of thought and those characteristic of the termination of that function. The second objective, then, has to do with the distinctive traits of situations within which the function of thought begins and eventually ends.

The two key concepts of Dewey's logical theory are *situation* and *inquiry*. The concept of the *situation* is, evidently, the most fundamental logically, for by means of it 'inquiry' is defined. On the other hand, in practice inquiry comes first, for it is only through inquiry that situations can be known or discussed at all.

As is generally the case with broad and abstractly drawn theories, we cannot hope to gain immediate acquaintance with the fundamental ideas by seeking

---

[15] On James's "functionalism," see § 27 above. James's criterion for establishing the presence of "mentality in phenomenon," quoted in § 27, is especially cited by Dewey as one of the influences upon instrumentalism. See Dewey's discussion in "The Development of American Pragmatism."

[16] *Studies in Logical Theory*, p. 13. Dewey may have borrowed the biologically directed phrase "life process" from Mead. See the letter to James (Perry, II, 520) in which Dewey mentions the phrase as one of Mead's. 'Life process' is often encountered in Dewey's later writings.

[17] Schiller, in particular, made excessive claims for this feature of the logical theory of pragmatism, so much so that he failed altogether to understand or appreciate the importance of deductive technique and mathematical logic. On this and on Schiller's philosophy, see below, Part III, ch. 1.

definitions of the first things first and then troubling ourselves over the second-ary details. We come to know what matters most only gradually when we have learned to make our way step by step through the theory and go back again to view it as a whole. Coming to the realization of what is basic to a theory is simi-lar to the process that characterized the thinking of those who first discovered and defined the basic ideas; as learners, we recapitulate that process. We can under-stand the fundamental definitions and concepts in retrospect, if at all, after we have grasped something of the superstructure, seeing how the definitions are fundamental to it and why.

We should not be surprised, therefore, that in Dewey's *Logic* the notion of *situation* is defined very broadly at the outset, but continues to be discussed and supplemented in the course of his analysis of the special features of logical theory. The definition runs:

> What is designated by the word 'situation' is *not* a single object or set of objects and events. For we never experience nor form judgments about objects and events in isolation but only in connection with a contextual whole. . . . In actual experi-ence there is never any such isolated singular object or event; *an* object or event is always a special part, a phase, or aspect, of an environing experienced world—a situation.[18]

That objects are to be construed as parts of a *context*, or aspects of an "environing experience world" implies that among the objects to be included in situations are living organisms, creatures experiencing situations. Logical theory will be con-cerned with human situations, or more accurately, with contexts in which human intelligence, purposes, and action affect what is experienced. But not every human situation is of concern or relevance to logical theory. Any one of these "context-ual wholes," because contextual and whole, exhibits some pervasive trait or qual-ity, according to Dewey. And it is only certain kinds of situations that can be said to *qualify* as logical, namely: those that are "indeterminate" or "doubtful" and in which *inquiry* is a natural development.

Dewey's conception of inquiry is heavily indebted to the theory of Peirce (§ 20).[19] For Dewey, as for Peirce, inquiry is a process by which doubtful or un-settled situations become settled. The goal of inquiry is the attainment of belief; the product or outcome of competent inquiries is knowledge.[20] More than does Peirce, Dewey describes the process of inquiry and the situations in which the process occurs in a language largely borrowed from the biological, social, and evolutionary movements of thought on the immediate historical scene.

---

[18] *Logic: The Theory of Inquiry*, pp. 66–67.

[19] To be fair and accurate on this matter, it must be added that Dewey had arrived at this general position before he began to see it clearly in Peirce. In 1903, the year in which *Studies in Logical Theory* was published, Dewey wrote James that he was reading and beginning to understand Peirce, who had earlier, he says, been "mostly a sealed book to me," Perry, II, 523. In the *Logic*, p. 9n., Dewey acknowledges his indebtedness to Peirce: "As far as I am aware he was the first writer on logic to make inquiry and its methods the primary and ultimate source of logical subject matter."

[20] *Logic: The Theory of Inquiry*, p. 8.

Inquiry is defined as:

the controlled or directed transformation of an indeterminate situation into one that is so determinate in its constituent distinctions and relations as to convert the elements of the original situation into a unified whole.[21]

One can scarcely help noticing the impersonal manner in which this definition of inquiry is formulated. As in his definition of a situation, one must look hard to find how it applies to, or includes, individual persons at all. Ordinarily we might suppose that *inquiry* is a mental activity persons perform usually evidenced by asking questions. We may, in philosophical moments, have doubts about what we mean by 'mental activities' and how we can know about them. But even in philosophical moments we would incline to assume that it is individual persons who engage in inquiries, singly or in groups, and who exhibit various degrees of intelligence in how they inquire and what they inquire about.

Dewey would not deny that it is human beings who carry on inquiries, and that it is persons, not situations, who ask questions and seek answers. In wondering why Dewey seems determined to exclude direct references to individuals in situations, or individual inquirers, in his theory, we come to a recurrent and dominant philosophic conviction, the crux of most of his positive and critical doctrines. In its critical form, the conviction is expressed in a rejection of *dualisms* in all of the many forms that dualisms have occurred in philosophy, both in methods of analysis and in subject matters analyzed.[22] The constructive counterpart of Dewey's criticism of the assumptions and consequences of dualisms lies in his attempts to develop a contextual and functional method of analysis and interpretation of subject matters.[23] Specific kinds of subject matters involve distinctions of specific kinds of objects and relations. But distinctions are made within contexts and operate (or are "operational") for certain purposes depending upon how the context has previously been identified and interpreted in the light of some problem or point of view.[24] In his logical theory Dewey's contextual and

---

[21] *Logic: The Theory of Inquiry*, pp. 104–105.

[22] Generally, the word 'dualism,' as Dewey uses it, seems to mean an irreducible separation in principle or in fact, in either the methods of knowing or experiencing things, or in the "natures" or "reality" of things themselves. Most characteristic of the dualisms he attacks are the allegedly separate functions of sense and reason, objects and ideas, action and thought, practice and theory; and of subject matters: body and mind, real and ideal, fact and value, man and nature, individual and society, organism and environment.

Dewey's unrelenting philosophic criticism of dualisms has its origins in his early attachment to Hegelian idealism. More specifically, it is due to the influence of G. S. Morris and T. H. Green (see Appendix 1, sec. C below), both of whom roundly renounced dualisms.

[23] The approach has been described variously as "organic," "genetic-functional," "naturalistic," and "holistic." Perhaps "contextualism" would serve as well as any. For some speculations about contextualism, see § 79 below.

[24] For example, Dewey comments on the oft-posed "problem" of the relation of objects as we experience them to the objects as interpreted by modern physical theory. Is the object we perceive "the same" or less or more "real" than the object as physical science construes it? Dewey's view is: "the table *as* a perceived table is an object of knowledge in one context as truly as the physical atoms, molecules, etc., are in another situational context and with reference to another *problem....*

. . . It is not just the thing as perceived, but the thing as and when it is placed in an

functional approach is made explicit in "the primary postulate" of that theory, the idea of continuity.[25]

So cautious is Dewey in avoiding the dualisms that result from identifying doubt, inquiry, and judgment as "mental states" or "personal traits," or from regarding the human organism and the environment as separate objects (or internal and external "worlds"), that he is willing to run the risk of being misunderstood at the other extreme as ignoring the individual altogether. Thus, for instance, Santayana was led to remark: "In Dewey . . . as in current science and ethics, there is a pervasive quasi-Hegelian tendency to dissolve the individual into his social functions, as well as everything substantial or actual into something relative or transitional."[26] A major reason for what is, unhappily, a labored and unduly difficult mode of expressing ideas in Dewey, for the tortuous stretches of discourse one encounters in his writings, is a resolute refusal to explore philosophic problems in the more familiar, customary language of traditional philosophizing.[27] For Dewey, that language and those procedures, for all their apparent reasonableness as *the* authoritative modes of philosophic expression, are treacherous vehicles; use them, and metaphysical or epistemological collisions called "problems" are inevitable. Indeed, the vehicles were partly geared for collisions, and hence the air of inevitability about the problems, or what the textbooks like to call their "perennial nature." The kind of mistakes and sources of confusion so ably discussed by Ryle in *The Concept of Mind* had been recognized by Dewey at the turn of the century, and, for better or worse, prompted the development of his own often arduous way of discussing thought and experience, in a vocabulary free of traditional entanglements. This refusal to use the usual philosophic language has been costly:[28] it has incurred some problems of its own and, oft times,

---

extensive ideational or theoretical context within which it exercises a special office that constitutes a distinctively physical scientific object." Schilpp, pp. 537–538.

[25] *Logic: The Theory of Inquiry*, p. 23. For this postulate and the idea of *continuity* in Dewey's thought, see, in addition to § 37 below, Appendix 1.

[26] "Dewey's Naturalistic Metaphysics," p. 217.

[27] Professor Costello tells of a conversation with Woodbridge: "I remember he said of Dewey, long his close friend and colleague: 'I ask Dewey from time to time some simple question, such as, "is there not something about the past that never again changes?" Surely the state before change begins cannot itself also change.' I said, 'What did he answer?' 'Answer!' Woodbridge replied, 'Dewey defined and distinguished and qualified, in such a maze of dialectic, that not only did I not get any answer, I didn't even know where my question went to. And do you know, when he gets that way, he thinks he is being empirical!' " Krikorian, p. 296.

[28] The "usual language of philosophy" here means the language of British empiricism. One difficulty in understanding Dewey rises from his use of language influenced by an idealism in which he was reared, but unfamiliar to philosophic readers these days. Dewey's use of the word 'experience' is a case in point. For in selecting it, Dewey was appropriating the most venerable and prized member of the vocabulary of British empiricism for his own un-British uses. Hence, the notorious difficulties and controversies that once went on over what Dewey meant by *experience* and his own difficulty in explaining what he meant. Dewey later remarked that if he had used the word 'culture' instead of 'experience' he would have avoided many misunderstandings. But 'culture' is hardly an unambiguous replacement for 'experience' in many important passages in his writings. We may note, too, that Dewey's early description of his position as "experimental idealism" would strike most of us as a contradiction in terms. As a matter of fact, "experimental idealism" aptly

a taxing obscurity where lucidity is most in demand. However, he seems to have thought this worth the expense compared to the philosophic price that must be paid for the other vehicle so finely machined for disaster.

§ 37.   Continuity: Growth and the Theory of Education[29]

The idea of continuity is the inclusive category of Dewey's philosophy.[30] For Dewey, continuity is characteristic of natural events; it is also a characteristic of the methods that have been developed for investigating nature. With a liberal tendency, Hegelian in origin, to seek and find continuity in things, Dewey speaks of continuity variously as an existential trait, a methodological hypothesis, a fact of nature, and a principle of inquiry. Whether the meaning of 'continuity' thus affirmed in these different contexts differs accordingly or remains the same is a moot point. Presumably, continuity is something seen and discovered as well as a way of seeing and discovering. In any event, affirming the presence of continuity seems to function for Dewey as an effective checking of dualisms and their protean reproductiveness.

Strangely enough, although the concept of continuity is markedly evident in his major writings, Dewey never specifically analyzed it. Its meaning is packed with moral, educational, even religious significance, in addition to functioning as a leading principle of logical theory. Just as fully packed is the familiar baggage of expressive words or metaphors that travel with (and sometimes for) 'continuity': 'unification,' 'growth,' 'progress,' 'integration,' 'whole'; and with discontinuity go 'rupture,' 'breaks,' 'gaps,' 'dualism,' 'fragmentation.' Like St. Augustine's two cities "in this present world entangled together," continuity conveys the spirit of development, completion, resolution, and value for Dewey, while discontinuity is of the flesh—destructive, partial, troubled, and problematic.

---

characterizes the later philosophy of G. S. Morris; and Dewey used the term *experience* in a sense widely current in his student days among idealists such as Morris and T. H. Green, both of whom influenced him (see Appendix 1, sec. C below). But even here, old associations can be treacherous, for Dewey's use of much of the language of idealism was as unidealistic in intent and diverged as much from traditional idealism as his use of the word 'experience' departs from traditional empiricism. Dewey might well have heeded the advice of Peirce that, when new ideas or new shifts in old ideas are at stake, the philosopher does well to coin new terms for them.

[29] A further discussion of continuity is to be found in Appendix 1. On the theory of education, see Childs. For the background, origins, and development of Dewey's educational philosophy, see ch. 11 of V. T. Thayer's illuminating historical study, *Formative Ideas in American Education.*

[30] Dewey once argued that the social is the inclusive philosophical category. But that category rests upon the idea of continuity, to which Dewey uncharacteristically assigns an almost "absolute" character in speaking of it as something like a necessarily true principle: "Upon the hypothesis of continuity—if that is to be termed a hypothesis which cannot be denied without self-contradiction—the social . . . furnishes philosophically the inclusive category," *Philosophy and Civilization*, p. 81. For this passage and a further discussion of continuity, see Appendix 1 below.

Dewey's own collection of metaphors presents us with a cluster of leading clues into his thought: as such, and for reasons commented upon earlier (in § 29) concerning the use of words, they are worth some attention. However, useful as metaphors surely are in the preliminary stages of formulating theoretical ideas, they tend to prove disadvantageous at a later stage when imprecise and indeterminately used language can become an obstacle. Just this happens to some of Dewey's fundamental ideas. The concept of continuity, since it is an important idea in his thought, is an important case in point.

In Dewey's writings the term most frequently associated with 'continuity' and most frequently used to designate a model of continuity is 'growth.' And it is growth as a form of continuity that provides the nexus and the beginning point of logical, ethical, and educational theory. Thus when he writes that continuity is "the primary postulate of a naturalistic theory of logic," his two fundamental illustrations contain references to growth:

> The term "naturalistic" has many meanings. As it is here employed it means, on the one side, that there is no breach of continuity between the operations of inquiry and biological operations and physical operations. "Continuity," on the other side, means that rational operations grow out of organic activities, without being identical with that from which they emerge.[31]

And again:

> the growth and development of any living organism from seed to maturity illustrates the meaning of continuity.[32]

Growth is the exemplar of continuity. Now, for Dewey, a paradigm, in turn, of growth is education. Education is growth.

> The educative process is a continuous [n.b.] process of growth, having as its aim at every stage an added capacity for growth.[33]

In directing the activities of the young, thus determining the course of their growth, society prepares for its own future. The very meaning of the words 'youth' or 'immaturity' entails a reference to the ability to grow and develop in certain ways. Dewey was well aware that 'ability' is susceptible of different connotations in different contexts. He points out, as Plato and Aristotle had in discussing the corresponding concept of dynamis (potentially, potency), that there are passive and active senses in which something is said to possess an ability. A thing may be said to possess an ability to receive changes, "mere receptivity,"[34] such as the wax has to be scratched and shaped. There is also the active sense in which 'ability'

---

[31] Logic: The Theory of Inquiry, p. 19.
[32] Ibid., p. 23. The fuller context of this passage is important; see Appendix 1, sec. A below.
[33] Democracy and Education, p. 63. Thus the main theme of ch. 4, "Education as Growth." But see also p. 12: "Education is thus a fostering, a nurturing, a cultivating, process. All of these words means that it implies attention to the conditions of growth."
[34] Ibid., p. 49.

refers to a power, a disposition to behave, such as the ability of animals to run or of men to think. The process of education, Dewey argues, is to be thought of as dealing with abilities in the latter sense. Immaturity is to be viewed as a state of active, if largely undirected powers and behavior, not mere receptivity. Thus,

> when we say that immaturity means the possibility of growth, we are not referring to the absence of powers which may exist at a later time; we express a force positively present—the ability to develop.[35]

It is worth noting that here, at the heart of educational theory, the group of disposition terms—'ability,' 'possibility,' along with 'growth,' 'change,' 'development'—so central in the pragmatism of Peirce and James has appeared again. These concepts are the coinage of pragmatic theorizing over meaning and action.[36]

The two senses in which growth is considered an ability of the young lead to two diverging conceptions of educational theory and practice. At one extreme the child is regarded as in a condition of privation. That condition is most markedly a receptivity to external forces. The child is not an adult but has the capacity to become an adult. The child *is*, potentially, the man. The educational process is then viewed as a program of external stimuli designed to produce internal responses. Society in the persons of parent and teacher exerts its pressure and the young respond. Schooling is the means of producing the socially approved response. In this manner the child eventually becomes a grownup.

At the other extreme childhood is conceived of as a state full of latent but readily unfolded powers. In the child the mature adult resides potentially waiting only to be educed (so that *educere* becomes *educatus*). Growth is the releasing of the adult from the child.

These are each extreme positions and not actually held or advocated as such by anyone. But they have each been approximated in the past. The first position derives from a literal and by no means definitive reading of Aristotle's doctrine of change as a passage of a subject from a state of potentiality (and *steresis*, incompleteness) to actuality. The second, Platonic position (and deriving from Leibniz) was held by Hegel and became especially influential with Froebel. Growth here is the stirring and movement of the Absolute, the perfecting whole, as a force immanent in human life. The two positions are instructive, and Dewey's approach, accordingly, is to strike a mean between them. The synthesis is articulated in the early chapters of *Democracy and Education*.

For Dewey, the most serious shortcoming in each of the above theories is that both make use of inadequate conceptions of human growth.[37] In each case

---

35 *Ibid.*, p. 49.

36 See Part Five, ch. 1, esp. §§ 100, 101 below. The concept of 'growth' would apparently require at the least some notion of *physical possibility* for its elucidation. For this later notion and its importance for pragmatism, see Appendix 7.

37 Connected with this, each of the theories employs an inadequate psychology of external stimulus and internal response. One of Dewey's major accomplishments was the setting forth of an empirical theory of the integration and interpretation of stimulus-response as phases within a large act. The theory is discussed in the next section, § 38.

"growth is regarded as having an end, instead of being an end."[38] On the first theory growth is the passage from a state of deprivation (*sterēsis*, to again invoke Aristotle) to a state of completion. Growth, education, is a movement to this perfecting end. The end (*telos*) completes and is the purpose of the activity. Dewey agrees that the child is "comparatively" (i.e., relative to conditions of maturity) incomplete and dependent upon environment and society. But "immaturity" is "a positive force or ability," not a negative feature (as *sterēsis* suggests). It is "the *power* to grow."[39] Moreover, *dependence* in this case also means interdependence, Dewey argues. Adaptation to environing conditions includes some *control* over them. "Adaptation . . . is as much adaptation *of* the environment to our own activities as our activities *to* the environment."[40] The degree of adaptability of a creature for growth is his plasticity. But this, for Dewey, again means not a passive faculty for receiving change.

> It is not a capacity to take on change of form in accord with external pressure. It lies near the pliable elasticity by which some persons take on the color of their surroundings while retaining their own bent. . . . It is essentially the ability to learn from experience; the power to retain from one experience something which is of avail in coping with the difficulties of a later situation. This means power to modify actions on the basis of the results of prior experiences, the power to *develop dispositions*. Without it, the acquisition of habits is impossible.[41]

Life, then, is growth, and growth is not something done to the young, or something put for them to do; "it is something they do."[42]

In many writings, all of them stressing the biological basis of behavior and clearly influenced by Darwinism and the biological emphasis in James's *Psychology*, Dewey formulated what he took to be the main characteristics of living behavior.[43] Organic life as a process of activity involves (and is continuous with) an environment.

---

[38] *Democracy and Education*, p. 60. The context of this quotation is Dewey's criticism of the first of the above views. Later, however, pp. 65 ff., he criticizes the second view, "Education as Unfolding," for the same reason: "logically the doctrine is only a variant of the preparation theory."

[39] *Ibid.*, p. 50.

[40] *Ibid.*, p. 56. For an important extension of this point in Dewey's ethical theory, see §§ 91, 92 below.

[41] *Ibid.*, pp. 52–53.

[42] *Ibid.*, p. 50.

[43] For educational theory, this biological emphasis is found in the first early chapters of *Democracy and Education*. See also the beginning of *Interest and Effort in Education*. The theory of behavior is found in *Human Nature and Conduct*, also *Conduct and Experience*, and below, § 38. For logical theory, see *Logic: The Theory of Inquiry*, ch. 2.

The influence of James's *Psychology* on Dewey is undeniable; Dewey has so testified. But the influence must not be overstated. As Mead has pointed out, in Dewey's early writing on psychology important features of his later position are worked out with no mention of James and no evidence of influences that came later. Thus, says Mead, in Dewey's *Outline of Ethics* (1891) we already find "the will, the idea and the consequences all placed inside the act, and the act itself placed only within the larger activity of the individual in society." "The Philosophies of Royce, James, and Dewey in Their American Setting," in *Selected Writings*, ed. Reck, p. 388.

It is a transaction extending beyond the spatial limits of the organism. An organism does not live *in* an environment; it lives by means of an environment.[44]

Every organic activity is "an interaction of intra-organic and extra-organic energies." In the course of life activities, the expenditure of energies is possible only when the energy expended can be replenished. The living creature in its expenditures of energy must therefore succeed in "making return drafts upon the environment—the only source of restoration of energy." The balance for life is precarious and important.

The energy that is drawn is not forced in from without; it is a consequence of energy expended. If there is a surplus balance, growth occurs. If there is a deficit balance, degeneration commences.[45]

The process of life activities is more or less successful depending upon interactions and balance—the expenditures and replenishments of organic and environing energies. Creatures may destroy these sources of energy in their surroundings or may fail to make use of them. But insofar as a life process does go on, organism and environment are integrally related: "they *are* an integration." Creatures with different organic powers and structures thus live in different and changing environments. The development of a new organ, or modifications of an old one, equally affects the environment.

It follows that with every differentiation of structure the environment expands. For a new organ provides a new way of interacting in which things in the world that were previously indifferent enter into life functions. . . . the environment of any fish differs from that of a bird. . . . the difference is not just that a fish lives *in* the water and a bird *in* the air, but that the characteristic functions of these animals are what they are because of the special way in which water and air enter into their respective activities.[46]

But with differentiations and changes occurring in the interactions of living organisms and their environments, "there comes a need of maintaining a balance among them," the need of unifying the environment. This, for Dewey, is the chief characteristic of living processes: maintenance (not always consciously) of a uniform integration with the environment.

Capacity for maintenance of a constant form of interaction between organism and environment is not confined to the individual organism. It is manifested also, in the reproduction of similar organisms. . . . As long as life continues, its processes are such as continuously to maintain and restore the enduring relationship which is characteristic of the life-activities of a given organism.[47]

The succession of life activities is thus teleological (purposive, but again not

[44] *Logic*, p. 25.
[45] *Ibid.*, p. 25.
[46] *Ibid.*, pp. 25–26.
[47] *Ibid.*, p. 26.

always endowed with conscious purpose). Earlier activities prepare the way for later ones. The order is not a succession but a series.[48]

> This seriated quality of life activities is effected through the delicate balance of the complex factors in each particular activity. When the balance within a given activity is disturbed—when there is a proportionate excess or deficit in some factor—then there is exhibited need, search and fulfillment (or satisfaction) in the objective meanings of those terms.

The more complex and differentiated the living structures and their activities become, the more difficult it becomes to maintain this balance. Dewey continues:

> Indeed, living may be regarded as a continual rhythm of disequilibrations and recoveries of equilibrium. The "higher" the organism, the more serious become the disturbances and the more energetic (and often more prolonged) are the efforts necessary for its reestablishment.

Dewey concludes this remarkably succinct and central philosophic account of the biological basis of life activities with a statement of the pattern of conditions that undergo transformation if life is to continue.

> The state of disturbed equilibration constitutes *need*. The movement towards its restoration is search and exploration. The recovery is fulfillment or satisfaction.[49]

Here the pattern of the integrating process between organism and environment is one of movement and reconstruction from an initial stage of disturbed action and need to one of recovery and satisfaction. The process from one stage to the other—the process of "search and exploration"—is characteristic of *inquiry*, as we shall see in pages to come (§ 39). But this pattern is also just that of the process of *growth* and the general course and form of the process of *education*.

Man shares with many living creatures the difficulty of establishing lasting integrations with the environment and thus achieving satisfactions, and only with effort is this reconstruction and fulfillment of experience made possible. His most valuable technique for successfully directing this effort is intelligence. Peirce had also so interpreted the purposive nature of thought and the origin and function of *inquiry* (§ 20). For Dewey, roughly, there are two main embodiments of intelligence in all human history: on the organic level, intelligence is manifested in habits; in a culture it is found in social institutions.[50] This is not to say that all habits and social institutions are intelligent. They are measures and the means of

---

[48] *Ibid.*, p. 27. The importance for Dewey of the idea of differentiations, stimulus, and response as integrated *within* acts, and integrations of acts with other acts, is discussed in the next section, § 38.

[49] *Ibid.*, p. 27. The importance of the quoted passage for Dewey's ethical theory is taken up in Part IV, ch. 3 below; see especially § 92.

[50] Thus, one can find Dewey often describing the function and value of social institutions and of habits in quite similar ways. He says, "the measure of the worth of any social institution, economic, domestic, political, legal, religious, is its effect in enlarging and improving experience," *Democracy and Education*, p. 6. The same measure applies to habits: "Habits give control over the environment, power to utilize it for human purposes," p. 62.

intelligence. Moreover, as the reader will by now suspect, for Dewey, habits and institutions are not sharply separate aspects of human life. There is a genetic and causal continuity between the development and function of organic habits and social institutions. Indeed, institutions are cultural and group habits.

The upshot of these remarks is that for Dewey the fundamental purpose of formal education is that of directing the capacity for human growth. This in turn means the formation of intelligent habits—especially the habit of assessing habits. Habits are the means of control over environing conditions; they are the way experience is assimilated and environments are interpreted as entering the activities of living creatures.

> Power to grow depends upon need for others and plasticity. Both of these conditions are at their height in childhood and youth. Plasticity or the power to learn from experience means the formation of habits. Habits give control over the environment, power to utilize it for human purposes. Habits take the form both of habituation, or a general and persistent balance of organic activities with the surroundings, and of active capacities to readjust activity to meet new conditions. The former furnishes the background of growth; the latter constitute growing. Active habits involve thought, invention, and initiative in applying capacities to new aims. They are opposed to routine which marks an arrest of growth. Since growth is the characteristic of life, education is all one with growing; it has no end beyond itself.[51]

One important implication of this biologically oriented social psychology, for educational theory, is that the genuinely educational process is "situational."[52] Habits are not injected into the child from without; they originate within the interactions of the child and his surroundings. Their function is instrumental. They are modes of adjustment, and inclination and dispositions affecting and directing action. "A habit means an ability to use natural conditions as means to ends. It is an active control of the environment through the control of the organs of action."[53] But control of things, and our getting to know them by getting used to them, is achieved by first using them.[54] The direction of formal education, then, begins in introducing the child to the uses of the materials of his surroundings. Generally, the directive influence would have to provide in the child's own experience the situations (with respect to given subject matters) of need, searching, and final fulfillment and satisfaction.[55] For this is the pattern of growth and

[51] *Ibid.*, p. 62.
[52] Keeping in mind the more technical sense of 'situation' discussed previously in § 36.
[53] *Democracy and Education*, pp. 54–55.
[54] *Ibid.*, p. 56.
[55] Such was the main theoretical point of Dewey's famous argument in *The School and Society*, p. 37, for a "child centered" school, in which "the life of the child becomes the all-controlling aim. All the media necessary to further the growth of the child center there." This point was often misunderstood as advocacy of anarchy or *kinder*-tyranny. The child is the center, for Dewey; growth the aim; but center and aim are both features *within situations*. The conditions of growth in situations are anything but arbitrary or haphazard.

learning that we came upon earlier.[56] The task of teacher and school so conceived is far less simple and routine than ordinarily supposed.

It would not be an accurate account of Dewey's conception of continuity,
growth, and the educational process if these were portrayed in exclusively biological terms. Later pages will make this clear. Interactions between organism
and environment are not only organic and biological; environments do not enter
into life activities only in biological ways. Interactions, environments, conditions of integration and growth are also significantly physical and social in content. Indeed, the biological form in which the life activities of interaction and integration of organism and environment take place already involves physical and
social conditions. The environment, the energies that sustain activities and forms
of control and balance among creatures and their surroundings are as much social
and cultural as biological.[57] Dewey's view of the social direction of education,
the social medium of growth—via gestures, language, common objects and situations and the modifying of "one another's dispositions"[58]—has its parallel in
Mead's theory of the social genesis of the self (see §§ 50–60 below).

Dewey summarizes the position we have been studying in these pages:

> We have been occupied with the conditions and implications of growth. . . . When
> it is said that education is development, everything depends upon *how* development
> is conceived. Our net conclusion is that life is development, and that developing,
> growing, is life. Translated into its educational equivalents, this means (i) that
> the educational process has no end beyond itself; it is its own end; and that (ii)
> the educational process is one of continual reorganizing, reconstructing, trans-
> forming.[59]

The statement that the educational process "has no end beyond itself" has
puzzled some and misled others to conclude that Dewey meant that the educational process has no end at all. But Dewey never intended to suggest that growth
or education are aimless. His statement above is an instance of his general view
that "growth itself is the only moral 'end.' "[60]

In saying that the educational process "is its own end" Dewey meant that this

[56] The pattern emerges clearly in Dewey's account of the method of thinking, as discovery and inquiry, in education, in *ibid.*, p. 192: ". . . thinking is the method of an educative experience. The essentials of method are therefore identical with the essentials of
reflection. They are first that the pupil have a genuine situation of experience—that there
be a continuous activity in which he is interested for its own sake; secondly, that a genuine
problem develop within this situation as a stimulus to thought; third, that he possess the
information and make the observations needed to deal with it; fourth, that suggested solutions occur to him which he shall be responsible for developing in an orderly way; fifth,
that he have opportunity and occasion to test his ideas by application, to make their meaning clear and to discover for himself their validity."
[57] See esp. *ibid.*, pp. 33 ff., with the emphasis on the social as the "medium in which an
individual lives, moves, and has his being."
[58] *Ibid.*, p. 38.
[59] *Ibid.*, p. 59.
[60] *Reconstruction in Philosophy*, p. 177, for the full statement. For a brief discussion of
the idea, see § 41 below. The larger theory is dealt with in ch. 3 of Part IV below.

process (like growth) is never finished or ended. As long as life continues, education continues. He also meant that the educational process is not subordinate to any other, nor a means to anything else, to any process or social institution; just as life has no other end but itself. In viewing the end within the process, Dewey was also rejecting any one fixed or "static" end as *the* goal of education.

The centrality of the idea of continuity in Dewey's philosophy, the related emphasis upon growth, and life activities in specific contexts as continuous processes, are also reasons for his preferring adverbial terms of analysis and description to nouns: "An adverb expresses a way, a mode of acting."[61]

An important adverbial role is given to the terms 'mind' and 'intelligence.' These do not express things but rather ways of acting.[62] Intelligence is a form of behavior in certain occurring situations, situations calling for inquiry, rather than a fund of prescriptions or formulas to be enacted. But then recipes for conduct, injunctions, and advice, the solutions to problems of educational, political, or economic practices are not forthcoming from Dewey or his philosophy. Since he is consistent with his theory of inquiry and the uniqueness of particular problem situations (§ 39), Dewey is able to suggest *how* problems are to be encountered and resolved but not *what* the solutions are or should be. For what to do, or what is the solution to a problem are matters that cannot be discovered prior to inquiry into the conditions in question. Disciples of Dewey have often found this the most difficult lesson to learn, and it has proved grievous for many of his hopeful converts. The temptation has been to search Dewey's writings for an answer to moral difficulties or intellectual doubts.[63] But no "answer" in the sense traditionally expected of the philosophic sage will be found. Those who demand final and readily available answers for such problems have not been favorably impressed with Dewey's philosophy.

[61] *Reconstruction in Philosophy*, p. 156. See his reasoning in such passages as: "It would be a great gain for logic and epistemology if we were always to translate the noun 'truth' back into the adjective 'true,' and this back into the adverb 'truly,'" *Influence of Darwin*, p. 95; "The adverb 'truly' is more fundamental than either the adjective, true, or the noun, truth," *Reconstruction in Philosophy*, p. 156. See the latter, p. 177, for a similar application of the point of view to moral concepts because "the process of growth, of improvement and progress, rather than the static outcome and result, becomes the significant thing." See § 41 below for more of this passage.
[62] Thus, in *Democracy and Education*, p. 155: "mind is not a name for something complete by itself; it is a name for a course of action in so far as that is intelligently directed; in so far, that is to say, as aims, ends, enter into it, with selection of means to further the attainment of aims. Intelligence is not a peculiar possession which a person owns; but a person is intelligent in so far as the activities in which he plays a part have the qualities mentioned."
[63] This has been particularly the case with Dewey's educational writings and his discussion of current social problems. In *Individualism Old and New*, the most pressing problems in American life are set forth with great clarity. But no simple "answer" to them is offered, other than stressing the urgent need for inquiry, a balanced, experimentally informed and scientifically inspired investigation of the problems and their possible solutions. This "answer" has disappointed some readers.
   For certain difficulties in this respect in social and political issues, see the critical discussion in § 105.

The core of Dewey's educational theory, we have seen, is the idea of continuity as exhibited by organic growth. Very much a part of this same theory and related to the reflections of the last paragraphs, is his conception of knowledge. This, says Dewey,

> may be termed pragmatic. Its essential feature is to maintain the continuity of knowing with an activity which purposely modifies the environment. It holds that knowledge in its strict sense of something possessed consists of our intellectual resources—of all the habits that render our action intelligent. Only that which has been organized into our dispositions so as to enable us to adapt the environment to our needs and to adapt our aims and desires to the situation in which we live is really knowledge.[64]

We would be well advised, in now taking a closer view of Dewey's instrumental theory of logic and knowledge, to consider one of the earliest critical formulations of his outlook. For this work continued to guide and influence much of Dewey's later theorizing. Some illumination of the latter is afforded by the historical perspective. Such, then, is the purpose of the next section.

§ 38. Sensation and Response: Reflex Arc and Circuit

For Dewey, we noticed, the chief task of modern philosophy is the integrating of human values and ideals with scientific knowledge, that is, establishing the *continuity* of methodological procedures, deliberation, and conceptualization that exist in the rational construction of evaluations and of propositions of fact.[65]

This task, at least as Dewey undertook it, required analysis of the kinds of experience that generate valuations and knowing and of the logical structures through which this experiencing emerges in judgments. The task and requirements, thus broadly conceived, call for considerable philosophic effort—what traditionally would have been felt as necessitating an ethic, a theory of knowledge, and a metaphysics. Dewey's early philosophizing was, we saw, a mixture of psychology and ethics. The metaphysics received fuller attention later. For the younger Dewey, *psychology* was *the* way to the successful completion of the philosophic task. The *worth* and *meaning* of the content of experience (thus already suggesting the fusing of value and knowledge) are determined in psychology. Dewey wrote:

> Psychology is the ultimate science of reality because it declares what experience in its totality is. It fixes the worth and meaning of its various elements by showing their development and place within this whole. It is, in short, philosophic method.[66]

[64] *Democracy and Education*, p. 400.
[65] The theory of valuation that Dewey developed to achieve this end is discussed below, Part IV, ch. 3.
[66] "Psychology as Philosophic Method" (1886), p. 153.

This early confident interest in psychology is important to us here, not as a revelation of the faith that Hegelianism could lead to, but because of the profoundly illuminating nature of Dewey's work in psychology for the formation of his later philosophy.

It becomes clear from his early writings in psychology, and in later continuous elaborations and reflections of their fundamental insights, that Dewey was gradually developing a general theory of human action. That is, the way he apparently envisaged an integration of moral values and scientific knowledge was to show how—on a theoretical level—these were related aspects of what in actual fact was the case when purposive human behavior took place. The theory of action became the matrix for resolving the most pressing problems of philosophy. But then what was needed first was the development of this theory. The theory would serve as a general explanation of the conditions initiating a process of reflective and active behavior—a coordination of activities—directed to establishing certain satisfactions and conscious changes in the relations between the acting individual and the environment. This theory of behavior, emphasizing both environmental pressures and changes and organic responses as phases in the process of successful coordination aimed at achieving successful issue, was first set forth in psychological terms by Dewey. Later the more formal and conceptual features of the same processes were formulated in the theory of inquiry. Thus, in the theory of behavior, the formal pattern of inquiry is clearly anticipated. Before turning to the latter we will glance at the former.

In the 1890's Dewey was the leader of the Chicago school of "functional psychology." Dewey's paper of 1896, "The Reflex Arc Concept in Psychology," was an important event in the history of American psychology as well as in the development of his own philosophy. The "functionalists" included James R. Angell, a pupil of James, and George Mead, who, like Dewey, was led to work out a general theory of action (see below, §§ 48 ff.). Functional psychology[67] had its origins in James's *Psychology*. This was a movement emphasizing the role of psychological processes (vs. events or elements) in their service to the adaptive functions of the organism. This was a biological and evolutionary psychology, opposed to a more traditional "structuralism," whose historical source was Locke's *Essay*, intent on a systematic description of the composition of mental states and elements of consciousness. Functional psychology took as its basic data not alleged psychic events, but behavioral processes in biological and social contexts.[68]

---

[67] A representative statement of "functional" psychology is Angell's *Psychology*, 1904. A sense of the movement and the time is found in Angell's "The Relations of Structural and Functional Psychology to Philosophy."

[68] Thus, Woodworth, p. 46: "Functional psychology sought to discover what needs of the organism were met by sense perception, by mental images, by emotion, by thinking. Taking the evolutionary point of view, it tried to divine at what stage in the development of the race the need for each mental process had become pressing enough to lead to the emergence of that particular process. In a general way, the higher mental processes were held to meet the need for a wider and more flexible control of the environment. Thus, functional psychology aimed to give psychology a place in the general field of biological science."

The Chicago group gave birth to what was to be known as "social behaviorism" (see below, § 50).

A Hegelian preference for wholes and processes, Darwinian evolution, and, particularly, James's view of mind as teleological (§ 28) and as an instrument for adaptation and control of the environment are the chief influences in the formation of Dewey's behavioral psychology. But it should be added that this formative period was one in which psychology was rapidly becoming an experimental science. Dewey had followed much of the experimental work, and had studied under G. Stanley Hall—a pioneer in American experimental psychology—while at Johns Hopkins.

The "Reflex Arc Concept" is interesting in what it presages of fundamental themes in Dewey's later instrumental theory of knowledge. It also sets forth some original and instructive methodological proposals for the analysis of behavior. Most important of these is Dewey's critical reinterpretation of the notions of *stimulus* and *response* and their roles in psychological explanations of human action.

The reflex arc concept had been brought from physiology into psychology as a way of accounting for the connections that existed between stimulated nerve structure and motor responses. It was to be an improvement over an atomistic philosophical psychology in which physical-physiological stimulus and "psychic" responses were so disparate that their supposed causal relationship was inexplicable. Dewey's objection to the reflex arc concept was that it did not sufficiently replace the older doctrine of sensation and activity; that the older psychology was concealed rather than routed by the new concept.

> The older dualism between sensation and idea is repeated in the current dualism of peripheral and central structures and functions; the older dualism of body and soul finds a distant echo in the current dualism of stimulus and response.[69]

Dewey proceeded to show how occasions of stimulus and response—"the character of sensation, idea, and action"—are to be interpreted as functions in (thus relative to) a whole and completed process of action. He found the reflex arc "not a comprehensive, or organic unity, but a patchwork of disjointed parts, a mechanical conjunction of unallied processes."[70] The arc idea, said Dewey,

> how much it may prate of unity . . . still leaves us with sensation or peripheral stimulus; idea, or, central process (the equivalent of attention); and motor response, or act, as three disconnected existences, having to be somehow adjusted

[69] "The Reflex Arc Concept in Psychology," pp. 357–358. This paper was reprinted under the title "The Unit of Behavior," with slight changes, in *Philosophy and Civilization*, pp. 233–248 (the better title "The Unity of Behavior" appears in the Table of Contents). For convenience, references below are to the original paper and also to its reprinting in *Philosophy and Civilization*. For the above passage, pp. 357–358; in *Philosophy and Civilization*, p. 249. A valuable but difficult companion study of Dewey's paper and generalization from it is Mead's "The Definition of the Psychical" (1903), reprinted in *Selected Writings*, pp. 25–59.

[70] "Reflex Arc Concept," pp. 357–358; *Philosophy and Civilization*, p. 234.

to each other, whether through the intervention of an extra-experimental soul, or by mechanical push and pull.[71]

The appeal to a soul with transcendental capacities for integrating these existences, or the reduction of stimuli and responses to mechanical interactions are both, of course, rejected by Dewey. The details of the rejection need not trouble us here—for these are now only of limited historical interest. It is Dewey's own theory, the explanatory view borne through these critically rejected alternatives, that concerns us.

Dewey's two underlying objections to the reflex arc concept lead directly to his own view. His first objection, as indicated above, is to the assumption that sense stimulation and motor response are "distinct mental existences." The stimulus and response, Dewey maintains, are "in reality . . . always inside a coördination." His second objection is to the treatment of the three parts of the arc, sensation or stimulus, the stimulation preceding the motor phase, and the activity following it, as "two different states." For Dewey, the state of stimulation and that of responsive activity are best thought of as a "development," a "mediation" of one experience. Instead of two successive states, argues Dewey, the last phase is "the first reconstituted."[72] The motor phase is a part of the mediation, a part of the reconstituting of initial experience.

An example may help. A child, seeing the flame of a candle, reaches for it, is burned, and quickly withdraws his hand. This process could be described thus: the sensation of light is the stimulus, reaching for the candle is the response; the burn received is the next stimulus, withdrawing of the hand the next response.[73] But Dewey points out that this description ignores a host of preliminary coordinated conditions of body, head, and eye, and of prior activity. The "real beginning" here was not a sensation of light, it was "the *act* of seeing."[74] The sensation of light is a constituent *within* this act, rather than an antecedent of the act. Moreover, that the act of seeing stimulates the act of reaching is partially explained by much past condition and coordinating of seeing and grasping. These are interrelated and interdependent activities—more or less smoothly and skillfully interrelated depending on past reciprocal executions. These activities support and reinforce one another as "functions" in a larger process of coordinated acts.

> The ability of the hand to do its work will depend, either directly or indirectly, upon its control, as well as its stimulation, by the act of vision. . . . The reaching, in turn, must both stimulate and control the seeing. The eye must be kept upon the candle if the arm is to do its work.[75]

Now it is in this coordination of activities taken as phases (or functions) of a larger process—for the candle is still to be reached and the burn experienced—

[71] *Ibid.*, p. 361; *Philosophy and Civilization*, p. 237.
[72] *Ibid.*, p. 360; *Philosophy and Civilization*, p. 236.
[73] I follow Dewey's discussion here, *ibid.*, pp. 358–359; *Philosophy and Civilization*, pp. 234–236.
[74] *Ibid.*, pp. 358–359; *Philosophy and Civilization*, p. 235.
[75] *Ibid.*, p. 359; *Philosophy and Civilization*, p. 235.

that initial stimuli become increasingly "reconstituted" with "more content or value."[76] That is, the initial act of seeing becomes enlarged and transformed into "seeing-for-reaching purposes." Or, we may put it, the act of seeing is supplemented with conditional anticipations and motivations. The candle flame seen is a sign (à la Berkeley[77]) of certain possible related experiences. When the act of reaching results in the child getting burned, a completion of earlier coordinated acts of eye and hand has occurred. The experienced burn is not to be construed as a simple sensation with an isolated content of its own. The sense of burn and pain has entered into the circuit of experience wherein are also optical and muscular activities. Only when the pain is recognized as a related feature of this whole process of activities "does the child learn from the experience and get the ability to avoid the experience in the future."[78]

Dewey summarizes this analysis of the occasions of stimulus and response as phases in a process of coordinated acts:

> The so-called response is not merely *to* the stimulus; it is *into* it. The burn is the original seeing, the original optical-ocular experience, enlarged and transformed in its value. It is no longer mere seeing; it is seeing-of-a-light-that-means-pain-when-contact-occurs.

The transformation of experience here is missed if one interprets the events as a case in which a sensation of burning and pain has, because of certain intervening motions, taken the place of a sensation of light.

> The fact is that the sole meaning of the intervening movement is to maintain, reinforce or transform (as the case may be) the original quale; we do not have the replacing of one sort of experience by another, but the development or . . . the mediation of an experience. The seeing, in a word, remains to control the reaching, and is, in turn, interpreted by the burning.[79]

Let us look, albeit briefly, at some of the explanatory consequences that Dewey derives from the foregoing analysis.

1) Considering the primacy, in fact and for analysis, of the behavioral *act* (or "sensori-motor co-ordination"), we begin to see that the distinctions of *stimulus* and *response* are relative to and dependent upon the act or circuit coordination. Stimulus and response, as Dewey says, "are not distinctions of existence, but teleological distinctions, that is, distinctions of function or part played with reference to reaching or maintaining an end."[80] Attributions of stimulus

---

[76] *Ibid.*, p. 359; *Philosophy and Civilization*, p. 235.
[77] See the last paragraph of § 7 above; and Appendix 5 below.
[78] "Reflex Arc Concept," p. 359; *Philosophy and Civilization*, p. 236.
[79] *Ibid.*, pp. 359–360; *Philosophy and Civilization*, p. 236, the first line of the previous extract reading: "the so-called response is not merely to the stimulus; it is, so to speak, *into* it."
[80] *Ibid.*, p. 365; *Philosophy and Civilization*, p. 242. Teleological distinctions are in bad repute in some philosophic quarters. But there are ways by which the teleological language can receive respectable reformulation in causal terms, or in non-teleological language, without loss of empirical content. See Nagel's discussion, "The Structure of Teleological Explanations," *The Structure of Science*, pp. 401–428.

events (or of response) are of little significance, therefore, without prior specification of a behavioral act with reference to some end. And, depending on the particular activities (like seeing or grasping) that constitute functions of a larger process of acts, the same events may function in one respect as stimuli, in another as response. In the example of the child, the particular act of seeing the flame is a *response* to prior actions of discovery and location; it may also be the *stimulus* to further acts.[81]

2) But suppose the child in past occasions of reaching for a bright light has sometimes experienced a pleasant play thing and sometimes the pain of being burned. Then, says Dewey, not only is the response uncertain, the stimulus is equally uncertain. The problem in this case is equally well stated: "either to discover the right stimulus, to constitute the stimulus, or to discover, to constitute, the response."[82] The question is: to reach or not to reach (i.e., how respond)? But this is also to question: what kind of bright thing am I looking at (i.e., what *is* the stimulus)? The stimulus must be "constituted," that is, interpreted for the response to take place. How the stimulus is interpreted determines the kind of response that will occur. How the response occurs and its consequences controls (or, in a sense, "verifies") the interpretation of the stimulus and future interpretations of like stimuli.

> It is doubt as to the next act, whether to reach or no, which gives the motive to examining the act. The end to follow is, in this sense, the stimulus. It furnishes the motivation to attend to what has just taken place; to define it more carefully.[83]

Here the discovery and interpretation of the stimulus is the response. The occurring stimulus conditions present *possible* responses, and until its quality is interpreted and acted upon, it requires attention, and the possibilities present uncertainty. What is suspended or doubtful is completion of the act; it waits upon further determination of the stimulus. Not any response, but a completing, successful response inhibits further action until the nature of the stimulus is determined.

3) Dewey has outlined the function of stimulus and response in the process of behavior as respectively exhibiting the pattern of *problem* and *solution*. This is the pattern that awaited further descriptive generalization in the theory of inquiry.

---

[81] An important augmenting argument of his analysis is Dewey's insistence that stimulus and response are not identifiable as or reducible to, sheer instances of sensation and movement: ". . . it is an act, a sensori-motor coordination which stimulates the response, itself in turn sensori-motor, not a sensation which stimulates a movement.
". . . Neither mere sensation, nor mere movement, can ever be either stimulus or response; only an act can be that; the *sensation* as stimulus means the lack of and search for such an objective stimulus, or orderly placing of an act; just as mere movement as response means the lack of and search for the right act to complete a desired coordination." *Ibid.*, pp. 366–367; *Philosophy and Civilization*, pp. 243–244, with 'act' in the first sentence italicized.
[82] *Ibid.*, p. 367; *Philosophy and Civilization*, p. 244.
[83] *Ibid.*, p. 368; *Philosophy and Civilization*, p. 245, with the first sentence reading: "Uncertainty as to the next act, whether to reach or not, gives the motive. . ."

Generalized, sensation as stimulus is always that phase of activity requiring to be defined in order that a coördination may be completed. What the sensation will be in particular at a given time, therefore, will depend entirely upon the way in which activity is directed. . . . The search for stimulus is the search for exact conditions of action . . . for the state of things which decides how a beginning coördination should be completed.

Similarly, motion, as response, had only functional value. It is whatever will serve to complete the disintegrating coördination. Just as the discovery of the sensation marks the establishing of the problem, so the constitution of the response marks the solution of this problem.[84]

Here we begin to see what is finally the fundamental philosophic idea in the above theory of action. This is more than the effective argument for an "organic" psychology, for a circuit and coordination of behavior instead of a "disjointed psychology."[85]

The important feature of Dewey's analysis is his careful application and development of the notions of "conflict" and "re-organization," "disintegration" and "reconstruction," "discord" and "successful co-ordination" in the context of organic-psychological behavior. These and like notions and the phases and characteristic conditions of behavior that they distinguish and describe are basic to Dewey's view of all forms of intelligent action. Indeed, as we have seen earlier, continuously occurring conditions of conflict and recovery or reconstruction characterize the maintenance of all life.[86]

The pattern of *conflict* and *reconstruction* is the organic counterpart of the logical pattern of *problem* and *solution*. In Dewey's analysis of purposive action, stimulus and response are finally construed as "minor acts serving by their respective positions the maintenance of some organized coördination."[87] The circuit of behavior in which acts of stimulus and response function to maintain and direct the course of further actions is, so long as experience runs smoothly, largely unconscious (or unattentive). For then no conscious distinction of sensory stimulus and motor response is made.

But there are occasions when the acts in a circuit come into conflict with each other. Seeing and reaching, in the above illustration, do not continue cooperatively in the carrying out of an action. Their joint work is disrupted because of prior hesitancy and inhibition of the tendency to reach: all of this because the *stimulus* —seeing a bright object—has become uncertain. This uncertainty and conflict is a state of trouble, and poses a problem to be resolved. When the circuit of acts is thus broken up into conflicting parts, then, in particular, the need for reconstruction of the conditions *in question* and for bringing action to a successful issue is most felt. These are the conditions that demand *inquiry*, as we shall see below. But, on the level of organic action, the disrupted coordination is the genesis of a

[84] *Ibid.*, pp. 368–369; *Philosophy and Civilization*, pp. 245–246.
[85] *Ibid.*, p. 360; *Philosophy and Civilization*, p. 236.
[86] The ethical import of this pattern for Dewey is discussed in § 92 below.
[87] *Ibid.*, p. 370; *Philosophy and Civilization*, p. 247.

conscious distinction of sensory stimulus and motor response, so Dewey argues.

The circuit is a coördination some of whose members have come into conflict with each other. It is the temporary disintegration and need of reconstruction which occasions, which affords the genesis of, the conscious distinction into sensory stimulus on one side and motor response on the other.

Here the distinction of what is taken to be the sensory stimulus and that which is the response is "functional": the distinction is instrumental to furthering the action that has become blocked and to assisting it to a satisfactory conclusion.

The stimulus is that phase of the forming coördination which represents the conditions which have to be met in bringing it to successful issue; the response is that phase of one and the same forming coördination which gives the key to meeting these conditions, which serves as an instrument in effecting the successful coördination. They are therefore strictly correlative and contemporaneous. The stimulus is something to be discovered; to be made out. . . . As soon as it is adequately determined, then and only then is the response also complete.[88]

This was the basic pattern of all purposive and conscious behavior in either relatively trivial or momentous circumstances. Dewey concluded his statement of the foregoing theory by deferring its application to questions of the development of mind and the nature of judgment.[89] But some of the later applications are not difficult to anticipate. Thus the theory of inquiry and especially of judgment as an "existential transformation" of problematic into resolved and coherent conditions has its outline in the above description of the response as a "constitution" and "reconstruction" of stimulus. And where, in the last quotation, Dewey speaks of the response as a forming of coordination which "gives the key" to the conditions that have to be met for a successful termination of behavior—the instrumental theory of truth is foreshadowed.[90]

Because of its historical philosophic importance for the growth of Dewey's instrumentalism, and also because of its merits as a contribution to philosophical psychology, the above pages have been devoted in considerable detail to Dewey's early paper on the reflex arc concept and the coordination of sensation and response. We must now turn to some of the philosophic consequences and developments deriving from the work in biological psychology.

§ 39. The Pattern of Inquiry

A brief look at what Dewey calls "the pattern of inquiry" will help fix our attention on what is important and so far only suggested in the theory of instrumen-

---

[88] *Ibid.*, p. 370; *Philosophy and Civilization*, pp. 247–248.
[89] The final paragraph, see p. 370; *Philosophy and Civilization*, p. 248.
[90] See § 40 below where, in Dewey's clearest statement of his "operational" theory of truth, he speaks of truth as correspondence, "namely, of *answering*, as a key answers to conditions imposed by a lock . . . as . . . a *solution* answers to the requirements of a *problem*."

talism being considered. Thinking, or the activity of inquiry, is a process having certain phases occurring within certain limits: it starts with a "perplexed, troubled, or confused situation at the beginning and a cleared-up, unified, resolved situation at the close."[91] The troubled situation in which inquiry begins has "biological antecedent conditions" in a "state of imbalance in organic-environmental interactions,"[92] a state of disturbed equilibration.[93] This situation of disequilibrium, or imbalance, is indeterminate "with respect to its *issue*"; it is *confused*, meaning "its outcome can not be anticipated"; it is *obscure* because its final consequences cannot be clearly foreseen; it is *conflicting* "when it tends to evoke discordant responses."[94]

Situations, it will be remembered, are "contextual wholes" possessing various qualitative traits. For Dewey, it is the "immediately pervasive quality" that makes any situation a "whole" and unique or individual.[95] While the list of experienceable qualities is endless, so that situations may be tragic, amusing, red, noisy, etc.,[96] the kind of situation with which we are concerned at present is one whose pervasive quality is *indeterminate* or doubtful. It is the whole *situation* which is indeterminate, doubtful, disturbed, or confused. For the reasons observed a few pages back, Dewey takes great pains to guard us from identifying the doubtfulness of situations with some allegedly subjective sense of doubt as a "state of mind" or an event in a human brain. He writes: "It is the situation that has these traits. *We* are doubtful because the situation is inherently doubtful. Personal states of doubt that are not evoked by and are not relevant to some existential situation are pathological."[97]

Inquiry proper commences when an indeterminate situation begins to yield "suggestions"; organic interaction, says Dewey, becomes inquiry when consequences begin to be anticipated. The first stage of inquiry consists in the recognition that the situation is a problem. "To see that a situation requires inquiry is the initial step in inquiry."[98] The indeterminate situation becomes a problematic situation. Formulation of the problem is the beginning of the transformation of the situation by inquiry. How and how adequately the problem is formulated has two major consequences: (1) it identifies the situation, correctly or not, as to the specific sort of problem it presents, and it interprets the situation as posing a question for which an answer is to be sought; (2) formulation of the problem suggests the scope and character of the ensuing inquiry necessary for the attain-

[91] *How We Think*, p. 106. See also, *Logic: The Theory of Inquiry*, p. 105.
[92] *Logic: The Theory of Inquiry*, p. 106; also see pp. 26–27.
[93] *Ibid.*, pp. 26–27: "The state of disturbed equilibration constitutes *need*. The movement towards its restoration is search and exploration. The recovery is fulfillment or satisfaction," p. 27.
[94] *Ibid.*, p. 106.
[95] *Ibid.*, p. 68.
[96] See Dewey's discussion of this in "Inquiry and Indeterminateness of Situations," *Problems of Men*, esp. pp. 326–329.
[97] *Logic: The Theory of Inquiry*, pp. 105–106. Some difficulties in this assignment of inherent doubt to situations are discussed in Thayer, *The Logic of Pragmatism*, pp. 75 ff.
[98] *Logic: The Theory of Inquiry*, p. 107.

ment of a solution. How the problem is conceived determines what data and suggestions are relevant, what irrelevant to the inquiry; "it is the criterion for relevancy and irrelevancy of hypotheses and conceptual structures."[99]

The second stage of inquiry consists of the formulation of hypotheses or possible relevant solutions to the problem. Hypotheses, or "ideas," are anticipations of consequences; they take a conditional form, being forecasts of what would (or will) happen if certain operations are performed with respect to certain conditions. Facts and observations will function as "suggestions"—i.e., to suggest ideas; and ideas will function as suggestions of possible operations and consequences. Ideas may even suggest other ideas and may suggest other facts and observations. The "function" of ideas here consists in their use, or suggested use, as means to the resolution of the problem. "Reasoning" is an examination of ideas in an attempt to discern the relevancy and pertinence of their function within inquiry and its movement toward a solution. Reasoning is thus called by Dewey an examination of meanings.[100] Reasoning operates with symbols, with propositions; and propositions develop the "meaning-contents of ideas in their relations to one another."[101] Reasoning is the third stage in the process of inquiry; it concludes in the fourth and last stage with an "experiment" or testing of the idea (or meaning) to which reasoning has led. The experiment may be immediately evident or may require more or less elaborate operations for its carrying out. The kind of experiment required and the success of its outcome will depend upon the initial character of the problematic situation and the inquiry that has taken place. Reason terminates with what is or is not an "answer" to the problematic situation. The "test" of that answer is whether it in fact is a solution of the problem. Inquiry then concludes or must retrace its steps or start over again. But a "successful" conclusion, when reached, marks a transformation of a problematic situation into one that is clear, untroubled, and settled.

§ 40.   Truth

In the foregoing review of the pattern of inquiry the word 'truth' has not been used. But the pattern enables us to make clear how considerations of truth or falsehood have a place in Dewey's logical theory.

It should not be thought that, in distinguishing the five stages of inquiry, Dewey was maintaining that every inquiry exhibits just these stages in the order described. The pattern is a generalization of the logical order of inquiry. In actual cases that order may not be evidenced without many special deviations from and

---

99 *Ibid.*, p. 108.
100 *Ibid.*, p. 111.
101 "This examination consists in noting what the meaning in question implies in relation to other meanings in the system of which it is a member, the formulated relation constituting a proposition. . . . Through a series of intermediate meanings, a meaning is finally reached which is more clearly *relevant* to the problem in hand than the originally suggested idea," *ibid.*, pp. 111–112.

rearrangements of the phases thus outlined. The pattern, however, is an impressive and careful attempt to make clear what happens when problems are investigated logically or methodically and of the means taken to reach solutions. Statement of the pattern is an illuminating account of what happens and where it happens when it is most cultivated: the practice of scientific method.

The settled outcome of inquiry is called "judgment" by Dewey. And while the comment that an inquiry concludes with a judgment is unlikely to shock the reader of Dewey's *Logic*, he will be surprised when he learns what is meant by a judgment.[102] As distinguished from propositions which are intermediate, representative, and carried by symbols, "judgment, as finally made, has *direct* existential import."[103] Inquiry concludes, we have seen, with the *transformation* of the initially problematic situation; "this resulting state of actual affairs—this changed situation—is the matter of the final settlement or judgment."[104] Judgment *is*, or is concerned with, the final consequences of inquiry, as the conditions that effect a reconstruction or transformation of the indeterminate situation.[105] The "existential reconstruction ultimately effected" is the ultimate ground of warranted judgment;[106] what judgment via inquiry warrants in this case, is belief or knowledge, or what Dewey prefers to call a "warranted assertion."[107]

The notion of *warranted assertion* is bound up with the idea (or theory) of inquiry, for Dewey. In a similar way, the notion of *truth* is bound up with the idea of warranted assertion. Having both witnessed and participated in the difficulties the pragmatists had run into in explaining the meaning of 'truth,' aware of divergent views among the followers of James (and in James himself) over this idea and of a general failure to make themselves understood, Dewey was tempted to give up the terms 'truth' and 'falsehood' altogether and replace them with less misleading equivalents, where equivalents were needed.

Another reason for giving up these words was that they had become the stock in trade of those who, like Russell, were exponents of the influential *correspon-*

---

[102] See especially ch. 7, *Logic: The Theory of Inquiry*.

[103] *Ibid.*, p. 120. That propositions are "intermediate in inquiry leads Dewey to view them as possessing the properties of *means* (relevancy, efficacy) but not those of truth or falsehood. Truth and falsehood are properties of the *end* or conclusions of inquiries. See *Problems of Men*, pp. 339–341; also, *Logic: The Theory of Inquiry*, pp. 118–119.

[104] *Ibid.*, pp. 121–122.

[105] It is uncertain (at least to me) whether *judgment*, for Dewey, *is* the "existential determination of the prior situation which was indeterminate as to its issue" (*ibid.*, p. 121); that is, whether it *is* the transformation, or is *about* or *refers* to that transformation. Or is judgment both? (1) Is it about the directives or consequences that emerge from inquiry and effect an existential change; or (2) is the very occurrence of judgment a part of these existential changes being wrought by inquiry? Different passages in the *Logic* support (1) and (2) and sometimes a combining of both. A way over, if not through, this difficulty is, in effect, followed above, distinguishing the *formulation* of judgment (judgment as expressed) from the *function* of judgment (judgment as enacted). Judgment, incidentally, is not only directed to the *outcome* of inquiry, but also goes on in the "estimates" and "evaluations" of the propositions within inquiry and their effectiveness as means to the furtherance of inquiry. "Final judgment is attained through a series of partial judgments," *Logic*, p. 133.

[106] *Ibid.*, p. 489.

[107] *Ibid.*, pp. 8–9.

dence theory, a theory of which Dewey was very critical and from which he was anxious to disassociate his own views on truth. Perhaps, also, Dewey saw, as James did not, an objection that could be fatal to many of James's arguments about truth, and which would leave the pragmatists, in their spirited controversy with non-pragmatists, without ground or even legs to stand on: namely, the objection (or at least the suspicion) that the doctrine of truth and falsehood, so ardently cultivated and defended by the pragmatists, on reflection was of doubtful use. James's religious and metaphysical interests, the problems for which he had adopted his doctrine of truth, were not the *sine qua non* of pragmatism or of being a pragmatist. Here the reflective suspicion begins and broadens. Given other interests and other sorts of philosophical problems, was it essential, was it even pragmatically advisable, to continue to talk about truth in the language of James and from his point of view? Was James's doctrine pragmatically necessary?

Whether or not these suspicions in fact occurred to Dewey, the *Logic* contains rather few references to truth. Whereas Dewey had once tended to define truth as the "working" or "satisfactory" produce of thought, "the verified" idea or hypothesis,[108] he later preferred to speak of *warranted assertibility*. The assertion warranted by inquiry is to be thought of as related to the indeterminate situation in much the same way that a solution is related to a problem. The conditions imposed by a problem must be met by an answer. The problem determines the conditions of an answer, but the answer resolves the problem. This occurrence of conditions *met* and *resolved* is the cardinal feature of truth for Dewey. To have *met* the conditions of a problem precludes chance and sheer guesswork and immediate knowledge as well; inquiry, the interpretation and analysis of the problem, will have intervened to produce an answer, a warranted assertion.[109]

---

[108] Thus, for example, *Reconstruction in Philosophy*, pp. 156–157: "The adverb 'truly' is more fundamental than either the adjective, true, or the noun, truth. An adverb expresses a way, a mode of action. Now an idea or conception is a claim or injunction or plan to *act* in a certain way as the way to arrive at the clearing up of a specific situation. When the claim or pretension or plan is acted upon *it guides us truly or falsely.* . . . Its active, dynamic function is the all-important thing about it, and in the quality of activity induced by it lies all its truth and falsity. The hypothesis that works is the *true* one; and *truth* is an abstract noun applied to the collection of cases, actually foreseen and desired, that receive confirmation in their works and consequences."

[109] Here we run into another verbal tangle. Is the warranted assertion true and the unwarranted assertion false? Or is it that warranted assertions (as true) are the products of "competent" inquiries (*Logic*, p. 8), while assertions warranted, but by incompetent inquiries, are false? Should we identify truth and falsehood with warranted and unwarranted assertions respectively, or should we identify truth and falsehood with the warranted assertions of sound and competent and unsound and incompetent inquiries, respectively? Either of the possibilities leads to difficulties. A further snare, like that encountered above (note 105), is found in the use of the word 'assertion.' Is a warranted assertion (the solving or solution of the problem situation) an *enactment* of the solution? Or is a warranted assertion a *statement* or description of the conditions that solve the problem? Is 'assertion' here intended in the sense in which conditions are projected and carried out, as when a man might be said to "assert himself," or is 'assertion' intended to convey the stating of conditions, as when one asserts a proposition?

Distinctions between the behavioral, organic, existential features of inquiry and the linguistic, symbolic features are often unclear in Dewey's exposition. Some of the main difficulties in the *Logic* occur where the line fades or fails to be drawn between words and objects or between what is said about things and processes and what is said about language

In general (and the idea of truth is a very general one for Dewey), truth is found in the relation between the first stage of inquiry (the problematic situation) and the final stage (that of judgment, resolution, transformation). *Truth* characterizes the relation that these two phases of particular inquiries bear to one another: the relation of problem (or question) and solution (or answer). The relation, we may add, obtains *in* a situation *between* that initial state of conditions whose pervasive quality is designated as *problematic,* and that later state of conditions whose quality is designated as *determinate, complete, closed, solved.* If we call the first state of conditions C_1 and the latter state C_2, then truth may be defined as the relation between any occurrence of the kind C_1 and C_2, such that C_2 resolves or answers C_1.[110] Here, C_2 is—or is formulated by—a warranted assertion. The warranted assertion represents, as an answer, a case of knowledge or true belief. His "analysis of 'warranted assertibility,' " Dewey said, "is offered as a *definition* of the nature of knowledge in the honorific sense according to which only *true* beliefs are knowledge."[111]

While Dewey tried to avoid using the words 'true' and 'false' and to keep clear of the correspondence theory, his attempts were not altogether successful. We may try to get along with other words in analyzing human knowledge, but the notions of truth and falsehood have a peculiarly fundamental position and continue to make themselves felt throughout any such analysis. Inventing linguistic substitutes for this pair of terms is a temporary expedient at best and of questionable value, since whenever the new locutions are themselves up for consideration they are explained and understood by reverting to the old. There is as well an obvious (if not obviously analyzable) sense in which ascriptions of *truth* contain, at the least, a reference to some correspondence between that which is *said* to be true and the conditions which are supposed as the prerequisites and criteria for anything to be true.

For, to call X true, whatever X may be, is to affirm that X satisfied certain conditions. Specification of these conditions is the business of a theory of truth. The earliest adumbrations of one theory, in Plato and Aristotle, confines truth to statements or utterances (or *logoi,* generally); truth is talking about things as they really are; what is *said* to be (the case) *is* (the case).[112] We could regard this view

---

and language uses. A reason, but no excuse, for this obscuring of much needed distinctions is Dewey's perseverance in the spirit of continuity (cf. § 37 and Appendix 1) to the extent of avoiding sharp distinctions between linguistic and non-linguistic subject matters within inquiry; and this, in turn, stems from Dewey's concern to retain the full force of the fact that, after all, language and the uses of words are behavioral, organic, and existential features, too, and are natural processes as well. So they are; but nonetheless distinct from other things and best distinguished if we are to avoid intellectual confusion. To draw a distinction is not always to invite a dualism.

[110] Knowing the meaning of 'true' here will, of course, depend on knowing the meaning of 'resolution' or 'answer.' Furthermore, so defined, truth is equally a property of two kinds of significantly different contexts: (1) truth is a relation between existing conditions C_1 and C_2, such that, given C_1, C_2 is the temporal transformation or solution of C_1; (2) truth is a relation between *statements* (or descriptions) of any conditions C_1 and C_2, such that C_2 is the statement of an answer to a stated question C_1.

[111] *Problems of Men,* p. 332.

[112] See, e.g., Plato, *Cratylus* 385b; Aristotle, *Metaphysics,* 1011b25.

as an approach to a "correspondence" theory wherein truth is attributed to statements that "correspond" to what *is*, and correspondence is the condition to be satisfied by statements. We know that a statement is true (corresponds) when we know that the circumstances *said* to exist do in fact exist. Thus, to say that the statement 'Socrates is walking' is true is to say that Socrates is walking. And generally, of any statement replacing S,

$$(1) \quad \text{'}S\text{' is true, if and only if } S.$$

Such, in rough, is Tarski's famous development of the semantic theory of truth.[113] The theory is neutral concerning epistemological questions of how 'S' is supposed to correspond to S. It is not neutral with respect to some metaphysical doctrines of truth, for it limits the meaning of truth to statements; a notable gain in clarity is achieved with this economy of usage. But Plato, Aristotle, and many succeeding philosophers have wished to predicate truth of various sorts of objects in addition to that of statements. Dewey, we have seen—and shall see immediately below— seems to permit senses in which the "things," or situations, or *conditions* of a solution are *true* of those constituting a problem. For this reason, the above comment on correspondence, initiating this paragraph, has necessitated an awkwardly general form. For even where truth is said to attach to nonlinguistic entities, we may still argue that (whatever the theory of truth in which truth conditions are specified) to say X is true is to affirm that X is correlated to certain conditions (conditions which X is said to conform to, match, fulfill, etc.); accordingly, X and the conditions in question are supposed to be co-respondent.

Tarski's theory holds for all *statements* so-called, explicating what is being said when statements are cited as true or false. The explication given by (1) does not conflict with Dewey's view of truth in any noticeable way except the following. The only statements Dewey would permit to be substitutable for S in (1) would be those warranted by inquiry. It is central to his notions of truth and propositions that only warranted assertions are true and that propositions are neither true or false.[114]

Thus, in the course of a series of critical exchanges with Russell,[115] and as a

---

[113] See Tarski.

[114] Cf. Thayer, *The Logic of Pragmatism*, pp. 119 ff. For a recent illuminating discussion of the semantic theory, some problems in it, and later appraisals of Dewey's view, see Ezorsky.

[115] Critical differences between Dewey and Russell found occasional expression from the turn of the century on. Some of Russell's sharpest criticisms of pragmatism were reprinted in *Philosophical Essays* (1910). A detailed critical analysis of certain of Russell's fundamental ideas came from Dewey in "The Existence of the World as a Logical Problem" (1915, reprinted in *Essays in Experimental Logic*, being a study of Russell's *Our Knowledge of the External World*, 1914). The controversy over truth is found in Schilpp, *The Philosophy of John Dewey* (1939), containing Russell's essay on Dewey's *Logic* and Dewey's rejoinder; from thence it is extended in Russell's *Inquiry into Meaning and Truth* (1940), ch. 23, and a reply from Dewey, "Propositions, Warranted Assertibility and Truth," reprinted in *Problems of Men*, ch. 10.

The philosophers summarized the grounds of their difference: "The difference between us has its basic source in different views of the nature of experience, which in turn is correlated with our different conceptions of the connection existing between man and the rest

result of pressure, Dewey was led to a restatement of his theory of truth, according to which a notion of correspondence was restored to grace. The statement remains one of the few and most direct of Dewey's pronouncements on truth.[116]

> My own view takes correspondence in the operational sense it bears in all cases except the unique epistemological case of an alleged relation between a "subject" and an "object": the meaning, namely, of *answering*, as a key answers to conditions imposed by a lock, or as two correspondences "answer" each other; or, in general, as a reply is an adequate answer to a question or a criticism—as, in short, a *solution* answers the requirements of a *problem*. On this view, both partners in "correspondence" are open and above board, instead of one of them being forever out of experience and the other in it by way of a "percept" or whatever.

Dewey concludes:

> In the sense of correspondence as operational and behavioral (the meaning which has definite parallels in ordinary experience), I hold that my *type* of theory is the only one entitled to be called a correspondence theory of truth.[117]

Nonetheless, we are obliged to note in passing that while this account of truth is clearer than others, it is not clear enough. Thus, the reader has a right to know precisely *what* it is that "corresponds" under this correspondence theory of truth. We are told that the correspondence is one of "answering"; but *what* is it that answers and to what does it answer? Is it a sentence (or sentence utterance)? Is it a proposition, a judgment, a belief that answers to—and thus corresponds with or to facts, or to other sentences (or utterances) or propositions? Dewey tells us that what *answers*, answers *as* a key, or *as* partners in correspondence, or in general *as* a solution answers a problem. He speaks of the partners in correspondence as—according to this theory—"open and above board." But he does not tell us *what* these partners are. We know only that they are related in ways similar to keys and locks, persons writing one another, and much as a solution answers a problem. This is an instance of Dewey's unfortunate inability to keep important philosophic convictions from working against and marring expository procedures. The reason why we come upon this awkward reticence in stating *what* it is that corresponds in this theory of truth is that Dewey is laboring to avoid attributions of truth to

---

of the world," Dewey, *Problems of Men*, p. 351. "The main difference between Dr. Dewey and me is that he judges a belief by its effects, whereas I judge it by its causes where a past occurrence is concerned," Russell, *A History of Western Philosophy*, p. 862. For the literature and discussion of the two theories, see H. S. Thayer, "Two Theories of Truth."

[116] —Even though Dewey had long made similar comments on truth. Thus, in a characteristic comment concerning the truth of ideas, Dewey writes: "suppose one uses the idea —that is to say, the present facts projected into a whole in the light of absent facts—as a guide of action. . . . one may say, my idea was right, it was in accord with facts; it agrees with reality. That is, acted upon sincerely it has led to the desired conclusion; it has *through action* worked out the state of things which it contemplated or intended. The agreement, correspondence, is between purpose, plan, and its own execution, fulfillment. . . . Just how does such agreement differ from success?" *Essays in Experimental Logic*, p. 240. This chapter of the *Essays*, "The Control of Ideas by Facts," was reprinted from an article of the same title, published in 1907.

[117] "Propositions, Warranted Assertibility and Truth," in *Problems of Men*, pp. 343–344.

propositions or sentences and utterances. *This* theory of truth is not linguistic—that is, truth is not (or not exclusively[118]) a property of sentences or linguistic behavior. Truth characterizes the conditions that correspond *as* a solution answers a problem.

What it is that corresponds is (to answer our own question above) a whole coordinated set of activities—either projected or actually carried out. This sense of "corresponding" conditions has come to us in earlier remarks and particularly in viewing, in § 38 above, Dewey's early theory of action. As remains to be suggested below, the correspondence relation in Dewey's theory is one holding among *situations*.

This statement of his theory of truth also casts some light on a cardinal doctrine of Dewey's theory of knowledge: inquiry effects an existential transformation of subject matters inquired into; knowledge brings about a change in the thing known.

Concerning this part of his theory Dewey has sometimes been compared with Marx,[119] who wrote: "It is in practice [*Praxis*] that man must demonstrate the truth, that is, the reality and power, the this-sidedness of his thinking . . . The philosophers have only interpreted the world in different ways; but what has become more urgent is to change it."[120] But it is not at all clear what insight this comparison is supposed to supply. For Dewey, philosophic interpretations *have* altered the world, often as obstacles to intellectual progress. And for Dewey, as for any sane thinker, the real problem is how to alter the world for the better. But the method Dewey proposes for this purpose is to be found in the writings of Dewey, not in those of Marx.

Dewey, like Peirce, once invoked a Biblical phrase in expressing his instrumentalist view of truth: "By their fruits shall ye *know* them."[121] However, in the present climate of Western opinion, critics of Dewey have found it convenient to classify him as a disciple of Marx rather than of Christ.

In any event, in speaking of knowledge (or the result of inquiry) as effecting a change in the things known, Dewey is not to be taken as arguing that knowing is an occult force mysteriously transforming the object of knowledge so that we are barred from "really" knowing what it is "in itself." Rather, our understanding of and relation to conditions that are *problematic* is not the "same" as our relation to those conditions when viewed according to a known or hypothesized *solution*. The conditions that make for a puzzle are not the "same" after we know the answer. For, before we know the answer, the conditions are puzzling; and after we know the answer, the conditions are not puzzling, and we may sometimes wonder why we thought them puzzling at all.

[118] This qualification arises because, since sentences and propositions are counted in among the means, the partial apparatus and techniques of inquiry, they may share in truth, i.e., in correspondence, but are not exclusive bearers of truth.

[119] E.g., by Russell in Schilpp, p. 143, and *Freedom Versus Organization*, p. 221.

[120] *On Feuerbach*, II–XI, pp. 70–72.

[121] In *Reconstruction in Philosophy*, p. 156.

But there is a more fundamental sense in which inquiry brings about an "existential transformation" of the constituents of a problematic situation. A problematic situation, we have seen, is one in which action and thought encounter obstacles in the execution of some course of conduct and the achievement of some purpose. To choose a simple illustration, suppose we are walking through the woods and we discover we have wandered from the path. We are lost and the problem is how to find a way to familiar terrain. Trees, stones, and shrubs confront us suddenly as the locus of our predicament; they are refractory impositions on how we are to proceed. But they are also the conditions to be reckoned with if we are to find our way out. Now on closer study of these same conditions, perhaps by retracing our footsteps and taking note of certain trees and stones we recall having passed earlier, the "same" constituents of the problem begin to serve as signs of possible directions to be taken—or avoided—in finding our way. The trees and stones remain the "same" as independently existing objects; but in the situation of which they are parts, and the relationships that become established among them in our deliberations, they acquire an evidential function serving to suggest a course of action. The erstwhile obstacles and elements of the problematic situation are now transformed in the process of inquiry into instruments which—in conjunction with other conditions—contribute to the formation of a solution of the problem.

Finally, as Dewey points out, in the operation of inquiry various features of the situation and its elements are selected and modified; certain traits become of heightened significance, others are relegated to the background in their bearing, accordingly, in utility and relevance for the developing inquiry. The anticipation of new data and observations, and the introduction of activities of observation and experiment, since these are existential operations, "modify the prior existential situation."

Truth, then, for Dewey seems to refer in general to those conditions which make the difference between what is a problem and what a solution; *truth* refers to just that set of conditions and operations which renders a problematic situation unproblematic.

§ *41.   Inquiry as Evaluation*[122]

James regarded truth as a species of *good.* Dewey agreed, with qualifications which cannot be adequately covered here (but see Part Four, Chapter Three), that establishing warranted conclusions of inquiry is an act of evaluation. The pattern of inquiry reviewed earlier can be interpreted as the stages of a reflective evaluation of a situation with a view to discovering what consequences, if insti-

---

[122] The present section describes how inquiry is an evaluative procedure. Later, in Part IV, ch. 3, the theory of valuation and moral judgment is discussed and examined in greater detail.

tuted, will answer to what is "needed" or "lacking." In this respect inquiry is a continuous activity of transforming existent situations, in which deficiencies and wants and specific moral perplexities are felt, by bringing about conditions that contribute to sufficiency, stability, and satisfaction. Relative to the former conditions, these latter are specific *goods*; relative to the situation in which deficiencies and ills are problems, inquiry is directed to finding "the right course of action, the right good."

Discovery of the right course of action, in such cases, requires an evaluation of inquiry itself. For Dewey, judgment, with which inquiry closes, involves an appraisal of the adequacy and "value" of the intermediate course of inquiry and of the propositions that are being prepared for a final settlement.[123] Judgment includes an evaluation of the means being formulated in inquiry (i.e., propositions) with respect to their relevance to the problem and to its solution. The warranted assertion of inquiry is the result of judgment; it is the evaluated solution terminating inquiry. In this sense inquiry concludes with what *ought* to be or is the *right* solution to the problem. In that sense, too, all inquiry is evaluative and aims at the establishment of a good. The good aimed for is "the meaning experienced . . . in a unified orderly release in action."[124] Not all situations are of an obvious "moral" character. But all inquiries are evaluations of situations and of the bearing of future consequences in the attainment of goods.

For Dewey, inquiry is not only essential to the moral reconstruction of experience; it is a paradigm of moral activity itself.

A moral situation is one in which judgment and choice are required antecedently to overt action. The practical meaning of the situation—that is to say the action needed to satisfy it—is not self-evident. It has to be searched for. There are conflicting desires and alternative apparent goods. What is needed is to find the right course of action, the right good. Hence inquiry is exacted. . . . This inquiry is intelligence. . . .

Moral goods and ends exist only when something has to be done. The fact that something has to be done proves that there are deficiencies, evils in the existent situation. . . . Consequently the good of the situation has to be discovered, projected and attained on the basis of the exact defect and trouble to be rectified.

. . . The process of growth, of improvement and progress, rather than the static outcome and result, becomes the significant thing. Not health as an end fixed once for all, but the needed improvement in health—a continual process—is the end and good. The end is no longer a terminus or limit to be reached. It is the active process of transforming the existent situation. Not perfection as a final goal, but the ever-enduring process of perfecting, maturing, refining is the aim of living. Honesty, industry, temperance, justice, like health, wealth and learning, are not goods to be possessed as they would be if they expressed fixed ends to be attained.

---

[123] *Logic: The Theory of Inquiry*, p. 122.

[124] *Human Nature and Conduct*, p. 210. But the full passage is important: "Good consists in the meaning that is experienced to belong to an activity when conflict and entanglement of various incompatible impulses and habits terminate in a unified orderly release in action."

They are directions of change in the quality of experience. Growth itself is the only moral "end."[125]

Inquiry is a sign and condition of human growth. It was not surprising that Dewey should find in inquiry the possibilities for a genuine religious outlook—one wanting only an imaginative projection of the essentially communal function of inquiry and its premium on socially shared experience. Nor was Dewey ineffective in giving expression to this intellectual deliverance; it was not a resuscitation of the eighteenth-century religion of Reason, but a reasonable faith in intelligence. In place of the divisive forces in modern society, effecting and preserving intellectual and social-class differences in the dry husks of orthodoxy, inquiry, as thus interpreted by Dewey, is a radical agent of unification and social cohesion. In inquiry men achieve communion.

In the very definition of inquiry, its role is cast as the bringing of order and coherence into otherwise conflicting and discordant experience. Coherent experience is communicative and communal. For Dewey, religion has its vital source and exercise in the shared experience of the community. Inquiry, since it is the compelling resource of human growth and renewal of values, is thus a fit object of religious reverence; just as its continuous workings are essential conditions of a humane and liberal existence.

§ 42. Some Problems in Pragmatism

It is hoped that this account of Dewey's theory of inquiry and truth is clear enough to dispel some of the more long-standing doubts as to what he was saying and what he attempted to achieve.

Two doubts, in particular, were expressed against Dewey's theory by critics of pragmatism: (1) he failed to explain judgments of past events; (2) he interpreted judgments of truth to be matters of personal satisfaction.

The first of these doubts rested upon misundertsandings concerning Dewey's notion of *experience* and his view of judgment as transforming or modifying the subject matters judged (§ 40). It was thought that if all we can know is what *we* can experience, we can never know anything of remote historical occurrences or of geological epochs before human life. In addition, if the conclusions of inquiry transform the subject matter inquired into, how does inquiry about, say, the date of Caesar's death "transform" that event? The answer to the last question is that inquiry into the date of Caesar's death has no effect on Caesar, his dying, or the time of death. What is transformed is the *question* (or, strictly, what is taken to be *questionable*) about that date and the conditions that made it a problem. It is *these* conditions that get transformed by inquiry (see the end of § 40). Dewey's reply to the first question was to point out that inquiry into remote past

---

[125] *Reconstruction in Philosophy*, pp. 163–164, 169, 177. The special moral significance of the idea of *growth*—an idea central to Dewey's theories of education (see § 37 above) and valuation (see Part IV, ch. 3 below), but often criticized—was derived primarily from T. H. Green. See note 76, § 98 below, and on Green, Appendix 1, sec. C below.

(or future) occurrences *begins* "in the actual presence of a problem." The alleged and remote event calls for inquiry if it is "an actual constituent of some experienced problematic situation."[126] Hypotheses concerning the event and the hypothetical solution to the question asked about the event are based upon what is at present known and the available information concerning the event. Any inquiry begins, after posing of the problem, with a fund of such available information. In the light of what is known and inquired into, an inquiry may conclude with a hypothesis (or extrapolation) concerning conditions that existed before men asked questions about them. We need not suppose that we are departing from experience or necessarily transcending the limits of what we now know in talking intelligently about portions of the universe or history where no human inquirer was, is, or will be present to make direct observations. Where we go astray is in supposing that because some unexperienced events do occur, and have occurred, we cannot acknowledge this much or treat it intelligently except by departing from what we know about experience. We forget that talk about unexperienced events makes sense only when it is prompted and controlled by what we do experience, that our talk about remote and unobserved happenings is neither remote nor compounded of unobserved happenings, that discussions of unobserved and once unrecorded facts attain a degree of plausibility only by many a side glance at facts recorded and observed.

It is the second of these doubts, concerning the pragmatist's view of truth, that has engendered a controversy running about as long as the history of pragmatism. Some of the movements of the controversy have claimed our attention several times in earlier pages and scarcely need going over once more. That unclear and debatable issues concerning pragmatic truth should have ever gotten so firmly entrenched as to go the whole way in the evolution of pragmatism is now a historical curiosity.

Dewey often used the language of James, saying that "the true is that which works," or that which proves "successful" or "satisfactory." He thus became the heir to many of the objections that had been made to James's doctrine of truth. Most of these objections can be summed up in one argument which, historically, represents the paradigm case against pragmatism: if ideas or beliefs are true or not depending on whether or not they "work" or their consequences are "successful" or "satisfactory," then (a) we can never know whether an idea is true or false, since we can never know *all* of the consequences or far-reaching effects; (b) the same idea can be both true and false, since it may prove satisfactory at one time, unsatisfactory at others, or may satisfy some persons while dissatisfying others; (c) we can never know whether the pragmatic definition of truth is justifiable or useful, since to try to judge that definition will require making true statements about it and its consequences—and true statements in this case will be ones that

126 "All that is necessary upon my view is that an astronomical or geological epoch be an actual constituent of some experienced problematic situation. I am not, logically speaking, obliged to indulge in any cosmological speculation about those epochs, because, on my theory, any proposition about them is of the nature of what A. E. Bentley, in well-chosen terms, calls 'extrapolation,' under certain conditions, be it understood, perfectly legitimate, but nevertheless an exptrapolation," *Problems of Men*, p. 351.

work or have satisfactory consequences, and this, for reasons (a) and (b), leads to an infinite regress and insuperable difficulties.

The paradigm case, if taken seriously, might lead one to suspicions about the sanity of the spokesmen for pragmatism.

Thus consider the following example. Suppose you are asked, "Did you have a poached egg for breakfast?" Most persons, when asked, will try to remember. But the pragmatist will have to take time out for an experiment. He will first try to believe that he *has* eaten a poached egg and observe the consequences of his belief. He will next believe the negative of his first belief and consider its consequences. He will then compare the consequences of the two beliefs and his answer to the question will depend on which of the consequences he finds most "satisfactory." This way of getting at truth is surely absurd. It is not only absurd, but impossible for the logical reasons (a), (b), and (c) just given. What is worse (for the pragmatist), this kind of example[127] is not only logically convincing as dissuading would-be pragmatists, it is very persuasive as rhetoric. For few philosophers could long stand the spectacle of that most austere and esteemed abstraction, a theory of truth, going to pieces over a mere matter of poached eggs.

On the larger social and ethical consequences of pragmatism, the paradigm case alarms us to these dangers: truth and falsehood will be determined by the desires and interests of men with power; the state, police, or politicians will decide what consequences of what ideas are "successful" or "satisfactory." Pragmatically, then, pragmatism is a socially disastrous philosophy.

The paradigm case, like the doctrine it opposes, is no longer a subject of much contemporary philosophic interest. As remarked, these are matters now of possible historical curiosity; not the least a curiosity because the paradigm case is a paradigm case of philosophical misunderstanding and confusion for which, and for reasons that have been indicated earlier, pragmatists and non-pragmatist critics were alike unwittingly responsible.

What is most wrong with the paradigm is an undeclared and uncritical use of the concepts of 'successful' or 'satisfactory' consequences of ideas or beliefs as somehow referring to private, willful, subjective episodes in the Mind.[128] But for

---

[127] Adopted from Russell, *History of Western Philosophy*, p. 825. The same kind of illustrative objection we saw taking place earlier, cf. § 32.

[128] Russell, who has long subscribed to the above paradigm case, and has most effectively helped to construct it, has also tried to clarify the pragmatist's position for him by showing that "satisfactory consequences" may be defined as "desired results": "A hypothesis is called 'true' when it leads the person entertaining it to acts which have effects he desires," Schilpp, p. 150; also p. 148. Russell has no difficulty showing the absurd consequences of the proposed clarification, Schilpp, pp. 152–153. It is essential, if the full effect of the resulting absurdity is to be preserved, that the phrase "effects he desires" be taken to refer to a *mental* (or emotional) event of approval or liking—i.e., a person's "desire"—supposedly related to a *physical* event, i.e., the "effects" of his "acts." Furthermore, we are to think of "mental events," such as willing, feeling, liking, as operating by a largely mysterious mechanism, vaguely analogous to physical subject matters, but capricious, mostly unobserved, and often apparently arbitrary in its workings. Desires are, in short, *subjective*; they are denizens of the internal world called *Mind*. It follows that to call something true because it has "desired results" is absurd because desires are too private, fleeting, and unruly, too ill-equipped to support or sustain judgments at all.

It does not seem to have occurred to Russell that Dewey's conception of "satisfactory consequences" was not to be explained by an eighteenth-century psychology of Mind and

Dewey, satisfaction and desiring are not "subjective" events and are not to be viewed according to an early and outmoded mentalistic psychology. The concept of 'satisfactory consequences' need not be construed as replaceable by concepts descriptive of mental conduct, 'desires,' 'wishes,' and the like: nor need it be construed as synonymous with certain expressions (like "effects someone desires") designating purely subjective mental events, as if the Cartesian concept of mind was the only available basis for a manageable and intelligible use of such language.

In Dewey's theory of inquiry it is a mistake to interpret "satisfactory consequences of ideas" as somehow entailing "subjective" or "private" items of behavior in contradistinction from something else called "objective." For ideas, or hypotheses, must *satisfy* the conditions of a *situation* which is problematic.[129] The consequences of ideas are satisfactory or not, relative to the conditions of some specific problem situation. This sense of 'satisfactory' does not call for trading on a theory of subjective mental events, nor does it call for a subjectively directed mental conduct language at all—no more so than when one is said to "satisfy" the requirements of an examination. When a man satisfies the requirements for military service, it would scarcely be credible to say that this means he has produced "desired effects" or an instance of *liking* in either his own mind or in that of his examining officer.

The trouble with the paradigm case against pragmatism lies in its defective strategy in relying upon defective assumptions. Yet to venture to remove the threat by exposing it in this fashion is not to abolish all lingering doubts about pragmatism. For there is even the unresolved question of why pragmatists should have such difficulty in exorcising the paradigm once and for all. It is ironic, considering that pragmatism began as a program for achieving conceptual clarity, that pragmatists should run into difficulties in making themselves understood. Conceptual confusion is always an ingrate; around most when least wanted and most effective when least suspected.

---

subjective mental events. A *desire* need not be construed as a *subjective* part of what Ryle aptly calls "the ghost in the machine." For a clear statement of his analysis of desire, see Dewey's *Theory of Valuation*, pp. 13 ff., and below, Part IV, ch. 3.

[129] In light of the discussion above, § 40, an idea has satisfactory consequences when, given conditions C_1, the idea leads to or describes conditions C_2, such that C_2 answers or resolves C_1. Thus, Dewey's reply to the paradigm case, as developed by Russell: "The interpretation Mr. Russell gives to consequences relates them to personal desire. The net outcome is attribution to me of generalized wishful thinking as a definition of truth. Mr. Russell proceeds first by converting a doubtful situation into a personal doubt, although the difference between the two things is repeatedly pointed out by me. I have even explicitly stated that a personal doubt is pathological unless it is a reflection of a *situation* which is problematic. Then by changing doubt into private discomfort, truth is identified with the removal of this discomfort. The only desire that enters, according to my view, is desire to remove as honestly and impartially as possible the problem involved in the situation. 'Satisfaction' is satisfaction of the conditions prescribed by the problem. Personal satisfaction may enter in as it arises when my job is well done according to the requirements of the job itself; but it does not enter in any way into the determination of validity, because, on the contrary, it is conditioned by that determination." Schilpp. p. 572.

CHAPTER FOUR

C. I. Lewis

§ 43. Conceptualistic Pragmatism

Peirce maintained that the fundamental hypothesis of "the method of science" is that "there are Real things, whose characters are entirely independent of our opinions about them."[1] This assumption, he argued, made the method of science unique and endowed it with its chief value and glory. For, in comparison with several other possible ways in which men have proceeded to form and defend their beliefs, only the method of science presents a real distinction between a right and wrong way of fixing them, and an objective criterion of their being true and false. In the process of investigating beliefs and in critical pronouncements upon single and competing beliefs, the assumption of Real things serves as an external condition of authentification and validation based on the coinciding of opinions with facts. And this is a standard uninfluenced by human opinion. Other methods of fixing our beliefs, lacking any acknowledged external standard of critical validation of beliefs, Peirce argued, were essentially arbitrary, and belief becomes settled by personal whim, by fancy, or by brute power.

Now granting that scientific progress is conditioned by some such commitment to an external and unassuageable condition of truth of beliefs, to Real things, nonetheless, Real things do not happen to be first encountered in a state of naked innocence unmolested by interpretive intrusions. Our contact with, our assumptions about, Real things do not have that immediate freshness given to a wanderer among the peoples of the South Seas. Our contact with reality is more devious and designedly complex, more like the coming of missionaries to the natives. Peirce stressed this fact as well, pointing out that what we suppose or assert to be *real* is the result of our socially shared, interpretive interactions with the world. What is thought to be real and the character of real things is determined by inquiry. It is the community, the community of scientific inquirers,

[1] "Fixation of Belief" (1877). See above, § 23.

that fixes the conception of the real. Of a supposed real itself "there" and "raw," we can say little or nothing at all: it "consists in the agreement that the whole community would eventually come to," says Peirce (§ 24).

These notions of a *reality* impervious to our declarations about it; of *experience* as a medium of vital sentient linkages to real things; and of *interpretation*, our socially evolved ways of talking about real things—these notions surely have been prominent in the reflections of philosophers. This we have viewed in Part One; and have also seen in those earlier pages why these notions, if they have not exhausted the modern philosophers' stock in trade, have been conspicuously in supply and in demand.

The same notions sustain the posing of the critical problem (or problems) of knowledge so central in modern philosophic thought guided by Descartes and Locke, Hume and Kant. After Kant's own way of stating and resolving the problem (§§ 10, 11) and his labors in behalf of a secure and equitable place for knowledge *and* faith—science and values—we noticed an onrush of new thought addressed to a new stating of the old problem and a trading again with the notions of reality, experience, and interpretation. Notably in Fichte (§ 16), a powerful form of voluntarism, practicalism, and signs of irrationalism replace or transform the Kantian apparatus of Pure and Practical Reason. In Schopenhauer, as in the whole Protestant tradition, the emphasis is upon Will. Will is primary and intellect is secondary, a means and servant of the Will. Intellect is necessary to Will in establishing relations with the external world. Thought and intellect are thus viewed as functions of an organism, as among the ways organisms survive and establish themselves and secure their satisfactions in the world. The evolutionary and biological usefulness of knowledge, of thought, is often stressed by the post-Kantian romantic philosophers. Nietzsche frequently expresses the idea: "knowledge works as an instrument of power"; "consciousness extends only so far as it is useful." For Nietzsche, logic and the categories of reason are "means to the adjustment of the world for utilitarian ends." Clearly it was not John Dewey who first invented the idea that thinking is a form of organic adjustment.

The pragmatism of C. I. Lewis is a major contemporary attempt to develop a theory of knowledge in which old dilemmas in the controversy between empiricists and rationalists could be avoided and, at the same time, new developments in logic and mathematics could be incorporated. Lewis drew significantly upon basic ideas in the analysis of thought, meaning, and experience worked out by Peirce, James, and Dewey. It is to Peirce, however, that he was most indebted and, perhaps through Peirce, to Berkeley. Lewis' "conceptual pragmatism," as he called his position, is not simply a return to Peirce; but it includes a carefully constructed projection of some of Peirce's sketched intentions to create a critical philosophy of knowledge and communication—a theory of signs and inquiry.

Peirce's emphasis on the interpretative character of thought (on signs and interpretants); his interest in the logical structures and behavioral patterns that constitute the *meanings* of ideas; his theory of meaning as carrying a futurative reference, a predictive component anticipative of future experience and a reference to conceived action—these themes are reflected and developed in Lewis' writings.

But Lewis, like Peirce, James, and Dewey, was also responsive to the reactions to Kant in German philosophy. The nineteenth century displayed a suggestive variety of interpretations of mind and thought as purposive and practical functions of the live creature maintaining itself in a changing environment. These, as has been suggested above (and §§ 15–17), were formative ideas in the evolution of pragmatism. In addition to these influences, Lewis, as Peirce before him, was aware of the merits of Berkeley's doctrine of ideas as signs, of his view of the data of experience as significant according to certain established modes of sign-ifying, and his evident anticipation and use of a verifiability criterion of the meaning of language (or linguistic signs).[2]

Lewis' long and distinguished teaching career at Harvard, his contact with Royce, his familiarity with the ideas and problems of the New Realist group, were all factors in the shaping of his philosophic outlook. But it is Lewis' own distinctive theory of knowledge which will concern us in the pages to follow.

§ 44. Logic and Order

Lewis' theory of knowledge and especially its cardinal and most novel doctrine— the pragmatic conception of the a priori—was the result of reflections and conclusions first arising within the study of mathematical logic. One of the many valuable results of the achievement of Russell and Whitehead's great Principia Mathematica was the impetus it imparted to further studies in logic. The first volume of Principia appeared in 1910, the second and third volumes followed in 1912 and 1913 respectively. A series of papers by Lewis, commencing in 1912 and culminating in 1918 as Chapter Five of his Survey of Symbolic Logic, set forth a critical reaction and alternative to a fundamental idea embodied in Russell and Whitehead's work. The alternative became a new system of modal logic known as "strict implication."[3]

Lewis' system of strict implication was, at least in part, initiated out of a certain confusion created by the authors of Principia concerning the notion of implication. Confusion is not usually the most promising source of good ideas; but sometimes it is, and this time it was. An added difference that ensued in the controversy between Russell and Lewis had its source in respectively disparate attitudes toward constructing a logical system or calculus of sentences. This was a difference obscure at the time but evident enough in retrospect. Russell was concerned solely with establishing the thesis that "all pure mathematics follows

[2] For these aspects of Berkeley's thought, see Appendix 5 below.
[3] For fuller statements, see Lewis and Langford, Symbolic Logic, pp. 136–147, and Appendix II, pp. 492–502; Parry, "Modalities in the Survey System of Strict Implication." But see, too, Curry, A Theory of Formal Deducibility.

from purely logical premisses and uses only concepts definable in logical terms."[4] Very important philosophical ideas, or ideas with important philosophical consequences which Russell developed in other writings, were made subordinate to this one express aim. Thus, the theory of descriptions, the theory of types, the notions of *individual, identity, extensionality*,[5] and the like, all of paramount philosophic interest, were treated according to the purpose stated. The philosophic defense of such philosophic commitments and theorizing as occurs in the course of *Principia* is negligible and passingly pragmatic: achievement of the end objective is the recurring justification. Lewis, however, had other and broader objectives in constructing his system. The derivation of mathematics from a system of logic, since *Principia* appeared as a realization of this ideal anyway, would count as but one among these. Lewis was interested in probing the nature of *systems*, the "analytic character and abstractness of exact systems" playing crucial roles not only in pure mathematics, but in physics and geometry and, though obscure and diffident at being uncovered, in ordinary knowledge of the world.

In taking up the study of logic, Lewis was encouraged and helped by Josiah Royce, which he later warmly acknowledged.[6] Royce had grown increasingly interested in mathematical logic as a way of investigating and neatly expressing types of order. Types of order, for Royce, were, as he put it, possible systems of the Theory of Order.[7] Royce constructed what he regarded as the Theory of Order in 1905. That system, which he called system Σ, he described as having "an order which is determined entirely by the fundamental laws of logic, and by one additional principle thus mentioned. . . ." The one additional principle was a version of Dedekind's definition of a dense continuous series which Royce saw applying to "facts," to activities, and to possible modes of action.[8] These, Royce pointed out, were not usually regarded as logical entities. "The whole system of the world," he wrote, "may be viewed as made up of various different systems." Feelings, deeds, persons, modes of conduct are interpreted as "series" interwoven into Systems of series.[9] The idea of *series* was for Royce the key to expressing order and relations among the facts of the world.[10] The system Σ was viewed as possessing a structure such that all types of order of wide variety might be

4 This is Russell's latest reminiscence on his motive in *My Philosophical Development*, p. 74. Similar statements can be found in his other writings.
5 See *Principia*, Vol. I, Appendix C.
6 Preface, *Mind and the World Order*, p. vii.
7 Royce's long chapter, "The Principles of Logic," in *Encyclopaedia of the Philosophical Sciences*, p. 120. Reprinted in Robinson, p. 373.
8 "Principles of Logic," pp. 130–131; or in Robinson, p. 373. Also, in the same context: "The principle corresponding to the geometrical principle which defines dense series of points . . . *does* apply to a set of objects. . . . This set may be defined as 'certain possible modes of action that are open to any rational being who can act at all, and who can also reflect upon his own possible modes of action.' " See also, *The World and the Individual*, 2nd series, pp. 90–91: "between any two facts there are to be found various series of intermediaries," etc.
9 *The World and the Individual*, 2nd series, p. 90.
10 *Ibid.*, p. 72: "To my mind, as I may at once say, our best single word for expressing what is essential to lawful order in the world of facts is the term series. Facts are subject to law in so far as they are arranged in definable series, or in systems of interwoven serial orders."

specifiable within it; it was to include "infinitely numerous continuous systems."[11]

In the supplementary essay to *The World and the Individual*,[12] Royce discusses some of the features of an infinite system of series. He speaks of the system as one in which the system is similar to a part of itself, or "self representative."[13] His well-known illustration of a self-representative system was that of a supposedly "perfect" and minutely detailed map of England, the map having been executed inside England. Since the map must be included in the area it represents in full detail, the map will contain a representation of itself. That is, one constituent part in the hypothetical map would be a map of England. But then, if the map, along with other details of terrain, contains a representation of a map, that second map will contain within it another map, and so on ad infinitum. A similar "system" is found in those cases where a manufacturer fixes a label on his product, and the label contains a picture of the product. Looking carefully at the picture of the product in the label, one sees a label on it with a picture of the product, and so on, as fine as print can get or the eye can see.

Part of Royce's concern in working out a general theory of Order, of which particular systems (of science, conduct, etc.) would be constituents, was the hope of discovering those concepts necessary to each of these systems and those necessary to them all. These latter, concepts necessary to all systems or all rational activity, would, if they could be disclosed, constitute the ultimate categories. These last would be the ultimate modes of action and meaning through which thinkers, in their otherwise individual ways, verge upon a common reality.[14] In

[11] "The Relation of the Principles of Logic to the Foundations of Geometry," reprinted in Robinson, pp. 379–441; for the passages quoted, p. 386. For discussions of the system, see C. I. Lewis, *Survey*, pp. 366–367, and his paper, "Types of Order and the System Sigma"; Joergensen, *Treatise*, Vol. I, pp. 260–266.

Royce stated his purpose in constructing system Σ, drawing upon the ideas of the English mathematician A. B. Kempe (see Royce's introduction to the above paper) as follows (Robinson, p. 386): "What I aim in the end to show is that all serial and other ordinal relations known to logic and to geometry, and all the operations known to both, so far as they are pure exact sciences, are ultimately reducible to assertions that certain entities do, while certain entities do not stand to one another in the perfectly symmetrical O-relation." The O-relation is "the relation in which (if we were talking of the possible chances open to one who had to decide upon a course of action) any set of *exhaustive but, in their entirety, inconsistent choices* would stand to one another," p. 385.

[12] I.e., 1st Series.

[13] "Self representative" or a system "similar" to a part of itself is Royce's way of using ideas analogous (though vaguely) to that of one-to-one correspondence in Peirce and Dedekind's method of defining an infinite series, viz., as a class having a one-to-one correspondence with a proper subclass. Dedekind, as Royce notes *The World and the Individual, 1st series* (p. 510), uses *ähnlich*, 'similar,' to refer to a one-to-one correspondence between systems or classes.

Roughly, the Peirce-Dedekind definition of an infinite class is this: If for any two classes *A* and *B*, all the members of *A* are members of *B* and at least one member of *B* is not a member of *A*, then *A* is a *proper subclass* of *B*. Now *B* is an infinite class when there is a one-to-one correspondence between it and its proper subclass (i.e., between the members of *B* and the members of *A*). See Church, p. 344.

[14] Thus, in Part III of his *Encyclopaedia* article, "The Principles of Logic," Royce begins by arguing that two concepts "absolutely essential to the Theory of Order" are *class* and *relation*. These are used in the definition of every type of order, and "their necessity depends upon the fact that without them no rational activity of any kind is possible," p. 120, or in Robinson, p. 363. Some pages on Royce describes the problem of the theory of Order as a new form of the Deduction of the Categories.

an address of 1908, Royce summed up this concern—this "absolute pragmatism" as he called it:

> As a fact our whole interpretation of our experience is determined, in a sense akin to that which Kant defined, by certain modes of our own activity, whose significance is transcendental, even while their whole application is empirical. These modes of our activity make all our empirical sciences logically possible. Meanwhile it need not surprise us to find that Kant's method of defining these modes of our activity was not adequate, and that a new logic is giving us, in this field, new light. The true nature of these necessary modes of our activity becomes most readily observable to us in case we rightly analyze the methods and concepts, not of our own empirical, but rather our mathematical sciences. For in these sciences our will finds its freest expression. And yet for that very reason in these sciences the absoluteness of the truth which the will defines is most obvious. The new logic to which I refer is especially a study of the logic of mathematics.[15]

This limited excursion into Royce's thought is not irrelevant to our gaining some view of the background of Lewis' philosophy of knowledge. It is not an accident that, but for the appeal to transcendental significance and absoluteness of truth, the above passage might have been written by Lewis. Lewis several times quotes with approval Royce's comment that the a priori or necessary categories represent our ways of acting.[16] At any rate, Lewis shows much agreement with Royce in construing categories—our fundamental principles of interpreting reality—as modes of initiative and action, and in stressing, in the theory of knowledge, the decisive role of certain a priori or necessary conditions of organizing and relating categorical modes of interpretation. But Lewis' analysis of knowledge, of the nature of abstract and systematic thought, emphasizes a pragmatic condition in all conceptualization in place of Royce's transcendental vision of ultimate significance and truth. To this pragmatism we shall shortly turn.

For the moment let us recall that Lewis' main criticism of the system of *Principia* was directed to the particular construction put upon the idea of *implication* between propositions. The critical issue, as suggested earlier, was confused. But that same confusion helped Lewis to recognize a plurality of logics and abstract systems by which subject matters could be ordered. Still, some systems and some a priori principles among all possible ones were viewed as more reasonable and natural. Why and how? A brief look at the original controversy over implication may throw light on these questions and Lewis' response to them in his later theory of knowledge.

The source of confusion in the initial controversy over implication was due to Russell and Whitehead's account in *Principia* of the horseshoe symbol, '$\supset$.' The symbol was described as the sign of "implication" or "material implication." Treating the letters 'p,' 'q,' etc., as propositional variables, the expression '$p \supset q$'

---

[15] "The Problem of Truth in the Light of Recent Discussion," p. 238; in Robinson, p. 89.
[16] E.g., *Mind and the World Order*, p. 101; "A Pragmatic Conception of the a priori," in Feigl and Sellars, p. 286.

was read "p implies q" or "p materially implies q." Material implication was, via a long tradition, given this construction: '$p \supset q$' to be taken as 'if p then q' or 'not (p and not q).' It happens that among the propositions or theorems that are "immediate consequences of the primitive propositions" of *Principia* are two resulting from this construction. One is

$$*2.02 \qquad q. \supset p. \supset q$$

and is explained: "*I.e.*, q implies that p implies q, *i.e.*, a true proposition is implied by any proposition." The other is

$$*2.21 \qquad \sim p. \supset p. \supset q.$$

This is explained: "a false proposition implies any proposition."

Lewis, among others,[17] rightly objected to these explanations on grounds of their excessive deviation from any ordinary sense of *implication*. The objection thus felt, that these were odd examples of implication, was well taken. The source of the oddity, however, escaped detection. Lewis went on to characterize the above as "paradoxes of implication."[18] This they were not. The air of paradox or abnormality attaching to the above theorems is due only to Russell and Whitehead's unfortunate choice of the phrase "material implication" and their reading of "implies" for the conditional sign between 'p' and 'q.' Russell and Whitehead had confused the conditional 'if . . . , then . . . ,' belonging between statements, and the verb 'implies,' most clearly belonging between the names of statements.[19] For example, consider the following. The statements

(1) 'if it rains every night then it rained last night' and 'it rains every night $\supset$ it rained last night'

make sense. So does

(2) 'it rains every night' implies 'it rained last night.'

But the statements in (1) are about rain and night, while that of (2) is about statements.

Not to recognize a difference between statements like those of (1) and that of (2), or not to keep the distinction clear, is to invite serious confusion over *using* expressions and *talking about* them. It was just this confusion that weaves through some of the informal discussion and explanatory passages in *Principia;* it does not affect the technical theory as elaborated.

---

[17] See G. E. Moore's comments, *Philosophical Studies*, pp. 295–297.

[18] For one of Russell's replies, see *Introduction to Mathematical Philosophy*, pp. 153–154. A clear statement of Lewis' objections to material implication in *Principia*, and a defense of strict implication, is found in his paper of 1917 (in reply to criticisms by Norbert Wiener), "The Issues Concerning Material Implication."

[19] The present discussion of the point derives from Quine, *Mathematical Logic*, pp. 31–33, and Carnap, *Logical Syntax of Language*, pp. 253–254. See also Quine's excellent historical essay, "Whitehead and the Rise of Modern Logic," esp. p. 141–142. A complicating factor in the controversy over implication is the obscure sense of 'proposition.' If 'implies' belongs between the names of statements, it is not entirely clear if and how *propositions* are capable of *implying* propositions, depending, of course, upon what these latter are.

Lewis, however, while objecting to Russell and Whitehead's interpretation of '$p \supset q$,' perpetuated the confusion over use and mention, i.e., the distinction illustrated by (1) and (2) above. He proceeded to construct a different interpretation of the conditional '$p \supset q$,' calling it "strict implication" and arguing that strict implication more accurately reflects the usual meaning of 'implies.' Lewis explained his sense of the conditional '$p \supset q$' as "p strictly implies q," explaining the latter as "It is not possible that p and not q" or "Necessarily not (p and not q)." For him, 'p strictly implies q' is taken to be the same as 'q is deducible from p.'

One result of Lewis' proposed system of strict implication was the interest it stimulated in modalities, in *possibility* and *necessity*, their meaning as operators on sentences and the roles they play in the organization of logical and linguistic systems.[20] Considering the prominence that modalities had in Peirce's analyses of signs, thought, and experience, Lewis' efforts to formalize a modal language constituted a partial continuation and clarification of Peirce's work. Another effect of Lewis' construction of his logical system was to impress its author with the fact that—as Royce within his monistic continuum of systems had seen—various possible abstract systems and "types of order" can be produced by the effort of thought alone. These systems in their a priori, definitive "logical integrity"[21] represent possible modes of action (as Royce would put it) or, for Lewis, possible concepts and modes of organizing and interpreting possible subject matters and aspects of experience. But the application of concepts thus delineated, indeed, the peculiar organization of some conceptual schemes and the selecting of certain concepts over others result from considerations that are not themselves a priori. A priori truth, Lewis holds, attaches to the analysis of and definitive interrelations among concepts. But working purposes, social needs, and intellectual ends sought and willed, are the *raison d'être* of conceptualization. These ends and working purposes govern crucial choices among and most constructions of conceptual forms and systems.

For Lewis, pragmatism is found in this sphere of conceptualization. The a priori element of knowledge is pragmatic, not the empirical.[22] This now calls for a closer look.

§ 45.   *Mind and World Order*

One of the oldest theories of the origin of language is preserved for us in Genesis 2:

[20] As Quine, in *Mathematical Logic*, p. 32, and *Word and Object*, p. 196, points out, when the distinction between use and mention is carefully observed, Lewis' modal logic becomes descriptive of a mode of statement composition, rather than a structure of implication relations between statements. The statement 'p strictly implies q' becomes a statement about statements: " '$p \supset q$' is analytic."

[21] Cf. Preface, *Mind and the World Order*, p. x.

[22] *Mind and the World Order*, p. 266.

And out of the ground the Lord God formed every beast of the field, and every fowl of the air; and brought them unto Adam to see what he would call them: and whatsoever Adam called every living creature, that was the name thereof. And Adam gave names to all cattle, and to the fowl of the air, and to every beast of the field.

We may notice that a certain arbitrariness and creativity went into this initial phase of naming. God and Adam match their respective repertoires; God made *things*, Adam created their names. Adam was free to give any verbal signs he pleased to the objects on display. But no such arbitrariness characterizes the objects themselves, nor the presentations of them. What the object was, say, a lion, was not Adam's doing; nor were the leonine shape, tawny pelt, tangled mane, and quite audible roar taken as stimulations of Adam's visual and auditory nervous system. We suppose Adam sensitive to stimuli, responding to wavelengths of light and sound. Identifying these stimulations, the sensuously given, with an object before him, we suppose he uttered "Lion!"[23] But neither the lion nor the passing shape and sound being experienced by Adam were made or determined by him. There is, then, in direct experience a given content, a brute immediacy, over which we can ponder and proceed to name, but cannot ponder or name away.

We may go on to suppose, improvising speculatively upon the story of Genesis, that having assigned the name 'lion' to leonine stimuli, thus naming the object the Lord put before him, Adam may gradually have advanced his rudimentary language and understanding of the things about him by certain interpretative modes of assessing repeated stimuli. For these, he finds, are ways of response through which patterns and regularities in the welter of sense impressions become detected and from which inferences and expectations concerning future sorts of experience become possible and irresistible. Adam commences, then, in the art of evolving a conceptual scheme: as the Lord had done before him, Adam makes order out of chaos—in this case, the chaos of immediate sense experience.

In order to construct even the simplest interpretation of some given elemental subject matter, one prerequisite is of particular importance: a prior settlement of certain principles of procedure, certain aims and techniques, necessary to guiding the construction at hand. These principles of procedure are prior to the interpretative scheme, for they represent basic decisions as to how that scheme shall be fashioned; just as in making a map, some procedural rules of mapping precede the drawing of the map, or in sketching a landscape, certain stipulations of horizon and vanishing point precede and guide the sketching. So, in general, the mind supplies the principles and categories by which we proceed to interpret the sensuously given elements of experience. These principles and categories are a priori, as Lewis, whose theory we are following and illustrating, writes:

[23] Since Adam had not yet eaten of the fruit of the tree of knowledge it is doubtful that he had constructed a theory of knowledge. Thus the favorite epistemological distinction over received stimuli and the inferred objects as causes had not occurred to him. 'Lion' somewhat ambiguously names either event.

the a priori is independent of experience, not because it prescribes a form which experience must fit or anticipates some preëstablished harmony of the given with the categories of the mind, but precisely because it prescribes *nothing* to the content of experience. That can only be a priori which is true *no matter what.* What is anticipated is not the given but our attitude toward it; it formulates an uncompelled initiative of mind, our categorical ways of acting.[24]

What the mind is compelled to accept is "given experience, brute fact, the *a posteriori* element in knowledge."[25] A priori truths, then, are necessary according to Lewis, but where 'necessary truth' is opposed to the factually contingent, not as opposed to the voluntary in conduct and thought.

Returning for a moment to our illustration of Adam and his first categorical ways of acting, one might find, among the a priori conditions of Adam's interpretation of experience, the principle of logic and "true no matter what": everything must either be or not be.[26] This principle and others on par with it represent a decision to pursue a certain mode of classifying and analyzing experience. But, as in his manufacturing of names, Adam has not imposed some restriction upon the nature of Eden by thus adopting this principle. True, the principle seems to exclude the very possibility of a lion both being and not being, or simultaneously both being and not being behind a given bush, or a bush at once both concealing and not concealing the lion. But this apparent restriction is due only to ambiguity in the notion of *possibility.* For what might be meant by the "possibility" of a lion both being and not being? (or being and not being behind a bush, etc.). Part of the answer depends upon clarification of the more general notion of 'possible experience,' or 'possible fact.' One influential answer derives from Hume;[27] a possible fact is one which, when asserted to *be* the case, does not entail a contradiction. It is customary to confine contradiction (like truth and falsehood) to *statements,* utterances, or linguistic forms; to what is *asserted* to be or not be, not to what *is.* Experiences or facts admit of neither contradiction nor non-contradiction, neither truth nor falsity. It is rather in what we say, or suppose, or how we describe facts and experiences that contradiction and con-

[24] *Mind and the World Order,* p. 197.
[25] "A Pragmatic Conception of the a Priori," in Feigl and Sellars, p. 286.
[26] I follow Lewis' argument and examples here, *ibid.,* p. 287. But we will see this occur later in another context, i.e., § 80. According to Lewis, "the law of the excluded middle formulates our decision that whatever is not designated by a certain term shall be designated by its negative," *ibid.,* p. 287.

The laws of logic, Lewis says, "are principles of procedure, the parliamentary rules of intelligent thought and action. Such laws are independent of the given because they impose no limitations whatever upon it. They are legislative because they are addressed to ourselves—because definition, classification, and inference represent no operation in the world of things, but only our categorial attitudes of mind." *Mind and the World Order,* p. 247. Cf. Feigl and Sellars, p. 287.

[27] E.g., *An Inquiry Concerning Human Understanding,* Sec. IV, Part I: "The Contrary of every matter of fact is still possible; because it can never imply a contradiction. . . ." And, going back to Aristotle, *De interpretatione* 13, 22b20: "A thing that may be may also not be," and 22b15: "From 'may be,' however, it follows that it is not impossible; and from that, that it is not necessary." Also, Diogenes Laertius, VII. 75 on Zeno the Stoic for this distinction of possible and necessary. The distinction is at work in Descartes's discussion of *conceivability,* noticed in § 21 above.

sistency are found. Hume's thesis may be debatable on several counts, but this lies aside from our present concern. If we agree (as Lewis would) to preserve the idea of contradiction for modes of discourse, classification, and analysis, then to exclude the possibility of a lion both being and not being is simply to impose a restriction upon our modes of discourse and classification. Such is the function and import of the principle: "a thing must either be or not be." This so-called law of contradiction legislates, not for being, nor experience, but for our interpretation and conceptualization of being. It does not characterize existence, but rather how we are to talk about things.

Thus the *possibility* of a lion, bush, or anything in Eden both being and not being turns upon the question whether (when 'possibility' is *defined* as 'not contradictory') it is contradictory to suppose or say that something both is and is not. The answer is obvious; obvious, that is, if one is holding to the principle of contradiction. To *assert* the being and non-being of something is contradictory and what is asserted is an impossibility. The law of contradiction and other logical principles, being accepted as the "uncompelled initiatives" and necessary to our conceptual scheme, are "true no matter what." They are true, or necessarily true, because once chosen they determine the system and conditions therein according to which necessary and possible truths are defined. The a priori is necessarily true, which is to say, in the system of which they are a part, a priori principles cannot *possibly* be falsified.

While a priori truth "is definitive or explicative" and rises exclusively from the analysis of concepts, this does not and could not explain why just certain a priori criteria rather than logically possible others have been selected and followed in the organization of our conceptual schemes for interpreting experience. "Mind makes classifications and determines meanings; in so doing it creates that truth without which there could be no other truth." But this process of creation is responsive to pragmatic considerations. Lewis thus recognizes a plurality of possible a priori concepts, their meanings (or definitions given to them) in the initial organizations of our conceptual schemes.[28] The a priori "has alternatives." Furthermore, the scheme of a priori principles and categories with which we order and interpret experience is itself evolutionary, not something fixed initially and for all time.[29]

[28] For the passages just quoted, see *Mind and the World Order*, pp. 231, 240. Lewis criticizes traditional conceptions of the a priori for arguing that "logically prior" principles (i.e., the "presuppositions" of system construction) are indispensable, self-evident, and compel us to use them (the other sense in which they are "necessary" rejected by Lewis, as we saw some pages above). Thus Lewis, like Peirce (cf. § 22), rejects the Aristotelian or Cartesian ideal of indubitable first principles of the system of empirical knowledge. "The supposed necessity, or logical indispensability, of presuppositions most frequently turns out to be nothing more significant than lack of imagination and ingenuity. The plurality of possible beginnings for the same system, and the plurality of equally cogent systems which may contain the *same* body of already verified propositions but differ in *what else* they include, dispel the notion of indispensability in what is logically prior." *Mind and the World Order*, pp. 204–205. Also see pp. 271–273.

[29] Lewis writes, *ibid.*, p. 235: "The *names* of our categories may be very old and stable, but the *concepts*, the modes of classifying and interpreting which they represent undergo progressive alteration with the advance of thought."

. . . The interpretation of experience must always be in terms of categories . . . and concepts which the mind itself determines. There may be alternative conceptual systems, giving rise to alternative descriptions of experience, which are equally objective and equally valid. . . . When this is so, choice will be determined, consciously or unconsciously, on pragmatic grounds.[30]

In recognizing the importance of the a priori element in knowledge, Lewis repudiates those forms of transcendental philosophy in which a priori conditions and the a priori character of knowing were so devoutly championed. These, as we have seen in Part One (§ 8), took the a priori as a *logos*, a formal pattern in knowing and in things known, a formal connection between mind and world—a concomitance that made knowledge possible. Or, alternatively and historically later, the a priori was conceived as a structure that mind brought to and imposed upon experience. Lewis' pluralism and his insistence that the a priori is not constitutive or determinative of the *content* of experience and the given is a rejection of both these transcendental theories of knowledge.

Philosophy proper is about the a priori, according to Lewis.

Philosophy is the study of the a priori. It seeks to reveal those categorial criteria which the mind applies to what is given to it, and by correct delineation of those criteria to define the good, the right, the valid, and the real.[31]

Important, however, as the a priori is in the *analysis* of knowledge, it is not all there is to the occurrence of knowledge. There is also "the given" in experience. And the a priori would be "empty" (to use Kant's language, § 11) without the given as the other component of knowledge. The concept and the sensuously given—conceptual interpretation and given presentation—are the two elements of our knowledge of objects. The given *happens*, and in happening is itself (if 'itself' makes sense as a characterization) the brute inarticulate stuff of knowledge. The *stuff of* knowledge, we may say; but this is not to be equated with the content of knowledge. For empirical knowledge, as Lewis maintains, and as we will see, is about experience, about the *real*, and is addressed to objects, all of which lead us beyond the sensuously given in experience.

The conceptual element in knowledge (or the "pure concept" according to Lewis) and the sensuously given are mutually independent; neither limits nor determines the nature of the other.[32] All empirical knowledge, our understanding of real objects and truths of experience, originates in and proceeds upon a conceptual interpretation of the given in experience. Now the given, Lewis, along with Peirce and Dewey, observes, in all felt, conscious immediacy, is not as such cognitive. "There is no knowledge merely by acquaintance. . . . Knowledge *always* transcends the immediately given."[33] Interpretation, essential to knowing,

[30] *Ibid.*, p. 271.
[31] *Ibid.*, p. 36.
[32] *Ibid.*, p. 37.
[33] *Ibid.*, p. 118. In a later paper, "Experience and Meaning" (1934), Lewis made this point emphatic. In criticism of some of the analyses of empirical knowledge by the Vienna

always goes beyond and involves more than what is presented in immediate experience. With Berkeley and with the other pragmatists Lewis shares this basic thesis concerning sense experience: the data or qualities of immediately occurring experience *become* knowledge (or enter into knowledge) only when interpreted (by language, classification, and habitual responses) as signs—and therefore predictive—of further possible experience.[34] Among these interpretive (thus conceptual) mediations of data is one that is common to us all and fundamental to empirical knowledge: the given is taken as a sign of the presence of an object, i.e., the given as object-*ified*. For, as Lewis points out:

> An object such as an apple is never given; between the real apple in all its complexity and this fragmentary presentation, lies that interval which only interpretation can bridge. The "objectivity" of this experience means *the verifiability of a further possible experience which is attributed by this interpretation*.[35]

Berkeley had advanced much the same analysis:[36] the given sensible impression (or 'idea' or sensation) is taken by the mind as a sign of other (possible) sense qualities. Objects are regular, predictable, "congeries" of sense impressions, and knowledge of nature rests on predicting the connections of qualities or ideas.

The immediate uninterpreted datum of sense experience is called by Lewis a "quale." Awareness or apprehension of a single presented quale is infallible, but only because awareness of a quale is not judgment nor is it knowledge.[37] The quale is the raw, uninterpreted, inarticulate item of direct experience. Qualia are what have sometimes been called "sense data" or "sensa," although these locutions are no more crisp or free from the vagueness that beclouds the primitives of epistemological theory than Lewis' language. Santayana preferred to caption these acts of immediate apprehension of some presentation as "intuition of essences." But this, too, is no apparent improvement in clarity. Qualia are, it seems, the ultimate raw material of sense (or of immediate) experience.[38] There are "qualitative

---

Circle and Russell, he wrote: "The conception that empirical knowledge is confined to what we actually observe is false. To know (empirically) is to be able to anticipate correctly further possible experience." Lewis adds, "What is anticipated, known or meant must indeed be something envisaged in terms of experience. . . . But it is equally essential that what is empirically known or meant should *not* be something which is immediately or exhaustively verified, in what I have called the moment of entertainment." In Feigl and Sellars, p. 137.

[34] See Lewis' comment on Berkeley's doctrine, *Mind and the World Order*, p. 133. See also, on Berkeley, Appendix 5 below.

[35] *Mind and the World Order*, p. 120.

[36] For sources and passages in question, see Appendix 5 below.

[37] *Mind and the World Order*, p. 125. Also, p. 121: "The quale is directly intuited, given, and is not the subject of any possible error because it is purely subjective."

[38] While immediate experience is *epistemologically* primitive or "first" in the analysis of knowledge, it is not first or the ultimate datum from which philosophic reflection starts. "It is indeed the thick experience of the world, not the thin given of immediacy which constitutes the datum for philosophic reflection," *ibid.*, p. 54. We begin with trees, houses, voices, etc., not patches of colors and sounds. Objects and full-bodied facts constitute the "preanalytic data" of epistemology. In this sense, *the given* is postanalytic, and an abstraction (*ibid.*, p. 54) of philosophic theory.

characters of the given"[39] capable of being repeated in different experiences; qualia are "a sort of universals."[40]

For Lewis, apprehension of a presented quale "being immediate stands in no need of verification."[41] But, he argues, knowledge of objects is a matter of judgment and verification concerning the various presentations of the objective properties of objects. There are difficulties here, for that which stands in no need of verification *can* be characterized as *necessarily* true (or false), or as never occurring or existing, or as incapable of being judged. The last possibility, in a special way, reflects Lewis' intention. Immediately presented qualia are "had" and in their having no conceptualization enters, but concepts are necessary to judgment and verification. Moreover, there are no concepts of immediate qualia. 'Blue,' 'round,' and the like denote no one immediate quale, but orders or "some stable pattern of relations."[42] Our concepts are of "objective properties," not immediate qualia.[43] Lewis is thus led to develop an important set of distinctions concerning our experience and judgments of objects. Presented qualia in some ordered relationship (not a momentary, single presented quale) provide the basic conditions for judgments of objects. The presented qualia function as signs of properties of objects. Judging and the assignment of properties to objects proceeds *via* presented qualia. How given qualia are interpreted as signs of objective properties can become quite complicated. The presented round shape and shininess may serve as signs of the properties of a coin. But so would an elliptical shape. One must recognize occasions in which we will say the penny now *looks* round (or elliptical) and those in which we will say it *looks* elliptical but *is* round. The elliptical presentation of the penny may function as a sign of a round object. In any case, predication of properties of an object is a matter of inference from presented qualia. Such inferences take a probable form, and certain patterns or orders of verifiable conditions constitute truth of a predication of a property to an object.[44]

> The predication of a property on the basis of momentarily presented experience, is in the nature of an hypothesis which predicts something definitely specifiable in further possible experience, and is something which such experience may corroborate or falsify. The identifiable character of presented qualia is *necessary* to the predication of objective properties and to the recognition of objects, but it is not *sufficient* for the verification of what such predication and recognition implicitly assert, both because what is thus asserted transcends the given and has the significance of the prediction of further possible experience, and because the *same* property

---

[39] *Ibid.*, p. 121.
[40] *Ibid.*, p. 125.
[41] *Ibid.*, p. 125.
[42] *Ibid.*, p. 129.
[43] *Ibid.*, pp. 128–130.
[44] Determining just what the conditions are under which a property *is* declared objective, "valid predication," from given qualia, is a matter of some perplexity. See Nelson Goodman's discussion of the point, *Structure of Appearance*, pp. 96–98. Thus, Goodman, p. 97: "to ascribe a property to a thing is in effect to affirm that the qualia it presents under different conditions conform to some more or less fully presented pattern." The difficulty lies in specifying the pattern, albeit more or less fully presented in actuality.

may be validly predicated on the basis of *different* presented qualia, and *different* properties may be signalized by the *same* presented quale.[45]

According to Lewis, ascribing objectivity to what is had as a presentation "is *the conceptual interpretation of what is presented.*"[46] Three important consequences follow directly from this view.

1) Knowledge of reality, judgments of objects, is carried on in a multitude of hypothetical propositions.[47] From this given experience, if I act in certain ways, other specifiable experiences will occur. Given this presentation of red and round as *apple*, if I bite it I will experience a sweet taste, etc.[48]

2) Experience presents us with possibilities of other or further experiences only some of which will be actualized. The apple seen *would* taste sweet, we say, but we may never taste it. "The whole content of our knowledge of reality is the truth of such 'if-then' propositions, in which the hypothesis is something we conceive could be made true by our mode of acting and the consequent presents a content of experience which . . . is a possible experience connected with the present."[49] Lewis' system of strict implication, commented on earlier, was partly motivated as an attempt to represent the 'if-then' relation between propositions true under certain possible conditions, that is, whose truth or falsehood is independent of the truth values of their antecedent clauses.[50] Moreover, our conception of the limits of possible experience is bound to just those 'if-then' propositions which, in our conceptual scheme, ascribe what is *conceivably real* or experienceable. "The limits of the possibility of experience are the limits of meaningful conception."[51] The possibility that reality is non-Euclidian, which is to say that a non-Euclidian reality is *conceivable*, is a "meaningful" possibility in the sense that an 'if-then' proposition can be given "in which the 'if' states some intelligible condition and the 'then' ascribes some content which supposedly would be *experienced* under the conditions of the 'if.' "[52]

3) *Reality*, for Lewis, is defined and understood as the result of certain operative principles in our conceptual scheme. Our scheme (or schemes) provides us with a criterion of reality; our concepts are criteria of reality. Exceptions to these principles and concepts, experiences which defy our conceptual interpretations, our predictions and verifications become classified (i.e., interpreted) as illusory or unreal. "In precisely the same sense that 'reality' is ascribed, in that sense some possibility of experience is predicated."[53] This is not to deny the *possibility* of

---

[45] *Mind and the World Order*, p. 131. See also p. 133.
[46] *Ibid.*, p. 133.
[47] *Ibid.*, p. 140.
[48] *Ibid.*, p. 140.
[49] *Ibid.*, p. 142. There are difficulties about what exactly a *possible* experience is; these are discussed in Appendix 7 below.
[50] See his footnote, *ibid.*, p. 142, and therein: "a material implication represents an "if-then' proposition the truth of which is *not* independent of the *truth* of its antecedent clause."
[51] *Ibid.*, p. 217.
[52] *Ibid.*, p. 217. Cf. also pp. 303–305.
[53] *Ibid.*, p. 217.

alterations, minor or major, in our schemes and among concepts when and if classification of reals and unreals proves unwieldy or unworkable.

In general, Lewis follows Berkeley in construing the criteria of reality as those of uniformity and predictability of experience. Objects are uniform orders of possible experience. They are orders that extend temporally beyond any one moment of presented qualia. When objects fail to behave according to categorically established uniform ways, they become classified as unreal. Walls that can be seen, but not touched, and through which one can walk to and fro, stones that float in the air, are cases of unreality. The given in experience contains both real and unreal. A priori criteria of the real are required before we can classify experience into that which is uniform and law-like and that which is not.[54]

A special and novel feature of Lewis' theory of the a priori is that while a priori principles are definitive and "true no matter what," such definitive principles can be altered or abandoned in the historical growth of knowledge. Logical principles are, perhaps, exceptions; these might be maintained "no matter what."[55] But while no given experience can force revisions of a priori principles—since these do not legislate the content of experience, and since they define the reality and unreality of given experience—still, these principles have an instrumental or pragmatic function in advancing knowledge. Thus, while we *can* categorize or interpret experience as we will, *what* categories will serve our collective interests best and our social arts of appraising and comprehending kinds of experience is not a matter of private fiat or uncoerced will. (This, by the way, is missed in the illustration of Adam above.[56]) Thus it is that fundamental principles and categories of some conceptual system might call for alterations if there should occur continued failure to render certain experiences intelligible or recurrent cases of unaccountable and unexpected (i.e., unpredictable) events. In the face of such experience, recalcitrant to explanation in our working conceptual scheme, one could continue to hold to his categories and plead illusion or unreality to whatever happened to defy or baffle those interpretative principles.

One of Lewis' examples of an a priori principle is "physical things must have mass."[57] The word 'must' gives the stated principle its definitive character so that (following Lewis) one is led to regard the principle, which we may call P, thus:

$$P: (x) \text{ (if } x \text{ is a physical thing then } x \text{ has mass)}[58]$$

P is true necessarily, analytically, or by definition. As such, Lewis points out, "no particular experience could upset this principle, because any experience in which

---

[54] For these points see "A Pragmatic Conception of the a Priori" in Feigl and Sellars, pp. 290–291.

[55] For doubts about this, see § 80, and Appendix 6.

[56] That conceptualization is a cooperative effort and our categories social products of interest and action is a weakness in the earlier illustration of Adam and his creation of language. The social, historical, and pragmatic contexts are missing: we inherit these with our conceptual scheme.

[57] *Mind and the World Order*, p. 26.

[58] Reading: "for anything x, if x is a physical thing then x has mass."

it should be violated would be repudiated as non-veridical or 'not correctly understood.' "[59] Or, putting it another way, no experience *could* violate P, because to
talk of what *could* be an experience is to talk of a *possible* experience, and P rules
over possible experience just to this extent: given P, it is impossible that something is physical and does not possess mass. No occasion or event of a counter-
instance of P being possible, P *could* be maintained forever. However, it is equally
possible or conceivable that phenomena of a kind occur which, while not in any
way characterized by mass (e.g., exhibiting no properties of gravity), do display
other traits of physical objects (e.g., predictable manifestations, persistence, independence, etc.). Such phenomena, while not falsifying P, might render P or the
category of *physical thing* useless in our coping with experience.[60]

It is possible, then, to preserve the a priori principles and categories of our
scheme of understanding without alteration, even if experience should "boil over."
A conceptual immunity can be maintained to all onslaughts of data, to unforeseen,
novel, or sudden expansions of experience. But such insular conservatism is
hardly likely where any practical interests or satisfactions are felt.[61] Alterability
of our most fundamental concepts and interpretive categories in the scheme from
which we view the world is, therefore, always a possibility. Such alterations occur
in the interest of increased understanding and control over experience, and when
they happen they happen pragmatically.

For these reasons, Lewis concludes that "It is the a priori element in knowledge
which is thus pragmatic, not the empirical."[62]

§ 46. Valuation as Empirical Judgment

There is one last observation yet to be made concerning Lewis' pragmatic theory
of knowledge. "Evaluations are a form of empirical knowledge."[63] Judgments of
value are thus subject to the same set of distinctions that Lewis works out for
empirical knowledge generally. Since this is not true, Lewis argues, in the case
of ethical judgments, *value* theory is sharply separated from *ethics* and ethical

[59] *Mind and the World Order*, p. 26.
[60] The general point of this argument follows Lewis, *ibid.*, pp. 26–27.
[61] William James, characteristically, was always critical of this conservatism. He saw in
the failure to recognize "unclassified residuum" of theory a moral and historical provincialism and dogmatism. "The ideal of every science is that of a closed and completed
system of truth. The charm of most sciences to their more passive disciples consists in their
appearing, in fact, to wear just this ideal form . . . when a consistent and organized scheme
of this sort has once been comprehended and assimilated, a different scheme is unimag-
inable. No alternative, whether to whole or parts, can any longer be conceived as possible.
Phenomena unclassifiable within the system are therefore paradoxical absurdities, and must
be held untrue. . . . Only the born geniuses let themselves be worried by these outstanding
exceptions. . . ." *The Will to Believe*, pp. 299–300.
[62] *Mind and the World Order*, p. 266.
[63] The whole statement is: "Evaluations are a form of empirical knowledge, not fundamentally different in what determines their truth or falsity, and what determines their
validity or justification, from other kinds of empirical knowledge," *An Analysis of Knowledge and Valuation*, p. 365.

judgment.[64] In his most extensive writing on this subject,[65] Lewis distinguishes three kinds of value predications, each with its own corresponding class of empirical judgments.

1) There are those cases of "apparent value" or "felt goodness"[66] which stand as reports of the character of given sense presentations. These, like reports of sensuously given data, are expressive statements. They are self-verifying and not subject to error. They function in the course of further evaluation as initial conditions and signs, the material of further evaluations; for without these directly felt instances of value (or disvalue), further evaluating of any kind would be unintelligible—not impossible, but vacant of experienced content. These reports of felt value might simply remain reports of the sensuously given—of a glass of wine, for example, that "this is good." As such, these do not constitute knowledge for Lewis, although in some cases they may lead to further judgments that do become knowledge. These reports, then, are like those of sensuous presentations, "this is red," "this is sweet" (said not of an object, i.e., not asserted as objective properties, but simply as had, a distinction discussed in § 45 above).

2) A second kind of evaluation Lewis calls a "terminating judgment."[67] These are predictions that in given circumstances, or like circumstances, on carrying out a certain mode of action, a value quality will result. These judgments are straightforward assertions of certain conditions as signs of other possible conditions to be realized (or not) when certain other conditions (i.e., actions) are fulfilled: thus, "if I taste this wine, I will enjoy it." Judgments of this kind are decisively verifiable but not (at the time of utterance) verified, and in becoming verified, their truth or falsehood is evidenced. By being capable of falsification they constitute knowledge.

3) Lastly, there are evaluations in which an objective property of "being valuable" is ascribed to an existent kind of thing, or a possible kind of thing.[68] These are often complex judgments, and among the complexities involved are the varied subtle differences in meanings among such ascriptions and in their validations. The cardinal feature of this sort of judgment, however, is its nonterminating form: at no one time, for no limited conditions, is it decisively verified. These judgments, like all judgments of *objective* fact (cf. § 45), are never more than probable. In this third class, judgments are determined more or less true, i.e., they achieve some degree of confirmation by means of the terminating judgments that are logically implied as consequences of them. That is, asserting that something possesses objective value implies (but is not equivalent to)

---

[64] For a further note on this separation of *value* and *ethical* theory, see § 87, note 1 below; also the papers of Baylis and Frankena. The present section concerns itself with Lewis' theory of *valuation*, not his ethics.

[65] *An Analysis of Knowledge and Valuation.* While his value theory was developed in this book, Lewis' full statement of his ethical theory, which he was working on, was left unfinished at his death. His manuscript is being prepared for publication. See Baylis, p. 560.

[66] *An Analysis of Knowledge and Valuation*, p. 374.

[67] *Ibid.*, p. 375.

[68] *Ibid.*, p. 375.

a multiplicity of terminating judgments each verifiable and each serving as a possible (degree of) confirmation of the original judgment. Insofar as the implied judgments turn out to be true, the initial judgment tends to achieve confirmation.

Lewis describes this third kind of evaluation as taking this approximate form:

> attributing value to an existent, O, means that under circumstances C, O will or would, or probably will or would, lead to satisfaction in the experience of somebody, S; or it intends the joint assertion of many such satisfactions.[69]

To say, for example, that O is beautiful is to assert an actual or possible experience: if somebody S (a connoisseur or critic, perhaps) sees or (under C) experiences O, he would be pleased[70] (waiving complications of esthetic theory over 'pleased' as the right predicate for describing test conditions of experience of *beauty*). The property of beauty in this case, say, of a piece of gold, is just as objective in its asserted status as the specific gravity or softness of the gold.[71] Harkening back to Peirce's method of explicating predicates like 'specific gravity' or 'softness' (§ 21), we recall the procedure:

> If *ExpS* (experiential situation of scales, or of instruments for scratch tests) and if O (operations of weighing gold in air and in water and its weight in air divided by the difference of the two weights, etc.; or scratching the gold), then such and such results (i.e., finding the quotient 19.3 its specific gravity, or that it is soft, is easily scratchable).

This same pragmatic procedure holds for warranting judgments of objective value. We noticed that Peirce held that "an innumerable series" of confirmations was implied in the meaning of the predicate. For Lewis, innumerable possible confirming (or disconfirming) instances are entailed by 'O is (objectively) beautiful.' It is not that *any* test or any person testing constitutes a genuine confirming instance of the judgment; "the test-observation should be made by an expert and under optimum conditions of the test-experience."[72] Earlier, we noticed problems in formulating the necessary conditions for ascribing objective properties to things. But the test cases or confirming conditions of the attribution of beauty as an objective property of O are evaluations of the second type distinguished above; they are decisively verifiable predictions, e.g., 'if an expert under such and such conditions experiences O he will be pleased (or affirm "O possesses beauty").'

Now the complicating notions that are nonetheless basic in delivering evaluations of this third kind are those (in Lewis' statement) of what "will or would, or probably will or would, lead to satisfaction . . . ," etc. The notions of what *will* or *would* be the case, Lewis recognizes, involve attributing a potentiality or

[69] *Ibid.*, p. 512.
[70] *Ibid.*, p. 514.
[71] *Ibid.*, p. 514.
[72] *Ibid.*, p. 514.

dispositional properties to objects, or to objects under certain conditions.[73] "There is the attribution of a potentiality for satisfactions which lies in the nature of the object."[74] The further notion of what *probably* will be the case calls for elucidation within a theory of probability, unless 'probable' is being used in some ordinary and informal sense of 'likelihood' or 'may be the case.' But not content with the easy resort to ordinary vagueness on such a fundamental idea as the *probable* character of empirical knowledge, Lewis outlines a theory of the probability of empirical beliefs and judgments (i.e., a specification of the meaning and justification of assignments of probability to beliefs or judgments) as a part of his general analysis of empirical knowledge and valuation.[75]

These items, roughly, of potentiality-for-satisfaction and probability-of-satisfaction, figure in this order of increasing complexity in evaluations. The assertion of a potential value (e.g., "if someone *should* find this diamond he *would* be gratified") takes a hypothetical form. The "potentiality is expressible by some if-then statement, in which the hypothesis will include reference to at least some circumstances affecting the object, and the consequent will assert satisfactions as following upon these hypothetical conditions."[76] For example: "if someone *should* find this diamond he *would be* gratified." The if-then statement may be true even if the hypothesis happens to be contrary to fact.[77]

To say the diamond is *valuable* in this case is to assert a fact about it: that, under such and such conditions, it *would* gratify. Here 'valuable' is one among other *disposition* terms, true (or false) of some object.[78] To say the diamond is 'valuable' is to say it *would* gratify; and to say it is 'hard' is to say it *would not* be scratched (see § 21 above).

But to assert the *probability* of satisfaction entails more than attributing a potentiality or value-disposition to an object; it carries as added content a statement of the actual or probable realization of the potential value under certain conditions. The distinction here is that between, for example, asserting the conditions under which this sugar would dissolve, and those under which the sugar probably will in fact be dissolved.[79] The first conditions are necessary but not sufficient conditions for the realization of the second. In the same way, that the diamond *would*, when found under certain conditions, gratify someone is a necessary condition in the judgment that it is now about to be found (or probably will be) and will gratify someone.[80] This latter sense of 'valuable' has reference to an actualization in experience of a potential value. And according to

---

[73] *Ibid.*, esp. pp. 519–520 ff.
[74] *Ibid.*, p. 519.
[75] *Ibid.*, cf. esp. ch. 10.
[76] *Ibid.*, p. 519. Or dissatisfactions, Lewis might have added.
[77] See *ibid.*, p. 519.
[78] Thus Lewis, *ibid.*, p. 520: "In this mode 'valuable' is just like 'soluble' and does not imply any actually realized satisfaction, any more than 'soluble' implies 'dissolved.' " For a complicating qualification, however, see *ibid.*, p. 380, last paragraph, to p. 388.
[79] Traditionally, the distinction is that of stating the potentiality, *dynamis*, of an object and that of formulating and predicting the actualization, *energeia*, of the potentiality.
[80] *An Analysis of Knowledge and Valuation*, pp. 519–520.

the latter sense of 'valuable,' the diamond that lies buried in the ground and probably will not be located has no value.[81]

It should be evident that each of these two ways of assigning objective value to objects takes the form of conditional statements, functioning as predictions, whose meaning and justification is no different in principle from other empirical judgments about objective qualities (discussed in § 45 above).

The structure of value predications, the three kinds of predication discussed, is the same structure that characterizes all empirical judgments. Judgments of immediate sense presentations, terminating judgments, and ascriptions of objective value-properties to objects—the first, second, and third kinds of evaluations commented upon in earlier paragraphs—is a pattern Lewis finds illustrated in all of empirical knowledge.

Finally, since a priori procedures and principles are a necessary part of the acquisition and organization of empirical knowledge, as we saw earlier, so a priori statements have a role in the determination of values. The definitive resolution that pleasure is the good is an example; or that a thing is good by being an object of interest; or that nothing is unqualifiedly good but a good will. These are judgments of the same kind as "the hard is unscratchable" or "a thing is hard by being an unscratchable object" or "nothing is unqualifiedly hard but a hard heart."[82] Such statements, says Lewis, "if true at all, can be certified by some analysis of meaning; their truth is determinable by reflection, without other evidence than that of logic and of what would be formulated in definitions."[83]

Such, in outline, is Lewis' theory of valuation and its relation, as a part, to his general theory of knowledge. The pragmatist's thesis that judgments of value are objective empirical judgments, not differing in kind from other judgments of fact, is reserved for more detailed consideration in another chapter (Part Four, Chapter Three). Here, for the moment, we shall pause to take stock of some themes discussed and some of the problems they raise.

§ 47.   Meaning and Mind

Much of the structure and the major doctrines of Lewis' philosophy of knowledge rest upon a theory of meaning. The theory of meaning, in turn, rests upon a

[81] *Ibid.*, p. 520.

[82] With some variations, the point and illustrations are Lewis', *ibid.*, p. 378.

[83] *Ibid.*, p. 378. Lewis' position here, as in his view of the a priori, generally in empirical knowledge rests upon the notion of *analyticity*. We will notice later (§ 80 and Appendix 6) that there have been some doubts about this. However, the main point at the moment is that there are analytic clarifications of meanings and intensions in value theory for Lewis. Furthermore, in the manner already viewed at the close of § 45 above, these analytic statements "are subject to debate, and determinably true or false; even though they are statements about meanings and not about any different kind of fact, and are open to decision by critical reflection only," *ibid.*, p. 379.

While he happens to regard "the question of justice" as distinct from that of the *summum bonum*—the former belonging to the peculiar province of ethics, the latter to the theory of values (p. vii)—Lewis cites as the fundamental a priori dictum or "tautology" of justice, "No rule of action is right except one which is right in all instances, and therefore right for everyone," p. 482. Cf. also pp. 481–483.

classification of truths or statements[84] into analytic and synthetic and of meanings into extensional and intensional modes.[85] We shall not attempt to reproduce the theory here nor to find our way through some of its difficult passages.[86] But it is worth remarking that Lewis' analysis of empirical knowledge, his conception of the a priori (or *analytic*) and pragmatic element in knowledge is guided and supported by the classification of truths or statements into *analytic* and *synthetic*. To the extent that this classification is questioned, or that the distinction upon which this basic separation is founded is called into doubt, the foundations of Lewis' philosophy of knowledge appear to be threatened. If the dichotomy in question should prove unable to withstand critical punishment, if it cannot be maintained at all beyond a confessedly vaguely felt attitude toward certain groups of statements,[87] how seriously is Lewis' philosophy in danger of a general crumbling into a few disconnected and fragmentary insights? Several answers are possible.

1) First of all, Lewis' analysis of the empirical content of knowledge, of the probable character of judgments of fact, of the inferential and predictive nature of our treatment of sense experience would all hold despite the rejection of the analytic-synthetic distinction. Some features of the analysis of empirical knowledge might be made more complicated as a result of this rejection. The notion of probability, for example, and those of possibility and actuality—each so important in the logic of judgments of objective qualities (§ 45)—are made more difficult without an appeal to analytic (or a priori) truths. For the concept of analytic, i.e., as *logically* or *necessarily* true, is useful in defining or partially defining 'possible,' 'actual,' and 'probable.'[88] Useful as 'analytic' is, however, there is no reason to suppose that it is essential to the definition and clarification of logical and physical modalities; nor is there reason to think that Lewis' analysis of how knowledge originates in immediate sense experience and how it proceeds from experience is incapable of formulation without the idea of analyticity.

2) It must be admitted that Lewis' conception of mind and the a priori *does*

[84] In the first four pages of ch. 3 of *An Analysis of Knowledge and Valuation*, Lewis speaks of analytic truths, analytic statements, and of a kind of catchall, *the* analytic. We may also observe that the notion of a priori, which occupied a central place in Lewis' earlier writings and which has been discussed above, is treated in this later work as roughly synonymous with analytic. Thus, p. 35, Lewis comments on his "thesis here put forward, that the a priori and the analytic coincide."

[85] For a brief account of these modes, see "The Modes of Meaning." For the fuller explanation with some changes, see ch. 3 of *Analysis of Knowledge and Valuation;* there the four modes are outlined on p. 39, where the modes of meaning hold for *terms*—but Lewis deals with traditional terms, propositions, and propositional functions each as kinds of terms.

[86] For the general theory the reader must consult *Analysis of Knowledge and Valuation,* esp. Book 1, pp. 35–161.

[87] Such is one possibility discussed in Appendix 6 below.

[88] See *Analysis of Knowledge and Valuation,* p. 123, for one example: "analytic truths are true of the all possible; and what is true of the all possible is *a fortiori* true of all actuality; but what is true of all actuality will not necessarily be true of all that is consistently thinkable. And what is true of all actuality but is *not analytic*, can no wise be assured except by induction from empirical observation, and belongs to natural science." For a related consideration, see Appendix 7, sec. B below.

depend on the analytic-synthetic distinction. To have to give up this distinction would inevitably call for considerable revision of theory in Lewis' account of the role of mind and a priori principles in the act of knowing. Let us try briefly to see why.

In acknowledging doubts as to a general definition of 'analytic' holding for natural and artificial languages alike, philosophers, notably Carnap, have taken to speaking of analytic statements for some given language L. L is either a deliberately constructed artificial language or a special portion of an ordinary language (which by virtue of being an explicitly special portion is in effect an artificial language). We do not have to deliberate over the merits of this procedure as a way of defining or of saving analyticity.[89] The appeal to given contexts in and relative to which certain constructions are interpreted according to certain purposes at hand is a general stratagem of pragmatism, as emphasized in § 79, and is welcome, therefore, to the pragmatist, in logical theory and semantics as in other matters. But Lewis happens to reject the confinement of analytic to some relativized specification 'analytic-in-L.' For one reason, having characterized 'analytic' as true, by reference to meanings alone,[90] Lewis argues that meanings precede languages.[91] Moreover, for Lewis, among the analytic (or a priori) principles we use in organizing our experience and in linguistic communication are those that express decisions and intentions of organizing a system and applying terms in the systems in certain ways.[92] These are, of course, prior to the systems they make possible and effective.

Lewis is thus committed to analyticity that precedes and is not always contained in language. This commitment is part of his conception of the concepts and interpretive categories that "mind brings to experience"[93] and of the a priori delimitations of reality wrought by mind.

Now it is this side of his theory of knowledge, one in which, as we have seen, Lewis puts some store, that is jeopardized most by doubts as to what can be meant by 'analyticity.' Such opacity as does, or is shown to belong inseparably to the notion of *analytic* has the deleterious consequent of obscuring Lewis' account of the a priori and of those acts of mind in which alleged a priori principles are brought to experience. The very nature of philosophy, indeed, is called into ques-

---

[89] For problems about this procedure of defining 'analytic-in-L,' by semantical rules of language L, see sec. 4 of Quine's "Two Dogmas of Empiricism," *From a Logical Point of View*, ch. 2. Also see Appendix 6 below.

[90] Cf. *An Analysis of Knowledge and Valuation*, pp. 35-37, 96.

[91] See *ibid.*, esp. pp. 72-73, 131. Also p. 36 for another basic objection to this method of keeping analytic relative to a language system.

[92] Thus, *An Analysis of Knowledge and Valuation*, p. 131: "The original determinations of analytic truth, and the final court of appeal with respect to it, cannot lie in linguistic usage, because meanings are not the creatures of language but are antecedent, and the relations of meanings are not determined by our syntactic conventions but are determinative of the significance which our syntactic usages may have."

Intension as a mode of meaning, productive of analytic truths in either of its forms, as "linguistic meaning" or "sense meaning," plays a major role in Lewis' theory of meaning. See pp. 37, 43-44, and esp. Book I, ch. 6, pp. 131-168.

[93] *Mind and the World Order*, pp. 36 ff.

tion with this uncertainty over the meaning of the a priori or analytic, for "philosophy is the study of the a-priori" according to Lewis.[94]

3) While, in Lewis' theory, the role of mind in knowing the world admits of increasing obscurity insofar as the meaning of 'a priori' is or remains obscure, there are other allied problems that should be mentioned.

We have seen earlier that Lewis thoroughly rejects some of the older and familiar interpretations of the nature of the a priori.[95] For him, a priori principles are alterable and their efficacy subject to critical evaluation in the light of changes in experience or evolutions in knowledge.

But in spite of this well reasoned radical departure from traditional hypostatizing of the a priori and Reason, Lewis does not entirely escape from the subtle and permanent influence of the transcendental philosophy of mind and knowledge (cf. § 8). This is evident in his language when discussing the function of mind in the acquisition of knowledge. And it is felt in the peculiar problems that result or appear to Lewis to result from his discussion of mind. Thus, any number of times in *Mind and the World Order*, Lewis uses the metaphor-burdened Kantian language of "the mind bringing to experience" concepts and a priori truths.[96] "The concept" or "the pure concept" is in mind, or a "product of the activity of thought,"[97] and is distinguished from "the sensuously given" or simply "the given."[98]

Metaphors, as we have noted before (§§ 29, 37), are valuable means of articulation, but they can also be sources of unwanted and unintended difficulties. Consider the famous phraseology that has been droned by philosophy teachers in countless lecture rooms: "The mind gives to experience concepts and principles of order," etc. This kind of elocution is helpful at an elementary stage of philosophical instruction or theorizing. But, it also happens, and under continued use, that such expressions as "*the* mind" and its "giving concepts to experience" may have unwanted aftereffects, breeding and nurturing a stock of epistemological problems mostly of dubious value. In "the mind" the definite article 'the' is a notoriously effective solicitor in behalf of hypostatization; *the* mind one fancies as an object of sorts, as is *the* chair or *the* body. And because 'the mind' by dint of a long intellectual tradition is customarily supposed to refer to all or most of what we are, of our very self, we drift naturally and imaginatively into a way of supposing and talking about mind as a kind of person or self within, or behind, the rest of our physical person. Taught by Aristotle that man is rational and animal, that "intelligence [*nous*] more than anything else *is* man";[99] guided by theologians and Descartes to picture mind (or soul) as separate from, but somehow connected with, the body, we easily come to imagine *the* mind as a kind of

[94] *Mind and the World Order,* p. 36. The fuller quotation is given in earlier pages of § 45 above. Doubts about the notion of analytic are briefly surveyed below in § 80 and Appendix 6.
[95] See *Mind and the World Order,* pp. 204–205.
[96] Cf. *ibid.,* p. 6, or pp. 36–37, for representative instances.
[97] *Ibid.,* p. 37.
[98] E.g., *ibid.,* p. 57.
[99] *Nicomachean Ethics* X. 7, 1178a.

individual person situated within and directing the bodily individual present before our eyes. Nor does this fancy, though wrought into a famous theory of the mind by philosophers and scientists (see §§ 4–6), have its origin in philosophy. In Egyptian painted and carved reliefs, or on Greek vases, the soul or the *ker* is depicted as a body with wings. Countless paintings from the Middle Ages onward show human souls in heaven or in hell as the very images of the fleshly bodily containers they have shed behind them in earthly graves.

The natural course under such infectious, imaginative, and philosophic pressures is to construe *the* mind both as a person and as a thing. The phrase "the mind brings (or gives) concepts to experience" becomes innocently, with little further taxing of imagination, affectionately envisioned as some helpful, homely act like that of the waiter bringing food to the table, or the doctor bringing his medical bag on his calls. But such associations, even when frankly fanciful, promise trouble, even when the language prompting them is acknowledged as metaphorical. For analogies support these figures of thought and speech, and the imputed presence of likenesses (between the mind bringing concepts to data and an object or person bearing something else) stubbornly persists despite disavowals of literalness and protestations of innocent intentions.

The effects of analogies, the actual metaphors and our willingness to entertain and be guided by them, even while disclaiming their hold on us are occasioned by the most arduous efforts at precise and unvarnished theorizing concerning the mind and knowing. Similes and illustrations aside, Kant's exposition of the mind (or Understanding) in his theory of how knowledge is possible is still carried by metaphors.[100] But this is not to condemn Kant, nor for that matter Lewis. The fact is that Western philosophizing about mind and knowing has always traded very heavily in metaphors and analogies derived from the activities of two organs, the eye and the hand. Knowing, accordingly, is spoken of as a "seeing" or "grasping," mind as a kind of eye or hand.[101]

There are disadvantages to these idioms, the mentalistic language and Kantian metaphors, that are not so numerously present in an alternative medium. Namely, instead of talking about mind, ideas, categories "which the mind itself determines," one can talk about *languages*, sentences, semantical and syntactical rules that determine in explicit ways the characteristics of what is said and sayable in a language. Thus, such transcendentally oriented phraseology as "the mind brings to experience . . ." or the "categorial criteria which the mind applies to what is given to it"[102] can be translated, or paraphrased, into the less noxious genre of discoursing of languages and linguistic rules or modes of language usage, without

---

[100] Kant gains many return benefits in his theories from such metaphors as the understanding *prescribes* (*der Verstand . . . Schreibt*, describes, writes) its *laws* (*Gesetze*) to nature, or as the political-legal suggestions in the *autonomy* of reason, etc. For instances, see §§ 11, 12 above.

[101] Two examples: "As sight is in the body, intelligence is in the soul," Aristotle, *Nicomachean Ethics* I. 6, 1096b30; and "The soul is like the hand; for as the hand is the instrument [*organon*] of instruments, so mind is the form of forms . . . ," Aristotle, *De anima* I. 7, 432a1.

[102] *Mind and the World Order*, p. 36.

serious loss of vital content. What gets lost in such paraphrasing is a number of seemingly irresoluble problems and metaphor-engendered perplexities encountered in using and reflecting upon the traditional idiom.

To be more specific. Lewis, as we have seen, is committed to a view of knowledge in which there are two components, "the concept" and "the sensuously given." The former is the product of thought or mind, while the latter is independent of these. But in the process of expounding his theory, Lewis feels obliged to wrestle with such "problems" as the following: Since concepts designate "psychological states," since the latter are "separate existences" never identical in quality, how can meanings be objective and shared?[103] Thus, *are* there objective or common meanings? And are there "pure concepts"? And how do we explain an affirmative answer, one presupposed by the sciences and "any other intellectual enterprise"?[104] What does it mean to "have a meaning in mind"?[105] With the question, "are there common meanings?" comes the companion query: "is there a common world, and if so, in what sense?"[106] Furthermore, since, in knowing, mind brings its categories to the materials of sense, how can mind know itself?[107] which is a question reserved for a fifteen-page appendix to *Mind and the World Order*.

Now while these questions, and especially Lewis' treatment of them, are not uninteresting, they are for the most part gratuitous. Gratuitous, that is, to the pragmatism and cardinal theses Lewis was concerned to articulate. In spite of his pronounced doubts that problems of meaning and analyticity (as we saw in earlier pages) can be best dealt with by resorting to languages and language rules, such a procedure might recommend itself if only as a way of avoiding the epistemological marsh of problems of the sort just cited.

We have frequently appreciated the fact in earlier discussions that a characteristic of recent philosophy is its readiness to deal with epistemological questions from the point of view of linguistic behavior and how concepts are used; to prefer to talk of utterances, statements, and expressions in situations and languages, rather than discourse of such traditionally conceived hidden units and mechanisms as ideas and the mind. In much the same preferred fashion, on grounds of increased clarity, one suspects that Lewis' discussions of the a priori in knowing

---

[103] Lewis is raising the notorious problem which we saw to be at least as old as Locke (§ 6; but for the specific problem and passages, see the first pages of § 21) which, in slightly altered expression, was: since meanings *are* ideas designated by words, how can two different minds (or, two different ideas in the same mind) yield the same meaning? See, e.g., *ibid.*, pp. 69–70: "Indeed, the question how meaning *can* be objective and shared, when the psychological states which are the bearers of this meaning are separate existences and not even identical is one of the important problems of meaning." For more on "are there common meanings," see *ibid.*, ch. 4.

[104] *Ibid.*, p. 70: "we shall define the pure concept as 'that meaning which must be common to two minds when they understand each other by the use of a substantive or its equivalent.' . . . That meanings may have this sort of objectivity, is a fundamental assumption of science or of any other intellectual enterprise."

[105] See *ibid.*, pp. 84–85.

[106] *Ibid.*, ch. 4.

[107] This Lewis discusses, *ibid.*, Appendix D.

could be recast into an account of analyticity in languages.[108] His somewhat mysterious Mind with its categorical issuings could be more empirically and suggestively accounted for as the socially conditioned structure of a language that is antecedent to sundry specific uses and to our learning how to use it. The structure is *prior* but not *a priori*. The structure of a language, while subject ordinarily to gradual changes, precedes our infantile and first attempts to learn and apply it in situations where the want is felt. Now such given situations, whether we are learning a language for the first time or learning a new one, are not determined by linguistic structure. They have all the independence of content that Lewis ascribes to the sensuously given. But that linguistic structure determines the possible and available ways that classification, interpretation, and analysis of the situation from speaker to speaker will occur. Lewis' philosophy of mind as determining the interpretation of experience by categories and definitive a priori concepts seems to be a misleading and metaphorically charged way of accounting for the fact that, to talk about the world and such experience of it as we wish to record or understand, we require a language, or conceptual scheme. And the latter already firmly conditions much of how we are to talk about the world and the ways we can and will record and classify experience.

There are occasions when Lewis points out that categories and the concepts we use in interpreting sense experience are social products, just as is the language we use. But he draws back at the point where one expects and most wants a thoroughly naturalistic and pragmatic analysis of mind, of knowing, and of language. The analysis wanted is one in which the function of mind, or mental behavior, and categories are exhibited as originating from and shaped under those social situations where communication is the achieved outcome of organisms cooperating in adjusting to and controlling their environment. Such a pragmatic account of mind and communication was developed by George Herbert Mead, to whose theory we turn next.

[108] Though this is not to overlook that undeniable problems remain concerning the sense of 'a language' and of 'analytic-in-a-language.'

CHAPTER FIVE

George Herbert Mead

§ 48. The Social Point of View

The most comprehensive and elaborate of the pragmatist theories of mind and behavior was developed by George Herbert Mead. Mead's social behaviorism is in full accord with Peirce and Dewey as to the biosocial origin and function of thought. It is farthest removed of the pragmatic philosophies from the individualism of James and, especially, the subjectivistic psychology of F. C. S. Schiller (§ 65). For Mead, the social point of view, the analysis of behavior as socially evolved and conditioned acts, pervades even the biological and physical subject matters relevant to accounting for human action.

When Aristotle stated the characteristically Greek conviction that man was a social animal (*zōon politikon anthrōpos*), he cited as primary evidence that man alone among animals possesses the faculty of language.[1] And language, surely, is a social art. Aristotle also said that society, or *polis*, is prior in the order of nature (not temporally) to the individual and family.[2] He meant, among other things, that human nature and the attendant abilities of speech and moral perceptions are not understandable without reference to the social contexts in which they achieve their function. In these respects, Mead's outlook is Aristotelian. The social context and social experience which play major roles in his thought have a priority for purposes of explaining human conduct and even a causal priority in affecting the growth of speech and intelligence. In no way, according to Mead, can an analysis of human behavior successfully suppose that society arises as the result of the expression of conscious selves.[3]

An illustration of the kind of influential position Mead was led to argue against

[1] *Politics* I. 2, 1253a.
[2] Cf. Mead, *Mind, Self and Society*, p. 7: "For social psychology, the whole (society) is prior to the part (individual), not the part to the whole; and the part is explained in terms of the whole, not the whole in terms of the part. . . ." The fuller context is quoted below.
[3] See *Selected Writings*, esp. p. 97, for this point.

will aid us in seeing how and why he came to place so much emphasis upon the social.

On the title page of the 1651 edition of Hobbes's *Leviathan* is engraved a human figure whose body is compounded of a multitude of individual men. The great Leviathan, Hobbes wrote, created by art, is "called a Commonwealth, or State ... which is but an artificial man."[4] This artificial man or commonwealth he described as "the Multitude so united in one Person."[5]

The engraved portrait of the commonwealth vividly illustrates one of Hobbes's theses, that society is an artificial body compounded of the matter and motions of atomic parts. This is Hobbes's mechanical, nominalistic, and thoroughly individualistic view of man and social organization. It further suggests that the social order is the effect, the collective result, of the coming together of individual men motivated by certain common interests. And that suggestion—that society is a mechanical state or system determined by the common properties of its individual parts—is indeed sometimes encouraged by Hobbes. But this is not an accurate representation of his theory, for Leviathan, we must recall, is a "mortal god," and a certain transformation in the moral and psychological condition of men, in the "parts," occurs with the addition of—or entrance into—social contract and community.[6]

However, the Hobbesian view of society as the conglomerate result of the joining of individual men, a view familiar to ancient spokesmen for the social contract theory,[7] serves as a point of critical reference in much of the philosophizing of Mead. An underlying assumption in the Hobbesian and ancient theories is that human nature, in wants and satisfactions, in modes of behavior, and even in consciousness of these modes and communication about them, preceded the existence of society. Society, in short, is derivative of human personality, sustained and shaped by the joint efforts and cooperative activities of separate selves.

It is this view of social structure, particularly its psychological and methodological consequences, of which Mead was most critical. His objection to its psychology was that it failed to provide an adequate explanation of mind. His objection to its methodology was directed to the reductive approach according to which social wholes or forms of behavior are analyzable as sums and products of individual selves. This methodology, Mead argued, leads to a false conception of reality and makes the analysis of meaning (and the evolution and function of language and consciousness) impossible.

Mead's theory of mind, meaning, and behavior is decidedly closer to idealism in emphasizing the social situation as primary than it is to reductivistic, mechan-

[4] See Hobbes's Introduction to *Leviathan*.
[5] Part II, the end of ch. 17.
[6] The doctrine is in Hobbes but becomes emphatic in Rousseau. Thus, see *The Social Contract*, I, 7, for the moral transformation that occurs in man as he passes from the state of nature into the civil state. He is turned from a limited and stupid mind into an intelligent being.
[7] Cf., e.g., Plato's *Republic*, Book II.

ical empiricism.[8] This outlook is revealed in one of Mead's early papers in which he discusses the teaching of science.

> The Weltanschauung of any age is at once the result of all its scientific achievements and a cause of each, by itself. We cannot finally understand any one without the comprehension of the whole, and it is the whole which is more comprehensible than any single science. . . . It may be a Hegelism, but it is good educational doctrine that the whole is more concrete than the part.[9]

For Mead the "whole" that is of fundamental importance to *social behaviorism* (for such is the appellation he gives to his own position[10]) is the social group and process.

> We are not, in social psychology, building up the behavior of the social group in terms of the behavior of the separate individuals composing it; rather, we are starting out with a given social whole of complex group activity, into which we analyze (as elements) the behavior of each of the separate individuals composing it. We attempt, that is, to explain the conduct of the individual in terms of the organized conduct of the social group. . . . For social psychology, the whole (society) is prior to the part (the individual), not the part to the whole; and the part is explained in terms of the whole, not the whole in terms of the part or parts.[11]

Indeed, in sharp and surprising contrast to the Hobbesian psychology and social theory, Mead holds that it is from the social process, the social acts that implicate the individual and other members of his group, that individuality emerges. Selves, self-consciousness, mind, thought, and meanings are "social emergents"; that is, social situations are preconditions in fact and for theoretical explanation of the genesis of the self and intelligent behavior.[12]

The dominant and leading idea in Mead's theory of mind and behavior is his conception of the development and function of language. For from the acquisition and use of language and from the conditions that determine its use, mind and self have their emergence. It is to this theory that we shall shortly turn.

§ 49.   A Problem of Materials

We must recognize at the very outset of our endeavor to study Mead's theory that while the attempt to develop a functional and behavioral account of mind was surely the most ambitious and painstaking effort ever made in American philosophy, Mead never completed the task.

The materials available for venturing to understand his theory are of three

---

[8] And not uncritical, too, of the idealism of Royce and his account of the emergence of meaning and social relationships. See *Selected Writings,* p. 101. In their social theories Mead and Dewey were indebted to idealism; there was, for example, the similar position worked out by T. H. Green that deeply impressed Dewey (see Appendix 1, sec. C below).
[9] *Selected Writings,* p. 68.
[10] See *Mind, Self and Society,* ch. 1.
[11] *Ibid.,* p. 7.
[12] Cf. *Selected Writings,* pp. 102–103, for this statement of "preconditions."

kinds:[13] first, a not very large literature of Mead's published papers;[14] second, a valuable collection of manuscripts and notes which, as is natural, range widely in length, clarity, and subject matter;[15] third, collections of notes taken by students in Mead's classes, which have been carefully organized into the substance of three published volumes.[16]

Mead's incomplete expression of his philosophic thought confronts us as something like an ambitiously projected but unfinished building. We see clearly enough much of the broad structure, and also patches of finely worked detail. But between the whole and some of its parts there are gaps that leave us guessing as to what the final construction would have been. We must then proceed by clues found mostly in the notes of the professor and his students. But even here there is guesswork in what to count or discount of ideas and emphases that may have been distorted for heuristic and pedagogical reasons or because of other academic obligations. We are left, alas, to reckon with interpretations of interpretations, the editorial assemblages of students' notes.[17]

To make things more difficult, Mead happens to have had what James complained of as the blunted literary sense of most American philosophers and their "uncouthness of form."[18]

There is a last reservation, of a more historical kind, about the state of the materials for studying Mead. In Mead's theory of the emergence of the intelligent self—or, in older language, the emergence of mind—one will discover echoes of Chauncey Wright's argument concerning the evolution of self-consciousness, set forth in a labored and well-known essay of that title. We can also witness the influence of Peirce on Mead. For Peirce's rejection of the Cartesian methodology of science (as discussed in § 22) was a part of his rejection of the Cartesian doctrine of mind. Peirce worked out a theory of the mind within his more general theory of signs and sign uses. Man is a cultural creature; he invents, modifies, and controls symbols. Man's essence, "His glassy essence," is in this communal exercise of signs, for man and thought *are* signs and the signs a man uses *is* the man. Thus Peirce wrote:

> in what does the reality of mind consist? We have seen that the content of consciousness, the entire phenomenal manifestation of mind, is a sign resulting from inference.

[13] I pass over but do not mean to undervalue secondary works and explanations about the philosophy of Mead.

[14] For a valuable selection of these papers see Reck, ed., *Selected Writings*, and also Strauss, ed., *The Social Psychology of George Herbert Mead*.

[15] Even the most complete manuscript, his Carus lectures—published as *The Philosophy of the Present* (1932)—was not intended for publication and required extensive editorial work.

[16] Published as *Mind, Self and Society* (1934), *Movements of Thought in the Nineteenth Century* (1936), and *The Philosophy of the Act* (1938).

[17] An example, itself trivial, but symptomatic of problems that lurk in the reconstructed text of an author, is found in *The Philosophy of the Act*, which has Mead citing Speusippos and Democritus (p. 386) when he quite clearly meant, and no doubt spoke of, Leukippos and Democritus. There could be passages where homonyms seriously damage the intended argument.

[18] For the passage and source see § 76 below. James had Dewey and the Chicago School particularly in mind in making the comment.

Words are signs, he continues, and we do not want to say that words are conscious, but men and words do "reciprocally educate each other," and

> there is no element whatever of man's consciousness which has not something corresponding to it in the word; . . . the word or sign which man uses *is* the man himself. . . . Thus my language is the sum total of myself; for man is the thought.[19]

The knower in knowing himself, or in knowing others is engaged in *interpretation*, and what is interpreted is a sign (as we saw in the final paragraph of § 19).

Mead's theory of mind and the evolution of the self from the social situation of the use of symbols is indebted to Peirce; his behavioristic social psychology applied to language, and the social situation in which his analysis of mind is centered has its philosophic reflection in Peirce's and Royce's theories of the community of interpretation and the realization of the self in that community. But there is also the impact of James, and there is Mead's study of more recent work in physiological psychology in Europe, his study of Darwin, Wundt and Dewey in shaping his theory of mind and the social act. In short, while thoroughly in the pragmatist tradition, Mead was an eclectic thinker, and the exact nature of his formative influences is not easily discerned. At present, with the lack of working materials commented upon earlier, the need for further research into his papers and correspondence, and into his biography, any judgment on the historical origins of Mead's thought is somewhat speculative. One must proceed largely by inference.

It is with some trepidation, then, that one approaches the task of representing and critically exploring Mead's thought. Extensive quotations from Mead himself are included at certain points in the present chapter rather than attempting paraphrases. In spite of the difficulties in the materials, however, the remarkable if fragmentary remains of Mead's philosophic views are worthy of great admiration. It is sincerely hoped that the pages to follow help support rather than detract from that fact.

§ 50.   *Social Behaviorism*[20]

All of the pragmatists were influenced by the doctrine of biological evolution. Mead was a heavily indebted but critical student of the work of Darwin and Wundt. The book that Mead cites as especially important in the history of social psychology (and the psychology of language) was Darwin's *Expression of the*

---

[19] For this and the earlier passage, *CP* 5.313–314. See also *CP* 313–315: "Again, consciousness is sometimes used to signify the *I think,* or unity in thought; but the unity is nothing but consistency, or the recognition of it. Consistency belongs to every sign. . . . Now the organism is only an instrument of thought. But the identity of man consists in the *consistency* of what he does and thinks, and consistency is the intellectual character of a thing; that is, its expressing something." For a further connection with Peirce, see below, § 61, note 125.
[20] "Our behaviorism is a social behaviorism," *Mind, Self and Society,* p. 6.

Emotions in Man and Animals.[21] This and "the more elaborate presentation of Wundt" were basic sources for his own social psychology.[22] Also of great importance was the functionalism of James's *Psychology* and his teleological conception of mind (see above, § 28). Dewey's analysis of stimulus and response as acts within a larger coordination of behavior (the Reflex Arc paper discussed in § 38), his evolving of a theory of knowing as a reconstruction of experience, and his descriptions of the phases and operations in the process of reflective conduct were also major influences in shaping Mead's outlook.

The starting point and basic subject matter for social behaviorism is the "social act." According to Mead,

> Social psychology studies the activity or behavior of the individual as it lies within the social process; the behavior of an individual can be understood only in terms of the behavior of the whole social group of which he is a member, since his individual acts are involved in larger, social acts which go beyond himself and which implicate the other members of that group.[23]

The direction of analysis, Mead then argues, is from "the social whole of complex group activity, into which we analyze (as elements) the behavior of the separate individuals composing it."[24] As we saw earlier, Mead contends that the whole is prior to the part and the "part is explained in terms of the whole."[25] Mead thus resolutely takes the Aristotelian rather than Hobbesian point of view (as lately contrasted, § 48).

Now this methodological point of view also happens to reproduce a genetic and *causal* order for Mead. It is the tracing and explanation of this order of events —namely, of the emergence[26] of the self and mind—that contains, as we shall see, some of Mead's most interesting and highly original theorizing.

§ 51.   Genetic Psychology and Social Theory

Dewey, among the group of social theorists at Chicago,[27] had stated the course to be taken by "genetic psychology" (that is, the "functional" psychology of the Chicago group, see § 38, notes 67, 68 above) in developing a social theory.[28]

---

[21] Cf. *Mind, Self and Society*, p. 15.
[22] *Ibid.*, p. 42.
[23] *Ibid.*, p. 6.
[24] *Ibid.*, p. 7.
[25] *Ibid.*, p. 7, and § 48 above for the larger passage.
[26] 'Emerge' is one of Mead's favorite words; it plays as characteristic a role in his philosophy as 'continuity' does for Dewey.
[27] The group included Mead, Albion Small, John Dewey, William James, H. Tufts, W. I. Thomas, and Thorstein Veblen. For a sketch of the background and position, see Schneider, ch. 33, esp. pp. 389–395.
[28] Dewey's paper "Interpretation of Savage Mind" (1902) was an influential formulation of the genetic-functional psychological approach in social philosophy. If one takes this paper in conjunction with "The Reflex Arc Concept" (see § 38 above), the structure of Dewey's educational and social thought emerges clearly.

The biological point of view commits us to the conviction that mind, whatever else it may be, is at least an organ of service for the control of environment in relation to the ends of the life process.[29]

If one examines any social group, Dewey then argued, the working or expressive functions of mind, in the sense of "mind" thus described, will be found in occupations.

Occupations determine the fundamental modes of activity, and hence control the formation and use of habits. . . . The occupations determine the chief modes of satisfaction, the standards of success and failure. Hence they furnish the working classifications and definitions of value; they control the desire process.[30]

Occupations, in Dewey's view, were given the same central place that "social acts" came to have in Mead's theory.

. . . They decide the sets of objects and relations that are important, and thereby provide the content or material of attention, and the qualities that are interestingly significant.[31]

Mental activity issues in occupations. But, Dewey continues, occupations direct and reconstitute[32] mental life.

The directions given to mental life thereby extend to emotional and intellectual characteristics. So fundamental and pervasive is the group of occupational activities that it affords the scheme or pattern of the structural organization of mental traits. Occupations integrate special elements into a functioning whole.[33]

Dewey proceeded to concentrate upon the hunting vocation—as a "psychophysic coordination"—among the Australian aborigines. His purpose was to show how the "mental pattern" developed in this occupation evolved and was carried over into other activities and institutions having nothing to do with hunting. This was a "psychological method for sociology," showing the evolutions and transformation of social institutions.[34]

[29] "Interpretation of Savage Mind." Originally published in *The Psychological Review*, 1902, Dewey's paper was reprinted in *Philosophy and Civilization*, pp. 173–187. Further references below are first to the original publication and then to the latter volume; for the above passage, p. 219; *Philosophy and Civilization*, p. 175.
[30] *Ibid.*, pp. 219–220; *Philosophy and Civilization*, p. 176.
[31] *Ibid.*, p. 220; *Philosophy and Civilization*, p. 176.
[32] I use this word deliberately in the Deweyan sense for the details of which see the latter half of § 38.
[33] "Interpretation of Savage Mind," p. 220; *Philosophy and Civilization*, p. 176.
[34] Dewey's express aim is interesting and deserves full statement here: "As a specific illustration of the standpoint and method I shall take the hunting vocation, and that as carried on by the Australian aborigines. I shall try first to describe its chief distinguishing marks; and then to show how the mental pattern developed is carried over into various activities, customs and products, which on their face have nothing to do with the hunting life. If a controlling influence of this sort can be made out—if it can be shown that art, war, marriage, etc. tend to be psychologically assimilated to the pattern developed in the hunting vocation, we shall thereby get an important method for the interpretation of social institutions and cultural resources—a psychological method for sociology." *Ibid.*, p. 220; *Philosophy and Civilization*, p. 176.

Dewey's answer to the question of the origins of society is suggested by his analysis of occupations. Society is an evolving network of occupations. But the person who first enters into occupations becomes transformed by them.

> . . . The adjustment of habits to ends, through the medium of a problematic, doubtful, precarious situation, is the structural form upon which present intelligence and emotion are built. It remains the ground-pattern. The further problem of genetic psychology is then to show how the purely immediate personal adjustment of habit to direct satisfaction, in the savage, became transformed through the introduction of impersonal, generalized objective instrumentalities and ends; how it ceased to be immediate and became loaded and surcharged with a content which forced personal want, initiative, effort and satisfaction further and further apart, putting all kinds of social divisions of labor, intermediate agencies and objective contents between them.[35]

Dewey was suggesting how, through a "genetic psychology," one might explain the formation of mental patterns operative in varied social occupations. The occupations and pursuits would be explained as "reconstructions" and "transformations" of some more original and primitive occupation. This was the genetic, psychological, and evolutionary method applied to the development of personality (or individuality) in society and to social institutions.

Mead's theory of the orgin of the self and mind complements Dewey's analysis of the social readjustment and reconstruction of original habits and immediate satisfactions and elaborates in considerable detail a feature only touched upon by Dewey. Mead was particularly concerned with this one very important kind of transformation of the person within social occupations—namely, the social process through which the participating individual becomes a conscious self. This is a formative process that cuts across, or is found within, all other social occupations. The process here, which Mead studied in detail, is that of language and symbolization. This is the most universal of social activities and its evolution eventuates in the most universal of institutions: science. The following statement expresses Mead's interests and his evolutionary viewpoint. In the idea of evolution, Mead says,

> We have a statement of the human animal as having reached a situation in which he gets control over his environment. Now, it is not the human animal as an individual that reaches any such climax as that; it is society. . . . The human animal as an individual could never have attained control over the environment. It is a control which has arisen through social organization. The very speech he uses, the very mechanism of thought which is given, are social products. His own self is attained only through his taking the attitude of the social group to which he belongs. He must become socialized to become himself. So when you speak of this evolution, of its having reached a certain climax in human form, you must realize that it reaches that point only in so far as the human form is recognized as an organic part of the social whole. Now there is nothing so social as science, nothing

[35] Ibid., pp. 229–230; Philosophy and Civilization, p. 187.

so universal. Nothing so rigorously oversteps the points that separate man from man and groups from groups as does science. There cannot be any narrow provincialism or patriotism in science. Scientific method makes that impossible. Science is inevitably a universal discipline which takes in all who think. It speaks with the voice of all rational beings. It must be true everywhere; otherwise it is not scientific. But science is evolutionary. . . . there is a continuous process which is taking on successively different forms.[36]

Dewey had pointed out that group occupational activities constitute "the pattern of the structural organization of mental traits."[37] Mead went further; he thought that the act of entering into a social occupation, becoming conscious of group attitudes and ways, is to become a mind and a self, an individual. How does this happen in a social process?

This question had occurred earlier. But in now coming to the details of Mead's answer, we are able to get rid of a certain clumsiness in how it has been asked. There is something unsettling about the phrasing when we speak of a human being "becoming himself"; or when we speak of a "self arising" or (perhaps) the mind of an individual "emerging." For surely by any ordinary criterion of identity, objects are identical with themselves and with nothing else. To say that a human being becomes himself is to say, then that *he* becomes what he is and nothing else; true, but not impressive. And how in other than trivial fashion can we speak of an individual self "arising" from a social process? What is *it* that is alleged to arise but a self? Yet this is to say no more than that an individual self *is* or becomes an individual self.

Mead's account is guided by some preliminary distinctions. Individual self and mind are not identical with (thus not the same objects as) the biological organism or physiological individual. Self and mind cannot occur without an organism and body. Bodies, that is, live creatures, *can* function without being selves. "The self is . . . entirely distinguishable from an organism that is surrounded by things and acts with reference to things, including parts of its own body."[38] The self, Mead argues, has one characteristic that marks it off from other objects and the body. The self "is an object to itself."[39] The word 'self' is *reflexive* it "indicates that which can be both subject and object.'[40] Now the reflexive character of the self occurs through communication. Communication provides that kind of behavior in which an individual can become an object to himself.[41]

The question, then, of how individuals become selves and minds is a question having to do with how certain kinds of animal organisms, through a certain

---

[36] *Movements of Thought in the Nineteenth Century*, p. 168.
[37] Above, and "Interpretation of the Savage Mind," p. 176.
[38] *Mind, Self and Society*, p. 137. Also cf. p. 136: "We can distinguish very definitely between the self and the body. The body can be there and can operate in a very intelligent fashion without there being a self involved in the experience." For more on this distinction see *The Philosophy of the Act*, pp. 445–453.
[39] *Mind, Self and Society*, p. 136.
[40] *Ibid.*, pp. 136–137.
[41] *Ibid.*, p. 138.

kind of social activity, become objects to themselves. We still must see what this means, but the question so understood is not anomalous.

§ 52. Social Gesture and Language

The social act in which a self emerges is the act of language or communication. A social act requires a cooperation of more than one individual;[42] language, then, for Mead, is to be viewed not as an affair of communicating private meanings or a way of conveying ideas or states of consciousness.

> We want to approach language not from the standpoint of inner meanings to be expressed, but in its larger context of co-operation in the group taking place by means of signals and gestures. Meaning appears within that process.[43]

The behavior that Mead held as fundamental to explaining the origin and use of language is that of gestures. Communication between animals and men has this origin: the gestures of one individual prompt responses in another, and the responses thus elicited prompt further gestures and responses between them. A conversation of gestures is the source of the language process.[44]

Mead found the importance of the gesture, as explaining the origin of language, partly in Darwin's *Expression of Emotions in Man and Animals.* Darwin described physical attitudes as well as physiological changes (e.g., blushing or growing pale) as expressive of emotions. The original function of some of these gestures, say, the baring of teeth originally for attack, had been lost; but the attitude or gesture served another function, as when baring of teeth is expressive of anger. The attractive aspect of Darwin's analysis to a man of Mead's predilections was that it suggested an evolutionary biological origin of the gesture of language. But the objection to Darwin was to his subjectivistic psychological theory: emotions are "inner states," and the gestures are outward expressions of these ideas or meanings. This is a theory of mind and psychophysical behavior that both Dewey and Mead had criticized in detail. Speaking of Darwin and psychologists who were interested, as Darwin was, in the study of how individuals communicate to one another through attitudes and acts, Mead adds:

> They assume that these acts had a reason for existence because they expressed something in the mind of the individual. It is an approach like that of the philologist. They assume that language existed for the purpose of conveying certain ideas, certain feelings.[45]

[42] Thus Mead writes: "I wish . . . to restrict the social act to the class of acts which involve the co-operation of more than one individual, and whose object as defined by the act, in the sense of Bergson, is a social object." *Ibid.,* p. 7, note 7. The quotation is from the article by Mead, "The Genesis of the Self," see *Selected Writings,* p. 279.
[43] *Mind, Self and Society,* p. 6.
[44] Cf. *ibid.,* p. 14.
[45] *Ibid.,* p. 16. In the same passage Mead observes that animals do not "undertake to express their emotions. They certainly do not undertake to express them for the benefit of

The idea of gestures as means for eliciting responses from other animals—thus as parts of a social act—was due to Wundt.[46] Mead's theory is an extension of Wundt's; but here, too, Mead rejected the "psychophysical parallelism" of Wundt, and argued that Wundt could not explain how the language of gestures arose.[47]

> The difficulty is that Wundt presupposes selves as antecedent to the social process in order to explain communication within that process, whereas, on the contrary, selves must be accounted for in terms of the social process, and in terms of communication.[48]

For Mead, language has its origin in gestures. The concept of *gesture* is thus basic to this social-psychological theory of the nature of communicative behavior. It is also, then, basic to the explanation of the emergence of selves, or minds, in the language process.

Now the essential characteristic of a gesture is (one might have suspected) its social properties. That is, a gesture affects and coordinates behavior among two or more individuals. In its simplest form, presumably, a gesture occurs as part of some action of one individual to which another individual responds. It is the act "as stimulations for the conduct of other individuals" that Mead especially emphasizes.[49]

Gestures and "conversations of gestures" occur among all kinds of animals, including man. For example, "the preliminaries of a dog or cock fight amply illustrate the sensitiveness of such individuals to the earliest perceptible indications of coming acts";[50] and human individuals engaged in a fencing or boxing match exhibit a like sensitivity to gestures, stimulating other gestures in response. Indeed, gestures occur between different kinds of animals, as between animals of prey and those they prey upon, or as in the dog's growl inducing the man to shrink back.

There are two important senses in which gestures possess *sociality* (if we can put it so), senses not always made clear by Mead. First, as we have seen, a gesture is the social phase of an individual act, that is, a cause of (and a reason for) a responsive act on the part of other individuals. In this sense the sociality of a gesture consists of a causal relation of behavioral acts among individuals; through gestures, individuals reciprocally influence one another's behavior. But the sec-

---

other animals." See also "The Theory of Emotion," the two important papers by Dewey in 1894–1895—drawing upon, but no doubt also shaping Mead's views—that set forth an analysis of emotion in which Darwin's theory and the James-Lange theory are brought "into some organic connection with each other."

[46] See *Selected Writings*, pp. 109–110.

[47] See *ibid.*, p. 42, n. 1, and ch. 7 complete for the criticism of Wundt. The psychophysical parallelism had come in for severe critical analysis in Dewey's "Reflex Arc Concept," for which see § 38 above.

[48] *Selected Writings*, p. 49.

[49] *Ibid.*, p. 109. Or cf. *Mind, Self and Society*, p. 46: "The gesture is that phase of the individual act to which adjustment takes place on the part of other individuals in the social process of behavior."

[50] *Selected Writings*, p. 110.

ond sense in which gestures possess sociality is a prerequisite of the first: gestures will have to be *significant* before they can function as stimuli to responsive acts (before they possess sociality in the first sense).

What is meant by calling gestures *significant* is difficult to make precise, yet the contention is not unclear. 'Significance' here refers to a socially organized and patterned act, one that has become established as a stimulus for which there are equally established responses.[51] Thus, in boxing, a certain movement is part of the coordinated act of delivering a blow to the opponent's jaw; the opponent recognizes this and responds accordingly. The initial movement has become a gesture; it calls forth a response from another individual. Of course, part of the skill of boxing consists in one's making use of gestures, or the established *significance* of gestures, to elicit a response that can be used to one's advantage. This, as we will see, is a new level of gesturing and of "meaning" for Mead. Thus the technique of boxing consists of a store of *feints*, gestures designed to be like other similar gestures; but these, too, are socially established and are therefore "significant." "That's an old trick, I should have known better," one says, as his opponent draws out a response that usually, customarily, is appropriate to the kind of act he initiated.

Thus in the performance of a gesture a socially established *type* of act elicits an established *type* of response. This sense of the *significance* of gestures is the basis for Mead's analysis of "consciousness of meaning" or for the emergence of meaning and selfhood. Imagine, however, oneself engaged in fencing or boxing with a child or a wooden post. The degrees of response to one's lunging or striking shade off from mostly uncoordinated, unpatterned acts to no response at all. In this case we have acts occurring between individuals, but not gestures— not until the child learns the appropriate response to the acts we are performing.

For a gesture to occur, then, entails the action of an agent and the response of another in which the response is an interpretation of the initial act. The pattern here is a coordination of acts in which a stimulus becomes constituted (or made significant) by a response—just the pattern Dewey had investigated in his "Reflex Arc Concept" (discussed above, § 38). But for a response as an *interpretation* of stimulus to occur, a social process is necessary. The amateur boxer, or the child, learns what and how appropriate responses follow the occurrence of certain kinds of acts.

Thus far we have been considering the gesture—or significant gesture—on a relatively elementary and primary level of occurrence. Here the gesture occurs when simply to the action of one individual there is an appropriate response from at least one other individual. We want now to turn to a more complicated form of gesture in which, for Mead, consciousness and meaning are found.

As long as one individual responds simply to the gesture of another by the appropriate response, there is no necessary consciousness of meaning. The situation is

[51] *Ibid.*, p. 110: "Gestures then are already significant in the sense that they are stimuli to performed reactions. . . ."

still on a level of that of two growling dogs walking around each other, with tense limbs . . . and uncovered teeth. It is not until an image arises of the response, which the gesture of one . . . will bring out in another, that a consciousness of meaning can attach to his own gesture.[52]

Gestures "take on meaning" or "consciousness of meaning" when the initial act in the gesture is performed with some reference to the response it produces. Treating *meaning* here as "consciousness of attitude" and, perhaps, of purpose, Mead is maintaining that when acts are performed with the purpose of effecting (thus in anticipation of, and to some extent conditional upon) a *response*, the gesture (i.e., act and response) includes "consciousness of meaning." To recall the examples earlier of boxing or fencing, these activities are instances of gestures with conscious meaning. The actions of the actors thus engaged are performed partly in order to produce certain kinds of responses and further actions.

§ 53. *The Significant Symbol*

For this second class of gestures, in which is included "consciousness of meaning," let us follow an alternative nomenclature of Mead's. We may call these gestures "significant symbols."[53] Although this is not entirely clear in Mead's writings, it would seem that significant symbols actually compose a subclass of the second sort of gestures, that is, of gestures that involve consciousness of meaning. The following illustration suggests these distinctions. Now and then a child screams, and on these occasions his parents rush to him. So far this scream is the initial act of a significant gesture of the first and elementary kind. After a while the child discovers that his scream produces the response in his parents. His scream, then, is the initial act in a significant gesture of the second kind; for the child has developed "consciousness of meaning" of the gesture. He screams *because* of the anticipated response or *in order to* produce the parental response. Now a further development in the child's "consciousness of meaning" is possible. This would consist of the child responding to his own scream with something like the quality of alarm, anxiety, and posture exhibited in the response of his parents. Here we have a gesture become a "significant symbol."

What has happened in the child's development is that his scream calls out the same response in himself as it produces in others. Presumably, also, as a phase in this development (or perhaps this is the very same development),[54] the child will respond as others do when someone else's scream is heard.

[52] *Ibid.*, pp. 110–111.

[53] "Significant symbol" is not to be confused with "significant gesture." For although Mead's terminology underwent some vicissitudes, it is consistent with his views to distinguish (as we have above) two classes of *significant gesture*. The *significant symbol* is found in all (or perhaps only some) of the second class of gestures. For details see "A Behavioristic Account of the Significant Symbol," *Selected Writings*, pp. 240–247; *Mind, Self and Society*, pp. 46–48, and esp. pp. 61–75.

[54] This is a minor but interesting feature of behavior that I do not find Mead discussing in any detail. I suppose—from indications found, e.g., in p. 134 of *Mind, Self and Society*—that

The notion of significant symbol is of considerable help to us in understanding Mead's view of *meaning* as referring to socially shared and uniformly conditioned attitudes and responses attaching to gestures. The especially important phenomenon here is the individual's becoming "conscious" of his own gesture, that is, his responding to his own gestures in much the same way as others respond. For then, Mead argues, the individual has come to be not only aware of others and the circumstances that prompt others to act in predictable ways, he has also "become an object to himself";[55] he has begun to respond to himself (i.e., his own gestures and attitudes).

This evolution of "consciousness," here meaning self-interpretation (i.e., interpreting one's own gestures), presupposes the social process in which the individual has first participated in conversations of gestures with others. But now a special "other" has become recognized as a stimulus and gesturer: namely, one's self. This lastly evolved process Mead calls "internalization." The social process of gestures, the process of acts and responses and further acts carried on among individuals, now becomes an internal process in the individual's own experience. On this fundamental idea and what it leads to for his analysis of language and mind, the following statement of Mead's is illuminating.

When, in any given act or situation, one individual indicates by a gesture to another individual what this other individual is to do, the first individual is conscious of the meaning of his own gesture—or the meaning of his gesture appears in his own experience—in so far as he takes the attitude of the second individual toward that gesture, and tends to respond to it implicitly in the same way that the second individual responds to it explicitly. Gestures become significant symbols when they implicitly arouse in an individual making them the same responses which they explicitly arouse, or are supposed to arouse, in other individuals, the individuals to whom they are addressed; and in all conversations of gestures within the social process, whether external (between different individuals) or internal (between a given individual and himself), the individual's consciousness of the content and flow of meaning involved depends on his thus taking the attitude of the other toward his own gesture. . . . In this way every gesture comes within a given social group or community to stand for a particular act or response, namely, the act or response which it calls forth explicitly in the individual to whom it is addressed, and implicitly in the individual who makes it; and this particular act or response for which it stands is its meaning as a significant symbol. Only in terms of gestures as significant symbols is the existence of mind or intelligence possible; for only in terms of gestures which are significant symbols can thinking —which is simply an internalized or implicit conversation of the individual with himself by means of such gestures—take place. The internalization in our experi-

---

Mead's view is that the very way one learns to respond (as others respond) to one's own gesture comes with (and is an integral part of the process of) one's responding to like gestures coming from others. Thus, our own responses to our own gestures are developed, i.e., "adjusted," "modified," "refined" (as Mead says), through a social process in which one also responds with other individuals to the gestures of others.

[55] *Mind, Self and Society*, p. 138.

ence of the external conversations of gestures which we carry on with other individuals in the social process is the essence of thinking; and the gestures thus internalized are significant symbols because they have the same meanings for all individual members of the given society or social group, i.e., they respectively arouse the same attitudes in the individuals making them that they arouse in the individuals responding to them: otherwise the individual could not internalize them or be conscious of them and their meanings. As we shall see, the same procedure which is responsible for the genesis and existence of mind or consciousness—namely, the taking of the attitude of the other toward one's self, or toward one's own behavior—also necessarily involves the genesis and existence at the same time of significant symbols, or significant gestures.[56]

When gestures become significant symbols, language is achieved. Language, for Mead, is something more and something else than the stage of conversation of gestures that we glanced at earlier. And, says Mead, "out of language emerges the field of mind."[57]

§ 54. Language as Gesture

Religion and philology are often coupled practices in primitive cultures; they seem to have conspired also in prompting John's account of Genesis: "In the beginning was the word." Faust (we happened to recall in § 14) decided that the text should be: "In the beginning was the *Deed*." Were we to demand from Mead an equally high deliverance on this solemn theme, we should get a perfect piece of liberal theology and a nice compromise. For Mead, in the beginning (of human language and self-consciousness) was the *word-deed*. That is, the *vocal gesture*.

There are numerous ways in which creatures engage in conversations of gestures; there are many kinds of gestures and always ample means for developing new gestures or modifying the old. But vocal gestures have a rather special place in Mead's theory and, according to the theory, in the evolution of the human race.

What distinguishes the vocal gesture from others, from facial expressions, bodily attitude or posture, movements of limbs? Obviously, the fact that vocal gestures are *heard*, while these others are *seen*. There are, of course, other obvious distinctions. The production of vocal acts and their reception requires organs and techniques different from those necessary to the other kinds of gestures. But more: the movements and objects that function as visible physical gestures are subject to familiar optical conditions and relations holding among observers and objects in space. Thus, the individual performing an action does not observe

---

[56] *Ibid.*, pp. 47–48.
[57] *Ibid.*, p. 133.

himself as others do (mirrors and feats of photography being ruled out for the moment); and, indeed, the observers of these actions are each situated in a different perspective, so that no two observers see quite the same performance. In the case of the vocal gesture, however, the conditions of optimum uniformity of reception of stimuli (i.e., of observations of acts, including the observation the individual acting makes upon his own acts) are usually easily attained. For one hears one's own utterances, and others hear them too, with a minimum of variations from observer to observer.

Now let us suppose—partly to summarize—that in the case of vocal gestures, the individuals sounding and those responding (with other sounds or actions) achieve a uniformity of stimuli and response not at all or not easily attained through other kinds of gesture. We recognize a norm of stimulus and response and a clustering about this norm with very little spread when vocal gestures operate. The mere fact of nearly identical patterns, of shared experience among all participants, is not all that Mead wants to argue. But it does point to the special importance of vocal gestures in this respect: the vocal gesture is the medium for one's becoming a self, or evolving and becoming aware of oneself as a self. The vocal gesture is the particularly apt and functional medium for using and developing the capacity to respond to one's own stimulus as others would and do respond.[58]

> The vocal gesture, then, has an importance which no other gesture has. We cannot see ourselves when our face assumes a certain expression. If we hear ourselves speak we are more apt to pay attention. One hears himself when he is irritated using a tone that is of an irritable quality, and so catches himself.[59]

When a man calls out "Fire!" he is "not only exciting other people but himself in the same fashion."[60] But supposing the man, or better, a child, calls "Fire!" and does not produce a response of excitement or alarm in himself. In this case he has not learned the vocal gesture as a significant symbol.

[58] The plausibility of Mead's contention of the social uniformity in response to the vocal gesture is not seriously diminished by inventing special counterinstances and caveats against it, easily manufactured as these are. But it is worth remarking upon the propensity among observers to want to achieve uniformity of observations, even to believing that uniformity was achieved in cases where it was not. Thus witnesses in trials sometimes are shown to believe (wrongly) that they have seen an event occur as others saw it, or as they believe others would have, and thus they should have seen it. Similarly, in conversations among persons, speech differences and variations tend shortly to become unnoticed—one thinks one's own and others' speech achieves uniformity. This propensity (not pointed out by Mead as far as I know) contributes to our establishing what Mead calls the "generalized other"—one sees oneself and others impersonally, as fulfilling a role; one thinks of a *kind* of person or agent (with individual variations cancelled out) taking and acting out a *kind* of role. Thus (as relating to the propensity I refer to here) consider one's surprise in hearing a recording of one's speaking voice. We are then acutely observing our own departure in speech behavior from a norm that we had believed we and other speakers all approximated.
[59] *Mind, Self and Society*, p. 65. A good presentation of this part of the theory is also found in *Movements of Thought in the Nineteenth Century*, pp. 375–385, cf. esp. p. 379.
[60] *Movements of Thought*, p. 380.

§ 55.   A Schematization of Gestures and Significant Symbols

A fairly simple set of symbols can be used to represent the main ideas in Mead's theory of gestures. The symbols allow us to sum up in a neat and less laborious way a number of the matters already dealt with; they also will prove convenient aids in the discussions of other issues to come. The machinery we require for this purpose is as follows.

We have been and will be considering groups of individuals—for Mead, individual biological organisms engaged in acts of communication. Let us symbolize the individual organisms by 'I' and the presence of two or more individuals simply by $I_1, I_2, I_3 \ldots$ etc.

Next, we recognize acts performed by groups of individuals. We are concerned, of course, with *gestures*, not with any sort of activity, but with *types* of acts performed by the individuals of a group. We are also concerned with *types* of responses that are called forth from individuals when acts are performed (or suggested). As Mead likes to put it: certain responses are "appropriate" when certain acts occur. And 'appropriate' here deliberately suggests that acts and responses are socially evolved and conditioned to conform to patterns of conduct. There are norm-*al* acts and responses to them. The acts may be designated by '*a*' and response by '*r*'; and various types of acts and responses by primes attaching to these symbols so that '*a*'' could symbolize the act of smiling, '*a*''' the act of screaming; '*a*'''' a bodily movement, etc. To each of these acts we shall suppose (skipping over vast stretches of complicating detail) there are appropriate types of responses, '*r*','r*'',' '*r*''',' etc.[61] The act of a certain individual I_1 and response of another individual I_2 can now be represented with the help of the arrow '→': thus, $I_1a \rightarrow I_2r$. But the act is of a type, say, screaming (or '*a*'') and the response is also, say, alarm (or '*r*''); so: $I_1a' \rightarrow I_2r'$.

Now it happens that a certain response *r*' from an individual may also serve as an act (or stimulus) calling out in turn other and further responses from other individuals. In a process of gestures, in "conversations of gestures," acts call out responses that then become stimuli (or acts) for further responses, etc.

---

[61] In thus letting '*a*' and '*r*' represent types of acts and responses, we happen, incidentally, to touch upon a subject of some interest to Mead. In actual performances, so he argued, actions and responses are unique. The particular stimulus conditions of one act and the particular circumstances in which the response from others occurs are local, individual, and never quite the same. The actual physical occurrence of *a* and *r* is "particular." But the particular stimuli and responses are also social. The act and response are significant symbols, thus organized and patterned communal modes of behavior. So the structure of the occurring expressions of *a*'s and *r*'s also possesses a "universal" character: the organized attitudes and roles of the group that are expressed in a social act or response. Thus, that individuals and objects perform *types* of acts and responses which call forth *types* of responses, treated then as *types* of objects—this led Mead to argue for a socio-behavioristic version of universals. See *Philosophy of the Act,* pp. 388–392; *Mind, Self and Society,* pp. 82–90.

Let us then symbolize a response r to an act that also serves as a stimulus for a future response as $'r(a).'$[62]

We can now apply this symbolism.[63]

1)   It was noticed earlier (in § 52) that *gestures* are *social* acts. Hence, two features, it was argued, distinguish gestures from simply *any* kind of behavior. A gesture relates the behavior of at least two individuals, one acting, the other responding. Gestures are "significant," that is, a certain kind of act is performed (as a cause or reason) in order to produce a certain kind of response. Now the simplest form of gesture (noted above at § 52) between two individuals I_1 and I_2 can be defined: $I_1d' \rightarrow I_2r'$. And, where a gesture is performed by one individual to which several other individuals respond, we have:

$$I_1d' \rightarrow I_2r', I_3r', I_4r' \dots, \text{etc.}$$

2)   A conversation of gestures between two individuals I_1 and I_2 may now be represented:

$$I_1d' \rightarrow I_2r' \text{ and } I_2d'' \rightarrow I_1r'' \text{ and } I_1d''' \rightarrow \dots \text{ and so on.}$$

A conversation of gestures among three or more individuals is easily extended from this pattern. Where the first individual acts and the second individual responds with a response that also serves as a stimulus-act to which the first individual responds and acts, we have:

$$I_1d' \rightarrow I_2r'(d'') \rightarrow I_1r''(d''') \rightarrow I_2 \dots \text{ and so on.}$$

3)   We come next to the *significant symbol*, that is, where an individual I_1 not only produces a type of r on other individuals but also responds (in the same way as others do) to his own act d':

$$I_1d' \rightarrow I_2r', I_3r' \dots \text{ and } I_1r'.$$

This may also be represented simply as:

$$I_1d' \rightarrow I_1r'.$$

---

[62] There are two observations to be made on this last paragraph of symbolism. First, the arrow '$\rightarrow$' simply reproduces Mead's way of saying that an act "calls forth" or "produces" a response. The convention of the arrow remains undaringly noncommittal and vague over the more subtle and extremely important distinction between a being a *cause* of r and a being a *reason for* r. Second, one recognizes that acts and responses occur in contexts and thus (quite in accord with the contextualism espoused in Part IV, ch. 1 below), relative to the contexts, an event of behavior can be construed from one point of view as a response, from another as a stimulus-act. Moreover, as we saw Dewey argue in § 38, in the course of behavior the character of a stimulus a can be "interpreted," "reconstructed" by a response r, and the kind of response to-be-made can function as an "object" and stimulus. So the above symbol of a response that also serves as a stimulus-act to further responses (viz., $'r(a)'$) avoids a host of further distinctions that might be called for in a more detailed analysis of behavior. Still, that the "same" event of behavior can function as a response of one type in context (viz., r') and can also serve as a stimulus-act of another type (viz., d'') can be symbolized thus: $r'(d'')$.

[63] Further niceties of specifying *contexts* or circumstances in which gestures occur, the time of a and r, are ignored here.

If we wish to consider an individual responding to his own acts and whose responses also serve as stimulus-acts to further response (i.e., for Mead, "internalization of conversation of gestures"), we have:

$$I_1 d' \rightarrow I_1 r' (d'') \rightarrow I_1 r'' (d''') \rightarrow \ldots \text{and so on.}$$

In this last scheme, if a and r be taken as vocal acts and responses, the whole pattern is one of vocal gestures internalized. That is, individual I_1 is talking to himself. Through this process, says Mead, the *self* emerges.[64] This we shall see shortly. The simple pattern representing an individual responding to his own acts,

$$I_1 d' \rightarrow I_1 r',$$

gives us a way of seeing what Mead means by an individual becoming "an object to himself" and the all important *reflexive* character of the notion of *self* which we came upon earlier (at the close of § 49 above).

Here we may take note of the fact that, for Mead, in a tradition going back to Peirce and to Berkeley, the r in these representations functions as an interpretation of an a; and the a is (under normal circumstances) a sign for and a prediction of[65] the occurrence of r. Now *signs* and *interpretations*, the acts and responses that go into gestures, are social institutions. It is in the social process that a's and r's become patterns of behavior; these are the norms and this is the process that precedes the emergence of particular individual selves. In short, the stages in the above scheme follow Mead's account of the genesis of mind and self: stages (1) and (2) precede stage (3) and the significant symbol. And prior to an individual I_1 responding to his own acts, the acts and responses—the a's and r's—have already evolved and function as types of conduct among individuals. The individual I_1 comes to them, or to take them up; they do not originally come from him. This, again, is the Aristotelian point of view commented on in § 48.

Before indulging in this symbolization of Mead's views, we were considering the importance of vocal-gestures. This now requires our attention further.

§ 56. An Actor Prepares

It is interesting that for illustrations of communication among individuals, either as conversations of gestures or conversations of significant symbols, Mead often resorts to instances of games, sports, hide-and-go-seek, boxing, fencing. Animals exhibit conversations of gestures; and some animals and birds master the significant symbol, i.e., respond to their own acts. Thus, a bird singing calls out a

---

[64] *Selected Writings,* p. 146: "The self which consciously stands over against other selves thus becomes an object, an other to himself, through the very fact that he hears himself talk, and replies."

[65] However, a is not in itself a prediction; a is an act that serves the purpose of carrying out a prediction, an anticipation and active attempt to produce a response r. See *Mind, Self and Society,* p. 73.

response in another—perhaps a song or physical movement. But the sheer act of singing can serve to produce responses in the bird to his own song, responses that act in turn to stimulate more song.[66]

The difference between the bird (say a parrot who quite skillfully uses vocal gestures) and man is the extent to which "internalization" takes place. Animals and birds are not responsive to those gestures they themselves act out, in the sense of responding as other creatures also respond (and responding to the fact that other creatures also so respond to the gesture).[67]

Birds engaged in the ritual preparatory to mating, animals hunting others, men dueling or boxing are dramatic enactments of conversations of gestures.

There is one human activity in which physical gestures are acquired and refined that is in many ways analogous to our developing vocal gestures. This is, as Mead points out, the fine art of acting in the theater. The training of an actor is very suggestive of the ways in which we become educated in vocal gestures. Perhaps because the education of an actor is an unusual process (beyond that point at which most of us leave off developing acting techniques) and the acquisition of vocal gestures is so native to us all, the analogy between processes is instructive. For the unusual and very attentive activity of the actor has its counterpart in our ordinary half-conscious learning of speech. In each case, the central feature is that of self-observation. The actor observes himself in a mirror; we hear our own voice.

The actor holds up a mirror and practices facial gestures. He recognizes, of course, that it is *his* face that he observes. He forms an expression, a grimace of pain or a smile of joy. He has two sources of experience to draw upon for developing this technique: he has seen other persons form these expressions and he has responded (with others) to the expressions; he has also formed these expressions in the past and observed how other persons have responded. With his mirror he is able to combine both of these otherwise distinct ways of learning how to form "appropriate" expressions. He is the actor as he forms the expression; but he is society and critic in his response to what he sees. His expression of pain may not be quite right; he wishes the expressive act to be of a certain character, that is, to produce a certain kind of response in his audience. He watches himself via the mirror, but he is also seeing himself as others would see him. He thus not only is critically appraising his own expression, but also

---

[66] Thus animals and birds may sometimes exhibit the pattern represented in (3) of the last section:

$$I_1 a' \rightarrow I_1 r'(a'') \rightarrow I_1 r''(a''') \rightarrow \ldots \text{ and so on.}$$

However, the extent of this series of acts and responses (the number of different a's and r's in the process) is very much limited for these creatures, and quite flexible and variable for humans.

[67] *Mind, Self and Society,* p. 81: "The conversation of gestures is not significant below the human level, because it is not conscious, that is, not *self*-conscious (though it is conscious in the sense of involving feelings or sensations). An animal as opposed to a human form, in indicating something to, or bringing out a meaning for, another form, is not at the same time indicating or bringing out the same thing or meaning to or for himself; for he has no mind."

is making some critical observations on a hypothetical audience. He is watching himself as others would watch him *and* he is simultaneously "watching" the "others" watching himself. He is imagining or hypothesizing that he is both watching his own performance on stage and watching the expressions of persons in the audience who are witnessing the performance. The process of studying one's gestures in a mirror is far from simple.

Our actor, dissatisfied with how he is expressing pain, modifies or accentuates the gesture. Here the initial act *a* is undergoing modification as a result of a response *r*.[68] Here Dewey's circuit coordination of stimulus-response (§ 38) is at work. The initial original stimulus-act *a* is being "reconstructed," and the original response *r* to *a* is serving as a stimulus to the modification of *a*. The pattern—to recall the scheme of (3) in the preceding section—is:

$$I_1 a' \rightarrow I_1 r'(a'') \rightarrow I_1 r''(a''') \rightarrow \ldots .$$

Here, the actor I_1 continues to modify his act a', a'', a''' as a result of a series of responses r', r'', r''', etc.

There are features of the actor's behavior here that set off what he is doing from ordinary performances of facial gestures. First, he is developing the ability to form expressions of pain and joy independent of any occurring experience of pain or joy. Much as the duelist or boxer, the actor learns to make use of socially patterned gestures for purposes that are other than those usually operative in gesturing. For acting in the theater is, of course, an art of simulating. Insofar as he is concerned to produce a certain response in those watching him grimace, the actor and the man really in pain have much the same motive. But the reasons why the actor grimaces and wants us to respond, why he gestures, are entirely different from those of a man who is grimacing in pain.

Now the actor with his mirror is a model of acute and deliberate attention to one's own performance of acts, while fully conscious of the social nature of the response of others. The actor is an impressive instance of an individual aware of himself as others see him.

If we were not in the possession of vocal gestures, Mead argues, it is unlikely that we would become aware of ourselves as selves to whom we and other persons respond alike. But Mead also notes: "If we exclude vocal gestures, it is only by the use of the mirror that one could reach the position where he responds to his own gestures as other people respond."[69]

§ 57. *The Discovery of the Self*

The way in which the actor critically educates himself in the performance of gestures is in many respects like the process of our learning how to produce vocal

[68] Of course, in the case of an actor this response *r* is doubly complicated; for *r* is the actor's critical response to his own gesture following a kind of test response which he supposes would be the average response of others to his gesture. His response (or responses) involves *his* response to his own act and his response to how he supposes others are (i.e., are imagined) responding.

[69] *Mind, Self*, p. 66.

gestures. The actor relies on himself, via his mirror, and also on the reactions of audiences for developing and improving his ability to gesture. The child is guided first by the reactions of adults to his babbling and gradually to his more distinctly formed utterances. Certain utterances are encouraged, praised, rewarded, and corrected by vocal gestures from adults. The techniques of reinforcement of kinds of behavior are put to work. The child in due course becomes a vocal participant in the community of vocal gesturers. He learns how to engage in conversations of gestures and eventually learns significant symbols. The process was illustrated above (in § 53), in the example of a child learning how to convert the sheer noise of screaming into a significant symbol.

The discovery of the self is thus an indirect and arduous outcome of a process of education in gestures that becomes increasingly intricate. That process is the transformation of a "biologic individual" into a "minded self." But the process originates not in private experience. For the supposition of "private" or personal experience is a late arrival in an individual's history of conscious experience. Rather, the discovery of the self originates in and from social activities.

> The individual experiences himself as such, not directly, but only indirectly, from the particular standpoints of other individual members of the same social group, or from the generalized standpoint of the social group as a whole to which he belongs. For he enters his own experience as a self or individual, not directly or immediately, not by becoming a subject to himself, but only in so far as he first becomes an object to himself just as other individuals are objects to him or in his experience; and he becomes an object to himself only by taking the attitudes of other individuals toward himself within a social environment or context of experience and behavior in which both he and they are involved.[70]

This discovery is itself a continuing feature of human behavior as Mead explains it.

> The self, as that which can be an object to itself, is essentially a social structure, and it arises in social experience. After a self has arisen, it in a certain sense provides for itself its social experiences, and so we can conceive of an absolutely solitary self. But it is impossible to conceive of a self arising outside of social experience. When it has arisen we can think of a person in solitary confinement . . . who still has himself as a companion, and is able to think and to converse with himself as he had communicated with others. That process . . . of responding to one's self as another responds to it, taking part in one's own conversation with others, being aware of what one is saying and using that awareness of what one is saying to determine what one is going to say thereafter—that is a process with which we are all familiar.[71]

The discovery of the self, Mead goes on to show, is the essential condition of intelligent behavior and significant speech. For what impressed Mead and receives

---

[70] *Ibid.*, p. 138. See also *The Philosophy of the Present*, pp. 176–195, and "The Genesis of the Self." This latter is a condensed version of a paper (1924) by Mead (perhaps his most important single philosophic paper) reprinted in full in *Selected Writings*, pp. 267–293.
[71] *Mind, Self*, p. 140. The following extracts are from pp. 140–142.

considerable attention in his writings is a process of individual behavior which, we can say, is *reflexive;*[72] that is, a process in which certain characteristic stages or constituent parts are elicited and controlled as responses to the process itself. We begin to explain the solution to a problem in mathematics; how we proceed, what we will say next is partly controlled by how the person listening to us behaves, by what he says and does. But in this case we are controlling the process of our own behavior by responses to our own conduct or speech—but the responses are *socially* conditioned in representing how other persons do or would react to what we are doing or saying.

> We are continually following up our own address to other persons by an understanding of what we are saying, and using that understanding in the direction of our continued speech. We are finding out what we are going to say, what we are going to do, by saying and doing, and in the process we are controlling the process itself.

We might, for example, find ourselves starting to say something unpleasant. The effect of this is our realization that we are saying something cruel and our response to what we have started to say stops us, or we might shift to saying something else.

> There is here a conversation of gestures between the individual and himself. We mean by significant speech that the action is one that affects the individual himself, and that the effect upon the individual himself is part of the intelligent carrying-out of the conversation with others.

One characteristic of intelligent behavior is, accordingly, behavior that is subject to modifications and controls determined by how the acting individual is responding to himself or to his own actions. But this presupposes the emergence and discovery of the self.

> That the person should be responding to himself is necessary to the self, and it is this sort of social conduct which provides behavior within which that self appears.

Communication—or "language" in some broad sense of gestures that have become significant symbols—is thus the all important means to the emergence and to the discovery of the self. Mead concludes:

> I know of no other form of behavior than the linguistic in which the individual is an object to himself, and, so far as I can see, the individual is not a self in the reflexive sense unless he is an object to himself. It is this fact that gives a critical importance to communication, since this is the type of behavior in which the individual does so respond to himself.[73]

[72] As far as I know, Mead does not use 'reflexive' to characterize certain behavioral processes. But I think this is in accord with his intentions.
[73] *Mind, Self,* p. 142. In addition to references here and below to *Mind, Self,* see "The Genesis of the Self," *Selected Writings,* pp. 284–285.

§ 58.   Play, Games, Roles,
and the Generalized Other

It was remarked at the outset of § 56 that Mead's examples of communication often refer to games and sports and the activities of individuals engaged in them. We can now understand this partiality.

While vocal gestures and communication are the most important means to the emergence and discovery of the self, there are other social activities that also have that outcome. These are the children's play and the organized and socially fixed form of play that becomes the "game."[74]

Children, at a certain early stage, not only talk to themselves, they also "play" or invent situations in which they communicate with imaginary companions. The companions also represent roles which the child will assume or "play at." Thus he may imagine that the situation includes soldiers or firemen, or fathers and mothers. He might assign these roles to objects around him. But he will also take these roles: he sets stimuli for himself, and his responses to the stimuli organizes them into the process of play.[75] He speaks to himself as a parent, or orders himself to act and obey as a soldier. He may act as a soldier and respond as a parent, but the parental response serves as a stimulus to himself in the role of the soldier. The result is a conversation between characters in roles. The roles are organized by the child, subject to all kinds of educative and formative influences from his environment.

The philosophically suggestive point here is that the child is organizing structures of stimuli and responses and these structures constitute the "meaning" of the roles he takes and acts out. The single child may determine the rules for organizing roles and acting them (rules, to be sure, that are largely socially produced and influenced). He may decide how the soldier role is to be acted, that is, what kind of acts and responses are to occur. He can change the rules and the roles at will. This is less so when children play together. Then rules for organizing and acting the roles are less flexible. The situation is reminiscent of social-contract theories of society. The child who doesn't observe the rules can be ostracized from the play by the others. Then play has evolved into a game. Here we can observe in group play the operation of significant symbols:[76] the children playing soldiers organize stimuli in their roles that call out the same responses (or structure of responses) in themselves that are also called out in their playmates. The role of *soldier* is an organization of acts which call out a

---

[74] Mead also considers the myths of primitive peoples, religious festivals, rituals and drama, as forms of organized play in the sense of 'play' now to be discussed. This part of his analysis need not concern us here, however. See *Mind, Self,* pp. 152 ff.

[75] I follow Mead's discussion of play in *ibid.,* pp. 150–151.

[76] And the pattern noticed in § 55. The child I_1 acts a role (or organizes stimuli) to which he responds as the other children I_2, I_3, I_4, etc., also respond. Thus:

$$I_1a' \rightarrow I_2r', I_3r', I_4r', \text{ and } I_1r'$$

class of responses that answers to something-being-a-soldier. That class of responses, r', r'', r''', etc., is the children's interpretation of what it is to be the soldier (in the game).

In games the selection of roles and the relation of roles to one another is more organized than in play. Moreover, in games, the individuals participating have to be able and ready to take up roles and attitudes of every other individual in the game. Roughly speaking, a game is a structure of roles, the acting out of which is fixed by certain rules and so interrelated that the performance of a role depends (via established rules) on how other roles are acted—on what is happening in the game. In tag, there are two roles: one individual is "it" and tries to catch any other member in the game; the other individuals attempt to avoid being caught. To play the game at all correctly, a player must know how to perform both roles. But notice that this is considerably more than merely knowing that there are two roles and that a player is permitted to perform but one role at a time and that only one player can be "it"; knowing how to play the game is knowing more than the rules that organize the game. In playing the game, each player is ready and, under appropriate circumstances, will take the attitude of other players. In order to avoid being caught, a player watches other players and the player who is "it." His acts of the moment are controlled by his responses to what he sees others doing. He avoids being tagged by momentarily assuming the role of the player who is "it" and then responding as a player who is not "it." One learns to catch others by learning how to avoid being caught and one learns how to escape from being caught by learning how to catch others. Tag is a simple game; but as in all games, the actuation and continuation of the game depends upon players learning how to take the roles of everyone else.

Applied to the game of tag, the scheme of § 55 brings out the features of acts and responses that Mead's theory is most concerned to emphasize and analyze. Suppose there are just two players, I_1 and I_2, and I_2 is "it." (In parentheses the acts a and responses r of the two players are explained.) Then:

I_1a' (runs) → I_2r' (pursues I_1) → I_1r'' (assumes role of I_2 — thus I_1 responds to I_1a' as I_2 — and modifies a' by a'', swerving, etc.) → I_2r''' (assumes role of I_1 fleeing — thus I_2 responds to I_1a'' as I_1 perhaps anticipating the move a'' — and accordingly modifies his manner of chasing I_1) → . . . , and so on.

The pattern illustrates this important idea: in the game there is an increasingly complex series of modifications and readjustments of the acts of I_1 and I_2 in relation to each other and to each other's roles.

Games will hence unfold in intricate sequences of coordinated acts and responses from and among players performing interdependent roles. A crucially important condition of interrelation of roles and cooperative performances of roles is the objective of the game—the individuals' act in consort to win, or to bring the game to its conclusion. In team games, such as football, the intricacy of conditions that call for "appropriate" actions and responses from each player moment by moment is extraordinary. Each player must know what every other player is doing and is going to do in order to carry out his own play.[77]

In the phenomenon of the game thus considered, we are brought again to the salient trait of gestures as significant symbols: individuals responding to their own acts as others also respond and whose responses stimulate and further actions. The team game exhibits greater complexity in the organization and determination of individual behavior (i.e., "appropriate" behavior moment by moment) than do the games of fencing or boxing noted earlier. (Or does it? for the latter gain complexity in the premium put upon the greater rapidity of acts and interpretive responses.) But it is not for the sake of repeating earlier ideas that we find ourselves dwelling on games once more. There is one important part of Mead's theory of the genesis of the self in vocal gestures and games that has yet to be stated.

Mead views the individual self as emerging from the development of the individual's ability to respond to his own vocal gestures and to assume the roles and attitudes of others in games. The *reflexive* condition (of § 51) is operative here. We have individuals speaking, hearing, and responding socially to their own speech; or acting and responding to their own acts (observing themselves) from the roles of other players in the game.[78]

Now let us make some enlargement of what is usually understood by 'game' to include clubs, political parties, corporations, and, in general, *social groups*.[79] The chief characteristic linking games with groups is, for our purposes here, the fact of organized social attitudes and roles and common objectives—which the individual group member (like the player in the game) takes or assumes. He may take on the attitude of his club or political party or business firm toward the rest of the community. There will be group roles and roles assumed by subgroups, officers and leaders, or the led, in which the individual may find himself participating. Whatever role he is active in, we have seen, is learned through taking the roles (if sometimes only in imagination) of others.

In modern societies, individuals assume various roles in a large variety of social groups. But it is by taking on a group attitude (as a player assumes the roles of other players in the game in order to play his role) in his attitude to himself and his acts that an individual becomes a self. Mead writes of this genesis:

the self reaches its full development by organizing these individual attitudes of others into the organized social or group attitudes, and thus becoming an individual reflection of the general systematic pattern of social or group behavior in which it and the others are all involved—a pattern which enters as a whole into the individual's experience in terms of these organized group attitudes which, through the mechanism of his central nervous system he takes toward himself, just as he takes the individual attitudes of others.[80]

[77] See *Mind, Self,* pp. 151, 153–154.
[78] Thus note the series of reciprocal and self-observations made by I_1 and I_2 in the game of tag schematically outlined on the previous page.
[79] Such is the course of Mead's discussion in *Mind, Self,* pp. 156–158.
[80] *Ibid.,* p. 158. See also *Selected Writings,* p. 288.

The attitude of others, of group or team, taken toward oneself introduces what Mead calls "the generalized other."[81]

The organization of personality and of selves consists in that structure of attitudes and responses common to the groups to which the individual belongs. The individual in a conversation of gestures with the generalized other (a conversation that he often has with himself) thus becomes himself.

> The structure, then, on which the self is built is the response common to all, for one has to be a member of a community to be a self. Such responses are abstract attitudes, but they constitute just what we term a man's character. They give him what we term his principles, the acknowledged attitudes of all members of the community toward what are the values of the community. He is putting himself in place of the generalized other, which represents the organized responses of all the members of the group. It is that which guides conduct controlled by principles, and a person who has such an organized group of responses is a man whom we say has character, in the moral sense.[82]

Lest we should fear that the individual self disappears altogether on this view, let us observe that selves become aware of their individuality and are marked off from other selves by virtue of differences of roles within the same groups and of membership in different groups.

But there is another condition of individuality and of the genesis of the self that requires our notice. This is Mead's analysis of consciousness as the integration of two phases of the social formation of the self.

§ 59. The Self as "I" and "Me"

A distinction paralleling that of the individual self and generalized other is that of the "me" and "I" contents of the self. This distinction is subject to changes in formulation and emphasis in Mead's thought, for it was a tentative principle of theoretical exploration. In general, the distinction is required to explain and elaborate the fact of two evident aspects and interchangeable roles of the self: we not only act and respond to our actions as others respond, we also often are

[81] See Mind, Self, p. 152. Insofar as an individual participates in different groups he recognizes different generalized others. But there are subordinate generalized others in the composition of a group or team, members or players recognized and calling forth our responses simply qua member or qua player. These others are "generalized": in the game we respond to the man running with the ball in his role as runner, not to his red face, his gambling reputation, his well-known wretched home life, etc. For us, in the game, he is more of a sign (that certain acts will occur under certain conditions) than a man. But even the part we play in games and groups has a generalized other. We play the part or role as we think the part would (or ought to) be played—as the Player.

[82] Ibid., pp. 162–163. As far as I know Mead did not develop at any length the ethical implications of the idea of the generalized other. But that part of Aristotle's theory in which it is argued that righteous actions are performed by agents who act as the (i.e., as a type of) righteous man would act, and Kant's categorical imperative and doctrine of moral autonomy are suggested by what would seem to be the function of the generalized other in moral conduct. See the interesting fragmentary reflections on this by Mead, Ibid., Supplementary Essay IV, pp. 379–389.

responding to the fact that we respond to our activities. We are aware at times that we are observing ourselves. This observer, says Mead, is the "I," "the response which one makes to his own conduct."[83] As such, the "I" is not an *object*, not a presented entity or subject in conscious experience. The object-self is the "me." But "a 'me' is inconceivable without an 'I.' "[84] The "me" appears in the process of conscious experience as the social empirical self, "that self which is able to maintain itself in the community, that is recognized in the community in so far as it recognizes the others."[85] It is thus "a conventional, habitual individual. It is always there."[86]

If selfhood were identified only with the "me," this would be a theory in which the individual is dissolved into a group of social functions.[87] The "me" *is* the group internalized, "that organized world which is present in our own nature. . . . It is to have those habits, those responses which everybody has; otherwise the individual could not be a member of the community."[88] But we also react to ourself as "me"—we respond to our own organization of attitudes, to our self as a communal, conventional individual. This responding aspect of ourself is the "I."

It is especially important to Mead that we also recognize that an individual's response to his organized attitude—the "I" responding to the "me"—changes the attitude.[89] The "I," accordingly, is the condition for novelty, creative advance, and reconstructions of social experience. Full individual self-expression comes through these responses of the "I" to the organized attitudes of the social, conventional "me."

We have seen earlier how the "me" is formed—the social process in which individuals internalize conversations of gestures. This formation of the "me" precedes the "I." The "I" has its genesis in memory.[90] Mead describes this genesis and the relation of "me" and "I":

> This analysis does reveal, then, in a memory process an attitude of observing oneself in which both the observer and the observed appear. To be concrete, one remembers asking himself how he could undertake to do this, that, or the other, chiding himself for his shortcomings or pluming himself upon his achievements. Thus, in the redintegrated self of the moment passed, one finds both a subject and an object, but it is a subject that is now an object of observation, and has the same nature as the object self whom we present as in intercourse with those about us. In quite the same fashion we remember the questions, admonitions, and approvals addressed

[83] *Selected Writings*, p. 145. The whole of ch. 12, "The Social Self," should be consulted for this distinction of "me" and "I." Also, *Mind, Self*, esp. pp. 192–222.
[84] *Selected Writings*, p. 142.
[85] *Mind, Self*, p. 196.
[86] *Ibid.*, p. 197.
[87] As Santayana complained of Dewey, see § 36 above.
[88] *Mind, Self*, pp. 196–197.
[89] *Ibid.*, p. 196: "The 'I' is the response of the individual to the attitude of the community as it appears in his own experience. His response to that organized attitude in turn changes it."
[90] Cf. *ibid.*, p. 196: "The 'I' appears in our experience in memory. It is only after we have acted that we know what we have done; it is only after we have spoken that we know what we have said."

to our fellows. But the subject attitude which we instinctively take can be presented only as something experienced—as we can be conscious of our acts only through the sensory processes set up after the act has begun.[91]

The "I" in this analysis is that remembered aspect of the self who observed, interrogated, chided, and praised, and, in short, "acted toward himself and is the same self who acts towards other selves."[92] Now since the response of "I" to "me" changes the organized attitude of the "me," the further activity of the "I" is also modified or qualified. Thus, a "dialectic" and internal reconstruction of attitudes and responses occurs within the individual self. This process becomes quite complicated, and in it, phase by phase, there is an interchanging or transition of roles of "I" and "me."

> . . . The stuff that goes to make up the "me" whom the "I" addresses and whom he observes, is the experience which is induced by this action of the "I." If the "I" speaks, the "me" hears. If the "I" strikes, the "me" feels the blow. Here again the "me" consciousness is of the same character as that which arises from the action of the other upon him. That is, it is only as the individual finds himself acting with reference to himself as he acts towards others, that he becomes a subject to himself rather than an object, and only as he is affected by his own social conduct in the manner in which he is affected by that of others, that he becomes an object to his own social conduct.[93]

Such, in outline, is Mead's account of the genesis of the self. In bringing this discussion of the development of the self (i.e., §§ 57–58) to a close, it is worth remarking that there is one abstract social group, according to Mead's analysis, that is all inclusive. All selves participate in it, and it is the most pervasive of conditions contributing to the emergence of selves. This group is the social institution of communication—the system of significant symbols.[94]

Now the language (or languages) of a group, the system of communication, presents a generalized other (to recall § 58), namely, the organized group responses, procedures, and attitudes that determine significant communication. It is this system with which the individual addresses himself and in which he expresses himself, to himself and to others. Moreover, to continue this speculation based on a fragment of Mead's,[95] if the system of communication contains certain a priori principles and categories and certain logical conditions of organization (all in the sense of Lewis, see § 45), then the generalized other as "the universe of discourse" is the subject matter of logic and theory of meaning. Formal logic, while not a prominent subject in Mead's writings, has this suggested place in his theory of language: logic studies what is common to all generalized others of all systems of communication.

[91] *Selected Writings*, pp. 142–143.
[92] *Ibid.*, p. 143.
[93] *Philosophy of the Act*, p. 432; see also pp. 152–153. Also, *Mind, Self*, pp. 268–269.
[94] See *Mind, Self*, pp. 157–158, where Mead calls this "the logical universe of discourse (or system of universally significant symbols)."
[95] See p. 432 of *The Philosophy of the Act*. The present paragraph admittedly is a speculative departure going far from Mead's text.

The organized group reaction to the physical environment would, in turn, find its current expression, within the group system of communication, in natural science; formerly, perhaps, in myth and religion. The most universal generalized other of the most universal systems of communication thus seem to be logic and empirical science.[96]

§ 60. Social Objects:
The Pragma of Things

So far we have been concentrating on Mead's explanation of the emergence of selves and minds within the social process. But there is another aspect of this theory which occupies a major part of Mead's attention: an environment of natural conditions, of biological and physical objects also enters into the social process. Moreover, the process and its parts exhibit spatial and temporal and emergent properties of a rather complicated kind.[97] Furthermore, both of these aspects of the process are involved in the event of the social act.

Mead's analysis of the social act is in basic harmony with Dewey's theory of the process of reflective behavior and the pattern of inquiry (§ 39). Mead distinguishes as phases of the act: *impulse* (a coordination of and sensitivity to sensory stimulation and the sensing of a problem); *perception* (the awareness of and selection for attention within a field of perceptual objects); *manipulation* (a stage of direct contact with or avoidance of the object of attention following the lead of perception); *consummation* (the stage in which the act moves from physical objects to that state in which "the adjectives of value obtain immediately").[98] Thought, or inquiry, is here depicted as instrumental to the development of the act in which the stimuli and problematic features in the stage of *impulse* become reconstructed and consummated. But Mead's analysis departs from Dewey's in its greater scope (thus calling for a philosophy of relativity physics, and concepts of physical and organic emergence) and in the intricacy of the details of the stages that require explanation.

For Mead, environing conditions, physical and organic objects, are as much parts of social acts as are the creatures and groups engaging in acts. Indeed, the line drawn between organism and environment is vague and at most of relative

---

[96] We noticed earlier, in § 51, Mead saying that "there is nothing so social as science, nothing so universal."

[97] Mead sketched but did not complete a general theory of the social act. He distinguished physical, biological, and reflective processes as these are constitutive of the act and give rise to "perspectives" and space-time systems into and among which man, as a social self, can enter in various ways. (Entering into perspectives is something like the process of assuming differing social roles. Cf. § 58 above.) Mead was then working out an elaborate cosmology. With the exception of Peirce, he was the only pragmatist to come directly to grips with modern science in attempting to elaborate this cosmology and theory of nature. His efforts in this respect place him very close to Whitehead, whose influence he felt but of whose doctrines he often was critical. For this part of Mead's thought see *The Philosophy of the Act* and *The Philosophy of the Present.*

[98] *The Philosophy of the Act*, p. 25. The order of stages is described on pp. 3–25.

and momentary convenience.[99] Mead is fully aware of how drawing that line has a long and prolix history of metaphysical and epistemological abuses.

Mead, like Dewey, emphasizes the interaction of organisms and objects within environments (or, within contexts, see § 37 and § 92). But this is all too easily said, and the value of the emphasis, if it has any at all, comes by way of careful explanation. This Mead (and Dewey) proceeded to undertake. How Mead proceeded affords us a clear view of his pragmatic conception of meaning, thought, and action. That conception controlled the development of the themes we have thus far been considering in Mead's social behaviorism; it is accordingly the subject with which the present attempt to survey Mead's pragmatism can be brought to a close.

We have several times now seen how for Mead (§ 52) and for Dewey (§ 38), the response to an object acting as a stimulus functions as a partial *interpretation* of the object. Organic reactions and coordinations "constitute" the "meaning" of the object, and given stimuli become "reconstructed" as signs of a certain kind of object under certain conditions.

Influenced by Peirce's contention that reality and the character of things are disclosed to us in what the community (of investigators) agrees to be,[100] Mead carefully incorporated this idea into his biosocial view of human attitudes to stimuli in the social process. As against some oversimplified conception of the nature of objects as "fixed" and "there," whose character comes to us, if deviously, through our impressions or via sense data, Mead took a contextualistic and relativistic approach. That is, he pointed out that existing relations between organisms and objects are themselves determining factors in some of the properties objects are in possession of and in what meanings we attach to them. Hence, while one in no way denies the presence of external conditions, of a physical world, the *existence* and the *nature* of some objects is due to kinds of attitudes, habits, and organized responses occurring in relation to them. Thus, Mead writes:

> There is a definite and necessary structure or *gestalt* of sensitivity within the organism, which determines selectively and relatively the character of the external object it perceives. . . . Our constructive selection of an environment—colors, emotional values, and the like—in terms of our physiological sensitivities, is essentially what we mean by consciousness.[101]

Here 'consciousness' and 'mind' are not words having reference to alleged psychical states. Rather, these characterize kinds of attitudes and modes of responsive behavior in relation to experienced objects.

[99] *Mind, Self*, p. 129: "It is a difficult matter to state just what we mean by dividing up a certain situation between the organism and its environment."
   By "relative and momentary convenience" here I mean only to suggest that the distinction is wholly one of contexts (see § 79). For example, it may be helpful, for some reason, to distinguish the man and the dinner before him as organism and external object respectively. But when and at what point in the man's eating of dinner does the external object become "internal" and indeed no longer object but organism?
   [100] See above, § 23. The idea is also found in Royce, see the beginning of § 62, note 7 below.
   [101] *Mind, Self*, p. 129.

The eye and related processes endow objects with color in exactly the same sense that an ox endows grass with the character of food.[102]

It is not that the ox projects this character into the object, or experience, as if he (and Mead) were proving a thesis of Kant's (§ 12). It is rather that the physiological and biological structure of the organism is a relevant causal condition for an explanation of the experienced content of the object. It is, then, Mead's view that the environment is "socialized" or endowed with meanings through the social process of group activities and attitudes. These attitudes, says Mead, "determine the environment . . . the appearance of the retinal elements has given the world color; the development of the organs in the ear has given the world sound."[103] Our organized responses *to* the world represent what exists for us in the world. "The particular phase of reality that is there for us is picked out for us by our response."[104]

There are objects, but *what* they are is conditioned by how we organize our responses to them. Among many other ways of distinguishing kinds of objects is this one: some objects more than others tend to stimulate uniform organized responses from groups of individuals. A chair, say, as against an exotic plant. Those objects that do call forth uniform responses and, indeed, toward which individual selves respond as others do (i.e., responding as the generalized other) are *social objects* of the group.[105] These represent permanent possibilities of standard ways of behaving and patterns of conduct from selves in the presence of the object. On a biologically based theory of the social process and group attitudes we come with Mead to conclusions that match Berkeley's analysis of "things" (Appendix 5) and Lewis' theory of objects (§ 45).

For Mead, our treatment of objects and how their significance becomes established follows the behavioral pattern of the game. Indeed, in games, social objects like dolls, bats and balls, and players *qua* players have prominent roles. The result is a conception of social objects as societies[106] of dispositional properties with which we engage in a language of gestures. The chair, becoming a known object of our experience, becomes so, not because we imitate it in our ideas or mind, but through our common responses to it; we recognize it as a thing with a role or group of roles; and it is by their roles that things are known.

Mead did not work out a theory of meaning in detail. Broadly speaking, for him, meanings occur in the field of gestures and communicated responses to stimuli; meaning arises in social conduct. Meaning thus occurs in relationships among organisms and objects, not in them nor in minds. Meaning occurs among

---

[102] *Ibid.*, p. 130.
[103] *Ibid.*, p. 128.
[104] *Ibid.*, p. 128.
[105] Cf. *ibid.*, p. 130, note 34: "A social group of individual organisms—constitutes or creates its own special environment of objects just as, and in the same sense as, an individual organism constitutes or creates its own special environment (which, however, is much more rudimentary than the environment constructed by a social organism)."
[106] Much like Berkeley's "congeries," see Appendix 5 below.

phases of the social act.[107] The attempt was to locate meaning in certain specifiable acts (or better, interactions) of behavior.

> The social process relates the responses of one individual to the gestures of an-
> other, as the meanings of the latter, and is thus responsible for the rise and existence
> of new objects in the social situation, objects dependent upon or constituted by
> these meanings. Meaning is thus not to be conceived, fundamentally as states of
> consciousness . . . it should be conceived objectively, as having its existence entirely
> within this field [of organized relations in experience] itself. The response of one
> organism to the gesture of another in any given social act is the meaning of that
> gesture. . . .[108]

Mead's conception of mind is also thoroughly behavioral, derived from the
same basic idea of the social process. When the social process is also present in
the attitudes and responses of participating individuals, mind has arisen. But the
"process as a whole enters into . . . the experience of anyone of the given individuals involved in that process"[109] through the condition of *reflexiveness* (cf.
§§ 51, 58 above). Individuals both adjust to and modify the course of social
processes by being able to take the attitude of others toward themselves.

> It is by means of reflexiveness—the turning-back of the experience of the indi-
> vidual upon himself—that the whole social process is thus brought into the expe-
> rience of the individuals involved in it. . . . Reflexiveness, then, is the essential
> condition, within the social process, for the development of mind.[110]

§ 61.   Social Pragmatism: Conclusion

In this chapter we have been occupied with Mead's pragmatic theory of the social
process and the genesis of the self and intelligent action.

It happens that in the progress of these reflections no special stress upon pragmatism, characteristic doctrines, or doctrinaire language has seemed necessary.
This is easily remedied, however, for the fact is that pragmatism pervades the
entire analysis and the conclusions of Mead's philosophy of mind and action. It
remains only to indicate how this is so.

1) To avoid a possible misunderstanding of Mead and of the foregoing pages,
it should be emphasized here (and was suggested in § 60) that the processes of
gesturing and response are themselves phases of a more inclusive activity, the *act*.
The general pattern of the act, we noticed above (§ 60), exhibits a set of co-

---

[107] Thus, *Mind, Self*, pp. 76–77: "meaning involves this three-fold relation among
phases of the social act as the context in which it arises and develops: this relation of the
gesture of one organism to the adjustive response of another organism (also implicated in
the act), and to the completion of the given act—a relation such that the second organism
responds to the gesture of the first as indicating or referring to the completion of the given
act." See also pp. 80–81, and *Selected Writings*, pp. 132–133.
[108] *Mind, Self*, p. 78.
[109] *Ibid.*, p. 134.
[110] *Ibid.*, p. 134.

ordinated movements initiated by *impulses* and terminating in *consummation*. But, as we took note of before, Mead, like Dewey, views the act as a "reconstruction" of experience, a changing and reorganization of the relations of organism and environment. Those relationships become endowed with new kinds of "meaning" as a result of the act.

The biological, evolutionary, and social point of view, each so much a part of the philosophic focus for Mead, leads one to interpret the human community and environment as related, basically, by conditions of determination and control. The acquisition of food and establishment of shelter are forms of direct control over the environment, and these kinds of control can be extended and complicated. Glacial epochs, seasonal changes, earthquakes, and the like are instances in which the environment controls the living form. But more complicated than these forms of direct control are the interrelationships that constitute *determinations* of the environment. As we saw (in the latter pages of § 60), Mead argues that how an environment is determined, that is, interpreted, given meaning, is relative to the sensitivity of organisms engaged in activities in that environment. The organism "selects and picks out what constitutes its environment."[111] The peculiar biological, physiological, and social character of the organism sets limiting conditions upon how the environment is determined and utilized by a living form.

> It selects that to which it responds and makes use of for its own purposes, purposes involved in its life-processes. It utilizes the earth on which it treads and through which it burrows, and the trees that it climbs; but only when it is sensitive to them. There must be a relation of stimulus and response; the environment must lie in some sense inside of the act if the form is to respond to it.[112]

Control of the environment by living things is thus a process of selection and organization. Sensitivity to stimuli, interpretation in the form of possible responses, and organization of responses in the furthering of conduct and the manipulation of the environment in rendering it favorable, is the life-process.

Man, as Mead points out, is distinguished from other animal forms by the range and variety with which he can respond to stimulation. Whereas animals make combinations of the stimuli-response conditions by trial and error, maintaining the successful combinations, man can select from the field of stimulation one stimulus rather than another; he can select the response that has been called out by given stimuli; and he can recombine that response with others. The ability to determine what kinds of stimuli *would* call out kinds of responses is a form of reflective consciousness for Mead. We are able to "break up" and suspend what are ordinarily routine complex acts by isolating stimuli and holding the responses and by recombining responses to build up another kind of act.[113]

---

[111] *Ibid.*, p. 245. Most of the comments of the above paragraph follow Mead's discussion. See, too, § 60 above.
[112] *Ibid.*, pp. 245–246.
[113] See *ibid.*, p. 94.

What takes place is an analysis of the process by giving attention to the specific stimuli that call out a particular act, and this analysis makes possible a reconstruction of the act.[114]

"We are conscious," says Mead, "when what we are going to do is controlling what we are doing."[115] Consciousness is the chief pragmatic instrument in our reconstructions of acts and of experience. And consciousness, or reflective intelligence, emerged from a pattern of social relations, especially that of communication by means of gestures functioning as significant symbols (§ 53).

2) Determination and control of the environment, in all the obvious but also myriad, subtle forms, is the function of thought and knowledge. For both Mead and Dewey, thought is a feature in the development of selves; specifically, in freeing conduct from confusion and blocked action, from problematic situations. Thought and knowledge thus become the effective cooperative and social forms of controlling the environment and future experience. In this manner, as we saw (§§ 52, 59), Mead regards science as the universal mode of cooperative effort.

Mead's conception of truth is formulated in and with reference to his theory of behavior. The "test of truth," he argued,

> is the ongoing of conduct, which has been stopped by a conflict of meanings—and in meanings I refer to responses or conduct which the characters of things lead up to.[116]

Truth, for Mead, and for Dewey, who was to work out the analysis more carefully (see § 40), is *tested* in "the ability to act where action was formerly estopped."[117] But the *meaning* of 'truth' turns upon the reconstruction of a problematic situation into one resolved and satisfied (in the sense of § 40). "Truth," Mead writes, "is then synonymous with the solution of the problem."[118] And this idea of truth is central to what Mead regarded as "the most distinctive mark" of pragmatism:

> the frank acceptance of actual ongoing experience, experimentally controlled, as the standpoint from which to interpret the past and anticipate the future.[119]

There are a few general comments with which this discussion of Mead can be brought to a close.

3) Mead's social pragmatism has not been influential in philosophy. This is hard to explain. His writing is not easy to read and often obscure, but in other men these deplorable traits have often been popularly heralded as proof of great profundity. Moreover, if one can survive the style, one can only admire how

---

[114] *Ibid.*, p. 95.
[115] *Ibid.*, p. xxi, note 12. That thought is directed to future experience and controls and modifies present conduct of present conduct is the unifying and dominant theme of the cooperative volume of "essays in the pragmatic attitude," *Creative Intelligence* (1917). Cf. Bode, "Consciousness and Psychology," on the anticipatory character of consciousness.
[116] "A Pragmatic Theory of Truth," *Selected Writings*, p. 328.
[117] *Ibid.*, p. 328.
[118] *Ibid.*, p. 328.
[119] *Ibid.*, p. 344.

some of the most firmly established problems in philosophy and psychology concerning the mind, learning, and language are either exposed as obsolete by Mead,
or are radically altered and shown to prompt strikingly original inquiries and
theorizing.

In social psychology and in psychiatry, however, Mead's work has not been
ignored. His theory of the genesis of the self from the social process and the
various concepts that we have studied above have been particularly effective in
the development of the interpersonal theory of psychiatry of Harry Stack Sullivan.[120] In Mead's theory of the self, taking roles, participating in various groups,
"a multiple personality is in a certain sense normal."[121] That is, Mead says: "We
carry on a whole series of different relationships to different people. We are one
thing to one man and another thing to another."[122]

In different social situations we are different selves—or different persons with
different social reactions and determining which kind of self we are going to
be.[123] The selves that we are and become are, normally, the outcomes, the attitudes,
and roles assumed in social relationships by a "unified self" formed in the community as a whole to which we belong.[124] Our different selves are the outcomes,
in given situations, of the conversation between the "I" and the "me."[125] In
forgetting, or in avoiding situations we relinquish or delimit our selves. But
there are cases where we say of someone that he is "not himself." There are
conditions in which disassociation of personality occurs, or where integration
of one's self becomes difficult or impossible or unsatisfactory. The disunification
of the self, and the distintegration in the social process, are the pathological
conditions that Mead recognizes as components in his empirical theory of the
development of the self. Clearly, the organization of roles and integration of the
self are among the more complicated factors in man's determination and control
of his environment.

Hamlet said: "What a piece of work is a man! how noble in reason! how infinite in faculties! in form and moving how express and admirable!"[126]

After coming through Mead's theory one is led to reflect, with something of

---

[120] See Sullivan's acknowledgment and discussion of this in *The Interpersonal Theory
of Psychiatry*, pp. 16–17 and pp. 18–19*n*. There is an interesting critical point in Sullivan's
discussion of Mead's theory, p. 17: "It showed very clearly that the unique individual person
was a complex derivative of many others. It did not quite serve for the purpose of psychiatry
. . . because there was, you might say, no source of energy presented to account for shifts in
roles, the energy expended in playing roles, and so on."

[121] *Mind, Self*, p. 142.

[122] *Ibid.*, p. 142.

[123] *Ibid.*, p. 143.

[124] *Ibid.*, p. 143.

[125] *Ibid.*, p. 335: "Thinking is simply the reasoning of the individual, the carrying-on of
a conversation between . . . the 'I' and the 'me.' "

It is worth noting that Peirce, in "What Pragmatism Is," 1905, was also expressing
this idea—so central, as we have seen, to Mead's analysis of the self. Peirce writes, *CP*
5.421: "a person is not absolutely an individual. His thoughts are what he is 'saying to
himself,' that is, is saying to that other self that is just coming into life in the flow of time.
When one reasons, it is that critical self that one is trying to persuade; and all thought
whatsoever is a sign, and is mostly of the nature of language."

[126] Shakespeare, *Hamlet*, II.ii.

Hamlet's admiration: what a piece of work is the gesture! Man is not the only creature who gestures; but he comes first in accomplishment and mastery. For he has achieved the supreme art of gesturing and responding: the use of significant symbols (§ 53). Still, having been led to ponder this phenomenon, one ought in propriety to appreciate something of the complexity of its occurrence.

For from Darwin's analysis on into Dewey (as we noticed in § 38) and Mead, one is struck by the marvelous intricacy and delicate organization and coordinations of cell structures, organs, and nerves in the passage of stimuli into responses, and in the organic motions that become gestures. Much past experience, marked by trials more or less successful in determinations of the environment, preparations for and rehearsals of activities, the almost endless distributions and combinations of responses in the central nervous system to incoming stimuli—all provide the initial tuition for the schooling of a creature in the art of gesturing. Further, consider the ordinary, simple act of vocal communication. The speaker has learned a language, in itself no mean accomplishment. In order to speak he has learned to take a certain posture (or select from a number of possible postures); he has learned to suspend or considerably modify the activity of breathing, to coordinate the activities of lungs and larynx and tongue. The speaker's eye, actively responding to and integrating the retinal radiation, in helping locate the audience being addressed, requires the coordinated turning of head and readjustments of bodily posture. And there is more, as Mead notes:

> Allow me to emphasize further the value of attitudes and the indications of organized preparation for conduct, especially in the change of the muscles of the countenance, the altered breathing, the quivering of tense muscles, the evidence of circulatory changes, in such minutely adapted social groups, because among these socially significant innervations will be found all these queer organic sensations about which the consciousness of the self is supposed to gather as a core.[127]

Mead's theory, to which these pages have been devoted, is remarkable. This is much to Mead's credit, but it is partly, also, that the live subject matter of the theory is, "in form, in moving, how express and admirable!" On this humanistic note it will be well to conclude the present discussion.

In Mead's pragmatic philosophy as we have studied it here, two subjects are paramount: the social process of communication, the related process of controlling future experience. Thus, we have found reflected in Mead, with many reverberations, the two major themes of *meaning* and *action* we have been concerned with in earlier chapters, and which we have seen guiding the pragmatism of Peirce, James, Dewey, and C. I. Lewis. Part Three, to which we turn next, has to do with some further variations on these themes.

[127] *Selected Writings*, p. 110.

PRAGMATISM IN EUROPE: ALLIANCES AND MISALLIANCES

Part Three

It was, of course, quite natural that the American pragmatists would state their ideas in a local philosophical idiom, and continue to reshape doctrines under the influence of academic and social pressures and the critical reactions of other philosophers. Still, the modification and adaptation of ideas to new conditions does not nullify the authenticity of their origins. American pragmatism had its roots in the European philosophic tradition.

In Europe, pragmatism had a circuitous development: it was initiated first as a response to the popular expressions by James, who was citing and quoting Peirce, and by Schiller's energetic advocacy of his pragmatic humanism; but it also derived from the complex background of post-Kantian romanticism and idealism and various forms of evolutionary thought. European thinkers, particularly the French, could and did immediately find many historical and contemporary European precedents in which James's pragmatism had been anticipated, or extended in new directions. Fichte, Nietzsche, Schelling, Renouvier, and Bergson[1] were all cited. As in America early in the century, so in Europe, pragmatism was expounded and "explained" in numerous ways. Because of the variety of intellectual traditions within pragmatism, because of the diverse classifications of their ideas by historically minded friendly and unfriendly critics, and because of James's habit of welcoming all sorts of apparently allied intellects into the pragmatic camp—the first quarter of the present century was to witness a profusion of often very different pragmatisms in Europe and America.

We took note briefly of this situation in § 2, remarking that at least thirteen kinds of pragmatism had been counted on the scene in 1908. To James, who liked variety, originality, and independence, this might have appeared an endearing trait and an omen of a glorious future. For us, attempting to gain a sense of the history of pragmatism and interested in scrutinizing some of its leading ideas, this multiplication is disarming.

However, we have in earlier discussions, and shall continue to do so here, invoked some criterion for judging what to include and exclude as authentic to pragmatism—a judgment to some extent arbitrary, but not wholly so. From earlier chapters, a definite pattern of philosophic problems and allied conceptual efforts emerges to impress us with a general understanding of the most significant historical and philosophic developments of pragmatism. One grants, of course, that pronouncements upon significance are relative— being relative to some criterion. But then it is some criterion that is needed, and one is better than none.

[1] Bergson made clear his esteem for, but the intellectual independence of the work of James. See Perry, II, 599 ff.

A summary statement of our earlier reflections, which guides the critical and evaluative discussion that follows, is to be found at the close of Chapter One of Part Five, specifically, § 101. While not preserving a dogged allegiance to that descriptive definition of *pragmatism*, we are still helped to find our way by it in taking a survey of the course of pragmatism in England, France, and Italy.

The range of this survey, it will be evident, is limited. A discussion of pragmatism in Germany is not included because the American philosophy had little or no impact east of the Rhine. This is not to deny that important lines of philosophic interest and communication occurred in various ways relating some of the ideas of Peirce, James, and Dewey with the thought of Simmel, Ostwald, Husserl, and Vaihinger. The work of Mach and the later Vienna Circle (as well as the methodological interests of Duhem and Poincaré) show certain strong connections (and some basic disconnections) with American pragmatism. But similarity of convictions and mutual interests do not constitute historical influences.[2]

In general, then, the following chapters take a less inclusive view of the spread of pragmatism than, say, did James, warmly eyeing the old country sixty years ago. Writing in 1904, he saw pragmatism vigorously rooting and spreading over Europe. He spoke of

> the pragmatism of Pearson in England, of Mach in Austria, and of the somewhat more reluctant Poincaré in France, all of whom say that our sciences are but *Denkmittel*—"true" in no other sense than that of yielding a conceptual shorthand, economical for our descriptions. Thus does Simmel in Berlin suggest that no human conception whatever is more than an instrument of biological utility; and that if it be successfully that, we may call it true, whatever it resembles or fails to resemble. Bergson, and more particularly his disciples Wilbois, Le Roy, and others in France, have defended a very similar doctrine. Ostwald in Leipzig, with his *Energetics*, belongs to the same school, which has received its most thoroughgoingly philosophical expressions here in America, in the publications of Professor Dewey and his pupils in Chicago University. . . .[3]

The review of pragmatism in Europe which occupies the next four chapters is not, however, wholly negative. In addition to the obvious historical place of Schiller (with finer qualifications to come in § 62), there is an interesting connection, and one awaiting further uncovering, between American pragmatism and the philosophic thought of F. P. Ramsey and Wittgenstein.

[2] In the program of logical empiricism of the last decade one sees the mutual settling in of pragmatism and positivism. For an early study of the relations between pragmatism and the logical empiricism of the Vienna Circle, see Charles Morris; also Joergensen, *The Development of Logical Empiricism*, pp. 55–57.
[3] *Collected Essays and Reviews*, pp. 449–450.

This is the subject of Chapter Two. There was also an important, if short-lived renaissance of pragmatism in Italy. There, the role of Papini is still well known; but the important work of Giovanni Vailati and Mario Calderoni is not.[4] The last two figures represent a very significant and genuine development of what is soundest and most enduring in pragmatism and in much recent analytic philosophy. Chapter Four treats of these developments.

[4] At least, not in Anglo-American philosophy.

CHAPTER ONE

England: F. C. S. Schiller

§ 62. Schiller and Pragmatism

The most famous pragmatist outside the United States was Ferdinand Canning Scott Schiller (1864–1937).[1] At the height of his influence early in the present century, Schiller was regarded the equal of James as leading spokesman for pragmatism. On the continent, far more attention was directed to the works of James and Schiller than to any of the other pragmatists.

Schiller's literary gifts and his active polemical bent against the contemporary mainstream of English philosophy brought him notice quite independently of his own philosophy. But his fame, which was once considerable, vanished. Unlike the other major philosophers of pragmatism, he is now scarcely read at all, and mention of his name is easily mistaken for a reference to the German poet.

In accounting for the history of pragmatism, it is usually said that Schiller was one of the originators of the movement, sharing a place with Peirce, James, and Dewey.[2] But this happens historically and philosophically to be doubtful. Schiller's general philosophic convictions and outlook, the substance of his *humanism*, were expressed, if in germinal form, before he had read or become familiar with James's writings.[3] Later, coming upon the work of James, he

1 For a time, perhaps, Papini of Italy (see § 76 below) was equally famous.
2 Such, e.g., was the allusion at the outset of § 2.
3 Schiller's first book, *Riddles of the Sphinx,* was published in 1891. Leroux, p. 119, note 1, quotes a communication from Schiller in which Schiller says that he had not read a word of James before 1891.
    In *Humanism* (1903), p. i, Schiller states that he was a pragmatist as early as 1892. In his "William James and the Making of Pragmatism," he says that while he had praised James's *The Will to Believe* in a review in *Mind,* Oct. 1897, "Still I could not then claim any status as a disciple of James," p. 84. I attach some importance to the word *'then'* in the phrasing of this sentence. Schiller adds shortly thereafter, p. 85: "Still, when the California Lecture on 'Philosophical Conceptions and Practical Results' baptized Pragmatism and flung it into the stream of philosophic controversy, I could in no wise set up as an authority on the meaning and the mind of James." James's lecture was delivered in 1898. While the lecture was printed in *The University Chronicle* in 1898, it did not appear to the general

greeted pragmatism as an ally. He attempted to persuade James to drop the name *pragmatism* in favor of *humanism*. For humanism, Schiller contended, represented the broader movement into which pragmatism fitted as a part.[4] Schiller's first consciously "pragmatic" piece of philosophizing was his paper "Axioms as Postulates," published in 1902.[5] While a significant contribution to the literature of pragmatism, it can scarcely be judged as an original and fundamental philosophic influence on the history of the movement.

Indeed, there is a curious fact about this, probably the best known of Schiller's philosophic essays. While Schiller professed in it to follow "the *Weltanschauung* which Professor James has called *pragmatism* and *radical empiricism*,"[6] a main part of the central argument had been anticipated and stated many years earlier by James and by Josiah Royce.[7]

---

philosophical world until reprinting, with slight changes, in the *Journal of Philosophy, Psychology and Scientific Methods*, 1904, with the title, "The Pragmatic Method." The passage containing the important reference to "Peirce's principle" was reprinted in the *Varieties of Religious Experience* (1902), and a larger portion was reprinted in *Pragmatism* (1907). But Schiller might have received a copy of the original 1898 lecture, for in 1897 he had become a friend of James, as James comments in a letter: "Schiller spent the Christmas holidays with us, and I find him a most peculiarly delightful fellow. His philosophy and mine run abreast in an altogether gratifying way to me," Perry, II, 166. Schiller, then, had "his philosophy" at this time. In the first paper referred to above, Schiller reminisces that it was in 1899, only after a critical discussion with Dickinson Miller over James's *The Will to Believe*, that he began to see clearly the significance of James's pragmatism and that he proceeded to develop it (i.e., the Will to Believe argument) in his "Axioms as Postulates," 1902.

[4] See his letter to James of 1903: "pragmatism will be a species of a greater genus—humanism in theory of knowledge," Perry, II, 498–499. See also *Studies in Humanism*, p. 16.

[5] According to his own account (see note 3 above) in "William James and the Making of Pragmatism," pp. 86–87: "I conceived my task as that of tracing throughout the established structures of the intellectual world the manifold operations of that volitional activity whose existence and potency James had revealed, under the name of the will to believe. . . . "The process of postulation . . . could be given logical status, and shown to enter into the operation of all our cognitive functions. It could be universalized like the will to believe, and identified with it, or traced to a common root with it in our volitional nature."

[6] "Axioms as Postulates," p. 63. Note that James's ideas, contrary to his own disclaimers, are here regarded as forming a *Weltanschauung*.

[7] See ch. 9, "The World of Postulates," in Royce's *The Religious Aspect of Philosophy* (1885), esp. p. 292: "The assumed world is no fixed *datum*, to which we are bound to submit at all hazards, but a *postulate*, which is made to satisfy certain familiar human needs." James also has a discussion of "metaphysical axioms" as essentially "postulates of rationality" in his *Psychology*, II, 669–670. Schiller, in "Axioms as Postulates," p. 118, refers to this account of James's. But, interestingly, James cites Royce's book in his *Psychology*, II, 316, and 317–318*n*., and he singles out for comment Royce's chapter on postulates, quoting p. 304 of Royce on "our will to have an external world." James's final remark is: "Chapters IX and X of Prof. Royce's work are on the whole the clearest account of the psychology of belief with which I am acquainted."

It is difficult to conclude that Schiller had not seen this reference or that he had not been led to look into Royce's book, though he does not acknowledge the influence of Royce. Ultimately, of course, both Royce and Schiller were influenced by the Kantian doctrine of the postulations of practical reason and by post-Kantian critical and romantic versions of the same. Schiller, like James, felt the attraction of Renouvier. But more directly, both Royce and Schiller must have been influenced by James. In his paper of 1878, "Spencer's Definition of Mind," James argues for the teleological function of mind in terms that directly anticipate both Royce's and Schiller's later views. (See § 28 above for this passage.) James's argument reappears in *The Will to Believe*, esp. p. 117 of "Reflex Action and Theism." And this was the book of James's that Schiller knew best and most admired.

Schiller's place in the history of pragmatism is not that of a founder; it is rather that of a friendly party and ready advocate in a cause which he felt in common with the pragmatists. His real link with pragmatism was his friendship with William James, and, philosophically, his admiration for *The Will to Believe*.

James directed Schiller's attention to Dewey and the Chicago School, and Schiller responded with respect but not untoward interest. Being the older man, James counseled Schiller on how properly to conduct himself in critical skirmishes with Bradley, and may have helped to shape the particular interests and direction of his later work. To Schiller, who was and felt himself to be something of an outcast in English philosophical circles, James's friendly encouragement must have meant very much. Schiller, on the other hand, was effective in strengthening James's feeling that pragmatism called for a cooperative effort against a "common enemy," absolutism or intellectualism. The existence of important doctrinal differences among the attackers was thus obscured in the spirit of unity against the foe. In America, absolutism and idealism were identified with Royce; in England, with Bradley. The effect of this militant critical spirit worked up by Schiller and James has since prevented most onlookers from recognizing that in very important respects, Peirce and Dewey stand much closer to Royce and Bradley than they do to Schiller.[8] Finally, it should be noted that primarily due to Schiller (and, some years later, to Papini, see § 76 below), James began to think that with *The Will to Believe* he had created a philosophy and started up a school of thought.

The importance of Schiller, then, is dependent upon what is lasting in his own philosophy of humanism and his critical essays on his contemporaries. Though Schiller's humanism merges with pragmatism at important junctures in the

[8] Bradley's critical reaction against T. H. Green's making particulars and qualities into relations and universals (for which see Appendix 1, sec. C below), Bradley's emphasis on immediate feeling as primary to thought, on feeling as a pervasive unity within which diversity occurs, a unified whole, are carried over into Dewey's theory of the situation as a pervasive qualitative whole (cf. § 39 and § 91, but see also § 97). For Bradley's one Whole, all-inclusive *experience*, the Absolute, Dewey has unique wholes, situations, each absolutely, i.e., qualitatively, what it is (§ 91). The route back for each thinker is to Hegel, but Dewey was influenced by this side of Bradley's thought. Dewey's criticisms of traditional logic and his analysis of the function of judgment have much in common with Bradley's views (both men having felt the influence of Green here, see Appendix 1, sec. C), and so, too, with Bradley's sense of satisfaction when used, e.g., to define truth as "that which satisfies the intellect," where error and contradiction produce unrest and dissatisfaction (cf. *Essays on Truth and Reality*, p. 1, and esp. ch. 1). Finally, Dewey's view that propositions are neither true nor meaningful independent of their place within the content, "the whole" of inquiry, his disavowal of separations between practice and theory, his insistence on the practical origin of thought have their counterparts in Bradley.

As for Royce and Peirce, both of whom had been deeply influenced by Schelling, see Peirce's letter to Mrs. Ladd-Franklin, criticizing James's sensationalistic nominalism (quoted in § 27 above) and adding: "Royce's opinions as developed in his 'World and Individual' are extremely near mine. His insistence on the element of purpose in intellectual concepts is essentially the pragmatic position . . . ," Ladd-Franklin, "Charles S. Peirce at the Johns Hopkins," p. 720. For Royce's indebtedness to Peirce, see his Prefaces to *The Problem of Christianity* and *The World and the Individual;* and Morris Cohen's account, pp. 727–728 in the Peirce commemorative issue of *The Journal of Philosophy, Psychology and Scientific Methods* (1916).

theory of knowledge, these are essentially independently developed philosophies.[9]

If historically Schiller's part in the development of pragmatism is not of great significance, there are, nonetheless, some important and interesting issues of his thought that are germane to pragmatism and current philosophy. It is these, rather than a review of the general content of Schiller's humanism, that will concern us in this chapter.

§ 63.   The Critical Orientation

Schiller was a Fellow of Corpus Christi College, Oxford. In 1893, as a young man of twenty-nine, Schiller had left Oxford to teach at Cornell and had studied for the Ph.D. degree. For reasons never fully known, he was not granted the doctorate, although his first book, *Riddles of the Sphinx*, was submitted as his thesis.[10] In the last ten years of his life Schiller taught at the University of Southern California.

Oxford was Schiller's residence for most of his lifetime, but it was never a philosophic home. Schiller was viewed with some distrust and scorn by the Oxford Idealists, the dominant philosophic movement in England during the last part of the nineteenth century. The leading figure at the time was F. H. Bradley (1846–1924), and before him, Hegelianism and idealism had been established in Oxford under the powerful influence of T. H. Green's few writings and persuasive teaching.[11]

9 In Schiller's own historical perspective he seems to have viewed himself and James as the two closest exponents of their particular pragmatism-humanism, and he the real disciple of James. Peirce, he thought, had foolishly disowned the movement. Indeed, Peirce never really invented pragmatism; James simply gave the credit to Peirce (see the account in Schiller's "William James and the Making of Pragmatism"). Dewey, according to Schiller's view, represented an independent movement. This impression of the alignment of forces and ideas, of where he and James stood in relation to the rest of the pragmatist movement, is revealed in Schiller's suggestion in a letter to James (1903) that they both "join forces with the Chicagoans," Perry, II, 498.

10 This, itself, might have been reason enough. The book is highly original, containing many fresh insights and novel bits of scholarship, and is gracefully written.

11 For some time it has been customary to refer to this school as the "Oxford Hegelians" or "Anglo-Hegelians." It has become clear, however, that while Green and Bradley knew Hegel thoroughly and encouraged younger men to study him (and while Bradley was fond of citing his opponents' latest ideas as all in Hegel), neither Green nor Bradley was a Hegelian in any obvious or informative sense. Green was more of a Kantian, though also a Platonist; and Bradley, while much influenced by the German, J. F. Herbart, was deeply indebted in method and conclusions in logic and metaphysics to Parmenides, Zeno, and the Plato of the *Parmenides* and *Sophist*. See Passmore, pp. 56, 59, who rightly comments on these influences. For a further statement of Green's thought, see Appendix 1, sec. C below; see also the perceptive essay on Bradley by W. H. Walsh.

Oxford idealism admits of no easy characterization, with its Kantian, German romantic, and classical ingredients. Thus it is noteworthy that Jowett, Master of Balliol, published an impressive translation of Plato in 1871, but also advised his students to read the German idealists. Jowett was succeeded by Edward Caird, a Scot, who produced a Hegelian version of Kant and a study of Hegel (1883) arguing that Hegel was concerned primarily to establish the religious nature of man's existence and the higher unity between religion and science. (We took note, incidentally, in the first pages of § 35 above, of Dewey's very favorable review of Caird's *The Critical Philosophy of Immanuel Kant* in 1890.)

The Oxford movement was usually described by Schiller as "English Absolutism." It was, for him, "the enemy" which he spent most of his life attacking.
The enemy is identified in this passage:

> Absolutism . . . has grown secure and strong and insolent. It has developed a
> powerful 'left wing,' which, as formerly in Germany has triumphed within the
> school, and quarreled with theology. Mr. F. H. Bradley, Dr. McTaggart, Prof. B.
> Bosanquet, Prof. J. S. Mackenzie are among its best-known representatives.[12]

Idealism in Great Britain, as in America, had a resurgence in the nineteenth
century, beginning as a reaction to materialistic and atheistic conceptions of life
encouraged by the advance of mechanical and biological science. The critical
reaction was carried under the cover of Hegelianism, which incorporated in
addition to Hegel, Kant, Schelling, German romanticism, and Platonism, and was
consolidated into the philosophies of idealism. Outright materialism also came
from Germany, almost in mid-century (in 1855). L Büchner's *Force and Matter*
became a source book for the "scientific" anti-theological, anti-supernatural point
of view. A more modified, agnostic, and skeptical outlook, again in the name of
science—this time Darwinism—was developed by T. H. Huxley. There were
quasi-scientific evolutionary philosophies of Spencer and of Ernst Haeckel (and
in America, John Fiske), within which religious values and idealistic longings
were, both surreptitiously and blatantly, given a pseudo-scientific standing.

The reaction of idealism to science or, more properly, to these philosophical
interpretations and popularizations of science in the nineteenth century was quite
simple: these philosophies neglected or denied everything that was of most interest and importance to human life. Religion, mortality, and, finally, truth are
not found in them, however "scientific" they might be. The idealists' alternative to materialism, to Mill's empiricism, or to evolution is not so simple. Elaborate technical dialectical argumentation was spent in showing that an evident,
or assumed, higher unity of science and religion is discoverable through reason.
Idealistic versions of evolution, the transformation of the self or nature into
higher manifestations of Mind or of Spirit, were worked out in different ways
by such men as Green, the Cairds, Andrew Seth, Bosanquet, and Royce.

The philosophic concern to establish a unification of science with religious
and moral values, as we have seen in Part One, was not new. Indeed, in England,
the Cambridge Platonists had undertaken much the same task in the seventeenth
century. But more, as we have observed before and shall argue in Part Five, this
quest for a theoretical continuity between the procedures for establishing empirical knowledge and ethical values is a basic aim in the history of pragmatism.
In this aim and motivation, pragmatism and idealism have a common history.

One of the popular forms in which the harmony between religion and science
was assured had been advanced by Lotze (1817–1881). Lotze's argument is less

---

[12] *Studies in Humanism,* p. 284. These names populate Schiller's writings (adding that
of H. H. Joachim and, in his earlier writings, A. E. Taylor), and are often found in his
polemical footnotes.

impressive than its timeliness and sweep.[13] But the spirit is, or was, attractive. Lotze elaborated upon the idea that our world is a mechanical system; this is his "realism." But this mechanism and its laws are the products of a universal soul, a will that uses these means to the realization of the Good; this is his "idealism." The world of mechanism and the realm of value are not separate spheres; there is unity of the two, Lotze affirmed, but this unity transcends knowledge and rational demonstration.

Lotze was carefully read and studied in England and America. His "logic," or analysis of the phases of thought from its initiation in simple judgments to its culmination in the systematic rendition of the concrete universal, was probably the greatest single influence in shaping the new idealist logic in the late nineteenth century. James often singles out for favorable comment Lotze's view of the difference that mind (or knowing) contributes to the ultimate character of reality.[14] Bradley's *Logic* and Dewey's instrumentalism are heavily, if critically, indebted to Lotze, although Germany also supplied, in addition to Kant and Hegel, the notable influences of Herbart and Sigwart.[15]

Not only were philosophers drawn to German thought in search of a defense of values threatened by skeptical empiricism and materialism; literary philosophers like Coleridge, Carlyle, and Emerson also had their reasons for urging the importance of Kant, Schelling, and idealism.[16] It was against this development that Mill had addressed his *Logic* and his *Examination of Sir William Hamilton's Philosophy*. Hamilton represented, wrote Mill, "the great fortress of the intuitional philosophy in this country."[17] 'Intuition' is Mill's pejorative term for

---

13 I refer here only to Lotze's general idealistic aim, not his specific analysis of thought—his "logic"—which struck men like John Dewey as the work of "one of the most vigorous and acute of modern logicians," *Essays in Experimental Logic*, p. 105.

14 See, e.g., *Pragmatism*, p. 256; also Kraushaar, for Lotze's influence on James's pragmatism.

15 Dewey's writings often contain references to Lotze, see esp. *Studies in Logical Theory* and *Essays in Experimental Logic*. G. S. Morris (1840–1889), under whom Dewey studied at Johns Hopkins in 1882 and who was Dewey's colleague two years later at Michigan (see the Introduction to Part II above), was a Hegelian whose impact on the young Dewey became a major force in Dewey's philosophical development. On this and Morris' Hegelianism, see Appendix 1, sec. C below.

As a part of our theme in the last few pages it is to be noted that in the 1890's Dewey was reading and praising Morris, T. H. Green, and Edward Caird for their ability to find a Hegelian and spiritual unification of science and religion. For more on this subject, and especially on the influence of Green, see Appendix 1, sec. C.

16 See Mill's explanation of this in his essay on "Coleridge," p. 108: "the Germano-Coleridgian doctrine . . . expresses the revolt of the human mind against the philosophy of the eighteenth century. It is ontological, because that was experimental; conservative, because that was innovative; religious, because so much of that was infidel; concrete and historical, because that was abstract and metaphysical; poetical, because that was matter-of-fact and prosaic. In every respect it flies off in the contrary direction to its predecessor."

17 *Autobiography*, p. 176. Hamilton was an exponent of the Scottish philosophy of Reid, but he also was an erudite advocate of German philosophy. Mill's *Examination* was a death blow to Scottish philosophy in England, but not in America, where it continued not only to develop but to thrive in universities and in textbooks. James McCosh (1811–1894), President of Princeton University, was a disciple of Hamilton and the most able proponent of the Scottish school. Dewey's first teacher in philosophy at the University of Vermont, H. A. P. Torrey, based his teaching upon the writings of the Scotch school (see Schilpp, p. 11). For Peirce's recognition of the influence of Scottish philosophy on his pragmatism, see § 27 above.

theories of a priori knowledge, transcendentalism, or higher instinct in morals, and, generally, defenses of conservative social institutions. His moral and social objective in these works he stated clearly:

> The German or *a priori* view of human knowledge, and of the knowing faculties, is likely for some time longer . . . to predominate among those who occupy themselves with such inquiries. . . . But the "System of Logic" supplies what was wanted, a text-book of the opposite doctrine. . . . The notion that truths external to the mind may be known by intuition or consciousness, independently of observation and experience, is, I am persuaded, in these times, the great intellectual support of false doctrines and bad institutions.[18]

This is the Mill, insisting upon the moral as well as scientific value of observation and experience, to whose memory James dedicated his *Pragmatism*. And in the course of the growth of Oxford idealism it was necessary for the leaders of that school to do for Mill what he had done for Hamilton. T. H. Green and Bradley sharpened and perfected the criticism of Mill's empirical, utilitarian philosophy and the positivistic system of Spencer.

Such was the historical setting into which Schiller brought his humanism. He was attempting to swing the balance of ideas back to the side of Mill. His own polemical sketch of the growth of English idealism is not without some accuracy:

> The history of English Absolutism . . . was originally a deliberate importation from Germany, with a purpose. And this purpose was a religious one—that of counteracting the anti-religious developments of Science. The indigenous philosophy, the old British empiricism, was useless for this purpose. For though a form of intellectualism, its sensationalism was in no wise hostile to Science. On the contrary, it showed every desire to ally itself with, and to promote, a great scientific movement of the nineteenth century, which penetrated into and almost overwhelmed Oxford between 1850 and 1870.
>
> But this movement excited natural, and not unwarranted alarm in that great centre of theology. For Science, flushed with its hard-won liberty, ignorant of philosophy

---

[18] *Autobiography*, pp. 144–145. The chief reason for his detailed refutation of Hamilton's philosophy is revealed on pp. 175–176:

> the difference between these two schools of philosophy, that of Intuition, and that of Experience and Association, is not a mere matter of abstract speculation; it is full of practical consequences, and lies at the foundation of all the greatest differences of practical opinion in an age of progress. The practical reformer has continually to demand that changes be made in things which are supported by powerful and widely-spread feelings, or to question the apparent necessity and indefeasibleness of established facts. . . . There is therefore a natural hostility between him and a philosophy which discourages the explanation of feelings and moral facts by circumstances and association, and prefers to treat them as ultimate elements of human nature; a philosophy which is addicted to holding up favorite doctrines as intuitive truths, and deems intuition to be the voice of Nature and of God. . . .

This latter philosophy, Mill adds, supports the prevailing tendency to suppose that human character distinctions are innate and indelibly fixed. This is a tendency against

> the rational treatment of great social questions, and one of the greatest stumbling blocks to human improvement. This tendency has its source in the intuitional metaphysics which characterized the reaction of the nineteenth century against the eighteenth, and it is a tendency . . . agreeable to human indolence, as well as to conservative interests generally. . . .

. . . was decidedly aggressive and over-confident. It seemed naturalistic, nay, materialistic, by the law of its being. The logic of Mill, the philosophy of Evolution, the faith in democracy, in freedom, in progress (on material lines), threatened to carry all before them.

Since word had come that in Germany there had been created a marvelous "metaphysical criticism of science," Schiller continues,

Emissaries accordingly went forth, and imported German philosophy, as the handmaid, or at least the governess, of a distressed theology.[19]

Schiller goes on to argue that absolutism, the "import," eventually bred an anti-theological spirit of its own and attempted to supplant religion by becoming a religion itself. In all this one must not suppose that Schiller is defending science against religion. His chief objection to "absolutism" is that it represents the nature of reality as a static, finished, inclusive system and human thought and life as compelled, on pain of illusoriness, to adapt to this closed system. What Schiller inveighed against, at least in his early writings (and this is reminiscent of Mill), is the aristocratic, unprogressive, and anti-individualistic metaphysics and social philosophy this form of idealism supported. As for religion, however, Schiller's objection to absolutism was that it encouraged irreligion in rendering religious values and God into dialectical theses or inconsequential mysteries. Schiller had his own religious philosophy which led him on occasion to be as hostile to materialism and scientifically proclaimed atheism as he was to absolutism.

The Hegel that fascinated and inspired Oxford was not the philosopher who saw reality as a historical process and truth as the intoxicating residue of a bacchanalian revel or raging battlefield of opposing forces. Nor was it the Hegel who spoke of the progressive realization of the Absolute in national states. It was rather the Hegel of dialectical process and categories, the Hegel who interpreted thought as necessarily limited and contradicted in each of its unfolding moments, but just as necessarily proceeding to a more complete synthesis, a "concrete whole," and higher realization of reality and truth. This was a rarified and assiduous tracing of the shortcomings, the inner contradictions and blind alleys of thought leading, however, inevitably to truth, coming to Spirit and the all-inclusive whole, the One, the Absolute—the absolutely simple Absolute of Bradley or the Community of McTaggart and Royce.

In the genteel philosophic atmosphere at Oxford, Schiller appeared as a truculent young man, rudely scornful of the carefully plotted hedges and intricate pathways that laced the approach to the temple of the Absolute. Moreover, it was made clear—indeed, Schiller was hardly to be restrained in his determination to make it clear—that his intent was to smash that idol in its home, to destroy the Absolute.

Now what disturbed Oxford and distinguished Schiller was not the zealous-

19 *Studies in Humanism*, pp. 277–278.

ness of his preparations against the Absolute. This, after all, could be dismissed as mere youthful defiance of established authority, something easily diverted or dissipated in cool-headed, official ways. But Schiller was more dangerous because he had a mission; he had his philosophy and sought to establish his new god in a new shrine. As to what this upstart philosophy was all about, Oxford, with few exceptions, avoided the effort of patient understanding. Schiller, unfortunately, announced in his Preface to *Humanism* that the older forms of philosophy are "flung aside with a contemptuous smile by the young, the strong, the virile." This kind of remark helped sustain the Oxford reaction to Schiller's philosophy. Heresy, after all, was forgivable; the great Bradley was heretical in his Hegelianism and in his theology. But Schiller was guilty of bad taste and, even worse, bad form. James had warned of this, advising Schiller of what seemed to others " 'bad taste' in the way of polemical jeers and general horse-play."[20] Oxford philosophy kept Schiller at a measured distance. His wit and philosophizing in behalf of humanism were received with suspicion and occasional offense. He was not ineffective as a teacher or even in influencing some of his colleagues. But he was made to appear as something like a peddler of patent medicines, loudly contemptuous of old-fashioned remedies and proclaiming the virtues of a marvelous new elixir that he and Doctor James had discovered.

In order to destroy the Absolute, or its philosophy, refuting Bradley was necessary. The march of attack moves through all of Schiller's writings and the polemical thrust is directed at Bradley even when spent on other men. Schiller was so occupied with what he once referred to as his "beloved *bête noire*, the Absolute,"[21] and so filled with the avenging spirit against Bradley that one wonders what he would have done if there had been no reigning Absolute or Bradley for him to defy. Still, even if the Absolute was an illusion, there was no doubt about the reality of Bradley; and here Schiller's critical faculties sometimes mislead him. Stung by Bradley's deliberate refusal to condescend to take him seriously, Schiller occasionally and at worst vent himself upon Bradley as if, in the white heat of distemper, Bradley, absolutism, and the Absolute had melted into a single abhorred object.

Bradley, who was no novice in dealing with critics, used the most effective weapon against Schiller. He maintained a lofty silence, knowing well, perhaps, that a man of Schiller's temperament could not bear to be ignored by his enemies. Schiller wanted to play St. George, slayer of the dragon of absolutism, but Bradley refused to cooperate. An aloof dragon who yawns rather than rages will trick a would-be St. George into becoming a Don Quixote. Piqued just once out of his silence, Bradley addressed a long critical article against Schiller, personal idealism, and pragmatism. In a footnote (Bradley was famous for sardonic and polemical footnotes) he quoted Schiller's claim that the "new" philosophy was represented by "the young, the strong, the virile," and added: "This is certainly

20 See the letter of 1904 in Perry, II, 503.
21 *Studies in Humanism*, p. 134.

young, indeed I doubt if at any time of life most of us have been as young as this." And in the same article Bradley advised James concerning Schiller: "it is certain that a writer can be discredited by the extravagance and the vulgarity of his disciple, if at least he does not see his way to disconnect himself from it."[22] But in his other writings Bradley never mentioned Schiller by name. His dislike for Schiller was genuine just as was his respect for James and his evident interest in the work of Dewey.[23] The antagonism between Schiller and Bradley, Schiller's outspoken opposition to Oxford absolutism, and the academic intrigue that operates in university life may explain why it was impossible for Schiller to be elected to a professorship at Oxford.[24]

It will not do to portray the quarrel between Schiller and Oxford philosophy as a vendetta or merely a clash of personalities. The differences were deeper. But devoting this much attention to the complicated combination of personal and philosophic incongruities that separated them may help to throw light on the motives and object of Schiller's long and continued onslaught upon what he referred to as "intellectualism," "formal logic," and "absolutism." For it has become painfully evident in recent years that without some grasp of what it was Schiller was criticising, and why his polemical sallies took a tiresomely repetitious form, one simply fails to appreciate Schiller at all. This is in fact what has happened, and is the main reason for the rapid eclipse of interest in him.

The "absolutism" Schiller was so devoutly concerned to destroy had begun to lose ground shortly after the turn of the century. It was under attack from other forces. G. E. Moore's now famous paper, "The Refutation of Idealism" (1903), was a signal of the change that he and Russell as well as James, Dewey, and Santayana were working to bring about. By the time of Schiller's death in 1937 (or Bradley's in 1924), there was little active interest in the writings of Green, Bradley, Bosanquet, and the other idealists. Schiller's "enemy" had ceased to be a power in philosophy.[25] There was also, except for the Personalist movement, a corresponding lack of interest in Schiller's ideas, and his work tended to be ignored even by the pragmatist disciples of James and Dewey.

To the reader innocent of the historical tradition that Schiller was opposing, many of his claims and lengthy arguments will appear mistaken and outmoded. His energetic wit which once gave color and crispness to his disputatious writings now contributes to the impression of a whimsical and crotchety earnestness in the airing of somewhat dated convictions.

22 "On Truth and Practice," *Mind*, 1904, p. 330. Bradley's footnoted comment on Schiller is on pp. 309–310, note 2. While they were both at Oxford, Bradley and Schiller evidently never spoke to one another. In a letter to Bradley, July 16, 1904, James wrote: "I was astonished when I was last at Oxford, to learn that you & Schiller had never met face to face. I imagine that you have never yet done so, and that your imaginations have been somewhat at work, representing mutual monsters," Kenna, p. 318.

23 It is clear from scattered comments in *Essays on Truth and Reality* that Bradley was one of the few distinguished British philosophers to take a serious interest in Dewey's thought.

24 There is Santayana's judgment concerning his "old friend": "Schiller, with the airs of a professed and shameless sophist, was an English Churchman, probably for that reason tolerated at Oxford where otherwise he might have been taboo." *My Host the World*, p. 98.

25 Recently there have been signs of a revival of interest in Bradley and idealism, but not in Schiller.

We can come, I think, to a more just assessment of Schiller's philosophizing and its bearing upon pragmatism than fáte has generally allotted him. But in doing so, some sense of the historical orientation, the philosophic climate in which Schiller's thought moved and against which it continued to address its hard-won wisdom is essential. We shall see why this is so in turning to some of the cardinal doctrines advanced by Schiller.

§ 64. Humanism, Butt-End-Foremost

William James once described Schiller's philosophy as "the butt-end-foremost statement of the humanist position."[26] This is the statement we now want to examine.

Schiller's philosophy is an inseparable blend of metaphysics and psychology. Over the course of his writing, one can notice an interest passing from metaphysical to psychological and logical topics. But even this observable change of direction can mislead us. For from the start, Schiller never abandoned the conviction that the knowing process, the human self responding to needs and purposes, is the fundamental fact with which philosophic wisdom (like human life itself) begins and ends. Thus the individual purposive self, man the measure and his measuring, becomes the immediate, permanent point of concentration.

Accordingly, for Schiller, analysis of the self in its cognitive activities implies metaphysical assumptions concerning the nature of the conditions generating and sustaining these activities. But the nature of the conditions, in turn, can be discerned only from within, through those very cognitive activities in which sustaining conditions become consciously acknowledged and interpreted.

Schiller described this fixing of his central point of view as his anthropomorphic philosophy, calling it "humanism," and later "voluntarism" and "personalism."[27] In commencing with what he maintained was "the certainty of our own existence on the basis and analogy of which the world must be interpreted,"[28] Schiller affirmed the reality of the self as an agent.[29] The self, as he put it, is "the master-key" with which all problems will be resolved, "when all things have been shown to be of like nature with the mind that knows them, then at length will knowledge be perfect and perfectly humanized."[30]

In thus declaring the primacy of the self and its cognitive operations as the initial and controlling condition for constructing a reasonable epistemology and

---

[26] *Pragmatism*, p. 243.
[27] Thus, see the important argument for the primacy and "reality of the Self," ch. 5 in *Riddles of the Sphinx*, in which Schiller calls "this unavoidable and salutary anthropomorphism *humanism*," p. 145. The chapter, significantly, is titled "Reconstruction."
[28] *Ibid.*, p. 147.
[29] Cf. *ibid.*, p. 142: "All experience is relative to a self, all acts of knowledge are performed by selves, the whole of our cognitive machinery, principles, axioms, postulates and categories, are invented by and modelled upon selves. The Self is the meeting-place of all antitheses and ambitions, the battleground of all theories and impulses, and their arbiter. It is in short a concrete fact."
[30] *Ibid.*, p. 147. Schiller later expressed doubts about this sanguine hope of a perfect and perfectly humanized knowledge.

metaphysics, Schiller would appear to be in full harmony with Dewey's emphasis upon the knowing process as the point of departure for theorizing about human nature, experience, and reality. There are similarities. Dewey's early writings on and preoccupation with psychology had Hegelian and idealistic roots, modified by "organic" biology and the progress of experimental psychology.[31] Dewey maintained (in 1886) that philosophy and psychology were one,[32] and, despite his break with idealism,[33] he continued to affirm the fundamental idea that "knowledge *is* reality making a particular and specified sort of change in itself."[34] In 1889, Dewey was arguing that "knowledge is the construction by the mind of a universe," which sounds initially like Schiller's view, but Dewey shortly goes on to describe the universal nature of mind and, indeed, of a universal mind which individual minds reproduce.[35] At first with an idealistic or mentalistic emphasis, later in increasingly biological, social, and cultural terms, Dewey described the objective, shared, common conditions of cognitive activity. Schiller, however, insisted on the role of private, unique, personal, individualistic factors in all occasions of thought and conceptualization. In contrast to Dewey's analysis of the function of thought as initiated in an objective situation,[36] Schiller begins with the Self and its inner perplexities and demands. His humanism is a subjectivistic and voluntaristic rendition of the transcendental philosophy of knowing reminiscent of Fichte and Schelling (discussed in Part One, §§ 13-16).[37]

James, in commenting on the differences (within the larger unity) that existed between Dewey, Schiller, and himself, rightly noted that

> Schiller's universe is the smallest, being essentially a psychological one. He starts with but one sort of thing, truth-claims, but is led ultimately to the independent objective facts which they assert. . . .[38]

And again:

> He starts from the subjective pole of the chain, the individual with his beliefs, as the more concrete and immediately given phenomena.[39]

James made a point of stressing Schiller's "realism"; that Schiller did indeed believe in an independently existing Reality and that this needed stressing is

[31] Dewey studied under G. Stanley Hall; see Schilpp, pp. 22–23; White, *Origin*, pp. 37–39. Also see above, Introduction to Part II and § 35, 38.
[32] See the passage quoted early in § 38.
[33] In 1907, writing to James, he described his pragmatism as, in contrast to Schiller's, "a reaction . . . against all idealism," Perry, II, 528.
[34] "The Practical Character of Reality," p. 40. For the fuller context, see the concluding portion of § 101 below.
[35] *Applied Psychology.* For the passage and a discussion of the background, see White, *Origin*, p. 55. But also see "Psychology As Philosophic Method" (1886), and "The Psychological Standpoint" (1886), pp. 3, 7, for illuminating instances of Dewey's early psychological point of view concerning knowing and reality.
[36] For Dewey's concept of the *situation* see § 39 above.
[37] Or, in Kallen's judgment: "Humanism is thus 'personal idealism,' pragmatism given a personal ego-centric or subjectivistic bias," "Pragmatism and its 'Principles,' " p. 630. See Abel, ch. 9, for a discussion of Schiller's subjectivism in metaphysics and psychology.
[38] Preface to *The Meaning of Truth,* next to the final paragraph.
[39] *The Meaning of Truth,* p. 169.

significant. For there is some obscurity, as critics have pointed out, over what it is that Schiller is committed to when he speaks of "reality." We have seen how important the notion of "Reals" was for Peirce. Scientific thought was based on the hypothesis of existing "Real things, whose characters are entirely independent of our opinion about them."[40] Peirce had argued that our conception of reality, our standing interpretation of what is real, is fixed by the community of knowers and inquirers.

Peirce can be misread as arguing that we, the thinking community, create and determine the nature of reality. But this is to fail to appreciate Peirce's insistence that real things "force" themselves upon our attention and their character is not dependent upon human thought. Peirce's "realism" is not to be denied. But Peirce also argued that real things do not make themselves known to us in some odd fashion of frank and absolute nakedness.[41] There are things, surely, given to us in our earnest grasping to know them. But exactly what there is, we can only think and discourse on by means of the articulation we have and trust most. We grant that there is *something*, a given, to which these intellectual efforts are directed, but *what* it *is* becomes dependent upon *how* we can express and record our taking of it in our conceptual scheme.

Now Schiller was clearly in agreement with this last point, but less clearly so with the first. That is, the assumption of Reals, independent of our taking of them, is not made, or not emphatically made, by him. James himself alludes to as much in the very moment of reassuring us of Schiller's realism. He comments that, for Schiller, so pervasive are the human elements and motives in all of our formulas, our answers, and intellectual products, "that Mr. Schiller sometimes seems almost to leave it an open question whether there be anything else."[42]

§ 65.   The Private Thinker
         and the Postulated World

The last three paragraphs reveal suspicions of philosophic difficulties in Schiller's affirmations, or attempts to affirm, the existence of a real world. But the suspected difficulties are of less interest to us here than the subject they direct us to look at more carefully, namely, the ontology that guides all of Schiller's philosophizing.

The ontology consists of two ultimate modes of being. There is first the human personality, the individual desiring and creative being, the irreducibly real fact

40 See above § 23 and the outset of § 43.
41 This has been discussed earlier, see §§ 23 and 24.
42 *Pragmatism*, p. 159. Or James in *The Meaning of Truth*, p. 243: "Schiller, remaining with the fallible individual, and treating only of reality-for-him, seems to many of his readers to ignore reality-in-itself altogether. But that is because he seeks only to tell us how truths are attained, not what the contents of those truths, when attained shall be."

of "human beings striving to comprehend a world of human experience by the resources of human minds."[43]

> Humanism . . . demands that man's integral nature shall be used as the whole premiss which philosophy must argue from wholeheartedly, that man's complete satisfaction shall be the conclusion philosophy must aim at, that philosophy shall not cut itself loose from the real problems of life by making initial abstractions which are false. . . . Hence it insists on *leaving in* the whole rich luxuriance of individual minds, instead of compressing them all into a single type of 'mind,' feigned to be one and immutable; it leaves in also the psychological wealth of every human mind and the complexities of its interests, emotions, volitions, aspirations.[44]

The other reality, or aspect of being, is that which serves as the material for our creative and cognitive manipulation. This is reality that we "make," and is always in the making, which receives considerable attention in Schiller's writings. In his first book, *Riddles of the Sphinx*, he argued against skepticism and pessimism and propounded a metaphysics of evolution. Later, in "Axioms as Postulates," while in no way abandoning the idea of evolution, he developed a rather special category for the mode of existence we are now considering, calling it *hylē:*

> The world . . . is essentially ὕλη, it is what we make of it. It is fruitless to define it by what it originally was or by what it is apart from us . . . ; it *is* what is made of it. Hence . . . the world is *plastic*, and may be moulded by our wishes. . . .[45]

Concerning this second condition, *hylē*, Schiller, who knew his Greek, followed Aristotle.[46] We can say *that hylē* is, but not *what* it is as such.[47] For to say what it is, e.g., bronze or wood, is already to have introduced distinctions of kinds of matter. Bronze and wood are materials, some of the ways that matter becomes

[43] *Studies in Humanism*, p. 12. One may enter one of the doubts lately alluded to in coming up against Schiller's use of expressions like '*the* human being,' '*the* mind,' '*the* individual human personality,' etc. How is the definite article 'the' to be taken here? One might argue that Schiller is affirming the reality of one and only one personality, or mind, or human being, but he clearly intends more than this. Or, true to his own subjective and egocentric starting point, we might have expected him to affirm, as Fichte, the reality only of *himself*, of *his* personality, *his* mind. But somehow his egocentric starting point allows him to affirm the reality of many individual persons; this is his intention despite our perplexity over how he can legitimately do so. In "Axioms as Postulates," p. 52, in answer to the question, If the world is experience, "*whose* experience is it"? he answers, " 'our experience' or if that imply too much among philosophers, and I may not take a common world for granted, more precisely, '*my* experience.' " But, undeterred, Schiller continues in the rest of the paper to speak of *our* experience, *the* world, *the* mind, and *its* (or *our*) wishes and purposes. For some of Schiller's arguments on and defenses of our ability "to create subjective worlds of objective reality," see *Riddles of the Sphinx*, p. 281, also pp. 262–265, and ch. 9; and *Studies in Humanism*, pp. 482 ff.

[44] *Studies in Humanism*, pp. 13–14. "*What we call reality* is bound up with our knowing and dependent upon our manipulations," p. 428.

[45] "Axioms as Postulates," pp. 60–61. This is the passage James selects for comment in *Pragmatism*, p. 159.

[46] "Axioms as Postulates," p. 60.

[47] Even this locution suffers an inaccuracy. For since *hylē* is *dynamis* (or *dynameis*) and "exists" in a state of potentiality and privation relative to form, *hylē* never *is* (is not as such complete); it is a becoming.

determinate, shaped or formed, and classified. Matter as such, *proto-hylē*, without form is not knowable according to Aristotle. Thus matter stands to form as potentiality (*dynamis*) to actuality. It is form that is the *kind* or *what* of which *matter* is the *this* or *this-here-existent*. For Aristotle, knowable objects, real existent things, are inseparable complexes of matter and form; each complex constitutes a being, a substance, *ousia*.[48] Aristotle also points out that matter, the *that* of something, is relative to form, the *what* the thing in question is and is known as. Thus, the what, the condition matter is in and how it is determined and how identified by us, will depend upon form. Wood remains wood whether we use and identify pieces as "firewood" or "wooden table." But what wood is as firewood and what it is as material of tables differs according to these *whats*. For the powers (*dynameis*) of wood in each case are different, and their selection and identification differs according to the differences of forms.[49] Wood can become many things, but to become fuel and to become a support of books, elbows, and vases are different becomings, different material careers for wood.

The Aristotelian concept of matter is not irrelevant to understanding Schiller's *hylē*. In the general idea of an indeterminate *that*, a becoming something, a *dynamis*, Schiller draws upon Aristotle. But Schiller is no Aristotelian respecting the nature and analysis of *form*. Aristotle viewed forms and actualizations in nature and regarded the world as a structure of processes and ends prior to and largely independent of human knowers. Schiller, however, attributed the origin of form and the process of forming *hylē* or matter to the activity of human beings.[50] He thoroughly humanized Aristotle's naturalism. *We* construct the world.

> The world, as it now appears, was not a ready-made datum. . . . If we have learnt enough philosophy to see that we must not only ask the ontological question, *What is it?* but also the profounder epistemological question, *How do we know what it is?* we shall realize that it is a *construction* which has been gradually achieved.[51]

Constructions and constructing, Schiller explains, are products of "trying," or "experiment."

---

[48] There are, of course, exceptions, i.e., objects wholly "actual," of form but not matter.
[49] Cf. *Physcis* II. 2, 194b10. "Matter [*hylē*] is a relative term, since for each form there is a different matter."
    Physics I. 9 is a good statement of the senses in which Aristotle understands matter to be in a state of privation and as potentiality, and as imperishable potentiality. There, too, 192a30, Aristotle defines 'matter' as the primary substratum (*proton hypokeimenon*) from which each thing is generated and which persists in the product in a way that is not incidental.
[50] There is a limited but suggestive resemblance between Aristotle's conception of *art* (*technē*) as a process of making (*poiēsis*) distinct from *natural* processes, and Schiller's view of our "constructing" the world. The artist, says Aristotle, differs from nature in making use of and forming materials outside himself. The *archē* of the process is in the artist, not (as with nature) within the materials. But Schiller's is a transcendentalist theory of knowing (as discussed in Part I, § 8), a subjectivistic Platonism and romanticism that comes closer, by comparison, to Locke's theory of property (see § 14) than to Aristotle.
[51] "Axioms as Postulates," p. 54.

I observe that since we do not know what the world is, we have to find out. This we do *by trying*. Not having a ready-made world presented to us . . . we have to make experiments in order to construct out of the materials we start with a harmonious cosmos which will satisfy all our desires (that for knowledge included). For this purpose we make use of every means that seems promising: we try it and *we try it on*. For we cannot afford to remain unresistingly passive, to be impressed, like the *tabula rasa* in the traditional fiction, by an independent 'external world' which stamps itself upon us. If we did that we should be stamped out.[52]

Experience is thus not the sum of our receptivity to a world acting upon us, but is, argues Schiller, experimental.

. . . Experience is always more than this: it is either experiment or *reaction*, reaction upon stimulation, which latter we ascribe to the 'external world.' But reaction is still a kind of action, and its character still depends in part on the reacting agent. Nor have we any independent knowledge of the 'external world'; it is merely the systematic way in which we construct the source of stimulation on which we feel ourselves to be reacting. Hence even our most passive receptivity to sensations can, and should, be construed as the effortless fruition of what was once acquired by strenuous effort. . . .[53]

Such experimental constructions, however, or reactions upon stimulation, do require acknowledging that "we never experiment *in vacuo*."[54] Conditions, says Schiller, limit our experimental activities. Our activity "always meets with resistance,"[55] and this existence of a resisting medium constitutes Schiller's "realism," for this medium is *hylē*. This is "the indeterminate potentiality" of "whatever form we succeed in imposing on it."[56]

William James, reflecting a British empirical conception of *matter* as *something* "there," determinate, although defying our efforts cognitively to absorb it —a limit approached but never reached—found difficulties in grasping Schiller's revival of Aristotelian *hylē*.[57] Commenting in a letter to Schiller on how Bradley and others had misunderstood pragmatism, James added:

I am sure that not one of us has any clear idea of what the ultimate *pre-human fact*, which we encounter and which works, through all our stratified predicates, upon us—the ὕλη as you call it—really is or signifies.[58]

But Schiller was not proposing the existence of a prehuman fact, a determinate but unknown "ultimate" working upon us. His argument was rather that our working, our predicates construct this fact.[59] To speculate about what this fact

[52] *Ibid.*, p. 55.
[53] *Ibid.*, pp. 55–56.
[54] *Ibid.*, p. 59.
[55] *Ibid.*, p. 59.
[56] *Ibid.*, p. 60.
[57] See *Pragmatism*, pp. 162–163.
[58] Perry, II, 503–504.
[59] Cf. James's query: "Isn't the ὕλη which you speak of as the primal bearer of all our humanized predicates, conceived by you epistemologically as an independent *that* which the

"really is or signifies" is to mistake the meaning of *hylē*. *Hylē* is plastic indeterminateness, not a devious, bewitching, and ephemeral substance given to
chamelion-like performances. *Hylē* is not the ingenious actor, there but inscru-
table behind his quick changes of costumes and masks as he assumes the roles the
audience requests of him. *Hylē* is rather more like the ability to respond and the
switching of masks than the actor hidden in these stratagems, for it is the performing abilities that have been called out, not the performer; it is the occasion of
thats which become *whats* with our urgings and cooperation: *we* make the performance.

James was aware of this much difference between himself and Schiller. He was
committed to an independent agent behind the mask, a realism that recognized
externality and independence of our objects, meaning "that even if *we* be annihilated they are indentifiable with objects that are still there for other people."
James summarized the important point over which he and Schiller differed:

> We both assume a situation to discuss, don't we? in the shape of someone claiming
> truth and getting there or not. Your procedure lets him get there all alone, mine
> [lets him] get there to someone else's satisfaction. . . . It seems to me really fantas-
> tically formal to ignore *that* much of the truth that is already established, namely,
> that men do think in social situations. . . . I *simply assume the social situation*,
> and I am sorry that . . . you balk at it so much.[60]

So far we have been reviewing Schiller's reinterpretation of the traditional
subject-object distinction in the theory of knowledge, namely, the distinction of
the knower and the general nature of the objects known. This distinction, for
Schiller, as we have seen, consists initially of demarcating in experience these two
conditions: a world of experience, and agents understanding that experience.[61]
Earlier, the manner in which Schiller develops this distinction was referred to as
guided by an *ontology* recognizing the existence of *persons* (or human minds)
and of *hylē*. Here it must be said, in fairness to Schiller and in accord with several
of his protests, that his intent and procedure was not to elaborate a theory of
knowledge from metaphysical assumptions or ontological commitments. Schiller
often insisted that his aim was fundamentally epistemological, and *humanism*
was originally intended to designate the central position of man in the theory of
knowledge.[62] The essay "Axioms as Postulates," in which these ontological principles are stated, was conceived by Schiller as "epistemological throughout" and

---

whats qualify, and which (in the ultimate) may be decided to be of any nature whatever?"
Perry, II, 509. Schiller thought this too much a concession to realism. I would guess that he
balked particularly at the word 'independent' in the above.

[60] Perry, II, 509–510. This view of knowledge as cooperative effort in and of a social
situation brings James close to Dewey and Mead. Dewey had even stronger reservations than
James concerning Schiller's egocentric theory of knowledge.

[61] "Axioms as Postulates," p. 52. Also p. 51: "the whole world in which we live is
experience and built up out of nothing else than experience."

[62] The term 'humanism,' he remarked, "is here used in a purely epistemological sense. It
was adopted by me, with very little philosophic precedent, in the year 1902, to designate a
point of view which emphasized the central position of man and of human enterprise in the
theory of knowledge," *Must Philosophers Disagree?* p. 308, note 1. See also Abel, p. 10.

not intended to be taken in any other sense.[63] Thus, the ontological commitments which we have been looking at in the above pages are themselves to be construed in an epistemological way for Schiller. The ontology is postulated from within and for the purposes of constructing a theory of knowledge. The purposive acting self and the world as *hylē* are, in short, methodological assumptions of the theory of knowledge and of actual conduct.

> . . . It is a *methodological necessity* to assume that the world is *wholly plastic, i.e.,* to *act as though* we believed this, and will yield us what we want, if we persevere in wanting it.[64]

With the assumption of a purely plastic world shaped and constructed by our *trying*, that is, our "experiments" in quest of a harmonizing and satisfying experience,[65] the distinctive and novel tenets of Schiller's humanism and personalism were expressed.

The notion of *experiment* continued to be central in the development of Schiller's outlook. The active experimenting of man results in the arts, sciences, and structures of social organization.[66] Experiment is here regarded by Schiller in a very broad sense, and, accordingly, scientific experimentation is but one special instance of this activity.[67] In general, an experiment is any trial or attempt to affect the materials of experience "from the most random restlessness and the most blindly instinctive adaptations, to the most clearly conscious testing of an elaborate theory."[68] All conscious human action is experimental, and it follows that, for Schiller, a theory of *experiment* or analysis of *experimentation* constitutes the fundamental philosophic conceptual scheme for discussing and understanding human nature and conduct. Though Schiller did not put the issue this way, this, I think, is how he envisioned the object of his endeavors and what he meant by his latter emphasis upon *method* as the substance, the focus, and the promise of humanism.[69] The *method* was the application and elaboration of

---

[63] *Studies in Humanism*, p. 16, note 1. See also p. 428, note 1: "I do not think that the text of *Axioms as Postulates* anywhere, even in isolated paragraphs, entitled critics to read it in a metaphysical sense. And certainly the whole method and purpose of that essay should have made it unmistakable that it was nowhere intended to be taken in any but an epistemological sense."

[64] "Axioms as Postulates," p. 61. *Hylē* and a "plastic" world, while essential features in Schiller's philosophy, are not crystal-clear concepts. For some doubts about this cardinal thesis of pragmatism—a world malleable, plastic, exhibiting physical *possibility*—see Appendix 7 below.

[65] See "Axioms as Postulates," p. 55.

[66] *Ibid.*, p. 56. The personality and goodness of God are also construed as methodological postulates by Schiller, p. 122.

[67] *Ibid.*, p. 57: "Of the 'experimenting' which builds up the cosmos the scientific experiment is only an extreme case."

[68] *Ibid.*, p. 58.

[69] Thus, *Studies in Humanism*, p. xvi: "we have a new method with inexhaustible possibilities of application to life and science, which, though it is not primarily metaphysical, contains also the promise of an infinity of valuable, and more or less valid, metaphysics. . . ." And p. 16: "Pragmatism will seem a special application of Humanism to the theory of knowledge. But Humanism will seem more universal. It will seem to be possessed of a method which is applicable universally, to ethics, to aesthetics, to metaphysics, to theology, to every concern of man, as well as to the theory of knowledge."

the concept of *experiment* in each and all of divers contexts of human action. A specially important feature of the method and essence of experimentation is the act of postulation.

> . . . The general structure of the mind and the fundamental principles that support it . . . must be conceived as growing up, like the rest of our powers and activities, that is, by a process of experimenting, designed to render the world conformable to our wishes. They will begin their career, that is, as *demands* we make upon our experience or in other words as *postulates*, and their subsequent sifting, which promotes some to be axioms and leads to the abandonment of others, which it turns out to be too expensive or painful to maintain, will depend on the experience of their working.[70]

We need not go into Schiller's detailed defense of the interpretation of axioms as accepted and working postulates. His attack upon the alleged a priori content and transcendental origin of axioms is not widely different from more recent critical doubts concerning the *analyticity* purportedly possessed by logical truths.[71] It is enough simply to take note of his pragmatic interpretation of man's postulational activity and the organized systems[72] of accepted, working postulates through which experience is made conformable to working purposes, demands, and desires.[73]

But the direction that Schiller gives to this pragmatic analysis of postulates was, as already remarked, subjectivistic and psychological. His doctrines of the plurality of truth and the individual "making" of truth and reality; his arguments for the primacy of psychology in logic and theory of knowledge; his humanizing of truth and of logic; and his criticisms of "formal" and "intellectualist" logic— these are all consequences of this theory of experiment and postulates which (as

---

[70] "Axioms as Postulates," p. 64.

[71] See § 80 below and Appendix 6. In "Axioms as Postulates" Schiller discusses several 'axioms,' notably one traditionally regarded as "the basis of all thinking in the strict sense of the term, the Principle of Identity," p. 95. Schiller rejects the a priori and transcendental necessity as sources of the axiom. He argues that from our own conscious "immediacy of felt self-identity" we proceed to postulate the identity of things and meanings as a practical demand and desire—we come to "the *recognition of the same* in the *recurrence of the like,*" p. 98. James was critical of this analysis of identity (see Perry, II, 497, and Appendix 1, sec. C below), in part no doubt because James was willing to entertain the idea of a pre-human reality, a real core of things independent of human thought, as we saw earlier. For Schiller we mold things, we demand that "A *shall be* A," p. 103. Both James and Schiller were troubled about how identity is possible in a "plastic" and changing world. What mars Schiller's analysis of identity—and has misled many other philosophers since Heraclitus—is the failure to appreciate how changes among parts of a thing do not destroy the identity of the whole with itself. This is at root a confusion of the sign 'is' or '=' relating the terms in statements (which are true when the terms thus related refer to the same object) with the *objects* referred to by statements. The 'is' in 'A is A' or the '=' in 'A = B' relate terms in statements, not objects in the world.

[72] The systems we in fact use and live by, Schiller notes, may not be tightly organized, and we may accept contradictory postulates, although protecting them from open conflict.

[73] "We must start from a psychical experience which suggests the postulate (= the previous fact suggesting the hypothesis); we must use the postulate (or hypothesis) as a means to an end which appears desirable; we must apply the postulate to experience (a postulate and a hypothesis not capable of and not intended for use are alike invalid); and the final validity of the postulate (or hypothesis) depends on the extent to which experience can be rendered congruous with it." "Axioms as Postulates," p. 107.

James said) began with a psychological universe and started "from the subjective pole of the chain."[74] Each of these developments and ramifications of Schiller's position was to lead him to the very antithesis of Absolutism and Bradley's idealism. We shall see why.

§ 66.   Psychology and Logic

A persistently argued theme in Schiller's writings is the dependence of logic upon psychology. This is, of course, to be expected in a philosophy that takes as its primary subject matter the human self in the activity of experiencing. Psychology is defined as "a descriptive science whose aim is the description of mental process as such" and, it is added, "the mental processes of individual minds are intended."[75] Psychology is then viewed as "the wider and lower" of the sciences, and logic is regarded as an *evaluation* of the processes of actual knowing, working upon the facts and materials made available by psychology.[76]

The extent to which psychology is basic to logic and to the theory of knowledge is made clear by Schiller:

> The definition we have adopted clearly assigns to Psychology a very extensive field of operations—practically the whole realm of direct experience. It recognizes *a psychological side also to everything that can be known*, inasmuch as everything known to exist must be connected with our experience, and known by a psychical process. In so far as any real is known, a process of experiencing is involved in it, and this process appertains to the science of Psychology. Thus all physical objects and questions become psychological, so soon as we ask how they can be experienced, and whether the psychical process of experiencing them warrants our claiming for them an 'objective reality.'[77]

Even the fundamental operation of postulation and the pragmatic trials and logical decisions whereby postulates become axioms is a matter primarily for psychology. For, Schiller argues, the postulate is itself a psychological fact, a process in which demands upon experience are made and evaluated: "Psychological processes are the vehicles of truth, and logical value must be found in psychological fact *or nowhere*."[78]

[74] Above, § 64.
[75] *Studies in Humanism*, p. 75. The entire third chapter, "Logic and Psychology," is a basic statement of Schiller's position.
[76] *Ibid.*, p. 78: Logic "may be defined as *the systematic evaluation of actual knowing*. . . . The same cognitive values occur twice over, first in Psychology as so many facts, then in Logic, as subjects for critical evaluation."
[77] *Ibid.*, p. 75.
[78] "Axioms as Postulates," p. 124. The whole passage is important for understanding Schiller:

> A postulate does not become axiomatic until it has been found to be workable and in proportion as it is so. But we deny that the two questions can be separated and logic can be cut adrift from psychology and dissipated in the ether of the unintelligible. Psychological processes are the vehicles of truth, and logical values must be found

Schiller then roundly affirmed his psychologism: "if 'psychologism' means a demand that the psychical facts of our cognitive functioning shall no longer be treated as irrelevant to Logic, it is clear . . . that Humanism is Psychologism." It was against much this same point of view, the British empirical tradition commencing with Locke and culminating in Hume and the Mills, that Bradley had directed his most powerful criticisms. The empiricist's conviction was that the aim of theoretical philosophy was to construct an explanation of knowledge, its characteristics and limits. And all agreed that the theory of knowledge took as its subject and materials the human mind and its workings. Bradley, however, argued for a rejection of psychologism and absolute separation of logic and psychology. In the _Principles of Logic_, he wrote:

> Both logic and psychology, if they are to exist at all, must remain each in principle independent. . . . And the subordination of one to the other, whenever seriously attempted, will never, I think, fail to make manifest in its result the absurdity of its leading idea.[79]

Bradley was not opposed to psychology as an empirical science. His point was rather that philosophy, and especially logic, must be freed from the empiricist's psychology of mental images and associations of ideas—the mechanism with which _judgment, inference_, and _meaning_ were reductively "explained." For that mental mechanism did not explain; it simply impeded investigations of these subjects. Schiller, while not at all an exponent of the traditional empirical view of mind and operations of thought, was convinced that logic had as its sole function the evaluation of those psychical occurrences that operated postulationally as claims to truth. The process of "criticizing, systematizing, harmonizing, and utilizing the claims actually made" is "the business of logic."[80]

The attempt to separate logic and psychology, Schiller maintained, represented a "dehumanizing" of thought. Moreover, he contended, the logical theory that resulted, by divorcing itself from psychological conditions and the purposes that initiate and control all cognitive occurrences, was useless (since it misrepresented the process of thinking). This is the burden of Schiller's onslaught against what he called "the Intellectualist" and "formal" logic. His indictment was severe, and it led him, intemperately, to reject the "new" mathematical logic of Russell along

---

in psychological fact _or nowhere_. Before a principle can have its logical validity determined, it must be tried; and it can be tried only if some one can be induced to postulate it. Logical possibilities (or even 'necessities') are nothing until they have somehow become psychologically actual and active. . . .

Hence it is impossible to treat the logical question of axioms without reference to the actual processes whereby they are established, and their actual functioning in minds which entertain the logical in close connection with their other ideals. . . . Here as elsewhere the ideals of the normative science must be developed out of the facts of the descriptive science.

See also _Studies in Humanism_, p. 72.

[79] Page 613. See Wollheim, ch. 1, for an account of the motives and the nature of Bradley's attack on psychologism.

[80] _Studies in Humanism,_ p. 76.

with the idealistic theories of Bradley and Bosanquet as alike species of "Absolutism."

Recent history and the progress of logic would seem to prove Schiller wrong. Certainly Bradley's strictures against identifying the concepts and operations of logic with the subject matter of psychology (especially the subjective mentalistic psychology of the past) was sage advice. Excepting a few almost deserted philosophic interpretations of logic, contemporary logical theory is not a representation of thinking at all, being concerned with implications among sentences rather than inferences and thought processes among mental events. One might be tempted to conclude that Schiller's critical objective was simply wrongheaded.[81] But this is too easy, and also wrong. For the chief obstacle to understanding and discerning any merits in Schiller's critical and positive views concerning logic is his frequent use of the notion of 'logic' in a rather unusual way. Schiller seems to have meant by 'logic' the method of evaluating our procedures of manipulating experience, not an analysis of judgment or a science of demonstrative reasoning. He was working his way toward the construction of a general methodology, in which scientific method would be included as an instance, of discovering and organizing workable postulates. This is the "logic," i.e., the methodology men employ in the process of making truth and reality.

§ 67.   The Critique of Logic

In maintaining the dependence of logic upon psychology, Schiller spent considerable effort criticizing the structure of contemporary logical theory and the accepted analyses of deductive arguments. Schiller was not the only pragmatist critical of "formal" or "intellectualist" logic; his antipathy was shared by James and Dewey. Both Schiller and Dewey were concerned to develop a logic of *inference* in place of an analysis of the structure of *implications*. Both sought to articulate a logic of inquiry, of the instruments and techniques of thoughtful behavior in instituting demands upon experience. Both attempted to show how this logic was related to the actual course of human thought, an evolved aspect of the natural history of thinking.[82] Both men were reflecting the historical aims of Bacon[83] in developing a "logic of induction and discovery" in contrast to a logic of deduction and proof.

These similarities between Schiller and Dewey are instructive, but so, too, are some of the differences. Dewey commented favorably on the fundamental point of view which Schiller (and he) took concerning logic, saying:

[81] On this point as on many others, one must do Schiller the justice of recalling the historical circumstances of his argument. His attack on "formal logic" as a false representation of *thought* was addressed to the idealist logicians Bradley and, in particular, Bosanquet, who explained that "logic" represents the thought process in its "fully self-consistent form," that "logic" is the perfect actualization of imperfect psychological cognitive processes. See Schiller's discussion of this thesis, with quotations, in *Studies in Humanism*, pp. 100–104.

[82] See § 36 above.

[83] See Dewey's chapter on Bacon, ch. 2 in *Reconstruction*.

The factual continuity of biological function and psychological operation with logical norm is one of the most significant things to be noted and described.[84]

But Dewey's logical theory was developed under the influence of an idealism in which thought emerges and functions in historical and social contexts. And Dewey was further influenced by developments in biology and psychology, by the biological point of view in James's psychology, the social psychology of Mead, and the idea of logic as inquiry advanced by Peirce. For Dewey, as for Peirce, "logic" becomes conceived as a thoroughly social art of cooperative inquiry and intelligent action. Schiller, however, developed his view of logic from a metaphysical interpretation of evolution and very much under the influence of James, not the James of the *Psychology* but the James of "The Will to Believe." His "logic," hence, was conceived as a study of how individual claims and satisfactions in experience were workable. Thus, Dewey's naturalistic logical theory with its emphasis on intelligence as a cooperative force and communal good is distinguished from Schiller's personalistic logical theory emphasizing the psychological origins and achievement of individual satisfactions.

Schiller's psychologism, personalism, and humanism are invoked in his criticism of what he regarded as the fundamental concepts of logic.[85] 'Necessity,' 'truth,' 'meaning,' he argued, not noticing that these concepts inhabit the metalanguage of logic and not its most characteristic and most valuable medium,[86] have reference to psychic processes. With much vigor he maintains that these concepts become meaningless when separated from the psychic processes, from interest, purpose, emotion, and satisfaction.[87] 'Certainty,' for example, "in its actual occurrence" is "accompanied by a psychical feeling of certainty in various degrees of intensity."[88] The feeling is basic: "if the *feeling* of certainty is eliminated the word becomes unmeaning."[89] But it is not easy to discover just how and to what extent Schiller intends to identify the *meaning* of logical concepts with particular feelings or "psychic" events. Does he seriously intend to say that 'certainty' (the word) meaningfully occurs in discourse only contingent upon the occurrence of a feeling? Schiller speaks of "the feeling" of certainty, but this is already a generalization. What actually occurs is, presumably, a unique, momentary feeling. This momentary feeling is hardly a stable anchoring for the word (or meaning?) 'certainty.' Does he intend to go so far as to hold that the word (presumably at the moment of utterance) is causally related to the occurring feel-

---

[84] In a review of *Humanism* in *Psychological Bulletin*, 1904, p. 337. But cf. Dewey's letter to James at this time, mentioning the intended review and stating important critical reservations about Schiller's philosophy, Perry, II, 525. See also Dewey's critical comment quoted in §69 below.

[85] "The most fundamental conceptions of Logic, like 'necessity,' 'certainty,' 'self-evidence,' 'truth,' 'meaning,' are primarily descriptions of processes which are psychical facts," *Studies in Humanism*, p. 83.

[86] I.e., these terms characterize *statements*—such and such a statement is *necessary, true, meaningful,* etc.—while logic ordinarily has to do with ways of compounding and establishing implications among statements.

[87] *Studies in Humanism*, p. 81.

[88] *Ibid.*, p. 83.

[89] *Ibid.*, p. 84.

ing, and that without this causal relation utterance of the word becomes un-meaningful? Schiller does maintain something like this, and his psychologism leads him, accordingly, into a disastrous theory of meaning. For the theory is one in which the actual occasions and causal conditions generating mean-ingful discourse are confused with what is supposed to be the meaning of dis-course. Language is thus conceived as the outward form "expressive" of inner psychic processes, and the meanings of words are bits of and links in those inner processes. But when we come to an analysis of these meanings we are not a whit closer to finding them out than we were when we stayed with words and sen-tences. We simply have in place of one ordinary language a multitude of private ones, to say nothing of a multitude of private psychic processes—thus a multitude of private meanings. Meaningful communication is rendered an utter mystery. Discourse being geared to the flow of psychic processes becomes as fleeting and inscrutably arcane as the very processes it is alleged to represent.

Two fundamental conditions of meaning, Schiller maintains, are those of the *context* and the *agent*. Thus the meaning of a statement or assertion depends upon the actual context in which these are made. "The actual meaning is always a psychical fact"[90] and is distinct from an "average" meaning that characterizes "a form of words" and how they will probably be used in a certain sense.[91] But more, the context of that meaning depends on and includes the purpose and the whole "concrete personality" of the agent making an assertion.[92]

Presumably, what gets communicated among human beings when language is used is "the *average meaning* of a form of words which will *probably* be used in a certain sense."[93] The meaning, argues Schiller, or what is "actually meant" remains a problem; and, indeed, it is difficult to see how "the meaning" can ever be known since it requires of us extraordinary powers: we should have somehow to "know" the actual context and psychical fact that led an individual to say something. Moreover, we should have to "know" the concrete personality of the agent making the statement. Finally, we should have to be, somehow, intimately aware of the assertor's interest, purpose, emotion, and satisfaction that prompted him to speak. Short of this knowledge, which seems possible only by a Berg-sonian intuition or mystical *sympathy*, we must fall back on "average" meaning. But this average meaning turns out to be "*infinitely ambiguous*," since a form of words may "be used in any sense in which anyone can convey . . . *his* meaning."[94]

[90] *Ibid.,* p. 86.
[91] *Ibid.,* p. 87.
[92] *Ibid.,* p. 86.
[93] *Ibid.,* p. 87.
[94] *Ibid.,* p. 87. In a footnote Schiller offers as an example of "infinite ambiguity" 'Smith is red-haired,' saying this "has as many 'meanings' as there are past, actual, and potential 'Smiths' of whom it can be (truly or falsely) predicated, and occasions on which it can be made," p. 87, note 1.
This is hardly an illustration of "ambiguity" due to how different persons may differ-ently intend to use the same form of words. But why, one wonders, must Schiller conclude because there are many Smiths of whom the above is false, many of whom it is true, and many occasions for making the predication, that the statement thus has many ("infinite"?) *meanings?* 'Smith is red-haired' is true of all red-haired Smiths, false of all others. Are we to

Schiller's emphasis upon contexts as relevant to issuances of meaningful language, and the analysis of them is welcome, at least in part. And, at least in part, it accords with the pragmatic contextualism espoused in § 79 below. One can raise questions about what (short of the whole universe) determines the *relevant* conditions and boundaries of contexts. What, if any, is *the* context of *the* meaning of a statement? But in principle contextualism is sound, since we are given a way of avoiding commitments to essences or esoteric objects as meanings and we can more easily recognize kinds of intentions, nuances, and shades of "meaning" accountable for by contexts but not by essences. But serious reservations about Schiller's procedure occur when the hypostatizing of meanings into essences is no worse in the end than the results of the counter tendency to hypostatizing contexts. In Schiller's case, hypostatizing of the private context of meaning as the "actual" context and this as the occurrence of "psychological facts" unique and never recaptured, leaves us unable to account for shared experience and social intercourse had through language. How meaningful language occurs in either its "actual" or "average" forms is a question we are left speechless to explain.

On the notion of *meaning* and the use, analysis, and clarification of the meaning of concepts, it will be noticed that there is very little in common between Schiller's outlook and the pragmatism of Peirce or Dewey. Schiller's pronouncements on conceptualization and meaning are close to the critical attitude of Bergson concerning abstractions and symbolism generally, and to James's outspoken antipathy to "intellectualism." Schiller's psychologism has these affinities. Also, it was in reacting against the idealist logic, according to which the meaning of a judgment implied or had reference to a reality or community beyond the judgment that Schiller overstated the role of personal peculiarities and private complexities and purposes as determining the meanings of language.

§ 68. Making Truth and Reality

Schiller's conception of the world as plastic, as *hylē*, and his interpretation of thought as postulation supplied him with the essentials of his theory of truth.

Once again in following Schiller we come back to—or must begin with—the human agent, the purposive individual. And in the theory of truth, as in Schiller's more general analysis of thinking, *purpose* is the fundamental concept. Truth and falsehood, Schiller says, "are the intellectual forms of 'good' and 'bad.' "[95] Like 'good' and 'bad,' the terms 'true' and 'false' are valuations and, like all valu-

---

identify the meaning of 'Smith is red-haired' with each instance of the extension of 'Smith,' i.e., with everything named by 'Smith'? But then if nothing happened to be named by 'Smith' the above predication would be meaningless (yet it is not), or if its meaning is that which it is true or false of, then, in being true of nothing, its meaning would be the same as 'Green-haired Achilles,' which is also true of nothing. *Meaning* must not be confused with *extension,* for these reasons.
[95] *Studies in Humanism,* p. 154.

ations, have reference to *purpose*.⁹⁶ This is clear in the sciences in which the "effective" truth or falsehood of answers depends on their relevance to the questions raised. And each science consists of a definite system of truths concerning a subject within which and relative to which questions and answers are put. All depends upon the *purpose* of the science: "for what we want to know in the science will determine the questions we put, and their bearing on the questions put will determine the standing of the answers we attain."⁹⁷ If the answers are "revelant to our questions and conducive to our ends, they will yield 'truth,'" otherwise they are "false."⁹⁸ Schiller continues:

> seeing thus that everywhere truth and falsity depend on the purpose which constitutes the science and are bestowed accordingly, we begin to perceive . . . that the predicates 'true' and 'false' are not unrelated to 'good' and 'bad.' For good and bad also (in their wider and primary sense) have reference to purpose. 'Good' is what conduces to, 'bad' what thwarts, a purpose. . . .
> Truth, then, being a valuation has reference to a purpose.

Schiller then proceeds to explain that "objective truth" is the result of social pressure and selection for common purposes and ends from among the wider fund of purposive, subjective "truths" held by individuals.⁹⁹

Schiller is accordingly led to formulate a doctrine of truth in outward respects very close to what the other pragmatists had argued.¹⁰⁰ He concludes:

> in all actual knowing the question whether an assertion is 'true' or 'false' is decided . . . by its consequences, by its bearing on the interest which prompted to the assertion, by its relation to the purpose which put the question. To add to this that the consequences must be *good* is superfluous. For if and so far as an assertion satisfies or forwards the purpose of the inquiry to which it owes its being, it is so far 'true'; if and so far as it thwarts or baffles it, it is unworkable, unserviceable, 'false.' And 'true' and 'false,' we have seen, are the intellectual forms of 'good' and 'bad.'¹⁰¹

In order, therefore, to discover and decide whether an answer to any question is true or false,

> we have merely to note its effect upon the inquiry in which we are interested, and in relation to which it has arisen. And if these effects are favourable, the answer is 'true' and 'good' for our purpose, and 'useful' as a means to the end we pursue.¹⁰²

The notions of 'workable,' 'serviceable' assertions seem to admit of no general definition. What is workable, to what extent and how, is measured according to

⁹⁶ *Ibid.*, p. 152.
⁹⁷ *Ibid.*, p. 152.
⁹⁸ *Ibid.*, p. 152.
⁹⁹ *Ibid.*, p. 153: "Whatever, therefore, individuals may recognize and value as 'true,' the 'truths which *de facto* prevail and are recognized as objective will only be a *selection* from these we are subjectively tempted to propound."
¹⁰⁰ The present account is drawn from *Studies in Humanism*, especially ch. 5. For Schiller's other explanations of truth, see *Humanism*, ch. 3; *Logic For Use*, chs. 6–9.
¹⁰¹ *Studies in Humanism*, p. 154.
¹⁰² *Ibid.*, pp. 154–155.

local circumstances, the specific inquiry occurring and the motivating purpose of it all. Schiller tried but eventually gave up the attempt to specify in a precise way a criterion of the *workableness* of assertions and truths.

Schiller went even further than James in not only suggesting, but outrightly affirming the individualistic and plural forms that *truth* (or falsehood) might assume. For, since truth is relative to purpose, being that which "forwards the purpose," then differences of purpose, disparities of interest concerning what effects are favorable, dictate fundamental differences over truth and falsehood. Since truths function in the realization of purpose, truth-claims are validated by their consequences when purposive activity is carried out.[103] The purposive action is an experiment (as noticed earlier, § 65, and the experiment proves successful or not.

> 'Success,' therefore, in validating a 'truth' is a relative term, *relative to the purpose* with which the truth was claimed. The 'same' predication may be 'true' for me and 'false' for you, if our purposes are different.[104]

The determination of truth or falsehood, then, is as various as the purposes and interests that inspire divers human interests and actions.

For Schiller, as we saw (in § 65), cognition is a matter of trying and experimenting with our experience according to our purposes and desires. Knowledge is a manipulating of experience, a shaping of *hylē*. Thus Schiller is led to couple the making of truth with the making of reality. If our beliefs and desires, he remarks, are essential features in "actual knowing," and if knowing is a deliberate changing and transformation of our experience, then beliefs and desires must be reckoned as among "*real forces*" which philosophy cannot afford to ignore.[105] These forces are effective in altering reality; "they affect our actions, and our actions affect our world."[106] Not only does knowing alter, or better, determine portions of reality (in our constructing *hylē*), but the knower, too, is altered. "Knowing always alters the knower; and as the knower is real and a part of reality, *reality is really altered*."[107]

But the thesis of reality in the making is not original with Schiller nor is his development of the theme of special importance. Once we have grasped the import of the concept of *hylē*, it follows that any effort—indeed, even spasms and automatic reflex movements of creatures—serve as alterations of reality.[108] Here Schiller remained primarily a disciple of James. The chief point, the spark and exhilarating insight for Schiller was that, quite the opposite of the Absolutist version of a fixed, static, or completed reality, human desires were taken as shaping

103 *Ibid.*, p. 186.
104 *Ibid.*, p. 193.
105 *Ibid.*, p. 199.
106 *Ibid.*, p. 199.
107 *Ibid.*, p. 439.
108 One of the controversies Schiller had with Bradley turned upon the sense of 'alteration' and Bradley's proposal to define 'practice' as 'alteration of existence.' See *ibid.*, pp. 129–130.

and moulding reality. Reality, in short, was the stuff of continued creative activity, not of a final beatific vision.

The initial impulses, the urgency, and surely the source of those tireless efforts in behalf of his theorizing about truth and reality were due, one suspects, to an early revelation that never ceased to lose its fascination and potency for Schiller. This was a metaphysical and moral illumination which, for him, provided a perfect complementation of wisdom and faith. In one of Schiller's better phrasings of the deliverance, for he wrought many variations from it—it being the *hylē*, as it were, of philosophic sagacity—he spoke of "the radically tentative tendency which runs through the entire cosmos."[109] This idea he continued to shape in technical arguments as to the operation of experimental knowing and the function of truth-claims, and the same idea feeds Schiller's militant and willful scorn of Absolutistic metaphysics and formal logic. For these latter outlooks, he was convinced, were infected with error, the error of intellectual and moral blindness, a refusal to see when shown that incompleteness, indeterminacy lie in the very core of reality, and are perhaps reality itself.

Such was Schiller's permanent inspiration. It glimmers through the pages of his first book, coming to warmth and full light consciously in the final chapter. The smile of the Sphinx is ambiguous, he wrote.[110] Now, that very same smile is the expression of reality. Indeed, Schiller's professed philosophic hero, Protagoras, had declared that there were always two *logoi*, two arguable sides to everything.[111] Hence settlement issues finally as an act of faith. "This faith in the rationality of things, in the light of which we must read the ambiguous indications of reality, is to be acquired by no reasoning," wrote Schiller.[112] But he discovered that this Protagorean approach to a sphinxlike reality had a beneficient moral in or behind it. For in a later writing, he observed:

> The world is always ambiguous, always impels us at certain points to say, 'it may be,' 'either . . . or,' etc. Nor were it well that it should grow rigid, unless we were assured that it would set in forms we could not wish to change.[113]

To some, the smile of this Sphinx would not be inviting. But Schiller saw, or believed he beheld there, a sign of promise and of sympathetic forces at play, insinuations of acceptance, even hospitality to human purposes flickering across the face of existence.

This was, of course, faith, a postulate of imagination and incitement to reason and action, an intuition of the ideal whose working radiance infuses all reality and all sundry finite human forms.[114] The ideal of a harmonious achievement of

---

[109] "Axioms as Postulates," p. 58.
[110] *Riddles of the Sphinx*, p. 435.
[111] *Diogenes Laertius* IX. 51.
[112] *Riddles of the Sphinx*, p. 436.
[113] "Axioms as Postulates," p. 56.
[114] Schiller's own quasi-theology of hope takes this form: "nothing is more reasonable than to suppose that if there be anything *personal* at the bottom of things, the way we behave to it *must* affect the way it behaves to us," *ibid.*, p. 63. He also put it more boldly in *Riddles of the Sphinx*, p. 471: "*God must sympathize with man*. This is the first and most enduring postulate of the religious attitude."

all ideals to which existence pledged efficacy and which all things cooperated to bring about—this seems to be the general substance of Schiller's faith. But translated into more intimately psychological terms and personal equivalents—which for Schiller would be nothing if not *the* meaning of this faith—its humanistic inspiration was that we do well to let our hesitant Protagorean sensibilities be routed by Promethean impulses and ambitions.

§ 69. *Final Reflections*

What conclusions are suggested in a final stock-taking of this lively but no longer living philosophy of humanism? One is instinctively wary in forming a critical position on Schiller's work, especially so if the critical impulse is tempted to earnestness and solemnity. For one always suspects a lurking mockery in Schiller's discourse and a trap readied to be sprung in those portions of his philosophizing that most tempt criticism. The trap one fears is that of being taken in, innocently and soberly made the prey of a jest and parody of philosophic seriousness. However, if this uneasy feeling is at all justified, nothing so thoroughly condemns a philosophy as the suspicion that it is not intended to be taken seriously.

It was Schiller's misfortune to indulge in excessively dramatic attacks upon Absolutism, formalism, and logic, to devote too much of his energy to forensic refutations of other philosophers, for it has obscured what is valuable and well worth attention in his philosophic thought. The source of most of the serious technical shortcomings and problems in Schiller's outlook is twofold.

First there is his deep-seated but errant mistrust of formal logic. Second, there is an incautious romantic subjectivism that, coupled with the horror of "formalism" and systematic thought, constantly misled Schiller at the most crucial stages in his attempt to construct an empirical theory of inquiry and intelligent behavior. This is not to dismiss romantic subjectivism as valueless, but to say that it is not the philosophic position from which to endeavor successfully to develop a scientific logic and theory of knowledge. What is needed and altogether missing in Schiller's theory of knowledge is a more careful and complete account of the relation of knowers to the natural world in which knowledge occurs. Dewey commented on this:

> 'Humanism,' as a technical philosophy is associated with Schiller; and while I have great regard for his writings, it seems to me that he gave Humanism an unduly subjective turn. He was so interested in bringing out the elements of human desire and purpose neglected in traditional philosophy that he tends . . . to a virtual isolation of man from the rest of nature.[115]

As for Schiller's criticisms of formal logic, we need not resuscitate these here. It is worth keeping in mind, however, that he had a somewhat unusual understanding of what was meant by 'logic.' This we will shortly consider further.

[115] Quoted in Lamont, p. 26.

Schiller's most frequent objection to formal logic was that it is inconsistent.[116] But this charge carries in it just the dogmatic spirit of absolutism that he otherwise deplored. To say that logic is inconsistent is like saying that weather is bad, or language is unclear, or statements are false. Some systems of logic are inconsistent. Some weather is bad, some language is unclear, and some statements are false. Schiller was unaware of any of the precise senses in which *inconsistency* (and well-known formulations of relative and absolute tests of consistency) have become established in modern logic. The failure to appreciate the more precise idea and the nature of tests of consistency (and the discovery of the limitations of tests among certain systems) adds to the air of intemperance in Schiller's condemnations of logic.

It is for these reasons that his philosophy has not impressed the contemporary generation. And along with these reservations, we have been given to some earlier expressed doubts about the propriety of classifying Schiller in the pragmatist tradition.

It was as a critical philosopher that Schiller will probably be remembered. His criticisms of logic, absolute idealism, epistemology, and psychology do, in spite of the polemical spirit, have merit. Thus, recent reconsiderations of the analytic-synthetic distinction;[117] the habit of philosophers of thinking of meanings as objects attaching to words, the confusion of formal logic with psychology, the supposition that scientific inquiry proceeds by "laws of thought" or formal rules of reasoning, the failure to appreciate how meanings and uses of language are contextually bound and relative to human purposes, or that logical meaning of expressions and their meaning in ordinary contexts are not the same—these are all sound critical thrusts found in Schiller's writings.[118]

There is, I think, in his thought, one idea especially that claims our attention and is deserving of continued admiration and commendation. This is a recurring motif in his philosophizing, though it was only half glimpsed and fragmentarily

[116] We should recognize here, in passing, that Schiller's mistrust of formal logic was shared by James and Dewey. Thus one of Peirce's complaints about James was the latter's unwillingness to absorb something of mathematics and logic. Dewey, on the other hand, announces in his *Logic: The Theory of Inquiry*, p. iv, that "I am convinced that acceptance of the general principles set forth will enable a more complete and consistent set of symbolizations than now exists to be made." But logic is not concerned with the consistency or completeness of *symbols*, but in some sense with what is symbolized (e.g., symbols *of* statements). Then, too, *consistency* and *completeness* are subjects of detailed scrutiny in modern logic and do not show prospects of improvements or advance in knowledge by means of any one "set of symbolizations."

[117] See § 80 and Appendix 6 below.

[118] In passing, one instance of what is at least arguably sound in these critical sallies of Schiller may be offered.

In defense of the view that "all meaning depends on purpose," *Studies in Humanism*, pp. 9–11, 86–88 (and cf. § 66 above), Schiller argues that it is a mistake to hold that for each expression, in term, or proposition there is "*only one* meaning," *the* meaning. There are, he says, "as many 'meanings' as parties to the discussion," p. 88. This was criticized earlier, in § 67 above. But in fairness to Schiller it should be said that (quite independently, and with no thought of Schiller's thesis) a *partial* defense of his pluralistic views happens to come coincidentally from Nelson Goodman's paper "On Likeness of Meaning" (see p. 73). Schiller's view is at least made plausible, i.e., the one part of Schillers' argument that, in effect, maintains that no two different words have the same meaning.

recorded. The idea was that of *method*. In Schiller's early writings this idea is partly operative in his suggestive generalization of the notion of his conception of the thinking process as postulational activity. In later years Schiller was approaching the same objective, the vision of method, through an attempted development of a theory of the "logic of discovery" and a "logic for use."[119] In this work Schiller is at his best and most interesting.

Schiller's idea of *method*, had he succeeded in articulating it in detail, would doubtless have resembled Dewey's theory of *inquiry*. For both men were alike interested in formulating the actual process of thought—the background, the phases of procedure and behavior, and the purposes that generate and sustain our reasoned manipulations of experience. But Dewey's theory of inquiry is confined to problematic situations and their solution (§ 39).

Schiller's vision of a general methodology of achieving purposes, a great organon for the expression of human interests of all kinds—poetic, religious, and intimately practical—is suggestive. It would have been a construction at least as broad and comprehensive in scope as Dewey's.[120] And it would, I think, have been, finally, a general theory not of inquiry but of practice. Here Schiller's sensitivity to the subtle roles and controlling effects of desire, of dreaming, of privately charged impulses, of play and sheer phantasmagoria in human conduct would have served him well. Here the subjective psychology, the literary sensibilities and insight, and the humanistic point of view might have been woven into a fitting expression of the human act of practice, the art of practical reasoning.

But all of this is, frankly, conjecture, a hypothesizing about something of excellence and intellectual fascination that never was brought to achievement by Schiller. Yet, to have us guessing and entertaining hypotheses is, if we can be sure about anything in Schiller, surely how he would have us take our leave of him.

---

[119] Here Schiller was working out a theory of the inductive procedures actually employed in scientific investigations. He was theorizing upon the subject and process of reasoning that Peirce called "abduction." For this work see Schiller's "Scientific Discovery and Logical Proof," and *Logic For Use*.

[120] Problem situations and *inquiry* characterize activities in the arts and social conduct as well as the sciences for Dewey.

CHAPTER TWO

England:
F. P. Ramsey and Ludwig Wittgenstein

§ 70. Some Missing Links

The present chapter is concerned with certain historical connections, some that
might be shown to exist between American pragmatism and the philosophic
ideas of F. P. Ramsey and Ludwig Wittgenstein. Unfortunately, the condition that
most persistently obstructs this effort and compromises our conclusions is that at
those points where the subject becomes of most interest, the amount of information we must depend on rapidly diminishes.

There are, however, some facts that are known, enough to indicate the existence
of a certain transmission of influences from Peirce and James to the developing
thought of these two brilliantly gifted young philosophers in England. In sketching these facts, we will proceed from what is most clearly known to what is less
certain.

Three questions concern us here. First is the historical question of how some
of the ideas of the American pragmatists came to the attention of Ramsey and
Wittgenstein. Second, were Ramsey and Wittgenstein at all aware of or influenced
by the work of the American pragmatists? Third, depending upon the answer to
the previous question—and I think an affirmative answer can be shown—in what
ways is that influence evidenced?

I propose now to consider each of these queries in turn.

By 1900 the work of James, especially the *Psychology*, was well known in
England. Peirce's writings were less familiar, but his modifications of Boolian
algebra (see the Introduction to Part Two), especially since discussed and followed by Schröder,[1] were familiar to mathematicians and logicians. Dewey had

---

[1] Thus, concerning the calculus of relations, Russell said: "Although a few hints for it
are to be found in De Morgan, the subject was first developed by C. S. Peirce," *Principles of
Mathematics*, § 27. Peirce's methods are treated at length in Schröder's *Algebra der Logik*,
Vol. III.
    Peirce's modifications of Boolean algebra, motivated by an interest in developing the

published articles in *Mind* and had attracted the interest of Bradley, among others.[2] F. C. S. Schiller had been proclaiming the importance of pragmatism in his writings. The American pragmatists were known, then, if not carefully studied in English philosophical circles. But this does not explain how pragmatism and especially the pragmatic analysis of meaning came to the attention of Ramsey and Wittgenstein.

The importance and extent of Peirce's work in logic would have been evident to Ramsey not only via Schröder, but through Russell's writings on logic, and through the more complete discussion by C. I. Lewis in 1918.[3] Perhaps through conversations with Russell, Ramsey learned something about Peirce's interests in the theory of signs and meaning. From Keynes,[4] if not also from Russell, he would have discovered Peirce's views of and papers on probability.

But there is also a more direct link from Ramsey to Peirce. When Ogden and Richards' widely read *The Meaning of Meaning* appeared in 1923, Ramsey read and must have noticed the attention given to Peirce's views on meaning and the theory of signs.[5] Ogden and Richards not only mention Peirce in their Preface, and several times thereafter, but also on the first page of the book remark about Peirce's interest in "language and its Meaning."[6] Most important, in an Appendix surveying the views of modern philosophers on the subject of meaning, the authors devote a section to the work of Peirce. They write:

> By far the most elaborate and determined attempt to give an account of signs and their meaning is that of the American logician C. S. Peirce, from whom William James took the idea and the term Pragmatism, and whose Algebra of Dyadic Relations was developed by Schroeder.[7]

How had Ogden and Richards come to this knowledge of Peirce? The explanation is that the forerunner of their own book was one by Lady Victoria Welby, called *What Is Meaning?* published in 1903.[8] Lady Welby had made a life study of meaning or, as she called her theoretical work, "Significs."[9] When her book appeared, Peirce wrote a warmly favorable and detailed review of it in *The Nation*.

---

calculus of probability (see §22 above), was recognized in Europe. Schröder incorporated this into his work called the "Boole-Schröder algebra of logic." Peirce's work is discussed in full by Schröder.
[2] This we saw in the previous chapter, § 62. Some of Dewey's papers in *Mind* interested Lady Welby, who appears in the next paragraphs below; see also below, note 21.
[3] Lewis' account in *A Survey* (1918), esp. pp. 79–114. Page 79 gives a forceful statement under three heads sketching the breadth of Peirce's interests and work in logic.
[4] Keynes, *Treatise on Probability,* references therein and the Bibliography.
[5] Ramsey reviewed the book in *Mind* (1924), and while critical of it, it is especially interesting in the present context to find him observing, p. 109, that "the excellent appendix on C. S. Peirce deserves special notice."
[6] See p. 1, and the additional comment about Peirce's poverty preventing him from continuing the study of meaning.
[7] *The Meaning of Meaning,* p. 279.
[8] Ogden and Richards acknowledge the import of the "independent studies" of Lady Welby, among others, including Peirce, *ibid.,* p. ix.
[9] Lady Welby wrote the article "Significs" for the *Encyclopædia Britannica,* 10th and 11th editions.

Lady Welby was pleasantly surprised. A correspondence with Peirce, which was to extend over the years 1903 to 1911, then commenced.[10]

It was a selection from the letters of Peirce to Lady Welby that Ogden and Richards drew upon, and quoted, in their presentation of Peirce's views of signs and meaning. Ogden was in correspondence with Lady Welby,[11] and when the authors of *The Meaning of Meaning* were preparing their work, they were partly guided by her earlier studies.

There is no question about Lady Welby's role as a center for the transmission of ideas, ideas mostly relating to her interest in language and meaning. She seems to have known almost everyone of intellectual note in England, America, and much of France. These luminaries who happened to write on the nature of knowledge or language or both, and were not acquainted with Lady Welby, soon found themselves engaged in correspondence with her and even visiting her home.

For our purposes it is Lady Welby's correspondence with Peirce, James, Russell, Schiller, and Vailati that is of special interest. It was a characteristic of her not only to keep up a large correspondence; she also deliberately and energetically kept the circle of her correspondents informed of one another's views. Discovering a basic harmony between her analysis of meaning and that of Peirce's theory of signs (a harmony that Peirce assured her existed), Lady Welby proceeded to inform many of her other friends of Peirce's work. She even copied portions of Peirce's letters and sent these on to other philosophically minded recipients.

Indeed, Lady Welby nearly succeeded in bringing together two of the great philosophers of our time: Peirce and Russell. What might have happened or resulted from a direct meeting, or from a correspondence between them, I do not venture to predict. But I dare say the consequences might well have been, to use the favorite idiom of Lady Welby, "significant."

Peirce's review of Lady Welby's *What is Meaning?* and the beginning of their letter-writing friendship was mentioned earlier. But Peirce's review was also concerned with a second book that had appeared in 1903, namely, Russell's *The Principles of Mathematics*. In fact, Peirce began his review with the remark: "Two really important works on logic are these."[12] He then briefly, in one paragraph, commented on Russell's book and devoted the far greater part of his review to Lady Welby's volume. In his third letter to Lady Welby, Peirce wrote that he found Russell's book "pretentious & pedantic."[13] Lady Welby, however, was enthusiastic over Russell's *Principles*, and Peirce's critical reservations about the same text are not very clear. Russell's frequent references to Peirce and his recognition of Peirce's important contribution to the algebra of logic are evident in the *Principles*. Whatever basic difference we might now find between the

---

[10] These important letters of Peirce to Lady Welby have been published. A selection is found in *CP* 8.327–379. For the main work, see Lieb. See, too, for selections from Lady Welby's answers, her *Other Dimensions*.

[11] Ogden apparently asked her about the works she had consulted in preparing her studies on meaning. For a letter to Ogden, see *Other Dimensions*, pp. 335–337.

[12] *CP* 8.171n. For the rest of the review, *CP* 8.171–175.

[13] See Lieb, p. 2.

philosophic outlooks of Peirce and Russell,[14] Lady Welby thought she saw possibilities of reconciliation—but this is really because the philosophic differences
had little moment for her. Her conviction was that the work of Peirce and Russell
jointly confirmed her semantical theories, the confirmation coming from the
rigorous and abstruse domain of mathematical logic.

Thus, characteristically, Lady Welby proceeded to keep Peirce and Russell informed about each other. She wrote to Russell about Peirce's critical attitude.[15]
Russell was interested and replied:

> I have always thought very highly of Dr. Peirce for having introduced such a method
> [i.e., this symbolism for expressing relations and his algebra of logic]. I should
> be interested to know what are the faults he finds with my book, as his criticisms
> would probably be instructive.[16]

In another letter Russell again wrote: "It would be the greatest interest and
pleasure to me to meet Dr. C. S. Peirce: he is a man for whose work I have great
respect."[17]

At this time, in 1903–1904, Lady Welby must have been urging Peirce to
visit some of the mathematically trained logicians in Cambridge. For there is a
letter in which he considers the attractive prospect of such an experience.[18] By
transmitting selected portions of Peirce's letters to her to Russell, by keeping
Peirce informed of Russell's comments and answers, Lady Welby hoped to establish a rapprochement, as she said, adding: "I am delighted to be the means of
conveying to the one the other's readiness for his criticisms."[19]

Lady Welby does not mention Peirce in *What is Meaning?* Schiller, with whom
she had an extensive correspondence and who kept her informed about pragmatism, and whom she probably kept informed about Peirce, "looked through"
her manuscript or proofs before publication.[20] But she does cite with approval
as "a first installment of the inquiry suggested" Dewey's comments on meaning in
an article he published in *Mind*.[21]

Through Lady Welby, C. K. Ogden came to know of Peirce's extensive work

---

[14] Russell, for example, did not take Peirce's doctrine of Firstness, Secondness, and Third-
ness very seriously, see *Other Dimensions,* p. 159.
[15] The details are not known, as the material of these letters has not been published. One
can infer from what has been published that Lady Welby softened Peirce's criticisms of
Russell in conveying them to Russell.
[16] From letters of 1903–1905, *Other Dimensions,* p. 159.
[17] *Ibid.,* p. 160.
[18] Peirce had visited Cambridge in 1875. See the earlier biographical sketch in the Introduction to Part II. Here to Lady Welby, Peirce expresses his interest in a visit with "Oxford
thinkers," *Other Dimensions,* p. 161.
[19] *Other Dimensions,* p. 159.
[20] *What Is Meaning?* Preface, p. xi. Schiller notified her of the review of her book in
Leonardo. For Lady Welby and the Italian pragmatists Vailati and Calderoni, see § 76 below.
[21] *What Is Meaning?* Appendix, p. 225. From an article by Dewey in *Mind* Lady Welby
quotes: "The meaning constitutes for us the whole value of the experience. . . . Even the
fact that there *is* an experience, aside from *what* it is, is not the sensation itself; it is the
interpretation of the sensation. It is part of the meaning." The Source she gives is *Mind,*
XLVII, 384. This is not correct. The passage, in a very suggestive early paper (1887), is to
be found in *Mind,* XII, 384.

in the analysis of meaning. In Ogden and Richards' *The Meaning of Meaning* Peirce's work receives some of the attention it deserves, and an important connection between American pragmatism and Ramsey and Wittgenstein was established.

If one surveys British philosophy in the twenty-year interval between the publication of Lady Welby's *What is Meaning?* and Ogden and Richards' *The Meaning of Meaning*, the impressive fact is how the subject of *meaning* became of increasing interest, puzzlement, and concern to philosophers. One reason, I suspect, for the waning of Hegelianism and the systems of Idealism is that while their spokesmen said a great deal about language and meaning, what they said appeared (rightly or wrongly) to shed very little light on the analysis of meaning. "The analysis of meaning" is itself an ambiguous phrase; it can refer either to a *technique* for analyzing meanings of various expressions, or to a general *theory* of what meaning is. The philosophers in the period described were interested in both of these matters, and, indeed, often made no distinction between them at all, treating them as aspects of a single task. But one main reason for dissatisfaction with the philosophic idealism dominating English and American universities was that its exponents did not seem capable of exhibiting a satisfactory technique for the analysis of logical, philosophical, and ordinary language, nor was the complex and grandoise idealistic theory—so ready at hand for explaining anything—a clear or relevant means of explaining the meaning of meaning.[22] G. E. Moore's defense of common sense and his own conception of analysis were part of the growing critical dissatisfaction with these tendencies of idealism. Contrary to a popular impression that the recent British philosophy of linguistic analysis has directed philosophers to concern themselves wholly with "meaning," this movement is part of the same critical reaction against just that concern as it was misconceived and mistakenly carried out by influential philosophers of the previous generation.

The above reflection has this bearing upon our present search for missing links. One English philosopher who helped focus the critical response to idealism, specifically by championing the importance of *meaning* and the inadequacy of idealism and most professional philosophers in dealing with the subject was F. C. S. Schiller. Schiller chastised his contemporaries, like Russell, for neglecting the importance of meaning.[23] And Schiller helped to prepare the increasing interest in meaning among philosophers with information about Peirce's and James's contributions to the technique of analyzing meanings and to the general theory of meaning. Schiller, then, is also a part of the line leading from Peirce and James to Ramsey and Wittgenstein.

---

[22] The more general critical reaction to idealism is suggested in § 17 of Part I, and § 63 of the previous chapter.

[23] Thus in *The Meaning of Meaning*, p. 160, note 1. Also Russell's comment in *My Philosophical Development*, p. 14: "There was another problem that began to interest me . . . about 1917. This was the problem of the relation of language to facts. . . . The problem had been dealt with by various people before I became interested in it. Lady Welby wrote a book about it and F. C. S. Schiller was always urging its importance."

§ 71.   F. P. Ramsey

Ramsey (1903–1930) spent almost all of his short lifetime in Cambridge. In his last years he was Lecturer in Mathematics in the University. Ramsey was a man of genius who combined, as G. E. Moore said, "exceptional brilliance with very great soundness of judgment in philosophy."[24]

In addition to his training and profession as a mathematician, Ramsey was very much interested in philosophy. His education in the latter seems primarily to have been formed under three influences: the philosophical work of Russell; *Principia Mathematica*; and Wittgenstein's *Tractatus*. In Ramsey's writings these are the three sources most frequently alluded to, but often in the spirit of a critical reexamination of issues and hypotheses. In mathematical logic, Ramsey considered himself an advocate of the "logical school" of Frege, Russell, and Whitehead, against the formalism of Hilbert and the intuitionism of Brouwer and Weyl.[25]

In 1922, when Wittgenstein's *Tractatus* appeared, Ramsey wrote a long critical review of the book for *Mind*. This was his first philosophical publication, and it shows both his analytical skill and his early recognition of the importance of Wittgenstein's work.[26] Ramsey became a friend of Wittgenstein, having helped in the translation of the *Tractatus*. One of Wittgenstein's convictions was that with the *Tractatus* he had solved all philosophical problems, and he accordingly abandoned philosophy to become a schoolmaster and architect. He was living in Austria at the time, since his release from the Austrian Army after the First World War. Ramsey visited him in 1923 and again in 1924 and attempted to persuade him to come to England.[27] The talks between the two men at this period were apparently stimulating and formative for them both.[28]

In Ramsey's 1922 review of the *Tractatus*, he acknowledges and makes use of Peirce's distinction of *token* and *type* in discussing one of Wittgenstein's theses.[29] Two questions thus occur in connection with our present subject: Had Ramsey read much of Peirce at this time? Did Ramsey and Wittgenstein discuss Peirce's

[24] In his Preface, p. vii, to Ramsey's *The Foundations of Mathematics*.
[25] See his account, *ibid.*, p. 3. In the last years of his life (i.e., in 1929), Ramsey was converted to a finitist position denying the existence of infinite classes of entities. Cf. *ibid.*, p. 252: " 'infinite collection' is really nonsense."
[26] The "critical Notice," reprinted as an Appendix in *The Foundations*, pp. 270–286, contains a number of philosophic insights and suggestions of great interest. Thus, a succinct anticipation of Tarski's theory of truth (cf. above, § 40), p. 275: "if a thought or proposition token 'p' says p then it is called true if p, and false if ~ p."
[27] For most of the facts here I follow the Biographical Sketch by von Wright in Malcolm's *Wittgenstein*.
[28] According to von Wright, *ibid.*, p. 12, one event that might have made Wittgenstein feel he could again do creative work in philosophy was his attending a lecture by Brouwer in 1928 on the foundations of mathematics. But one would guess that matters of this kind were discussed by Ramsey and Wittgenstein in their meetings in 1923 and 1924.
[29] *Foundations of Mathematics*, p. 274.

thought during Ramsey's visits in 1923 and 1924? The answers to either of these questions are not known.

In the latter years of his life, from 1927 to 1930, however, the interest in and influence of Peirce is quite clear in Ramsey's work. Thus, in a paper, "Truth and Probability" (1926), Ramsey quotes Peirce several times and in the latter pages develops an analysis and pragmatic justification of habits of inference, observation, and memory, "almost entirely based on the writings of C. S. Peirce."[30] Ramsey argues that induction is a habit. The habit does not require a general "justification" —for none can be given without employing induction—but its "degree of utility" in specific cases is subject to continual examination. That is, some habits of inference are good, some are not. Ramsey follows Peirce in distinguishing good from bad habits generally, according to whether or not the consequences, the opinions, or actions they lead to are satisfactory or not. Specifically, he writes:

> This is a kind of pragmatism: we judge mental habits by whether they work, i.e., whether the opinions they lead to are for the most part true, or more often true than those which alternative habits would lead to.[31]

Ramsey's pragmatic view of induction is that induction is a most useful habit "and so to adopt it is reasonable."[32] In a spirit akin to Peirce, but also not unlike F. C. S. Schiller, he speaks of the "inductive or human logic" as a study of methods of thought and an evaluation of them: "what degree of confidence should be placed in them, i.e., in what proportion of cases they lead to truth."[33] The "justification" of induction is not to be found in some formal defense, or as Keynes had held, in the theory of probability.[34] But induction is not less reasonable for that. Its reasonableness as a "human logic" is pragmatic.

In a paper of 1927, Ramsey also maintained an admittedly vague pragmatic criterion of the meaning of a sentence as "defined by reference to the actions to which asserting it would lead, or, more vaguely still, by its possible causes and effects."[35]

In addition to a Peircean pragmatism of belief and of the analysis of both the meaning and justification (or "reasonableness") of habits of thought, Ramsey developed an instrumentalist interpretation of laws and theories (see Part Four, Chapter Two below). Instead of treating general propositions as conjunctions of simple or atomic propositions, Ramsey advanced an analysis of them as "variable hypotheticals." Variable hypotheticals, he argued, "are not judgments but rules for judging."[36] These are not true or false; they are good or bad rules for judging and acting. Thus the sentence "All men are mortal" can, as Mill said, in effect, be taken as a rule that such and such a man will die.[37] The "rule" here is

---

[30] This is his acknowledgement, "Truth and Probability," p. 194, note 2.
[31] *Ibid.*, pp. 197–198.
[32] *Ibid.*, p. 198.
[33] *Ibid.*, p. 198.
[34] In the *Tractatus*, Wittgenstein had said (6.3631) that the process of induction "has no logical foundation but only a psychological one."
[35] "Facts and propositions," in *Foundations of Mathematics*, p. 155. It should be added, however, that in the same passage Ramsey ascribes this pragmatism to Russell.
[36] *Ibid.*, p. 241.
[37] *Ibid.*, p. 245. For more on Mill's argument, see § 84 below.

the interpretation of "All men are mortal" as a connection (and expectation for action) of "there is a man" with "he will die." As Ramsey puts it, "Variable hypotheticals or causal laws form the system with which the speaker meets the future."[38]

As a result of this interpretation of laws, Ramsey was led to regard theories not as descriptive of facts, but as ways of deriving statements from statements and developing expectations for the future. He called his view "a *forecasting* theory" of science.[39] (This view is discussed somewhat more fully in Part Four, Chapter Two, and we need not go into it here.[40]) While at many points in his working out of this conception of general propositions and universals Ramsey is critically departing from the ideas of Wittgenstein in the *Tractatus*, it happens that in his later thought Wittgenstein also held much the same kind of instrumentalist interpretation of general statements as rules or directives.

The pragmatism of Ramsey is clear. It is derived mostly from Peirce, but perhaps also from James's discussions of the connection between belief and ways of acting. It was Wittgenstein, however, who took considerable interest in James.

§ 72. Ludwig Wittgenstein

Next to Russell, Wittgenstein (1889–1951) is probably the most famous figure in contemporary Anglo-American philosophy. I do not propose to say a great deal about his philosophic development nor to attempt to interpret his ideas, a hazardous venture in any case. The intention is only to point to a few suggestive facts, for the known facts here are few, having to do with the theme announced above in § 70.

Wittgenstein visited friends in England in 1925. From 1929 to 1935 he spent almost all his time at Cambridge, having become a Fellow of Trinity College in 1930. In about 1933 a new period in his philosophy came about which marks a break with most of the *Tractatus*, and even with ideas he had been working out up to 1930. Two important forces in helping to stimulate this new direction were Piero Sraffa, an Italian economist residing in Cambridge,[41] and Ramsey, with whom Wittgenstein had "innumerable conversations during the last two years of his life."[42]

The key question for us here (again an unanswerable one) is how and to what extent, if at all, did Ramsey's pragmatism affect Wittgenstein? Several of Witt-

---

[38] *Ibid.*, p. 241. On this topic see above, the latter part of § 22 and below, § 86. At § 85 I have suggested that the variable hypothetical is a prescription, thus (in the above example) "all men are mortal": infer if 'x is a man' is true, 'x is mortal' is true.

[39] *Ibid.*, p. 255. See, too, Ramsey's reference to Peirce, p. 194, note 2, and his development of a Peircean theory of truth and probability, pp. 194–198.

[40] It is worth noting, however, that a similar "instrumental" interpretation of scientific theory and of laws as "our method of representing . . . phenomena" was developed by W. H. Watson, cf. esp. pp. 50–52. Moreover, he attributes the initial insights of this interpretation to Wittgenstein.

[41] Von Wright's Biographical Sketch, in Malcolm, *Wittgenstein*, p. 15.

[42] Preface, *Philosophical Investigations*, Xe. But see G. E. Moore, "Wittgenstein's Lectures," p. 253, note 1, for a question about this.

genstein's major rejections of earlier theses of the *Tractatus* are in accord with the criticisms Ramsey made in his last papers.

Wittgenstein's later philosophic thought, say from 1933 to 1947 when he retired from Cambridge, was brought to difficult expression in 1948. For he then completed the *Philosophical Investigations*, published after his death in 1953.

There are three major subjects of interest in this later period of Wittgenstein's philosophical work. Each constitutes a marked departure from the *Tractatus*.[43] Each is represented in the complex course of analysis in the *Investigations* as a focal point of study. Each brings the philosophy of Wittgenstein into very basic harmony with pragmatism.

1)   In the *Tractatus* Wittgenstein held that below our deviating and varied uses of significant language there resides a single logical structure. It was the chief object of logical analysis to uncover this structure. Once made clear, the structure would determine what can and cannot be meaningfully said in language. Thus, in a now famous sentence Wittgenstein writes: "what can be said at all can be said clearly; and whereof one cannot speak thereof one must be silent." This, says Wittgenstein in his Preface, is the "whole meaning" of his book. But the *Investigations* contain no vision of one logical structure determining what can and what cannot be said and symbolized significantly. The emphasis in the *Investigations* is much less on formal structure, techniques, and logic; much more on language, language uses, actual as well as specially constructed illustrations (i.e., language games) of the varieties of unsystematic, un-universally patterned uses of language.[44] Uses, it should be added, that, in contexts, decide what is and can be significantly said.

2)   In the *Tractatus*, Wittgenstein set forth a "picture" theory of the meaning of propositions. "The meaning" is descriptive. It is the reference of the sign to things, the relation of the proposition to the world.[45] There is one such relation, the meaning, and the goal of analysis is arriving at this: "there is one and only one complete analysis of the proposition."[46] Moreover, all propositions, not themselves elementary, are generalized from elementary propositions,[47] and the elementary propositions consist of names[48] true or false of atomic facts.[49] Now, while

---

[43] The contrast between the *Tractatus* and the *Investigations* is no simple matter of an entire change of mind or complete break. Certain ideas in the later book are to be understood in and by contrast with the earlier. Thus Wittgenstein's hope was that the *Tractatus* be republished along with the newer work; the new thoughts, he said, "could be seen in the right light only by contrast with and against the background of my old ways of thinking." Preface, Xe, to the *Investigations*.

[44] Quinton, whom I have followed here, describes the difference, p. 540: "Where the *Tractatus* saw language as a logically rigid essence concealed behind the contingent surface of everyday discourse . . . in the *Investigations* language is accepted as it actually and observably is, as a living, unsystematic, and polymorphous array of working conventions for a large and not simply classifiable range of human purposes."

[45] E.g., *Tractatus*, 4.01: "The proposition is a picture of reality," and cf. 2.1511.

[46] *Ibid.*, 3.25.

[47] *Ibid.*, 4.52.

[48] *Ibid.*, 4.22, 5.55.

[49] *Ibid.*, 4.25.

Wittgenstein does recognize the concept of *use* as the key to meaning in the *Tractatus*,[50] in the *Investigations* the logical structure and picture approach is abandoned. Instead, analysis of the meanings of expressions considers the uses of expressions among users in certain kinds of situations—uses exhibited in fact, in real discussions, and in model cases, i.e., "language games" constructed for the study of uses.[51] Instead of regarding language as taking place within a formal structure whose units "picture" the world, this is an approach to a behavioral analysis of expressions. There are no ultimately simple units of language on this view; there are more or less simple ways of using words relative to and dependent upon purposes of users in various contexts (or "games").

3) Finally, a subject of considerable discussion in the *Investigations* is that of how language about mental behavior is used. Here Wittgenstein exposes the mistakes and confusions that follow from the traditional view (and way of speaking) of mind as "inner" mental processes accompanying physical acts of the body. With remarkable skill and sensitivity he examines words that, on the dualist theory, "name" or "designate" private internal mental states or experiences. Wittgenstein shows that concepts like 'understanding' or 'pain' have their meaning not as names of inner entities, but in how they are applied in situations and how ascribed among users and speakers. How, in short, the words fit in with the observable behavior and continuing uses of language among speakers is where their "meaning" is looked for and found.

The resulting inquiries in the *Investigations*, in both their critical and positive conclusions, are very much in accord (sometimes coinciding remarkably) with the outlook and writings of Dewey and Mead. I do not say that Wittgenstein had consciously shifted toward the pragmatist theories of meaning, mind, and methods of analysis. But the direction Wittgenstein took, whether it was wholly independent of pragmatism or partly or largely worked out in response to Ramsey's pragmatic views, is evident enough in his last writings. But if there was influence, this would not have been solely the effect of Ramsey, for Wittgenstein often referred to James in his lectures, and for a time James's *Psychology* was the one book that he kept in his sparsely furnished rooms.[52]

It is to be hoped that a future historian will make clear the relation of the work of Ramsey and Wittgenstein to American pragmatism.

[50] *Ibid.*, 3.326, 3.262.
[51] Wittgenstein once described his procedure as directed to "the morphology of the use of an expression," see Malcolm, p. 50. His idea of a "language game" came to him, writes Malcolm, p. 65, when Wittgenstein was passing a field where a football game was being played: "in language we play *games* with words" was the thought that then occurred. I suspect that, unlike some of his less tolerant disciples, Wittgenstein would have been very much interested in Mead's theory of language taking place in conversations of gestures, and Mead's sensitivity to and interest in games as forms of communication and action according to certain rules and objectives (see above § 52–54).
[52] See Passmore, p. 428, note 2, for the source of this.

CHAPTER THREE

France

§ 73. Pragmatism and *Pragmatisme*

In the Preface to his *Pragmatism* (1907), James spoke of "the pragmatic movement" as apparently having "rather suddenly precipitated itself out of the air."
He regarded "the movement" as a collective and combined expression of "a
number of tendencies that have always existed in philosophy," this expression
coming from "so many countries, and from so many points of view, that much
unconcerted statement has resulted." In supplying the reader with references to
the literature of pragmatism, James mentions books and articles by Dewey and
Schiller and also cites articles by Le Roy and by Blondel and B. de Sailly.

Maurice Blondel (1861–1939) was the author of the book *L'Action. Essai
d'une critique de la vue et d'une science de la pratique*, published in 1893. In this
work Blondel argued for the primacy of will and action in the furtherance of
life, a voluntaristic and activistic philosophy of knowledge and reality addressed
against what he took to be intellectualism and rationalism of the past century.
Blondel was the founder of a school, the "philosophy of action," which became
the center of a liberal catholic group in France and of which Le Roy was a member. This group was in turn part of the movement of French Catholic Modernism.[1] The school of action flourished in the years between 1900 and 1906, and
its organ was the *Annales de philosophie chrétienne*; but its popularity was suddenly put to an end when, in 1907, Modernism was condemned in the Encyclical
Pascendi dominici gregis, issued by Pope Pius X.[2] The Modernist movement in
France was an attempt to reconcile the tradition and faith of the Catholic church
with evolutions in science and historical and Biblical criticism and research, with
a radical democratic social movement, and with the new philosophy of action

[1] On the philosophy of action and its relation to pragmatism and Modernism, see
Berthelot; Horton, pp. 290–296. On Modernism, see Tyrrell.
[2] See Tyrrell for the Encyclical and the Modernists' response.

314

(with its metaphysical and theological doctrines, its reinterpretation and defense of religious belief). In the condemnation of Modernism, the philosophy of action was held to be the agnostic source of the errors of modernism as a whole.

The articles by B. de Sailly, which had interested James and are mentioned by him in his Preface, were an exposition of the program and aims of the philosophy of action school. According to de Sailly, the philosophy of action contained five elements:[3] (1) a critique of immediate consciousness or common sense; (2) a critique of science; (3) a critique of traditional epistemology; (4) a new moral and metaphysical dogmatism; (5) a philosophic "apologetic" for the Christian faith. As for the first element, the philosophy of action agreed with Bergson (in his *Les données immédiates de la conscience*) that consciousness cannot be treated as a material, spatial, and mechanical object; that a true philosophy of reality must correct this falsification of the data of sense and consciousness. The second critical element is an interpretation of science having affinities with the views of Poincaré and Duhem. Here the position argued was that scientific theories are schemes and points of view the purpose of which is to solve certain practical problems. A scientific construction is true if it fulfills the purpose for which it was made. According to Le Roy (in the articles cited by James), scientific truth is "the growing success of our conquest of the world," and thus "scientific truth resembles moral good: one does not receive it from without, one acts it and makes it."[4]

The third element of the school of action, its critique of epistemology, is of special interest here for two reasons, one historical and the other philosophical. The interesting philosophical point is the repudiation of the theory of ideas as copies, representations, or images of objects. This is also a criticism of those traditional theories of truth according to which truth consists in the correspondence of an idea with an object. In this critical rejection of the notion of ideas as (faithful or unfaithful) copies of objects, Blondel and his school and American pragmatists are agreed.[5] The agreement seems to have been arrived at independently and in different ways with different consequences in each case, however. There is no evidence of a route of influence between the school of action and pragmatism. Instead of regarding ideas as copies of objects, Blondel construed them as phases or integral parts of the totality of action that characterizes the development of life. An idea is a "movement, a means, in the development of life, which it illuminates and furthers."[6] Ideas may function as ways of furthering life, and the truth of an idea depends upon its so functioning. The point of historical interest in this critique concerns this version of ideas, their function and truth. For it was this theory that Blondel called *pragmatisme* as early as

---

[3] "Les éléments de la philosophie de l'action." See the brief account given by Horton, pp. 291–294.
[4] "Science et philosophie," VII, 562. Horton, p. 292, draws attention to these passages.
[5] Again except for James, who vacillated on this point; he sometimes affirmed the representative and "copying" nature of ideas.
[6] Quoted in Horton, p. 293.

1888;[7] and this name he evidently abandoned when he discovered how James was advocating "pragmatism."

However, when one looks a little closer for some account of the meaning of 'action,' there is not, in the philosophy of M. Blondel, anything of a striking resemblance to American pragmatism. Blondel remains somewhat vague as to the nature of action.

> I understand by action . . . that which envelopes the intellect, preceding it, following it, and surpassing it; that which, consequently, in thought is an internal synthesis rather than an objective representation.[8]

In explaining his view of the relation of thought to action, Blondel writes:

> Theory and practice are not identical nor does one exclude the other. . . . This is because action and the idea of action are not equivalent, because nothing exempts the one who practices from thinking nor the thinker from practicing. . . . Thinking constitutes effective progress: it realizes in fact a form of existence that would not occur without it, but a form of existence that becomes an integral part (aspect) because it is a normal expression, an essential condition, of the development of being and of the truth of the beings in us. For man, life is not life without thought, no more so than thought is thought without life. We must make use of what we are and what we have, in order to know, and to use what we know in order to be and in order to become more.[9]

But here, too, in the light of our understanding of the distinctive features of pragmatism (in § 101), there does not appear very much in common between *action* and *pragmatism.*

The fourth element in the philosophy of action emerges from the critique of common sense, of science, and the theory of knowledge. This is the conviction that since reality is not discoverable by reason or by the traditional techniques of intelligence and science, it is attained by and through *action.* Instead of ending in skepticism as to what can be known about reality, instead of accepting a relativistic analysis of knowledge (which one might have anticipated from the second and third "elements"), the philosophy of action affirms a new moral and metaphysical thesis. The Absolute is revealed to us through action. We discover the

---

[7] On this point, see Lalande; Stebbing; Hébert, p. 72, note 3. It is to be noted that James had critical reservations concerning Hébert's book, although on points other than those that are cited in the next pages. James's review, reprinted in *The Meaning of Truth,* ch. 12, concluded, however, p. 245, that M. Hébert's "little book, apart from the false accusation of subjectivism, gives a fairly instructive account of the pragmatist epistemology."

[8] *Bulletin de la société française de philosophie,* July, 1902. Cited in Hébert, p. 55.

[9] *Annales de philosophie chrétienne,* 1906, p. 241, and see Hébert, p. 71-72, who quotes Blondel: " 'La theorie et la pratique ni ne font double emploi, ni ne sont extérieures l'une à l'autre. . . . C'est parce que l'action et l'idée de l'action ne sont pas équivalentes, que rien ne dispense le pratiquant de penser, ni le penseur de pratiquer.' '. . . La connaissance constituce un progrès effectif: elle realise en effet une forme d'existence qui ne serait pas sans elle, mais une forme d'existence qui devient une partie intégrante parce qu'elle est une expression normale, une condition essentielle du developpement de l'être et de la verité des êtres en nous. Pour l'homme, la vie n'est pas la vie, sans la pensée, pas plus que la pensée n'est la pensée, sans la vie. Il faut se servir de ce qu'on est et de ce qu'on a, pour connaître, et se servir de ce qu'on connait pour être et pour avoir davantage.' "

ultimate nature of the universe in the process of discovering what attitude we should take in the world as it confronts us. This attitude is the result of an act of will and faith. The right philosophy is the product of the right practical attitude toward the world and our way of acting; one who takes a wrong attitude ends with an erroneous philosophy and way of thinking.[10] It remains simply to add, as a moral and metaphysical corollary in this philosophy, that the "right" practical attitude to take is a Christian faith in God.[11] Thus, the fifth element in the philosophy of action is a defense of the truth of Christian faith, drawn from the other four philosophic points.

In his essay "Pragmatisme et Pragmaticisme," Lalande comments on the difference between pragmatism and Blondel's philosophy of action.

> M. Blondel's pragmatism rests on an entirely different principle than Peirce's: it consists of choosing, through action, something of the supra-phenomenal, from which we cannot free ourselves, and the analysis of which inevitably carries us, if we wish to be logical, even to the necessity of religious faith. "By his voluntary action, man transcends phenomena; he cannot equal his own exigencies; he has in himself more than he alone can make use of (*L'Action* 324)." This apologetic undoubtedly rejoins, definitively, what has been gathered from Anglo-American pragmatism. It seems to me, however, to differ from the latter in a profound way in its spirit and its method. That is why I do not seek to class it in the course of doctrines in question. These are two parallel currents which are only joined at their source.[12]

While Blondel was the most important figure in the history of the philosophy of action,[13] Édouard Le Roy was closer to James than any of the other French

---

[10] Cf. Horton, p. 293, on this and on the background of the argument.

[11] *Ibid.*, pp. 293–294.

[12] Lalande, p. 123, n. 1. "Ce pragmatisme de M. Blondel repose sur un tout autre principe que celui de M. Peirce: il consiste à montrer, dans l'action, quelque chose de supraphénoménal, auquel nous ne pouvons nous soustraire, et dont l'analyse nous entraine forcément, si nous voulons être logiques, jusqu'à la nécessité de la foi religieuse. 'Par son action volontaire, l'homme dépasse les phénomènes; il ne peut égaler ses propres exigences; il a en lui plus qu'il ne peut employer seul (324).' Cette apologétique rejoint sans doute, en définitive, celle qu'on a tirée du pragmatisme anglo-américain. Elle me semble pourtant en différer d'une façon profonde par son esprit et sa méthode. C'est pourquoi je ne cherche pas à la classer dans le courant des doctrines en question. Ce sont deux fleuves parallèles qui ne se rejoignent qu'à leur embouchure."

[13] F. C. S. Schiller, in 1911, was urging the importance of M. Pradines. Pradines' *Critique des Conditions de l'Action*, Schiller wrote in a review of it in *Mind*, was a work ranking with those of Renouvier, Boutroux, Bergson, Poincaré, and Le Roy.

M. Pradines' work is an attack on rationalism (but not on reason) and intellectualism (but not on intelligence). "His fundamental position," says Schiller, "is that every thought (and so every cognition) is an *act*. . . . Action is all including, and the source of all knowledge. Knowledge indeed is 'nothing but a form of action, which has to forget its own nature' (*L'Erreur Morale*, p. 499)," *Mind*, pp. 423–424. All forms of thought, laws, necessity, truth, ends, goods, mathematics, and novelty are the creations and instruments of action. But action "as such is as free and undetermined as all reality. We and our thoughts are thus only acts of the universe (*Principes*, p. 152) freely directing our course," *Mind*, p. 424. For M. Pradines, acting involves *risking*, and so does knowing. Scientific knowledge is not, then, an attempt to copy reality with exact certitude. Rather it lives in its doubts (see *L'Erreur Morale*, p. 501), and "it is doubt which creates certitude, and hypothesis truth," *Principes*, pp. 7, 299. Science is the perfect expression of reason, and this is practical, and

thinkers. Le Roy called his philosophy by the name *pragmatisme* as late as 1907, when the other members of the philosophy of action school had ceased to use the term.[14] Schiller characterizes Le Roy as an "ultra-pragmatic" follower of Bergson.[15]

James often expressed his debt to French voluntarism and Renouvier. He was an admirer of Bergson and surely felt the attraction and fascination of some of Bergson's most characteristic doctrines. James read Blondel and Le Roy. Both James and Le Roy were keenly interested in the nature and validation of religious belief in ways that avoided the reduction of belief to muscular tensions or ended in agnosticism and suspension of belief. Both emphasized the practical effect, the working consequences of religious belief as a condition of "truth."

It should be noticed, however, that James in all of these respects stood alone among the American pragmatists. Neither Peirce nor Dewey had carefully studied or responded to these currents of French philosophizing. We must also recognize the fact that James characteristically welcomed expressions of thought that bore even a superficial resemblance to his pragmatism and his conception of the function of moral and religious beliefs, and tended to ignore what might be important differences of detail among them. Thus, while he hailed the work of Le Roy, James was in fact engaged in an overhauling of older notions, and in setting forth a new theory of truth not at all countenanced by Le Roy. Le Roy held that a test of practical benefit was relevant to determining the truth of religious belief. But he, like the rest of the school of action, maintained that *if* an idea or belief were really true, practical and beneficial consequences served as evidence of that truth. He did not, like James, try to identify the truth of an idea with its operative practical working consequences (or the performance, cf. § 34). Indeed, Le Roy was committed to a doctrine of an absolute objective truth—an idealistic entity or realm—to which religion has chief access. Religious truth is the highest order of truth for Le Roy; then, on a descending scale of less and less inclusiveness in ends-in-view, come science and finally common sense. Philosophy that becomes realized and perfected through action approaches truth, or the Absolute, but never penetrates the depths. Religion carries the willing knower into reality and truth: "A St. Vincent of Paul comes nearer than a Spinoza to the depths of veritable reality."[16] Le Roy stated what he took to be the difference between his own position and that of pragmatism:

---

has as its aim the overturn of Nature to liberate man. See *L'Erreur Morale*, pp. 690–691; Schiller, review of Pradines in *Mind*, p. 424.

Pradines thus represents an interesting alternative philosophy of *action* to that of Blondel. While he was critical of pragmatism for employing "action to ruin reason" (*Principles*, p. 79), Pradines did not read the American pragmatists, and his criticism was addressed to a "pragmatism" he found in Bergson and Le Roy. Schiller, however, regarded Pradines as expressing a position much like his own; see his account in *Mind*, p. 425.

[14] Horton, p. 295.

[15] *Studies in Humanism*, p. xiv. Interesting critical discussions of Le Roy's "pragmatic" theories of science can be found in Duhem, and in Poincaré, "The Philosophy of Le Roy," pp. 321–339.

[16] "Science et Philosophie," *Revue*, VIII, 71. Quoted in Horton, p. 296.

You will please note the difference between the doctrine I defend and contemporary English "pragmatism." The latter it seems puts . . . in place of the desire for *truth* a preoccupation with mere *utility*. I propose nothing of the sort. All I say is that the true must be acted and lived as well as thought out.[17]

In spite of James's singling out of this movement in French philosophy as one of the points of view of pragmatism, a close look reveals only rather general and superficial resemblances with what Peirce and he and Dewey had been advancing. There was the critical reaction to an earlier rationalism; an interest in the function and behavioral aspects of belief; a recognition of the purposive and practical character of thought; a concern with the relation of scientific knowledge and moral beliefs. But as to how each of these issues was conceived and resolved and especially the last, American pragmatism and the French school of action have little in common.

The philosophy of action, by invoking an Absolute and higher religious truth, was headed, before its demise, in the direction of an idealism novel only in its terminology and its emphasis upon will and action over the intellect. But one wonders what would result from a pragmatic analysis of the meaning of 'Absolute' or 'the truth' or, most important, 'action' as central conceptual units in the doctrines of this school. De Sailly was so impressed with the importance of the philosophy of action that he regarded Anglo-American pragmatism and Bergson's philosophy as aspects, or in the first case, a lame and inadequate instance of the philosophy of action infected with utilitarian, naturalistic, and empirical influences. As Horton says, "Actually, we have in Pragmatism and the Philosophy of Action two closely related but relatively independent trends within a larger, world-wide movement for which we have no name in English, but which is often referred to in French by the term *pragmatisme*."[18] The terms in French or English, we have had occasion to observe before, are easily liable to misunderstanding.

It was not the pragmatic maxim of Peirce nor Dewey's instrumentalism that related American pragmatism and French *pragmatisme*, nor was it James's more controlled discussions of pragmatism as a critical method in philosophy. It was rather James's defense of the will to believe, taken as an affirmation of willing and acting as the creative life of man, James's romantic suggestiveness and the very language he used to describe our activity of "making reality," of beliefs that create their verifying facts (cf. §§ 33, 34), of how we "make truth," that captured the attention of the continent. It was this aspect of James's temperament and philosophizing which Schiller and Papini most appreciated and Peirce and Dewey were most critical of that, merging with Schiller's humanism, presented itself as *pragmatisme*.[19]

In 1905 Bergson set forth an explicit denial of the existence of any influences

---

[17] *Dogme et Critique,* p. 331. Quoted in Horton, p. 296. See, too, Hébert, p. 88.
[18] Horton, p. 294.
[19] Berthelot makes a similar distinction, though with a different and dramatic emphasis. The creation of the idea of pragmatism he credits to Nietzsche and Peirce; but to James and Schiller, "la vulgarisation de l'idée et de l'équivoque pragmatistes," I, § 3, p. 11.

between himself and James that might have seemed to have affected the evolution of their respective philosophies.[20] In so doing he pointed out what can rightly be said to be, not the link, but the climate and temperament that invited associations between pragmatism, *pragmatisme*, and Bergsonianism. He spoke of

> a movement of ideas which has for some years been in evidence everywhere and which arises from causes that are general and profound. In every country and with many thinkers, the need has been felt for a philosophy more genuinely empirical, closer to the immediately given, than the traditional philosophy, worked out, as the latter has been, by thinkers who were primarily mathematicians.[21]

In France, Renouvier and other members of the neocritical school of Boutroux and Bergson, while having important differences among them, united in a reaction against Hegelianism and science, the traditions that had dominated French philosophy since the decline of the metaphysical movement led by Victor Cousin.

§ 74. Georges Sorel

There is one other manifestation of something resembling pragmatism—and often so identified—in the lively vicissitudes of recent French intellectual history. This is the political philosophizing of Georges Sorel (1847–1922).

Sorel's best-known work, *Réflexions sur la violence* (1906), sets forth the position of revolutionary syndicalism. The chief theoretical idea Sorel was concerned to articulate was that of the social, or class, *myth*. The chief practical and moral inspiration that guides Sorel's conception of myth is that of *action*. Myths have their function and value in their capacity to be incitements to action. If they do not prompt immediate action they still retain value as insistent stimuli to action and as keeping the *ideal* of action vivid and alive. A myth, for Sorel, draws men together in collective efforts; myths give *élan* and direction to political and social life, they sharpen and focus the aims of the class struggle. Why some myths are more valuable and successful in their function is not entirely clear. All myths, Sorel pointed out, make their appeal and have their real effects in, not reason, but emotion. The myth, he argued, as a whole, in its entirety, is a body of images evoking sentiments in a people, party, or class, and portrays a future "in some indeterminate time," but arouses hopes and encourages immediate action for realizing that future.[22] Myths are to be judged as means of acting on the present.[23] And through myth, men act upon the present and shape the future—though the future thus shaped may not, is usually not, what was intended or suggested in the myth.[24] The organ, or means to the human reception of the images of myth, and

---

[20] For the occasion, see Perry, II, 599–600.
[21] Quoted in Perry, II, 600.
[22] *Reflections on Violence*, pp. 133, 137.
[23] *Ibid.*, p. 135.
[24] "Psychologists say that there is heterogeneity between the ends in view and the ends actually realized: the slightest experience of life reveals this law to us . . .," *ibid.*, p. 135.

through which the sentiments are arranged, is *intuition*. Intuition precedes any "considered analysis"[25] of myth images.

In all this, Sorel draws upon a variety of sources: Marx, Proudhon, Bernstein, Durkheim, and Bergson.[26] To the latter, in particular, Sorel was indebted for the idea of instinct and intuition as sources of insight, energy, and a feeling for action, as opposed to scientific analysis of ideas. There are clearly certain broad similarities between Sorel's view of the function of myth for social groups and James's argument in *The Will to Believe* concerning the benefits of belief to certain individuals.

Sorel took a special interest in one myth: the idea of a general strike of the workers. This myth was the core of socialism for Sorel.[27] "The myth of the general strike dominates all the truly working class movements."[28] Myths give social action the only moral value it can possess. The myth of the general strike gives to these actions that are prompted by it the special moral character, *violence*. Proletarian violence, thought Sorel, would bring about self-consciousness in all classes and regenerate all phases of society. Bourgeois ideals of parliamentary procedures and peaceful administration of states would be swept away by violence and the faith in direct action, and the system of production would be given to "free men," men who could run it without needing masters. Sorel took the view that the state was an enemy of the proletariat and that political parties were a method by which it exploited the working class. Men would be organized by occupations, not by parties.

A noteworthy feature of Sorel's social philosophy is its anti-scientific outlook and its rejection of "conceptual" thought and analysis. In place of the latter, Sorel appealed to the function and value of *intuition*. His view of the myth of the general strike as evoking noble and deep sentiments in the proletariat concludes on a very Bergsonian note: the myth, he says, enables us "to obtain that intuition of Socialism which language cannot give us with perfect clearness—and we obtain it as a whole, perceived instantaneously. . . ."[29]

§ 75. *Sorel and Mussolini*

Sorel may be credited with having given an emphatic (though hardly original) statement of the fact that men are moved to social action by other than rational or even conscious considerations. This, of course, is a ubiquitous theme in "mod-

[25] *Ibid.*, pp. 130–131. See also p. 37.
[26] Thus, *ibid.*, p. 131: "this method has all the advantages which 'integral' knowledge has over analysis, according to the doctrine of Bergson."
[27] "The general strike is indeed what I have said: the *myth* in which Socialism is wholly comprised, i.e., a body of images capable of evoking instinctively all the sentiments which correspond to the different manifestations of the war undertaken by Socialism against modern society," *ibid.*, p. 137.
[28] *Ibid.*, p. 36.
[29] *Ibid.*, p. 37.

ern" political theory reacting to what was supposed to be the excessive rationalism of eighteenth-century liberalism. It is a discovery, however, that would not have surprised Hume. And after all, as Sorel notes, collective myths have a long history; the doctrine of the second coming among early Christians is one example. He might also have added that the entire theory of the social myth is enunciated in Plato's *Republic*. But this insight into human nature and social action and his harshly delivered rationale of syndicalist action by no means classified Sorel as a pragmatist. Nor are the several doctrines in which action or its imminence are celebrated, or a morality of violence which has its source and appeal in the irrational—in the romance and depths of the "heart" of man—in any special sense pragmatic inspirations. Sorel himself would have disclaimed such associations. Sorel's pragmatism—if so we may call it—had its expression after these other parts of his thought had been long familiar. It was in 1921, in *De l'utilité du pragmatisme*, that Sorel stated his partial acceptance of James's pragmatism and argued for its "usefulness" as a means of settling controversies.[30] But Sorel also pointed out that Jamesian pragmatism suffered from both the Protestant and academic American limitations of its author and from James's European disciples who, like Papini, were given to mystical and fantastic renditions of otherwise important ideas. Sorel undertook in consequence to rethink and reformulate the idea of pragmatism in a sober manner; it needed, he said, a European mind to thus elicit and direct what was of value and use in this philosophy.

While it is unlikely that Mussolini became acquainted with pragmatism through Sorel, he acknowledged the importance of Sorel's teaching: "were it not for Sorel, I would not be what I am,"[31] he once wrote. And he cited Sorel and James as two of his philosophical mentors. In an interview in 1926, Mussolini is reported to have said, after remarking on the influence of Sorel and Nietzsche on his intellectual development:

> The pragmatism of William James was of great use to me in my political career. James taught me that action should be judged rather by its results than by its doctrinary basis.* I learnt of James that faith in action, that ardent will to live and fight, to which Fascism owes a great part of its success. . . .[32]

James's argument for a *right* to *believe*, given a liberal misinterpretation, thus issues in a declaration of *faith* in *action*. It was probably in 1908, through contact with the group of Italian intellectuals who had founded the journal *Leonardo* in Florence,[33] that Mussolini first learned about James and, perhaps, some of the doctrines of pragmatism. In the *Leonardo* group, James's pragmatism, Schiller's

[30] The *Avantpropos* was written in 1917. See Perry, II, 577.
[31] Quoted in Catlin, p. 716.
[32] The interview is reported in the London *Sunday Times*, April 11, 1926. The pertinent passages are given in Perry, II, 575.
[33] See Perry, II, 577. *Leonardo* was founded in 1903 and lasted until 1907. It was succeeded by *La Voce*, administered primarily by the *Leonardo* group, but which was more of a political organ than was its philosophical predecessor. Mussolini contributed occasionally to *La Voce*.

pragmatic humanism, Sorel's syndicalism with its theory of violence and myths of the class war (*una interpretazione will-to-believe-istica* of Marxism, said Papini[34]) were topics of interested discussion. The group was sometimes called "The Pragmatic Club," and this contact may have supplied Mussolini with what he knew about pragmatism. At any rate, through the efforts mainly of Papini, *pragmatismo* was launched.

[34] See Perry, II, 576, for the source. Sorel, as Perry notes, p. 577, note 23, was publishing articles in Italy in 1903 anticipating the *Reflections on Violence*.

CHAPTER FOUR

Italy

§ 76. *Papini, Prezzolini, Vailati, and Calderoni*

When James was attending the Fifth International Congress of Psychology in Rome in 1905, he met and conversed with a "little band of 'pragmatists.'"[1] James was very much impressed. "It has," he wrote,

> given me a certain new idea of the way in which truth ought to find its way into the world. The most interesting, and in fact genuinely edifying, part of my trip has been meeting this little *cénacle*, who have taken my own writings, *entre autres*, *au grand sérieux*.[2]

Speaking of this "band," James remarked that they "publish the monthly Journal *Leonardo* at their own expense, and carry on a very serious philosophic movement, apparently *really* inspired by Schiller and myself."[3] The philosophic membership of the *Leonardo* group included Giovanni Papini and Giuseppe Prezzolini, the spokesmen for a romantic, or, in Papini's phraseology, an imaginative and "magical" version of pragmatism. Also in the group were Giovanni Vailati and Mario Calderoni who represented a medicinally salutory logical, analytical, and scientific development of pragmatism, and Giovanni Amendola, another moderate and later editor of *L'Anima*, which started publication in 1911.

Pragmatism in Italy flourished with great vitality and promise in roughly the first ten years of the century. But the movement did not last. The Church's condemnation of the Modernist movement (see § 73 above) made pragmatism suspect, for some alliance between pragmatism and Modernism had been established in Italy as well as in France. Against Catholic tradition, and the increasingly influential idealism of Croce and Gentile, Italian pragmatism did not survive. But probably the main cause of this decline was a loss of direction due to

---

[1] *Letters*, II, 227, to Mrs. James. He mentions "Papini, Vailati, Calderoni, Amendola, etc."
[2] Letter to Santayana. *Ibid.*, II, 228.
[3] *Ibid.*, II, 227.

increasing philosophic dissension among the "magical" and "logical" tendencies of the parties in the group, and the untimely death of Vailati at the age of 46 in 1909, and of Calderoni at 35 in 1914. *Leonardo* died in 1907, James in 1910.[4] Prezzolini became converted to Crocian idealism. Amendola became a statesman and liberal; he died in 1926 as a result of beatings by Fascist agents. Papini continued to write on pragmatism, but he was responding to other influences. When his book *Pragmatismo* appeared in 1913, as a revised edition of a collection of earlier articles, it had the air of a reminiscence rather than an argument for a new philosophy. In the latter part of his lifetime Papini became converted to Christian mysticism. This, according to many critics of pragmatism, was surely living proof of the failure of pragmatism to answer the philosophic needs of man.

When James encountered the *Leonardo* group he recognized the importance of his own influence and that of Schiller. What he apparently did not then see nor later appreciate was the influence of Peirce and even Dewey on the thinking of the "logical" pragmatists, Vailati and Calderoni. We shall turn to this more sober, yet philosophically more important development of pragmatism in Italy after first considering the work of the "magicians."

Evidently, it was James's "Will to Believe" that had most inspired Giovanni Papini (1881–1956), the leader of the *Leonardo* group.[5] Papini in turn came in for more than a fair share of James's abundant enthusiasm. Although Papini was only in his twenties at the time of their meeting, James addressed him in a letter one year later as "My dear friend and master, Papini," and commented, "What a thing is genius! and you are a real genius!"[6] To this ardent salutation the young Papini replied:

> To hear the master whom I have studied and whom I admire say to me things that seem too flattering even for my pride (which, I might say, is not inconsiderable) has been for me one of the most intense joys of my intellectual life. . . . I am still quite young, dear master—only twenty-five years old—and I am eager to go on working in your path. I *hope* that you will continue to support me—your confidence in me will be one of my sustaining forces.[7]

What was it in Papini that drew such warm praise from James? Papini was, James thought, "a brilliant, humorous and witty writer"; his was a refreshing contrast to the literature that American pragmatists—indeed American philosophers generally—were encouraged to grind out.[8] James was repelled by the

---

[4] Some of these events are recorded in the Avvertimento in Papini's *Pragmatismo*.

[5] See Perry, II, 574, no. 13, for one source. The influence of James' essay and the book of the same name is evident in Papini's writings.

[6] Perry, II, 571.

[7] *Ibid.*, II, 572–573. Papini's letter, written in French, is translated by Perry.

[8] Thus James commented in his report on "G. Papini and the Pragmatist Movement in Italy," pp. 459–460: "To one accustomed to the style of article that has usually discussed pragmatism, Deweyism, or radical empiricism in this country . . . the Italian literature of the subject is a surprising, and to the present writer a refreshing, novelty. Our university seminaries (where so many bald-headed and bald-hearted young aspirants for the Ph.D. have all these years been accustomed to bore one another with the pedantry and technicality, formless, uncircumcised, unabashed, and unrebuked, of their 'papers' and 'reports') are

"uncouthness of form" of American philosophic writing. With his feeling every reader of the literature must sympathize (including the philosophers responsible when they are not writing). There are very few who escaped the "blunting of the literary sense"; James was one and Schiller another. There is, as we have noticed before, some special irony in pragmatists suffering from expository uncouthness while in the very act of espousing the ways of clarifying meanings.

While it would be folly to praise the recondite style of most philosophers, it can be said that a brilliant style is not always the concomitant of brilliant or even clear thought. The trouble with James and Schiller and Papini is that a superior literary ability often produced a kind of façade, darting with colors and flashes, which had an unclarity of its own, for it too facilely led over what was solid as well as what was knotty and cracked beneath the surface. James's impatience with detailed analysis, Schiller's preference for polemical exchanges, and Papini's lack of discipline were as unfortunate for the later history of pragmatism as was the inelegant literature of Peirce, Dewey, and Mead.

But it was not merely because of his style that Papini attracted James: the style was an accurate expression of Papini's philosophic person, and to this James responded as to something favorable and permanently assertive in himself. Papini was the embodiment of that restless, defiant strain in James, a source of intermittent energies which might have had its most complete employment in the arts, in painting, but which led philosophically to his express convictions of the novel and plastic possibilities in reality, to his disdain for closed systems, "scholastic" or "intellectualistic" tendencies and finality in theorizing—characteristics we have taken note of earlier (in the latter pages of § 34). In acutely sensing and praising these traits in Papini, James comes close to describing an incontinent and romantic streak of his own, often in rebellion against the rest of his nature. He says in a letter to Papini:

> Here have I, with my intellectual timidity and conscientiousness, been painfully trying to clear a few steps of the pathway that leads to the systematized new *Weltanschauung* and you with a pair of bold strides get out in a moment beyond the pathway altogether into the freedom of the whole system—into the open country. It is your *temper of carelessness*, quite as much as your particular formulas, that has had such an emancipating effect on my intelligence. You will be accused of extravagance, and *correctly* accused . . . but the program . . . *must* be sketched extravagantly.[9]

There is one other fact about Papini that explains James's unusual interest in him. This is indicated in the above letter where James speaks of the *Weltan-*

bearing at last the fruit that was to be expected, in an almost complete blunting of the literary sense in the more youthful philosophers of our land. Surely no other country could utter in the same number of months as badly written a philosophic mass as ours has published since Dewey's *Studies in Logical Theory* came out. Germany is not 'in it' with us, in my estimation, for uncouthness of form."

[9] Perry, II, 571–572.

schauung, and shortly afterwards refers to "the program."[10] As against earlier and more cautious statements about pragmatism as a method, James had now, in 1906, one year before *Pragmatism* was published, begun to think of pragmatism as a philosophy, a program, a world-wide intellectual movement of which he was a founder; and after meeting the Italians, he was suddenly fully conscious of being the leader.

James proceeded to write an article on Papini and pragmatism in Italy. He described the band of Leonardists as possessing "a frolicsomeness and impertinence that wear the charm of youth and freedom."[11] He mentions in particular a paper by Papini in which "he states the whole pragmatic scope and program very neatly."[12] Fundamentally, says James, following Papini, *pragmatism* means an "*unstiffening*" of our theories and beliefs,[13] and recognizing their *instrumental* value.

Papini's conception of pragmatism does not commit him to any one specific philosophic tenet or require of him a defense of certain doctrines. He said that it would be antipragmatic to attempt a definition of pragmatism, but then, characteristically, proceeded to do so anyway, stating that it is "nothing but a *collection of methods for augmenting the power of man*."[14] He made it clear that pragmatism as a way of philosophizing about philosophic ideas could lead men of differing temperaments and interests in quite different philosophic directions. Pragmatism functions for Papini, not as a theory, but as a theoretical attitude toward theories—it brings together into a common scope these tendencies:

1. *Nominalism*, that is, the appeal to *particular* facts for the significance of words.[15] Pragmatism, from a particular point of view, is none other than nominalism applied to an entire sentence rather than to the word itself, to the theory rather than to the general term.

2. *Utilitarianism*, which has directed intellectual activity toward practical prob-

10 Schiller also spoke of James's pragmatism as a *Weltanschauung*, see § 62.
11 "G. Papini and The Pragmatist Movement in Italy," *Essays and Reviews*, pp. 460–461. Schiller praised the band in similar terms: "In Italy Florence boasts of a youthful, but extremely active and brilliant, band of avowed Pragmatists, whose militant organ, the *Leonardo*, edited by Signor Giovanni Papini, is distinguished by a freedom and vigour of language which must frequently horrify the susceptibilities of academic coteries," *Studies In Humanism*, pp. xiv–xv.
12 "G. Papini," in *Essays and Reviews*, p. 462.
13 *Ibid.*, p. 462; Papini, *Pragmatismo*, p. 91: "il disirrigidimento delle teorie e delle credenze."
14 "Introduzione al pragmatismo," p. 26. Papini recognizes that this definition "includes too much." In this paper he formulates a definition of pragmatism which, he says, is most satisfactory to its friends: "the meaning of a theory consists wholly in the consequences that may be expected to follow from it."
15 Papini seems to incline towards "nominalism" here, maintaining that the *meaning* of a word is the particular fact the word designates: *"ill nominalismo, cioè l'appello ai fatti particolari per dar significato alle parole," Pragmatismo*, p. 91. This version of "meaning" may be close to James or Schiller, but was a nominalism repudiated by Peirce and certainly questioned by Vailati who, as will be seen below, criticizes the entire supposition of defining single words in isolation from linguistic contexts.

lems, that is, toward those whose solution is influential in making changes in some of our actions.

3. *Positivism*, in which is found opposition to verbal and useless questions (called by antonomasia, *metafisiche*), and in which is also found the presentiment of the provisional character of scientific theories.

4. *Kantianism*, with its primacy of *practical reason*, that is, of will. It is the only known source for those who do not know pragmatism well, but is not the most important [source].

5. *Schopenhauerian voluntarism*, which has insisted on the influence of the will (including also sentiment) exerting itself on intelligence, that is, also on science.

6. *Fideism*, as well as the religious apologetic of Pascalian origin, is interested in establishing the importance of faith, and in looking for the best way to create, develop, and restore religious faith.[16]

Pragmatism is thus a collection of methods and a refining and perfecting of the ideas just listed. The chief characteristic of pragmatism, says Papini, is its preservation of an "armed neutrality" (*neutralità armata*) amid these other methods.[17] Here Papini developed the illustration so appreciated by James in which pragmatism was held to be "a corridor theory" (*una teoria corridoio.*)[18] As James summarized it, pragmatism

is like a corridor in a hotel from which a hundred doors open into a hundred chambers. In one you may see a man on his knees praying to regain his faith; in another a desk at which sits someone eager to destroy all metaphysics; in a third a laboratory with an investigator looking for new footholds by which to advance upon the future. But the corridor belongs to all, and all must pass there. Pragmatism, in short, is a great *corridor-theory.*[19]

But the main idea in pragmatism, to which the other methods contribute and toward which the corridor leads, is *action*. Papini defines philosophy as "one of the instruments created by man for the appropriation of the world."[20] Action may take many different forms, and pragmatism, in inspiring activity, will motivate different men in different ways. Papini preaches pluralism. In fact, he urged the importance of complete involvement in any collective or individual activity; and he espoused, especially, the moral ideal of becoming a martyr or hero in any cause. This was a youthful, romantic and idealistic philosophy of action—remindful of the philosophic spirit and subsequent lessons in the drama of Goethe's *Faust* and in the teachings of Fichte (cf. § 14 above). Papini does not emphasize the consequences of action as fundamental morally to an evaluation of action

---

[16] *Ibid.,* pp. 91–92. Or see James, "G. Papini and the Pragmatist Movement in Italy," in *Essays and Reviews,* p. 462, which summarizes the statement. The above follows Papini's Italian text.

[17] *Pragmatismo,* pp. 96–97.

[18] *Ibid.,* p. 97.

[19] "G. Papini and the Pragmatist Movement in Italy," *Essays and Reviews,* pp. 462–463. James enlarges upon the same idea in *Pragmatism,* p. 54.

[20] *Pragmatismo,* p. 36. 'Appropriation' here, *appropriazione,* can connote *seeing* and *gathering in* as well as taking from the world.

or to deliberation over possible actions. He is thus neither pragmatic nor utilitarian in this sense.

On the contrary, it is the action itself that is viewed as consequential by Papini. By being a consequence of need and of passion and having its value determined esthetically and passionally, action transforms reality so as to realize more fully our ideal and desire. Art, religion, science, philosophy—each is the instrument of change and way of acting upon reality. Reality is malleable; it stands as a kind of specious material to be molded according to the ideals, myths, and concepts that men have created for this purpose. As James put it for Papini:

> Tristan and Isolde, Paradise, Atoms, Substance, neither of them copies anything real; all are creations placed above reality, to transform, build out, and interpret it in the interests of human need or passion.[21]

Those intellectual instruments and ideals are not to be judged by some assessment of their approximation to reality. Rather, these are all "*ideal limits* towards which reality must evermore be approximated."[22] It is reality, not thought or passion, that must be molded and made to adapt to human interests. In this Papini was following James's doctrine of reality "in the making" and of truth that becomes "real-ized" (see §§ 33, 34), and Schiller's views on reality as *hylē* which men shape and give meaning to through postulates developed and guided by our particular purposes and needs (see § 65). Papini was simply completing the romantic interpretation of thought that James and Schiller had been reviving in psychological rather than in the dominantly esthetic terms of earlier German romanticism (as surveyed above in § 14).

The note that needed piping in this all but lyrical rendition of the willful and practical nature of thought was, for Papini, the note of *passion*, of feeling.[23] Passion is essential to creativity, and the corridor of pragmatism, in leading to suggested forms of action, guides us at the same time to the ways by which passion can receive conscious expression. Thus, the doors opening off the corridor are not merely incitements to action; they are in this *grande albergo*, this grand hotel of pragmatism, invitations to passionate action.

James had no difficulty in hearing and recording what Papini was sounding in this "pragmatic," this theory of action. "In our cognitive as well as in our active life we are creative," wrote James.

[21] "G. Papini," *Essays and Reviews*, pp. 463–464.
[22] *Ibid.*, p. 464.
[23] In his Preface to *Il Crepuscolo dei Filosofi*, Papini describes his work as one of passion. Of his *24 Cervelli*, Papini says his essays "are impassioned, subjective, partial—lyric in a sense—and not critical." Papini is at his literary best in this vein. And there is something to be said for his view of what is required to *understand* some philosophic theories. Papini's essay on Berkeley in *24 Cervelli* is one of his best; in it he comments, pp. 217–218: "I believe that it is not enough, even in the domain of philosophy, to know [*conoscere*] a thing. One must engage in living it and feeling it with the entire soul—must infuse all of one's thought with it, at least for some time, as the content, the coloring and the significance of one's existence."

The world stands ready, malleable, waiting to receive its final touches at our hands.
. . . Man *engenders* truth upon it.

To some thinkers, James adds, this proves an inspiring notion.

> Signore Papini, the leader of Italian pragmatism, grows fairly dithyrambic over the view that it opens of man's divinely-creative functions.[24]

If we presume to inquire, as perhaps we should not in the case of dithyrambic enthusiasms, what the idea of *action,* "passionate" and "creative," is really supposed to convey, we will receive no clear answer from Papini. Perhaps this may seem as it should be, that is, as fully in harmony with a philosophy of action not to pause to catch a breath of reflection or to ponder upon what actions have to teach us. Insofar as action is an end in itself, and this seems to be one of Papini's convictions, the exercise of thought would assume a secondary role as contributory to action and, maybe, to such consciousness of action as is necessary for our appreciation or awareness of acting at all. Still, one has a right to expect of a *philosophy* of action some explanation of its leading ideas. But, as we have discovered before, the hope of encountering theoretical clarity on fundamental ideas in "practical" philosophies of action is bound to be disappointed. It seems a fixed trait of the more practically inspired philosophies to be impatient over matters of conceptual clarification and elucidation of principles, as discomfiting impracticalities.

For Papini philosophy is "a pragmatic," that is, "a general theory of human action."[25] To the question of what is *action,* James's answer is:

> By 'action' Signore Papini means any change into which man enters as a conscious cause, whether it be to add to existing reality or subtract from it.[26]

But this is so accommodating as to allow under the heading of *action* merely growing and moving and most of the ordinary functions of living. And while these activities are not to be dismissed as unimportant, they do not constitute or call for a philosophy to insure our continued observance and regular performance of them.

In an attempt to meet certain difficulties that Bradley had found in the pragmatists' conception of *practice* and the *practical,* Schiller was led to define 'practice' as "*the control of experience,*" and "to define as 'practical' whatever serves, *directly or indirectly,* to control events."[27] It is in this same general spirit that

---

[24] *Pragmatism,* p. 257. In Jerusalem's German translation of *Pragmatism* (1908), James's reference to Papini as "the leader of Italian pragmatism" comes out as "der Führer der italienischen Pragmatisten," p. 164. Later, when 'Führer' acquired its despicable associations, some critics of pragmatism found it convenient to quote James—as if he were a German professor tinged with Nazism—as benignly calling Papini the Führer. For example, Chiocchetti, p. 55, note 3.

[25] James, "G. Papini," in *Essays and Reviews,* p. 464.

[26] *Ibid.,* p. 463.

[27] *Studies in Humanism,* p. 130. In a letter to Schiller, Peirce comments on the "neat" definition and says, *CP* 8.322: "By 'practical' I mean apt to affect conduct; and by conduct, voluntary action that is self-controlled, i.e., controlled by adequate deliberation."

Papini conceived of *action*. The value of pragmatism, its purpose, and unifying idea, says Papini,

> is that of action, that is, of increasing our power of modifying things, but to act it is necessary *also* to foresee and to foresee with surety it is necessary to have adequate knowledge, that is, convenient and verifiable. From induction by *Will to Believe*, there is given a single aim: aspiration to be able to act (*Wille zur Macht*).[28]

It is not surprising that, after delivering this version of pragmatism, Papini should have moved on to other views. After all, if a philosophic apostle of the merits of action is to succeed in being believed, or in believing himself, his endeavors in behalf of the ideal he espouses must issue in some form of action. To continue theorizing and restating the doctrine, or to go on repeating injunctions and arguments, would be a pathetic exhibition of one's own loss of confidence and belief in that very ideal of action or the *Wille zur Macht*. It does not augur well for those who are most devoutly convinced of the superiority of the deed over the word to spend too much time discoursing upon the subject. Such is the paradox of philosophies of action generally: the more they are true the less philosophical they are, and the more philosophical they become the less they are true— a paradox that would have had Hegel's approval. For Hegel would have detected, in this paradox of a philosophy that proceeds either to refuting or denying itself, that form of self-annihilation by which spirit (whose essence is *action*) passes into some higher phase.

The spirit of this paradox must have also moved Papini. The image that he had created of pragamatism as a corridor theory aptly reinforces the moral of the paradox. For one values corridors according to where they lead; and once they have led us, corridors are usually forgotten. Papini, whose talent was that of a literary artist and who wrote several volumes of critical essays, two novels, and poetry, was led eventually into mysticism and returned to the faith. His *Storia di Cristo* (1921) was a great success. In the end it was the word, not the action, that proved the power and reward.

What is best in the imaginative and "magical" pragmatism of Papini and Prezzolini is of a distinctively literary and artistic quality.[29] This version of Italian pragmatism thrived in ateliers and among groups of poets and artists. Its one sig-

---

[28] *Pragmatismo*, p. 95. "Lo scopo commune è quello di agire, cioè di aumentare il nostro potere di modificare le cose, ma per agire bisogna *anche* prevedere e per prevedere con sicurrezza bisogna avere delle scienze ben atte, cioè comode e verificabili. Dall' induzione al *Will to Believe* c'è una data dallo scopo unico: l'aspirazione a poter agire (*Wille zur Macht*)." James, "G. Papini," *Essays and Reviews*, p. 463, quotes Papini: "The common denominator to which all the forms of human life can be reduced is this: the quest of instruments to act with, or, in other words, *the quest of power*."

[29] Artistic ability is undoubtedly Papini's chief merit. But alertness of mind, if unsystematic in expression, led him to be responsive to what was going on intellectually all over Europe. Thus in his *24 Cervelli*, in the chapter on Eucken (written in 1909), Papini comments on the fact that in Jena there dwelt three great men, Haeckel who was celebrated, Eucken who was slightly known, and Frege "absolutely unknown in Jena and outside." He adds, "there are possibly not ten persons in Europe who have read and understood his works, but that detracts nothing from his glory," pp. 331–332. Frege's greatness is recognized these days, but it was not generally so among philosophers in 1909.

nificant historical connection is in the arts and the movement of Futurism, sup-posedly originated by the Franco-Italian poet Martinetti.

But there is more to say about other philosophically important developments of pragmatism in Italy.

Of the others in the "little band" of *Leonardo* pragmatists, Giuseppe Prezzolini was philosophically closest to Papini. He not only helped to clarify and develop some of Papini's more impressionistically sketched intuitions, he also initiated and influenced some of the doctrines supposedly characteristic of Papini. It was Prezzolini who first advanced the man-god, *Uomo-Dio*, idea that Papini was to make famous as a doctrine.[30] This was the idea that through *action* man acquires power and through power he becomes molder and master of reality. Man then achieves complete satisfaction of desire, and cessation of driving desire and of the activity that springs from desire. But with the end of desire and activity, man becomes both godlike and dead, his dying being a divine death.

For all of his emphasis on action, Papini could also argue that the end of action is divine inaction and that the "true greatness of man consists in his doing the useless exactly because it is useless."[31]

Prezzolini was a disciple of Bergson and an enthusiastic follower of Schiller. Like Schiller he conducted vigorous sallies against the "miseries" of formal logic and logicians. The better part of human thought is not to be found in logic, and the best use of language is not to serve thought but the will. Persuasion, as an art whereby the will is able to exert power over men, especially interested Prezzolini. The beauty of language in creating an effective parable and the power of rhetoric is of greater human importance than a valid syllogism. Prezzolini was fascinated by the esthetic effects and the volitional force of language. In this he is like Sorel. Prezzolini wrote a book on the art of persuasion expressing these interests and the main idea of how language can be used to gain control over men. Vailati described the book as "a manual for liars" (*un manuale per bugiardi*).[32]

We noticed earlier that Papini distinguished two forms of pragmatism: one which he described as *pragmatista majica*, and the other, social-minded and positivistic, which he called *pragmatista sociali*. Associated with the latter was the *pragmatista logica* of which Giovanni Vailati (1863–1909) and Mario Calderoni (1879–1914) were the leaders.

Vailati was a mathematician, widely read in the history of science and having a keen interest in the analysis of language. His work displays a meeting of intel-lectual currents that were to determine the later character of modern philosophy: Peirce's pragmatism and his interest in signs and the analysis of concepts; the interest of the Vienna Circle, 1923, in formulating the methodology of verifica-tion and a criterion of meaningful (i.e., the cognitive use of) language; the mathematical, critical, and analytical investigations of language, logic, and science

---

[30] Gullace points this out, p. 95.
[31] *L'altra meta,* p. 203.
[32] The title of his review of Prezzolini's *L'arte di persuadere* (1907), *Scritti,* pp. 770–776.

by Ramsey and Wittgenstein. Had Vailati lived longer he might well have become one of the most powerful and interesting philosophers of our time.

As it is, Vailati's work well repays study, and it is a pity that he has been hitherto almost entirely ignored in Anglo-American philosophy.[33] Because he is still so little known, and because there is scarcely any writing in English on Vailati, the following discussion quotes rather substantially from one of his most important papers on pragmatism.[34]

Vailati and Calderoni were good friends and had planned to collaborate on a book in which they were to set forth a complete statement of logical pragmatism. Unfortunately when Vailati died, Calderoni did not himself have time to complete the project, for he died five years later.

Calderoni was a lawyer and political scientist. He had some correspondence with Peirce.[35] His understanding of pragmatism as fundamentally the analysis of ideas in terms of predictive consequences (prevision and verification, to be discussed shortly) applied to the administration of the law and the behavior of judges, is in many ways strikingly like Oliver Wendell Holmes's "predictive" theory of the law.[36] Vailati and Calderoni had a lively visit with Lady Welby (for whom see § 70 above) in the summer of 1903.[37] According to her account, both men were enthusiastic about her work on "significs," the study of meaning.[38] They regarded significs as a way of bringing "Plato and Aristotle into line with all that is most modern in knowledge." After "unsparing criticism of the obscurity and confusion" in the philosophies of Kant, Hegel, Schopenhauer, materialists,

[33] James's essay, "G. Papini and the Pragmatist Movement in Italy," merely mentions the names of Vailati and Calderoni. The only other study of the subject known to me in English is the brief and not very sympathetic sketch by Gullace, and that is mostly concerned with Papini and why pragmatism failed as a movement in Italy. His few remarks on Vailati and Calderoni are enticing but not very informative.

An English translation of the important papers of Vailati and Calderoni is a major desideratum these days. For the reader who may be interested, there are several papers by Vailati in English; references to five of these will be found below; for the full reference, see the Bibliography.

[34] "Pragmatismo e Logica Matematica," *Leonardo,* 1906; reprinted in *Scritti;* I follow this text in the next pages. An English translation of this paper can be found in the *Monist,* 1906. I have been guided by this translation, but have made revisions.

Basic to the study of Vailati is Rossi-Landi, "Materiale per lo studio di Vailati." See also Santucci, ch. 4 and bibliographical references therein. Vailati's writings were collected by Calderoni, *Scritti.* This large volume is invaluable for what it presents concerning the scope, diversity, and analytical powers of Vailati's mind. Among the distinguished names of the subscribers who made this publication possible are William James, Russell, and Lady Welby; see *Scritti,* Nota Die Sottoscrittori. There is also a *Scritti* of Calderoni's writings. There is a selection of the writings of both men, edited by Papini. See also Papini's *24 Cervelli,* ch. 8, pp. 115–131, for a sketch of Vailati, and his *Stroncature,* ch. 13, on Calderoni.

[35] For an important letter from Peirce to Calderoni see *CP* 8.205–213, part of which is quoted above in § 21, note 57. Also see Vailati's interesting short review of Peirce's *Monist* paper, "What Pragmatism Is," in *Leonardo* (1905), *Scritti,* pp. 639–640.

[36] Noted by Gullace, p. 100. The subject and the relation of these developments in legal philosophy well deserves study.

[37] This was the summer preceding the appearance of Lady Welby's book *What is Meaning?* which was reviewed by Peirce in the *Nation;* see *CP* 8.171–175.

[38] On the visit to Lady Welby and this conversation, see her letter describing it, *Other Dimensions,* p. 126, also pp. 142–143. She refers to the visit as in the summer preceding the review of her book by Peirce, and his review appeared in October 1903.

pantheists, and others, they proceeded to express their great admiration of Locke and Mill.[39]

Lady Welby was much impressed by Russell's *The Principles of Mathematics* (1903),[40] and noticed the frequent mention of Vailati in that book.[41] She would scarcely have missed the importance of Peano,[42] and Vailati's contact with Peano must have interested her. She carried on a correspondence with Vailati about mathematical logic, among other topics.[43] Through Lady Welby, Vailati and Calderoni must have received information about Peirce and Russell, with whom she also kept up a correspondence (cf. § 70).[44]

Among the Italian pragmatists generally, there was a sense of liberation from the tradition-bound philosophic history of Catholicism.[45] For Calderoni and Vailati this new sense of freedom and exploration was realized less in the romantic action and anarchic myths of Papini; it was rather felt as a breaking out from sterile formulas and the mechanical, repetitive methods of rationalism, and a directing of thought about science, society, and religion in concepts relevant to and guided by experience, in the manner so successfully practiced in the sciences.

Vailati made important contributions to mathematics and the foundations of geometry.[46] He was one of the group of mathematical logicians, led by Giuseppe Peano (1858–1932), whose main interest lay in showing how all of arithmetic and algebra can be derived from a meager set of logical concepts. (The activities of this group were one of the precursors of the great *Principia Mathematica* of Russell and Whitehead.) One of the distinguished collaborators who compiled Peano's main work, *Formulaire Mathematique*, Vailati, in his own writings on the analysis of scientific and philosophic problems, often makes effective use of techniques and distinctions developed by Peano in mathematical logic. Vailati thus stands as one of the very few early pragmatists who, like Peirce, had a command of mathematics and an appreciation of the formal techniques of mathematical logic.[47] Vailati's "logical pragmatism" is a singularly interesting and important philosophic occurrence. It embodies the formal techniques of logic and

[39] Vailati often stated his admiration of Locke and Mill. In a letter to Lady Welby of 1903, he describes himself as a fervant admirer of Mill who was, he says, the most exact and profound philosopher of the century. This interesting letter is discussed in the pages below.

[40] Peirce's review of 1903 also included Russell's book. Peirce devotes only a few sentences to Russell's volume and occupies the rest of the review with Lady Welby's work.

[41] She notes that Russell cites Vailati and Peano, and remarks that Vailati is introducing her work to Peano, in a letter to E. B. Tichner, *Other Dimensions*, p. 142.

[42] Russell's Preface, p. xvii, states his obligation in mathematics to Cantor and Peano.

[43] See *Other Dimensions*, pp. 143–144. She comments on points in the paper "Pragmatismo e Logica Matematica," which will be discussed at some length in the pages below.

[44] James received articles from Vailati and Calderoni and passed them on to Peirce, and encouraged the Italians to send their work directly to Peirce. See *CP* 8.260.

[45] Santucci, p. 200.

[46] Russell, in *The Principles,* as noticed two paragraphs back, makes seven references to Vailati. See especially his § 376. For a reference to Vailati's work in descriptive geometry as a science of class relations, see Whitehead's *Encyclopedia* article, "The Axioms of Geometry," the first paragraph of the section "Descriptive Geometry" and note 2.

[47] C. I. Lewis, twenty years younger than Vailati, is also to be included in this judgment and, of course, Ramsey (§ 71), insofar as he can be classified as a pragmatist.

mathematics, the logical analysis of language, the pragmatic approach to the explication of the meanings of concepts, and the pragmatic analysis of the purposeful character of conceptualization.

In marked contrast to Papini and Prezzolini, the pragmatism of Vailati and Calderoni represents a veering away from James and Schiller toward Peirce and Dewey.

I come now to one of Vailati's valuable and characteristic discussions of the relation between pragmatism and mathematical logic, his essay "Pragmatismo e Logica Matematica."

Vailati acknowledges the work of Peirce as an "initiator and promotor of an original trend in logico-mathematical studies."[48] But he announces his intention of starting from the work of Peano in developing the view of the pragmatic characteristics of modern logical theory. He finds four basic points of contact between pragmatism and logic.

1) Vailati argues first that pragmatism and logic are agreed that the value and meaning (*significato*) of an assertion is

> intimately related to the use which can be made, or which one may desire to make of it, for the deduction and construction of determinant consequences or groups of consequences.[49]

This, he continues, is characteristic of the procedure of mathematicians in choosing and determining postulates. The choice of postulates depends on an *end* in view.[50] And the end desired determines the relations of dependence and connections between the postulates and the rest of the propositions of a theory.

Vailati is fully aware of the relative character of a postulate: some statements are postulates relative to other statements derivable from them, under certain logical conditions.[51] We may say that one set of statements is "dependent" on

[48] "Pragmatism and Mathematical Logic," p. 481; *Scritti*, p. 689. In this and the references that follow I first cite the pages of the English translation by H. D. Austin, then of the Italian text in Vailati's *Scritti*.
Vailati's familiarity with the work of Peirce, his full acceptance and employment of the methodology of pragmatism—as discussed in §§ 21, 101, and 106—is clearly expressed in his "A Study of Platonic Terminology," p. 475, where he emphasizes the value of the rule
that . . . advises us to determine the meaning of every phrase or abstract proposition by means of the examination of the *consequences* which are involved in it, or the *applications* which are made of it, and to regard two phrases or propositions as equivalent, or as two ways of saying the same thing (Peirce), whenever they are employed, by any one who adopts them, as a means of arriving at the same particular conclusions.
[49] Page 482; *Scritti*, p. 689.
[50] Page 482; *Scritti*, pp. 689–690.
[51] A point, incidentally, but for reasons far removed from those above, made by Quine in *From A Logical Point of View*, p. 35. Vailati also offers illuminating comments on the "relativity" of phases in the deductive process and acute observations on the roles of the metaphors we use to describe these processes. Thus in "On Material Representations of Deductive Processes," p. 312, he writes:
The relation between premises and conclusion of a piece of deductive reasoning would not . . . be correctly described by saying that the latter is "supported" by the former, unless the common image of one object "supported by another" be substituted by the more general and more scientifically precise one of bodies which are "attracting each other," and which, when in contact, do support each other by reciprocal pressure. Of a pebble resting on a rock it is equally correct to say that the whole earth does support it as to say that the whole earth is supported by it.

others. But just how dependency is established and what statements are to be made dependent upon others is largely a matter of how we wish to organize a system of statements. This, in turn, depends upon what purposes we want to accomplish with the system.

Vailati states this last idea picturesquely. The relations of postulates to the rest of the propositions dependent on them was formerly thought to be like an aristocratic regime, like the relation of monarch or princes to the rest of the social order. The work of mathematical logicians is then revolutionary in overthrowing the old order and establishing in its place a constitutional democracy. Under this new regime

> the choice of rulers depends, at least theoretically, upon their recognized ability to exercise temporarily determined functions for the public interest.[52]

Postulates thus lose any claim to rule by "divine right" and are put to work as *"servi servorum,* as simply *employees,* of the great *associations* of propositions" that compose the various branches of mathematics.[53]

2) There is a critical agreement between pragmatists and mathematical logicians in their mutual repudiation of

> the vague, imprecise, generic; and in their care to analyze every assertion into its simplest terms, whether referring directly to *facts,* or to *connections between facts.*[54]

As a result, a great deal of traditional logic and philosophy is brought under a powerful critical examination from which it emerges "transfigured, restored, enriched with new and more important significances."[55]

It is to be noticed that the new critical spirit, for Vailati, is not hostile to nor a rejection of the scientific and philosophic theorizing of the past. Rather, he sees the intellectual past illuminated by the methods of analysis; instead of pedantic obfuscation, the past is made relevant and alive to present interests and becomes a suggestive source, even, for new theoretical developments.

One of the "enrichening" benefits of the above method of analysis, for Vailati, was in its application to the time-honored intellectual art of making *distinctions,* of framing *definitions,* and of analyzing *propositions.* These are peculiarly prevalent activities of philosophers and scientists. Pragmatism and mathematical logic have rescued this art from a scholastic rigidity and narrowness, and have brought about a new understanding of the subtle, flexible, and powerful exercise of these intellectual techniques. We will return to Vailati's view on definitions shortly.

3) The third connection between pragmatism and mathematical logic is the importance each attaches to historical research in the development of scientific theories. Research of this kind has disclosed the interesting fact that what

---

[52] Pages 482–483; *Scritti,* p. 690.
[53] Page 483; *Scritti,* p. 690.
[54] Page 483; *Scritti,* p. 690. "Simplest terms" here is not to be misunderstood as a call for absolutely simple or primitive terms from which all other words are defined. Vailati repudiates the notion of single, ultimate terms, uniquely defined once and for all. This will be evident in part of the discussion to follow.
[55] Page 483; *Scritti,* p. 690.

were supposed to be very different theories in different fields of study, or in different periods of development from ancient to modern times, can often be shown to possess identical features. Modern mathematics, Vailati observes, has shown us that what has sometimes appeared to be a new discovery or radical development, may only be a new method or notation for techniques formerly used under other names and other symbolizations by our predecessors.

The interest in the identical content of theories under differences of expression, symbolism, and methods of representation, is also an "interest in linguistic questions."[56] Such was Couturat's project of *Ido*, the "Universal language," or Peano's *latino non flexo*.[57] In these references, presumably, Vailati has in mind the idea of representing or expressing theories in a single universal language as a way of discovering identical features and a continuity of content under otherwise seeming diversity. From Peano's interests in historical data in the *Formulario*, says Vailati, we have learned to see theories not as static structures,

> not in the conventional attitudes of stuffed animals . . . but as organisms, which live, eat, struggle, reproduce . . . with some naturalness of progression and development.[58]

4)   We are brought back to the topic of definitions. For here, too, pragmatism and mathematical logic have affinities. The logical structure and functions of definitions was a subject of considerable interest to Vailati.

Vailati maintains that the traditional method of definition, that is, the search for *genera* and *species*, is but a special instance of a much more inclusive procedure. For the traditional method essentially consists in determining a class from which the class to be defined results as a logical product. The broader procedure is a method of obtaining the class to be defined as a *function* of known classes by means of logical operations. In addition, the older method is itself broadened so that what is defined

> is not an isolated word but a group of words or phrase in which this word appears (*implicit definitions*).[59]

The idea that we define single words in isolation from others, or in isolation from contexts of their uses, is a misunderstanding often commented upon by Vailati. Sometimes, as in the paper we have been following, he argues that a definition of a single word is possible, but only as a special case, and the simplest, in a more vast field of "implicit definitions." But often, in other writings, Vailati denies that definition is ever of single words isolated from uses and from other words—or phrases—in which the word in question acquires meaning. He thus anticipates a number of recent doubts about the possibility of isolating *the* meaning of single words abstracted or distilled from the rest of language and the circumstances of utterance.

The techniques of mathematical logicians, Vailati remarks, show that for "a

56 Page 485; *Scritti,* p. 691.
57 Page 485; *Scritti,* p. 692.
58 Page 485; *Scritti,* p. 691.
59 Page 486; *Scritti,* p. 692.

given word, taken by itself, a definition in the ordinary sense cannot be given."[60]
He writes:

> to speak of the "definability" or "non-definability" of a given word or concept is to use a meaningless expression, so long as no precise indication is supplied as to what *other words* or concepts may be employed in the desired definition; but it has also afforded an explanation of the fact that among many of the most important terms of science and philosophy are to be found those very ones for which it is unreasonable to ask for a definition in the scholastic sense.[61]

By "scholastic sense" Vailati means a definition of terms in isolation from all others based on an alleged capacity "of the human mind to penetrate to the 'essence' of things."[62]

In an interesting letter to Lady Welby,[63] with whom Vailati had been corresponding on the topic of meaning, he develops the following points. The question of meaning, he writes, is really the question of the meaning (or import) of propositions.[64] The common view according to which only *words* are defined, happens to leave out an important class of *definitions*, namely, *phrases* composed of words which, taken by themselves, would have no meaning at all. He cites, as examples, the meanings of prepositions such as 'in,' 'out,' 'of,' 'from,' and especially their use in metaphorical contexts "as is nearly always the case in metaphysical discussion." Can we determine the meaning of these, or like instances, "without determining the meaning of the propositions into which they enter to connect other words?"[65] A similar consideration applies to expressions like 'to be,' 'to act,' 'to reproduce,' 'to represent,' 'to manifest.' These words can be given meaning, says Vailati, by attributing some meaning to the propositions "in which we use them in connection with other words." And these words, he points out, may in turn have no meaning except to call "their meaning the meaning of the phrases into which they enter."[66] Defining the phrases, or classes of them, saves us from the danger of ambiguity and even the meaninglessness of words,

> while, on the contrary, our definitions of words would serve no useful purpose if by them we were not enabled rightly to interpret the meaning of the propositions in which such words are combined.[67]

---

[60] Page 486; *Scritti,* p. 692.

[61] Page 487; *Scritti,* pp. 692–693. Many of the important distinctions made in the sciences also have this character, Vailati argues in "The Attack on Distinctions," p. 707. He says of terms like *mass,* or more complicated notions of physical theory that presuppose certain contexts and points of reference for the distinctions we make, that "The special feature of such distinctions is that the words which we use to express them can only be defined indirectly, i.e., by stating the meaning of a whole sentence in which they appear, as is the case, for instance, with the word 'ratio' *(logos)* as used by Euclid, which he only defines by explaining the meaning of the assertion that the two quantities 'have the same ratio to each other' as two others."

[62] P. 487; *Scritti,* p. 693. For some other suggestive comments on definition, see Vailati's "On Material Representations of Deductive Processes," pp. 314–315.

[63] This especially valuable letter is found on pp. 82–84 of *Other Dimensions.*

[64] *Ibid.,* p. 83.

[65] *Ibid.,* p. 83.

[66] *Ibid.,* pp. 83–84.

[67] *Ibid.,* p. 84. For an interesting development of this point in the context of mechanics, and with respect to the law of inertia, see "The Attack on Distinctions," pp. 706–707.

Vailati stresses the relative and hypothetical nature of definitions. Definitions formulate a possible representation of certain kinds of properties—or possible applications of concepts. The logical consequences of these possible definitions will be truths, "truths for the definition," but the value of the definition will be determined by how the consequences drawn from it and the operations it prescribes add to the rest of our knowledge. It may be useful in given domains to construct various possible definitions, partly or wholly mutually exclusive, for the purpose of tracing out their consequences and arriving, perhaps, at interesting and novel results. Possible definitions, says Vailati, of properties possessed by a given mathematical object clearly exhibit the relative nature of the distinction between the object's "essential" properties and its other properties. In general, possible definitions seem to be propositions affirming "the *possibility* or *non-absurdity* of the co-existence of two or more facts."[68]

Closely related to possible definitions are those that Vailati, following Peano, calls "definitions by abstraction." These represent possible formulations *via* the inductive construction of new concepts, developed from the observation of certain sets of properties or operations.

> Particular interest, in the relations they have to pragmatism, is presented by what were called (Peano) *"definitions by abstraction"*; in which, from the fact that a given relation presents some of the characteristic properties of equality, occasion is taken to fashion a new concept: as, for example, from the fact that two straight lines parellel to a third are parallel to each other, is drawn the concept "direction"; or, from the fact that two amounts of merchandise exchanged for one and the same amount of a third commodity are mutually exchangeable, is evolved the concept "value," etc.[69]

Hypothetical or possible definitions are a special case of the more general and equally important class of hypothetical propositions. The source of Vailati's interest in the importance of hypothetical propositions was Peano's distinction (in 1888) between *categorical* and *conditional* propositions. Jourdain described this as "the beginnings of those reforms in mathematical logic by which Peano made it capable of expressing all mathematical propositions."[70] Vailati praised the distinction as "the first time that symbolic logic was presented as an instrument shaped with a view [*forgé en vue*] to its immediate application to a definite branch of scientific investigation."[71]

A categorical proposition, for Peano, expresses a relation between definite

---

[68] "Pragmatism and Mathematical Logic," p. 484; *Scritti,* p. 690. The use of possible definitions seems to be related logically to a type of reasoning that Couturat, "The Principles of Logic," p. 147, says is due to Vailati: the *reductio ad absurdum,* "if A implies not-A, A is false." Any possible definition A must, of course, not imply not-A. The utility and interest of a possible definition A will depend on the *kind* of consequences that follow from A; the *reductio* is only a necessary condition of the utility of A. The determination of logical *consequences* is one form of *prevedere, previsione,* "foreseeing" so essential to science and all intelligent activity, for Vailati and Calderoni, as we shall notice in the latter part of the present section.

[69] Pages 486–487; *Scritti,* p. 692.

[70] Quoted in Joergensen, Vol. I, p. 175.

[71] *Scritti,* p. 236; Joergensen, Vol. I, p. 175, note 88.

objects and is therefore either true or false. A hypothetical proposition states a relation between indefinite or variable objects and hence is only verified for some of them.[72] Certain implicit restrictions operate with the use of conditional or hypothetical propositions. Recognition of

> the hypothetical nature of general propositions has also helped to turn attention to the "tacit restrictions," or unspecified limitations upon which their validity depends. A good example is the observation of Maxwell . . . that even the simplest propositions as to areas, e.g., that "the area of a triangle is given by one-half the product of the base by the altitude," would cease to be true if, instead of taking as the unit of measure of areas the square with the side of unit length, we were to take the triangle having such unit as base and altitude.
>
> These considerations are intimately connected with those by which the pragmatists have been led to a more precise determination of the difference expressed in ordinary language by opposing "laws" to facts; and to form on an entirely new basis the classic controversy between determinists and contingentists [contingentisti].[73]

Vailati explains the point of this last comment in another writing.[74] Assuming that "there are no facts that *repeat* themselves,"[75] and that there are only certain resemblances among facts, the "principle of causality" comes to this: effects which resemble one another constantly succeed causes which resemble one another. To say that an effect of a given cause is "determined" is to say that *some* of its characteristics are determined; that is, in *some* (but not every) respect the effect or fact belongs to the class of things for which the principle of causality holds.[76] But in *other* respects, the effect or fact in question may not be determined. Thus Vailati attempts to steer between the extremes of determinism and indeterminism. It should be added that which of the characteristics of groups of facts are to be singled out as the basis of a *resemblance* feature, and thus what will be determined as "causes" and "effects" among facts (in short, how we apply the principle of causality) are matters of selection to be justified pragmatically. In any given application of it, the causal principle thus takes the form of a hypothetical proposition.

A number of the foregoing observations may be read as particulars of a general trait of definitions, and one which Vailati opposes to the "scholastic" attempts at definition of essences. This general feature he calls "definition by postulates."[77] Mathematical logic and pragmatism, he says, have another issue in common here.

---

[72] Joergensen, Vol. I, p. 175. Joergensen gives Peano's illustration: The statement 'X² − 3X + 2 + 0' is *conditional;* the statement 'X² − 3X + 2 = 0 has the roots 1 and 2' is *categorical.* Peano's distinction between conditional and categorical propositions is related to his equally important distinction of *real* and *apparent* variables. See e.g., Russell, "Mathematical Logic," p. 65 and note, and Joergensen, p. 175.

[73] "Pragmatism and Mathematical Logic," p. 484; *Scritti*, pp. 690–691.

[74] "The Attack on Distinctions."

[75] *Ibid.*, p. 708. Vailati does not discuss the puzzling question of what this frequently made statement *means*, or how we really know that "no fact repeats itself."

[76] *Ibid.*, p. 708.

[77] "Pragmatism and Mathematical Logic," p. 487; *Scritti,* p. 693.

For definition by postulation is to see how the significance of a sign or operation is made evident by "enunciating a certain number of norms which, by hypothesis, are to regulate its operation."[78] This, he says, is the procedure of pragmatism; for the norms, functioning as postulates and definitions and governing the uses and meanings of the concepts of some discipline, are themselves "arbitrary." The norms are propositions

> which possess the function of determining, in view of given ends or applications, the various fields of research; that is, as propositions whose sole justification consists in the importance and utility of the *consequences* which it may be possible to deduce therefrom.[79]

5) We come to the last of the various interrelations Vailati finds between pragmatism and modern logic: he works out a very suggestive interpretation of the emphasis in pragmatism upon particular facts. And in this interpretation, Vailati is much closer to Peirce than to James, Schiller, or Papini.

Vailati construes the appeal to "the concrete" and "particular" as the testing ground of thought to be, in effect, an appeal to *models* for studying and assessing formal constructions. He notes that the search for and construction of "particular interpretations" or "concrete examples" is an important way of determining the "mutual independence, or compatibility, of given affirmations or hypotheses."[80] Hence he sees the role of particular facts as that of providing a model of some sort for verifying (or rendering probable) the premises of a logical system and of its consistency.

This procedure Vailati characterizes as the need of pure logic to derive strength, like Antaeus, from occasional contacts with the earth. In the meeting between a formal system and its concrete interpretation, he explains, we can discern the real meaning of the alliance between " 'extremes of theoretical activity' (the intuition *of the particular* and the impulse to abstraction and generalization),"[81] which, pragmatists have argued, characterizes all our thinking.

This version of the role of particular models, along with the recognition of the instrumental function of theories, is a way of keeping the latter trim and healthy. Mere plenitude and increase of propositional content is not always a condition of richness of theoretical scope. For this may also be a "fatty degeneration" says Vailati. And against degeneration, pragmatism offers this therapy by insisting

> on the *instrumental* character of theories—affirming that they are not an *end in themselves*, but *media* and "organisms" whose efficacy and potency is rigorously dependent upon their agility, upon the absence of encumbrances and hindrances

---

[78] Page 488; *Scritti,* p. 693.

[79] Page 488; *Scritti,* p. 693.

[80] Page 488; *Scritti,* p. 693: "Un altro carattere della logica matematica, per il quale essa, ancora più forse che per qualunque dei precedenti, si manifesta affine al pragmatismo, è quello che riguarda l'ufficio che in essa sono venute ad assumere la ricerca e la construzione di 'interpretazioni particolari' o di esempi concreti come criteri per decidere della ricproca indipendenza, o della compatibilità, di date affermazioni od ipotesi."

[81] Page 489; *Scritti,* p. 694.

to their movements, upon their resemblance rather to lions and tigers than to hippopotami and mastodons.[82]

While Vailati was especially interested in setting forth the kind of methodological and analytic pragmatism of the foregoing pages, he did not ignore other important philosophic aspects of meaning and human action. Thus, while he saw the advisability of distinguishing the moral and psychological pragmatism of James's *Will to Believe* from Peirce's work in the clarification of concepts and the theory of signs, Vailati (and Calderoni) recognized the role of will and belief in affecting conduct and determining ends, so well described by James. Vailati took pains to separate the logical and empirical significance of James's views from what appeared as paradoxical, irrational, and an apologetic for traditional religious and metaphysical faith.[83]

The propensity to believe is as natural to man as the interest in deduction and the anticipation of consequences of ideas. Vailati, Calderoni, the American pragmatists, and Hume[84] agreed on this. Vailati and Calderoni were led to view the systems in which knowledge is organized and explained as shaped by more than just the concern to describe and predict experience and to verify the predictions. For moral interests and values also work to affect the selection and formation of concepts. Value judgments resulting from human desires are woven in among the verified propositions of our working system of knowledge. Predictions are in part the outcome of human desires; that is, the systems which enable predictions to be made, and the particular predictions thus made, achieve their importance and the particular weight assigned their outcomes partly from considerations of human desire and purposes. These subjective conditions of desire and hope make up what Vailati and Calderoni call "the arbitrary in the working of our psychical life."[85]

If the arbitrary promptings of desire affect some of the choices we make of definitions and postulates and concepts in our system of knowledge, desire does not determine truth. We may will this or that possible definition and make choices among possible conceptual constructions and operations, and this may be "arbitrary," that is, motivated by subjective interests.[86] But the products of such arbi-

---

[82] Pages 490–491; *Scritti,* p. 694. Vailati fully appreciated the pragmatic interpretation of theories as instruments—the position discussed below, Part IV, ch. 2. In "A Pragmatic Zoologist," p. 150 (*Scritti,* p. 734), he comments on "the pragmatic conception of scientific theories as expressions of conditional expectation or instruments for the forecasting [*la previsione*] of possible experiments [*di possibili esperienze*]."

[83] See Santucci, pp. 200–201 for a discussion of this response of Vailati to James's views. See also *Scritti,* pp. 269–272 and 273–277 for two of Vailati's reviews of James's *The Will to Believe.*

[84] See Hume's explanation of the view: "that all our reasonings concerning causes and effects are deriv'd from nothing but custom; and that belief is more properly an act of the sensitive, than of the cogitative part of our nature." *Treatise,* Book I, Part IV, sec. 1.

[85] See the article written by Calderoni from notes left by Vailati, "L'Arbitrario nel funzionamento della vita psichica."

[86] Dewey, of course, as we will see in §§ 93–94, would have been critical of this psychology and concept of *desire* and the alleged "subjectivity" of the origin and expression of desires in value judgments.

trary selections and choices are neither true nor false. They become true or false when, in conjunction with the other propositions of the system of which they are parts, they are brought to verification. Verification thus limits the range of acceptable and useful arbitrary choices.

Vailati and Calderoni were thus led to state and make use of, as a central feature of their logical pragmatism, a verifiability principle of meaning and truth suggested by Peirce (in (8) of § 21). In this their position anticipates the logical positivism of the later Vienna Circle. In certain respects Vailati's and Calderoni's use of this principle was more sophisticated and certainly more tolerant than was the practice in its later Viennese days. Vailati recognized that the "same" term or proposition might have different meanings in different contexts (as we observed in the discussion of the third and fourth points above). The concept of 'moving body,' for example, has widely different senses for a problem in astronomy and for one in engineering. The procedures of verification of a proposition will also vary in differing contexts. Now this forces us to conclude that it is a mistake to seek *the* one meaning of a term. But also it is a mistake to suppose that there is just one kind of operation of verification for a proposition.

Vailati was aware, however, of other subtle forms in which *meaning* occurs and defies any simple or uniform analysis. Thus he points out that we can always make adjustments in our conceptual schemes, especially those of ordinary and scientific knowledge, for the locution and accommodation of idioms that might have even sentimental or traditional values for us.[87] Moreover, Vailati was sensitive to the shift in roles, sometimes imperceptible, that concepts can take. Like Dewey (as noticed in § 80 below) he observed, for example, how a seemingly synthetic statement can be gradually transformed into an analytic truth, and how these transformations if not recognized can breed philosophic confusion.[88]

Cognizant of the fact that sometimes various possible theoretical constructions, the multiple results of arbitrary choice, might all be meaningful and verifiable, and indeed verified, Vailati and Calderoni resorted to a second methodological principle to accompany that of verifiability. This was the familiar Occamite razor, or Mach's principle of the economy of thought. Foresight and predictions are to be mediated by the simplest hypothesis and constructions. Simplicity is a condition of effective theorizing; simpler hypotheses are superior to more complicated alternatives, other things being equal,[89] in utility and our control over them.

---

[87] See Santucci, pp. 208–209. There is also a very suggestive study by Vailati on the role of metaphors and "images" representative of "mental activities" in "On Material Representations of Deductive Processes."

[88] One main source of confusion, Vailati held, was the notion of *essential* properties of objects, so that if that property is lost or is unknown, the object ceases to be, or becomes unknowable. Locke's doctrine of substance (see Part One, §§ 6–7 above) and the dubious nature of propositions about *substance* are cases in point.

[89] This is, it must be confessed, a rather facile phrase, but convenient as a way of avoiding a host of complicating details. The notion of theoretical simplicity, moreover, is far from simple.

344 III. PRAGMATISM IN EUROPE

The arbitrary workings of value interests and beliefs are then subject to this criterion: the choices of conceptual instruments, of postulates and theories are good or bad, wise or foolish, to the degree that these help us to foresee and predict effectively. But then—and this was a point of some importance to Vailati and Calderoni—sheer utility of a belief or proposition is not, as such, its truth.[90] Rather, the truth of a belief or proposition is just the value or utility foreseen or predicted from its tentative acceptance. It is not merely any utilities that happen to follow from the acceptance of a hypothesis that constitute its truth. The truth of a hypothesis turns upon its determinate logical consequences. Thus, the relation between real coercive conditions that do happen and those predicted or foreseen from a given proposition determines the proportion's truth.

Ultimately our desires have their origin in the will to power. And this is addressed to transforming and controlling the natural world in which we find ourselves. We seek then, and naturally so, the most powerful and effective instruments for this purpose. But this is to say that the will to power and science are related to the important extent that stable, accurate, and reliable anticipations and predictions of reality are wanted. Whether or not science should be viewed exclusively as a way of enabling us to increase our control over nature, it surely does do this much. In this respect, if not in all others, Vailati and Calderoni agreed with Papini's description of the pragmatist.

> His sympathies will be with the study of the particular instance; with the development of prevision; with precise and well-determined theories; with those which serve as the best instruments for the most important ends of life; with conciseness, with economy of thought, etc.

The pragmatist is enthusiastic

> for . . . all that shows the complexity and multiplicity of things; for whatever increases our power to act upon the world; for all that is most clearly bound up with practice, activity, life.[91]

Vailati and Calderoni would have subscribed to this, but not the the harsh utilitarian form and fascistic mold into which these ideas could be pressed. "Logical pragmatism" had too good an understanding of logic and sciences and too sound an appreciation of the central and most valuable contributions of the American

---

[90] As James sometimes seemed to suggest (§ 31, but also see § 32). A good statement of the position that all knowledge is addressed to the future and that the truth or falsity of our instruments and system of knowledge becomes manifest in their uses and consequences, is found in Calderoni's "La prévision dans la théorie de la connaissance." Calderoni cited Berkeley's *New Theory of Vision* as the source of the theory of *prevision*. (On this, see the comments of Renauld, pp. 208–209; for Berkeley, see Appendix 5 below, and on this point, the notion of (i) discussed there.) One reason for Vailati's and Calderoni's emphatic and frequent appeal to a verifiability criterion of meaning and the concept of *prevision* is that they were impressed with the Peircean pragmatic thesis that meaning carries a futuritive reference (§ 21), "that the rational meaning of every proposition lies in the future," *CP* 5.427. Vailati quotes this passage in his review of Peirce's article (see note 35 above), *Scritti*, p. 640.

[91] "What Pragmatism is Like," pp. 352–353.

pragmatists to go the way of romantic irresponsibility on the one hand, or fanaticism on the other.[92]

While they were acutely responsive to the pragmatism of Peirce and James, to the diverse kinds of philosophizing in Europe, and to science and history, Vailati and Calderoni were never imitators. They adapted the important ideas of pragmatism to their own developing philosophic outlook. They were engaged in projecting the most original philosophy in Italy since the Renaissance, a philosophy with a thoroughly responsible interpretation of reason, but liberal enough in scope to allow attentive consideration of the various manifestations of human reason in human actions and institutions. At the root of this version of scientific and practical reason was a sanity deriving from the Greeks.

The more the pity, then, that the two architects of *pragmatista logica* did not have enough time to complete their work. One year after Calderoni's death, Italy was swept into the first world war.

§ 77. Summary

This sketchy survey of pragmatism in Europe is in the main negative. What has passed as pragmatism in European philosophical thought has not been distinctive of the essential and most important features of American pragmatism.[93] American pragmatism and European analogues in various forms of voluntaristic and practicalistic moral and psychological interpretations of experience and reason have the same roots in earlier post-Kantian philosophy. But it was the pragmatism of James, specifically his views on truth and the function of belief, combined with Schiller's humanism, that presented itself as pragmatism in Europe, and easily merged with similar movements on the continent. This general movement of ideas, anti-intellectualistic, anti-scientific, often proliferating in varied apologias for religious and mystical values, violent social or individual action, and ethical illiberalism and subjectivity, was one with which pragmatism has been associated, as progenitor or equivalent, unfortunately even among European intellectuals. The very different and technically more proficient pragmatism of Peirce, of James in his less popular writings, of Dewey and the Chicago School, of Mead and Lewis has hardly made itself known at all in Europe. And where this main body of American pragmatism has been studied and understood,[94] it has not proved very influential.

It must be acknowledged, finally, that James's failure to undertake a less popularly directed but more precise exposition of his pragmatism had some curious and undesirable consequences. Among his more enthusiastic disciples, the thesis

---

[92] See the important account by Vailati, "Le Mouvement Philosophique en Italie" (1907), *Scritti*, pp. 753–769. Also see the paper by Calderoni and Vailati, "Le origini e l'idea fondamentale del Pragmatismo."
[93] Excepting the work of Vailati and Calderoni.
[94] E.g., as by Lalande or Leroux. Again, Vailati and Calderoni are exceptions.

of the right to believe (like James's theory of truth to which it is related) seemed to be an invitation to intellectual irresponsibility, subjectivism, and fanaticism. That the will to believe could be loosely interpreted as a version of the will to power explains how and why Mussolini subscribed to pragmatism. Ironically, the democratic, pluralistic James, for whom the rights and pursuits of individuals are sacred, the James who hated "bigness" in all its forms, was thus mistakenly credited with being one of the spiritual ancestors of totalitarianism.

SOME PRAGMATIC CONSEQUENCES OF PRAGMATISM

Part Four

From its inception, pragmatism was never intended as a philosophy, or as a school or a new orthodoxy.

By those who contributed most to its development, it was conceived as a way of philosophizing, a method for dealing with problems. Peirce usually described pragmatism as a method of analysis (as we saw in § 21); on occasion he claimed that pragmatism "invokes a whole system of philosophy" (see Appendix 3). James envisioned pragmatism as a theory of meaning and of truth (§ 26), although, as we have several times noticed in Part Three, he did eventually think of it as a new philosophic "movement" and a "mission."[1] Dewey made limited use of 'pragmatism' in referring to his views; he preferred 'instrumentalism,' in which the methodological emphasis over the substantive, the regulative over the constitutive, is uppermost.[2] And much the same may be said of Mead and C. I. Lewis. Pragmatism, then, was neither at first nor thereafter mainly proposed as a system of philosophy or a calling for devotees and disciples. Indeed, much of its influence is to be found in disciplines other than professional philosophy.

The following chapters discuss the several ways in which pragmatism continues to be operative as one among other philosophic approaches upon the current intellectual scene. Specifically, the three main philosophic contributions that have come from pragmatism invite our attention in the next three chapters.

[1] See his Preface to *Pragmatism*, first paragraph.
[2] Thus his comment in Lamont, p. 26: "I have always limited my use of 'instrumentalism' to my theory of thinking and knowledge; the word 'pragmatism' I have used very little, and then with reserves."

CHAPTER ONE

The Methodological Spirit

§ 78. Fallibilism

Pragmatists neither invented nor are the sole subscribers to the doctrine that statements about matters of fact can never be known with certainty to be true. Let us deliberately bypass some of the problems accompanying this doctrine, including the difficulty in stating it clearly. For it is not always evident whether, as stated, the thesis purports to be an *argument* about the nature of empirical assertions (as it was for Plato, the ancient skeptics, and Hume), or a *definition* of empirical assertions (as it has come to be regarded since Kant).

Strictly speaking, for Peirce, fallibilism commits us to holding that any statement (or belief) contains an element of error—any, that is, except the assertion of fallibilism itself (see § 24). But the message of fallibilism extracted from the particular setting of Peirce's philosophy advised that no interpretation of facts is self-warranting, that every conceptual organization of experience is in principle subject to revision.[1] It is always possible, as James argued, and Lewis explained (§ 45), that new experience borne in on us may force us to readjust our working conceptual schemes.

Briefly, the principle of fallibilism has helped to activate the following approaches to three kinds of philosophic problems.

1) In our systematizing of knowledge, fallibilism enjoins us to acknowledge the presence of "conventional" procedures, and, thereby, of pluralities of possible constructions. That is, no one point of view (nor any part of one view) can claim to be unique and definitive in the codification of a subject matter.

An exemplary case of this recognition of conventional and plural possibilities in the conceptualization of experience is found in James's famous essay, "Does Consciousness Exist?" There James initiates a fundamental revision of the tra-

[1] "There are three things we can never hope to attain . . . , absolute certainty, absolute exactitude, absolute universality," CP 1.141.

ditional concepts of object and subject (or *thing* and *thought*). He reinterprets these as "functional attributes," or relations of a single postulated primitive stuff: "pure experience." The specific argument does not concern us at the moment, but the procedure does. James nowhere claims that he has drawn a "true" representation of the facts. He does claim, however, to have succeeded in avoiding the many notorious difficulties in the traditional concepts and their use while retaining what is useful in them. The effect is to preserve what is worth preserving of the older notions by providing them with their "pragmatic equivalents," while what does not need preservation, in this case *consciousness* (not *thought*, but the un-thing-like thing called "soul"), gets eliminated as a gratuitous obstacle to knowledge. This essay of James is a model of his interpretation and use of the pragmatic method of analysis.

2) Another effect of fallibilism is its promotion of inquiries concerning the *justification* of statements and claims of knowledge. A working suggestion of pragmatism is that questions of justification and justificatory procedures are not of one fixed kind; rather, they vary with the contexts peculiar to different areas of investigation in which such questions may arise.

Since fallibilism maintains, at the least, that our knowledge of facts is inexact and uncertain, it follows that, in addition to investigations of facts, there are always questions that can be raised about the justification of the procedures and the conclusions of inquiries. Where knowledge is prized and sought, fallibilism encourages inquiries into how knowledge-claims are established and justified. But how justificatory queries are elicited, if they are not to be dismissed as mere philosophical sport, is a function of the specific contexts in which they may illumine or be germane to actually occurring problems.

Philosophers have often demonstrated a knack for finding "problems" in the validation of statements in the sciences. As philosophic activity, this is innocent enough. But it becomes irresponsible when some of these problems and their grandiose or ingenious solutions are passed off as essential to conceptual clarity within science. There is cause for wonder, to choose a classic example, over the vast philosophic literature on induction and the "justification" of inductive inference which, purporting to be crucially relevant to the procedures of science, has been largely ignored by practicing scientists. Somehow science seems to have evolved on its own, even to the extent of being inductive when necessary, without philosophic crutches. This is not to deny all value to philosophic investigations of science. But if the suggestion of pragmatism is right, it behooves the philosopher of justificatory interests to familiarize himself with problems and procedures in those disciplines where these interests have reasonably practical consequences. This is to recognize the contexts and forms in which issues of justification come naturally rather than as superimposed gambits of logic.

3) One other effect of fallibilism, related to those just mentioned, is its function as a principle of caution and tentativeness in moral judgment and decisions of policy. For pragmatism, this is meant to convey something more than Peirce's oft-expressed imperative: "Do not block the way of inquiry" (a worthy injunc-

tion, alas, too often unheeded). It means more than that ethical commitments are subject, in principle, to modifications hinging upon their foreseeable practical consequences. It means that decisions of policy and value are open to critical revision and that their *justification* is a matter of inquiry—not the sheer tenacity of belief or closed conviction.

The process of justification, we noted above, depends in part upon the kind of situation in which a question of justification arises. Thus, very roughly, the quality and amount of information available in particular cases as to how moral ideals will function to produce certain satisfactions, the kind of problem and the urgency of the decision, the foreseeable consequences and their character—all figure in specific moral judgments and their critical evaluation.

In short, moral ideals function as hypotheses for *suggested* conduct in situations.[2] Moreover, a moral ideal characteristically conveys a permanently general suggestion of conduct, while moral situations are transient, particular occurrences.[3] Thus one of the tasks in making and evaluating moral decisions lies in establishing the relevance of proposed ideals to the specific conflicts of interests or uncertainty of aims that generate moral problems. The task is analogous to establishing the relevant initial conditions for which a hypothesis or law is applicable in constructing a scientific explanation. Viewing ideals as fallible, the validation of them in practice operates not so much through abstract critiques of idealisms or competitive ethical theorizing, but rather as an assessing of hypotheses. The assessment is of the relevance of ideally suggested conduct to the problem at hand, the applicability of an ideal and the predictable consequences were it to be acted upon and the effectiveness (or "value") of these consequences viewed in connection with the immediate problem and possible future moral deliberations.

Those human activities that happen to comprise what is called scientific method and judgment can be summed up synoptically as a way of *evaluating claims to knowledge*. So, at least, pragmatists have argued, holding that this is a lesson to be drawn from science if not from textbooks on methodology. The emphasis, for the moment, should be placed upon the notion of *evaluation*.[4] From this observation pragmatism has put forth a claim of its own: the objective procedures of evaluation in science do not differ in kind from those that govern moral decisions when those are rational or at all accountable. It is, of course, not denied that men come to moral decisions in any number of ways. The claim made by pragmatism is that responsible and rational moral decisions can be made[5] and that the logic of such decisions, the rationale for them, is the same as that of decisions in science.

---

[2] For the sense in which *suggestions* occur and function in inquiry, see § 39.

[3] Borrowing from Mill's famous definition of 'matter,' one can conjecture a rephrasing of the above: moral ideals are promises of permanent possibilities of satisfaction.

[4] For a related earlier context, see above, § 41 and § 46.

[5] The claim is bolder than simply holding that moral decisions should be rational or objective (this being a moral judgment itself). The claim is that in fact when moral judgments occur in any thoughtful or deliberative fashion, they exhibit a pattern common to all modes of judgment. The pattern is that of inquiry for Dewey (§§ 39, 41); for Lewis, see § 46. The full theory of valuation is the subject of ch. 3 below.

The difference is only a difference of subject matter, not of procedure. For the subject matter encountered in moral judgment consists of a complex and over-lapping variety of "facts": human interests, energies, and institutions; biological, social, and historical conditions, and so on. But the method of inquiry, judgment, and validation is not for this reason unempirical or of a categorically different kind.

How is this claim to be substantiated? Surely not by attempts at a *reductio ad absurdum* of all counterclaims. Accordingly, it was long a major concern of Dewey to develop the logical structure and exhibit the leading principles of moral judgment and inquiry (Dewey's theory of moral judgment is treated in Chapter Three of the present Part), and one need not be a devotee of his philosophy to appreciate his fundamental and suggestive contributions to this end. For Dewey (as we saw at the outset of § 35), the most challenging problem facing con-temporary philosophy was the establishment of continuity and possibilities of mutual enrichment between natural science and morals.

More recently, as we saw in Chapter Four of Part Two, C. I. Lewis undertook in a major work this same task of developing the theory and objective principles of moral judgment.[6] However, in candor, this claim of pragmatism stands as an unfinished and theoretical program, one deserving of further investigation and patient elaboration.

But there are other live consequences of pragmatism yet to consider.

§ 79.   *Pragmatic Contextualism*

Our experience in and of the world is an active affair to which we contribute (even by the least *reaction*)—an affair mostly of discernible things happening mostly in discernible ways. For while our directly encountered experience is not always in-telligible and may require considerable detours of thought to become so, that our species has survived is reason enough for refusing to regard ordinary experience as a gross deception. Now, things observed happening in observed ways occasion our talk about them. But how we proceed to talk and what we talk about depends, too, upon the problems and purposes we have in mind.

This is to affirm again the inescapable relevance of contexts to our under-standing of talk, of thought, and of experience. What is experienced and how, what is said and how, are understandable relative to a context. Supplying the references of 'what' and 'how' in each case specifies a context. Consider the ex-ample (drawn from Lewis[7]) of a pen on a desk. The pragmatist feels no sting of conscience in believing something to be there. It was never the purpose of pragmatism to deny that the world exists.[8] Nor was the aim to show that common-

---

[6] See above, § 46.
[7] See *Mind and the World Order*, p. 49.
[8] Dewey was occasionally accused of being an idealist, because, it was alleged, he denied the "reality" of the external world, or "external" objects. The accusation was based on what Dewey said about *experience* (for troubles over this notion, see § 36 above). To say we

sense realism is discredited in theory if not in practice. But pragmatists have argued that a consistent and well formulated realism, one that does not come to grief upon its own assumptions and procedures, one that is able to account for experience rather than be driven to wholly skeptical conclusions, must be particularly careful about the kind of assumptions it makes and uncommonly sensitive to how they are stated and what they imply.[9]

It is not the external world that pragmatists have found impossible to accept intellectually, but rather the habitual conclusions to which philosophers have been led by how they used the words 'the' and 'external' in purporting to talk about the external world. Those uses and their habitual consequences are treacherous, which much of the pragmatic critique of various philosophies of realism has been aimed at exposing. The critique was not undertaken to "save" the world from philosophic skepticism or from idealism or to "justify" common sense. It was to save philosophy from itself and its periodic tendency to take some of its irresponsibilities too seriously.

The pen on the desk will make concrete what these generalizations do not, and protect us from the seduction of platitudes. We say "here is a pen," pointing or otherwise expanding the directive for 'here.' A geometer, with purely professional interests for the moment, might report his observation of a cylinder; geometry knows no pens. A psychologist will see a stimulus object or perhaps a phallic symbol. A sociologist will see a structured situation with a high potential of utility for manually patterned communication—who knows what sociologists see? A schoolboy, with the wrong kind of schooling, may see an enemy there.

Each of these direct encounters with something experienced is real. It would be folly to dispute whether the object encountered was "really" a pen or a cylinder. For this would be an undeliberately deliberate confusion of object and point of view, a confusion soon seen to inspire the mistaken principle that since each single experienced object or each collection of them is one, there is but one way of interpreting objects or our experience of them. The word 'really' does a yeoman's service in behalf of this misleading principle. To say the pen is "really" a

---

can only know things *by* experience and can only know *what* we experience was mistakenly supposed to imply that all we know *is* experience, that what we experience is experience. For an effective answer from Dewey that *what* we experience is objects and portions of the world, see *Experience and Nature*, p. 4a.

As we have seen in Part I, especially §§ 5, 6, the problem of how we know there is an "external world" is clearly stated by Descartes in the *Meditations*, and results from Locke's analysis of ideas and knowledge. In our own time the problem is stated by Russell in *Our Knowledge of the External World*. See Dewey's acute critical analysis of Russell's argument in *Essays in Experimental Logic*, ch. 11. Dewey's detailed analysis is initiated from a question he puts earlier in the book: "Under what conditions is the [question of the] relation of knower to known an intelligible question?" (p. 268). A major part of his analysis consists in showing that the "problem" results from unnoticed assumptions and confusions as to *how* it has been formulated. For further comments on Dewey's argument, and its historical background, see Appendix 1, sec. C below, notes 54, 56.

[9] The classical instance is Locke; for the issue, see § 6. Locke's *Essay* commences with the assumptions of seventeenth-century science, a world of material particles obeying mechanical laws, and a tribute to "the incomparable Mr. Newton." Analysis of those assumptions leads Locke later to conclude we can have no "scientific" (i.e., certain) knowledge of bodies.

354 IV. SOME PRAGMATIC CONSEQUENCES

cylinder, or "really" a collection of subatomic particles is a sly way of assigning a priority to a context and point of view while seeming to uphold the sacred obligation to respect, come what may, the objectivity of objects and the truths of experience.

The pragmatist, not overly impressed with the revelation that objects are objective, suspicious of the undeclared motives that have led to the weighting of priorities in favor of certain contexts over others (these days, those of physical theory), views the consequences of all this as especially sorry. To see why, we need go back once more to the pen on the table.

We have observed how the encounter with the simple fact "there is a pen" invests a possible variety of different contexts with widely different interpretations of the fact. That *something* is experienced is not for the moment in question. If it were, if in each context in which x is said to be a pen, a cylinder, etc., the statement asserting x to exist is false, then all of the statements about what x is are false. But outside of outright falsehood in every context, what is of importance pragmatically is not a futile declaration of probity or superiority between contexts, but the grounds and validation of judgments within the respective contexts. The contexts thus acknowledged do not have to be taken as mutually competitive attempts to dominate the market of reality.

We can make our choices among the conceptual schemes that have evolved and proved effective in different contexts, the schemes of common sense, geometry, psychology, and the like. Generally, this choice of schemes will be a bit like choosing to invest in enterprises doing business in a common market, and more like choices of different economic systems—systems to be sure impinging upon one another at points and whose points of contact may require various special arrangements for avoiding conceptual friction. Each system has its overall merits and disadvantages viewed according to one or another of our overall purposes and interests. The choice is thus pragmatic, as between systems and contexts, just as in the narrower sphere of contexts once chosen, the ensuing choices of certain conceptual procedures as against others is similarly pragmatically motivated.

The illustration of the pen suggests one sort of point of contact between several differing interpretive schemes. The pen represents one directly encountered experience in each of a variety of contexts. The pen is a single object. Its encountering is a single event taking each of the contexts singly, but many events taking contexts collectively. Each context provides a legitimate way of encountering the pen, subject to internally applied critical standards. Abstracting and systematically avoiding contextually bound references to what the pen is and how it is encountered, we call it 'object' or 'datum.' These are attempts to talk in or over contexts while remaining neutral as to the contexts themselves and to the sundry specific modes of encountering and interpreting experience. The techniques of modern logic are especially helpful in enabling a contextually neutral discourse to function with ease and precision.

There are, of course, other philosophic positions than the one we have been picturing in a necessarily very general way as pragmatic contextualism. There have been various attempts to find in certain contexts and types of conceptual schemes an authoritative preeminence among the ways man encounters the world. One has given the crown and scepter to the language of modern physical theory; another has hoped to enthrone a language of sense-data or conceptually innocent blow-by-blow reports of raw experience.

The first position, and probably the most popular, has exhibited a remarkable penchant for courting intellectual disasters. One discovers, for example, that not only is the language of physics made preferential, but somehow that language *falsifies* all others. By obscuring distinctions between language (or conceptualization) and objects (experienced), the very objects and contents of ordinary experience are falsified as well. "Common sense imagines that when it sees a table it sees a table. This is a gross delusion."[10] Russell's skill built, but did not save, the famous two tables with which Eddington began his Gifford Lectures. One table is the solid, familiar object of common sense, the other, the whirling particles of physics. Only the latter table is real, or "really there."[11] The table of common sense is an "inherited prejudice." But Eddington luckily did not follow logically the implications of his analysis all the way. If he had, he could not have delivered his lectures. For, logically, there were two Eddingtons, and only one, the common-sense Eddington, could write and lecture. But it is that Eddington, unfortunately, who must be relegated to the limbo of unreals, a mere shade of inherited prejudice discoursing among shadows.

We saw this form of Democritean intolerance guiding a reflection of Galileo's, in Part One, § 5. The modern expressions of this "scientific" point of view scarcely deviate at all from the old. But this is curious when one considers how much science itself has changed since the fifth century B.C. or the sixteenth century.

This first position reduces essentially to the following claim: No statement purporting to be about matters of fact can possibly be true unless made in or translatable into the vocabulary of modern physics. This leaves one wondering how true statements about the world were ever uttered prior to the present century (or even how the thesis of the first position can be stated by its advocates). But since there appears to be no justification whatever for this claim, we need not pursue it further here.

The second position, quite the other extreme of the first, consists of several differing but similarly motivated and allied forms of phenomenalism. Thus, priority of interpretive scheme and context is sought in immediate sense impressions (sometimes construed as recurring clusters of single sense stimulations, sometimes as recurring responses to types of stimulation[12]), or, alternatively, in immediately observable objects. The former, a more radical phenomenalism, is

---

[10] Russell, *The ABC of Relativity*, p. 213.
[11] Eddington, *The Nature of the Physical World*, p. xii.
[12] I.e., either where one or more monetary stimulus events are taken as fundamental, or where qualities are basic. On the former view, 'red' (for example) is the name of a class of sense events; on the latter it names an individual (and pervasive though scattered) quality.

distinguished from the latter, physicalism, by its refusal to countenance such inferential constructs as hypothetical physical objects *of* impressions among its ultimate materials (or in its primitive vocabulary). In any case, this second position differs from the first of the previous paragraph in its ingenuous methodological spirit. Whereas the first, in effect, condemns all contexts but one, the other seeks a pooling of the empirical content of all other contexts into one. And this primary phenomenalistic context is treated in a language descriptive solely of immediate experience or by observational terms.

While we are not concerned here with the detailed development of these alternative points of view, we can note that this second position is also confronted with problems, problems not like those of the first position, but of comparable seriousness. The paramount difficulty is that there is little evidence for, and many reasons against the thesis that a phenominalistic context or language can be made to accommodate the empirical content of all (or many possible) others. The bank of immediate sense impressions—or the "language" thereof—is simply not able to provide the cash value equivalent in meaning for many expressions of undeniable import in stating and establishing empirical knowledge.[13]

As an experimental program, instructive and inventive, the position of phenomenalism is to be welcomed. How far and in what ways can our several ordinary and scientific interpretations of experience be systematically absorbed, without loss of significance, into a presumably simpler and unified scheme of sense experience? But taken as a general criterion of empirical significance, i.e., where program leaves off and pogrom begins, the second position becomes a very expensive luxury.

For instance, since most of the fundamental concepts of theoretical physics do not seem likely ever to be brought under this criterion, we are obliged to treat them as devoid of empirical significance. For this reason alone it is not difficult to guess where the sacrifices will finally be made. A philosophic criterion of meaningful sentences will hardly prevail against the established utility of theoretical concepts in science. And against scientific needs, philosophic luxuries must give way. Where necessity is the mother of invention, delinquent fancies are doomed to perish.

Let us not fail to recognize, in this cursory survey of other points of view, the existence of two others receiving much attention these days: that of the existentialist, which finds the ground of human experience or the world as such "absurd" or "meaningless"; and a psychoanalytic view of "irrational" and "unconscious motivations" affecting man's attempts to interpret and conceptualize his experience.

Pragmatically, both views deserve to be taken seriously. Both at least claim to provide valuable insights and information concerning human nature and experience. Where the pragmatist becomes a critic is in his demand that the *contexts* in

---

[13] For more on this topic see Carnap; Hempel, *Fundamentals of Concept Formation,* pp. 20 ff.; Nagel, *The Structure of Science,* pp. 117 ff.; Quine, *From a Logical Point of View,* ch. 2.

which these claims are made be carefully specified. Without some prior understanding of the specific kinds of conditions for which these claimed insights are relevant and informative, and of the criteria determining them to be so, one is at a loss to know what these points of view convey or communicate. The need for contextual references becomes more obvious when one reflects that to assert of any subject whatever that it has the character of being "absurd," "meaningless," or "irrational" tacitly presupposes *some* criterion of non-absurdity, meaning, and rationality. For surely the judgments that the world is meaningless or that men are subject to irrational motives are not themselves to be taken as meaningless in the one instance or irrational in the other. But this request for a criterion is simply another way of asking about the kind of contexts in which these claims to knowledge purport to inform and be of value. It is asking for the point of these points of view.

Our survey of pragmatic contextualism can be summed up thus: Our experience of the world yields many possible distinctions and possible forms of conceptualization; the stuff of experience is rich with potentialities (Aristotelian *dynameis*).[14] Which potentialities of what experienced things happen to engage our attention and prompt appropriate modes of discourse is largely a matter of past conditioning and future expectations. The points of view from which we judge objects and our encounters with them are socially conditioned. The language we use and the habitual responses we have learned to rely on are socially inherited instruments of interpretation. Conscious of this much or not, we adapt as best we can to the pressure of continuing experience, taking this point of view or that depending on the context—that is, depending upon what ways of accounting for experience are available to us and which among these ways seems most called for. In context, what we at any time take to be happening is a function of past experience, available interpretative equipment, and the gentle force of continuously felt purposes.

The methodically sound respect for contexts, it was argued, discourages misdirected and fruitless controversy between philosophies or converging philosophical perspectives, and between philosophers unaware or unable to acknowledge that, pragmatically, truths of fact are gained in a plurality of ways. Whether the pen is pen or cylinder was a deliberately simplified case. Whether certain "data" of behavior are to be interpreted as physical or mental, and how these interpretations proceed, is less simple. Applied to the traditional setting of the mind-body problem, pragmatic contextualism has its critical parallel in the currently popular doctrine of the category mistake.[15] Mistaking categories is confusing contexts. The procedures relevant and justified pragmatically in one context are wrongly supposed to be relevant and justified in another.

[14] And rich with *possibilities*, it might be added, while recognizing serious difficulties in being clear about the important concept of physical possibility, a subject discussed in Appendix 7.
[15] See Ryle, ch. 1.

§ 80.   The Given, A Priori, and Logic

The pragmatist's fidelity to contexts has not proved so absorbing as to lead him to overlook other important theoretical matters. There is, for example, the fact of the continuity of certain contexts and recurrent kinds of experience. And this has led some, notably Dewey, to try to formulate how and in what ways the operations involved in making judgments in a given situation are related to (or "coextensive" with) operations developed in others. For Dewey, there is a continuity of operations within inquiry and also a genetic and historical continuity of operations (or "logical forms") among inquiries.

Dewey was interested in the historical fact that in the evolution of knowledge, certain kinds of general propositions seem to undergo a logical evolution with respect to their function in inquiries. That is, the logical character of some propositions becomes reinterpreted or "transformed" in the course of successive inquiries and the general advance of knowledge. Thus, in the relatively youthful stages of a science, a certain proposition may have emerged as an experimental result of inquiry. But in later stages, and in later inquiries, the once experimental hypothesis may function as a formal condition to be satisfied, as a procedural rule (or criterion) of successful investigations. What was once a contingent result of inquiry is preserved as a necessary condition in some further inquiries. The history of science supplies examples of such—propositions that at one time were viewed as empirical statements while at another functioned in a definitional capacity as standards of organization and adequacy in the acquisition of knowledge. For example, the statements 'The sum of the angles of a (Euclidean) triangle equals two right angles' and 'A whale is a mammal' can be imagined at one time to have been understood as empirical assertions based upon observation and experiment. At a later date, within the developing structure of scientific knowledge, these statements may function as partial definitions and among the logically necessary conditions to be fulfilled when something is said to be a *triangle* or a *whale*.[16]

[16] There is a large body of literature, explanatory and controversial, on this subject. The classical example of the issue is that of interpreting Newton's second law of motion. When the law is expressed in the form of the equation '$F = ma$,' the question of interpretation is whether the law is a statement of empirical fact or a definition of 'force.' For Dewey, presumably, this law would now be interpreted as a guiding principle of inquiries in mechanics, when the motions of bodies are under consideration (for the logic of the propositions in question here, see Appendix 6, sec. C below). It is thus not a simple truth or falsehood of *fact*, nor a nominal definition of 'force,' but an informative principle whose use may contribute to the organization of inquiry by helping to determine the selection of relevant suggestions (ideas and facts, cf. the latter part of § 39) and by directing investigators to certain features of the motion of bodies to be expected in the course of analysis. The law, thus, viewed, is relevant or not depending on the kind of inquiry taking place. But if it is relevant as a guiding principle, it also functions as one necessary condition of the success and adequacy of inquiry. In fact, however, Newton's second law has not proved to be indispensable or irreplaceable as a guiding principle.

For a discussion of the above issue, see Nagel, *The Structure of Science*, pp. 186–192; cf. also his analysis of scientific laws, ch. 4. For more on guiding principles, see the chapter that follows.

Let us notice in passing that the suggestion in the foregoing and following paragraphs, concerning the transformation of propositions, has its origin in Kant's doctrine of regulative Ideas (see § 12). The insight that impressed Dewey and Lewis was that in certain stages of the evolution of knowledge some propositions once enjoying a "constitutive" status might undergo a loss of this, while simultaneously gaining a "regulative" function in the process of continual revision and reorganization of the system of empirical knowledge.

We cannot here go into the details of this apparent transformation. The change of function of propositions is often construed as effecting a corresponding transformation of meaning. The statement of fact is reinterpreted as an a priori truth.

The same or closely analogous reasoning guides Dewey's conception of a priori principles and the formal character of logical propositions. In the past, Dewey observes, a priori propositions were regarded by most philosophers as distinctive on account of their supposed possession of self-evident truth, their self-certification, or their truth simply by virtue of their meaning. But Dewey's theory of truth, and his acceptance of fallibilism, denies this. Instead he argues for what he calls a "functional" interpretation of the a priori content of propositions. Briefly, the argument consists in reviewing the role of such propositions in and among inquiries. Even the "laws" of logic, on this view, are regarded as postulates and guiding principles of inquiry. A priori principles represent stipulations and rules of procedure whose central function is to clarify and expedite the particular operations occurring in particular inquiries by formulating the most general "conditions to be satisfied" and to be observed in every successful inquiry.

Lewis (as we saw in Part Two, Chapter Four), impressed with the inventiveness of our rational powers and the variety of different consistent formal systems the mind is able to construct, has taken a different view of the a priori. Human experience as *given*, can be *taken* and interpreted in any one of a number of possible conceptual schemes and categories. A priori propositions, "purely" logical implications, provide connecting links between interpretive categories and establish the sentential interconnections of completed schemes. A priori truths thus occur within and through the analysis of conceptual schemes. But what is said to be the case about experience (indeed, what is sayable and how experience is interpreted) is relative to one or another conceptual scheme. Outside of esthetic preferences or a speculative interest in exploring ideas, our choices of the conceptual schemes we use for talking about and analyzing experience represent decisions of convenience and utility. The choices are pragmatic.[17]

Alive to the world in which he finds himself, man is distinguished from other animals by his skill in communicating his experience. Not all communication is scientific; explanations and predictions of experience are not the only uses of language, important though these are. Furthermore, some explaining and a great

---

[17] Lewis writes: "The truths of experience must always be relative to our chosen conceptual systems," and the choices we make "will be determined, consciously or not, on pragmatic grounds." For this expressed view and a further discussion of it, see § 45.

deal of predicting goes on in communicative forms not even vaguely classified as scientific. But what is common to all communication of experience is the occurrence of experiences and acts of interpretation. Generally, then, empirically directed discourse and knowledge continues by means of two continuously occurring conditions: sense experience and conceptual interpretation.

The two conditions just noted represent, philosophically and analytically, distinct aspects of what is perhaps in fact a single behavioral process. In any event, there is evidence of the revival and influence of pragmatism in recent discussions of this kind concerning the nature of empirical knowledge.

Pragmatists from Pierce onward have maintained that sense data in their most immediate and raw form are at most a necessary but not sufficient condition of knowledge. The position derives not from Hume but from Berkeley. That sensations do occur and that we may often be aware of their occurrence is a fact not denied by the pragmatist. But when stimulations or data become more than given or simply had, when they become recognized or identified, they have undergone interpretation. The difference consists in what distinguishes the pinprick on the finger and neural responses, with their identification as "pain occurring in finger." Stimulus events become cognitive events as well when the stimulus *given* is *taken* as a sign *of* certain conditions. But for something to be a sign presupposes some principle of interpretation; habits, biological, cultural, and linguistic, provide the interpretants. Here as well, for the pragmatist, is the root of the probable and predictive element in all empirical knowledge. Stimulus events when interpreted, when taken as signs, occasion predictions:[18] from "I feel a pain" to "something is pricking my finger"; or from compound inferences "I see an apple" to "that apple will have a sweet taste." The signs and the predictions need not, and usually do not, take a consciously expressed form—as when I see the apple and my mouth waters.

The pragmatist is hence led to reject the notion of simple sense-data experience of a non-inferential sort. If he grants that such sense events do at all occur, he argues against the view that these occurrences in themselves have any cognitive significance.[19] And he argues as well against the claim that classes of these events constitute the content of empirical knowledge. Indeed, the notion of pure sense experience, the real thing before becoming sicklied o'er with the pale cast of thought, is doubtful in principle and in fact. In principle there is a question of whether the notion itself or evidence for it is suspectible of formulation at all in a way that admits of test cases. There are problems in knowing how to interpret what is described as an undescribed and uninterpreted subject matter. And, in fact, there is considerable evidence that events of sense experience, either as stimulus or response or both, do not occur as simple sense atoms nor as pure streams.

---

[18] This is a basic theme in all the pragmatic analyses of knowledge; hence, it pervades the chapters of Part II. But that the predictions based on sense experience take a *probable* form (stated clearly by Berkeley, cf. Appendix 5) and hence, that an empirical theory of knowledge calls for theory of probability, was set forth most carefully by Peirce and C. I. Lewis. This was also a special interest of Ramsey (§ 71).

[19] James sometimes did not subscribe to this view.

As to the other aspect of our experiential pursuits, that of conceptualization, we find logic enlisted along with matters of fact. With good reason, we prize a coherent and efficient organization of our conceptual gleanings from and predictive dealings with the continually experienced world. Where logical interests are operative, order and economy are introduced into our conceptual frameworks. Needless excrescences of structure, recondite and circuitous channels of inference are thus eliminated or replaced by something simpler. Logical interests will also often effect disclosures or otherwise hidden connections and unsuspected stretches of conceptual implications.

For some time it has been generally agreed that where logical interests are paramount in the organization of conceptual systems, logical necessity and a priori truths are to be found. The truths of experience may be relative to various conceptual schemes, but are in any case the same in resting upon matters of fact. These are "synthetic" truths. As statements, they are thought to be distinct in kind from those of an "a priori" or "logically necessary" character. For the latter have their truth anchored in the meanings of their terms, and are hence true independently of matters of fact. These latter are *analytic* truths.[20]

The distinction between *synthetic* and *analytic* truths, meanings, or statements is a familiar enough doctrine in modern philosophy. Advanced by Leibniz and Hume, and urged by Kant, it tends to be taken for granted, but has recently been challenged. It is argued, most forcibly by Quine,[21] that the synthetic-analytic distinction fails to be clearly drawn; and that the remedy lies not in a search for a definitive criterion of discreteness of kinds, but in abandoning the assumption that we are faced with anything more than a difference of degree.

Thus what was once held to be the essentially impervious, hence essentially unrelated content of analytic statements to matters of fact, is viewed not as an inevitable dictate of the nature of things, but as a human contrivance. Analytic statements turn out to be those segments of our conceptual schemes which are most protected and least likely to be revised in the event that internal simplifications or unforeseen occurrences of fact stimulate conceptual repairs.

It happens that the most striking effects of this proposed reconsideration of the synthetic-analytic distinction are not the most relevant to us here. What is especially surprising, judged by the now customary interpretations of logical and mathematical laws, is that these so-called logically necessary statements are not immune from possible revisions, rare as the possibility may be.[22] Logical and mathematical laws are pictured by Quine as the centrally situated statements of our conceptual schemes for interpreting experience. And these statements are remotely connected, via a spreading network of intermediate statements, to those more directly conditioned by experience. Still, there is some question as to what sort of repercussions or readjustments, begun among statements about

20 This topic, beyond the few observations made here, is resumed in Appendix 6.
21 *From a Logical Point of View*, ch. 2. See also Appendix 6 below.
22 In addition to the aforementioned book, see Quine's lucid statement of his view in *Methods of Logic*, Introduction. Also see Appendix 6 below.

facts, would eventuate in revisions of the laws of logic and mathematics.[23]

But what is relevant for us here is the renewed suggestion that logical principles, the a priori forms of discourse, are both discerned and appraised, not according to certain inherent characteristics in their possession, but according to their value and function in the continuous organization and interpretation of experience. Whatever the specific difficulties may be in an outright rejection of the synthetic-analytic distinction, for this is a matter of controversy at present, one indirect side effect has been to philosophize anew concerning the subject matter of logic in a way that harks back to Dewey's instrumentalism. For in giving up any hard and fast "absolute" separation of statements or truths into two classes or kinds, proponents of this new view remind us that we are not thereby deprived of the lingering uses and left-over descriptive value of the old distinction. We can still continue, though confessedly in a vague way, to describe those portions of a conceptual scheme that have been adjudged a highly protective status against revisions—by reason of their crucial role within the system as a whole—as logically "necessary." We can describe those statements of a less central sort, whose possible revisions would not entail vast disturbances of the entire system, as "contingent" or "synthetic." But in so viewing logical structures, we are guided by considerations of their definite and related *functions* within systems and in systematically organized investigations of experience. We are making critically pragmatic distinctions, in given contexts, of the forms of conceptualization. But these are in large part distinctions of the instruments and operations necessary to the overall aim of conceptualization: effective and reliable communication.

We can bring this review of some of the methodological issuings of pragmatism to a close with a final observation.

Pragmatic contextualism, we have seen, is in part a defense of the legitimacy of the plurality of modes by which men experience and describe the world. It is in part an attempt to develop a consistent and inclusive set of philosophic distinctions for interpreting and clarifying recurrent and dominant—because socially conditioned—modes of experience and expression. Ideally this attempt would issue in a philosophic critique, a comprehensive theory of experience and communication.

[23] This is to ask, making use of the traditional distinction, how a logically possible statement (of fact) could contradict (or necessitate a revision of) a logically necessary statement. The example Quine offers is an allusion to proposals for the construction of a logical system of quantum mechanics. The proposal involves abandoning certain familiar "laws," e.g., that of excluded middle, and the development of a many-valued logic. While this is cited as an instance of the revision of logical laws for achieving conceptual simplicity (in this case, simplicity in the scheme of quantum mechanics), it is not clear how the evidence supports Quine's view. For is this a *revision* of a law of logic, somehow necessitated *within* a conceptual scheme; or is it the construction of a scheme in which a law, familiar to other schemes, is deliberately abandoned altogether? There is an additional difficulty in contemplating, say, the revision of excluded middle in the system of *Principia Mathematica*. Would this be a revision of the system, or simply its replacement by another system? At any rate, one wonders how the decision not to make use of a (so-called logically necessary) law in one system—for whatever reason—is evidence of the "possibility" that statements of experience might occur within some system S_1, and prove to be incompatible with the logical laws of S_1 and thereby force the latter to be abrogated.

The ideal, were it seriously entertained, calls for an obviously ambitious effort. It would require an extensive empirical study of the conditions and kinds of contexts that occasion characteristic types of experience. And it would require investigation of the characteristic modes of expression that function in these contexts: in ordinary situations, in the sciences, in the arts, and in philosophy. It would require an analysis of what is common and peculiar to how these "languages" or modes of expression function and to the procedures of evaluation that occur in each and are common to them all.

To this end, and to the even more general goal of understanding man and the world and the arts of rational improvement, pragmatism has not advanced in one grand sweep. Its movements have been sporadic, often disconnected, and increasingly hesitant. Allied more than not with the critical spirit of modern British "analysis" concerned with the morphology and phenomenology of the philosophic uses and misuses of language; allied, too, with logical empiricism in its pursuit of a responsible philosophic grasp of the structure and procedures of scientifically warranted knowledge; proposing to extend the objective procedures for evaluating knowledge-claims to evaluating social and moral experience and ideals—pragmatism contains latent possibilities for important syntheses of current trends in philosophy. Whether synthesis is to be looked for in philosophy as a renewal of vitality or avoided as encouraging ersatz products is an open question.

CHAPTER TWO

The Instrumentalist Interpretation

of the Structure of Knowledge

§ 81. Logic and the Structure of Science

It is possible to give an illustrative and perhaps more pertinent bent to some of the comments on pragmatic contextualism in the previous chapter. This can be done by turning to one or two issues in contemporary philosophizing over the framework of science. We may thus hope to pass from the ingenuous description of several ideas and attitudes of modern pragmatism to an application of the same in a context—a move from soliciting insights to testing them in use.

Logicians scrutinizing the logical structure of scientific knowledge are in general agreement that formulations of scientific laws and theories constitute a subclass of universal statements of the form: 'All A is B,' or 'For any x, if Fx then Gx,' where the terms 'A' and 'B' or predicative terms 'F' and 'G' may be quite complicated, and call for considerable expansion and subtleties of interpretation. Indeed, thus stated, these are deliberate oversimplifications of what might and could serve as formalizations of most scientific laws. But the simplifications conceded, we are afforded an access over otherwise troublesome and difficult matters of logical analysis so necessary to a fully adequate formalization of laws but unnecessary to us here. It is conceded, also, that other issues rooted in the same soil as to varied kinds of universal statements that do not qualify as laws shall quietly be ignored, an insular attitude all but unforgiveable except that it keeps us from getting bogged down before half way to our destination. The destination here, it should be explained, is the instrumentalist[1] and pragmatic interpretation of laws

---

[1] A variety of thinkers, often of quite different philosophic persuasions, have contributed to what will be called in this chapter the *instrumentalist* view of theories, laws, and theoretical terms. We are, of course, concerned with the pragmatists here. But, in general, in addition to references cited in pages to come, see: Ramsey, *The Foundations of Mathematics*, pp. 194 ff. (and § 71); Ryle, pp. 120–125; Toulmin, chs. 3–4; W. H. Watson, ch. 3. For further references to and discussion of the position, see Nagel, *The Structure of Science*, pp. 129–140.

and theories in scientific inquiry and explanation. It is convenient, but not necessary, to confine our attention to scientific subject matters, narrowly construed as natural science, while recalling Dewey's liberalized conception of "science" as the attainment of any kind of knowledge through the process of inquiry.

It may be noted first, and in passing, that such seemingly innocuous, ordinary, and "unscientific" pronouncements as "here is a glass of water" or "there is a stone" or "the knife is rusty" are theory-laden and delivered within and through an established conceptual fabric of laws and lawlike generalizations. Thus in using the word 'stone' in "there is a stone," a tacit assumption is made as to a certain kind of existing substance exhibiting certain invariant characteristics (among these, certain dispositional properties such as *hardness*, i.e., *would not be scratched* under such and such conditions, the elaboration of which, following Peirce—§ 21 above—invokes theoretical principles and general conditionals). Hence, what have sometimes been supposed to be simple and direct statements of observed facts come in for their share of theoretical complexity. And the supposedly sharp cleavage between *theoretical* and *observational* statements (e.g., see §§ 27, 79) in all but an artificially constructed linguistic taxonomy is a dubious fiction.[2] In use, "there is a stone" is made sense of through the supplementary, if tacit premiss, '(x) (if x is stone, then . . .)' which, when filled in, stands as a law of natural kinds or substances.[3]

It is the instrumentalist conception of the status of laws chiefly with respect to their function, i.e., their uses in scientific procedure, that now concerns us. The pragmatic or instrumental view of the controlling logical features of scientific inquiry and explanation was motivated in large part by an attempt to resolve several longstanding philosophic problems as to the logical warrant and reliability of scientific laws and theories taken as assertions about the world and what there is.

These problems are the following. Historically, philosophers have uniformly had recourse to some conception of *truth* in defining and explaining the nature of knowledge. Uniformity and agreement does not characterize these conceptions of truth, nor, accordingly, the versions (or senses) of 'knowledge.' But despite this record of intellectual vicissitudes, general agreement has prevailed this far: in some sense of 'truth' (employed in reference to what constitutes a true thought, or statement), truth is to be counted as a necessary (but not sufficient) condition of knowledge. Thus, whatever constitutes *knowledge* of some subject matter, to possess that knowledge is to be in possession of some truth (i.e., variously considered residing in thoughts, statements, relations, etc.) concerning it. The problems already alluded to above are now stated simply: In what sense are

[2] I am suggesting here that any alleged absolute cleavage between theoretical terms and observational expressions is a mistake. But I do not object to *distinctions* of these relative to certain levels of scientific language. Thus, relative to quantum physics, the theoretical language of classical physics could be taken as an observational language. For the source of this idea, see Bernays.
[3] See, e.g., Campbell, ch. 3; Nagel, *The Structure of Science*, pp. 31n., 75–76. The symbolic formulation is to be read: 'For anything x, if x is a stone, then. . . .'

the laws and theories of science true?[4] Laws and theories, as we have sketchily suggested so far, are to be construed as universal statements, and sequences or logical concatenations of the same. Under what conditions, then, are these said to be true, true of the world? To make more sense of the question and also to cut it down to manageable size for our present purposes, let us take a brief look at a few historical factors in its emergence—thus indicating some of the reasoning behind it and how we intend to pursue it.

§ 82.   Some Historical Factors

When Aristotle began to analyze the kinds of logical structures by which men reasoned from premisses to conclusions, he drew attention to two sorts of premisses, *universal* and *particular*. Thus, the universal affirmative (taken note of some pages back) is 'All *A* is *B*' (or negative, 'No *A* is *B*'), and the particular, 'Some *A* is *B*' (or negative, 'Some *A* is not *B*'). Aristotle argued that a necessary condition of any valid deduction in a syllogism required at least one universal statement among the premisses of the syllogism. Moreover, in the case of scientific knowledge (i.e., scientific demonstration, which always takes a syllogistic form), the premisses of demonstration had to be true, to be known to be true, and to be prior to and better known than the conclusions derived from them.[5] These logical conditions of scientific knowledge are related, but not identical with, Aristotle's dictum noted much earlier (§ 19) that scientific knowledge is of the universal, perception is of particulars. Related also, in stemming from Aristotle and Plato, is the long-adopted view that, given some exceptions, the whole body of scientific knowledge at any time is expressible through two interconnected modes grading off from one another respectively in universality and particularity. Thus arose the long-established precedent for thinking of the system of "science" as comprising stretches of universal discourse, "purely theoretical" assertions, "abstract laws" on the one side, and particular statements "of facts" on the other. "System," wherein proof and explanation are made possible, is thought of as the logically ordered linkage of universal statements with one another and with the sets and portions of particular statements grounded in turn in experience.

The source of inspiration in this classical vision of science is the spirit of de-

---

[4] For the purposes of this discussion, no attempt to demarcate clearly laws and theories is needed here. Examples of laws as universal statements, of theories as logically interconnected sets of universal statements, are readily found in the sciences. But so, too, are less easily discountable exceptions, of universal statements that are not laws, and interrelated sets of such statements that are not theories.

[5] *Posterior Analytics* I. 2. Actually Aristotle does not state these conditions so much in the spirit of conditions to be satisfied as simply the essential features of what it is to be a scientific demonstration.

For Aristotle, '*A*' and '*B*' symbolize non-empty classes of individuals, and the above statement-forms are schematic representations for affirming that all (or some) individuals of class *A* are (or are not) included in—or members of—class *B*. Difficulties of obscurity have been long noted, of needed distinctions concerning individual, class, and the nature of classes possessing only one member and the relations of inclusion and membership.

duction. Historians of science have often remarked that Aristotle's conception of demonstration and the logical structure of science was primarily influenced by geometry. Traditionally geometry was thought of as "the science of space," a notion that may be seriously wrong, but is worth our attention as accounting, possibly, for the frequency with which spatial metaphors have played a role in so many philosophic disquisitions on the nature of science. Perhaps, to speculate, the very procedures elaborated in space (on various surfaces) by which the first acquaintance with geometry is acquired have contributed to this production of metaphors. At any rate, the systems of scientific knowledge have long been conceived in spatial terms: "higher level" laws and theories are thus "built-up" from particular statements "resting or grounded" upon facts.[6] The deductive pattern is envisaged as commencing with definitions, axioms, and postulates, suitably formed via a vocabulary of fundamental definitions and rules of composition and inference.

While this classical model of the logical structure of science has impressed itself upon later thought as an ideal expository pattern in which scientists and philosophers have conceived the nature of knowledge, it has met with a number of serious difficulties. These, it may be noted, derived not so much from the assumptions and conditions controlling Aristotle's own analysis of science; they occurred, rather, when the formalized, logical pattern of science set forth by Aristotle was bent and stretched to accommodate a mathematical and mechanical science of nature (a physics, optics, and astronomy) in many ways rather alien to Aristotle's conception of the subject matter and techniques of natural science.

In the seventeenth century the Aristotelian *archai* or basic truths of scientific demonstration received formulation as the mathematical principles of natural philosophy. Newton called these the "axioms, or laws of motion."[7] They retain much of the Aristotelian logical flavor, that is, the condition that the premisses of the system of science are "better known" than the conclusions deduced from them, and that they are universal statements and are "true." Aristotle had given a sketch of how the basic truths are arrived at and "known" in Book Two, Chapter Nineteen of *Posterior Analytics*. He there describes the process of sense perception, memory, and experience in which, from single sensations and classes of similar sensations, "the universal" is elicited and stabilized in the soul. The process commences in sense experience but culminates in *nous*, intellectual insight or intuition, whereby a universal *archē* is apprehended. Newton spoke of deducing these basic propositions from phenomena and generalizing them from experiments by induction.[8] Still, in spite of important differences in their respec-

---

[6] Neurath's well-known picture of science as a boat at sea, being rebuilt while still afloat, fits the geometrical image. But even more so is Hempel's vivid and useful figure in *Concept Formation*, p. 36, of science as a spatially extended net, floating above the base of experience. Metaphors of higher and lower levels, we noticed in § 22, also derive from architecture.

[7] *Principia*, Book I.

[8] See some of his letters (e.g., to Cotes and Oldenburg), his Rules of Reasoning in Philosophy, Rule IV, and the last two paragraphs of the *Optics*. See my *Newton's Philosophy of Nature*, pp. 5–8, 178–179 for these passages.

tive conceptions of the structure and subject matter of natural science, the formal pattern of that structure for Newton as for Aristotle was much the same: it took the axiomatic form of geometry for its model.

We are encouraged then, by history and eminent authorities, to contemplate the conceptual system of science in very simple outline. There is:

First, an order of universal statements, definitions, laws, theories of varying degrees of generality, which we can call "θ."

Second, an order of particular statements of fact, which we will call "O."[9]

Third, the order of experience, our contact with the world, to be called "E."

Now portions of θ are so coordinated with portions of O by means of so-called correspondence or semantical rules[10] that, once given certain conjunctions of θ and O as true premises, further portions of O can be deduced. Selecting from θ a fragmentary item, 'For any x, if x is iron and heated x expands,' and from O, 'x_1 is a piece of iron, and x_1 is now heated,' one can deduce the further portion of O: 'x_1 now expands.'

So viewed, one utility of the system of science is that it permits us to anticipate reliably (to predict and explain) events of experience in this way: Given some true statements St of θ conjoined with statements So of O, other true statements $So_1, So_2, \ldots$ are logical consequences of St and So. All that is needed is that St and So are true. Given this much, then statements of the sort $So_1, So_2, \ldots$ are necessarily true. The steps that permit us to infer from conjunctions of θ and O further truths of E stated in O—that is, the conceptual system of θ that enables us to move from some true statements of fact to others—may indeed be recondite and sometimes tortuous. But that the steps are possible at all and rationally directed is the important thing. We are assured of a way of continuously and cumulatively progressing from once attained truths of experience to new ones.

Passage from truths to truths in the manner indicated depends on a crucial logical condition: the conjunctions of θ statements and O statements must be true, thus their components must be true. Therefore scientific knowledge advances and informs us of E under circumstances where we affirm statements of θ (truly) and O (truly) and infer other statements of O truly. We are led at length back to the question: In what sense are θ statements true? As an example of a θ statement, consider Newton's first law of motion: "Every body continues in its state of rest or of uniform motion in a right line unless it is compelled to change that state by forces impressed upon it." We recognized earlier that there are contexts and occasions of strategy in which "laws" might function not as statements of fact, but in a definitional capacity (§ 80). In some cases, perhaps Newton's law could be construed as a partial definition of *bodies* on a par with Euclid's definition of 'point' (§ 24). But let us now think of this law as a universal statement, purporting to be a truth of E, and from which, connected with O statement "There

---

[9] Here the letters 'θ' and 'O' are to suggest vaguely 'theoretical' and 'observational,' despite certain doubts registered some pages back as to sharp boundaries between theoretical statements and so-called observational ones.

[10] See § 24 above, and the illustration from geometry.

is a moving body at such and such a time and place," we can deduce another O statement "That body is moving in a right line unless it is compelled . . . ," etc.

For Hume, an analysis of how it is that the human mind ever arrived at comprehending laws of the above kind, reveals an inescapable uncertainty on our part as to their truth.[11] For beginning with E and O statements of E (or, for Hume, beginning with simple sense *impressions*) as singular reports of singular facts, and conjunctions of reports, there is no mechanical or rational procedure for arriving at universal θ statements. The mind by dint of customary past experience and reiterated stimulations and by a "force" (not unlike the momentum that operates among Newtonian bodies) of expectation and belief makes its impulsive leap from the finite data of experience to universal affirmations; from "body b_1, body b_2, body b_3 are (under appropriate conditions) observed to move in straight lines" to "for any body b, if b moves . . ." of Newton's law. The latter affirmation, a θ statement, is of a different logical and epistemological order than the conjunction of particular O statements. Such accumulations of O statements as "b_1 moves in a straight line," "b_2 moves in a straight line," "b_3 . . . ," etc., will indeed be said to count as *evidence* for Newton's law. But θ statements, expressing the laws of science, are most impressive in point of informational value and theoretical content partly by virtue of their assertorial breadth and scope—a scope unmatched by finite compilations and recordings of evidence. The universal statement exploits, as it were, the 'etc.' attaching to, but not contained in, the series of particular affirmations about particular moving bodies.

§ 83. Interpretations of the Theoretical Structure of Science

Philosophers impressed with Hume's critical probings into the genesis and justification of our belief in causal laws and inductive thinking have sought various ways in which to supply answers for Humean doubts. One proposal, we noticed earlier (§§ 27, 79), was a kind of Humean oriented attempt to dispel Hume's skeptical conclusions as to our "right" to believe in θ statements. This was to show that θ statements are reducible to those of O. This procedure, were it successful, would certainly strengthen the view of such nominalistic empiricists as Berkeley and Mach and sometimes James (§ 79) that the abstract terms and theoretical structure of science are conventions, linguistic and conceptual conveniences, whose usefulness in the systematic organization of knowledge does not commit us to affirming the existence of anything beyond the evidence of immediate experience.[12] For, since O statements geared directly to E are sufficient for

11 An issue sketched briefly in historical context in Part I, § 11.
12 See Berkeley's attack upon the doctrine of abstract ideas, e.g., *man, triangle,* as a confusion of particular objects and general names—a confusion, as he says, of *language*: "words came to produce the doctrine of abstract ideas," *Principles,* Introduction, esp. secs. 18–19. For Mach, see *Popular Scientific Lectures,* esp. p. 209, and *Analysis of Sensations.*

translating and defining all other scientific concepts, the theoretical language of θ is dispensable at will or if the need be felt. But we have already seen some of the limits of this proposed procedure.

The opposite extreme from the conventionalist interpretation of science, and historically older, is a realist-descriptive view held by Aristotle, Descartes, and Newton, among others. Here the conceptual system of science, embodying as it does true universal affirmations of the sort '(x) (if x is a body ...)' is taken as implying (or assuming) a corresponding structure of general traits, a structure manifest in E or, for some thinkers, since not directly experienced, assumed as a real order under or behind E. The system of science is thus taken as corresponding to, thus true of, reality.

To skeptical doubts like Hume's, as to the warrant for our believing that laws are and will be true, different tactics for solution have come from the realist-descriptive tradition. In addition to Aristotle's appeal to a rational intuition as disclosing basic truths and thus anchoring the resulting system of science in first truths, there is Descartes's similarly inspired Platonic appeal to clear and distinct conceptions (see § 8). There is the notion of the first principles of science as necessary or analytic truths, argued by Hobbes (who in other respects was something of a conventionalist) and Leibniz. Other realists, like Newton, wishing to keep empirical (i.e., to "deduce from phenomena") while requiring concepts and laws that pretty clearly contain general assumptions and inductive affirmations concerning experience that go beyond the experimental evidence for them, have set forth explanatory or justificatory principles—in this case not to "save phenomena" but to salvage theoretical generalization. Thus, in Newton's *Rules of Reasoning in Philosophy* (Rule III), for example, it is proposed as a rule and "foundation of all philosophy" that where all bodies we have observed are extended, hard, impenetrable, etc., we conclude that these are universal properties of all bodies whatsoever. Or, there have been many attempts to derive and justify assertions of causal laws and inductions from some single principle of the Uniformity of Nature. But in general, these appeals to ulterior principles of scientific thought as licensing the assertions of science have not been successful. Mill's famous statement of the principle of the Uniformity of Nature (i.e., the principle of causality) runs, in effect: if in circumstances C an event e occurs, then if conditions similar to C occur, e (or an event simlar to e) will occur.[13] Presumably some scientific law of the form "all A is B" is "grounded" on this principle: where 'this A is B' is true once, then in all circumstances similar to the occurrence of A, B (or A is B) will occur. But this simply postpones or defers the questions raised by Hume. Instead of questioning the grounds of our belief

---

[13] Mill, *A System of Logic,* Book III, ch. 3, sec. 1: "There are such things in nature as parallel cases; what happens once, will under a sufficient degree of similarity of circumstances, happen again." Note that this principle seems to contain two features: (1) if under conditions C, event e occurs, then when conditions C^1 are of "a sufficient degree of similarity" to C, e^1 will occur (where e^1 is similar to e); and (2) what happens once, will happen again.

in some law, "A is B," we are led to question in the same way the grounds of our belief in this principle of causality.

§ 84. The Instrumentalist Point of View

Let us turn without further ado to the pragmatic-instrumentalist approach to the questions we have been considering, questions concerning the truth and interpretation of the abstract and theoretical structure (the θ statements) of science. This view lies between the realist-descriptive and conventionalist outlooks touched on above. Historically, it derives from several quite different philosophic antecedents; from Berkeley's analysis of the immediate data of experience as signs (via a system of interpretation) of other determinate data; from Kant's doctrine of regulative ideas and the romantic and Fichtean interpretations of the nature of thought and purposive conceptualization; from the Hegelian, Darwinian, and evolutionary doctrines of the social, biological, and "organic" character of knowledge. (For a view of this part of the background themes, see Part One.)

But an especially important source of the instrumentalist position is to be found in Mill's interpretation of syllogistic reasoning in his *System of Logic*. A common charge against the value of the syllogism is that since there cannot validly be anything contained in the conclusion that is not contained in the premisses,[14] the conclusion is always sterile. That is, the conclusion never informs us of anything that was not already known in the premisses. Moreover, when a syllogism is regarded as an argument designed to prove the conclusion, since the conclusion is "contained in" the premisses,[15] it is already presupposed in the "proof." Thus, the syllogism as a proof is a *petitio principii*, a begging of the question.

Mill, operating with a characteristic distinction between how we do in fact reason and formal proofs of the correctness of our reasoning, defended the syllogism this way: we do not in fact reason syllogistically, but the syllogistic form of argument is a valuable *test* of reasoning, a form into which reasoning can be translated and thus tested.[16] But as to the actual process of reasoning, Mill argued, "all inference is from particulars to particulars,"[17] not from a general premiss to a particular conclusion.

Mill here follows Berkeley.[18] "He for the first time saw to the bottom of the Nominalist and Realist controversy, and established the fact that all our ideas are

[14] This principle, we shall see in § 89 below, has had an interesting application in ethical theory, viz., as the thesis: One cannot derive *ought* from *is*.

[15] Much depends here on a clarification of the sense of 'contained in'; a clarification not easy to make, but when made, tending to dissipate the charge of *petitio principii*. Vailati (see § 76) has some interesting comments on this in his "On Material Representations," p. 313.

[16] He developed this point in his *Examination of Sir William Hamilton's Philosophy*. Also cf. the *Logic*, Book II, ch. 3, sec. 5.

[17] *Logic*, Book II, ch. 3, sec. 4.

[18] See his essay on Berkeley and the second of the important discoveries he attributes to Berkeley's philosophy.

of individuals,"[19] wrote Mill. Language, argues Mill, in effect (i.e., "general names") enables us to signify "class-attributes" and formulate universal propositions. Mill then maintains:

All inference is from particulars to particulars; general propositions are merely registers of such inferences already made, and short formulae for making more. . . .

Then Mill states the essential feature of the instrumentalist position:

the major premise of a syllogism, consequently, is a formula of this description, and the conclusion is not an inference drawn *from* the formula, but an inference drawn *according* to the formula. . . .[20]

I pass over here some difficulties and dubious points in Mill's account of the inductive nature of the major premiss as a formula. The vital issue, for us, is Mill's interpretation of the major premiss of the syllogism, or general propositions in reasoning, as formulas or rules of procedure *by which* inferences are made rather than from which they are drawn.[21] The proposition "All men are mortal," Mill says, "shows that we have had experience from which we thought it followed that the attributes connoted by the term 'man' are a mark of mortality."[22]

Peirce rejected Mill's nominalism. In part he transformed Mill's psychologically based interpretation of formulas, or general propositions, into a logical analysis of the "leading principles" of reasoning. But he also argues, in his theory of inquiry (§ 20), that these formulas are of the nature of habits. It is in these that the nature of reasoning and belief was found; it is the kind of particular conclusions that followed in accordance with the formula that determined its meaning (§ 21) and truth (§§ 21, 23). But we shall return to Peirce's conception of leading principles below.

The realist-descriptive position, we have seen, treats laws of the form 'for any x, if x is a body . . .' as, when filled in (say, as Newton's first law of motion), true statements—true, in the sense of corresponding to reality.[23] Usually, if not always, abstract terms like 'atom,' 'electron,' 'probability wave,' are supposed by the realist to "correspond" also to reality. The realist thus supposes the ontological query, "do electrons exist?" to be a significant request for information about the world, one addressed to—if not within—theoretical science.

By contrast, the instrumentalist (while working, be it recalled, with a different concept of *truth*) sees little point, if considerable confusion abetted, by piling up of analogies between "surely the stones we see exist" and "surely the sub-visible atomic parts of the same stones exist" to the ontological question as ordinarily

19 "Berkeley's Life and Writings," p. 276.
20 *Logic,* Book II, ch. 3, sec. 4.
21 Mill, of course, argues for this interpretation not as a logical construction but as an empirical fact of psychology: "Not only *may* we reason from particulars to particulars without passing through generals, but we perpetually do so reason," *Logic,* Book II, ch. 3, sec. 3.
22 *Ibid.,* Book II, ch. 3, sec. 4.
23 For this view of truth as correspondence, see § 40 above, also the comments in § 79.

framed, i.e., "do electrons, etc., exist?" Nor does the instrumentalist countenance the notion of laws and theories as ensconced in true statements.[24] Here, too, for the instrumentalist, room for exceptional cases remains, committed as he is (and as we have stressed in § 79 above) to the plurality and relativity of contexts in which questioning and conceptual interpreting goes on. But roughly and generally, the instrumentalist treats laws and theories to be best construed, when heeding the actual practice of scientific thought, as conditional expressions.[25] That is, guided by the Peircian analysis of the meaning and function of beliefs, ideas, and concepts as habits of action, explicated pragmatically in conditionally articulated constructions (as we studied earlier in § 21), the pragmatic instrumentalist sees laws, theories, and theoretical terms of science in a similar light. These, too, have to do with matters of belief, but in a regulative rather than constitutive capacity (to recall Kant and the observations of § 12).

For the instrumentalist, then, laws and theories are not affirmations of *what* we believe about the world, and thus supposed to be express truths of the world, but rather are *how* some of our beliefs are related to others as conditionally organized consequences and expectations. This shift in point of view leads, for example, to construing laws and theories (in general, θ statements) not as premises of scientific knowledge but as rules of inference or guiding principles of knowledge and warranted belief. Accordingly, the deductive pattern, lately noticed, in which, say, "this piece of iron expands" comes through from the premises "all iron expands on heating" and "this piece of iron is heated," is revised by the instrumentalist in the following way. The "law" "all iron expands on heating," or "for any x, if x is iron and heated x expands," is conceived in the spirit rather of a leading principle permitting us to infer from 'x is iron' the consequent 'x expands when heated'; or from 'x is iron and heated' the consequent 'x expands.' Here the law functions not as a *premiss* in an argument but as a *rule of inference*, not as a statement but as a way of relating statements. Such, as we saw earlier, was Mill's view of syllogistic reasoning.

Reference was made some pages back to such elementary "laws of substances" of common sense as are conveyed by the terms 'stone,' 'glass,' 'water,' etc. Each of these terms refers to an invariant association of certain kinds of properties with

---

[24] I.e., 'true' here in the correspondence sense.
[25] The straightforward assertorial "all ravens are black" may be rendered 'anything raven (and it) is black' or the apparently less bold '(x) (if x is a raven then x is black).' Distinct from the conjunction 'A and B' is the conditional 'if A then B.' The realist, as now imagined, will regard laws as bold true statements: "all iron expands when heated." The instrumentalist, as now imagined and to be shortly explained, has a preference for conditional forms: "if something is iron, then. . . ." But it is instructive to note that the preference is guided by more formal considerations. For, by well-known ways, statements of the form 'A and B' 'either A or B,' 'if A then B,' involving the connectives 'and,' 'either—or,' 'if—then,' respectively, are each reducible to and definable by a single mode, *joint denial*, to be read as 'neither—nor.' Thus let the stroke '|' symbolize 'neither—nor.' The conjunction 'A and B' is defined: '$[(A|A) \mid (B|B)]$.' The conditional 'if A then B' is defined: '$[((A|A) \mid B) \mid (A|A) \mid B))]$.' This technique and its symbol is known as Sheffer's stroke, set forth by Sheffer in 1913; but it was developed earlier by Peirce, see *CP* 4.12–20; 4.264.

others under certain conditions. Thus, as we saw, use of the word 'stone' involves and presupposes some such generalizing as 'if x is stone, x is heavy, solid, hard ...,' etc.—generalizing which, in ordinary common-sense parlance, remains tacit in using the word 'stone' and inexplicit as to boundary conditions and the precise sense in which the relative terms 'heavy,' 'solid,' 'hard,' etc., are intended. These conditions are usually evident in given contexts of communication. The law, or lawlike generalization operative in using the word 'stone' is vague; the conditions in which the vague term 'stone' is intended along with its lawlike association of vagaries 'heavy,' 'solid,' 'hard' remain unspecified in ordinary discourse. Yet communication succeeds often by virtue of this very vagueness. Unencumbered by elaborate specifications and qualifications, ordinary discourse succeeds because the wit, experience, and the social context in which speakers and listeners gather, cooperate in effect to specify and supplement in behavioral ways the open stretches of otherwise vague language. Sometimes occasions of ordinary discourse do not succeed; communication fails. Philosophers have been prone to make much of these occasions and have pointed to the comparative rarity of such occurrences in science, a language painfully developed for, among other things, avoiding just such confusions as sometimes beset common sense—hence one reason for the pejorative note heard in philosophic circles in references to "common sense," as, e.g., "cocksure, vague, and self-contradictory."[26]

The case is different with θ terms of science such as 'atom,' 'electron,' and the like. For whereas 'stone' in its status of a law of substances is vague, and usefully so in its service to common sense, 'electron' as couched in physical theory is not vague, nor, if and when vagueness should creep into transactions with θ terms, would this be prized. Still, while of very different orders of conceptualization, 'stone' and 'electron,' for the pragmatist, do partake of this same general pattern of distinctions. In many uses 'stone' functions as a law; thus (pragmatically) "this is a stone" is to be taken not as a statement true of some fact (not as asserting '$(\exists x)$ $(x$ is stone$)$'), but as a compendious way of saying, 'if certain conditions are fulfilled for something x to be stone (and they are), then other conditions are fulfilled, namely, x is heavy, solid, hard, etc." "This is a stone" then serves as a leading principle for inferring certain kinds of conditions from others. Similarly with 'electron'; its use in physical theory warrants inferences from certain theoretical conditions to others—inferences conducted in mathematical form supplemented by any number of physical laws and portions of theory culled for the purpose. Nonetheless, despite the abstract character of the conditions in question, and the complexity of inference, 'electron' provides a kind of inferential mechanism—or principle—helping, along with laws and theory, to make calculations and inferences of a certain determinate kind possible.

Ultimately, of course, such inferences if sound eventuate in some testable experimental consequences. But this we noticed was one of the uses of theory: to guide us from truths to truths of experience, a matter on which realist, conventionalist,

[26] Russell's famous characterization of it in *Philosophy*, p. 1.

and pragmatist agree. At the moment, it is not this thought, but rather interpretation of the logical character of abstract terms in science that concerns us. For clarity, let us dogmatically summarize the points of view. In the realist-descriptive outlook, a term like 'electron' is taken as a name[27] of an object, or, since there are thought to be many such objects, 'electron' is the name for each. In this view, as we saw, the ontological or metaphysically directed question "do electrons exist?" makes sense and is usually given, with an appeal to the authority of modern physics, a "yes" answer. Curiously the vaguely similar question "do stones exist?" or even "do ordinary physical objects exist?" receives the opposite answer from some philosophical realists. The reasoning here was reviewed earlier (§ 79), namely, that modern physical theory disconfirms the assumptions and data of common sense. Other realists more kindly disposed to the untutored and rash ways of common sense take a conciliatory view in holding that stones and other "ordinary physical objects" are collapsible into electrons, charges, and fields, and the other media of physics. This is to hold that stones exist as among sundry other crudely conceived and archaic ways of referring to the objects of physics. This kind of realist-descriptive philosophizing betrays its own form of conventionalism. For here it is ordinary objects and sense data that are regarded as conventions, convenient modes of interpreting reality, generated from primeval human experience but inviting physical theory to exorcize them of their fictional elements for the sake of a first-hand literal view of reality.

The conventionalist interpretation of 'electron' has also on occasion treated that term as a name, but then the object named is thought of as a fictional entity, a character in a drama of theory, useful in helping to speed and simplify the labor of thought and to stimulate invention, but not a "real" existence. Pressed to explain what 'electron' means, the conventionalist makes a case for a useful fiction. But this in turn is but a vivid way in which to say that 'electron' does not really name anything (as 'stone' does), and is short for an elaborate set of operations and theorizing by which we organize in conceptual outline the data of sense experience.

For the realist, then, the laws, theories, and abstract terms of θ somehow mirror or correspond to reality. For the conventionalist, the θ order of science is a convenient and compendious labor-saving way of recording, reproducing, and ordering our perceptual experience—assuming, always, that an observational language O can replace the theoretical statements of θ and, save for simplicity, without loss of meaning or scientific content.[28]

---

[27] A general name or general term, i.e., *naming* or *true of* each of all of those objects known as electrons.

[28] For the conventionalist is committed to E and the language thereof (i.e., O). He has to recognize some controls over his inventive, shorthand transcriptions of experience. His theories have to square with experience—are short for descriptions of immediate experience. This means that theories, laws, and θ terms are reducible to, or translatable into the observational language. Such reduction of all θ terms to the O language assures the conventionalist of the warrant of the θ language. But the possibilities of this reduction being successfully carried out we have, several times before (§§ 27, 79), had occasion to doubt.

§ 85.   Leading Principles

To the pragmatist, the conspicuous and significant feature of the abstract terms, the definitions, laws, and theories of θ, in view of the evolution of science and in scientific inquiry, is the role they perform as leading principles. In general, as we have seen in § 21, the pragmatic analysis and interpretation of the meaning of theoretical terms (or signs) consists of a general description of the experimental conditions in which a certain kind of operation produces a certain set of empirical (i.e., practical, conceivable) consequences. The description (formulated as a conditional statement, see § 21) serves as a "prescription" or "precept," as Peirce often said, or, as we might say with Peirce and Kant in mind, as a formula or schema directing us to the kinds of conditions in which a term (or sign) has its significant use and application. This view of meaning as located and clarified in resolutions, habits, formulas, and rules of (conceived) action and consequences has direct bearing upon how Peirce and Dewey undertook to explain the logical character of scientific laws and theories. For the universal statements constituting laws and theories are meant, or supposed by the pragmatist to function, as formulations of policy or resolutions. Specifically they operate as decisions to permit certain kinds of inferences from certain formulated conditions to others.

Peirce developed the idea of a leading principle as follows:

> It is of the essence of reasoning that the reasoner should proceed, and should be conscious of proceeding, according to a general habit, or method, which he holds would either (according to the kind of reasoning) always lead to the truth, provided the premises were true; or, consistently adhered to, would eventually approximate indefinitely to the truth; or would be generally conducive to the ascertainment of truth, supposing there be any ascertainable truth. The effect of this habit or method could be stated in a proposition of which the antecedent should describe all possible premises upon which it could operate, while the consequent should describe how the conclusion to which it would lead would be determinately related to those premises. Such a proposition is called the "leading principle" of the reasoning.[29]

The reasoning process from a premiss, or premisses P to a conclusion C, occurs by means of "a habit or rule active within us."[30] Let us refer to the habit, rule, or leading principle as "Lp." Any Lp, according to Peirce, determines a class of inferences, that is, all of those inferences that would be made, according to Lp, when "once the proper premises were admitted."[31] The Lp that governs a class of inferences seems to be the logical analogue of the belief (or habit) that gov-

---

[29] CP 2.558. One of Peirce's clearest and most revealing statements of the nature of a leading principle within the context of his theory of thought and inquiry is "On the Algebra of Logic" (1880), CP 3.154 ff., from which are taken the following quotations and paraphrases.
[30] CP 3.163.
[31] CP 3.163.

erns a class of actions, in Peirce's theory of inquiry (see § 20). In any event, Peirce recognizes that some Lp's will be good, some bad; and indeed different persons may use different Lp's expressing different habits or routes of inference, although proceeding from the same premisses and terminating in the same conclusion. But for Peirce, a good habit and Lp is one that would never (or in the case of probable inference, seldom) lead from a true premiss to a false conclusion, otherwise it is logically bad.[32]

In his analysis of the notion of a leading principle, Peirce was not only attempting to emphasize and formulate what he took to be "the essence of reasoning," the philosophic core of logic and scientific method. He was also concerned to give a logically precise account of the general pragmatic thesis concerning the regulative and leading function of thought (as against a copy-theory of ideas): concepts carry a futurative reference; ideas are plans and tools of action and expectation with which we face and deal with future experience. Dewey's instrumentalism (see § 36) was similarly motivated. Dewey's description of the most general kinds of leading principles and ways in which they function, concentrated upon the biological and cultural conditions generating and shaping thought. Peirce was concerned with the formal character of leading principles and with their roles as signs as part of a general theory of signs.[33]

Following Peirce and Dewey, pragmatic instrumentalism thus construes the laws and theories of science[34] as leading principles for understanding the objects of experience, where *understanding* is taken to include prediction, interpretation, discovery, and (sometimes) modifications of things experienced. Fundamental for Peirce and Dewey, and for this conception of leading principles, is the part played by particular experienced cases—or, as Peirce put it, the "possible premisses" and conclusion of reasoning. Dewey writes:

> The individually observed case becomes the measure of knowledge. Laws are intellectual instrumentalities by which that individual object is instituted and its

[32] *CP* 3.163. Also: "every possible case of the operation of a good habit would either be one in which the premiss was false or one in which the conclusion would be true; whereas, if a habit of inference is bad, there is a possible case in which the premiss would be true, while the conclusion was false."

[33] In the course of his analysis Peirce distinguished *formal* and *material* leading principles. A leading principle "whose truth is implied in the premisses of every inference which it governs" (*CP* 2.588) is a "logical" or "formal" leading principle. A leading principle whose truth is not implied in the premisses is "factual" or "material." A formal Lp does not "state" or "add" anything in addition to the premisses it governs. It simply states a rule of inference and permits symbolic transformations and operations within a system. Different systems will contain different formal leading principles. The *material Lp,* however, does state something and its (pragmatic) truth depends upon the conditions and premisses of inference it governs. Thus: from 'x is a man,' if true, we may infer 'x is mortal,' by a material Lp permitting that inference (i.e., the leading principle 'all men die'—cf. *CP* 3.166). On the other hand, if 'mortal' is taken as a defining trait of man, then a formal Lp permits the analytic or definitional "inference" from 'x is a man' to 'x is mortal.' Peirce's discussion of the leading principle 'all men die' at *CP* 3.166 reads like a commentary on Mill's argument of § 84 above.

Peirce's distinction of two types of leading principle was to be reflected in Dewey's analysis of two kinds of universal proposition, *universal* and *generic,* in his *Logic: The Theory of Inquiry.* See Appendix 6, sec. C below.

[34] Indeed, all intelligent activities, including art, for Dewey.

meaning determined. This . . . involves a reversal of the theory which has dominated thought since the Newtonian system obtained full sway. According to the
latter, the aim of science is to ascertain laws; individual cases are known only as
they are reduced to instances of laws.[35]

Against the Newtonian conception of laws as true statements of "the ultimate and
rigid uniformities of being," Dewey argues that developments in modern physics
point to a new view:

> laws on the new basis are *formulae for the prediction of the probability of an ob-
> servable occurrence*. They are designations of relations sufficiently stable to allow
> of the occurrence of forecasts of individualized situations. . . .[36]

And of the regulative, instrumental nature of laws, Dewey writes that, as general
statements, laws serve to direct observation "of the particular case so as to discover
what it is *like*."[37]

> The eventual purpose in knowledge is observation of a new phenomenon, an
> object actually experienced by way of perception. Thus the supposed immutable
> law supposed to govern phenomena becomes a way of transacting business effec-
> tively with concrete existence, a mode of regulation of our relations with them.
> There is no difference in principle between their use in "pure" science and in
> an art.[38]

In this interpretation of laws and theories the pragmatist-instrumentalist
claims to have retained all of the benefits, while avoiding most of the shortcomings of the other two views, the realist and conventionalist interpretations. He is
not committed to the dubious attempts of the realist to provide a reality, hidden
or naked, of "facts" to which the universal statements of science "correspond" by
virtue of their truth. The instrumentalist has sometimes been criticized for not
being able to talk about the *truth* of scientific laws, since, by his own admission,
instruments or tools, etc., are not true or false. But this is not an impressive objection, even when supplemented by the observation that scientists usually speak of
the truth or falsehood of theories or laws. For what scientists might mean by referring to a law as false (or as true) is quite easily accommodated in the instrumentalist's idiom of referring to leading principles as sound, useful, good, workable (or unsound, useless, bad, unworkable). But further, the instrumentalist can
even talk of the truth or falsity of laws or theories, 'truth' or 'falsehood,' however,
being understood and defined pragmatically. The pragmatist thus avoids the other
extremity of conventionalism, according to which the whole system of science is
a fiction or myth or a convenient if artificial way of making sense of sense data.
To treat the structure of science as a huge fiction does raise questions of truth
over the sense in which this "myth" as distinct from others is believed to be true.

35 *The Quest for Certainty*, p. 205.
36 *Ibid.*, p. 206.
37 *Ibid.*, p. 207.
38 *Ibid.*, p. 207.

The so-called "myth" of natural science has evolved in ways determinate and explainable; its statements or components have been developed and accepted under known uniform conditions of experiment and critical assessment. This evolution and the pattern it exhibits is so different from the unevolving or haphazardly changing "myths" of literature, anthropology, and religion as not to warrant the same appellation.

The "law" that iron expands on heating, regarded instrumentally as a leading principle, could be taken as facilitating and governing inferences as follows: referring to the law simply as *Lp*, we are advised, accordingly, that:

1) Conditions where '*x* is iron' is true, are (via *Lp*) conditions where '*x* expands when heated' is true.

Or, more simply:

2) Whenever '*x* is iron' is true or warranted, '*x* will expand when heated' is also true.

In more ordinary contexts of human behavior, leading principles may function as warnings or signals:

3) Whenever 'This is iron' is true, expect, look out for, expansion when heated.

We must notice in each example that the leading principle stated as (1), (2), or (3) operates over and among statements. In short, leading principles may be represented as meta-language expressions concerning the permissibility of inferring some statements from other statements, or stated conditions from other stated conditions.

To a considerable extent modern philosophizing about science has been indebted, in its problems and schooling, to Hume's analysis of the grounds of our belief in causal laws and in knowledge of matters of fact.[39] That analysis, we have noticed in past pages, precipitated a flood of perplexities, real and imagined, and much ambitious thought concerning induction and the truth or reliability of universal statements about the world.

One advantage of the instrumentalist view of the theoretical structure of science is that while it represents a way of understanding the intellectual procedures employed in attaining and organizing scientific knowledge, it also provides a solution to some of the philosophic problems that have troubled many thinkers since Hume's critical analysis of knowledge.[40] By regarding laws and theories as intel-

---

[39] Modern thinking about science, in technical and speculative forms, of course has a history before Hume, as the sketch of Part I attempts to illustrate.

[40] One pragmatic defense of the instrumentalist thesis has occurred in discussions of the "problem" of the "justification" of induction. Since the conclusions of an inductive argument are more or less sound depending on how sound the premises are, since the premises are generalizations about classes or orders of events based on some study of a subclass or proportion of those events, and since the laws of sciences are universal statements arrived at inductively but the *evidence* for them is finite, is there some way of *justifying* this inductive procedure? We have seen above that the view of laws as inductive generalizations is questionable.

Peirce argued (§ 22, and also Ramsey, § 71) that there is no "problem" of induction or "justification" needed of the scientific *method* of making synthetic inferences beyond the

lectual tools for the exploration of experience, tools that may be used and guided differently depending on the context being inquired into, questions such as we have seen as to the truth of these principles, or what ideal and abstract terms (like 'frictionless surface' or 'instantaneous velocity') refer to among existing things, are rendered pointless. It is not that the questions need detailed answers or that they could be answered. It is rather that any hoped for answers are vain, because the questions are misguided.

§ 86.   Some Critical Issues and Conclusion

Two issues, I think, require our attention in bringing this account of the instrumentalist conception of scientific knowledge to a close.

1) Let us go back for a moment to the analysis suggested earlier of concepts like 'stone' and 'electron.' The proposal was that each of these, despite enormous differences in the complexity of theoretical contexts between them, could be treated as a leading principle. That is, 'stone' is short for a formula of kinds of conditions that can be inferred from others. The formula is a principle *by which* inferences are guided, not *from which* they are drawn. Thus, 'stone' represents a lawlike conditional construction:

'For any *x*, if *x* is a stone, then *x* is hard, heavy . . . , etc.'

As for 'electron' the same logical interpretation is advanced by the instrumentalist. Thus, with respect now not to ordinary objects of observation, nor the familiar activities of eye and hand, 'electron' as well as the laws and theories of quantum physics in which this concept is used are also interpreted as leading principles. 'Electron' then in the actual conduct of inquiries in physics provides one with a way of inferring certain conditions of subatomic physical states from others. Thus, under such and such conditions, specified by means of quantum

---

application of that method itself to specific problems. Thus, as Nagel writes:

> A theory is "better established" when we increase the number and kinds of its positive instances, because the *method* we thereby employ is one which our general experience confirms as leading to conclusions which are stable or which provide satisfactory solutions to the specific problems of inquiry. . . . While no probability in a frequency sense can be significantly assigned to any formulation of our method (because it is that very method which is involved in estimating and testing such probabilities), scientific inquiry is based upon the assumption, which is supported by our general experience, that the method of science leads to a proportionately greater number of successful terminations of inquiry than any alternative method yet proposed.

Nagel concludes with a clear statement of the instrumentalist position of Peirce, Ramsey, and Dewey, among others:

> no antecedent principle is required to justify the procedure of science . . . the sole justification of that procedure lies in the specific solutions it offers to the problems which set it in motion, and . . . a *general* problem of induction in its usual formulation does not exist.

This is also Nagel's own position as stated in *Principles of the Theory of Probability,* from whence the above quotes, pp. 72–73.

theory, if *x* is an electron present among those conditions, then such and such conditions are present or inferrable from other conditions. The electron *is* the conditional conditions—or, more accurately, it is our formula and leading principle for inferring the conjunctions of certain kinds of specified conditions.

Now against the instrumentalist interpretation of laws, theories, and especially θ terms like 'electron,' one can imagine this objection. Suppose that a very special electron microscope were constructed, so that peering into it at a material object one saw a cloud of electrons around their nucleus.[41] Thus, looking at a sodium atom, one "sees" eleven electrons surrounding the nucleus. In this case the instrumentalist treatment of 'electron' would seem to have been refuted. 'Electron' would name the particles under observation. There are answers to this.

The electron "observed," that is, the decision to regard the observed phenomena *as* electrons involves a complicated superimposition of theory upon what is observed. The theory, by which what is seen is interpreted as evidence for the presence of electrons, is clearly prior to and accepted on grounds other than the observations being made. The observed data, *interpreted* as evidence for the presence of *electrons*, are already theory-laden (much as we noticed in § 81 above). There is a considerable stretch of imagination, theorizing, and hard scientific study intervening between the act of seeing specks or dots on a ground and the decision to regard what is seen as electrons. Electrons are more than what does or can meet the eye. The instrumentalist and pragmatist response to this example, then, is to argue that observed data of any kind, if these are to function in a cognitively significant manner, serve as *signs* of certain kinds of inferable conditions.

As such, the electrons of our example are no more directly seen than the stones of ordinary experience. For the stone of ordinary experience is, we have noticed before, a construction too. When we say we see a stone, we infer (as Lewis, § 45, and Dewey point out) that what we *are* perceiving fulfills certain conditions: that what is seen is also hard, heavy, etc. The stone as a substance fulfills one of our elementary laws of substances (§ 81). The electron observed, in the qualified, inferential, ànd theory-intrusive sense just noted might equally classify as a "substance." But like all *things*, according to the instrumentalist view, it too would serve as an instance of a law or of lawlike conditionals.

From this part of our discussion the following moral is to be drawn. If the instrumentalist position can be successfully sustained, it must be held radically and all the way. The interpretation of laws, theories, and θ terms as guiding principles, and the corresponding view of *things*, objects, as conjunctions of properties,[42] has to be held *in toto*. When this is not heeded, the instrumentalist is found shifting inconsistently between his own view and the realist-descriptive position—between espousing the instrumental character of the structure of science

---

[41] The example happens to depend upon ignoring some very serious theoretical difficulties. It is also dependent on metaphors, i.e., the word 'particle' with its ordinary associations applied to electron, and models of "miniature solar systems," etc.

[42] Or Berkeley's "congeries" of events, see Appendix 5 below.

382 IV. SOME PRAGMATIC CONSEQUENCES

and entertaining "realist" questions as to whether any thing exists corresponding to this structure.[43]

2) Another and more effective criticism of the instrumentalist thesis of leading principles is the following. Mill and Peirce show how a general premiss in an argument can be converted into a rule of inference. Thus, the inference 'if x is a man x is mortal' proceeds by the rule 'everything man is mortal.' But we can also always convert leading principles into premisses of a deductive argument. Thus, the leading principle 'everything man is mortal' can be taken as a premiss from which, with 'x is a man,' the conclusion 'x is mortal' follows. The formal difference between leading principles in accordance *with* which inferences proceed, and premisses *from* which conclusions are deduced, is thus a matter of convenience only.[44] To this the only answer possible is that the preference for the ruling-principle interpretation of the structure of science as against the deductive pattern is extra-logical. That is, the preference for one over the other will turn on advantages other than formal considerations. It is true that finished expositions of scientific theory are usually stated as premisses from which deductions are made. But the instrumentalist could concede that the deductive pattern of the structure of science has its uses in some contexts, heuristic and clarificatory, while still claiming that more important insights into the use and meaning of the language of science and the avoiding of dubious metaphysical and epistemological problems favor his point of view in other contexts. It is not that the two points of view are always at odds that matters. It is rather a question of which point of view is assumed with respect to what sorts of problems. And in such cases the decisions will be pragmatic.

Emphasizing the instrumental character of theoretical concepts of science obliges and entails an emphasis upon the "concrete" factual materials, the contexts in which intellectual instrumentalities promote, direct, and effectively contribute to experimental inquiry and observation. These contexts and the purpose of inquiry constitute the test conditions of leading principles as intellectual tools. When rightly understood, therefore, the instrumentalist viewpoint shares with any other responsible analysis of scientific thought a concern with critical testing, validation, and appraisal of laws, conceptual schemes, and theories. And while instruments are not easily characterized as true or false (except pragmatically), the instrumentalist is not bereft of a vocabulary with which to articulate critical judgments upon the relevance and utility of this or that bit of scientific theory, for given purposes in given situations.

---

[43] For this kind of shift and a critical comment on it, see Nagel, "A Perspective on Theoretical Physics," pp. 310–311. The criticism is directed against Toulmin, cf. esp. p. 136. Toulmin, taking a Wittgenstein-Watson view of laws and theories as "methods of representation," or rules for representing phenomena (see Watson, ch. 2), does nonetheless raise and discuss the question, "Do neutrinos exist?" The argument of the above paragraphs is close to C. F. Presley and one of his conclusions, p. 102: "It is a mistake . . . to say that all the evidence for the existence of molecules or mesons is indirect, for in this context it is impossible to describe evidence which would be, in contrast, direct."

[44] See Nagel, *The Structure of Science,* pp. 138–140, 150–152 for this point.

CHAPTER THREE

The Construction of Good

§ 87. Constructing the Good

A major achievement in the history of pragmatism, and a matter of conscious effort on the part of Dewey, C. I. Lewis, and Mead, was the construction of an ethical theory. The theory was to be an integral part of the pragmatic conception of meaning and knowing as ways of interpreting experience with respect to future experimental consequences. It was centered in the pragmatic analysis of intelligent action as a deliberate anticipation and realization of selected modes and possibilities of experience.

The pragmatic ethic or theory of valuation accordingly deserves careful consideration. While it has called forth controversial appraisals, it has been influential. The theory is also of considerable intrinsic importance as the most comprehensive attempt ever made to show the logical interrelations of empirical knowledge and valuations.

The two writers who have done the most to develop the pragmatic theory of ethics are Dewey and Lewis. With the exception of one important point of difference,[1] their theories are very much alike. Lewis' views were discussed earlier (§ 46) and references to them will be made in pages to follow. But Dewey first stated the theory at the turn of the century and continued in many writings to defend and modify it under criticism, and to elaborate its historical and philo-

---

[1] Unlike Dewey, Lewis makes a fundamental distinction between *ethics* and *valuation*. "The problem which delineates the field of ethics is not that of the empirically good or valuable but that of the right and morally imperative. To be sure, there is essential connection between rightness of action and goodness in that which this action is intended to effect." But, he adds, "we should be careful that we do not illicitly connect the right and the good, before ever we have distinguished them." *Analysis of Knowledge and Valuation*, p. 552. Also, p. 554: "Valuation is always a matter of empirical knowledge. But what is right and just can never be determined by empirical facts alone." Another basic difference will be brought out in the discussion to follow. The fundamental context of *values* for Dewey is the *situation*. Lewis might have subscribed to this, but in fact speaks instead of satisfactions of some organism O with respect to objects.

sophic relevance in the development of scientific knowledge. Accordingly, with some occasional references to Lewis, it will be Dewey's formulations of the ethic that will occupy us in this chapter.

§ 88.   The Problem of Ethical Judgment

The notion that the human mind is in some way contained in the head, being in or a part of the brain, and that ideas are contained in the mind, posed (as we have surveyed in Part One) a very troublesome philosophic problem. If the materials and units of knowledge are our own ideas, how do we ever know anything about objects outside of our own minds?

In the sixteenth and seventeenth centuries a number of influential scientists and philosophers had assured the philosophic world that, on the authority of science, this picture of ideas in a mind in a head was the correct way to think and talk about mind and knowing. Of course, since science does give us knowledge of the world, it follows (if mysteriously) that we *do* have access from some of our ideas to certain "primary" "real" objects. Galileo, Descartes, Newton, and Locke all affirmed this much. However, given these assumptions and this picture, the fact that we do have scientific knowledge is utterly mysterious. This was pointed out by many, but by none more accutely than Berkeley.

This problem of knowledge, so called, the problem of understanding the existence of science, has been sketched earlier. But very much a part of the history of this problem was that of accounting for the origin of morals and the nature of values. Indeed, this latter problem of understanding exhibits far more complexity and variety of analyses and speculation, and more of a sense of importance by the seventeenth- and eighteenth-century philosophers (excepting Descartes), than the other of understanding science. Yet the problem of knowledge, unadulterated epistemology, usually receives more attention in textbooks on the history of modern philosophy. Perhaps this is due to contemporary predilections. Or perhaps it is because the other part of the story is a more intricate and complicated subject to expound. At any rate, an important moment in the history of thought arrived when Kant argued that scientific and moral experience alike were doomed to remain unintelligible unless certain assumptions, certain indemonstrable conditions were accepted (see § 11). In short, Kant seemed to have established that both science and ethics rested on beliefs that were not demonstrable but were to be taken on faith, a not unreasonable faith, but faith nonetheless.

The details of the Kantian argument do not concern us here. It suffices to observe that a separation between science and ethics appeared to be, by Kant's argument, a theoretical necessity. In this respect Kant was more of a "dualist" than Hume. For while Hume argued for a sharp distinction between reason and passion, he saw a place for reason in enlightening moral sentiment and he had, after all, hoped to apply "the experimental method of reasoning into moral subjects."[2]

Looking back over the development of modern thought and at its current perplexities and uncertainties, Dewey pointed out at length that the deeply driven philosophic wedges, the splitting of mind and bodily world, of ethics from natural science, of values from facts, of evaluations from scientific methods of establishing empirical judgments, had had the most noxious of influences, and that they most urgently demanded critical philosophic reconsideration. Having touched upon much of this earlier in Part Two, Chapter Three, we turn now to a fuller discussion of Dewey's own ethical theory, in which he is especially concerned to show that valuations can be "empirically grounded propositions" of an experimental empiricism.

§ 89. Ought and Is

In a celebrated passage of his *Treatise*, Hume writes:

> In every system of morality, which I have hitherto met with, I have always remark'd, that the author proceeds for some time in the ordinary way of reasoning, and establishes the being of a God, or makes observations concerning human affairs; when of a sudden I am surpriz'd to find, that instead of the usual copulations of propositions, *is*, and *is not*, I meet with no proposition that is not connected with an *ought*, or an *ought not*. This change is imperceptible; but is, however, of the last consequence. For as this *ought*, or *ought not*, expresses some new relation or affirmation, 'tis necessary that it shou'd be observ'd and explain'd; and at the same time that a reason should be given, for what seems altogether inconceivable, how this new relation can be a deduction from others, which are entirely different from it.[3]

What is "inconceivable" about an *ought* being deduced from an *is*? It is the simple logical principle, whose violation breeds inconceivables, that an expression containing one kind of terms (or "relation") cannot be logically derived from an expression containing a different kind of terms. Thus, a deductive argument in which the conclusion contains terms not contained in the premises is not logically valid. If it always rains on Sunday, it follows that it rained last Sunday and will rain next Sunday; but not that there has been or will be snow on Sundays.

To continue this line of reasoning a bit further, suppose we were confronted with some philosophic observations of varying profundity, as "all men desire

---

[2] Hume's subtitle to his *Treatise of Human Nature.*
[3] *Treatise*, Book III, Part I, sec. 1. The point is of importance in Rousseau's *Social Contract*, I.2. Rousseau comments on those whose "method is to derive Right from Fact. It might be possible to adopt a more logical system of reasoning but none that would be more favorable to tyrants."

pleasure," "everyone worships God in his own way," "historical change exhibits a pattern of development toward increasing consciousness and freedom." It does not follow that men *ought* to desire pleasure, or that one *ought* to worship, or that, because historical change is patterned, any part of the pattern is *right, good,* or *ought* to have occurred. The *ought* expressions are not implied by those expressing what *is* the case.

One cannot, then, *deduce* moral conclusions from premises that contain no moral terms. This is no more possible than to deduce theorems about masses in motion from the premises of geometry.

It is doubtful that anyone would disagree with Hume's critical comment if it is understood in the manner just indicated. That is, schematically, let us consider any deductive argument as consisting of:

First, a finite number of premises P.

Second, the class of all those words or other signs that are found in the sentences of P and which we will call *the total vocabulary* V of P.

Third, one or more *conclusions* C, derived from P according to established logical principles.

Now Hume's point is simply that C does not follow deductively from P if there are terms in the vocabulary of C not contained in V. It is unlikely that anyone would seriously question this argument. But the reason for giving this much attention to it is that, in spite of his characteristic lucidity, what Hume actually says is not entirely clear or entirely convincing. Hume was advancing an idea of major importance in ethical theory, an idea that happens to run counter to a number of ethical systems ancient and modern. While defenders of these systems might readily agree that it is fallacious to suppose that C follows from P if C contains terms not contained in V of P, they would nonetheless want to maintain that Hume was wrong in holding that no logical connection between *is* and *ought* can be established.

There is a serious question as to what is meant by a *connection* or 'logical connection.' In those ethical systems containing some supposed or asserted relation between what *is* and what *ought to be,* the precise nature of this relation is often obscure. In some of these systems it appears to be of a metaphysical kind. That is, statements of what *ought* to be (or prescriptive statements of what one *ought* to do) are deducible from statements of what is, because the valuable, desirable, and obligatory are in some way inherent traits of reality. Plato's Good is an example. In fact, each of the moral Forms (or Ideas), justice, courage, temperance, etc., *is* (real) and is or prescribes what *ought* to be as sources of value and ideals of conduct. Philosophers such as Plato and Aristotle have also argued that if we know what man *is,* what his function is, what his nature is, we can determine how he *ought* to live and behave. It is a commonplace that the word 'nature' when used by classical philosophers and their followers often has normative as well as factual significance. One might say: "it is the nature of fire to heat things," i.e., this is what fire does. But "it is the nature of man to think," i.e., this is what few men do and all ought to do.[4] When the ghost asks Hamlet to

> Revenge his foul and most unnatural murther,[5]

"unnatural" means that the causes of his murder were not normal (i.e., usual) even for murder, and his murderer is more than usually wicked. In these senses of the word 'nature' we have a good example of the logical or ontological linking of *is* and *ought*. A similar linkage is found in the idea of the will of God, where it is believed that what God in fact wills, commands or obliges man's acts and attitudes.

It will not do to conclude that in the examples considered, moral expressions are supposedly deduced from expressions containing no moral terms. For this, we saw, is fallacious. What, then, is the rationale, in these systems by which some relation between *is* and *ought* is established? Or, rephrasing the question in the language of the scheme lately sketched: if among the premises P of an ethical system we find statements about what *is* and conclusions C are drawn about what *ought* to be, how is this possible? At least three answers can be given.

To begin with, in the vocabulary V of P there might be moral terms ('ought,' 'is good,' etc.) in addition to expressions about what *is* the case. But this is simply to say that among the premises of a system containing factual sentences about what *is*, there are also moral sentences or premises containing an *ought*.

Secondly, there is a possibility that the *ought* expressions in C while not found in P are definable by the terms contained in V. This suggests that in some ethical systems, given certain rules and techniques of definition, the moral terms 'good,' 'ought,' or expressions of the form 'x is good,' 'x ought to be done,' etc., are defined by certain terms or expressions in V.[6] In Neoplatonistic ethics, 'good' is defined by 'being,' 'evil' is 'non-being.' The procedure for accomplishing this follows either the first method above, or the present one. St. Augustine, for example, usually characterizes God as "immutable being"; 'goodness' (and 'evil') is supposedly explained or defined by means of this concept of *being*.[7]

Thirdly, C might contain moral expressions like 'ought,' and P contain no such expressions, yet C might be deduced from P by means of a rule permitting the inferences. As a trivial example, the statement "the world is a sphere" might imply "the world is good" on the rule that whatever is said to be spherical may also be said to be good. Rules allowing terms or sentences to imply other terms or sentences can be established sheerly by fiat, or by much or little argument for their

---

[4] Cf. Aristotle, *Politics* I. 2, 1252b32ff.: "The nature [*physis*] of a thing is its end [*telos*]. For that which each thing is when its development is fully completed, we call the nature of that thing, whether it be a man, a horse or a family. Again, that for the sake of which a thing is, and its end, is the best."
[5] Shakespeare, *Hamlet*, I.v.
[6] Once again, but in a new context, we have come upon the thesis of *reducibility* touched upon in § 27 and § 79. Here the point of the claim is that ethical terms in expressions containing them are reducible by certain logical constructions to terms of a descriptive kind.
[7] Cf. *Enchiridion*, 10–14.

388   IV. SOME PRAGMATIC CONSEQUENCES

reasonableness, or both. In a special and untrivial manner now to be studied, this way of relating evaluations and ethical judgments to statements about matters of fact is found in the theory advocated by Dewey and most pragmatists. Here, however, it is not by means of some simple rule by fiat that certain true statements about what *is* the case may imply statements about what *ought* to be or be done.

The special way in which Dewey may be said to hold that ethical judgments are logically related to (and indeed, contain) empirical statements of fact is that of offering a general theory of valuation. The theory attempts to explain how "valuation-propositions" partly consist of and are related to propositions about facts. Basically, the theory is an analysis of what a valuation-proposition is. The analysis is characteristic of Dewey's "genetic-functional" method of dealing with philosophic ideas: Dewey describes the conditions in which valuations arise and are formed, as well as the function, the purpose, and consequences of valuational judgments.

Dewey's theory of valuation is concerned to show how valuation-propositions take place within empirical contexts and have empirical consequences. In a vague way, his can be called an empirical ethic, if one has a liking for the nomenclature. But in one respect Dewey's theory is not empirical at all. And this, while easily missed because of the emphasis in Dewey's exposition on things empirical, is the purpose Dewey had in mind in constructing the theory itself. That is, Dewey's theory is not empirical, if by 'empirical' is meant a faithful description of how in fact men moralize and evaluate things. Dewey's theory itself makes this much of a normative departure from hard facts: the theory explains how the circumstances for valuations *do* occur and how men *ought* to (or will best) proceed to formulate and judge value-propositions. But much of Dewey's energy is devoted to critical comparisons between how men do and how they should evaluate their present and future experience. In this one respect, the theory is offered, normatively, as a model of how intelligent value judgments can be made where "empirically" dulled habits, powerful authorities, fanaticism, and fantasizing have hitherto prevailed.[8]

In sketchy anticipation of ideas to be explained shortly, we may say that for Dewey, valuation-propositions contain in their formulation a descriptive empirical component (i.e., an *is*) and an imperative moral component (i.e., an *ought*). The theory of valuation in which this relation is developed incorporates and is dependent upon Dewey's conception of *situation* and *inquiry* (cf. § 39). The underlying principles, for Dewey, are as follows:

1)   The conditions in general that occasion and generate moral judgments are no different from the kind of conditions that give rise to any judgment: these conditions are a problematic situation.

---

[8] In answer to Stevenson's criticism of his views in *Ethics and Language,* this was Dewey's line of reasoning. See his "Ethical Subject Matter and Language" and the last pages of § 96 below. Men may in fact use ethical language in purely "emotive" ways, and make judgments accordingly, but this is not how they ought to make valuations or regard their function. Dewey's theory would be justified (by him) on the same pragmatic and empirical test of satisfactory consequences that the theory is concerned to articulate.

2) The procedure of formulating and testing (or validating) moral judgments does not differ from that employed in forming any kind of judgment: the
procedure of formulation and testing is inquiry.

3) The conditions that bring moral judgments and inquiry to an end, the
"good" with which such efforts terminate, are no less real and objective than the
kinds of conditions in which any inquiry terminates. They are objects and possibilities that resolve a problematic situation.

As a *situation* and as *inquiry*, moral situations and inquiries do not differ logically or ontologically from other kinds of situations and inquiries. According to
this view, then, judgments and expressions containing no moral terms can be
related to those containing distinctively moral terms. The relation here is a
logical one within inquiry and an existential one with reference to the *situation*.
As we shall see more clearly below, the "facts" or conditions that compose a moral
situation are describable in propositions that contain no moral expressions in
any peculiar sense.

§ 90.   *A Modified Naturalistic Ethic*

The passage in Hume prompting the above reflections provides us with a way of
classifying a group of ethical systems. Let us, following the fashion, call "naturalistic" any ethical theory that maintains that "moral judgments are equivalent
in meaning to statements of non-moral fact."[9] Let us say, according to naturalism,
that any expressions or terms found in moral judgments are *synonymous with*
or possess the same meaning as terms or expressions or combinations thereof of a
purely factual or descriptive kind.[10] This is to deny, then, any unique and special
"meaning" to ethical expressions that cannot be translated into descriptive
language.

Now naturalism, thus described, is not how Dewey's theory can be characterized.
For Dewey does not argue that value-propositions are synonymous with factually
descriptive ones. As we shall see below (§ 96), Dewey attributes a *de jure* quality
and imperative meaning to valuation-propositions marking them off from *de
facto* and empirical judgments generally. But it is possible to see Dewey's theory
as exemplifying a modified version of naturalism in the following way. For
Dewey, a valuation-proposition occurs in relation to other propositions of a descriptive and predictive empirical kind. As we will see, at least three stated predictions are necessary to and are included in any completely formulated valuation. In addition, statements of observed fact of and about the context in which
value-propositions are forthcoming are necessary to the formulation of a distinc-

[9] This, very nearly, is Hare's way of putting it. See *The Language of Morals*, ch. 5, esp.
p. 92. The passage quoted is from the excellent article on ethics in Urmson, p. 139; I assume its author is Hare.
[10] We can defer to Appendix 6 the questions that have been raised recently about a
criterion for or definition of *synonymity*.

tive value-proposition, according to Dewey. Thus the thesis of modified naturalism comes to this: moral judgments are not synonymous with statements of nonmoral fact, but (a) a moral judgment includes in it statements of nonmoral fact, and (b) a moral judgment is discredited, invalidated, unwarranted, if the statements of fact included in it are false.[11]

It is in some such sense, I believe, that Dewey construed the relation of moral and purely factual judgments within inquiry. Empirical propositions, on this view, serve not only as *reasons for* a moral judgment; they are among the logically necessary conditions of a moral judgment (and the "warrantability" of certain empirical propositions, cf. §§ 39–40, necessarily affects the warrantability of moral judgments). But the matrix for the relation between given propositions of fact and propositions of valuation is that of *inquiry*. It is the occurrence of a specific inquiry that determines just what judgments of fact and value will be relevant, and what propositions will be related and how, in bringing inquiry to a conclusion. And inquiries, in turn, originate because of the occurrence of those *situations* that expressly require inquiry.

While he does not deny a distinction between moral and nonmoral propositions, the point of the distinction, for Dewey, is not driven in upon an alleged special logic or component of meaning separating moral assertions and language from assertions and descriptions of fact. Rather, Dewey directs the distinction between moral or ethical and nonmoral to be one of kinds of *contexts* of human activities and purposes. In short, 'moral' and 'ethical' characterize *situations* for Dewey, a distinct class of situations possessing certain distinguishable features marking them off from other kinds of situations. In this sense, where a situation is regarded as *moral* in quality and outcome, *all* propositions relevant to and effective in the resolution of the situation, all propositions effecting the institution of judgment and an active transformation of the situation are of a "moral" nature.

But we must now turn to the theory itself and to Dewey's analysis of judgment and evaluation.

§ 91.   *Situation, Value, and Valuation*

For Dewey, values originate, are located, and persist or pass away among the relations of human beings to one another and to environing conditions. 'Value,' as Dewey points out,[12] is used both as a verb ("I value his friendship") and a noun ("It was a choice between values," "Pack your valuables"). The verb 'to value' may be used in the sense of *prizing* something or *appraising*. The noun 'value' may designate an object or a goal of action, or quality of object. In any of these cases, however, 'value' has reference to types of objects and conditions—

---

[11] It remains only to add that, for Dewey, the nonmoral statements of fact are true or false of "existential situations," i.e., empirical conditions—thus distinguishing this modified naturalism from possible others in which nonmoral facts could also be nonempirical.
[12] *Theory of Valuation*, p. 4.

to complex conditions, not to simple properties of objects or simple feelings of persons or states of mind. That which has value, or is valued, is in possession of these characteristics by being a part of a complex whole of conditions—a situation.[13]

A situation, it will be recalled, "is not a single object or set of objects and events" but a "contextual whole."[14] Dewey adds that it is as an aspect *of* situations that any object or event is discriminated and becomes knowable. We do not experience or judge "of objects or events in isolation but only in connection with a contextual whole."[15]

At the moment, there are two important features of Dewey's theory of the situation as a contextual whole which most concern us.

First, these contexts consist of "an environing experienced world," and thus physical and organic conditions are among the properties contributing to and making up situations. That is, situations include living creatures and material conditions organized and interacting in various intricate physical-chemical and biological ways. The substratum of situations, we may say, is a level of physical, biochemical, physiological events, structures, and processes. But more, a situation in which experience occurs includes a pattern of habitual behavior and organic adjustments on the part of persons involved. Thus psychological and social components, or in a broad sense, cultural factors, are also to be counted in as aspects of situations. Moreover, behavior directed to certain interests or ends-in-view as goals is conditioned in fairly elaborate ways by past experience, failures, and successes, and socially approved modes of action. Thus an anticipated future and patterns of past experience impinge upon occurring situations to give the present a historical character and temporal depth in which past and future events relate to those presently happening. In short, situations are complicated not only as temporal processes of events, i.e., as a process is of greater complexity than any one of its parts or stages, but also because of the element of human behavior in which past and future (possible) events serve to influence present conduct.[16]

Second, according to Dewey, every situation "is a whole in virtue of its immediately pervasive quality."[17] The pervasive quality identifies the situation, for us, *as* a situation and as *the* individual situation it is. Perhaps, although Dewey does

[13] On Dewey's theory of *situation*, see § 39 above.
[14] *Logic: The Theory of Inquiry*, p. 66. For the full quotation, see § 39 above.
[15] *Ibid.*, p. 66.
[16] " 'Present' activity is not a sharp narrow knife-blade in time. The present is complex, containing within itself a multitude of habits and impulses. It is enduring, a course of action, a process including memory, observation and foresight, a pressure foreward, a glance backward and a look outward. It is of *moral* moment because it marks a transition in the direction of breadth and clarity of action or in that of triviality and confusion." *Human Nature and Conduct*, p. 281.
[17] *Logic*, p. 68. On the same page Dewey adds: "The pervasively qualitative is not only that which binds all constituents into a whole but it is also unique; it constitutes in each situation an *individual* situation, indivisible and unduplicable. Distinctions and relations are instituted *within* a situation; *they* are recurrent and repeatable in different situations." See also Dewey's discussion of this aspect of situations in *Problems of Men*, pp. 327–328. The "pervasive quality" of a situation is a notion that Dewey felt to be true in Bradley's criticism of Green. We took note of this earlier in § 62.

not say, different qualities may be judged as pervasive under differing conditions, or by different observers. But in ·such possible cases it is not one situation that exhibits differing qualities from differing points of view. The differing points of view constitute different situations. And different qualities serve to identify different situations.

One kind of pervasive quality that characterizes situations wanting inquiry is that of *indeterminateness*. This is a kind of situation that ordinarily is questionable and evokes inquiry; the doubtful situation becomes identified as problematic and inquiry has begun.[18]

From the two observations just made we are led to two general conclusions:

1) For Dewey moral judgments occur in and have to do with situations whose characteristics and constituent parts are of considerable complexity. This should not, of course, suggest that because the conditions causing situations to occur exhibit great variety—ranging as we noticed from physics through biological and culturally conditioning habits and impulses, etc.—a moral judgment is *about* or *entails* references to this multitude of conditions. This would be like saying that when a man makes a comment on the weather, since he is a physico-chemical-biological system, and since he could not have commented at all if he were not a material organization of a certain kind, his comment entails or "includes in its meaning" references to these physicochemical conditions. It is unlikely that anyone would wish to maintain that in order to understand our neighbor's remark, "it looks as if it will snow," we must know something about the anatomical and psychological properties of our neighbor. There have been, however, those who argue that in order to understand any statement one must know something about the history, psychoanalytic background, and culture of the person making the statement. But this contention need not detain us; it invites fatal objections in resting on a peculiar sense of 'understanding,' and applied to itself, it is self-refuting.

Supposing, however, in the example offered, when our neighbor happens to say "it looks as if it will snow," it is afternoon on a hot summer's day. We should be surprised. And while nonetheless understanding *what* he has said, we might take an interest in some of the causal conditions, even anatomical and psychological, that we suppose might explain *why* he has made this comment. In this case, we would be concerned to consider various formative and causal conditions relevant to *how* and *why* a certain statement was made (i.e., what led to its selection and utterance, or *how* it was arrived at). We still need not argue that a certain fairly simple comment about possible snow entails, or "involves" references to what may be very complicated psychological and neurological phenomena, such as the causes of sunstroke and the like. Where utterances may be relatively simple, the occasions of utterance may be exceedingly intricate.

Similar considerations apply to Dewey's ethical theory and distinctions to be made in it and its uses. Thus the occasions (i.e., situations) of moral judgment

[18] *Logic*, pp. 105, 107.

are never simple, and inquiry into *how* or *why* a moral judgment is rendered in a given situation will comprise the many sorts of conditions noted earlier. In general, that kind of empirical inquiry will be guided by theoretical and factual information drawn from physics, biology, psychology, social, and historical conditions, and so on. The inquiry is aimed at investigating and explaining *how*, in a given situation, one or more expressions of value or value judgments happened to be made. The inquiry might also result in critical evaluation, that is, in an appraisal of the specific valuations that occurred in the specific situation. The appraisal would be directed to discerning and judging how effective and satisfactory, relative to the situation in which they occurred, were the valuations in question. The controlling principles of this other kind of inquiry into and appraisal of a given valuation will be discussed shortly. Here, for the moment, we want to recognize one form of ethical inquiry and, according to Dewey, its wholly empirical character.

> Valuations are empirically observable patterns of behavior and may be studied as such. The propositions that result are *about* valuations but are not themselves value-propositions in any sense marking them off from other matter-of-fact propositions.[19]

Dewey's theory of valuation is proposed as an attempt to explain (*a*) how valuations, as patterns of behavior, occur; (*b*) how informative and accurate empirical propositions *about* valuations can be constructed; (*c*) how empirical propositions about the *warrantability* of valuations or judgments, and assessments of valuations can be made.

2) Dewey's conception of a moral situation was described in an earlier chapter (§ 41). One part of his own description bears repeating here.

> *Moral* goods and ends exist only when something has to be done. The fact that something has to be done proves that there are deficiencies, evils in the existent situation. . . . Consequently the good of the situation has to be discovered, projected and attained on the basis of the exact defect and trouble to be rectified.[20]

This passage, in relation to the remarks of some pages back, illustrates the essential pattern of Dewey's ethical theory and rightly emphasizes the import of the *situation* as basic to the ensuing theory.

§ 92. *The Biological Basis of Desire: The Origins of Valuation*

Basic as the concept of *situation* is to Dewey's ethical theory it is necessary to notice in addition, if we are to appreciate the rationale of the position, how the situation is construed (focusing upon the human agents) in a biological fashion.

[19] *Theory of Valuation*, p. 51.
[20] *Reconstruction in Philosophy*, p. 169.

Organic shock, disequilibrium, imbalance—all characterize the "disrupted" "distorted" relations of the live creature and its environing conditions. Impulse and habits, and organic energies are called into play in these circumstances of stimulus irregularity, irritation, blocked action. In man alert to trouble, to something gone wrong, to a sense of need, a vital *difference* is instituted in operations of sensation and thought. Where these might in moments of relative stability operate quiescently, even aimlessly and enjoyably, in troubled situations they become functional and directive: attention transforms passing sensations into signals of existing conditions, and ideas become projections and anticipations of future conditions under hypothetically calculated courses of action.

Theorizing thus, as Dewey does, we find the categories of *conflict* and *adjustment* fundamental in the analysis of behavior (as reviewed in §§ 37, 38). Conflict and adjustment describe phases of the life process of organisms in their environments. So viewed, environments are not containers of life but mediums and means of life.[21] The situations in which conflict and adjustment occur are interactions and integrations of organic and inorganic conditions and energies. With changes that come in organic and environing conditions, writes Dewey, "With differentiation of interactions comes the need of maintaining a balance among them; or, in objective terms, a unified environment."[22] Balance, or maintenance of a unified environment, is the distinct *need* and *objective* of living creatures.[23]

> Indeed, living may be regarded as a continual rhythm of disequilibrations and recoveries of equilibrium. The "higher" the organism, the more serious become the disturbances and the more energetic (and often more prolonged) are the efforts necessary for its reestablishment. The state of disturbed equilibration constitutes *need*. The movement towards its restoration is search and exploration. The recovery is fulfillment or satisfaction.[24]

It must be remembered that the predicates or those qualitative aspects of situations conveyed by 'conflict,' 'disequilibrium,' 'doubt,' and 'adjustment,' 'equilibrium,' 'integration,' etc., are not to be taken as references to internal states of organisms *in* situations, but as descriptive *of* situations as wholes.[25] It is situations that exhibit conflicting tendencies or components, or adjustment and integration. Allowing for differences in selective points of view and analytical distinctions in

[21] *Human Nature and Conduct*, p. 296: "Human nature exists and operates in an environment. And it is not 'in' that environment as coins are in a box, but as a plant is in the sunlight and soil. It is of them, continuous with their energies. . . ."
[22] *Logic*, p. 26. The entire chapter "The Existential Matrix of Inquiry: Biological" repays study.
[23] The "need" and "objective" do not necessarily have to be taken as conscious or reflective.
[24] *Logic*, p. 27.
[25] Thus, as noted in § 39, "The *situation* has these traits. *We* are doubtful because the situation is inherently doubtful. . . . The habit of disposing of the doubtful as if it belonged only to *us* rather than to the existential situation in which we are caught and implicated is an inheritance from subjectivistic psychology." *Logic*, pp. 105–106.

contexts (as argued in § 79), one can say that in situations as a whole where disequilibrium and equilibrium, respectively, are exhibited, from the point of view of organic behavior *need* and *satisfaction*, respectively, are exhibited.

The relevance of the foregoing ideas to ethical theory must now be considered.

For Dewey, valuations are defined as acts of desiring. Now there is a sense in which value is identified with enjoyment, and an object (or condition) of enjoyment is said to be valued as "prized," "cherished," "cared for," etc. In one sense 'enjoyment' may refer to cases where gratification is received from an object or events already in existence. Moreover, in some cases, no concern may be felt to produce, protect, or sustain the conditions of enjoyment—for example, the sense in which a man is said to enjoy life, or an afternoon is declared enjoyable. These might be classified as instances of something valued and where declarations or expressions of value are made. But these are not cases of *valuation*, on Dewey's theory. Wishing for something, cherishing, enjoying, as activities that do not involve an effort to *produce* the conditions valued, or to *perpetuate* the same, are not valuations. Valuation includes as a necessary condition of its occurrence a causative or productive effort. That effort is an organic biologic tendency[26] in a situation,[27] mediated by habits and social conditions—with an outcome in some way (significantly, successfully, or the reverse) affecting or modifying the circumstances in which it arose. This effort, or tendency, as a causal condition of results, actively affecting the interaction of organism and environment, is *desire*.

> When we inquire into the actual emergence of desire and its object and the value-property ascribed to the latter . . . it is as plain as anything can be that desires arise only when "there is something the matter," where there is some "trouble" in an existing situation. When analyzed, this "something the matter" is found to spring from the fact that there is something lacking, wanting, in the existing situation as it stands, an absence which produces conflict in the elements that do exist. When things are going completely smoothly, desires do not arise, and there is no occasion to project ends-in-view, for "going smoothly" signifies that there is no need for effort and struggle. It suffices to let things take their "natural" course. There is no occasion to investigate what it would be better to have happen in the future, and hence no projection of an end-object.[28]

§ 93. The Rational Element in Desire: Valuation-Propositions

Desire originates, we have seen, in disturbances or conflicts in organic-environing relations. But desire is distinct from impulses, automatic reflexes, or routine

---

[26] Dewey's expression, *Theory of Valuation*, p. 18.
[27] Or as Dewey often puts it, in "existential contexts." Cf. *ibid.*, p. 16.
[28] *Ibid.*, p. 33.

actions that might be occasioned by troubled situations. Desires contain a directive, anticipatory, "projective" component, in addition to sheer energetic tendency or drive.[29] Dewey seems to interpret it as similar to sheer impulse or appetite in origin, but containing, or modified by, references to ends-in-view.[30]

It must be observed that for Dewey, desire and desiring are not occasions of allegedly simple mental or psychological events nor simply units of behavior. Rather, Dewey's treatment is about processes of behavior and rather complicated organic operations and coordinations making up phases of these processes (see § 38 above). Response to disequilibrium or need, the end-in-view suggested, will be detected by when, where, and how a need is felt, the occurrence of other desires, and judgments of what is and will be happening, etc. All of the complexities that enter into the genesis of a *situation* (§ 91 above) bear upon the genesis and outcome of desires.

Let us for a moment contrast this view of desires, as basic causal conditions of evaluations, with one original and influential ethical analysis advanced by Russell. Russell argued that in asserting that something had *value*, we are giving expression to our emotions, i.e., wishes and desires. He wrote:

> It is obvious, to begin with, that the whole idea of good and bad has some connection with *desire*. *Prima facie*, anything we desire is "good," and anything that we all dread is "bad." If we all agreed in our desires, the matter could be left there, but unfortunately our desires conflict.[31]

Russell describes ethics as an unsuccessful attempt to escape from the subjectivity and irresolvability of differences over what men desire.[32] Ethical sentences, Russell argued, *seem* to be statements; indeed they are often deliberately uttered as if they were statements. But unlike statements such as 'this is square,' the sentence 'this is good' is neither true nor false. What the sentence means reflects some desire on the part of the person making it:

> When a man says "this is good in itself" he *seems* to be making a statement. . . . I think that what the man really means is: "I wish everybody to desire this" or rather "Would that everybody desired this."[33]

---

[29] There are difficulties in the role of the little word 'contain' here; we saw a similar difficulty in a quite suggestively analogous analysis by Peirce of belief 'containing' a habit, signs and meanings 'containing' a futuritive reference. There are problems as to whether 'contained' is to be given a logical, or (here) psychological construction. Dewey's view of *desire* as "containing" or "involving" an "ideational" element, viz., "end-in-view," and Peirce's doctrine of a futuritive reference of beliefs, ideas, and signs, are significant theoretical linkings in the pragmatic analysis of behavior and thought.

[30] "Sheer impulse or appetite may be described as affective-motor; but any theory that connects valuation with desire and interest by that very fact connects valuation with behavior which is affective-*ideational*-motor. This fact proves the *possibility* of the existence of distinctive valuation-propositions." *Theory of Valuation*, p. 52.

[31] *Religion and Science*, ch. 9, "Science and Ethics," p. 231.

[32] Ibid., p. 231: "If I say 'what I want is good,' my neighbor will say 'No, what *I* want.' Ethics is an attempt—though not, I think, a successful one—to escape from this subjectivity."

[33] *Ibid.*, p. 235.

For Russell we have two possible interpretations of the sentence "this is good": taken as a statement it asserts something about the speaker (i.e., what he truly does or does not desire); or "interpreted in a general way, it states nothing, but merely desires something."[34]

In general, by Russell's analysis, sentences of the form 'x is good' are translatable into either (a) 'I desire x' or (b) 'would that everybody desired x.' Of these latter sentences, (a), when the context of utterance is clear, is an autobiographical statement; (b) is an ethical assertion about desires, strictly, that it is desired that everybody desire x, or, as an imperative, 'desire x!' It follows, for Russell, that ethical sentences are not empirical statements at all and that no scientific justification for or adjudication of ethical assertions is possible.

I am not concerned here with the merits of Russell's view,[35] only with what it illustrates by comparison with Dewey's theory. Both theories emphasize in their respective ways the place of desire in expressions of value and acts of valuing. But the interesting difference is that while Russell takes as ultimate the existence of desires ("existing" as "private," "subjective," personal "state of mind"[36]), for Dewey the existence of desires is neither ultimate[37] nor self-explanatory. And, as we have seen, determining what is a desire (like what is desired) is a rather elaborate task of analysis, and dependent upon a theory of situation, human energies and conduct. Russell's analysis rests on assumptions concerning the meaning of 'desire' that are themselves parts of a traditional theory of mind, a subjectivistic psychology and epistemology largely stemming from Descartes (as indicated in Part One).[38]

The point here is not so much that Russell's analysis of ethical sentences is wrong, for we might agree with the main thesis that expressions of valuation *are* the results of desires. The point is rather that Russell's assumptions concerning the nature of desire and his use of the concept of 'desire' are empirically questionable and conceptually confused, and thus one of Russell's main conclusions is not decisive. That conclusion is:

[34] *Ibid.*, p. 236.

[35] Thus I pass over many difficulties in Russell's analysis as not germane to the present discussion. It can be noticed that while Russell might be right that *sometimes* 'x is good' could mean 'would that everybody desired x,' this leaves out a very important ethical use of 'good,' viz., one in which it often might be held that (1) 'x is good in itself' is not to mean (2) 'I wish (or, would that) everybody desired x' but (3) 'x *ought* to be desired.' The sentences (2) and (3) are not always used as equivalents, for ordinarily (3) would be said to *follow* from (1) but not from (2), yet if (1) and (2) were equivalent, (3) would also follow from (2).

[36] Cf. Russell, *Religion and Science*, pp. 236–237.

[37] Thus, as Dewey says, "The confusions and mistakes in existing theories . . . arise very largely from taking desire and interest as original instead of in the contextual situations in which the arise." *Theory of Valuation*, p. 55.

[38] The background of this theory has been sketched in Part I and we have also come upon it in the beginning of the present chapter and earlier in § 42. Many of Dewey's writings are directed to exposing the dubious assumptions of this Cartesian theory of mind and their disastrous consequences for ethics, epistemology, and philosophy of science as the Cartesian theory was gerrymandered into the empirical philosophies of Locke, Hume, Mill, and Russell. A more recent lucid critical analysis of the doctrine is in Ryle, and on its epistemology, Austin.

Since no way can be even imagined for deciding a difference as to values, the conclusion is forced upon us that the difference is one of tastes, not one as to any objective truth.[39]

It is this conclusion that Dewey's theory is concerned to deny.

We can now begin to see how Dewey argues that desires and ends-in-view *are* subject to appraisal, how valuations can in turn be subject to critical evaluation.

In maintaining that 'desire' has reference to behavior-patterns, to operations and processes, rather than to things or psychic states, we may—to follow Dewey—note those analytically discriminable phases of the organic pattern or process: (*a*) and initially felt or threatened irritation or shock, or need, deficit, conflict; (*b*) a predicted, forecasted, projected "good" or end "answering" or satisfying conditions (*a*); (*c*) efforts, or a series of more or less related and organized efforts to bring about (*b*) or institute (*b*) in place of (*a*). I do not mean to suggest that Dewey would have held that a *desire* is irritated, that *it* anticipates or forecasts, that *it* strives to achieve satisfaction, etc. This would be to personify desires, or worse, to confuse desire with the creature and situation in which desire occurs. Thus (*a*), (*b*), and (*c*) should be taken as roughly demarcated phases of human behavior under the influence of or manifesting desires.

The rational aspect of desiring is suggested by phase (*b*). Behavior that under conflict and tension, i.e., "need," projects and anticipates an "end" or possible satisfaction is rational (or "ideational" in Dewey's terminology). It is just here that critical canons and assessments of desiring are possible, namely, as to degrees of rationality or reasonableness of what (end-in-view) is desired, of what may be the projected goal of actual effort.

§ 94.   Intelligent Desiring: Ends-Means

The Greek word *aitia*, rendered into Latin as *causa*, from which our word 'cause,' when used by Greek poets and philosophers could mean *reason, explanation, motive, responsibility, blame*. Plato, in a famous discussion of *aitia* in the *Phaedo*, argued that human conduct could not be adequately explained by mechanical or physical kinds of *aitia* alone. My anatomical properties, bones and muscles, may be among the "causes" of my sitting or walking. These causes help to make my action possible. They might also be included in an *explanation* (a causal account) of my behavior. But there is another *aitia* to consider as the "motive" and factor "responsible" for what I do. There are purposes, goals, ends that I seek. This kind of *aitia* is not of a mechanical or physical nature. Man acts partly in response to future goods. Plato argued that the good is a most important kind of *aitia* for explaining human nature.

Explanations of goal-directed or purposive behavior take a teleological point of view. An end, *telos*, or goal is one kind of *aitia* (a "final cause," to use Aristotle's

[39] *Religion and Science*, p. 238.

term) of the behavior of live creatures. Now the Greeks liked to point out also that man differed from the other animals not by having purposes, but by possession of a sense of *right* and of *law*[40] and of *good*.[41] That sense of law and good thus figures as a central "cause," *aitia*, in human conduct, and man is viewed as a creature whose purposes and motives are distinctly ethical.

Ethical theory and ethical behavior have thus been construed in teleological terms.[42] Action and choice aim at some good, and the good is defined as that at which all things aim. Since the end or aim is "that for the sake of which" we act, action without an end is blind and futile.[43] This point of view, which has dominated ethical theory since Plato and Aristotle, leads to a conclusion that has permeated all later theory as well: there must be some ultimate end, or aim, to all action and desire, something intrinsically good, the Good. Without such a Good, the activities of life seem aimless, and ethically meaningless; experience is then conceived as the labors of Sisyphus in the absence of a focal Good to deliver and consummate all action.

It is against this classical tradition of separating end from means and hypostatizing ends, and absolutizing a Good, that Dewey developed his conception of norms and ends as "ends-in-view." He insisted that 'end' in ethical theorizing was ambiguous. The term could mean, first, an actual result of the effort undergone, the successful completion of action and satisfactory termination of desire; second, that which guides effort, which is the projected "good" of a situation as a directive *means* to organizing effort in reaching a satisfactory conclusion. In the first sense, *end* is a completion of activity, a state of satisfaction, (or otherwise). In the second sense, *end* is a plan or guide for activity and thus functions as a *means to* an end in the first sense. The end or goal of health in medical practice, for example, can be described as what the efforts of the physician (if successful) come to, how they terminate. Or it may mean a general guiding principle or way of planning and organizing the treatment of a patient. The physician, says Dewey,

> does not have an idea of health as an absolute end-in-itself, an absolute good by which to determine what to do. On the contrary he forms his general idea of health as an end and a good (value) for the patient on the ground of what his techniques

[40] Hesiod, *Works and Days*, 276–279: "The son of Kronos ordained this law for men, that fishes and beasts and winged fowls should devour one another, for right [*dikē*] is not in them; but to mankind he gave right which proves far the best."

[41] Aristotle, *Politics* I. 2, 1253a15: "what distinguishes man from other animals is that he alone has a sense of good and evil, of right [*dikē*] and wrong, and the like."

[42] In connection with themes discussed in Part I and § 88 above, it can be added here that, when the teleological point of view was abandoned in physical science (i.e., explanations invoking "final causes" were renounced), the separation of science and ethics, natural and moral philosophy, physics and psychology, body and mind seemed an inevitable result of "scientific" procedure. Descartes' dualism of two orders, body and mind, is an apt symbol of this. The teleological formulation of behavior, we happened to note in § 38, note 80, can be reconstructed in causal terms.

[43] Thus, Aristotle, *Nicomachean Ethics* I. 2, 1094a20: "if, in other words, we do not make all our choices for the sake of something else—for in this way the process will go on infinitely so that our desire would be futile and pointless—then obviously this end will be the good, that is, the highest good."

of examination have shown to be the troubles from which patients suffer and the means by which they are overcome.[44]

Basically, it is the situation, the particular privations and the existing "need," that constitutes the empirically objective conditions relative to which desires and ends-in-view are reasonable (i.e., productive of a satisfactory solution) or not.

The "value" of different ends that suggest themselves is estimated or measured by the capacity they exhibit to guide action in making good, *satisfying*, in its literal sense, existing lacks. . . .

Ends-in-view are appraised or valued as *good* or *bad* on the ground of their serviceability in the direction of behavior dealing with states of affairs found to be objectionable because of some lack or conflict in them. They are appraised as fit or unfit, proper or improper, *right* or *wrong*, on the ground of their *requiredness* in accomplishing this end.[45]

The function of ends-in-view in guiding action and deliberation toward a satisfying terminus of effort, is analogous to the role of leading principles, theories, and laws in the organization and execution of scientific inquiries (whch we studied in the previous chapter). Now definitions of 'health,' 'wealth,' 'honesty,' 'courage,' and other virtues can be found in dictionaries, and these excellences might seem to have some object-like status as ends-in-themselves. But on the pragmatic interpretation of leading principles, these "virtues" are not *what* is desired, but general suggestions of *how* desire can be guided in specific situations. The virtues are not objects or *things*. They represent possible *ways*, generalized from past experience, of encountering and acting with things in existing situations. 'Health' or 'justice' are adverbial, interpreted as suggestions or leading principles for anticipating and inferring certain kinds of conditons from others and acting accordingly; "they are modifiers of action in special cases." "To say that a man seeks health or justice is only to say that he seeks to live healthily or justly."[46] The class of traditional virtues—health, wealth, temperance, courage, etc.—pragmatically or instrumentally viewed, function as hypotheses. They

suggest possible traits to be on the lookout for in studying a particular case; they suggest methods of action to be tried in removing the inferred causes of ill. They are tools of insight; their value is in promoting an individualized response in the individual situation.[47]

§ 95. *Propositions and the Criterion of Valuation*

We are now in a position to appreciate and examine the logical structure of Dewey's ethical theory.

[44] *Theory of Valuation*, p. 46.
[45] *Ibid.*, pp. 46, 47.
[46] *Reconstruction in Philosophy*, p. 167.
[47] *Ibid.*, p. 169.

The problem-situation, we have seen, is fundamental both to the occurrence of desires and valuations, and as the criterion of relevance and adequacy of ends-in-view. It is in actual existing situations that a need or conflict occurs and it is those particular situations that objectively determine *what* is needed. Thus while desires and valuations occur, the specific desire-efforts to sustain or to bring about certain conditions (i.e., what is valued) are "warranted" or not depending on the degree to which the conditions desired are in fact the conditions that will and do *satisfy* the situation in *question*. We have seen this pattern before (§ 40). For a troubled situation S_1, one in which there is conflict and need, there exist certain active operations and certain conditions S_2 such that if S_2 is brought into existence, it corresponds to S_1 as a solution or satisfactory resolution of S_1. We can observe the pattern a little more carefully and witness the working of valuation-propositions.

1) S_1 is the situation in which conflict (or threat of same) and "tension of need" seem to occur. That *something* is occurring, is, for purposes of the theory, undeniable. But *what* is occurring, what in fact *is* wrong, is a matter for examination. Suppose that observations on what seem to be the conditions of the trouble, and interpretation and judgment (in the form of statements about what is happening and what is wrong) are made. Any number of true or false, sound or unsound empirical statements about the situation are possible. Eventually, we suppose, a general concluding judgment about what the source and nature of the conflict is, is arrived at. Dewey calls this a determination of what is lacking or needed.[48] Since 'need,' for Dewey, seems to refer both to the existence of deficiency or lack, and to the way a thing is lacking (therefore *what* is needed), to determine *that* something is needed (i.e., a problem) is also to be venturing suggestions of *what* is needed (i.e., a solution). How accurately the need is understood clearly affects the reasonableness of *what* is desired and valued, of what is thought needed and anticipated as promising satisfaction.

2)   With the desires that arise in the troubled situation, come "ends-in-view" or projected goods or satisfactions. The problem is how to transform S_1 into S_2. Now this problem, or its resolution, is the locus for what Dewey regards as "value-propositions of the distinctive sort."

The problem of this transformation requires, for its solution, additional propositions (based upon and related to those already advanced concerning what is needed, or what is lacking); it requires judgments concerning the available means to the solution of S_1, and the amount of effort required; and the weighing of various possible ends or goods in relation to these means and to other long-range purposes and interests. Ends-in-view, possible goods and relevant future purposes, serve as partial plans of action (conceived action, as Peirce would say):

48 'Need' is a somewhat ambiguous term; it can be used to designate a state of deficiency or lack without including a suggestion of what is lacking or needed, e.g., "I am in need," "What do you need?" But it is also often used in the latter sense to assert not only *that* something is wanting or needed but *what* is needed: "Give to the needy," "Your country needs you now."

"desires . . . and environing conditions as means are modes of action."[49] Desires *and* environing conditions are to be thought of as energies. These energies and their possible coordination and direction constitute the problem for and process of valuation and moral action.

We may represent the process of valuation as a pattern or series of propositions:

1) S_1 occurs.

2) S_1 exhibits such and such condition of need or threatened loss.

With the operation of desire-effort to get rid of S_1 and produce an acceptable situation, further propositions are forthcoming

3) S_2 (as a projected, anticipated good, i.e., *what* is valued) will satisfy, or is the solution to S_1.

4) Such and such energies, existent (and possible) conditions and actions, are means or ways to the institution of S_2, as the transformation of S_1.

Now each of these four stages might include many further propositions supporting or warranting the general propositions thus stated. Stages (1) and (2) are (for Dewey) to be determined empirically, on inquiry, as being the case or not. There either is a troubled situation of a certain kind, or there is not. Propositions making up and supporting (1) and (2) in this case will be empirically verifiable. The propositions in stages (3) and (4) are also (Dewey argues) subject to verification, at least in principle. That is, given conditions asserted (truly) to exist in (1) and (2), there *is* a satisfactory solution to those conditions, or there is not, and some proposed "end" S_2 *is* that solution or it is not. The same logical conditions hold for (4); certain actions and conditions will or will not produce S_2. Thus the propositions represented by (1), (2), (3), and (4) are (all or some of them) warranted empirically or not. A process of valuation, in case S_1 occurred, might be symbolized, then, as the general propositional assertion Π, viz.:

The propositions (1), (2), (3), and (4) are true,
i.e., warranted.

Either Π is warranted by the facts or it is not. A valuation *of* a process of valuation could consist of an inquiry into the warrant for Π. One might conclude that some of the prepositions under Π were not warranted, or that alternative possible steps in place of those asserted in (3) and (4) would prove less frustrating and less apt to occasion further problems. In turn, this last valuation would be at least theoretically subject to critical inquiry and verification in further valuations.

§ 96.   Desire and the Desirable

Dewey has sometimes been accused of failing to indicate how, in his theory, any distinction between desires and the desirable can be made. Unless we believe

49 *Theory of Valuation*, p. 53.

(mysteriously) that what *is* ought to be, if we recognize no difference between 'x is desired' and 'x ought (or ought not) to be desired,' we seem to have no theory or sense of moral judgments. As should be clear from earlier pages, however, Dewey emphasizes just this difference in kinds of judgments and statements. In his terminology, not every desire, not every end-in-view, not every object valued *ought* to be desired, pursued, or valued.

For Dewey, that desires occur, that some objects or events are valued are facts about the world that are in themselves no more "moral" in import than any other empirical facts. Nor is the fact that desires or feelings of enjoyment or liking in themselves exist, to be identified with the existence of objects of *value*.[50]

The way in which we come to know increasingly more about the world we live in exhibits an important transition between our immediately had or given experience of objects and controlled experimental operations upon those objects. "The scientific revolution" writes Dewey, "came about when the material of direct and uncontrolled experience was taken as problematic; as supplying material to be transformed by reflective operations into known objects."[51] We have seen how Lewis developed essentially the same distinction in his discussion of directly presented and objective properties of objects (§ 45). This difference between directly *experienced* and *known* objects is used by Dewey in constructing an important analogous distinction in his analysis of value.

> Formal analogy suggests that we regard our direct and original experience of things liked and enjoyed as only *possibilities* of values to be achieved. . . .

> The formal statement may be given concrete content by pointing to the difference between the enjoyed and the enjoyable, the desired and the desirable, the satis*fying* and the satis*factory*.[52]

To say that something is enjoyed or desired is to report (truly or falsely) some existing fact. According to Dewey, this report is on a par with statements that something is sweet, or red. "But to call an object a value is to assert that it satisfies or fulfills certain conditions."[53] To call an object a value, Dewey argues, is more than a statement of fact. It is a judgment, and specifically one in which a prediction is made *and* an attitude or intended action or policy is declared.

> To declare something satis*factory* . . . is, in effect, a judgment that the thing "will do." It involves a prediction; it contemplates a future in which the thing will

---

[50] Dewey writes in "Construction of the Good," pp. 264–265 (Sellars and Hospers, pp. 278–279):

> Values . . . may be connected inherently with liking, and yet not with *every* liking but only with those that judgment has approved.

> A *feeling* of good or excellence is as far removed from goodness in fact as a feeling that objects are intelligently thus and so is removed from their being actually so.

Dewey's important statement of his position, "The Construction of the Good," appeared as ch. 10 in *The Quest for Certainty*. It also has been reprinted in Sellars and Hospers' anthology.

[51] *The Quest for Certainty*, p. 258; Sellars and Hospers, p. 275.
[52] *Quest*, pp. 259, 260; Sellars and Hospers, p. 275.
[53] *Quest*, p. 260; Sellars and Hospers, p. 275.

continue to serve; it *will* do. It asserts a consequence the thing will actively institute; it will *do*. That it is satisfying is the content of a proposition of fact; that it is satis-factory is a judgment, an estimate, an appraisal. It denotes an attitude *to be* taken, that of striving to perpetuate and to make secure.[54]

To say of some object *x* that *x* is satisfactory is to (*a*) predict that *x* will satisfy and fulfill certain conditions, and (*b*) declare that a certain attitude and action will be taken in the future to secure or perpetuate *x*. As for this latter part of the judgment, in which Dewey says "an attitude *to be* taken" is denoted, how are we to interpret the sense of '*to be*'?[55] Not simply as a prediction; not, for example, saying "at some future time *t* an attitude will be taken, and striving to secure *x* will occur at *t*." This would be to predict the future occurrence of an attitude and striving. Dewey does not mean this, although he apparently does not notice that a prediction of this kind, as well as the prediction in (*a*), *is* involved in what he does mean. For what Dewey does mean by '*to be*' is, as we noticed, a declaration of intention or announcement of policy with respect to *x* and its securance. But intentions, or policy announcements, *do*—unless uttered as lies—include pre-dictions, viz., that given certain conditions, one will perform and one (and per-haps others) can expect the performance of certain acts.

For Dewey, a judgment that *x* is satisfactory, in addition to containing a predic-tion that *x* "will do," also possesses "a claim on future action."[56]

A judgment about what is *to be* desired and enjoyed is . . . a claim on future action; it possesses *de jure* and not merely *de facto* quality.[57]

Following the analogy remarked upon a moment ago, Dewey cites the differ-ence between the proposition "that thing has been eaten" and the judgment "that thing is edible."[58] The difference, he says, "between the desired and the desirable . . . becomes effective as just this point." The statement about something eaten is a simple report of fact. The judgment that something is edible involves predictions and is based on "knowledge of its interactions with other things sufficient to en-able us to foresee its probable effects when it is taken into the organism and produces effects there."[59] So Dewey argues:

To assume that anything can be known in isolation from its connections with other things is to identify knowing with merely having some object before percep-tion or in feeling, and is thus to lose the key to the traits that distinguish an object as known. It is futile, even silly, to suppose that some quality that is directly present constitutes the whole of the thing presenting the quality. It does not do so

[54] *Quest*, p. 261; Sellars and Hospers, p. 276.
[55] I am indebted to Stevenson, *Ethics and Language*, pp. 256–257, for pointing out some problems in a critical discussion of this phraseology of Dewey's.
[56] Dewey early derived the idea that desires are claims upon the future from William James. See his letter to James in Perry, II, 520. See, too, § 28 above.
[57] *Quest*, p. 263; Sellars and Hospers, p. 277.
[58] *Quest*, p. 266; Sellars and Hospers, p. 279.
[59] *Quest*, p. 266; Sellars and Hospers, p. 280.

when the quality is that of being hot or fluid or heavy, and it does not when the quality is that of giving pleasure, or being enjoyed.[60]

Dewey's analogy is designed to help us note likenesses and unlikenesses among the following sorts of statements in the following ways:

a)   'x is desired,' 'w has been eaten,'
        'y is hot,' 'z is dissolved'

are collectively analogous and are as a whole unlike

β)   'x is desirable,' 'w is edible,'
          'y is heat-producing,' 'z is soluble.'

The a statements are *de facto*, reports of the ongoing show; the β statements are not. By the tail endings 'able' and 'ble' in the language in β we can recognize (from § 21 and § 46) the presence of disposition terms.[61] These expressions carry with them futurative references and *indicate* possible expansion into predictions and formulation as conditionals (e.g., 'z is soluble in water' as 'if z were placed in water, z would dissolve.')

But now the question is, if a statements are *de facto*, then following Dewey's analogy, how are β statements to be construed as *de jure*? The contrast of 'x is desired' as an a *de facto* with 'x is desirable' meaning 'x ought to be desired' or 'is *to be* desired' as a β statement *de jure*, in Dewey's exposition, seems to depend on a like contrast between, say, 'z is dissolved' as *de facto* and 'z is soluble' as *de jure*. But in what sense are 'z is soluble' and 'w is edible' *de jure*? It seems absurd to say that these last statements have a *de jure* quality, i.e., that 'z is soluble' is synonymous with 'z ought to be dissolved,' or that 'w is edible' is synonymous with 'w ought to be eaten.' It is absurd, too, to treat all predictions and disposition terms as possessing a normative role. But then Dewey's entire analysis of the difference between 'desire' and 'desirable,' his attempt to suggest the *normative* role of the latter term, if not absurd, is hardly successful.

To the question raised and the criticism it actuated, several answers are possible, for several misunderstandings of Dewey inspire the objecting paragraph. Yet, because it represents a fairly prevalent dissenting argument to Dewey's ethical theory, answers are called for, even if only briefly.

1) The question as to how β statements, such as 'w is edible,' or 'z is soluble,' can reasonably be interpreted as possessing a *de jure* quality presumes an extension of analogy not intended by Dewey. That is, Dewey does not argue that in *every* respect, or that in all significant roles and uses, expressions like 'w is edible'

---

[60] *Quest*, p. 267; Sellars and Hospers, p. 280.

[61] Dewey draws attention to the distinction in *Quest*, p. 266, citing along with the β-like terms ending in 'able,' 'worthy,' and 'ful,' "Noted and notable, noteworthy; remarked and remarkable; advised and advisable, wondered at and wonderful; pleasing and beautiful." We might include in a 'x is valued,' and in β 'x is valuable,' to get Lewis' comment (cf. § 46 above or *An Analysis of Knowledge and Valuation*, p. 520): " 'valuable' is just like 'soluble' and does not imply any actually realized satisfaction any more than 'soluble' implies 'dissolved.' "

and 'x is desirable' are analogous. Dewey is not the clearest of writers, and he does in unguarded moments perhaps suggest this identification. For those who do not countenance the claim that valuations are true or false empirical judgments and thus "scientific" in principle, it is most tempting to read Dewey as saying that no basic difference is to be found between the valuations 'x is desirable,' 'x is valuable,' and such predictions as 'it will rain' or 'iron will expand on heating.' But Dewey does make it clear in some important passages that a moral judgment is not only a prediction or merely a conditional statement of fact.[62]

There is, as we have been seeing, *some* analogy for Dewey between 'x is desired' and 'w is eaten' on the one hand and 'x is desirable' and 'w is edible' on the other. And we have studied that analogy earlier. But in the central passage in question, Dewey does not assign a *de jure* quality to all predictions nor to all true disposition statements. What he does say is that what is to be pursued as *desired* and *enjoyed* possesses a *de jure* quality. The expression 'to be desired,' recalling Dewey's analysis of *desire*, differs from, say, 'edible' or 'soluble,' in just that crucial *moral* meaning of the former not found in the latter. The statement 'w is edible' Dewey takes as a judgment about the nature of w; it involves knowledge of the interactions of w with other substances and organic processes "sufficient to enable us to foresee its probable effects when it is taken into the organism and produces its effects there."[63] Thus 'w is edible' is interpreted as an assertion

[62] The critical points of discussion in the foregoing and immediately following paragraphs have been occasioned partly as a response to Morton White's trenchant objection to the portion of Dewey's analysis here under consideration. For White's critical discussion, see "Value and Obligation in Dewey and Lewis," and *Social Thought in America*, pp. 212–217. White correctly points out, as Dewey does not, the difference between the disposition terms 'soluble' and 'red.' Everything that dissolves is soluble, but not everything that appears red is *objectively* red. The world appears rosy if we wear rose-colored glasses. (We saw, incidentally, in discussing Lewis in § 45 above, the distinction between immediately appearing and objective qualities of objects.) White approves of Dewey holding that 'x is desirable' is not implied by 'x is desired.' Just so, 'a is objectively red' is not implied by 'a appears red.' But the main criticism of Dewey is "that the relation between 'desirable' and 'desired' is allegedly identical with that between 'objectively red' and 'appears red,' " "Value and Obligation in Dewey and Lewis," in Sellars and Hospers, p. 336. White argues that the statements about red do not exhibit *de jure* and *de facto* traits respectively while 'desirable' and 'desired' certainly do. He writes, "the fact that a is objectively red . . . is no more *normative* than the fact that a appears red now. And since the fact that a is desirable (as Dewey construes it) is related to the fact that a is desired in precisely the way that the fact that a is objectively red is related to the fact that a appears red, it would follow that a is desirable is no more normative than a is desired."
One could reply according to much that Dewey says about *norms* that 'a is objectively red' *is* normative. With respect to certain investigations, 'a is objectively red' could function as a standard governing certain experimental procedures, expectations, and rulings upon statements such as 'a appears red' or 'a *ought* to appear red,' etc. But the more basic dissent comes in at those points where White attributes to Dewey the allegation of an *identical* relation between the pairs 'desirable—desire' and 'objectively red—appears red.' Again, White says, "as Dewey construes it 'a is desirable' is related to 'a is desired' in *precisely the way* that the fact that something *is* red is related to the fact that something appears red," Sellars and Hospers, p. 336. But this is to turn Dewey's analogical illustration of some likenesses holding for these relations of terms into an argument for identical relations. Dewey simply does not maintain that the same relation holds between 'is objectively red' and 'appears red,' between 'is edible' and 'is eaten,' or between 'desirable' and 'desire.'

[63] Cf. above, and Dewey, *Quest*, p. 266; Sellars and Hospers, p. 280.

of the form: '*w* possesses such and such chemical and biological properties and if *w* is eaten, it will produce such and such effects in the organism.' This fulfills *one* but not all of the conditions of moral judgment outlined on page 402. For there, we noticed, that in addition to containing a prediction, there was also a declared intent and policy prediction-assertion.

It is clear that the β statements '*w* is edible' and '*z* is soluble' do not have all of the characteristics of '*x* is desirable' or '*x* is enjoyable.' Judgments or propositions that '*x* is desirable' or '*x* is enjoyable' are (true or false) declarations that effort is being taken to produce *x* (i.e., bring *x* into existence) or to secure its continuance. It is this aspect of valuation that constitutes "a claim on future action" and makes a moral judgment "about what is to be desired or enjoyed."[64] A stated valuation contains a rule or principle "for determination of an act to be performed, its reference being to the future and not something already accomplished or done."[65] But, as against taking this reference in a predictive sense only:

> The future act or state is not set forth as a prediction of what will happen but as something which *shall* or *should* happen. Thus the proposition may be said to lay down a norm, but "norm" must be understood simply in the sense of a condition *to be* conformed to in definite forms of future action.[66]

2) The distinctive features of valuation-propositions we have seen so far are the predictive ('*x* will have such and such effects'), and the reference to the future act or state as something that *should* happen (*x* is *to be*). But there is a third feature, one that Dewey mentions but might well have said more about. For the language of "*x* is *to be* desired," and Dewey's *de jure* judgments do not seem to have the robust emotive, hortatory quality characteristic of much ethical language.

I draw attention to this third feature of valuation-propositions for two reasons: the first is that it helps us to see another kind of answer to the earlier stated objection to Dewey's theory—and such is the purpose of the present pages—and the second is that it completes our analysis of what the constituents of moral judgments, or valuation-propositions, are in Dewey's theory.

[64] As described earlier, and Dewey, *Quest*, p. 267; Sellars and Hospers, p. 277.
[65] *Theory of Valuation*, p. 20. Note the 'to be' phrase in this sentence, and the Peircian, pragmatic cast of thought.
  In his way of viewing the distinctive character of value-propositions, Dewey is remarkably consistent in his writings over the years. Thus, in *Theory of Valuation* of 1939, he writes: "Value-propositions . . . are not about things or events that have occurred or that already exist . . . but are about things *to be* brought into existence," pp. 51–52. Almost half a century earlier he had written (and we notice 'to be' appearing): "in the degree that any consequence is considered likely to result from an act, just in that degree it gets its moral value, for it becomes part of the act itself. . . . *The conceived results constitute the content of the act to be performed*. They are not merely relevant to its morality, but *are* its moral quality," *Outlines of a Critical Theory of Ethics* (1891), pp. 8–9. For a discussion of the background and importance of this work in the growth of Dewey's thought, see White, *Origin*, ch. 7 and p. 111. Also on his new analysis of *desire* in the *Outlines*, see Dewey's letter to James, Perry, II, 520.
[66] *Theory of Valuation*, p. 21.

The third feature of the sort of propositions or judgments we have been study-ing is also a prediction taking the conditional form, viz.: what is *to be* brought into existence, or maintained, *will not* occur unless intermediate personal action is taken. In recognizing this third 'aspect of value-propositions, we are able to sum up the present part of the discussion with a definition. According to Dewey's theory, in asserting the *value* proposition '*x* is desirable,' the following conditions are (or are purported to be) fulfilled:

i) In a conflicting and deficient situation S_1, x, in its predictable conse-quences and relations to other conditions, *will* integrate, satisfy the ob-jective conditions of need in S_1.

ii) x *shall* be brought about, produced, realized, and *should* be.[67]

iii) Without some personal intermediate effort, x *will not* take place or be realized.

These three conditions, if I am not mistaken, define what is necessary for a proposition to be a value judgment for Dewey. But of course the actual forma-tion and final deliverance of value-propositions occurs in a context of related propositions. Presumably, other normative considerations, plus propositions of observed facts and predictions all bearing upon the realization of x, will condi-tion the value-propositions finally made.

This last feature of value-propositions is the vehicle for the characteristically *prescriptive* and emotive language of moral discourse. Imperatives would of course have a role in the '*should*' of (ii), i.e., '*x* should exist.' But the hortatory, imperative, emotive urgency[68] of ethical language would function primarily in connection with (iii): if such and such is not done, then *x* will not *be* (i.e., either not be brought into existence or its existence will not be maintained). Here is the place of commanding, pleading with, prompting, exhorting oneself or others.

Dewey does not have very much to say about these emotive, persuasive uses of ethical language. He does argue that the emotive theories of ethical expressions (such as Russell's, for one, as reviewed some pages back) are not so much wrong as incomplete, and are absorbable or reinterpretable within his own theory.[69] I

---

[67] This condition, discussed earlier and commented on in the next paragraph below, is the declaration of intention and policy announcement with respect to securing x.

[68] The terms are Stevenson's, *Ethics and Language*, esp. p. 258.

[69] See, e.g., *Theory of Valuation*, pp. 6–13, "Value-Expression as Ejaculatory." On Dewey's own careful analysis of what is meant by describing language as '*expressive*' and his conception of the behavioral conditions of *feeling*, ethical sentences as "expressions of feelings and commands" (so-called or theoretically alleged) do have a cognitive role and are empirically warranted or not. Cf. *Theory of Valuation*, pp. 12–13, where Dewey in-terprets the content of simple utterances, "fire!" or "help!" in his pattern of valuation-expressions, thus:

When analyzed, what is said is (i) that there exists a situation that will have ob-noxious consequences; (ii) that the person uttering the expressions is unable to cope with the situation; and (iii) that an improved situation is anticipated in case the assistance of others is obtained. . . .
. . . The expressions noted are employed as intermediaries to bring about the desired change from present to future conditions.

suspect that Dewey's reluctance to consider the emotive function of ethical expressions in detail was due to his rejection of the psychological theory of mind and emotions that most of the emotivists employed.[70] But Dewey may also have thought that hortatory emotive uses of ethical language, while real, are variously conditioned by the situations occasioning ethical judgment, and that the hortatory, emotive character, etc., is not of central importance to a general theory of valuation.[71] He might have thought this for reasons that, analogously, leave us unconcerned with the phenomena of inflections and phonetic peculiarities with which the premises of a syllogism can be uttered, even screamed, when it is the general theory of how conclusions are implied by premises that we are after.

But that there is a place and a significant one for the existence of norms and normative language in Dewey's ethic, for *de jure* judgment of the desirable conditioned by and operating with judgments of fact, the foregoing pages have attempted to show and explore.[72]

§ 97. Some Last Observations and Questions

Before we bring this lengthy discussion of Dewey's ethical theory to a close, some comments are necessary on matters insufficiently dealt with earlier.

An easily recognizable, and to some a disturbing trait of Dewey's analysis of valuation is the absence of the Good, *to agathon*, the *summum bonum*. Instead of that absolute and unconditional Good so dear to moralists, Dewey substitutes goods, possible and actual in their varied forms and relationships to human desires and moral situations. There is no Good, except as a symbol of endeavor and progress in the cultivation of intelligent desiring (§ 94 above) and shareable enjoyments, a symbol of moral activity itself. There is no ultimate object of desire, for no object of desire and no desire exists independent of all vital attachments in or references to particular situations. But the conspicuous absence of the Good does not dispossess the relative goods of existing situations of all moral significance or possible glamor, for these are nonetheless authentic objects of valuation.

For Dewey, we saw (§ 94 above), general aims, norms, and ends-in-view may be suggested in particular situations. But this ethical theory, based on what Dewey often describes as the logic of concrete, particular situations does not and can not issue in a set of imperatives or recipes for conduct. One might argue that some vague injunctions, such as "Be intelligent!" or "Always inquire!" are implied in all that Dewey says concerning the process of evaluation. But these are hardly comparable to the categorical imperative, Mill's principle of Utilitarianism, or

[70] See his paper "Ethical Subject-Matter and Language," esp. pp. 707–708, this being Dewey's reply to criticisms of his theory by Stevenson in *Ethics and Language*.
[71] Such is the spirit of his paper mentioned in the previous footnote.
[72] Some of the points in these last paragraphs are intended to bear on the critical discussions of Dewey's theory by White (cf. note 62) and by Stevenson. For a criticism, in turn, of White and Stevenson and a defense of Dewey, see the paper by Hook which takes a rather different line from the one I have argued here.

appeals to intuition or the heart for moral instruction. Because of his conception of the situation and the actual genesis of desire that define the conditions of moral (or valuational) activity for Dewey; because he regards ethical judgment and action as a *process*, a deliberate transformation of a given situation; and because "action is always specific"; Dewey quite consistently does not attempt to set forth an ethic of general rules and imperatives.

> The blunt assertion that every moral situation is a unique situation having its own irreplaceable good may seem not only blunt but preposterous. For the established tradition teaches that it is precisely the irregularity of special cases which makes necessary the guidance of conduct by universals, and that the essence of the virtuous disposition is willingness to subordinate every particular case to adjudication by a fixed principle. It would then follow that the submission of a generic end and law to determination by the concrete situation entails complete confusion and unrestrained licentiousness. Let us, however, follow the pragmatic rule, and in order to discover the meaning of the idea ask for its consequences. Then it surprisingly turns out that the primary significance of the unique and morally ultimate character of the concrete situation is to transfer the weight and burden of morality to intelligence. It does not destroy responsibility; it only locates it.[73]

In a related passage Dewey adds:

> the special moral perplexities where the aid of intelligence is required go unenlightened. We cannot seek or attain health, wealth, learning, justice or kindness in general. Action is always specific, concrete, individualized, unique. And consequently judgments as to acts to be performed must be similarly specific. To say that a man seeks health or justice is only to say that he seeks to live healthily or justly. These things . . . are adverbial. They are modifiers of action in special cases.[74]

The moral life is seen as movement, with conflict, recovery, and integration marking its phases. The movement is not linear, aimed at one fixed and beckoning Good and seeking consummation there. The end or aim for Dewey is not a fixed state to be achieved; it is the continual process of transforming existing situations, directing and controlling experience as the means to increasing the richness and refining the quality of experience. This is growth, and "Growth itself is the only moral 'end.' "[75]

We are brought back to the idea of the situation and its progressive transformation as the reasoning of cardinal importance in Dewey's theory. It is the existing situation, its qualities and conditions as problematic or satisfactory, that provides the criterion and authenticity of moral judgment and action. For while actions

[73] *Reconstruction in Philosophy*, p. 163.
[74] *Ibid.*, pp. 166–167.
[75] Cf. § 41 above and *Reconstruction in Philosophy*, p. 177. While often a point of confusion and criticism concerning Dewey's ethical theory, the idea of growth as an "end" is basic to his rejection of "fixed ends" and "one *summum bonum*, one supreme end" for morality, *Reconstruction in Philosophy*, p. 166. The idea of growth as the "continual process" of transforming existing situations (p. 177) and of the moral life as the institution of this process, Dewey derived in the main from T. H. Green. For this, see Appendix 1, sec. C below.

are specific, purposes and valuations selective, these do not occur in isolation from other conditions in a context giving them their peculiar significance. Ultimately it is situations that are valued and that are the objects of valuation.

Because of the central role of the idea of *situation* in Dewey's theory, one would expect that it would occupy most attention in probative deliberations over the theory. In fact, however, this has not been the case. The concept of situation, of serious import for an accurate assessment of Dewey's views, has been relatively neglected in favor of controversies over other matters, such as Dewey's "naturalism," or to what extent valuations are predictions, the absence of intrinsic values in this outlook, and the like.

Without needlessly prolonging the present discussion it will be well to take note briefly of some questions that arise in connection with Dewey's account of *situations*. These, if I am not mistaken, are indications not so much of error as of incompleteness in Dewey's views and consequently of the need for further work.

To begin with, one might ask, How thoroughly empirical is Dewey's conception of situations? He appeals convincingly to biology and psychology (of a behavioristic kind) in describing what situations are and how human conduct is a function of them. At the same time, he keeps insisting that every situation is "unique" and "individual" in its occurrence, problematic quality, and outcome. The question is not how this is known, but what it means. It means something more, surely, than the mere tautology that every individual is unique (i.e., individual). But writing of a doubtful situation, Dewey says, "it is a unique doubtfulness which makes that situation to be just and only the situation it is."[76] It would be unique to discover any one doubtful of the truth of this sentence. But its informing us that a unique quality makes a situation just what it is, is hardly an empirical truth.

Insofar as Dewey's view of situation is an empirically based and developed construction, it has the admirable result of making his ethical theory largely testable and defensible on empirical grounds. But when Dewey comes to explanations of the "logic of concrete, individual situations" and their existential transformations, he seems strangely often to have reached the limits of articulate discourse. Like a wave tossed back from a breakwater, Dewey's language then falls back upon itself with nothing but its own immediate resources, in a stream of tormented reiterations. It is then that we find ourselves reassured that each situation is what it is, that its quality is uniquely just what it is, and so on.

Another question concerns the reasons leading Dewey to suppose that since situations have a uniquely doubtful quality, there is *one* unique *solution* or resolution for each doubtful situation. Or does Dewey assume this? He certainly suggests as much and does not discuss the interesting possibility of situations in which several warranted valuations, several possible and equally satisfactory value-solutions present themselves. Final choice of an outcome—valuational judgment in this case—would seem to be purely free, spontaneous, and willful. But this

---

[76] *Logic*, p. 105.

would mean that sometimes, *after* a certain amount of inquiry has taken place, valuation may *proceed* in a-rational, unthinking ways.

A last question arises over the agents in situations. This is simply to ask if Dewey has not so overemphasized the situation as to neglect individual agents who, after all, transact the business of morals. Is Dewey guilty of dissolving the individual into a situation, to paraphrase Santayana's remark (§ 36, note 26).

To this question there is an answer. The whole of Dewey's theory is constructed on the idea of agents in situations. Valuations are the products of desiring, and it is in situations that desires occur. But agents, persons, do the desiring. They *do* this in conjunction with and partly by means of environing conditions and energies. Desiring, like any human activity, is a transaction between organism and environment. All of this is rendered impersonal in Dewey's *theory* of valuation. But in actual valuations, in practical application of what the theory abstractly formulates, it is the person, the individual, or group of individuals, in ethical deliberation who becomes the ruling party in achieving a satisfactory state of affairs in place of those where conflict and need are felt. It is the agent who directs and constructs the good and for whom valuation is a conscious achievement.

§ 98.   Conclusion

One of the chief merits of Dewey's ethical theory is the establishment of lines of communication between the philosophic theory of valuation and the empirical sciences of human behavior.

> Moral science is not something with a separate province. It is physical, biological, and historic knowledge placed in a human context where it will illuminate and guide the activities of men.[77]

The Socratic conviction that virtue, *aretē*, is knowledge has its modern expression in Dewey. If Dewey is right, the study of ethics—the conditions that are relevant and formative in making moral judgments and the critical standards for assessing judgments—is enormously enriched with information available from the behavioral and natural sciences. Ethical philosophy has traditionally conceived its function as the construction of ethical systems. But in place of this dialectical system-building and defense of certain norms and imperatives of conduct, Dewey's conception of the subject matter of ethics and ethical judgment cuts across the special sciences, drawing upon them all for information concerning the agencies men employ in living and in planning future experience. In so viewing the subject matter of ethics, the philosophic systems of ethics of the past constitute but a small part of the study of ethics. It is an additional, urgently expressed hope of Dewey's that when the subject matter of ethics is seen as drawing from and integrated with scientific knowledge, the actual judgments men continue to

[77] *Human Nature and Conduct*, p. 296.

make will exhibit increasing intelligence, foresight, and stability concerning the ends and satisfactions sought and pursued.

We have seen how, in Dewey's theory, an evaluation, a *de jure* judgment, is supported by and operative within a context or network of empirical propositions. These latter serve as means of information concerning the nature of the situation, and the possibilities it presents for transformation (employing therefore predictions and judgments of the potentialities of conditions and results of hypothetical actions, etc.). Two important consequences of this theory of empirically *informed* valuation deserve to be mentioned.

First: Value judgments, especially on matters of human conduct and aims, do not receive authority from some special source, office, or administration of ethics, such as a sacred book or code or profession. There is nothing analogous to the divine right of kings, the command of the sovereign, the cross or the sword or Reason that establishes itself as the authority in ethical matters. The familiar habit of politicians and ministers of pronouncing moral judgments with a ring of finality has no theoretical justification because, for Dewey, as is the case with all empirical judgments, valuations are never self-certified or exempt from reevaluation and inquiry. The source of authority in forming and testing ethical judgment is the objective, troubled situation within which need is felt, desires occur, and a good is realizable. A turning point in his philosophic development occurred when Dewey came to believe that all of the forces and institutions of society—being moral in function as influencing action and mediating desire—were to have their authority subjected to the authority of free inquiry.[78]

Second: Rather than interpreting valuation-activities as possessing some special quality separating them from other cognitive endeavors, Dewey regards valuations as permeating all intellectual conduct. The characteristics of situations in which valuations occur may differ; they may be literary, political, scientific, and so on. But in each case where the future is modified by purposive action, where selection and realization of some among many possible consequences of action occur, acts of valuation have taken place. For Dewey this view leads to

> doing away once for all with the traditional distinction between moral goods, like the virtues, and natural goods like health, economic security, art, science and the like. . . . the experimental logic when carried into morals makes every quality that is judged to be good according as it contributes to amelioration of existing ills. And in so doing, it enforces the moral meaning of natural science.[79]

Here Dewey expresses a lifelong philosophic concern (cf. § 35) and, as we have seen in Part One and several times since, a fundamental theme in the history of

---

[78] It was a newspaperman, Franklin Ford, whose influence upon Dewey in 1890, concerning the ethical and social implications of scientific intelligence, or method, was of great importance in the development of Dewey's ethical philosophy and his break with idealism. See Dewey's letter to James concerning Ford, in Perry, II, 517–519, and White, *The Origin of Dewey's Instrumentalism,* pp. 100 ff. for a discussion of the importance of Ford for Dewey.

[79] *Reconstruction in Philosophy,* pp. 172–173.

modern philosophy:[80] the integration or resolution of conflicts between scientific knowledge and ethical beliefs and practices.

> When the consciousness of science is fully impregnated with the consciousness of human value, the greatest dualism which now weighs humanity down, the split between the material, the mechanical, the scientific and the moral and ideal will be destroyed. Human forces that now waver because of this division will be unified and reinforced.[81]

To this declared end Dewey's theory focuses and articulates the predominant intellectual intent of what was virtual and potential and nurturing in the development of American pragmatism.

[80] A theme basic in the development of pragmatism also, as argued in Part V, ch. 1 below.
[81] *Reconstruction in Philosophy,* pp. 173–174.

SPECULATIONS

Part Five

There continues to be an interest in the philosophies of Peirce, James, Dewey, Mead, and C. I. Lewis. But pragmatism as a philosophic movement or body of ideas, as surveyed in Part Two, cannot be said to be alive today. However, it can be remarked that pragmatism succeeded in its critical reaction to the nineteenth-century philosophic background from which it emerged: it helped shape the modern conception of philosophy as a way of investigating problems and clarifying communication rather than as a fixed system of ultimate answers and great truths. And in this alteration of the philosophic scene some of the positive suggestions of pragmatism were disseminated into current intellectual life as practices taken for granted to an extent that no longer calls for special notice. Pragmatically, this is all that a pragmatist could have asked for.

In the chapters that follow there will be no further detailed and technical scrutiny of pragmatism. Rather, it is my purpose in these final pages to comment on some of the broader historical and intellectual aspects of our subject.

I will begin with an attempt to describe and explain what, I believe, is the essential motivation and aim effecting the development of pragmatism and shaping its distinctively *philosophical* outlook. Here, of course, pragmatism is taken as more than a principle of analysis and strategic procedure for achieving successful communication and sound conceptualization. We are now to regard pragmatism as a general philosophical position in which this principle is embedded as the initially evolved part.

From the endeavor in Chapter One below to draw a general portrait of this philosophy, thus making explicit a number of earlier allusions, we are led in the second chapter to consider some of the conditions of American life that relate to the genesis of pragmatism. The third and final chapter is a summing up of themes in this Part and in this book.

If I am right in my interpretation of the moral basis of pragmatism,[1] it is not at all difficult to see how recent expressions of concern over the division in our age of "cultures"—of the sciences and humanities, or of scientific technology and human values—have been thoroughly anticipated and the problem carefully weighed in the philosophical history of pragmatism. Pragmatism began, indeed, as a conscious, attentive, and, in time, increasingly more comprehensive response to that very problem. But that problem, still so much with us, as I have tried to show in Part One, has roots going back into the early sixteenth century.

It must be admitted at the outset that much of what is said in these ensuing pages is speculative—hence, the title of this Part. Moreover, the range is wide and equally controversial—as speculations are apt to be. On such matters it is hard not to be

[1] The phrase refers to § 99 below, but the theme pervades all three chapters that follow.

slapdash and dogmatic; I plead partly guilty to both, but with the excuse that my interest in this Part is less that of demonstrating certain ideas here concerning pragmatism, philosophy, and American culture, and more that of using and illustrating them, and drawing conclusions from them. It is left to the reader to assess the reasonableness of the case.

The Meaning of Pragmatism

§ 99. The Moral Basis of Pragmatism

What *you* want is a philosophy that will not only exercise your powers of intellectual abstraction, but that will make some positive connexion with this actual world of finite lives.

You want a system that will combine both things, the scientific loyalty to facts and willingness to take account of them, the spirit of adaptation and accommodation, in short, but also the old confidence in human values and the resultant spontaneity, whether of the religious or the romantic type. And this then is your dilemma: you find the two parts of your *quaesitum* hopelessly separated. You find an empiricism with inhumanism and irreligion; or else you find a rationalistic philosophy that indeed may call itself religious, but that keeps out of all definite touch with concrete facts and joys and sorrows.[1]

William James's description of the "present dilemma in philosophy" in 1906 illustrates a pattern visible in earlier pages. The word 'dilemma,' however, does not accurately convey what James was (or this book has been) describing, for, strictly, a dilemma constitutes a rigid fixing of two separated and ununifiable points, as the two points of a bull's horns are wont to be; over or between the horns of a dilemma we may go like the acrobats of ancient Crete. But James was proposing pragmatism as a mediator, a way of resolving the "dilemma" of scientific hard-headedness on the one side, and tender-minded concern for religious and moral values on the other. And that sense, that fact of separated and diverging interests and of needed reconciliation, has impressed us before. It has been remarked that pragmatism emerged and was elaborated as an attempt to provide an integration of the two traditionally separate provinces of thought and action in modern philosophy—those of values and scientific knowledge. The whole of Part One is devoted to showing how, in what ways, and why a separation of moral values and

---

[1] *Pragmatism*, p. 20.

knowledge is characteristic of modern thought since the seventeenth century. This concern to harmonize morals and science (more accurately, to establish and justify an interpretation of valuing and knowing as logically common modes of intelligent action) was not the only historical motivation of pragmatism—one grants multiple causative conditions and impulses in the philosophizing of men. Moreover, "harmonizing," "bridging," "reconciling" the alleged separations of "morals and science" are all quite vague descriptively, or as attributive of causes and motives; the expressions help express, but do not go very far to identify historical facts. That pragmatism was born in a Metaphysical Club some of whose members were "men of science" (see Peirce's description, § 19), however, aptly symbolizes the historical thesis. Further, it is clear that Peirce regarded his maxim of pragmatism as a sound and familiar technique of scientific *practice*. In articulating this practice, he was not directly proposing it to scientists or to the advancement of science; he was addressing philosophers. While he found his logical maxim of pragmatism "of signal service to every branch of science,"[2] it was because of this that he urged its employment in philosophy. Use of the maxim, Peirce argued, would further "reasonableness" or "clearness of thought," and this was to contribute to that "ultimate good," "concrete reasonableness."[3] Pragmatism, Peirce noted, is a philosophic method concerned with "the purpose of the ideas it analyzes, whether these be of the nature and uses of action or thought."[4] And he leaves little doubt that he saw a normative role for this maxim of logic:

> if, as pragmatism teaches us, what we think is to be interpreted in terms of what we are prepared to do, then surely *logic* or the doctrine of what we ought to think, must be an application of the doctrine of what we deliberately choose to do, which is Ethics.[5]

As we saw in § 31, an almost exclusively moral interpretation and application of Peirce's maxim was developed by James. In his *Pragmatism*, James argues for the pragmatic maxim in the same order as does Peirce. James says, "the pragmatic method is primarily a method of settling metaphysical disputes that otherwise might be interminable."[6] But his evidence for the usefulness of the principle consists of references to practices in the sciences.

The point I now wish to suggest is that while the history of pragmatism commenced as an attempt to construct a "maxim" of meaning, the ultimate purpose of the maxim—or pragmatism—was moral: to render the substantive content, the very "meaning" of ethical and metaphysical beliefs and decisions of conduct into terms capable of analysis and verification by established norms of scientific judgment. Though this goal might appear similar to the occasionally expressed

---

[2] *CP* 5.14.
[3] *CP* 5.3. Peirce does say the maxim would be useful in clearing up metaphysical muddles, *CP* 4.2, and see § 20.
[4] *CP* 5.13 *n.* Peirce believed "the ultimate good lies in the evolutionary process in some way" and this process was "the growth of reasonableness." See *CP* 5.4.
[5] *CP* 5.35.
[6] *Pragmatism*, p. 45.

hope of making ethics and all philosophy "scientific," such a view reverses what in fact and historically is the proper emphasis. The pragmatists were led from Peirce's maxim of meaning to develop a general theory of knowledge according to which knowing is an evaluative activity. It was not that morality was to become scientific; it was rather that scientific knowledge is a paradigm of moral activity.

The history of pragmatism, then, consists of two main phases of development:

1) The first is the early formulation of the maxim by Peirce—partly as intellectual residue of the Metaphysical Club's discussions (see §§ 19, 21) and the revival of Peirce's ideas by James.

2) Second is the more comprehensive development of pragmatism into a theory of inquiry, knowledge, and valuation as "instrumentalism" by Dewey, and by Mead and Lewis.

Something must now be said about each of these.

1) As we have seen in § 2 and § 19, pragmatism in the distinct sense of a discernible idea was first projected by Peirce as a "maxim of logic," a method of philosophic analysis. This was the "principle" which, in earlier pages, has been under study as a theory of meaning or a technique for clarifying the meaning of certain classes of terms.

As to this maxim and the precise scope of its application, Peirce vacillated, as we have seen. Sometimes he confined pragmatism only to a way of analyzing general concepts (§ 21); sometimes he spoke of the principle as relevant to and clarificatory of the concepts of reality and truth. James, however, in "reviving" this maxim, made it quite clear that he viewed it as a theory of meaning (or meaningfulness) and a theory of truth. The usual judgment is that James misunderstood, misapplied, and misdirected Peirce's pragmatism. Peirce certainly had a right to protest against what James was doing with the ideas James even attributed to Peirce. But in emphasizing (or inventing) the moral significance of pragmatism, that is, in arguing for the purposive and practical character of thought, for the *valuation* of ideas as effective or ineffective ways of coping with experience (subject to the qualifications of relativity noted in § 78) and of interpreting and controlling environments, James was expressing the dominant historical spirit—the origins and future of pragmatism as an American philosophy.

Writing about pragmatism as a moralist (cf. §§ 26, 31), James was responding to what he took to be the immediate dubious inheritance of modern philosophy in 1906. To men drawn to, even needing a philosophy, he wrote: "what kinds of philosophy do you find actually offered to meet your need? You find an empirical philosophy that is not religious enough, and a religious philosophy that is not empirical enough for your purpose." This was "the present dilemma in philosophy." It was, as we have been suggesting, one phase in the long-evolving philosophic problem of the relation between morals and knowledge. James believed and argued that pragmatism was "just the mediating way of thinking you require"[7] to establish and preserve a cordial relation with facts and religious and moral convictions.

While heavily indebted to James's conception of the moral role of pragmatism, the later pragmatists, especially Dewey, Mead, and Lewis, found serious short-comings in the way James viewed the wider philosophic scene into which pragmatism was introduced. James's anti-intellectualism in philosophy, his distrust of scientific abstractions, and his inability to see the significance of scientific method as a vital part of philosophic inquiry and of the interpretation of behavior were not shared by Dewey.

An even more salient critical contrast to James's intellectual pluralism, social individualism, and radical empiricism was Dewey's Hegelian way of seeing thought and behavior as expressions of social contexts and historically evolved in-stitutions. James never developed a social philosophy. His championing of indi-vidualism—"live and let live" (§ 34)—while of undoubted sincerity and while one desirable part of a social outlook, did not go very far in confronting the facts of industrial organization and conflicting economic forces in American society, or in illuminating a way of dealing with these same facts. Dewey, on the other hand, devoted most of his philosophic endeavors to examining the ways of controlling and directing social conditions through education and through critical revisions of the institutions of society.

The role that James helped most to create for pragmatism, the moral function, was retained in the later history, but how it was conceived and how performed was altered. James thought of pragmatism as a way in which man's otherwise dis-parate and dilemmatic interests in religious beliefs and hard scientific facts could be linked together. Guided partly by ideas that James himself had stated but not developed, the later pragmatists revised this conception. Instead of being viewed as an instrument for connecting science and values, pragmatism was envisioned as one theory of intelligent action within which scientific facts and moral values were interpreted as instruments and agencies for controlling the content and enrich-ing the quality of experience.

2) The second phase in the historical development of pragmatism was the enlarging of Peirce's maxim and a tightening and critical revising of James's views of meaning and truth into a general theory of knowledge. Some though not all of the main parts of the theory clearly derived from Peirce and James, but its fuller statement came with Dewey, Mead, and Lewis. Having already studied this theory in some detail (Part Two), even to recognizing certain differences in out-look and direction affecting its elaboration under Dewey, Mead, and Lewis, we can omit repeating this here. We shall instead confine ourselves to the broad features and aims of this theory, and thereby come as close as possible to a defini-tion of the general meaning of contemporary pragmatism.

There is no question of the moral basis and aim given to pragmatism by each of

[7] *Ibid.,* p. 40.

these thinkers. For their whole conception of knowing—so prominent in pragmatism—has a moral function. Dewey has written:

> Certainly one of the most genuine problems of modern life is the reconciliation
> of the scientific view of the universe with the claims of the moral life. . . . There
> is no occasion to expatiate on the importance of the moral life, nor upon the
> supreme importance of intelligence within the moral life. But there does seem to
> be occasion for asking how moral judgments—judgments of the would and should
> —relate themselves to the world of scientific knowledge. To frame a theory of
> knowledge which makes it necessary to deny the validity of moral ideas, or else
> to refer them to some other and separate kind of universe from that of common
> sense and science, is both provincial and arbitrary. The pragmatist has at least tried
> to face, and not to dodge, the question of how it is that moral and scientific "knowl-
> edge" can both hold of one and the same world. And whatever the difficulties in
> his proffered solution, the conception that scientific judgments are to be assimi-
> lated to moral is closer to common sense than is the theory that validity is to be
> denied to moral judgments because they do not square with a preconceived theory
> of the nature of the world to which scientific judgments must refer. And all moral
> judgments are about changes to be made.[8]

It is desirable here to indicate more carefully the sense in which, for pragmatism, knowledge is valuation.

§ *100.   Knowledge as Valuation*

The primary importance of knowledge is as a guide for action. "Knowing exists
for the sake of doing," writes Lewis,[9] and Dewey surely would concur.

Action, deliberate, and guided by much or little reflection, is the result of valuation. For to act deliberately is to intend to realize certain possible events or states
of affairs. Actions have consequences, and deliberate actions have (usually) foreseen and anticipated consequences. Such characterizes intelligent action generally;
sought and anticipated possible results of acting do in fact occur. Here predictions
and judgments of fact become verified not haphazardly or by wild surmise;
rather, what is wanted, planned, and hoped for is actively brought to realization.
Means, including action, have been taken to secure the ends desired—the very
essence of moral activity, according to Dewey (§§ 93, 94 above). Such active
real-izing of some among many foreseen possible acts, and some of many possible
consequences of action is the substance of intelligent behavior, or certainly the
manifest expression of it. For this is behavior in which choice, interest, and
valuation are operative.

The intent to effect and deliberately shape some portion of the world and the
planning of future experience is both to apprehend (however meagerly) and

---

8 "The Practical Character of Reality," in *Philosophy and Civilization*, p. 43.
9 *An Analysis of Knowledge and Valuation*, p. 3.

assign value to something in the future. To assign value to something in the future and to commence pursuit is to entertain predictions that, under certain describable conditions, such and such an object (or objects, or states of affairs) *would* be satisfactory to someone (or in some situation) in some way, and such and such efforts *would* (or would not) bring the satisfaction about. Action upon predictions of this kind is aimed at the selection of some possible results, some experiences, over others. In this sense, intelligent action is an evaluation of the future. The same may be put negatively thus: a deliberate action is undertaken in order to nullify all but some of many possible future happenings. Indeed, to act at all (or not to act) is to include some events and exclude others from happening. To act intelligently is, at least, to plan and select the happenings of future events; that, again, is to evaluate the future. Thus, portions of reality are molded by human desire, and men seek to know the future in order to modify and control its possibilities.

Lewis summarizes the outlook well:

> To know is to apprehend the future as qualified by values which action may realize; and empirical knowledge is essentially utilitarian and pragmatic.
> . . . The utility of knowledge lies in the control it gives us, through appropriate action, over the quality of our future experience. And such control will be exercised in the interest of realizing that which we value, and of obviating or avoiding what is undesirable. Such considerations but serve to emphasize the essential relations between the knowledge we seek of objective facts, the values we hope to realize in experience, and the actions which, guided by the one, move toward the other.[10]

Taken in conjunction with the theme of the foregoing pages, the moral basis of pragmatism, the above passage not only helps aptly to confirm our previous contentions. It also, in part explicitly and in part by allusion, contains the cluster of ideas peculiarly characteristic of the evolution of pragmatism: the relation of knowledge to action; the futurative reference of thought and ideas (thus meanings, cf. § 21); the predictive character of knowing; the difference that conceived action would make in future experience as one criterion of meaning; knowledge as a modification of the world or as an existential transformation of the materials of experience.

The course of the present discussion brings us to the following general characterization of what are, apart from that of a technique of analysis and scientific practice, the essential philosophic features of pragmatism.

§ 101.   *What Pragmatism Is*

Mutability and transitivity are traits of nature and of all life in it. Change, as an ultimate characteristic of existence, is not precluded by relative conditions of

[10] *Ibid.*, pp. 4–5.

stability, organization, and structure, nor expunged by a fairly persistent hankering of men to see things *sub specie aeternitatis*. The latter aspiration may have its source in the very omnipresence of transient experience from which, in due course, one yearns to escape, or which one tries to render intelligible. James described our first encounter with the world as a "blooming buzzing confusion"; witness at close range the vicissitudes of the perpetual onslaught of sensation, the separate distractions of irritated surfaces and nerve fibers of our animal selves. The human impulse, if not to take flight from existence, then to philosophize, is germinal in all thought or conceptualization, since these, along with more native habits, have as a natural function the ordering of the otherwise discordant chaos of experience.

The mark of intelligent life, perhaps the root of reason, is the maintenance of life itself through continuously changing environments by evolving techniques of adaptation and control, i.e., efficacious modification and direction of existing conditions. Reason, thus portrayed in the service of life, is to be understood as a natural function with a natural history like those of breathing and digestion. There are other theories of knowing whose ideal issue is just the viewing of all existence *sub specie aeternitatis*, according to which to "know" is to be illuminated by,[11] to image, or to picture reality. Indeed, this is the etymological import of 'theory,' *theoria*—a seeing or beholding of things as a spectator would in the *theatre*. The details of this spectator theory of knowing do not concern us. The reason for alluding to it at all is to illustrate by contrast with pragmatism how mind, or knowing, is viewed as passively receiving and reflecting the show of things going on. Pragmatism, on the other hand—and this is a thesis of some force for our summary—emphasizes the practical character of reason and of reality.[12]

The obvious question now is: What is meant by the practical character of reality and knowledge? Preparatory to an answer, it must be said that by 'practical' the pragmatist does not mean only the most urgent and fundamental needs and utilities. Pragmatism is not to be condemned for holding that only "practical thinking" about food, shelter, family, and business affairs is "real."

What pragmatism argues as 'the practical nature of thought and reality' is that, since existence is transitional, knowledge is one of the ways of effecting transitions of events, and the only reliable way of guiding them.[13] Logically, this is

---

[11] Or, alternatively, to cast a "searchlight" on things—as Ayer has described it, pp. 23–24. This metaphorically molded theory, by the way, leaves out just what is to the point in the above considerations, viz., that in theory the light beam of a searchlight does materially modify or affect the surfaces of the object illuminated.

[12] The phrasing is deliberate as an allusion to the title of one of Dewey's important studies of the leading ideas of pragmatism, "The Practical Character of Reality."

[13] Cf. Dewey, *ibid.*, p. 38: "If one is already committed to a belief that Reality is neatly and finally tied up in a packet without loose ends, unfinished issues or new departures, one would object to knowledge making a difference just as one would object to any impertinent obtruder. But if one believes that the world itself is in transformation, why should the notion that knowledge is the most important mode of its modification and the only organ of its guidance be *a priori* obnoxious?"

part of the conception of knowledge as valuation, discussed a moment ago. And it is in this connection that the familiar and much emphasized pragmatic analysis of thought as directed to consequences and action rather than antecedents and origins finds its place.

> Pragmatism, thus, presents itself as an extension of historical empiricism, but with this fundamental difference, that it does not insist upon antecedent phenomena but upon consequent phenomena; not upon the precedents but upon the possibilities of action. And this change in point of view is almost revolutionary in its consequences.[14]

There are three related claims involved in what pragmatism contends is the practical character of thought and reality.

1)   Insofar as knowledge and action can be addressed to future possibilities, *possibility* is in some sense a trait of reality. Dewey writes:

> Pragmatism thus has a metaphysical implication. The doctrine of the value of consequences leads us to take the future into consideration. And this taking into consideration of the future takes us to the conception of a universe whose evolution is not finished, of a universe which is still, in James' term, "in the making," "in the process of becoming," of a universe up to a certain point still plastic.[15]

It is not at all easy to state precisely what this doctrine of a future "in the making," of a "plastic" universe, really asserts. The notion had also been argued by Peirce as "objective chance"; and for Peirce (as we noted in § 21), the modality of possibility is real.[16] But the present thesis is not a contention that future events are uncaused or occur at random, i.e., without any determinate antecedents.[17] For then the whole point of pragmatism in championing inquiry addressed to future consequences, or in thought directed to future possibilities would be lost. Disposition terms (the future is *makeable, malleable*, etc.) figure in as expository aids in stating the doctrine, and so, too, do varieties of counterfactual statements ("If we had more knowledge, the future could be made more hospitable to our interests"). But, presumably, this language carries something beyond mere expository convenience in its use. Presumably, affirming the truth of some counterfactual statements, or employing statements containing disposition terms entails certain metaphysical commitments for the pragmatist (certainly for Peirce). That stones are hard, i.e., *would* not be scratched under certain conditions; that my planning and acting to build a house affects the future of the wood and brick I use, delimiting their other uses—these point to the existence of real potentialities in the first instance and to physical possibilities in the second. Thus, one notices how disposition terms and counterfactual statements are foreshadowed in the metaphysical orientation of such reflections as this:

[14] Dewey, "Development of American Pragmatism," p. 24.
[15] *Ibid.*, p. 25. The concept of physical possibility or *potentiality* is crucial in Schiller's philosophy: "it is a *methodological* necessity to assume that the world is wholly plastic, i.e., *to act as though* we believed this," "Axioms as Postulates," p. 64.
[16] "Possibility is sometimes of a real kind," *CP* 5.453. See § 21 above and Appendix 7.
[17] Absolute randomness is itself a complicated and dubious thesis.

reason, or thought, in its more general sense, has a real, though limited, function, a creative, constructive function. If we form general ideas and if we put them in action, consequences are produced which could not be produced otherwise. Under these conditions the world will be different from what it would have been if thought had not intervened. This consideration confirms the human and moral importance of thought and of its reflective operation in experience.[18]

The notions of a world "in the making" or of a "plastic" universe hint of something more than the metaphors can convey. These augur vaguely of a principle of certain equi-possible, but mutually exclusive classes of events, some of whose actualization at one time is a causal condition of the actualization of only some of a class of possible events at a future time.[19] Far from making an appeal to objective chance, this stated principle holds that the actualization of some (as against other) present possible events "determines" the future actualization of some (as against other) events.[20] But, obviously, the entire thesis of a "world in the making" needs an explicit and detailed formulation. While it is not on the face of it unreasonable as a philosophic idea, it is both vague and ambiguous as enunciated by James and Dewey, so that without redoubling our analytic efforts, we will have scarcely advanced into the subtleties or profundities of metaphysics.

In the latter part of his life James devoted his attention to just this problem, of clarifying what is meant by a "growing world." He had moved from an earlier espoused tychism to a view of the emerging of novelties that, unlike tychism, did not leave novel events irrelevant to and unnaturally discontinuous with the rest of nature.[21]

What is surprising, when we consider how basic the idea of possibility as a trait of reality is to pragmatism, and recall the initial devotion of this philosophy to the clarification of ideas, is that pragmatists have done little to throw light upon this cardinal thesis.[22]

2) The other idea supporting the interpretation of the practical character

[18] Dewey, "Development of American Pragmatism," p. 25. But also quite in accord with Dewey's comment and the course of discussion in these pages is a statement from Mead, *The Philosophy of the Present*, pp. 3–4: "I am proceeding upon the assumption that cognition, and thought as a part of the cognitive process, is reconstructive, because reconstruction is essential to the conduct of an intelligent being in the universe. This is but part of the more general proposition that changes are going on in the universe, and that as a consequence of these changes the universe is becoming a different universe. Intelligence is but one aspect of this change. It is a change that is part of an ongoing living process that tends to maintain itself."

[19] Peirce, it may be noted in passing, found the idea of equally possible cases "thoroughly unclear," preferring the notion of "cases equally frequent," *CP* 2.673.

[20] This is not wholly unrelated to "principle A" stated by Lewis (derived from Keynes), and explained in part: "every possible experience is *ipso facto* a possibility of experience, but it is not possible that all possibilities should be actual. Any possibility is a possible actuality, but it is not possible that all possibilities should be concomitantly real," *Mind and the World Order*, p. 368.

[21] See Perry, II, 664: "This notion of a 'really growing world' is the general theme of the latter part of the *Problems of Philosophy*, the theme which bound him closely to Bergson, and the theme with which he was increasingly occupied during the last years and months of his life."

[22] Appendix 7 has been reserved for a further discussion of *possibility*.

of thought and reality has already been stated in the passage quoted above, viz., "the world will be different from what it would have been if thought had not intervened." I will not dwell upon this point here, since it has already received attention in this and earlier chapters.

What has yet to be sufficiently emphasized concerning this notion of the practicality of thought is that it is largely based on a *behavioral* interpretation and analysis of mind and thinking.[23] There is also a rather important metaphysical generalization made upon the pragmatic conception of thought.

The behavioral approach of pragmatism to a theory of mind is, negatively, a rejection of the Cartesian doctrine of mind as an immaterial substance joined to a material body, and a rejection of introspective psychology stemming from Descartes. The critical literature of the pragmatists' attack on these doctrines and their examination of later "empirical" theories of mind, impressions, and sense-data ideas, has been neglected (but see, however, § 28, § 38, and Chapter Five, Part Two). But it makes interesting reading, especially when, quite independently, the most influential English philosophers today have come to remarkably similar critical conclusions.[24] Americans, drawn to English ways, may suddenly be reassured of the respectability of their own neglected philosophic past, since a substantial part of that past has by coincidence been rediscovered in Oxford.

Aside from critical rejections of earlier influential theories of knowledge, the pragmatists also addressed themselves to the positive task of constructing a new theory. This theory had as its objective an explanation of mind and mental conduct language which was (*a*) to avoid bogging down in the traditional dialectical problems (i.e., the problem of knowledge discussed in Part One); and (*b*) to stand up as an empirical theory capable, at least at crucial stretches, of receiving empirical verification. The theory in question, then, was evolved as a number of related hypotheses concerning the motivating and mediating factors of reflective or intelligent conduct in biological and socially conditioned situations. The theory has been briefly described by Dewey:

> The adaptations made by inferior organisms, for example their effective and co-ordinated responses to stimuli, become teleological in man and therefore give occasion to thought. Reflection is an indirect response to the environment, and the element of indirection can itself become great and very complicated. But it has its origin in biological adaptive behavior and the ultimate function of its cognitive aspect is a prospective control of the conditions of the environment. The function of intelligence is therefore not that of copying the objects of the environment, but rather of taking account of the way in which more effective and more profitable relations with these objects may be established in the future.[25]

[23] Both Mead and Dewey had jointly developed a "behavioral" analysis of mind and intelligent behavior before Watson's *Behaviorism* appeared.

[24] The reader can easily verify this claim. Ryle's *Concept of Mind,* in its critical function and in its proposed constructive approach to the analysis of mental conduct language is very close to Dewey's writings on the same topic. An even more striking resemblance, recommended for comparison, is to be found in Austin's *Sense and Sensibilia* and Dewey's critical analysis of Russell's epistemology, ch. 11 in *Essays in Experimental Logic.*

[25] "The Development of American Pragmatism," p. 30.

The metaphysical conclusion that was drawn from this behavioral conception of mind and thought was that these are not empirically null or irrelevant to an adequate theory of reality; indeed, under the critical and explanatory norms of the theory, if intelligence is real as a form of behavior, it follows that intelligence is one of the forms in which reality behaves.

> If reality be itself in transition—and this doctrine originated not with the objectionable pragmatist but with the physicist and naturalist and historian—then the doctrine that knowledge *is* reality making a particular and specific sort of change in itself seems to have the best chance at maintaining a theory of knowing which is in wholesome touch with the genuine and valid.[26]

3)   The third claim guiding the pragmatic interpretation of the practical character of reality is one with which the history of pragmatism began and for which the name 'pragmatism' was first invented. (The details are given in § 27.) This is the contention, as Peirce put it, "of an inseparable connection between rational cognition and rational purpose."[27] It is what Peirce, James, Dewey, and other pragmatists have all agreed to as the purposive character of conceptualization.[28] This subject has appeared with some frequency in previous chapters and does not require reiteration here, but for one important point which has not been sufficiently dealt with earlier.

When it is maintained that conceptualization is purposive,[29] or that thought is teleological,[30] or that ideas are instruments,[31] the methodological principle these doctrines suggest is that the analysis of meanings (of signs, i.e., ideas, concepts, statements[32]) is an analysis of certain kinds of action in certain contexts. Language is an instrument, even in its purely esthetic and intrinsically appreciated uses. One understands instruments by getting to understand their uses. This is to understand the purposes that instruments are used to achieve; it is also to understand why certain materials and their organization and operations are necessary to instruments if their purposes are to be achieved. In the case of concepts, then, a necessary condition of the elucidation of a concept is an analysis of its use—or the purpose of its use—in acts of communication. But actions are performed and observed in particular contexts with particular outcomes conditioning them.

For the pragmatist, therefore, meaning has reference, if sometimes only remotely so, to the ordinary situations and conditions in which actions occur. "There is no distinction of meaning so fine as to consist in anything but a possible

---

[26] "The Practical Character of Reality," p. 40.
[27] *CP* 4.12. For the context, see § 27.
[28] See esp. §§ 20, 28, 38; also 45, 60, 65, 84–85, 93–94. The idea being central to pragmatism is accordingly ubiquitous in the foregoing pages.
[29] Peirce, see § 20.
[30] James, see § 28.
[31] Dewey, see § 36.
[32] In keeping with the large sense of *sign* registered in the discussion of Peirce, § 21, note 39.

difference of practice," wrote Peirce.[33] The relation of meaning to action, that is, of the analysis and interpretation of the meanings of signs as a part of and with reference to actions, has at least two major philosophic consequences in the empirical methodology of pragmatism.

First, there is no sharp cleavage between the language and conceptualization of men in ordinary situations engaged in ordinary activities, and communication for more specialized purposes in less familiar and more "theoretical" contexts. For it is in and by means of ordinary language in most ordinary situations that, when the need is felt, one proceeds gradually to acquire and use the language of theoretical science. Moreover, it is in the ordinary language of us all that the understanding and clarification of scientific thought (even its more extraordinary conceptualization) is carried out for the most part, and for the most part terminates. The evolution of ordinary language and an accompanying evolution in our conceptualization over what we count as ordinary objects, is another and supporting part of this contention. Thus the ordinary language of today, given to such parlance as 'nuclear fission,' 'genes,' 'schizophrenia,' is partly made up of the formidable language of theoretical science of yesteryear.

Second, particular contexts in which actions occur, since qualified by particular working purposes and aims, provide a more or less definite and continuous range of the possible uses of language and of roles for concepts to perform.[34] Words for concepts may remain the same, but this fact must not bewitch us from recognizing that variations in the uses of concepts, sometimes even deliberate departures from norms of usage, will and do happen and often suit our sundry purposes.

Roughly, in the act of communication (in writing or speaking), the available normal structure of language and occurring purposeful experience meet. The system of language is then made to accommodate and facilitate action; it is even plundered and bent to the purpose. The act, in this case, is that of *utterance*, and in the utterance is incorporated the full generality of language with the individuation of intentional uses in particular contexts. Indeed, acts of utterance are *concretions*, not the "concrete" of slabs of pavement, but literally *concretus* = "grown together," as in Aristotle's doctrine of individuals as concretions of logical structure and material possibilities. In any event, the varied uses of conceptualization for descriptive, prescriptive, and explanatory purposes, and the meanings of concepts in given uses, will be conditioned by the coercion of reality, of rational purposes and possible differences of practice.[35]

[33] In "How to Make Our Ideas Clear" (1878), CP 5.400. But cf.: "the possible practical consequences of a concept constitute the sum total of the concept," CP 5.27, and, "The intellectual significance of all thought ultimately lies in its effect upon our actions," CP 7.361. For a speculative development of one of Peirce's suggested insights here, see the last pages of § 22 above.
[34] These two points, forming the previous and the present paragraphs, were often elaborated by Dewey. For a recent clear statement of them addressed to the methodology of behavioral science, see Kaplan, pp. 45–47.
[35] These last phrases allude to James's and Peirce's doctrine of the practical and efficacious nature of reality over our thinking. The expression of this view—historically among the first statements of pragmatism—came from Peirce in "How to Make Our Ideas Clear"

To sum up, we have been concerned to describe and trace the aim and formative doctrines of pragmatism. The results of this survey can be stated in outline as follows:

PRAGMATISM: 1.   A maxim or procedural principle in philosophy and science for explicating the meanings of certain concepts (see § 21).

2.   A theory of knowledge, experience, and reality maintaining: (*a*) that thought and knowledge are biologically and socially evolved modes of adaptation to and control over experience and reality; (*b*) that reality possesses a transitional character and that thought is a guide to the realization and satisfaction of our interests and purposes; (*c*) that all knowledge is evaluative of future experience and that thinking functions experimentally in anticipations of future experiences and consequences of actions—thus in organizing conditions of future observations and experience. Thought is a behavioral process manifested in controlled actualizations of selected, anticipated, and planned possibilities of future experience.[36]

It remains only to append one further note to the survey in order to bring the contents up to date.

3.   In recent literature, under the influence of Dewey and Lewis as well as F. P. Ramsey, Rudolf Carnap, Ernest Nagel, W. V. Quine, *et al.*, "pragmatism" connotes one broad philosophic attitude toward our conceptualization of experience: theorizing over experience is, as a whole and in detail, fundamentally motivated and justified by conditions of efficacy and utility in serving our various aims and needs. The ways in which experience is apprehended, systematized, and anticipated may be many. Here pragmatism counsels tolerance and pluralism. But, aside from esthetic and intrinsic interests, all theorizing is subject to the critical objective of maximum usefulness in serving our needs. Our critical decisions in general will be pragmatic, granted that in particular cases decisions over what is most useful or needed in our rational endeavors are relative to some given point of view and purposes.

The three parts of this outline comprise a general definition of pragmatism.

---

and from James in "Spencer's Definition of Mind." On these see §§ 23, 24, and 28; the final paragraph of § 28 treats of them together. It is interesting and not insignificant to notice that publication of both papers occurred in the same month of the same year, January 1878.

[36] The emphasis on future experience does not deny historical knowledge, for the pragmatist argues that historical inquiry and the results of historical knowledge have future consequences. See the suggestion of § 42 above.

CHAPTER TWO

Pragmatism and American Life

§ 102. The Import of Some Ideas

Pragmatism has sometimes been praised and often condemned as a typically American philosophy. Certainly as a movement it stands thus far as the major achievement of American philosophic thought. But in referring to it as typically American, what is usually meant is that pragmatism is the characteristic expression of American life, its civilization, and its mind.

Undoubtedly there are some relations between the forces and conditions that shape a civilization and the philosophy that takes place therein. But relations are not always or exclusively *causal* connections, and as was hinted at much earlier in § 2 and § 19, and will be contended below, the easy and familiar generalizations occupying the above paragraph are something less than edifying. This is not to deny some grain of truth at the bottom of these diagnostic pronouncements. But that truth is all but buried under a profusion of misdirected inferences and captious moralizing that the subject has usually prompted.

The origins of American pragmatism are not primarily to be looked for in America. They are an integral part of the whole uninterrupted course of European philosophy, surveyed in Part One. Pragmatism is one late development alongside others in the history of modern philosophy. As for the originators of pragmatism, Peirce, James, and Dewey, each was educated and thoroughly immersed in the traditions of English and continental philosophy and literature. Each had read and felt the impact of British empiricism, neo-Kantian idealism, and romanticism. And they were not alone in drawing upon European thought, for such has always been the lot and the schooling of the American intellectual. The diversity and profusion of ideas and intellectual movements in American history, the moral and religious heterodoxies, the fanaticisms, controversies, and changing enthusiasms are not to be attributed to an unusual vigor for inventiveness and variety in the American people or climate. The fact is that the conglomerate manifestations of the American mind are the result of local adaptations, graftings, and crossings of the older loyalties and ideas that migrated from Europe.

There have been, of course, occasions in which this transplanting and subsequent inbreeding produced curious and exotic offshoots. Quaint eccentricity, melancholia, and profoundly sensitive and original moralizing have conspired in ways and under varying circumstances to flower in genius—in a Lincoln, Whitman, Thoreau, or Poe. But what characterizes the expression of these men, especially the latter two, is the unstudied, the unsystematic nature of their thought. Philosophy tends inevitably toward systematic expression and scope. And systematic philosophizing in America has always had to take its initial problems, vocabulary, and conceptual instruments from the one available resource: the history of philosophy. And that history, it needs no repeating, was to be found in Europe, not in America.

In any sense of analytical concepts, technical doctrine, and systematic organization, pragmatism is neither typically American nor American at all. Yet there is a sense in which pragmatism does sharply reflect something of American life, and this sense remains to be considered.

§ *103. The Dilemma of American Philosophy*

The observations of the last pages lead to a rather interesting historical problem of American philosophy in general and thus also of pragmatism.

It is a characteristic of philosophy, more so than in the other intellectual arts, to live on its past. Each generation of philosophers has made use of the materials, methods, and insights that immediate or remote forebears have developed—even when the form was outright rebellion against the past. For it is the past that makes rejection of it possible, and, moreover, suggests the very form that it might take. Even the antihistorical spirit has quite a long history and could learn something from the past—if only how to avoid repeating itself.

This trait of philosophy, to indulge and trade upon its past, has endowed philosophizing in America with a rather special problem. For, as we took note earlier, in origin American culture is a European import—diverse, heterogeneous, and necessarily modified to adapt to rather un-European circumstances and experience. Americans, or Europeans in the new country, soon learned to modify and to exploit and invent new uses for English corn, French cattle, German beer. And they made ingenious readaptations of religions, customs, languages, and laws, brought from the old countries.

Unlike the English, French, and Germans, Americans can not look back upon a long philosophic tradition of their own. Immediately behind the American philosopher is his prototype the clergyman and theologian, steeped in Protestant puritanism and caught in the coils of Calvin, Hume, and Fichte. During the latter part of the nineteenth and the first part of the present century, the academic homeland of American philosophy was Germany. More recently, it has been Cambridge and Oxford. Young Americans went overseas to become proficient in literary or scientific research techniques and to acquire a scholarly education. They returned to teach what they had learned. A Ph.D. earned in one of these sojourns abroad was a promising condition of advancement in American universities. These days the American university, with business acumen and available funds, is proceeding rather more directly to the *fons et origo* of learning by attracting the European professor himself—which perhaps is the unexpected fulfillment of the prophesy of Hegel, who declared that the future of history was to take this route, the *Weltgeist* itself was going to travel to America. But for Americans, the pattern still continues to be less Hegelian and more after the fashion of the heroes of Henry James's stories, who go to Europe in order to find themselves.

From this cursory noting of the biography of American philosophy, we are led to the following general observations.

First: The main problem of American philosophical thought, quite aside from differing doctrinal positions, is how to bend and exploit its European heritage to the conditions of American culture. This is a problem, of course, only insofar as American philosophers are interested in influencing social and political life. This is something like the economic problem of converting and allocating raw materials and capital goods imported from abroad. (A striking historical example of the modification of ideas in adapting them to American conditions and interests is witnessable in the way in which the doctrines of Locke appear in the Declaration of Independence.)

Second: The *dilemma* confronting American philosophy is that the more systematically philosophical it becomes, the less peculiarly American it is; and the more it concerns itself with the idioms, currents, and events peculiar to American life, the less philosophical in a technical sense it becomes.

Now both the problem and dilemma thus stated are of passing historical interest only for these reasons. To begin with, philosophy, insofar as it survives in the future, is becoming increasingly eclectic and less and less a product of single traditions of ideas. It also happens that the world is growing smaller, the arts of communication more effective. More philosophers know more about one another and the philosophic past than in any previous generation. Finally, the existence of national boundaries and of indigenous peculiarities that thrive within them are rapidly becoming things of the past. The problems of a social and political nature that call for philosophic thought are more urgent, but less local and unique than ever before. The problems and the culture of one part of the world are increasingly the business and interest of the whole race. The atomic age is also the age of one world, and this latter development renders obsolete both the problem and dilemma of American philosophy.

Philosophically this is all as it should be. For in no ultimate sense is a philosophy typical of a time or a nation. Climate, locale, and national boundaries are utterly irrelevant to philosophic truth. Indeed, these are mere artifices which, insofar as they affect a philosopher's vision and perhaps his language, are distractions and encumbrances that he is best rid of or made impervious to if possible.

What we have now to ask ourselves is, What *is* the relation of American pragmatism to American life and culture?

§ *104. Pragmatism: Wit and Philosophy in America*

The reader is to be reassured quickly that my intention is not to digress upon the subject of humor (if any) in philosophy. Nor should the title be thought to imply, maliciously, that one must take American philosophy with a sense of humor. By 'wit' I follow a different and characteristically humorless usage deriving from Aristotle. 'Wit' refers to the ability and readiness to discern how and why certain facts or statements are the effects or consequents of others.[1] It is, among other manifestations, a grasp of the connection between a particular conclusion and general premisses. Now it is the notion of *wit* in this distinctive operation that encourages the following reflections on the historical nature of pragmatism as an expression of American intellectual life.

American philosophic thought, we observed a moment ago, has been reared upon a problem and brought, if only half-consciously, to a dilemma. The same problem has shaped the efforts of American artists, painters, writers, and poets: they, too, have had to reckon with the problem of how to incorporate the European heritage and schooling in artistic forms relevant to and meaningful within American social experience. Although by the nature of his materials—by the premium on originality and experimental genres in which the arts thrive—the artist has not faced quite the dilemma thrust upon the philosopher, yet they both alike have had to invent ways of deploying the adopted foreign tradition while avoiding slavish imitation and artificial reproductions of it. Interestingly enough, the American artist, unlike the philosopher, has been vocal and eloquent about this difficulty. He has felt the problem by an afflatus of culture and sensibility, and there are any number of critical studies devoted to this "problem" (especially in tiresome abundance, to the "problem" of the American novel). One senses, to choose but a single illustration, full awareness of the problem in these reflections by Walt Whitman:

> Plenty of songs had been sung—beautiful, matchless songs—adjusted to other lands than these. . . . The Old World has had the poems of myths, fictions, feudal-

[1] Thus, Aristotle, *Posterior Analytics* I. 3, 89b10: "Quick wit is the skill of hitting upon the middle term without a moment's reflection, as when one sees that the moon has the bright side always turned to the sun, and immediately realizes the reason for this: because the moon's brightness is due to the sun."

ism, conquest, caste, dynastic wars, splendid exceptional characters, which have been great; but the New World needs the poems of realities and science and of the democratic average and basic equality. . . . As for native American individuality, the distinctive and ideal type of Western character (as consistent with the operative and even money-making features of United States humanity as chosen knights, gentlemen and warriors were the ideals of the centuries of European feudalism) it has not yet appeared. I have allowed the stress of my poems from beginning to end to bear upon American individuality and assist it—not only because that is a great lesson in Nature, amid all her generalizing laws, but as counterpoise to the levelling tendencies of Democracy.[2]

Whatever we may think of the solution he comes to or the convictions generated, the passage shows very clearly Whitman's full cognizance of what we have been calling "the intellectual's problem."

But the passage also reveals in it the exercise of *wit*. Discerning what the New World needs by contrast to the tradition of the Old World, discerning what principles (in this case of poetic subject matter) are to be applied, and how, to American life, are instances of that kind of rational wit we took notice of in commencing this discussion.

For purposes of convenient identification, let us refer to the problem of these pages as "the problem of a two-part culture," fully acknowledging that this descriptive appellation is a tag, uninformative except as roughly indicative of certain conditions—not an explanatory hypothesis or sociological theory.[3] The 'two-part' symbolizes the mixed product of American culture. One part is the indigenous, evolving community begun in a wilderness, become colonized, and most of whose organization and mores were (and in very complex ways continue to be) determined by conditions of survival and, in due course, conditions of prosperity on the cleared land or seaport. The other part is the whole imported, variegated intellectual, moral, and religious European tradition already commented on. One recognizes, surely, that in the course of American social history, these two parts interpenetrate. Basic to the organization of the earliest settlements, in economic patterns and communal habits, in the very language spoken, were efficacious second-part, ideological assumptions and convictions.

---

[2] Quoted in Auden's essay "American Poetry," pp. 364–365. Auden's study of the American poet in many ways illuminates in parallel fashion the theme of these pages devoted to American philosophy.

[3] This idea and phraseology of a "two-part culture" has obvious antecedents, from which it partially derives, in the familiar analysis of cultures into a *technological* aspect (i.e., the arts and institutions of survival and economic organization, corresponding to what I have called "the first part" of the culture), and an *ideological* aspect (the ethical, religious, political, philosophic ideals and norms, corresponding here to what is referred to as "the second part" of the culture). For Marxists, this is designated as the economic base and ideological superstructure of a culture. For Hegelians, much the same analytical distinction is found in the momentary historical manifestation of the World-Spirit in the material conditions it must use. I should add, however, that in suggesting the notion of two-part culture, I have in mind no simple scheme of pure economic structure adjacent to or supporting a pure ideology. The parts are mixed and interdependent. The history of medicine is a good example of an important technological art, but initiated and often influenced by ideological (i.e., moral and religious) considerations.

§ *105*.   *Our Two-Part Culture: Angelic Impulses and Predatory Lusts*[4]

Let us grant that ours is a two-part culture, subject to interactions and modifications among the parts, and subject also to regional and periodic variations in the contents of the parts, that is, in the local and spreading manifestations of culture across this continent. The fundamental problems of American society have their origins in divisions of interest and conflicting values, that attach to each of the two parts of the culture and are due to both. Visitors from other countries have often commented on the strikingly paradoxical nature of the American character and way of life. We espouse our religion on the weekends, and practice quite a different set of ideals during the business week. We hold that all men are morally and politically equal and that life, liberty, the pursuit of happiness are inalienable rights, yet we have a history of slavery; the Negroes, Orientals, American Indians, and Mexicans have never enjoyed these inalienable rights. We believe in law and order and equal justice for all, yet many of our folk heroes are outlaws; and in movies and television, crime and violence are subjects of prolonged fascination. Some of these and many other aspects of the paradoxical American are well portrayed by Gunner Myrdal, whose controlling theme is paradox in his book entitled *The American Dilemma.*[5] We are quite as paradoxical as anything to be found in the eighteenth-century Enlightenment (as depicted in § 7), and the similarities are not hard to find.

Now for many practical purposes, paradoxes, even to living a double life, are of no crucial moment. Not, at least, as long as convenient means of correlating roles and switching parts are available, as a certain material thickness of coin supports the pair of Janus faces. Crises occur when roles conflict, or the wrong part is enacted, or when the two parts of the culture diverge or call for necessarily divergent loyalties, when one side of the coin wears into the other to threaten Janus faces and coinhood altogether.

In nineteenth-century America, just past midpoint, there occurred just such a loss of correlative roles and a separating of two parts: the Civil War was a clash between cultures. But the Civil War was an extreme instance of more generally felt frictions and separations. During that century, enormous changes in the first part of the culture, in the economy, and in daily experience were unmatched by the relatively ossified second-part religious, ethical, and philosophic beliefs. In

---

[4] The words are drawn from James's address to the Anti-Imperialist League in 1903. The passage is apropos our present theme: "Angelic impulses and predatory lusts divide our heart exactly as they divide the hearts of other countries. . . . Political virtue . . . follows the eternal division inside of each country between the more animal and more intellectual kind of men, between the tory and liberal tendencies, the jingoism and animal instinct that would run things by main force and brute possession, and the critical conscience that believes in educational methods and in rational rules of right. . . ." Perry, II, 313.

[5] See especially the first chapter of *The American Dilemma.*

contrast to the fairly static pattern of second-part traditional ideals, an increase in population and the settling of the West was changing American life. The population almost doubled in a twenty-year period: in 1840 the population was estimated at 17,000,000; in 1850 that figure became 23,995,000; and in 1860, slightly over 31,000,000. After the Civil War, from 1865 to 1900, with the coming of. the railroads, the great plains west of the Mississippi were occupied. Accompanying this settling and the resultant rise in population was an equally rapid increase in manufactures in the east, so that after the war, in the twenty years from 1860 to 1880, the value of domestic manufactures more than doubled; and after 1880, this continued to increase at a phenomenal rate.

Given this period of enormous economic activity and expansion, and its continual transformation of the social conditions and standards of living in America, the second part of the culture, the European heritage, appears more and more remote from the practical, ordinary, everyday life. The heritage was kept alive primarily by the influx of immigrants from the old country and by those who, having achieved prosperity, could recultivate tradition and educate their children in it. Still, from the viewpoint of the mass of Americans in the nineteenth century, the European heritage had the appearance of a pious memory sustained by a few intellectuals, and encountered, if fleetingly, in that rather isolated and elite institution of learning, the college.

In the absence of an effective critical and directive morality, there emerged an ethic, shrewd in practical injunctions, clear, uncomplicated, and uncompromising in its enunciation of the techniques of success. This is the ethic of collective competition for individual commercial success. The goal, in a peculiarly American idiom, is called "making good." This evolved as the business ethic: not an articulation of the mores of business, but a very clear reflection and application of that ethos and its values to all other aspects of life. This Fichtean rugged individualism in the arena of commercial realism, where and when possible, might be grafted upon or made to pass for the sentimentally revered tradition, the older orthodoxy—that felt but only vaguely discernible metaphysical body of ancestral values and ideals.

Thus Americans have been endowed with two moral traditions connected tenuously at best, and often only by the sheer sophistry of clerics and politicians. We are taught the old tradition in our schools and churches, but it is the newer, viable, exhortatory morality of striving and success that we soon learn in the world. It is this education in and commitment to two moralities that gives the American character its paradoxical and often contradictory expression.

In the newer ethic, success is delineated as the rational and predatory acquisition of wealth, mostly for irrational and lavish consumption. In its practice this has usually led to a crass commercialism, to cheap and ostentatious pecuniary displays, to compulsive expenditures, and, under the conditions of mass production, to uniformly bad taste and an obsession with profitable things, i.e., activities or articles that in some way "pay" or prove useful. The idea of a perfectly useless good, or something intrinsically valuable but not a means of or use to anything else—such as music, or metaphysics, or poetry—has no place in this ethic. For value is largely identified with market price, and thereby the value of anything tends to be conceived as a commercial function, the equivalent in labor or in goods that the article could bring if sold or exchanged. Music, or metaphysics, for example, would be thought of as profitable activities, if at all, only because cultural polish can "pay" in business and social connections and command esteem from other persons.[6]

It is this ethic, so pervasively a part of the American culture, so finely attuned to the business spirit and the art of making and spending money, that has often been called the pragmatism in American life.[7] We must not fall into quarreling over words. But the philosophic ideas we have been examining in this book as constituting *pragmatism* are most certainly not to be identified with this ethic, geared to the growth of industry and big business in America. On the contrary, much of the philosophizing of pragmatists in America has been a criticism of the commercialism and money-haunted pursuits of Americans, of our double standards deriving from our two ethical and ideological traditions, of our split and divisive two-part culture.

Here, I think, we come to what can be regarded as the historical occasion and the formative cultural conditions of the origins of American pragmatism. It was argued in the previous chapter that the central technical motivation of pragmatism was that of synthesizing and integrating ethical values and empirical knowledge, and that this was gradually worked out in the pragmatic theory of knowledge as a practical and valuational activity (§ 100). This technical philosophic aim, however, appears in some part to have emerged and received stimulus from the climate of philosophic thought and social conditions in America in the last decade of the nineteenth century.

James, as we have seen (§§ 26, 31), conceived of pragmatism as providing a method for determining the meaning, value, and truth of beliefs. He also thought that pragmatism supplied a "mediating way of thinking" by which empirical and religious philosophies might be united, or "concrete facts" and "human values" could be brought into "definite touch" (see § 99). James's view of the function of pragmatism reveals, if we study it, something slightly more complicated than the establishment of a synthesis of otherwise antithetical religion and science, or moral values and concrete facts. For there is a third dimension of the synthesis all-important to James, without which the synthesizing operation remains a purely "intellectual" matter, significant, but wanting in vital results and full "meaningfulness." This latter part of the synthesis is its direct and positive connection with live experience, its application to specific action and individual lives. Thus, the

---

[6] Or, as Veblen argued in *The Theory of the Leisure Class*, these activities are valued as providing evidence of pecuniary ability to afford idleness.

[7] Even by Veblen, although he does not identify this pragmatism as a peculiarly American phenomenon, and argues that the Middle Ages were more pragmatic than the modern age. See "Science in Modern Civilization."

mediating role of pragmatism, for James, exhibits a kind of triadic route: a mediation of· moral values (religious or romantic, see the passage quoted at the start of § 99 above); a further application of this synthesis in the lives of individuals; and, finally, the specific enactments of the mediated values in life situations. The emphasis here, and in James's writings, is on the individualistic function of pragmatism, on the variety and diversity of the mediating forms that pragmatism could and would take in what was, for James, the thoroughly pluralistic character of human experience and society.

The most powerful support of James's philosophizing came from Dewey and the "Chicago School" in 1903.[8] James described this movement in a letter to Schiller in the same year:

> it appears now that, under Dewey's inspiration, they have at Chicago a flourishing school of radical empiricism of which I for one have been entirely ignorant, having been led to neglect its utterances by their lack of "terseness," "crispness," "raciness," and other "newspaporial" virtues, though I could discern that Dewey himself was laboring with a big freight, towards the light. They have started from Hegelianism, and they have that temperament (that is, such men as Mead and Lloyd have it strongly) which makes one still suspect that if they do strike Truth eventually, they will mean some mischief to it after all; but still the fact remains that from such opposite poles minds are moving towards a common centre, that old compartments and divisions are breaking down, and that a very inclusive new school may be formed. Once admit that experience is a river which made the channel that now, in part, but only in part, confines it, and it seems to me that all sorts of realities and completenesses are possible in philosophy, hitherto stiffened and cramped by the silly littlenesses of the upper and lower dogmatisms. . . .[9]

Now the important historical fact for us at present concerning this movement is revealed in James's comment above that "They have started from Hegelianism, and they have that temperament." Indeed, James's further words about "minds moving towards a common centre" and "old compartments and divisions . . . breaking down" are themselves in that Hegelian spirit.[10]

---

[8] The "Chicago School" began as a group forming around Dewey at the University of Michigan and moved later to the University of Chicago. See the Introduction to Part II on Dewey and Mead. The year 1903 marks the publication of *Studies in Logical Theory,* dedicated to James, containing chapters by Dewey as well as by a number of graduate students: H. B. Thompson, S. F. McLennan, M. L. Ashley, W. C. Gore, W. H. Heidel, N. W. Stuart, and A. W. Moore.

Dewey had been in correspondence with James as early as 1888, see Perry, II, 514–533. Although certain of Dewey's leading ideas had been in a stage of development and transition earlier, 1903 is as good a date as any to indicate the start of "Instrumentalism" as a philosophic movement within pragmatism. Dewey describes the position of the school and of the volume *Studies in Logical Theory* to James in a letter (1903) thus: "As for the standpoint,—we have all been at work at it for about twelve years." Perry, II, 520.

[9] For the full letter, see Perry, II, 374–375. Mead is discussed above, Part II, ch. 4. Alfred H. Lloyd was a professor at the University of Michigan. Dewey wrote James from Chicago, in 1903: "Did you ever read Lloyd's *Dynamic Idealism?* I can't see much difference between his monism and your pluralism. . . ," Perry, II, 520. See the study on Lloyd by Evelyn Shirk.

[10] Breaking down of compartments and divisions is very much the language of Hegelian continuity. For the spirit, and some remarkably similar uses of the language in Dewey, see Appendix 1, sec. A below.

The difference in philosophic orientation and temperament between James and the new supporting school is significant. James phrased the difference thus: "You have all come from Hegel and your terminology *s'en ressent*, I from empiricism, and though we reach much the same goal it superficially looks different from the opposite sides."[11] But there was something more below the surface that separated James's pragmatism from Dewey's instrumentalism. This is seen not so much in stated doctrines as in how these doctrines related to the circumstances that called for intellectual clarification; how in their respective ways they suggested the course that intelligent action might take in troubled and perplexed times; how, in sum, the rather different philosophic backgrounds from which James and Dewey had come in "moving towards a common centre" led each to quite distinct reflections and conclusions concerning the applications of pragmatism to American social conditions at the close of the nineteenth century.

James was always a champion of individualism. Social problems, insofar as philosophic thought applied to them at all (since James seems never to have shared Dewey's view of a philosophic-scientific method of resolving social and political problems), were to be settled in local contexts with specific individual benefits the uppermost consideration. "Damn great Empires! Including that of the Absolute. . . ," said James. "Give me individuals and their spheres of activity." James, unlike Dewey, never attempted to work out his social views in a systematic way[12] (as we observed briefly in the previous chapter, § 99). But James had convictions and loyalties, to which his pluralism and individualism led him, and he could be fully expressive about these. He was an ardent spokesman for small countries, the underdog, the minority point of view. He spoke out against what he took to be the most dangerous of growing tendencies in American life, the fighting instinct, mob hysteria, and bigness. He saw these effectively at work in the Venezuela incident, the Spanish-American War, and our interest in and treatment of the Philippines.[13] He also saw these as factors in the psychology of a lynching mob, concerning which he wrote a long letter to the *Springfield Republican* in 1903.[14] James's major political activity was devoted, for some years, accordingly, to the Anti-Imperialist League. Imperialism seemed to him to absorb and carry in it the worst of the tendencies just noted along with "the passion of military conquest" and of mastery masked by false ideals of benevolence. In a letter, James set forth a characteristically deft and frank statement of his individualistic social point of view:

I am against bigness and greatness in all their forms, and with the invisible molecular moral forces that work from individual to individual, stealing in through the crannies of the world like so many soft rootlets, or like the capillary oozing of water, and yet rending the hardest monuments of man's pride, if you give them time. The bigger the unit you deal with, the hollower, the more brutal, the more

11 Perry, II, 521–522.
12 Perry, II, 315.
13 For these and other aspects of James's view, see Perry, II, ch. 68.
14 Perry, II, 317.

mendacious is the life displayed. So I am against all big organizations as such, national ones first and foremost; against all big successes and big results; and in favor of the eternal forces of truth which always work in the individual and immediately unsuccessful way, under-dogs always, till history comes, after they are long dead, and puts them on top.[15]

(One finds some difficulty in reconciling this statement of James's with the frequent identification of his pragmatism as a philosophy reflecting and justifying the growth of big business in America.)

Now the contrast between James and Dewey is clearest and most significant at just this point. Whereas James believed that "individuals and their spheres of activity" were the fundamental units, the pragmatically meaningful terms which social problems and ideals were to be reduced to and appraised by, Dewey focused his philosophic analysis upon the individual-in-context, in a cultural and historical set of relationships with other individuals in a common environment. Dewey was to emphasize the individual, but what received this underscoring was the individual *situation*, the context or qualitative whole.[16]

James might have sensed in Dewey's approach the Hegelian influence, and worse yet, for James, the tendency to lose sight of the concrete individual through a screen of abstractions and intellectual relations. But 'concrete' and 'individual' are difficult and charged terms. For Dewey, the individual-in-context is not an abstraction, but the full, robust, empirical reality; accordingly, it is the conception of a concrete individual, sharply delineated from all supporting relations and natural connections with physical, organic, and socially environing conditions, that constitutes an abstraction. Indeed, if we were to force the difference between James and Dewey here, Dewey would have characterized James as a spokesman for the "old individualism" of an eighteenth-century laissez-faire, atomistic, pre-industrial social philosophy. James's hatred of bigness, of large organizations, and his prizing of individual action in a "plastic" and "growing world" is suited to conditions in the first but not the second half of the nineteenth century in America. His America and his social outlook ally him with Walt Whitman.[17] And one is tempted to see in James's metaphysical doctrine of reality in the making, and of a "growing world,"[18] a reflection of the open frontier and the beckoning adventuresome West.

Dewey, however, regarded this older individualism as a thing of the past. Big business, big cities, big organizations were inevitable developments of the modern world. The question of concern for Dewey, therefore, was how to arrive at a "new individualism." This was the question of working out the ways in which persons might engage in intelligent and imaginative occupations with a sense

[15] *Letters*, II, 90; also Perry, II, 315–316.
[16] For the character of a *situation*, see earlier, §§ 39 and 91.
[17] James read and often praised Whitman. Cf. a letter of 1900 to Palmer: "Always things burst by the growing content of experience. Dramatic unities; laws of versification; ecclesiastical systems; scholastic doctrines. Bah! Give me Walt Whitman and Browning ten times over. . . ." Perry, II, p. 320.
[18] We took note of this doctrine in the previous chapter; some pondering over it occupies Appendix 7.

of purpose and value in a social order becoming increasingly organized, collectivistic, and economically deterministic.[19] The older ideals of rugged individualism or Jamesian pluralism, of spontaneity and freedom of action were inadequate to the changed social and technological scene. Significantly, Dewey described the new individualism as calling for "organic" conditions of "growth" and integration.[20]

My subject is not, however, that of simply noting philosophic differences between the social views of James and Dewey. At the moment, aware that fundamental differences of perspective did exist and that James and Dewey accordingly philosophized over the same scene in different ways, I want to follow the announced intention of discerning the historical connections of pragmatism with that American scene.

Dewey's instrumentalism was initiated and painstakingly directed to articulating the formal aspects (the concepts, ideas, conditions, and kinds of inference and judgment) of intelligent action (see § 36). The entire theory is an interpretation of thought or reason as a form of social behavior. For inquiry is a socially disciplined activity and, like the language and habits so vital to it, a cultural inheritance and communal institution. Moreover, for Dewey, the workings and results of inquiry assume a thoroughly social character: inquiry issues in "resolved" unified wholes, in organic and existential "equilibration" and "integration"; gaps, conflicts, dualisms are "transformed," and unification, continuity, and growth are the outcome.[21] This philosophic emphasis on the social and the community puts Dewey much closer to Peirce and Royce than to James. The social, Dewey has argued, is "the inclusive philosophic idea."[22]

A theory of knowledge in which social and cultural considerations have prominent roles is not thereby shown to have any specific or revealing linkages to the actual social conditions at the time the theory was born. That the historical, organic, cultural point of view is foremost in Dewey's analysis of thinking tells us little about the historical and cultural circumstances that may have stimulated that analysis. There is, however, a rather important way in which Dewey's instrumentalism is related historically to a general movement of social thought in America—the relation is an intellectual one. Dewey's instrumentalism has its origins, its driving spirit and aims, in common with several parallel developing ideas and attitudes, advanced respectively by Oliver W. Holmes, Jr., Thorstein Veblen, James Harvey Robinson, and Charles Beard.[23] The common movement is described by Morton White:

[19] This is the main theme of Dewey's *Individualism Old and New*.
[20] On the importance of the idea of *growth* in Dewey's thought, see § 41 above and Appendix 1, sec. A.
[21] See Part II, ch. 3, and especially Appendix 1, sec. A, for references to *inquiry, continuity*, and the *social* as the "inclusive category of philosophy."
[22] This is the title of his essay, p. 77, in *Philosophy and Civilization*. For a further note on this, see Appendix 1, sec. A below.
[23] Here and in the next pages I am indebted to Morton White's illuminating historical study, *Social Thought in America*. However, for the reasoning that has led up to citing this book and that will lead on to other consequences, Professor White is not to be blamed.

Pragmatism, instrumentalism, institutionalism, economic determinism and legal realism exhibit striking philosophical kinships. They are all suspicious of approaches which are excessively formal; they all protest their anxiety to come to grips with reality, their attachment to the moving and the vital in social life. Most of those who founded or represented these movements started their serious thinking in the eighties and the nineties of the last century. . . . The eighties and nineties saw the growth of science and capitalism, the spread of Darwinism, socialism, industrialization, and the monopoly. Holmes was directly confronted with truculent capitalism in cases involving concrete social questions. Veblen, interested in unmasking the effects of absentee ownership upon industry, and the role of the leisure class in American life, was brought face to face with the pattern of exploitation. Dewey met it when he examined the touchy relations of science, morality, and society and urged the scrapping of outworn theological and metaphysical creeds. Beard was the scholarly product of a progressive age bent upon raking muck and fulfilling the promise of American life.[24]

Professor White further characterizes the parts played by the men most involved in the movement.

They are all under the spell of history and culture. Holmes is the learned historian of the law and one of the heroes of sociological jurisprudence; Veblen is the evolutionary and sociological student of economic institutions; Beard urges us to view political instruments as more than documents; Robinson construes history as the ally of all the social disciplines and the study of how things have come to be as they are; Dewey describes his philosophy alternately as "evolutionary" and "cultural" naturalism. All of them insist upon coming to grips with life, experience, process, growth, context, function. They are all products of the historical and cultural emphases of the nineteenth century, following, being influenced by, reacting from its great philosophers of change and process.[25]

Such was the intellectual milieu, the climate of intentions with the background of Hegelianism and Darwinism, and foreground of social engineering, in which instrumentalism came of age. But while these intellectual critics and progressive reformers of American life were emphasizing process, growth, context, function, the social sciences, the practical arts of control and the enriching of public experience, the American scene itself was exhibiting not these but other traits—traits, it must be added, that brought forth the critical efforts, the appeal to and reliance upon the historical, organic, cultural approach to social problems. The conditions of American life that captured the attention and heightened the energies of these students of cultural experience, of these spokesmen for understanding the present as a means of controlling the future, were the conditions (so they thought) that worked against process, growth, social unification, and cultural integration. Indeed, in retrospect, when one looks over the library of writings produced by these men, one is struck by the dominance of the critical spirit: often detached, occasionally passionate, acutely and often formidably unfolding its argument over the inade-

[24] *Ibid.*, pp. 6–7.
[25] *Ibid.*, pp. 12–13.

quacy of this or that institution or ingrained social habit or policy attesting to
long-lost functions whose continuance positively jeopardizes evolution. But,
alongside the critical exercise of reason, one finds rather meager and vague suggestions of how and in what ways the future is to be planned and established.

To recall our earlier discussion, if the picture of a two-part culture and a
double morality is at all accurate, pragmatism is to be viewed historically as a
critical response to the widening cleavage between economic expansion and
powerful and elaborate technological advances on the one side, and on the other,
deepening divisions between the laboring classes and the owners and directors
of business: an increasing separation between the realities of social and political
experience and the traditional ideals of American democracy. The general historical role of pragmatism insofar as it reflected these conditions was that of
proposing an experimental method directed to mediating between conflicting
forces and interests. The ultimate aim, in the practice of the pragmatic method,
was that of a social reconstruction of the two-part culture. The projected ideal was
a new integration of the separate currents of American life. This was the task in
which creative intelligence would pave the way, and social engineering would
accomplish the result.

The exercise of pragmatism in behalf of this ideal of social reconstruction
demanded a twofold effort: (*a*) a new and continuing critical understanding of
our technological skills, our economic structures, materials, and possibilities, so
that reorganization and planned changes might take the place of disorganization
and recurrent catastrophies; (*b*) a new and continuing reorganization of beliefs
and ideals appropriate to the technological, political, and social problems and
changes that continue to be encountered.

In all, the pragmatic ideal of social reconstruction and unification called for a
new technological and moral education, namely, the scientific acquisition and
application of the skills of political technology.[26]

We come back to the idea of wit. In the sphere of social problems and their
solution, where existing institutions and policies are to be understood and
appraised by their effects upon future experience of the community of men (the
"whole" community), Dewey's instrumentalism functions as a form of critical,
experimental wit. In essence this pragmatic wit consists of establishing or anticipating the consequences of existing states of affairs, customs, general ideas, or
behavior. The consequences, actual or reasoned (as predictions), are measured by
specific practical social effects observable in the community and in the lives of its
members. For Aristotle, wit may seize upon how a conclusion is related to premisses. For Dewey, instrumental analysis experiments with the kinds of future
consequences that flow from (or *would* be effected by) such and such an institution, such and such a belief or action.

[26] On this important point in the political philosophizing of Dewey, see Randall's critical observations in Schilpp, pp. 84–99, and Dewey's answer, p. 522. For some further
critical reflections, see White, *Social Thought in America*, pp. 244–246. For an excellent
study of recent currents in pragmatic social philosophizing, see Myers.

§ 106.   Conclusion

In this chapter we have been studying the sense in which pragmatism is a reflection of American life. That reflection, it was argued, is nothing like a mirror image. For the *technical* core of pragmatism has European not American origins, and the *social* philosophy that pragmatism has infused has been in large part critical of much of American culture.

There are many serious philosophic questions that arise in reviewing the history of pragmatism and its connections with American society. It is clear that pragmatic social thought, advanced in its most influential intellectual form by Dewey, operated with certain ulterior moral assumptions never made wholly explicit nor of evident justification. Thus, for Dewey, as for many thinkers, organically related, unified, integrated social conditions are more *desirable* than conflicting ones. This might be true, but it is not pragmatism, or instrumentalism, that assures us of this truth. We should not confuse a method of examining and testing ideas with ideas and claims that may be tested. These assumptions, like Dewey's preference for situations and cultural institutions as the basic units of social analysis, or his emphasis upon growth, remained to be explained and defended on other grounds, ultimately on a theory of human nature and experience.

But more serious as a practical and analytical question is how one proceeds to determine just what are the organic, integrated conditions of growth that make for wise social policy in given cases. We know Dewey's general answer: inquiry, reflective intelligence, discloses the liberal and fruitful course for future action. The answer is right, but much too general to inspire great confidence in particular undertakings. "Intelligence" led Dewey early to condemn war, then to vacillate and eventually, in 1917, to support the war, and later to become a spokesman for peace and socialism.[27] What was wanted but never forthcoming from pragmatists practicing intelligence was a social program, something more concrete and pragmatically meaningful than "growth" or "intelligence." For without some program of specific objectives, social engineering is hardly possible. Yet his fear of absolutizing ends, his philosophic rejection of static goals, and his practical mistrust of inflexible social programs led Dewey to draw back at this crucial point. One suspects that the Hegelian and Darwinian heritages, the belief in the reality of continuity, organic relations, and growth supplied Dewey with a basic, quiet inner faith in the almost inevitable pro-gressive assertion of the forces of liberal civilization.

It is, I think, to be regretted that Dewey and the pragmatists did not attempt to work out a program of social aims as leading ideas and hypotheses for organizing and directing our technological abilities. Dewey's uncovering of social problems, critical needs, and shortcomings in American culture is brilliant. But a serious

[27] See White, *ibid.,* pp. 161-172.

weakening of the influence of pragmatism, beginning in the period of the first world war, is due to this failure to suggest what might be the specific intelligent objectives of American productive power in the reconstruction of American culture.

The later problems and drifting of pragmatists, their resort to a defensive strategy—defending the legitimacy of the method while exhibiting indecision as to aims and witnessing a certain paucity of results and achievements—and the tendency of pragmatic social thought to spread and ally itself with other movements are matters that lie beyond the scope of the present chapter. For we have been concerned with how the history of pragmatism is a part of American history.

CHAPTER THREE

Conclusion

§ 107. The Revolutionary Point of View

The attempt to give a general statement of the fundamental theoretical ideas of pragmatism in § 101 may have been felt to be too general and too theoretical. In bringing this study to an end, I will recapitulate briefly some of the earlier conclusions, and at least suggest how some of the theoretical points in earlier pages can be matched with more practical applications of the same *in concreto*.

There is no question about the influence of American pragmatism on the study of the sciences, law, political theory, education, art, and religion. So much was remarked at the very beginning of the present volume (in § 1, and in the Introduction to this Part). To just the extent that pragmatism has made a practical and theoretical *difference* in our intellectual history, its significant content and value is determined and to be appraised. Such, at least, is James's functional test (in § 27) of ideas.

It could be argued that pragmatism *is* the sum of its dispersion of influences in these diverse extra-philosophic disciplines. Thus, subtract the net result of the varied receptions and manifestations of pragmatic doctrine from the doctrine itself and we are left, not with the residue of pure pragmatism, but with nothing at all. This is a thesis I can understand, but do not accept (thus see Parts Two and Four). However, one reason for the outward-bound influences of this philosophy was the pronounced intention of the pragmatist philosophers to regard non-philosophical subject matters as posing the most serious challenges for philosophic thought. Given this conviction of the primacy of nonphilosophic contexts as the initiating and terminating setting for philosophical analysis, given also the disavowal of any sharp cleavage between philosophic theory and practice, and the breadth of stimulation is not to be wondered at.

What, we may ask in summary spirit, is the kernel of this doctrine that has rooted, spread, and flowered in so much of contemporary thought and practice?

448

It is surely not, for reasons insisted upon and argued before, the vague and capricious pronouncements that the true is useful, or that value and use are identical, or that only practical pursuits are important. A more studied response to this question occupies § 101. But, in brief, the answer is to be found in that major shift in methodology and criticism at the end of the nineteenth century that Dewey described as an almost revolutionary point of view. The description is worth repeating.

> Pragmatism . . . presents itself as an extension of historical empiricism but with this fundamental difference, that it does not insist upon antecedent phenomena but consequent phenomena; not upon the precedents but upon the possibilities of action. And this change in point of view is almost revolutionary in its consequences.[1]

The major historical factor responsible for this change of view was the impact and rapidly radiating influence of Darwinism.[2]

The methodological importance of the change was not simply that experience or organic responses to the environment is the "original of knowledge." For that thesis, as the language indicates, is the heir of the historical empiricism of Locke.[3] The new point of view counsels a method as revolutionary as was Locke's appeal to experience as the source of ideas.

For in making experience the "original" of knowledge, Locke and his most enthusiastic readers exploited a principle that was not so evident in earlier but equally impressive affirmations of experience as the source of knowledge—as it was affirmed, say, by Aristotle or St. Thomas. In Locke's age, the championing of experience meant a discrediting of claims to social power and intellectual authority based on divine rights, heredity, or allegedly favorable traffic with transcendant agencies.[4] In this respect, John Stuart Mill was a direct descendant of Locke. A growing commercial and industrial class saw in Locke's *experience* the theoretical instrument for a critical defense of new ideas (i.e., new middle class interests) against those venerable and established ways of sovereignty and landed aristocracy.

Time is the scourge of revolutionary movements, and the end is superannuation. Youth's a stuff will not endure. Locke would be dismayed to learn that we now classify him as an "early modern," a traditional empiricist. The change in empiricist methods and in the very conception of experience in the nineteenth century was from the emphatic proclamation of *experience* as the original and

---

[1] "The Development of American Pragmatism," p. 24. See § 101 above for more on this passage.

[2] See Part I, § 17, and for Peirce's view of the same, § 22, point 4. See especially Dewey's *The Influence of Darwin on Philosophy*, particularly ch. 1. He regarded the central "transformations in philosophy" as "wrought by the Darwinian genetic and experimental logic," p. 18.

[3] In the *Essay*, Introduction, sec. 2, Locke announces his intention of inquiry "into the original, certainty, and extent of human knowledge."

[4] This is one reason for Locke's long attack on the doctrine of innate ideas in the first book of the *Essay*. These days the first book is difficult to appreciate and is usually neglected, while the larger work continues to be widely read.

genesis of knowledge to a view of experience as the future resolution and terminating condition of thought. This is a much more radical extension of the critical spirit of the Lockean empirical tradition.

It is worth pausing for a moment to consider why, since the nineteenth century is generally held to be more historically minded than any previous period, it would not have continued in the Lockean manner to emphasize the *origins* of knowledge as the primary way of understanding knowledge at all. Surely this century was interested in origins. Certainly with Darwin (as in earlier evolutionary doctrines going back into the eighteenth century) the ancestry of human intelligence and culture, the evolution of ideas from their primitive beginnings, were subjects of immense interest and stimulating inquiry. Would not the presumably "empirical" method then consist in performing a kind of Darwinian analysis of our current system of knowledge? Ought we not go back to trace the fascinating careers of concepts in the manner of Frazer's *Golden Bough* and thus get at the meanings of current ideas by investigating their ancestral lineage and somewhat shady past? The explanation of this is that while the nineteenth century undoubtedly was a historically minded period, its evolutionary outlook and philosophical idealisms all encouraged the major conviction that it was the future that carried the promise of enlightenment and value. Progress lay in the future. The past was a clue to the present and future; but the very nerve of evolutionary doctrine was that the present and future was not reducible to the past—*growth* is not merely a derivation from the past.

Now Locke and his followers had also taken a historical approach to the analysis of knowledge. Locke characterized his manner of inquiry as a "historical, plain method." But Locke and his enlightened contemporaries were much impressed with the idea that science had no use for final causes. Ends, purposes, goals are not to be found outside of organic behavior. From Lucretius, through Galileo, Descartes, and Spinoza, the scientific philosophers declared that final causes were obsolete. Thus Locke's method is "historical" in a purely mechanical sense;[5] that is, the original of knowledge is not viewed in an evolutionary way—and certainly not in a way allowing for novelty and emergence. It is a purely reductive analysis (see §§ 27, 79, 83) of thought: the ultimate origins in sense experience are the mechanical state, the material conditions of particles and motions (and our observations of our intellectual operations). This is the *complete* state, from which, in Locke's words, "all our knowledge is founded; and from that it ultimately derives itself."[6]

---

[5] Locke's model, as we noticed in Part I, is Newtonian mechanics. But note also the logical-mechanical analogy in the *Essay*, Book II, ch. 2, sec. 2, where Locke speaks of simple ideas as never created or destroyed—an old axiom of atomism—and the materials of the understanding "being muchwhat the same as it is in the great visible world of things."

Sometimes, however, Locke's appeal to experience is simply to ordinary acquaintance with environing conditions, ordinary common good sense. This is an important, if conflicting strain in his philosophy of experience in the *Essay*.

[6] *Essay*, Book II, ch. 1, sec. 2.

The new emphasis on experience—as Dewey remarks above—is concerned not with "antecedent phenomena" but with "consequent phenomena." One manifestation of this is that instead of proposing a causal explanation of how ideas are generated,[7] the new empiricism proposes a method of critical testing and evaluation of the significance of claims to knowledge. This in turn is an alteration in the interpretation of experience: experience is not an initial stuff of sensation and reflection nor the motions of matter from which intellection is derived. 'Experience' designates the conditions to-be-satisfied by thought. And these conditions include the need of establishing and maintaining organic-environmental equilibrations[8] and the pursuit of various kinds of purpose and interest. The purposive nature of thought, we have seen in earlier chapters, is a cardinal thesis in the pragmatic theory of inquiry and action.

Traditional empiricism conceived the testing of ideas, that is, validation and the determination of meaning, to consist of an introspective process of matching ideas against their origins. We have several times before taken note of objections to this entire conception of testing. A mechanical or geometrical determination of how ideas "fit" or "copy" their sources, managed somehow by the selfsame creature whose only access to the originals are the very ideas under test, is hardly a defensible position, nor, for all we know, is the presumption that ideas or mental events are "images" in any understood sense of that term.

Short of abandoning empiricism altogether, as doomed to confusion, the only course of action to be taken by those who felt some truth in the empirical tradition was to overhaul the concept of *experience*. This Kant and the romantic idealists started to do, and it was further carried out by the evolutionary and idealist philosophies of the nineteenth century. The result was that instead of experience being the stuff from which ideas are derived, it became a way in which ideas have a function and their significance is elicited. Experience thus interpreted is a process rather than substance. It is not what we know (as it is sometimes for Locke), nor the cause of ideas; it is how we know certain kinds of objects and a method of controlling and assessing ideas. In short, experience becomes experimentation.

It was the prospects of this new form of empiricism, with its emphasis on consequent phenomena, that captured the interest of many students of the natural and social sciences, history, and law. Crises and revolutions in physics, the natural science *par excellence*, and the rapidity of the development of the social sciences have cooperated to make modern science method-conscious. In no other time has so much effort been devoted to understanding and clarifying the methods of analysis, the concepts, and the methodological procedures of science. The new empiricism was a part of this general drift of thought. But it received atten-

---

[7] Of course, in their philosophical psychologies, both Peirce and Dewey offered a hypothesis about the causal origins, not of ideas, but of thinking, or inquiry. See §§ 20, 38, 39.
[8] As we observed Dewey to argue, in §§ 37, 39, and 91–92.

tion also because it seemed to many to be the orientation for a sound grasp of scientific methodology and a fruitful way of approaching unresolved issues in the current thinking of men, scientists and non-scientists alike.

The methodological change we have been touching on here is from what Locke called his "historical, plain method" to what Peirce, James, Dewey, Mead, and the other pragmatists described as the clarification and analysis of ideas through determination of their conceivable practical consequences. The center of this change, as we have been observing and as we found Dewey to say, is from antecedents to consequent phenomena. Meaning, verification, and the evaluation of thought have a "futuritive reference." The spirit of the nineteenth century and the technical elaboration of this methodology are both responsible for the notions of *time, contingency, development,* and *continuity* being serious and basic subjects in the philosophizing of pragmatists. These are among the conditions that determine experience and are to be reckoned with, therefore, in the determination of future experience.

Knowledge, pragmatically construed, is one of the ways in which presently occurring experience becomes the means of instituting future experience, a future qualified by values and realized by action. But this version of knowledge as essentially valuation (see §§ 41, 46, 79) also makes of knowledge something inescapably experimental in its function. Knowledge is control over and selection of future experience. But then future possibilities enter in as controlling factors in present behavior.

Now it was this new analysis of thought, this mode of criticism and evaluation —the pragmatic critique—that exerted itself and found applications in the diversity of subject matters commented on earlier. To choose an illustration almost at random, we can see the new point of view reflected in this description of the operation of the Supreme Court.

> We see not black robes but men in the flesh, laboring not only with intellect but with feeling, and sometimes with passion, toward balanced reconciliation of competing values. We see the intense pragmatism (revealed most clearly in verbatim quotations from oral arguments) with which the Justices and counsel probe for the practical consequences of one position or another. If devotional Bible-reading in public schools is unlawful, they ask, does it follow that we must give up "The Star Spangled Banner," "In God We Trust," military chaplains and the invocation of divine grace that opens sessions of Congress and the Court itself? Contrariwise, if it is lawful to devote five minutes a day to the Bible, why not five hours?[9]

Under this new experimental methodology, as in Locke's championing of experience, intellectual orthodoxies and institutional ossification come in for fairly severe punishment. The law, so often regarded as a precedent-bound discipline (focusing on "antecedent phenomena," in Dewey's words), is thus an interesting case in point here.

[9] Professor Louis Lusky in *The New York Times* Book Review, July 5, 1964, p. 16.

A further illustration may help elicit a final important feature of the new point of view. Supposing one wanted to determine how thoroughly a book had been understood by a group of readers. One venerable technique for this purpose is that of the recitation of the text. The accuracy of a recitation, with its premium upon direct quotation and close paraphrase, is measurable in quite automatic ways. To "know" the book, by this standard, is a measure of reportorial matching with the "original." The book, or a mimetic retention of it, is the "original," and knowledge is a mental and verbal copy of the same. Here, then, is a correspondence theory of knowledge and truth very much a part of traditional empiricism (for which, see §§ 6, 27 above). The reportorial skill has its place, especially when the "original" is not easily accessible to public scrutiny, as when travelers report on far-off lands, or, as was the case in classical and medieval times, when books are scarce items. Nonetheless this skill is not an exclusive criterion of knowledge, nor ought it be allowed to dominate our thinking about the nature of knowledge; its issue in a "spectator" theory of knowledge has been the object of considerable criticism from the pragmatists.

Let us suppose the book in question was a manual for constructing a machine. Clearly, whether the book had been understood or not would be brought to the test by determining its effect upon behavior: its role in contributing to the assembling of the machine. Knowledge of the book, in this case, is taken as the degree to which the reading informs and guides conduct in the efficient control of action with pieces of machinery directed to the elaboration of the machine—assuming the book to be a reliable guide. Here we have an instrumental conception of knowing (as reviewed in §§ 100–101). Admittedly, not all books are manuals or guides for action. More subtle adjustments and forms of behavior enter into the ways of understanding a poem. But recitation, correctness of verbal report (i.e., "correspondence") is not a crucial test here either, for parrots and phonographs can be made to quote Shakespeare.

The main point of these reflections is this: on the traditional theory, knowledge is interpreted as a copy, a geometrical or pictorial representation—a correspondence—within an agent and of a subject matter. For the pragmatist, the fundamental relation characterizing knowledge is temporal and behavioral. Knowledge is an interpretation of given situations as means to deliberate future consequences under hypothetical or anticipated conditions. The act of behavior with its projected consequences is here taken as the fundamental unit, the "original," rather than an idea, image, or proposition. The very discernment of objects, the operation of perception and interpretation are thus determined by the acts of which they are parts in environments exhibiting fluid centers of resistance and manipulation, functioning alternatively as obstacles and instruments to actions and their completion (see § 38 above).

Such, then, is the "revolutionary point of view" brought about at the turn of the century and receiving its philosophic formulation in pragmatism.

§ 108.   The New Organon:
A Theory of Meaning and Action

A daimonic pragma, he said.
Rather it is useful, I said, for seeking
the beautiful and good.
PLATO, Republic 531c

There was a certain justice in John Dewey's ascription of the prophetic beginnings
of pragmatism to Francis Bacon (see § 2 above), for Bacon was inspired with the
idea of a new method of knowledge, inductive and experimental. Bacon's conception of the inductive method of science was seriously defective. But the interest in method, and an inductive, scientific one at that, is a trait of the modern
age, as we have been observing in the foregoing pages.

In these pages and in earlier chapters, we have been viewing pragmatism primarily as a method. What it is a method of and for has been dealt with in the
course of this book. Now of all the artificial ways of classifying philosophers, one
of some interest is this: There are philosophers who believe that a method of
analysis and critical evaluation of ideas does entail metaphysical and moral commitments as well; and there are philosophers who deny this. The pragmatists, despite Peirce's inconsistent pronouncements (e.g., § 32 and § 19 above, also Appendix 3) are members of the first group. Thus, in subscribing to a certain
method of analysis—so it would be argued—one is obligated to accept certain
consequences of a theoretical sort about the kind of world in which that method
is successful (or the only appropriate one for the purposes it accomplishes), and
the kind of creatures and conditions of behavior for which that method is of use
and importance. How the initially methodological focus of pragmatism was wid-
ened into a larger philosophy is an evolving subject of Part Two and is brought
to more conscious scrutiny in the first chapter of this present Part.[10]

The main problem of modern philosophy, as we explored it in Part One, has
been that of finding some way of integrating in one conceptual scheme a sound
interpretation of natural knowledge and of moral values. This has been the ideal
of restoring a harmony between the increasingly divergent disciplines of what
once was called natural and moral philosophy. The problem had its origin in a
continuing conflict between the growth of scientific knowledge and technology,
and traditional ethical patterns and conceptions of the moral life. The continuing
conflict was furthermore part of the rapidly expanding and changing economic
and social conditions of Europe since the Middle Ages.

The Darwinian theory of evolution, and the resultant controversy in the latter
half of the nineteenth century was the immediate historical setting in which

[10] Especially §§ 99, 100.

pragmatism originated.[11] The Darwinian controversy was a dramatic instance of what appeared to be an irreconcilable division between scientific knowledge and traditional moral conceptions of human nature and history. If the position taken above in §§99–100 is correct, the new method of pragmatism emerged as a way of critically analyzing the assumptions and concepts of the prevailing intellectual traditions in which the division between scientific empiricism and moral and religious belief appeared as an inevitable and permanent crevice in the nature of things. Thus, initially, it was practiced as a way of mediating among and salvaging something from the warring faiths of materialistic scientism, anti-scientific idealism and metaphysics, and Protestant theology.

The most important specific problem in Anglo-American philosophy in the late nineteenth century was made more challenging by Darwinism, yet predated the evolution controversy. This was the problem of explaining the nature of *belief* and knowledge, subjects that, since Hume's probings, continued to concern philosophers and that, on the continent, had undergone the powerful critique of Kant and a vast synthesis in Hegel.

The approach taken by Mill, as by the major British tradition before him, was to set forth a philosophical psychology for the explanation of belief and knowledge. This "psychologizing" method was one main object of Bradley's criticism of empiricism; yet that method, unforeseen by Mill and his powerful critics, T. H. Green and Bradley, led directly into the British Idealism—the very position that Green and Bradley were engaged in articulating.[12] In America, Mill's *Examination of Hamilton* (1865) was carefully read by Chauncey Wright[13] and Peirce, each of whom reacted in different ways. Wright, in reviewing Mill's book, called the definition of external objects (i.e., "permanent possibilities of sensation") "among the most important contributions to psychology which have been made in modern times." But he criticized Mill for neglecting to discuss carefully "the distinction of knowledge and belief."[14]

Mill and Bain, Venn, and Chauncey Wright each worked upon a theory of belief as a mode of action, or motive to act.[15] At first the analysis seems to have been directed to how the presence of belief is manifested and how its occurrence is tested; later it merged into a theory of the *meaning* or content of belief. James and Peirce actively participated in continuing this quest of a philosophic analysis of belief and knowledge—one that would do equal justice, it should be added, to science, a moral evolutionism, and to the phenomena of human conduct.

---

[11] For this background, see Wiener's book.

[12] On this transition, see Randall's "Mill and the Working-Out of Empiricism," and his conclusion, p. 88: "British Idealism is the continuation, the next stage, of British Empiricism." For more on Green and Bradley, see § 63 above, and on Green's philosophy, see Appendix 1, sec. C.

[13] See Appendix 2, sec. B.

[14] *The Nation* (1865). For this source, see Fisch, "A Chronicle of Pragmaticism," p. 444 and note 11.

[15] Mill and Bain cooperated in this task. See Mill's *Logic* (8th edition), Book 6, ch. 3, sec. 3, note to the third paragraph. For Bain, see § 19 above. On Venn, see § 22 above, notes 100, 101.

In Part One I have tried to suggest how in responding to the serious problem of interpreting scientific knowledge, philosophers have drawn upon one of more earlier philosophies of knowledge. The past has served philosophers, even if only with the language and distinctions necessary for them to express current problems. But philosophizing at its best has never been a slavish imitation of the past. Rather, the history of philosophy has been one fertile source of hypotheses, of theoretical and analytical procedures that can be made to illuminate present problems and inspire creative ways by which solutions might be sought.

The pragmatists were no exception to this. It was to Berkeley and Mill, Kant, Fichte, Schelling and romantic idealism, Hegel and Hegelianism, that Peirce, James, Dewey, and later pragmatists turned—supported by contemporary advances in psychology, biology, physics, and logic—in working out the pragmatic solution to the problem of the split between scientific knowledge and ethical values. That solution issued as a theory of knowledge as valuation (§ 100).

How the pragmatists went about this task has been the substance of preceding chapters. It suffices to observe finally that pragmatism began as an analysis of the purposeful and selective nature of the processes of thought and belief and of the effect upon these of a clarification of the concepts of reality and truth. Such is the scope and intent of the two papers,[16] one by Peirce and one by James, that appeared simultaneously in 1878, and which together mark the historical point of origin of pragmatism.[17] However, the initial analysis was deepened and broadened into a general philosophical theory, a theory comprising a philosophical psychology of the organic genesis and function of thought in transitional and problematic environments, an interpretation of the instrumental and logical structure of inquiry, knowledge and ethical judgment, and an empirical methodology of the use and effectiveness of cognitive language—in short, a theory of meaning and action.

Since each of the component parts of the new method thus described happen to be topics of renewed interest in recent philosophy, there are, contrary to the somber impressions registered in the introduction to this Part, signs of change in the winds of philosophic doctrine. There is reason for supposing that the future may well be with Dewey, Lewis, and Mead.

Pragmatism was, after all, engaged in a critical effort to formulate a theory of intelligent action, partly transcriptive and reportorial, and partly prescriptive of how human action, guided by knowledge, might continually realize and make more effective and stable the satisfactions and ideal goods of experience. The task, then, was to develop a comprehensive philosophy of experimental method and a critique of action. In our age this effort required at least a technically competent interpretation of scientific knowledge, but one rendered humane and luminous, including in its scope a place for liberal values, imagination, and human wisdom.

---

[16] See the last paragraph of § 28 and § 101, note 35.

[17] That is, the origin of its written history. The Metaphysical Club, § 19 and Appendix 2, had met earlier. For some further details, see § 101 above, note 35.

To a historian or poet, given to seeing the present in prophetic or dramatic images drawn from the past, the pragmatic theory of inquiry as a process of transforming experience in instituting belief, or truth, might have introduced itself as a modern reenactment of Dante's fable: Dantesque man guided by the Human Reason of Virgil through earthly perils toward Beatrice, divine Love, and consuming faith, *l'amor che move il sole e l' altre stelle*. In what pragmatism was attempting, there are muted strains of the past, the ancient acknowledgment of human predicaments and the precariousness of existence, the long-sought reintegration of technical skills and ideal aims. There are accents, too, of the classical celebration of the life of reason, although altered and sounded in a new key, and more deliberately proclaiming the supremacy of method and the critical faculties in the successful conduct of human affairs.

In earlier pages we have found much to be critical of, much remaining to be completed, but little to condemn. The incompleteness in some of the philosophizing of pragmatists is not wholly a negative condition.[18] For it also means that the development of certain intuitions and doctrines remains unfulfilled, that interesting possibilities wait further exploration. This is especially true, I think, for pragmatic method of the analysis of concepts, the instrumentalist interpretation of the structure of science, and the naturalistic theory of valuation. The most then that a critical history of pragmatism can hope to accomplish is to provoke renewed study of the subject matter, and thereby of the philosophy itself, and of its philosophers. The value of this philosophy and what is finally to be learned from and possibly inspired by it, remain—and in this case not inappropriately—to be settled in the future.

The future brings its judgments and its vengeance upon those systems of thought which have flourished in ways other than in truth. Yet the notion of one final adjudication resting in the future is an illusion. Each age makes its own critical judgments, and unmakes others, according to the intellectual atmosphere and pressures of the time. But in philosophy as in other good things of the mind there is scope for diversification. Works of art and philosophy have a way of outliving their critics; and final judgments have a way of becoming temporary and sometimes vanishing entirely. One must settle, then, for something more relative and less ruthless in these matters of the intellect, asking, say, for no more than sanity in the pursuit of the ideal—whatever the conception of that ideal may be —and liberality in its election. This is to ask enough!

The pragmatists have taught us this much, seeing, more clearly than ever had been, the senses in which knowledge is power. Like all power, knowledge is dangerous; but unlike all other forms of power, it carries in its very operations, in its natural and habitual practice and its logical functions, a working good. Such is the *method* of knowing, a self-corrective process, one that is critically reflexive and demanding in its own conditions of adequacy and warrant, as Peirce and Dewey

---

[18] A point that occurred coincidentally in another context in § 37. A major project calling for completion was sketched in the last three paragraphs of § 80.

labored to show. The method, the new organon, was envisaged by the pragmatists as man's chief access to all other goods, enabling us to see our moral and practical anxieties and subsequent accomplishments as relative to and occurring within the surrounding immensity of nature; enabling us to increase our knowledge of this world and to better enlighten our restless goings up and down in the earth.

APPENDIXES

Dewey: Continuity—Hegel and Darwin

A. Continuity

Ultimately, Dewey has maintained, the role of philosophy is criticism: criticism of all phases and institutional administrations of social life for the purpose of intelligent control of experience. He stated this as the aim of his *Experience and Nature*:

Philosophy . . . is a generalized theory of criticism. Its ultimate value for life-experience is that it continuously provides instruments for the criticism of those values —whether beliefs, institutions, actions or products—that are found in all aspects of experience. The chief obstacle to a more effective criticism of current values lies in the traditional separation of nature and experience, which it is the purpose of this volume to replace by the idea of continuity.[1]

Note the emphasis upon continuity. As early as the turn of the century Dewey had argued:

The postulate of moral science is the continuity of scientific judgment.[2]

And he seems to have meant:

The intelligent acknowledgment of the continuity of nature, man and society will alone secure a growth of morals. . . .[3]

Continuity is basic to Dewey's conception of a "naturalistic theory" of logic. He writes:

The term 'naturalistic' has many meanings. As here employed it means, on the one side, that there is no breach of continuity between operations of inquiry and biological operations and physical operations. 'Continuity,' on the other hand,

---

[1] Preface, p. ix.
[2] *Logical Conditions of a Scientific Treatment of Morality*, in *Problems of Men*, p. 244. Later, p. 249, he calls this "the postulate of the continuity of experience."
[3] *Human Nature and Conduct*, p. 13.

means that the operations *grow out of* organic activities, without being identical with that from which they emerge.[4]

The words "grow out of" are important. They indicate the essential point of a statement made later in the *Logic*:

> The primary postulate of a naturalistic theory of logic is continuity of the lower (less complex) and the higher (more complex) activities and forms. The idea of continuity is not self-explanatory. But its meaning excludes complete rupture on one side and mere repetition of identities on the other, it precludes reduction of the 'higher' to the 'lower' just as it precludes complete breaks and gaps. The growth and development of any living organism from seed to maturity illustrates the meaning of continuity.[5]

The last lines, while valuable as suggesting what 'continuity' means for Dewey, also introduce tones of a moral approbation of continuity. And if we overlook that kind of continuity that occurs after growth, namely, the gradual death and degeneration of organic processes, we will be tempted to identify continuity with the morally valuable, desirable, and good. We may also recall that Dewey once declared that "Growth itself is the only moral 'end.'"[6] It is interesting that growth should happen to occur to Dewey as a paradigm case of continuity.

In keeping with the critical aim noted in the first quotation above (i.e., replacing the traditional separation of nature and experience with the idea of continuity), Dewey also criticized the separation of the *natural* and *social*. He argued:

> A denial of the separation is not only possible to a sane mind, but is demanded by any methodological adoption of the principle of continuity. . . . Upon the hypothesis of continuity—if that is to be termed a hypothesis which cannot be denied without self-contradiction—the social . . . furnishes philosophically the inclusive category.[7]

One does not often find Dewey philosophizing with hypotheses that cannot be denied without contradiction, i.e., with analytic or a priori principles for, presumably, empirical purposes. And one suspects that this is as close as a duly chastised and disillusioned Hegelian can come to maintaining a belief in an absolute.

This inclusive category of philosophy rests upon the more inclusive notion of continuity. The idea of continuity, surely, is the inclusive category of John Dewey's philosophy.

B. *The Background of Continuity: Hegel*

A crude way of describing Dewey's idea of continuity is to say that it is a vigorous application of the ancient maxim, "Nature abhors a vacuum." For Dewey the

[4] *Logic: The Theory of Inquiry*, p. 19.
[5] *Ibid.*, p. 23.
[6] See above, §§ 37, 41, 97, and *Reconstruction in Philosophy*, p. 177. The theory behind this statement is discussed in Part IV, ch. 3 above. The idea of good as growth—for which Dewey has often been criticized—was derived primarily from T. H. Green; see sec. C below.
[7] *Philosophy and Civilization*, p. 81.

scope of this maxim is broadened to cover not only nature, but all life in nature. Every phase and institution of social existence, in art, science, in thought and conduct, exhibits this pervasive trait. Indeed, these latter are viewed as complex extensions evolving from less refined organic materials of a biological level of nature in which they have prehensile roots. In the very nature of things there are no breaks, no interstices or cleavages. Where there are apparent separations and disconnections, say of the kind that differentiate men and animals, or ancient civilizations and modern, or the myriad delineations of ordinary experience into more or less distinct qualitative features such as love or hate, war or peace, laughter or tears, these are for Dewey at most *demarcations within* a more ultimate and inclusive subject matter; they are like ripples or waves of water, separated, and even significant on their own, but never wholly discontinuous with the totality of which they are part.

All of this is evident, I think, in Dewey's gradually worked out theory of the *situation*. Every situation, he insists, is unique, and given situations may be characterized by conflict, tensions, or unity and equilibrum. Though there are distinctive conditions in a situation which can be noted and described, yet each situation and the conditions making it up is just what *it* is, says Dewey on pain of tautology; each situation is a whole related internally and emerging without complete break from the past into the future, from situation to situation.

Thus the idea of continuity is fundamental in Dewey's conception of the *situation*. For the parts of a situation—experience, doing and suffering, acting and reacting—constitute one continuous process in which there are no gaps, no "vacuum." And not only is there a continuity among the constituent parts within a situation, and among situations; there is also a temporal continuity of past and future in which things, parts, and whole situations are to be viewed as subsidiary phases. This temporal continuity is found in all developments in anything that pro-gresses, in all growth. And these lead to considerations of an ethical kind and possess a religious value for Dewey. Like Nature, Dewey abhors a vacuum; but unlike Nature, his abhorrence comes from what is ultimately a moral protest and an ethical commitment.

For a naturalist looking at nature, a vacuum will mean, if anything, a place in which nothing *is* or is happening. But the moral equivalent of such a material lacuna will mean the absence of any good. At any rate, for Dewey, where we find nothing happening, we must expect to find either nothing at all or a case of arrested development. Cleavages, breakages, or gaps in natural processes, if they are acknowledged to occur at all, are viewed with a certain alarm, as is, for example, that which is "static"—while it might not be a positive evil, it may be an obstacle to change, to continuity, and to growth. "The process of growth, of improvement and progress," Dewey writes, "rather than the static outcome and result, becomes the significant thing."[8]

8 *Reconstruction in Philosophy*, p. 177.

Certain vital moral interests, then, are at work in this conception of continuity as a pervasive trait of nature. They help to explain why Dewey is far less interested in the fact, only reluctantly acknowledged, of discontinuity on the one hand, and of death in lieu of growth on the other. To these equally objective manifestations of nature, life, and experience, only a sentimental moralist—which Dewey is not—could be blind. Nature is impassive to any and all of these traits, but on this score Dewey and Nature part company.

How did Dewey come to put such stock in this idea of continuity? A look at his philosophic development reveals the answer, and it may carry us somewhat further to an understanding of what 'continuity' really means for Dewey, thus succeeding where the above reflections fail.

The idea makes an early appearance in Dewey's thought, and is evidenced there with much of the significance it was to have for him later. In an article describing the appeal which Hegel's philosophy had for him as a young man, and the "permanent deposit" left on his thinking by that acquaintance, Dewey refers to "the demand for unification that was doubtless an intense emotional craving." Hegel's thought supplied the sought-for solution. Commenting further on the "permanent deposit" left by Hegel, Dewey says: "the Hegelian emphasis upon continuity and the function of conflict persisted on empirical grounds after my earlier confidence in dialectic had given way to scepticism."[9] This early impact of Hegel is described:

> Hegel's synthesis of subject and objects, matter and spirit, the divine and the human, was, however, no mere intellectual formula; it operated as an immense release, a liberation. Hegel's treatment of human culture, of institutions and the arts, involved that same dissolution of hard-and-fast dividing walls, and had a special attraction for me.[10]

The spirit comes through: the demand for *unification*, the dissolution of *walls*, the emphasis on *continuity*. Each is an exorcism of the "vacuum."

This philosophic emphasis upon unification and synthesis was first impressed on Dewey in the 1880's while a student at Johns Hopkins. Yet the impression lasted. It is both significant and revealing of this side of Dewey's thought, though it has not to my knowledge been much discussed, that we can discover him somewhat later finding no difficulty in relating the Hegelian "continuity and function of conflict" to Darwinian theory. T. H. Huxley in "Evolution and Ethics"

[9] See Jane Dewey, "Biography of John Dewey," in Schilpp, *Philosophy of John Dewey*, p. 18.
[10] "From Absolutism to Experimentalism," p. 19. In § 62 I suggested certain philosophic affinities between Dewey and Bradley. On this score it is interesting to compare Dewey's account of the importance of Hegel for his own thought with an informal statement by Bradley, in a letter to Lady Welby, on the same subject. In expressing his great indebtedness to Hegel, Bradley said: "Hegel had no doubt too great a bias in favor of thought and tried too much to make a logical law, or what he considered such, the main principle of the universe. But this is but one feature of Hegel and unfortunately the one most dwelt on. To see the world and man as a whole that makes 'de' differences as mere means to its fuller unity; to show that all abstractions and onesidedness live only in and through the concrete living whole; this was his inspiring principle." Welby, *Echoes of Larger Life*, pp. 167–168.

had described the cosmos as a process of conflicts and struggles and civilized man
as opposed to that process and combatting it;[11] Dewey's criticism of this lecture
(*Monist*, 1898) is illustrative of how he brought to bear, in defense of his own
conception of Darwinism, principles and convictions which he had inherited not
from the study of Darwin, but from Hegelian idealism. In place of Huxley's conflict and combat between man and nature, Dewey argues for *conflicts* viewed as
tensions and subsequent "modifications" of conditions in environments. We do
not have a conflict between man and nature, he says; "We have rather the modification by man of one part of the environment with reference to another part."[12]
In terms of existing social structure, he also argues, our conception of the "fittest"
will change. The techniques of animal struggles which might once have determined the fittest of the beasts become outmoded with the development of human
society. The "fittest" and the "best" are relative to and become meaningful in
the light of the maintenance of society. "The unfit is practically the anti-
social."[13]

Whatever one may think of Dewey's version of Darwinian theory and the interpretation he gives of such key terms as 'conflict' and 'fittest' is beside the point
in the present discussion. What is to the point is that we can witness the settling
down, so to speak, of the "permanent deposit" left by Hegel upon Dewey, and in
particular that emphasis upon continuity (even more than conflict).[14]

Dewey is not alone in coming to Darwin with certain prior commitments and
established philosophic convictions, only, with some trepidation, to find these
same convictions "there" and thus warranted in the name of the new biological
science. Nor is he among the most guilty of this hazardous inclination of philosophers, as the record of extravagant claims in the name of Darwinism will show.
That he did see *continuity* there is clear; and it is less clear but equally important
that Dewey was to impart this idea and its conceptual framework into his interpretation of Darwin. The procedure looks suspiciously unempirical. It comes

[11] Huxley's lecture, given in 1893, is reprinted in his *Evolution and Ethics and Other Essays*.
[12] "Evolution and Ethics," p. 325.
[13] *Ibid.*, p. 326. See the chapter in White, *The Origin of Dewey's Instrumentalism*, pp. 119 ff.
[14] To avoid misunderstanding here it should be added that Dewey did at this time, and for the rest of his philosophic career, take *conflict* seriously. Thus, in the 1890's, Dewey was to see and state succinctly the role of conflict, tension, and friction as the initial con-dition of thought and human action. It was later that this version of conflict became gen-eralized as the "problematic situation," the beginning of *inquiry*. What I am concerned to suggest is not the absence of the notion of conflict in Dewey's thought, but the primacy of *continuity*. Continuity is seen as a deeper and more pervasive trait of things; indeed, it underlies or is a feature of conflict. For the conflict that initiates human deliberation and inquiry is itself "continuous" with conditions (material, organic, and social) that precede it and with those that are to follow. For Dewey, the occurrences of conflicts and tensions in general have a natural history; they do not arise *ex nihilo*. And that history, whatever its specific characteristics may be, like all histories, exhibits continuity.
If this emphasis upon *continuity* for Dewey is rightly taken, it does not minimize his critical views of "organic-whole" theories of society, for example (see *Reconstruction in Philosophy*, ch. 8), nor his explicit assignment of "discreteness" as a trait of things in his comment, "I lay no claim to having invented an environment that is marked by both dis-creteness and continuity," Schilpp, *Philosophy of John Dewey*, p. 545.

close to being a case of verifying Darwin according to prior principles rather than verifying the principles according to Darwin.[15]

I do not mean to suggest that continuity in some sense is not to be found in Darwinian theory, but only to indicate that in some of the forms in which Dewey understood and articulated the idea of continuity, it is very difficult to discern just what empirical conditions would constitute a relevant test of either its application of verification. The problem is quite simple and quite serious. Does the idea of *continuity* as Dewey then or subsequently understood it assume the form of some metaphysical principle, wholly ubiquitous and possessing an unlimited range of applicability, so that it can be extended or discovered to be present in any and all subject matters and any order of facts? If it holds in any case, if it is always true, it in fact tells us nothing. That Dewey found and championed continuity in evolutionary biology has had considerable influence among his followers and in the position known as naturalism. It was perhaps because of this uncritical enthusiasm for continuity that Ernest Nagel recently warned the naturalists not to make "a fetish of continuity."[16]

While Dewey was to see what he took as confirmation of his views in evolutionary theory, there were, at this same time, around 1891, the signs of his freeing himself from wholesale idealism. Outwardly, this break with the past is manifested in criticisms of T. H. Green, whose thought had dominated Dewey in the eighties (see the section to follow). A significant feature in that critical break with idealism is the influence of William James. In a letter in 1891 Dewey mentions a class of four graduates he has reading the *Psychology*.[17] In the most "philosophical" sections of James's *Psychology* there is a sustained criticism of the "transcendental self" of Hegelianism and of Green, and we know that Dewey responded to that criticism. In one paper he commented that James "has given that theory the hardest knocks it has received from the psychological side."[18]

This section of the *Psychology*, preceded by the famous "stream of thought" discussion, is called "Consciousness of Self." Shortly after his criticism of idealistic views of consciousness, James turns to the topic of "Discrimination and Comparison." There he considers the question of experience interpreted or analyzed by the English psychologists' principle of association, or the alternative principle of disassociation. He argued: "The truth is that Experience is trained by *both* association and disassociation, and that psychology must be writ *both* in synthetic and

---

15 Seeing Darwin through Hegel may also have been encouraged by the earlier conviction that "Hegel . . . is the quintessence of the scientific spirit," "The Present Position of Logical Theory" (1891), p. 10.

16 "Naturalism Reconsidered," in *Logic Without Metaphysics*, p. 10.

17 Perry, II, 517. Also see sec. C, note 63 below.

18 "The Ego as Cause" (1894), p. 340, note 1. The comment is in the context of a more general criticism of James. Dewey cites James's *Psychology*, I, 360–370, as containing the passages that deliver the "hardest knocks" to the theory of the transcendental self. In these pages James discusses the Kantian theory of Self, but also, in passing, supports his interpretation with a reference to G. S. Morris (p. 365n.), and considers Green's version of the self. The views of Morris and Green are discussed in the section that follows below. For a later study of James's concept of the self, see Dewey's "The Vanishing Subject in the Psychology of James."

analytic terms."[19] James asks, is experience of and thinking about objects a sum of simpler discriminated parts, or is it an unbroken unit? The question and its answer could not fail to interest Dewey. James proceeds to maintain that "each thought is within itself a *continuum*, a *plenum*. . . ."[20]

In 1922, in "The Development of American Pragmatism," Dewey refers to this section of James's *Psychology*, saying that it constituted one of the influences in the forging of "Instrumentalism."[21]

Idealism, Darwinism, and William James were three sources of Dewey's discovery and appreciation of the idea of continuity. But in the interest of accuracy something more must be said about the first of these influences.

C. G. S. Morris and T. H. Green

When a philosopher acknowledges an intellectual debt to Hegel—and Dewey, we have seen, has—it is tempting to attribute almost any of his doctrines to "the influence of Hegel." For much, perhaps everything, can be found in Hegel or in his "influence."

In the development of Dewey's philosophy a number of "Hegelian" forces were important. It remains here to consider two of these: first, and briefly, the part played by George Sylvester Morris (1840–1889); and secondly the very significant, although hitherto neglected figure in this history, Thomas Hill Green (1836–1882).

Morris[22] was appointed lecturer in the history of philosophy and ethics at Johns Hopkins in 1878. There, in 1882, Dewey was one of his students. We took note in the Introduction to Part Two, above, of Dewey's close association with Morris. Both men happened to be born and raised in Vermont, Morris in the village of Norwich. It was Morris, Dewey said later, who led him to Hegel and who "left a deep impress on the mind of his student."[23] Morris was well read in classical

---

[19] *Psychology*, I, 483.

[20] *Ibid.*, p. 489.

[21] Pages 27–29. Dewey speaks of what he regards as the central influence of James's *Psychology* on his own thought. James, he says, denies that sensations and ideas are discrete units, and replaces that idea with "the stream of consciousness." This makes relations "an immediate part of the field of consciousness," equal in status with qualities. Dewey then mentions James's criticism of the "atomism of Locke and Hume as well as the *a-priorism* of the synthesis of rational principles by Kant and his successors, among whom should be mentioned in England, Thomas Hill Green, who was then at the height of his influence," p. 28. This influence, I think, is what James here helped Dewey throw off. Dewey also goes on to mention the "biological nature" of James's *Psychology*. Among other chapters he cites that of "Discrimination and Comparison," which he views as a discussion of "the way in which ends to be attained and the means for attaining them evoke and control intellectual analysis, pp. 28–29.

[22] On Morris and his place in the development of Dewey's philosophy, see White, *Origin*, ch. 2. The standard and valuable work on Morris is by Wenley (1917); this must be read critically, however; thus, see the more recent study (1948) of Morris by Jones. Dewey's sketch of Morris as a teacher and philosopher, "The Late Professor Morris" (1889), is especially illuminating. Also his later reminiscence (1915) in Wenley, pp. 313–321. See also Schneider, pp. 474–477.

[23] "Biography of John Dewey" in Schilpp, *Philosophy of Dewey*, p. 16. Also see Dewey's "From Absolutism to Experimentalism."

and German literature and was a thoroughly competent scholar of the history of philosophy. He translated Ueberweg's history of philosophy, an accomplishment in which he demonstrated a complete mastery of the German language and also of the sources of Ueberweg's work. In several respects the English translation is to be preferred to the German original in style and for the accuracy of its historical references.

In his youth Morris had been a follower of the British school of the Mills, Bain, and Spencer. But in his late twenties (1867–1868) he studied under J. E. Erdmann and Herman Ulrici at Halle and Friedrich Trendelenburg in Berlin. Ulrici was a stimulating critic of Hegel; but it was from Trendelenburg that Morris was led back from Hegel to Kant and was impressed with the relevance of Aristotle. The impact of Trendelenburg on Morris' education can be witnessed in the able essay Morris later wrote on the philosophy of his former teacher.[24] Morris treats of Trendelenburg's doctrine of motion as the primitive (thus in itself unanalyzable and undefined) basis for explaining the relation or "identity" of thought and being. The activity that infuses mind and sensible objects is "the *prius* of experience" and "the *a-priori* before experience."[25] Trendelenburg's teleological theory of organic process, "the notion of purpose, inherent end, as manifested in organic existence,"[26] particularly impresses Morris. All things, including knowledge, are parts of this process; this is an "organic conception of the universe of thought and being."[27] With warm interest Morris discusses Trendelenburg's view that all things are to be understood as parts of an "organic whole," that truth is the whole, and that thought and ideas are not real "except as belonging to the whole *organism* of knowledge."[28] For Morris, as we shall notice, the "organic" point of view leads to a new "experimental" interpretation of thought and nature.

Dewey recalled the position taken by Morris:

> He effected in himself what many book-scholars would doubtless regard as impossible—a union of Aristotle, Fichte and Hegel. The world, the world truly seen, was itself ideal; and it was upon the ideal character of the world, as supporting and realizing itself in the energy of intelligence as the dominant element in creation, that he insisted. That the struggle of intelligence to realize in man the supreme position which it occupies ontologically in the structure of the universe was a moral struggle, went without saying. The teleological metaphysics of Aristotle thus found a natural complement in the moral idealism of Fichte.[29]

Aristotle, Fichte, and Hegel, it should be observed, were each formative in Green's philosophic development, as we shall see below.

[24] "Friedrich Adolph Trendelenburg" (1874).
[25] *Ibid.,* p. 321.
[26] *Ibid.,* p. 324. On a matter quite relevant to the subject of the present Appendix, Morris was one of the many thinkers who seemed to find philosophic antecedents of Darwinism. Thus, inspired by Trendelenburg, he wrote "Darwinism today unwittingly confirms . . . even . . . reaffirms the fundamental Aristotelian conceptions concerning nature," "Philosophy and Its Specific Problems," p. 216*n.*
[27] "Trendelenburg," p. 298.
[28] *Ibid.,* pp. 298, 331.
[29] Quoted in Wenley, p. 316.

Morris taught a course in the history of British thought at Johns Hopkins. He published a book, *British Thought and Thinkers*, 1880, which was a popular statement of the substance of his more "technical course" of lectures to his students.[30] The keynote of the book, as also of his academic lectures, was the severe rejection of the main tenets of British empiricism, "a constant depreciation of English thought when compared with the German."[31] This rejection is not the result of a detailed critical analysis. Although presumably in his class lectures Morris did engage in careful scrutiny of the ideas in question and in the development of arguments against them, his book, on the other hand, is more polemical than soberly argumentative; it is a summary of Morris' critical convictions and conclusions. Only occasionally a critical weakness of confusion in his subject is fully exploited and the steps of argument made bare. Rather, the general spirit predominates: British philosophy is the perpetuation of errors in misconstruing the nature of mind and the act of knowing and in its hedonistic ethic so untrue to the idealism that is the essential "constituent and necessary element of human nature."[32] In the introductory chapter of the book, Morris is led to declare: "In the British poets . . . we find the best British philosophy."[33] Again and again the critical sallies depart from a comment by "a German thinker"—Schopenhauer, Heine, Goethe.

Morris' enthusiasm for German philosophy is not disguised in his approach to British thought. He even prophesied some hope for the latter from the former: "Under the influence of German precedents," he wrote, we see developing a movement which might "realize our hopeful expectations for a more brilliant future of English philosophy."[34] The brilliant future, as Morris saw it, was being prepared by the Cairds, Andrew Seth, Bosanquet, and T. H. Green.

As might be expected, a study of British philosophy inspired by German idealism will direct its sharpest thrusts against Locke, Hume, and Mill. This Morris does. Berkeley, who was after all a Bishop, and whose "idealism" encompassed a "celestial" and "moral interest" in the attempt to show how the lover of mind (Philonous) conquers matter (Hylas), is favored in Morris' assessment as "the truest, acutest philosopher that Great Britain has ever known."[35] On the other hand "Mill's greatest personal misfortune was that he was born the son of James Mill, and not of Johann Gottlieb Fichte."[36]

The point of special relevance to us here, in considering Morris' work, is the basic agreement in positive and critical doctrines which he shared with Green and the definite assimilation of these in the early formation of Dewey's outlook.

Like Green, as we shall soon see, Morris protests against the "mechanical," in-

---

[30] The book is the result of "public lectures" delivered to an "audience of ladies and gentlemen" at Johns Hopkins. See the Preface, p. 3.
[31] Dewey's comment quoted in Wenley, p. 315.
[32] *British Thought and Thinkers*, p. 12.
[33] *Ibid.*, p. 28.
[34] *Ibid.*, p. 29.
[35] *Ibid.*, p. 233.
[36] *Ibid.*, p. 336.

consistent, and "dualistic" conception of experience in British philosophy.[37] Locke, Mill, and Spencer, he argues, are representatives of "the essentially *static* view of mind and knowledge."[38] It is not insignificant that in his "technical" academic course on this subject, Morris used Green's edition of Hume with its long critical *Introduction* as well as his own book on the British thinkers.[39] In his book, Morris espouses a conception of mind and consciousness that is also close to Green's idealism. "Man is mind, is spirit," says Morris, "and all the products of these his characteristically spiritual, i.e., human activities" point to norms of truth and judgment "independent of subjective or purely individual prepossessions."[40] In a passage that may well have impressed the young Dewey, Morris adds:

> Further, Mind is conscious intelligence. Intelligence is an active function, not simply a passive possession: strictly passive, it were no longer intelligence, for then, inactive, it would not have intelligence of itself.[41]

Much of Morris' language, the characteristic terms he uses in approving or disapproving certain doctrines, survives in Dewey's writings. Many of these key terms are also found in Green's manner of expressing himself. Morris champions the "vital," "organic," and "dynamic."[42] In contrast to Spencer's view, "Mind," Morris holds, is "a reality . . . , is dynamic, synthetic, vital, and knows itself in active self-consciousness."[43] Whereas the empiricists had been led to make a complete separation between the knowing agent and the world—so much so that the very existence of that "external" world became problematic—Morris, in language identical with that of Green, argued for the view that "knowledge and being are correlative terms."[44] Nature, Morris declares in Hegelian fashion, "is grounded in spirit." Nature is thus an "organic" process embodying a purpose, namely, the

---

[37] His paper, "Philosophy and Its Specific Problems" is particularly explicit on this, as we shall see in the next pages.

[38] *British Thought and Thinkers*, p. 194. In his chapter on Locke, Morris remarks that while Locke started with a " 'white paper' theory, so far as it seemed to imply that mind was blankly passive and receptive, and only that" (p. 196), in the progress of Locke's inquiry it was necessary—in order to account for knowledge—to shift to another conception: "the 'white paper' turns out to be capable of 'operations' and to possess 'powers.' " Here, Morris says, Locke is "on the track of a conception of mind as an ideal value, a living power, an energy of intelligence" (p. 196). It is interesting to note that this critical comment very clearly anticipates the central theme of Dewey's suggestive study, "Substance, Power, and Quality in Locke" (1926).

[39] In his course on Ethics he made "especial reference to F. H. Bradley's *Ethical Studies,*" Wenley, p. 145.

[40] *British Thought and Thinkers*, p. 12.

[41] *Ibid.*, pp. 12–13.

[42] Thus, his comments on the "vital element," *ibid.*, p. 23; "vital experience," p. 23; "synthetic vital reason," p. 26; "vital self-consciousness," "dynamic, . . . living . . . consciousness," p. 385.

[43] *Ibid.*, p. 367.

[44] *Philosophy and Christianity*, p. 70. Green's use of this expression is given in pages below. The use is Hegelian. Dewey notes that Trendelenburg had incorporated in his teaching the main achievements "of the great philosophic movement which began with Kant and closed with Hegel—the ideas, for example, of the correlation of thought and being, the idea of man as a self-realizing personality, the notion of organized society as the objective reality of man," although, Dewey adds, Trendelenburg had become critical of these ideas as stated and taught by Hegel. "The Late Professor Morris," p. 113.

realization of Absolute Spirit. But in particular, this advance to the ideal is expressed in

the explicit development of finite self-consciousness, as in man, as the approximate end to which all her varied activity is (again) but 'instrumental.'[45]

As Dewey has observed, Morris' rejection of materialistic empiricism "was something more than a logical conviction of the purely theoretical short-coming of these forms of philosophy that made him so strong . . . an opponent of them." There was also "the conviction, which personal experience had brought home to him, of their failure to support and inspire life."[46] Dewey could well appreciate Morris' motives and his attempt to find a union of intellectual and moral interests in a philosophy where "those internal divisions, which eat into the heart of so much of contemporary spiritual life, and which rob the intellect of its faith in truth, and the will of its belief in the value of life, had been overcome."[47] Dewey had felt these demands keenly himself. Led by Morris, Dewey first discovered this unifying outlook in Hegel, not merely as an abstract thesis, but worked out in great detail in the philosophy of art, society, religion, and history, as well as the theory of knowledge. For some time Dewey was to agree with Morris' statement that Hegel "was the most profound and comprehensive of modern thinkers."[48]

Finally, Morris came to consider the main problem of philosophy to be the problem of determining the nature of *experience*. In this, too, Morris was philosophically very close to Green. For Morris, "Philosophy . . . is nothing but the examination of our whole and undivided experience, with a view to ascertaining its whole nature, its range, and its content."[49] In thus focusing on the concept of experience, Morris argued that the alternative to a skeptical empiricism was a more "experimental" conception of reality, sense, and intelligence, taking its lead from Kant. The experimental position would show that intelligence is not "merely subjective and formal" but also "objective," embracing

not the dark phantom of the 'unknowable' or of the inaccessible, because non-sensible, Ding-an-sich, but an intelligible, rational, self-illuminating, and self-explaining world of living, present, effective reality.[50]

[45] *Philosophy and Christianity*, p. 84; Wenley, p. 274. Morris occasionally uses the word 'instrumental' in contexts that strongly suggest the origins of Dewey's nomenclature for his philosophy (for which, see § 36). Thus, in addition to the above, he also argues that real numenal objects are not "shut out from us" by a screen of phenomenal objects. Rather, for the act of *knowing*, the former leads the latter: "to thought it instrumentally reveals the true object," *Philosophy and Christianity*, p. 45. In *British Thought and Thinkers*, p. 385, Morris espouses a more "experimental" philosophy than empiricism (a view to be discussed shortly, and see note 51 below), and in so doing affirms the presence in things of *reason* operating instrumentally: "the necessary *means*, or instrument, through which the unchanging *ends* of perfect reason . . . must be reached."
[46] "The Late Professor Morris," p. 112.
[47] *Ibid.*, p. 115.
[48] *Ibid.*, p. 113. At the same time it is worth noting that, according to Dewey, p. 114, the two writings which Morris "most often quoted were the Dialogues of Plato and the Gospel of St. John."
[49] "Philosophy and Its Specific Problems," p. 212.
[50] *Ibid.*, p. 222.

As Wenley, Morris' biographer, points out, often throughout this article, "Philosophy and Its Specific Problems," Morris uses the terms 'experimental' and 'experiment' for 'experiential' and 'experience.'[51] This same terminology made its way into Dewey's vocabulary. But an especially interesting feature of this essay, in its bearing on the early history of Dewey's thought, is Morris' attempt to express an "experimental" theory of mind and experience that would overcome the difficulties of "mechanical" empiricist versions of the same. Philosophy, Morris writes, is "in form" knowledge of the universal, but in substance it is knowledge of the "nature of experimental reality."[52] Indeed, "All our knowledge consists of nothing but the interpretation and comprehension of experience."[53] Morris launches a particularly forceful criticism at the traditional problem of the existence of the external world. His entire argument is very much in the vein taken by Dewey in discussing the same problem thirty-three years later.[54] Morris refers scathingly to the fact that in British empiricism

> the problem respecting the existence of the external world could become, in the language of Mr. Bain, the "great problem of metaphysics in the eighteenth century," as it still is for Mr. Bain and other metaphysicians, the Mills, Spencers, and their like of the nineteenth century.[55]

As Dewey argued later, and as some contemporary analytic philosophers have reiterated more recently, Morris points to the purely verbal character of the "problem" and its built-in impossibility of solution.

> . . . Since all ground of evidence upon which to solve the "problem" is cut away by the dogmatic theory of knowledge or experience adopted at the outset, it follows that all discussion of it, all ostensible weighing of evidence concerning it, can

---

[51] Wenley, p. 260n. As alluded to earlier (above, note 45), in *British Thought and Thinkers* Morris had sketchily affirmed a new "experimentalism." There, in criticism of Spencer's "mechanical" psychology "of automatic . . . unreasoned processes," Morris argued that this analysis is "neither required nor justified by pure science," and is "in direct contrast with experimental truth," p. 384. He proceeds to advocate a "Positive, affirmative, reasoned philosophy, resting on the only true substantive *experience* (= etymologically, *trial, proving*) possible for man," p. 384. This is to recognize "rational, spiritual power" as part of experience. In *Philosophy and Christianity*, in criticizing the empiricists for being unable to properly direct philosophy to a living reality "like that of Self," he notes that "the method . . . in which . . . they put all their trust, and which they style 'experimental,'" is not this but "abstract, partial, incomplete." What is wanted is "a larger and more liberal, but not less strictly scientific, method, which is not unknown to philosophy and which, not being arbitrarily conceived and forcibly imposed on experience, but simply founded in and dictated by the recognition of experience in its whole nature, is alone entitled to be fully and without qualification 'experimental,'" p. 287. In this last work, as in the article "Philosophy and Its Specific Problems," Morris was advancing a philosophy that is best characterized in the words Dewey used to describe his own early position: "experimental idealism" (see § 36, note 28 above). For further developments of this position, see, e.g., Lloyd's *Dynamic Idealism* (and the study by Shirk); also Dewey, "An Empirical Survey of Empiricisms."
[52] "Philosophy and Its Specific Problems," p. 217.
[53] *Ibid.*, p. 212.
[54] "The Existence of the World as a Problem" (1915). For an earlier reference to this essay, see § 79, note 8 above.
[55] "Philosophy and Its Specific Problems," p. 214.

really only consist in a dialectical beating of the air . . . pompously uttering words and phrases which have a solemn sound but convey no meaning.[56]

Morris' own resolution of this problem is characteristically direct:

The external world, the question concerning whose existence furnishes so much employment to sensational "metaphysics," is given in man's experience.

But this is not man's "sensible experience," as even the sensational metaphysicians discover,

but given in his whole experience, which is not merely and exclusively sensible. It is no work of philosophy, it is not one of philosophy's "specific problems" to justify our belief in the external world, or to prove the "real existence" of the latter, but to comprehend it as it is given.[57]

The real problem of philosophy, Morris proceeds to argue, if it is not to be absorbed in physical science—the science of sensible reality—is to establish a "complete science of knowledge or—what amounts to the same thing—of conscious experience."[58] This had been started by the "brilliant movement" of Kant, Fichte, Schelling, and Hegel."

The core of this new science, as Morris outlines it, is an "experimental" theory of the relation of the knowing subject and external objects. This is to be a definite contrast to the view of a "simply mechanical" separation of subject and object in experience. The latter ends in skepticism; the objects of thought become matters of professed ignorance. For Morris

The distinction of subject and object is experimentally real; and it is within, not behind, the veil of consciousness.[59]

Subject and object "confront each other and meet together." The relation between subject and object must be given more than "mechanical or sensible meaning." For "the relation between them is organic."[60]

[56] *Ibid.*, p. 214. Dewey's 1915 paper on Russell (see note 54 above) parallels Morris' argument. "There is no problem, logically speaking, of the existence of an external world" is Dewey's thesis, stated in his first paragraph. "The very attempt to state the problem involves a self-contradiction." That attempt to generate the problem requires assuming the very point being questioned, is Dewey's main argument.
   In the same year this paper was written, Dewey also wrote an appreciative reminiscence of Morris (quoted in Wenley, pp. 313–321). He refers specifically to Morris' view of the above "problem": "I remember the scorn with which he alluded to Bain's reference to the problem of the existence of an external world as the great problem in metaphysics," Wenley, p. 317. White, *Origin*, p. 30, note 45, rightly notes this. It should be added, in the light of the present pages, that Green also found the empirical tradition contradictory in its conception of reality, and in the relation of mind to the world (see *Works*, I, 112, 134 ff., calling it "a doctrine founded on the testimony of the senses, which ends by showing that the senses testify to nothing," *Works*, I, 132. Locke's attempt to determine "the relation of such outer things to the mind, cannot be spoken of without contradiction," I, 112. Also see his essays on Spencer, in *Works*, I, 373–441.
[57] "Philosophy and Its Specific Problems," p. 214.
[58] *Ibid.*, p. 221. In addition to a science of knowledge, the article also outlines a science of Being, Nature, Society, Art, and Religion.
[59] *Ibid.*, p. 224.
[60] *Ibid.*, p. 225.

The "identity" of subject and object is organic identity or oneness of nature. Subject and object are parts of a whole, and each part at once implies and reveals the other.[61]

This whole, he adds, is "one concrete, organic universal,"[62] which illuminates and imparts significance to each of its parts. In the working out of Dewey's philosophy, this "whole" was to become the "situation."

The new critical interest in experience that Morris was developing had already been more clearly and effectively introduced by Green. Dewey was responsive to both these men, but finally and most profoundly to Green.

Both Green and Morris set forth a critique of traditional empiricism which drew heavily upon the philosophic heritage of Aristotle, Kant, and Hegel. Both men were familiar with this historical heritage. In each case the critique was conducted in behalf of an idealism of "universal consciousness" and emphasized continuity instead of dualism between thought and things, self and environment, man and world, spirit and nature, the ideal and the real. Green was less of an outright Hegelian than Morris. His critique was the more comprehensive, scrupulously subtle, and difficult of the two. Some of Dewey's most interesting and serious early writings exhibit a patient reading of Green, a reverence and eventually a friendly wrestling with Green's ideas as he proceeded to work out his own philosophy.[63]

The object of these next pages is to consider the philosophy of Green as Dewey responded to it and found in it resources and perspective.

There were two Greens—although he (or they) would protest this "dualism." The first Green was the penetrating critic of the British empirical tradition from Locke through John Stuart Mill. However, this detailed, acute, and accurate critical endeavor also reveals certain novel and influential convictions directing its course. Occasionally Green turned from the critical task to develop some luminous insight or powerful idea. Sometimes he did this in separate essays; sometimes, as is the case in his long Introduction to Hume or the essay on Aristotle, sudden moments of radiant philosophic reflection interrupt the determined critical pursuit. Thus, throughout the tightly constructed argumentation on the faults of empiri-

[61] *Ibid.,* p. 226.
[62] *Ibid.,* p. 226.
[63] Dewey's early essay, "The Philosophy of Thomas Hill Green" (1889), reviewed in the next pages, is entirely favorable to Green. So, too, the final pages of his interesting study of the idealistic versions of self in "Some Current Conceptions of the Term 'Self' " (1890). The critical wrestling with Green's thought occurs in "Green's Theory of the Moral Motive" (1892) and "Self-Realization as the Moral Ideal" (1893). The break with Green and resurgence of an increasingly critical examination of fundamental parts of Green's philosophy and idealism occurred generally in 1891–1892. It is worth noting that James's *Psychology* appeared in 1890 (although many of its fundamental themes had appeared earlier in articles). As argued in the previous section, the *Psychology* was probably the main stimulus for Dewey's departure from Hegelian and Greenian idealism. We took note in the previous section of Dewey's letter of 1891 to James about a class of four graduates going through the *Psychology,* see Perry, II, 517; in 1903 he wrote James that "your *Psychology* is the spiritual progenitor of the whole industry," i.e., the Chicago movement of pragmatism of which Dewey was the leader, see Perry, II, 521. James's criticisms of Green will be discussed below.

cism, there lurks the presence of a substantial and yet finely tempered philosophy of human experience and action. However, this latent philosophy, so promising in its moments of illumination and its disparate expression, Green never explicitly articulated. Moreover, when he did come to suggesting his own ideas he fell back upon the language and traditional locutions of German idealism and especially of Hegel. The choice of tongues was unfortunate; it tended to conceal the genuinely novel and suggestive direction of Green's thinking. Only his more perceptive readers, such as Dewey or Bradley, saw through the stylistic conventions and avoided the error of taking Green to be restating Hegel. What they saw instead makes up the second Green.

Both Greens are present in most of his writings; the dual presence is also reflected in Nettleship's attempt to expound Green's thought and to describe his intellectual life in the long memoir included in the *Works*.[64]

The two Greens are important. The first, the critical philosopher, would impress any audience and certainly, considering Morris's predilections and his influence over young Dewey, must have had Dewey's sympathy. The second Green, the idealist making use of the German tradition primarily as a means of expression and as material for the development of his own ideas, for a time profoundly captured Dewey. Both aspects of Green's philosophizing, both Greens, can indeed be viewed as jointly contributive to one philosophy, namely, a form of critical idealism. This philosophy, had it been sufficiently developed, would have been very close to that which Dewey eventually brought forth as instrumentalism. The discussion that follows will make this clearer.

Green had one main philosophic objective, the reconciliation of science and religion.[65] This, as we have noticed before, was of paramount interest to Dewey in his early philosophic years; and, as argued in § 99, this same concern to find an integration of scientific procedure and knowledge with moral values was central to the history of pragmatism. Edward Caird stated this concern at the time when idealism was the reigning philosophy:

> Any one who writes about philosophy must have his work judged, not by its relation to the intellectual wants of a past generation, but by its power to meet the wants of the present time—wants which arise out of the advance of science, and the new currents of influence which are transforming man's social and religious life.[66]

Peirce, James, and Dewey would have subscribed to this criterion.

Green is an excellent example of a philosopher whose thought in general, even in its most theoretical moments, is consciously related to the conduct of human affairs in the world at large. James characteristically admired this in

---

[64] In the *Works of Thomas Hill Green*, III, xi–clxi.

[65] See Dewey, "The Philosophy of Thomas Hill Green," p. 339.

[66] Preface, pp. 2–3, in *Essays in Philosophical Criticism*. See also Wenley, p. 253. The *Essays* contains contributions from many thinkers in widely different fields of interest, all affected by idealism. The book is dedicated to the memory of Green.

Green.[67] Dewey, in his early laudatory essay on Green, emphasized that "it is impossible to hold his philosophy as a mere speculative theory apart from its applications to life."[68] Dewey comments on Green's intense social and political convictions. He notes that Green's philosophy was in the service of these convictions, not as a rationalization of impulse, but as their more complete and rational expression.[69] This, Dewey adds, makes Green's philosophy, despite the "logical and impersonal" form, "vital and concrete."[70]

Green's liberal, democratic social convictions and political activities are intimately part of his idealistic ethic. In this respect Green differed from most of the English idealists of his time. He was a "radical," a dedicated spokesman for the moral and economic rights of the poor. One example of the kind of position Green took on the many urgent issues of his day is his siding with the cause of the North during the American Civil War. He was fearful of the possibility, after the capture of Confederate commissioners on board the *Trent*, of a break between England and the northern United States. "A war with them," he commented, "would make England a wretched country to live in for the term of our lives at least."[71] In a speech of 1863, in answer to those who had urged that the war had been caused by northern aggression, Green replied: "It is not a republic that is answerable for this war, but a slave-holding, slave-breeding, and slave-burning oligarchy, on whom the curse of God and humanity rests."[72] His shock at the assassination of Lincoln was severe, far more so, it may be added, than was William James's, ordinarily that most human of men. For Green, this was "a fitting consummation of the greatest political crime of modern times," and he was not above seeing some of the responsibility extended as far as the English newspapers.[73]

As a teacher, Green's influence was remarkable. In his position at Oxford, as Randall has said, Green

> had an extraordinary influence in moulding the ideas of a generation of English political leaders—those who triumphed in 1906 with the Neo-Liberalism of Henry Campbell-Bannerman and Herbert Asquith, including their philosophical leader, Viscount Haldane. His social criticism had far wider repercussions, however, on the leaders of more radical movements. It is hardly too much to say that his social thought dominated the British Labour Party, in its non-Marxian divisions, down through G. D. H. Cole and Harold J. Laski; and Green was the chief influence in the early social philosophy of John Dewey in America."[74]

[67] See James's comment in *Psychology*, II, 11n., on Green as "this apostolic human being but strenuously feeble writer."

[68] "The Philosophy of Thomas Hill Green," p. 338. This also impressed G. S. Morris, who, during his journey to Wales and Oxford, according to Wenley, p. 167, noted a "distinct direction of Green and Caird, and their men, to practical and social life."

[69] "The Philosophy of Thomas Hill Green," p. 338.

[70] *Ibid.*, p. 339. For Dewey (and for Morris, as we saw above, note 42), and also for Green, 'vital,' 'concrete,' and 'growing' are terms of strong commendation.

[71] Nettleship's Memoir, in *Works*, III, xliii.

[72] *Ibid.*, p. xliii.

[73] *Ibid.*, p. xliv.

[74] "T. H. Green and English Thought," pp. 217–218.

One of Dewey's motives in presenting his account of Green's philosophy was to correct the picture in Mrs. Humphry Ward's then popular novel, *Robert Elsmere* (1888), where Green appears as "Mr. Grey."

Green's attempt to demonstrate the essential—if much unnoticed—harmony between science and religion, by showing that the common source of science, religion, and ethics is a "spiritual principle," *reason*,[75] or *consciousness*, has long been regarded as a rejection of science and an appeal to a higher metaphysical wisdom. But this is a mistake; he fully accepts the existence of the growing body of scientific knowledge. The seemingly anti-scientific spirit is to be understood, rather, as going against the "scientific" British empirical tradition in philosophy represented by Locke, Hume, Mill, and Spencer. That tradition had developed its own philosophic interpretation of scientific knowledge; and this had been argued well enough to be received in many quarters as the authentic voice of science itself. To Green, the empirical philosophy could explain neither science nor any kind of knowledge. His criticism is addressed to revealing the shortcomings of this empiricism, not of empirical science.

Not only did this same empirical philosophy fail in its analysis of knowledge, so Green argued, it also encouraged a hostility to religion and an agnostic and skeptical outlook generally, which, it unjustifiably alleged, were derived from the very nature and conclusions of science. Moreover, no adequate conception of moral action and social ideals could be constructed on the basis of this confused philosophy of *experience*, which held that knowledge originated in sensations and that morality originated in feelings of pleasure and pain, and that the former was the "slave" of the latter.[76]

Thus the first Green—the critic—subjects the doctrines of Locke and Hume to an exhaustive and withering examination. Much the same critical energy was directed with devastating effect, in his lectures, to Mill, and later to the views of Spencer and Lewes.

Green's fundamental criticism of empiricism was Kantian in origin. In holding that knowledge was grounded in single sensations (i.e., Locke's simple ideas of sense—see § 6 above—or Hume's impressions), empiricism could not adequately acknowledge the *structure* of experience, the relations and conjunctions without which sense experience is an unintelligible barrage of single stimulations. Thought or Mind has a crucial role here, as we have seen Kant argue (§ 11 above). However, thinking is assigned a derivative, rather than constructive function in the theory in question. This, Green and all subsequent Kantians argue, is the dilemma of empiricism: it cannot avoid giving certain "constructive" and integrative functions to intelligence,[77] yet it cannot account for these operative powers "empiri-

---

[75] *Prolegomena*, Book I, ch. 1, sec. 33. See also "Faith," in *Works*, III, 267: "reason is the source alike of faith and knowledge."

[76] See Green's comment in *Works*, III, 105, on Hume's statement, *Treatise*, Book II, Part III, sec. 3, that "Reason is, and ought to be only the slave of the passions."

[77] Dewey, "The Philosophy of Thomas Hill Green," p. 342: "Empiricism must either make intelligence a mere product or deny it all constructive function, as a matter of fact it cannot get along without ascribing certain powers to intelligence."

cally" in terms simply of sense stimulation. So Dewey comments, in following Green's powerful exposure of the problem. The role of intelligence in ordering and discovering *relations* among sensations cannot be explained by sensations alone. The claim that "every relation is the product of mere sensations" is "a contradiction essential to the very method of empiricism."[78] Green himself made much of the argument that, put simply, single sensations of themselves produce no *sense* of order. He also effectively pointed out that sensations, or impressions, constituted one order of experience; but *objects*, the very stuff of scientific interest, are not sensations. But then the relation that linked sensations to the objects they were to represent could not be explained by means of these same sensations. Clearly empiricism was suffering from a faulty conception of experience. This, Green set out to correct.

In his *Prolegomena*, says Dewey, Green raises "the real question of philosophy": What is experience? How is it constituted?[79] The answer, as Green develops it, and as we have already begun to see, is that it is structure, order, relations that most constitute experience, rather than irreducible units of sensation or feeling. Experience, or "reality," is the connected whole of things, and what is illusory and therefore unreal is something that cannot fit in as a member of this unified whole.[80]

Like Green, William James also took notice of the failure of empiricism to account for order and "connexion among distinct existences."[81] But the contrast between the two thinkers in how each proposed to overcome the empiricists' difficulty is interesting; the contrast is one of the sources of diverse currents of thought within the development of pragmatism, the radical empiricism and nominalism of James versus the Kantian and experimental "realism" of Peirce, Dewey, and Mead. Unlike Green, who departed from sensation and feeling to locate relational principles and activity in thought, James advanced a more "radical empiricism" in which he argued that the relatedness of our perceptual experience is as immediately evident as is distinctness and diversity.[82] James maintained that relations were as much an immediate part of the content of sense experience as were the units being related. Experience, James held, is neither all unity nor all diversity; rather, it exhibits "fringes," "threads," and the "stream of consciousness."[83] It followed that

[78] Dewey, *ibid.*, p. 342.
[79] *Ibid.*, p. 344. Also see Green, *Prolegomena*, Book I, ch. 1; *Works*, I, 373 ff.; "Mr. Spencer on the Relation of Subject to Object" and "Mr. Lewes' Account of Experience," pp. 412 ff.
[80] *Prolegomena*, Book I, ch. 1, secs. 22–23.
[81] The words are from Hume, *Treatise*, Appendix to Book I. James quotes the passage: *"all our distinct perceptions are distinct existences* and *that the mind never perceives any real connexion among distinct existences,"* from Green's edition of the *Treatise*, in "The Sentiment of Rationality," *Collected Essays and Reviews*, p. 100. See also James's *Psychology*, I, 352.
[82] This brought James close to Bradley, but with important qualifications. See his "Bradley or Bergson?"
[83] *Psychology*, Vol. I, ch. 10, esp. p. 239. James was advancing a theory of experience that comes very close to Berkeley's interpretation of sensations as *signs,* or as significant,

The unity of the parts of the stream is just as 'real' as a connection as their diversity is a real separation.[84]

For Green, however, the fundamental and "ultimate" fact in this recognition of ordered experience is thought or consciousness. Green rejects the "dualism" between thinking and the objects of thought, between *ego* and *non-ego*.[85] The thinking subject and the object known are correlative:

> Neither of the two correlata in his view [the "true idealistic view"] has any reality apart from the other. Every determination of the one implies a corresponding determination of the other.[86]

It was remarked earlier that Green has often been viewed as an anti-scientific philosopher, and that this was a misunderstanding of his critical objectives. But it is true that he thought there was an intelligible principle, and source of knowledge, that science itself required yet could not disclose. Still, even here, Green reasoned that this principle, the rational source of knowledge, values, and action, was to be sought within rather than outside of science. This was Green's "metaphysical analysis" of scientific knowledge. That analysis would yield what science, by its very nature, could not: a principle which transcends all nature and is "spiritual" in essence.[87]

This principle is referred to in different ways by Green. He calls it "ideal," "thought," "reason," or "spiritual principle." He also calls it *consciousness*, and the idea of *self-consciousness* is the fundamental concept in his positive idealistic philosophy. A self-conscious being, Green contends, by the very act of *self-*awareness, is also aware of something *else*, or non-self. Fichte, whom Green had read and absorbed in his student days.[88] had called this the non-ego, "posited" by the ego (see § 16 above). But Green makes a far more ambitious claim. First, to be self-conscious is necessarily to be conscious of something other than oneself. That something else is not merely posited, it is a rational necessity. Second, for

---

of other sense experience (see Appendix 5 below). He, and indeed Berkeley, were motivated in this respect by critical considerations of the sort clearly stated by Green. Green's insistence that sense experience requires the force of thought—the relational element—to be intelligible is not far from Berkeley's doctrine of sensations as *signs* (where particular sense data have the "arrow-function" discussed in Appendix 5 below) nor from James's view of "felt" connections and leading interests and purposes guiding and weaving through sensations. See above, note 21, for a further related comment.

[84] *Ibid.,* 5, 353. James had begun to develop this alternative to "ordinary empiricism" in his critical analysis of Spencer, 1876 (see § 28 above). See also his "The Sentiment of Rationality," 1879.

[85] E.g., his study of Spencer, *Works*, I, 432.

[86] *Works,* I, 387.

[87] See Green's *Prolegomena,* Book I, ch. 1, secs. 18–19 and 52–54.

[88] In his Memoir, in *Works*, III, xxv, Nettleship says of Green: "The writers from whom he seems at this time to have assimilated the most were Wordsworth, Carlyle, Maurice, and probably Fichte in his lectures on the 'nature' and 'vocation' of 'the scholar' and of 'man.' In them he found the congenial idea of a divine life or spirit pervading the world, making nature intelligible, giving unity to history, embodying itself in states and churches, and inspiring individual men of genius." For Fichte, see § 16 above. Morris also had been deeply impressed by Fichte.

a "true idealism" there is no "dualism" of ego and non-ego; they are "correlative factors of one reality."[89] Third, the one reality for Green is thought or self-consciousness. As Dewey says of Green's fundamental principle: self-consciousness is "the only thing that is real in its own right; the only thing of which the reality is not relative or derived."[90]

The agency of self-consciousness is central to Green's interpretation of knowledge and the moral life. Knowledge is not an interpretation of experience (as, for example, Romanticism advised, see § 14); it is an act of discovery. The mind does not legislate the order of nature—here Green departs from Kant—but discovers that legislation ordered by a supreme Consciousness. Nature is a system, a whole of related appearances, and the relations are inexplicable except—since all relations are the workings of thought—as "the action of an intelligence." In individual rational beings the eternal reason or consciousness is operative. This eternal self-consciousness is "constitutive" (in the Kantian sense discussed in § 12 above) of both nature and our understandings. Knowing is a progressive realizing of the ideal, the intelligible order—or logical structure—of nature.[91] Man, since he is an animal as well as a spiritual organism, is limited by his dependence upon the sensible as well as the intelligible conditions of experience. But in this limited being there is the reproducing action of eternal rational consciousness. In Hegelian fashion, Green argued that the eternal consciousness sought to realize itself; and in this quest all partial selves served as means (Morris' word was 'instrumental') to this end, yet they are participants also in the progressive realization of the end, the whole.

The growth of knowledge on our part is regarded not as a process in which facts or objects, in themselves unrelated to thought, by some inexplicable means gradually produce intelligible counterparts of themselves in thought. The true account of it is held to be that the concrete whole, which may be described indifferently as an eternal intelligence realised in the related facts of the world, or as a system of related facts rendered possible by such an intelligence, partially and gradually reproduces itself in us, communicating piece-meal, but in inseparable correlation, understanding and the facts understood, experience and the experienced world.[92]

The synthesizing and constructive function of thought in ordering experience is assigned to a universal intelligence. The most serious objection to Green's position was put by William James in his *Psychology*. Concerning Green's prin-

[89] See his critical essay on Spencer, *Works*, I, 432.

[90] "The Philosophy of Thomas Hill Green," p. 345. Cf. Green's *Prolegomena*, Book I, ch. 1, secs. 51, 54, and Book III, ch. 2, sec. 182. See also Green's review of John Caird's *Introduction to the Philosophy of Religion*, in *Works*, III, 145, for an illuminating statement of the one "unifying principle." Also, Green's essay on Aristotle, in *Works*, III, 69; his Introduction to Hume, sec. 129, in *Works*, 109–110.

[91] "Logical structure" is Randall's neutral and more acceptable term for what Green was expressing in idealistic language as the "order of thought," "T. H. Green and English Thought," p. 220.

[92] *Prolegomena*, Book I, ch. 1, sec. 36.

ciple of a consciousness whose "action" is to "hold appearances together,"[93] James remarks:

the connection of things in our knowledge is in no whit explained by making it the deed of an agent whose essence is self-identity and who is out of time.

This, James proceeds to point out, is to "explain" phenomena

as results of dramas enacted by entities which but reduplicate the character of the phenomena themselves.[94]

To say that we are enabled to know the world by means of the unifying and correlating action of a universal intelligence is not really to explain how we or that intelligence actually acquires knowledge. The introduction of the mechanism of an Intelligence adds no further information about the operation of knowing than the phenomenon from which we began.

James's criticism later impressed Dewey as giving "the hardest knocks" to Green's theory (as we saw in the last pages of the previous section). However, in 1886, Dewey was actively restating Green's view of the self. In a paper devoted to clarifying how psychology provides philosophy with a method for the analysis of experience and the relation of knowing subjects to objects known, a paper commencing with a tribute to Green,[95] Dewey concluded:

The case stands thus: We are to determine the nature of everything, subject and object, individual and universal, as it is found within conscious experience. Conscious experience testifies, in the primary aspect, my individual self is a "transition," is a process of becoming. But it testifies also that this individual self is conscious of the transition, that it knows the process by which it has become. In short, the individual self can take the universal self as its standpoint, and thence know its own origin. . . . All consciousness, in short, is self-consciousness, and the self is the universal consciousness, for which all process is and which, therefore, always is. The individual consciousness is but the process of realization of the universal consciousness through itself.[96]

Green's principle of "eternal self-consciousness" as discerned through the analysis of science, and as basic to an adequate conception of knowledge, is also fundamental for his moral theory. The action of eternal consciousness in us and upon the passage of sensations constitutes them, in Dewey's words, "into an experience of what *is*, so the same consciousness, acting upon transitory impulses,

---

[93] *Ibid.*, Book I, ch. 2, secs. 62, 64 ff. For the quote, see the second paragraph of sec. 64. Note here also Green's use of Berkeley's word "congeries" (see below, Appendix 5) in: "every object we perceive is a congeries of related facts."

[94] *Psychology*, I, 368–369.

[95] "The Psychological Standpoint," pp. 1–2. Also see his "Psychology as Philosophic Method" (1886), which continues to clarify the "Psychological Standpoint." In the second paper a sympathetic but critical comment on Green's reasoning that *what* consciousness is cannot be positively stated, is developed by Dewey. Of "the late Professor Green," says Dewey, "the writer would not speak without expressing his deep, almost reverential gratitude," p. 161. For an interesting attempt to combine an evolutionary analysis of the relation of mind and body with a strong moral idealism, see Dewey's "Soul and Body" (1886).

[96] "The Psychological Standpoint," p. 19.

creates our practical world, our conception of what is not, but *should* be, *ought* to be."[97] Indeed, according to Green, the divine consciousness recognizes no "dualism" between *ought* and *is*, nor any distinction between the *real* and *ideal*. As consciousness—or thought—transforms "mere" feeling into intelligible perceptions *of* objects, so it also illuminates our impulses and wants so that *wants* become intelligible as *of* something and directed to something. In this latter case, by transforming "mere" wanting into something rational—which for Green always means the supplying of *relations*, and here the relating of a want to other desires and to the future state of affairs wanted—divine consciousness leads us to form an ideal of completion and satisfaction. We form then a conception of an "ideal self," and this becomes for us an ideal Good and a standard of moral obligation.[98] The moral life is then viewed as a continual but never entirely complete realization of the ideal self. How, we may ask, does this ideal make itself clear to us? Green's answer is that the content of the ideal becomes progressively clarified within moral activity itself. The ideal is not to be defined abstractly or separately from activity; its expression is in moral activity; its consummation is in love and self-sacrifice. This consummation is the projection of one's self into the absolute, perfect self.[99]

It is worth pausing here to note how these last features of Green's theory must have impressed Dewey. For the notion of *wants* as becoming intelligible by a disclosure of the states of affairs and objects they are *of* or related to; the conception of an ideal of completeness and satisfaction as the criterion for evaluating wants; and the idea of moral ends as defined within moral activity itself[100]— these are central to the ethical theory that Dewey was to work out over many years (see Part Four, Chapter Three above).

A moral action, says Green,

Whatever else it may be, . . . is at least an action determined by desire for an object which is not merely presented to the agent, but which he presents to himself as his own end. . . . Now to act for an object which I present to myself, or make my object, is to identify myself with it, and thus to desire to be something which I am not, but which I conceive myself as able to become. Moral action, then, as determined by such a desire, is an expression at once of conscious contrast between an actual possible self, and of an impulse to make that possible self real; or, as it

[97] "The Philosophy of Thomas Hill Green," p. 346. See Green, *Prolegomena*, Book II, ch. 1, sec. 85.
[98] *Prolegomena*, Book III, ch. 1, secs. 171–173, 175–177; Book III, ch. 2.
[99] "Faith," in *Works*, III, 269.
[100] On this point, particularly, see Dewey's later critical reflections in "Green's Theory of the Moral Motive" (1892), esp. pp. 599 and 608, where Dewey argues that Green has set off and abstracted the unifying and wanted ideal of moral experience from the actual process of moral effort and expression. Thus the ideal Self is not within the activity of particular self-activity nor does it define that activity even as an end; it remains forever "behind, set off" from moral action. In "Self-Realization as the Moral Ideal" (1893), Dewey further criticized Green's hypostatized Self, saying, pp. 661–662: "It is not action *for* the self that is required (thus setting up a fixed self which is simply going to *get* something more, wealth, pleasure, morality, or whatever) but action *as* the self. To find the self in the highest and fullest activity possible at the time, and to perform the act in the consciousness of its complete identification with self (which means, I take it, with complete interest) is morality, and is realization."

is sometimes put, it is a process of self-realization, i.e. of making a possible self real.[101]

Green explains that the moral content of the ideal self, the Good, is developed and evidenced in individual persons and in social relationships. The "concrete" significance of the ideal is found in history and the institutions that have worked to the betterment of human life. These institutions are vehicles and embodiments of "the consciousness of the ideal."

This ethical doctrine leads directly to Green's humane and liberal social philosophy in which the ideal of growth and self-realization of persons in society, and by means of society, is emphasized. It is this philosophy that Dewey apparently regarded as Green's major positive contribution to ethical thought. Green's doctrines are clear in Dewey's enthusiastic exposition of them and, later, are reflected in Dewey's own social philosophy. It is thus worth quoting Dewey's account of Green's conception of social self-realization; it is the most eloquent expression of Green's argument in Dewey's essay, "The Philosophy of Thomas Hill Green," and the harmony with Dewey's later thinking is interesting. Dewey puts Green's view as follows:

since the principle which is reproducing itself in us is a self-conscious personality, we may know that its reproduction must also be a self-conscious personality.[102] Of one thing we may be sure: "Our ultimate standard of worth is an ideal of *personal* worth. All other values are relative to value for, of, or in the person."[103] This ideal cannot be found, then, in impersonal humanity, in some national or world consciousness, in some organization of society, nor in some far off event, however divine, towards which the world is supposed to be making. "The spiritual progress of mankind is [thus] an unmeaning phrase, unless it means a progress *of* personal character, and *to* personal character,—a progress of which feeling, thinking, and willing subjects are the agents and sustainers."[104] But, on the other hand, this progress can be only realized in society. While its beginning, its process, and its end is in an individual, yet without society, and the conditions afforded by it, there can be no individual, no person. "Society is the condition of development of a personality."[105] "Social life is to personality what language is to thought."[106] "Human society presupposes persons in *capacity*, [. . .] but it is only in the intercourse of men, each recognized by each as an end, not merely a means, and thus having reciprocal claims, that the capacity is actualized, and that we really live as persons."[107] ". . . It is through the action of society that the individual comes [at once] practically to conceive his [own] personality [. . .] and to conceive the same personality as belonging to others; [so] it is society [also] that supplies all the

[101] "The Word is Nigh Thee," *Works*, III, 224.
[102] See Green, *Prolegomena*, Book III, ch. 2, sec. 182.
[103] *Ibid.*, Book III, ch. 2, sec. 184.
[104] *Ibid.*. Book III, ch. 2, sec. 185. The 'thus' in square brackets is Green's, omitted in Dewey's quotation; the word 'sustainers' is Green's, Dewey uses 'substainers.'
[105] *Ibid.*, Book III, ch. 2, sec. 191.
[106] *Ibid.*, Book III, ch. 2, sec. 183.
[107] *Ibid.*, Book III, ch. 2, sec. 183. 'Capacity' not italicized in Green's original; ellipsis in square brackets not given in Dewey's quotation.

higher content to this conception, all those objects of a man's personal interest, in living for which he lives for his own satisfaction. . . ."[108]

For Green, moral conduct has as its end the perfection of human personality. But this is, as Dewey says, "the perfection of persons living as persons, that is, living in society." According to Green's theory of knowledge, thought invests sensations with order and the real is the logical structure of experience. Here, in the social theory, the communal structure and relatedness of personalities is the basic reality.

The full moral force of this theory, which proved so attractive to Dewey, is its identification in one ideal good of the rights and interests of individual persons *and* their common development. Dewey expressed this idea first in Green's theological language:

> Each being in whom God so communicates himself is a person, an end in himself, and has the rights of personality. An ideal so constituted cannot be exclusive, cannot be other than common.

But then, characteristically, the same point is developed from a more "psychological" point of view.

> If we put it in a more psychological way, the person who is to realize his capacities has interests in persons; not merely interests in them so far as they are *means* to his own gratification, but interest in them as in himself—interest in their good as in his own. Man cannot be thought as man without this fundamental social interest. This social interest cannot by any possibility be developed or evolved from forms of life which do not already in germ possess it. . . . A unity of interest, a conception of well-being common to a number of persons, however small the number, the idea of community is the necessary presupposition of all human history. Once given this community, this number of persons who conceive themselves and one another as persons, as ends in themselves, and any conceivable development of morality is possible. Without it, morality has no existence.[109]

The foregoing pages make clear, I think, the fundamental nature of Green's influence on Dewey. Green's objective, the harmonizing of science and religion in a comprehensive theory of human "consciousness," that is, a theory of thought and action centered in a liberal social philosophy, has its later historical parallel in Dewey's own philosophical development. It remains, briefly, to note some other aspects of Dewey's indebtedness to Green.

1) Green's penetrating criticism of the classical British empiricists, Locke, Berkeley, Hume, and Mill, is the main reason why, unlike James, Dewey always had strong reservations concerning this tradition. The same critical orientation guides Dewey's discussions of the more recent extensions of empiricism in Russell, Moore, and the Vienna Circle. Furthermore, the basic course of Green's critical

[108] *Ibid.,* Book III, ch. 2, sec. 190. Dewey's quotation of the original is corrected in square brackets. The words 'own' and 'also,' in square brackets, are not in Green's original. The full extract is from "The Philosophy of Thomas Hill Green," pp. 348–349.
[109] "The Philosophy of Thomas Hill Green," p. 350.

analysis of empiricism concentrated on the mechanical and sensationalistic and subjective notion of *experience*, on the "dualism" between knowing subject and external objects, on the assumption that the mind is a passive receptacle of discrete sensations; each became a point of departure for Dewey's critical assaying of that same tradition.

2) Green's detailed examination of the psychology of the empiricist, the theory that sensations or impressions were, in some inexplicable sense, images of objects, and that sensations were the basic units of knowledge, also influenced Dewey. He followed Green in regarding "feeling" or sheer sense stimulation not as knowledge until incorporated into larger acts of attention and adjustment that might issue in knowledge (see § 38). Sensations viewed as constituents of acts of behavior have a teleological factor; for Green this was the purposive operation of consciousness in the organic materials of sense; for Dewey it was the mediating and interpretive effect of the purposive *act*. Intelligence and interest work to render sensations significant of certain conditions, signs of certain events taking place whose function is to guide and suggest possible avenues of action. What Peirce, James, and C. I. Lewis learned from Berkeley on the analysis of sensations, Dewey derived from Green.[110]

3) Green's conception of logic was, despite his other criticisms, partly due to Mill. He was led to view traditional logic as "formal" and empty and an inaccurate representation of how we actually think.[111] Morris also, as we noticed earlier, had sharply contrasted formal logic with a "real logic" of practical thinking. And Dewey was responsive to these idealistic critiques of the formal in behalf of the "concrete" and "organic" in logical theory. In Green's essay on Aristotle, he states very clearly some of his main objections to traditional logic, namely, that it separates sense and reason and relies upon a faulty notion of the nature of abstraction and the relation between particulars and universals, matter and form. Throughout the essay Green insists that the universal, conceptual, the relational and abstract are not separate from nor the outcome of an analysis of sensible experience. These are *in* the very materials of "intelligent experience." Sense experience without thought is blind (to recall Kant, and § 11 earlier). But the awareness of a sensation as *of* something *here*, as preceded and followed by other sensations, introduces stable and determinate relations to the self and into experience. Thought is then at work; logical structure is the result. "The 'sensible thing' thus reappears, no longer, however, as a 'sensible' but as a 'cogitable.' "[112] In a manner very much like that of Dewey later, Green's conclusion is:

110 For this reference to Berkeley see Appendix 5 below.
111 Green thus anticipates a characteristic critical trend in pragmatism against "formalism" (see Appendix 6, sec. D below). Schiller (see especially §§ 66–67) seems not to have been aware of his kinship with Green in this respect.
112 *Works*, III, 52. Green's use of 'cogitable' here is much like Dewey's 'logiscible,' which he used on occasion to refer to the knowable, relational, and statable aspect of things. Another word that became quite characteristic in Dewey's writing is 'reconstruction'; Green occasionally uses this term, e.g., in speaking of the "reconstruction of moral ideas," *Works*, III, 117.

The antithesis between thought, as that in which we are active, and experience, as that in which we are simply receptive, vanishes, for thought appears as a factor in experience even in its remotest germs. Thought again appears as a process of concretion, at least as much as abstraction. . . . By a succession of judgments, each manifesting in the copula the presence of the same unifying and distinguishing agent as the most primary, the chaos of sense is resolved into definite elements. One indeterminate sensation after another is determined by comparison and contrast with others, and as determinate is referred as a property to a thing, to become in its turn the subject of other predicates. . . .

. . . All thinking . . . is of this kind. It is not a progress from the less to the more abstract, but from the less to the more determinate. It does not begin with determinate attributes which it abstracts from each other, but has itself to create them.[113]

Thought, then, is a unifying action by which experience becomes concrete and determinate.

The process of thought appears as one not of abstraction but of concretion. It 'integrates' just so far as it 'differentiates.'[114]

Finally, Green observes:

Such a theory of the process of thought does away with the false antithesis between experience and reasoning, between induction and deduction, between relations of ideas and relations of things. The first act of experience is the same in kind with all reasoning not simply rhetorical, and thought is active in the creation of its materials as in their arrangements.[115]

For Green, then, thought—or consciousness—reconstructs and makes determinate the initially ephemeral and unstable flux of feeling. In the next generation, Bradley was to argue against Green that thought falsifies experience. Thought is not the unifying agent that Green supposed; it is disintegrative, and truth is to be found in a supra-empirical unity transcending thought altogether. This was a return to feeling, a level of experience thoroughly disowned by Green, but restored to respectability by subtle logical argumentation from Bradley.

For Dewey, Green's self and consciousness are replaced by situation and inquiry. Situations are qualitative wholes, and inquiry is the transformation of indeterminate situations into those that are determinate and become unified wholes (as we have seen in § 39 above). The interpretation of thought as the progressive, determinate, integrative and unifying recreation of conditions of experience, as set forth by Green, is one of the main sources of Dewey's instrumentalism (see § 36 above).[116]

---

[113] *Ibid.*, III, 52–53.
[114] *Ibid.*, III, 63.
[115] *Ibid.*, III, 63.
[116] While other influences also helped shape Dewey's logical theory, it is worth noting that Dewey's analysis of universal propositions (see Appendix 6, sec. C below) is close to Green's theory of these as relational, and to Green's interpretation of the Aristotelian concepts of matter and form as "correlative determinants" proposed instead of the "false dualism" in Aristotle (see Green's essay on Aristotle, *Works*, III, 46–91, esp. 62–89).

These were the dominant ideas in Green's idealism that were carefully and critically assimilated by Dewey in the development of his instrumentalism and naturalism.

I turn now to one further and final aspect of our subject.

D. Nineteenth-Century Philosophizing and the Concepts of Continuity, Possibility, and Identity

Historical periods in the course of philosophy can be specified by the dominant problems and forms of conceptualization, or themes, as well as by the names of famous philosophers. Were one to attempt such a specification of the latter part of the nineteenth century, one fundamental conceptual earmark would be *continuity*. This we have reviewed in earlier pages. But associated with continuity are two others: *identity* and *possibility*.

The three concepts became focal in the philosophizing of men who, in general heavily influenced by German idealism (and especially Hegel), were accustomed, when driven, to analyze subject matters in a historical spirit. That is, the approach taken to any kind of "facts" requiring analysis relied upon and stressed notions of development, growth, passage in time, movement in time and sometimes in space. Men, institutions, and thought were thus scrutinized within theoretical frameworks of the conviction that developmental or processive traits of the subjects under analysis were the most relevant and informative for knowledge.

This same point of view received vigorous reinforcement from Darwinism—processes or processive traits were viewed then as evolutionary phenomena. Moreover, both idealism and Darwinism guided philosophers to regard evolvings, processive traits, and developments as continuous processes. This we noticed earlier; no "breaks" or "gaps" characterize the evolution of the subject matter under analysis (e.g., men and their behavior or thinking, institutions, historical epochs, etc.). The philosopher thus looked at the subject of his theorizing and attempted to state how its earlier and later, or primitive and advanced, or lower and higher, conditions characterize the course of or contribute to or are manifested by the evolving subject.

The evolutionary mode of analysis thus works with the concept of continuity, in some form, and also with the idea of the "end" or higher "phase" or "completion" of the evolutionary process as not the same or reducible to the initial stages of the process. Thus arises an appeal to novel and possible outcomes of processes, to future conditions and possibilities whose complexion and constituents are (in some sense) radically different from and not "contained in" those of the past. This notion rests upon that of *physical* possibility, a concept vital to pragmatism, or any conception of evolution, and discussed in Appendix 7.

One problem occurring in the framework in which these concepts operate is how and in what sense things retain *identity* in evolving from lower stages to higher, or in passing from one stage of development to another. Faced with this problem, philosophers in the late nineteenth century struggled to make sense of identity. Hegel had explained in his "Doctrine of Essence" how the Ground is a unity of identity and difference. Bradley, criticizing and rejecting what he argued was assumed to be the "indisputable basis of all reasoning" that "what seems the same is the same," worked out a famous theory of "Identity-in-difference."[117] Schiller objected, and offered instead a theory of identity as a postulate.[118] James was most critical of this argument in Schiller's best-known essay "Axioms as Postulates."[119] James worked long and hard in the latter part of his life to provide a meaningful accommodation in the conceptual framework of his pragmatism and radical empiricism for continuity, novelty, possibility, and identity.[120]

This note on continuity began with some references to Dewey's characteristic emphasis on continuity, and on growth as a paradigm of continuity. Now in the idea of *growth* the notions of *continuity*, *identity*, and *possibility*—so central in the philosophy of the nineteenth century, as we have observed—are directly implicated. Peirce, fully sensitive to this, made a pertinent comment on the urgent importance of and philosophic fascination with *growth:*

> As this Century is drawing to a close, it is interesting to pause and look about us and to ask ourselves in what great questions science is now most interested. The answer must be that *the* question that everybody is now asking, in metaphysics, in the theory of reasoning, in psychology, in general history, in philology, in sociology, in astronomy, perhaps even in molecular physics, is the question *How things grow*.[121]

[117] See Wollheim, esp. pp. 152–159.
[118] See *Studies in Humanism,* p. 85, and on Schiller's conception of postulates, § 65 above.
[119] In a letter to Schiller of 1902, see Perry, II, 497, James writes: "I don't think that you have quite succeeded with the example of identity which you have taken. I wish you hadn't tackled that example, or else treated it a little differently, for the enemies will make the most of it and ignore the rest of the article." For Schiller's argument, see § 65, note 72 above.
[120] See Appendix 7 for a further notice of this.
[121] *CP* 7.267, note 8.

The Background of Peirce's Pragmatism

A more precise and explicit statement of the origins of pragmatism than that contained in the chapter on Peirce and in § 19 is in order here as a supplement to those earlier pages. Two topics require comment: (*a*) the exact data concerning the first statement of pragmatism from Peirce; (*b*) the role of Chauncey Wright in the founding of pragmatism.

A. The First Statement of Pragmatism

There are two valuable accounts by Peirce of how pragmatism came to light. One of these has been quoted in part above (§ 19) and is found in *CP* 5. 12–13. The other is the subject of a long letter to Mrs. Ladd-Franklin, part of which she presents in her paper in the Peirce issue of *The Journal of Philosophy, Psychology and Scientific Methods*, Dec. 21, 1916, pp. 715–722. The letter in question is found in pages 718–720. A part of this is quoted below. From these two documents the following picture emerges.[1]

The first statement of pragmatism came in a paper that Peirce read to "The Metaphysical Club": "I drew up a little paper expressing some of the opinions that I had been urging all along under the name of pragmatism."[2] The Club had its meetings in "the earliest seventies."[3] Peirce indicates that the "little paper" was read to the Club in 1871.

[1] Since this Appendix was written, a paper by Max Fisch, "Was There a Metaphysical Club?" has appeared which is a definitive account of the historical facts and of Peirce's accounts of the founding of the Metaphysical Club. For the full facts the reader should consult this paper. See also Fisch's "Chronicle of Pragmaticism" for further valuable information; on the philosophic background of the members of the club, see Wiener's *Evolution and the Founders of Pragmatism*.

[2] *CP* 5.13. In the letter to Mrs. Ladd-Franklin, Peirce says of the Club: "It was there that the name and doctrine of pragmatism saw the light," p. 719.

[3] *CP* 5.12. But in the letter to Mrs. Ladd-Franklin, Peirce writes: "In the sixties I started a little club called the Metaphysical Club," p. 719. In a letter, James tells a story about the meeting of the Club in 1874, *Letters*, II, 233.

This paper was received with such unlooked-for kindness, that I was encouraged, some half dozen years later, on the invitation of the great publisher, Mr. W. H. Appleton, to insert it, somewhat expanded, in the *Popular Science Monthly* for November, 1877 and January, 1888. . . . The same paper appeared the next year in a French redaction in the *Revue Philosophique* (Vol. VI, 1878, p. 553; Vol. VII, 1879, p. 39).[4]

The original paper that Peirce wrote for the Club, unfortunately, is not among his surviving manuscripts. The published paper was the result of some reworking of the original.[5]

It would appear, then, that in the years 1871 and 1872, Peirce's theory of meaning and the maxim of pragmatism received statement. Peirce's review of Fraser's edition of the *Works* of Berkeley, written in 1871, already contained some of the leading ideas of his pragmatism.

It was the first two papers of a series of six published in *Popular Science Monthly* that have come to be regarded as the major expressions of Peirce's pragmatism. The series was called "Illustrations of the Logic of Science." The first paper (published in 1877) and the second (published in 1878) were, respectively, "The Fixation of Belief" and "How to Make Our Ideas Clear."

In his University of California lecture of 1898, "Philosophical Conceptions and Practical Results," James first drew public attention to 'pragmatism' and to Peirce's role in the development of a theory of meaning. James's lecture was printed in 1898; but not until portions of the lecture discussing "Peirce's principle" appeared in James's other publications (in 1902, 1904)[6] did pragmatism really attract attention.

In the lecture James mistakenly said that Peirce introduced the term *pragmatism* in the 1878 paper, "How to Make Our Ideas Clear."[7] James may have been thinking of Peirce's original Club paper, or discussions at the time in which 'pragmatism' apparently was used. It is worth noting that Peirce did not at first use the word 'pragmatism' in a titular or emphatic way to designate some special doctrine; the pragmatic maxim was then regarded as part of a larger theory of inquiry and the study of signs. It was later that Peirce had some regrets that he had not made more of the word—and doctrine—in earlier days. It was later also, by some twenty years, that Peirce was encouraged to recall and describe what his earlier doctrine was—a fact that advises us to preserve some caution about Peirce's explanations and later reminiscences concerning the origins of his pragmatism. He wrote:

---

[4] *CP* 5.13.
[5] Peirce says in the letter to Mrs. Ladd-Franklin, p. 719: "I employed some Sundays in putting that piece into a literary form. . . . I patched up the piece I speak of . . . and it appeared in November, 1877." For a less famous but very illuminating statement by Peirce, see Appendix 3, sec. B below.
[6] 1902: *Varieties of Religious Experience*. In 1904, the lecture was reprinted with slight changes in *Journal of Philosophy, Psychology and Scientific Methods*. *Pragmatism* appeared in 1907.
[7] See *Pragmatism*, p. 46.

As late as 1893, when I might have procured the insertion of the word pragmatism in the *Century Dictionary*, it did not seem to me that its vogue was sufficient to warrant that step.

But he added privately in 1902:

> It is a singular instance of that over-modesty and unyielding self-underestimate on my part of which I am so justly proud as my principal claim to distinction that I should have omitted *pragmatism*, my own offspring, with which the world resounds.[8]

B.   Peirce and Chauncey Wright

In drawing attention to the remarkable thinker Chauncey Wright (1830–1875), Morris Cohen overstated Wright's influence on the development of Peirce's pragmatism. According to Cohen:

> There can be little doubt that Peirce was led to the formulation of the principle of pragmatism through the influence of Chauncey Wright.[9]

Cohen had in mind, primarily, Wright's view that "the principles of modern mathematical and physical science are the means through which nature is discovered, that scientific laws are the finders rather than merely the summaries of factual truths."[10] This is to quote Wright himself:

> Nothing justifies the development of abstract principles in science but their utility in enlarging our concrete knowledge of nature. The ideas on which mathematical Mechanics and the Calculus are founded . . . the theories of Chemistry are such working ideas,—finders, not merely summaries of truth.[11]

This conception of the general principles of empirical science as *means* to rather than summaries of truth, and whose functioning is that of prescribing certain operations for attaining new experimental truths, is certainly an expression of the instrumentalist version of the logical structure of science (see Part Four, Chapter Two). But the instrumentalist point of view had also been stated by Mill (see § 83 above), and Wright's comment above does not add anything exceptional to Mill's formulation of the idea. Moreover, Wright was a critically

---

[8] *CP* 5.13.
[9] Preface to *Chance, Love and Logic*, p. xvii. For Peirce's own account of this association with Wright and the founding of the "Metaphysical Club," see his letter to Mrs. Ladd-Franklin, Peirce commemorative issue of the *Journal of Philosophy, Psychology and Scientific Methods*, p. 719, or *CP* 5.12–13. Peirce's account does not confirm (or disconfirm) Cohen's statement above.
[10] Preface to *Chance, Love and Logic*, pp. xix–xx. Cohen also cites Wright's doctrine of "cosmic weather" as a source of Peirce's tychism. But see Madden's discussion and doubts on this, *C. Wright and the Foundations of Pragmatism*, pp. 82–91.
[11] "The Philosophy of Herbert Spencer" (1865), p. 436; *Philosophical Discussion*, p. 56; *The Philosophical Writings of Chauncey Wright*, p. 14.

able but thoroughly and fundamentally sympathetic student of Mill's empiricism.[12] Wright's instrumentalist empiricism, and his familiarity with scientific work and thought led him to note with special interest the relation of the logical structure of science to the conditions of experience and the procedures for linking theoretical principles to their verification in sensible experience. Wright was a critical empiricist, and was fully aware, in the furthering of scientific inquiries, of the use and value of ideally interpretative and hypothetical constructions of a subject matter, constructions not themselves directly confirmable by "sensuous tests." He thus refused to accept a narrowly positivistic view of the verifiability of scientific concepts, or an empiricism that failed to account for and appreciate these techniques. But ideal and theoretical constructions, he argued, while not directly subject to sensuous test, must satisfy a minimum requirement of providing consequences of a verifiable sort or supplying such consequences when conjoined with other constructions which are verifiable. Thus in the course of an extensive criticism of Spencer's "scientific" philosophy for its unscientific conception of the logic of science, Wright made an acute statement of this methodological insight:

> The *value* of scientific theories whatever their origin can only be tested by an appeal to sensible experience; by deductions from them of consequences which we can confirm by the undoubted testimony of the senses. Thus, while ideal or transcendental elements are admitted into scientific researches, though in themselves insusceptible of simple verification, they must still show credentials from the senses, either by affording from themselves consequences capable of sensuous verification, or by yielding such consequences in conjunction with ideas which by themselves are verifiable.[13]

From all this, however, and from what is known about the influence of Wright upon Peirce and James,[14] there is no evidence of a direct and precise connection between Wright's critical empiricism and the maxim of pragmatism (§ 21) of Peirce.[15] In regarding Wright as one of the founders of pragmatism, we are obliged to view his contribution as that of a penetrating, informed critical mind, the elder of Peirce and James, who in discussions undoubtedly affected and helped shape the thought and clarify the intent of Peirce's early expressions of pragmatism. As suggested in § 19, pragmatism was born in and resulted from a cooperative effort. A group of original and able thinkers in discussion produced this doctrine through the interchange of ideas. The major credit for inventive, first articulation must go to Peirce; much credit goes to·Wright and, of course,

[12] See Kennedy, pp. 482–484; Madden, *C. Wright and the Foundations of Pragmatism,* pp. 8 ff. For Peirce's account, *CP* 5.12.
[13] "The Philosophy of Herbert Spencer," p. 427; *Philosophical Discussions,* p. 47; *The Philosophical Writings of Chauncey Wright,* p. 7. For a discussion of the statement, see Kennedy, p. 497; Madden, *C. Wright and the Foundations,* pp. 74–77.
[14] For a recent and full survey, see Madden, *C. Wright and the Foundations.*
[15] Such was Kennedy's conclusion, pp. 498–503; and more recently, Madden's careful study and summary, *ibid.* cf. esp. pp. 79–81.

James. But other members of the Club were active. In a letter to Mrs. Ladd-Franklin,[16] Peirce records that Wright

> had a mind about on the level of J. S. Mill. He was a thorough mathematician. . . . He and I used to have long and very lively and close disputations lasting two or three hours daily for many years.

When he started the Metaphysical Club, Peirce says,

> Wright was the strongest member and probably I was next. Nicholas St. John Green was a marvelously strong intelligence. Then there were Frank Abbot, William James and others. It was there that the name and doctrine of pragmatism saw the light. There was in particular one paper of mine that was much admired and the ms. went around to different members who wished to go over it more closely. . . .

That paper, reworked and "patched up," as noted in section A above, became the first statement of pragmatism; "The Fixation of Belief" and "How To Make Our Ideas Clear" became the first two of a series of six papers published in the *Popular Science Monthly*, 1877–1878.[17]

Wright, then, was the "penetrating intellect" and philosophical "boxing master"[18] of ideas, but not the one influence that led Peirce to his pragmatism.[19]

[16] In the Peirce commemorative issue of *The Journal of Philosophy, Psychology and Scientific Methods*, pp. 718–720. The quoted passages here are from p. 719.
[17] *CP* 5.13 for Peirce's history of this event. For the papers, see *CP* 5.358 ff. and above, §§ 20, 21.
[18] *CP* 5.12.
[19] For a recent and informative study of the place of Abbot in Peirce's intellectual development, see the essay by Daniel D. O'Connor.
In defense of the thesis of Wright's influence on Peirce, it should be mentioned that Fisch in "A Chronicle of Pragmaticism," p. 444, finds that in Wright's review for the *Nation*, 1865, of Mill's *Examination of Hamilton*, Wright's own analysis of "belief and doubt, knowledge and ignorance, in terms of motives of action . . . is a nearer approach to that in Peirce's pragmatic essays of 1877–78 than anything so far in Peirce's own writings" (i.e., up to 1865).

APPENDIX THREE

Peirce on Pragmatism

A. Peirce's Statement

There exists among Peirce's papers a draft for a review of a book in which, in one very long paragraph, he expounds the meaning of *pragmatism*.[1] This is a particularly noteworthy document, this one long paragraph. It is, I should judge, the clearest and most complete single statement of what pragmatism is that Peirce ever wrote.[2] One sees here, in an integrated and summary form, each of the leading ideas that for Peirce form the matrix or follow as consequences from the "maxim" of pragmatism. Thus the relation of the maxim to a theory of signs, which it is "grounded upon," is made clear, and so too is Peirce's conception of the nature of *thought*, of the *real*, and of how the latter includes not only existent objects but the realism of "general types and would-bes."

There are two points in this statement that call for special notice because of their bearing upon the exposition of Peirce's pragmatism in the text (§ 20 above). First, in contradistinction to what he often claimed in other writings, Peirce here says that *pragmatism* as a "maxim of logic . . . as was shown at its first enouncement, involves a whole system of philosophy." Second, it should be observed that in describing the maxim as furnishing "a method for the analysis of concepts," Peirce goes on to draw the reader's attention to the "exclusion from this statement of all reference to sensation." He thus takes pains to divorce his pragmatism from the practicalism and nominalism of James and his followers and from their emphasis upon pragmatic meaning as referential to objects and sensations. Thus for James (as we saw in §§ 27, 30) "the maxim of pragmatism is directed to objects, practical reactions and sensations;"[3] for Peirce the maxim leads

[1] See *CP* 8.191. The draft was for a review of Nichols' *A Treatise On Cosmology* (1904). The review appeared in *The Monist*, XV (April 1905).
[2] I have not examined the unpublished MSS of Peirce.
[3] Thus, the whole of "our conception of the object" is "what conceivable effects of a practical kind the object may involve—what sensations we have to expect from it, and what reactions we must prepare," *Pragmatism*, pp. 46–47. See § 27 above.

to an analysis of concepts, which, quite unlike sensations, have "the mode of being of a general type."

The following is Peirce's remarkable statement entire.

B.   Peirce's Description of Pragmatism

Our standpoint will be pragmatism; but this word has been so loosely used, that a partial explanation of its nature is needful, with some indications of the intricate process by which those who hold it become assured of its truth. If philosophy is ever to become a sound science, its students must submit themselves to that same ethics of terminology that students of chemistry and taxonomic biology observe; and when a word has been invented for the declared purpose of conveying a precisely defined meaning, they must give up their habit of using it for every other purpose that may happen to hit their fancy at the moment. The word *pragmatism* was invented to express a certain maxim of logic, which, as was shown at its first enouncement, involves a whole system of philosophy. The maxim is intended to furnish a method for the analysis of concepts. A concept is something having the mode of being of a general type which is, or may be made, the rational part of the purport of a word. A more precise or fuller definition cannot here be attempted. The method prescribed in the maxim is to trace out in the imagination the conceivable practical consequences—that is, the consequences for deliberate, self-controlled conduct,—of the affirmation or denial of the concept; and the assertion of the maxim is that herein lies the *whole* of the purport of the word, the *entire* concept. The sedulous exclusion from this statement of all reference to sensation is specially to be remarked. Such a distinction as that between red and blue is held to form no part of the concept. This maxim is put forth neither as a handy tool to serve so far as it may be found serviceable, nor as a self-evident truth, but as a far-reaching theorem solidly grounded upon an elaborate study of the nature of signs. Every thought, or cognitive representation, is of the nature of a sign. "Representation" and "sign" are synonyms. The whole purpose of a sign is that it shall be interpreted in another sign; and its whole purport lies in the special character which it imparts to that interpretation. When a sign determines an interpretation of itself in another sign, it produces an effect external to itself, a physical effect, though the sign producing the effect may itself be not an existent object but merely a type. It produces this effect, not in this or that metaphysical sense, but in an indisputable sense. As to this, it is to be remarked that actions beyond the reach of self-control are not subjects of blame. Thinking is a kind of action, and reasoning is a kind of deliberate action; and to call an argument illogical, or a proposition false, is a special kind of moral judgment, and as such is inapplicable to what we cannot help. This does not deny that what cannot be conceived today may be conceivable tomorrow. But just as long as we cannot help adopting a mode of thought, so long it must be thoroughly accepted as true. Any doubt of it is idle make-believe and irredeemable paper. Now we all do regard, and cannot help regarding, signs as *affecting* their interpretant signs. It is by a patient examination of the various modes (some of them quite disparate) of interpretations of signs, and of the connections between these (an exploration in which one ought, if possible, to provide himself with a guide, or, if that cannot be, to prepare his courage to see one conception that will have to be mastered peering over the head of another, and soon another peering over that, and so on, until he shall begin to think there is to be no end of it, or that life will not be long enough to complete the study) that the pragmatist has at length, to his great astonishment, emerged from the disheartening labyrinth with this simple maxim in his hand. In distrust of so surprising a result he has searched for some flaw in its method, and for some case in which it should break down, but after every deep-laid plot for disproving it that long-working ingenuity could devise has recoiled upon his own head, and all doubts he could start have been exhausted, he has been forced at last to acknowledge its truth. This maxim once accepted—intelligently accepted, in the light of the evidence of its truth,—speedily sweeps all metaphysical rubbish out of one's house. Each abstraction is either pronounced to be gibberish or is provided with a plain, practical definition. The general leaning of the results is toward what the idealists call the naïve, toward common sense, toward anthropomorphism. Thus, for example, the *real* becomes that which is such as it is regardless of what you or I or any of our folks may think it to be. The *external* becomes that element which is such as it is regardless of what somebody thinks, feels, or does, whether about that external object or about anything else. Accordingly, the external is necessarily real, while the real may or may not be external; nor is anything absolutely external nor absolutely devoid of externality. Every assertory proposition refers to something external, and even a dream withstands us sufficiently for one description to be true of it and another not. The *existent* is that which reacts against other things. Consequently, the external world, (that is, the world that is comparatively external) does not consist of existent objects merely, nor merely of these and their reactions; but on the contrary, its most important reals have the mode of being of what the nominalist calls "mere" words, that is, general types and would-bes. The nominalist is right in saying that they are substantially of the nature of words; but his "mere" reveals a complete misunderstanding of what our everyday world consists of.

Peirce on Truth and Some References

to Boole

Our reflections on Peirce's version of truth as an ideal limit of inquiry prompt the following brief speculation.

Where information is lacking from Peirce himself as to the origins of his ideas, guesses are hazardous. Peirce was a widely read, eclectic thinker and student of the history of science and philosophy. The idea of truth as a limit approached by inquiry is a case in point. The idea, or something resembling it, had been conspicuous in idealist circles since Hegel, and was to be found in a number of earlier conceptions of the "unity of truth" (or truth as the unification of opposing ideas and philosophies)—in Hellenistic thought, in Arabic philosophy, in Pico della Mirandola, Leibniz, and Hegel. In the nineteenth-century belief in progress, the idea of exhaustive scientific truth ever coming closer to completion, also had a place.

It also happens that certain striking similarities can be found between Peirce's pronouncements on truth and some of the ideas expressed by Boole in *The Laws of Thought* (1854). One of the fundamental principles in Boole's algebra is that of '1' and '0' representing the two classes, Universe (or everything), and Nothing (or the null class).[1] Now these are the "two limits of class extension,"[2] and thus any classes of individuals, represented by the letters 'x,' 'y,' 'z,' etc., will be equal to either 1 or 0.[3] Further, classes that differ by differences of their members—say, the class of men and class of non-men—are simply represented as 'x' (or '1x') and '1 — x' (where the element x is taken as the class of men). The principle of contradiction is derived from one fundamental "law of thought"[4] and becomes:

$$(1) \quad x(1 - x) = 0$$

[1] *The Laws of Thought*, ch. 3, sec. 13.
[2] *Ibid.*, ch. 3, sec. 13.
[3] Classes are "equal" if their members are the same. The sign '=' means 'is' or 'are' in Boole's exposition.
[4] *The Laws of Thought*, ch. 2, sec. 9.

496

Thus, taking 'x' as the name of the class of men, (1) reads: "the class of things that are men and not men $= 0$" or, generally, "nothing is both x and not-x."

But it is not a difficult transition from construing '1' and '0' as the universal and null classes respectively to construing them propositionally:[5] '1' then represents the class of true propositions and '0' the class of false propositions. Here '1' and '0' still represent classes, but the elements of these classes for which the letters 'x,' 'y,' 'z,' etc., were names, under the new construction no longer serve as names of classes but rather as names of propositions. In this vein (1) becomes a principle holding for propositions or statements, disallowing any proposition x to be both true and false. Now a further possible move lies in injecting into this framework, or superimposing upon it, the more recondite philosophical notion of (for us) indeterminate propositions (or beliefs in propositions) whose status (for us) will be located somewhere between 1 and 0. The propositions x, y, z, etc., still fall exclusively into the classes 1 or 0. But a kind of surrogate proposition, 'our belief in x,' or 'our knowledge-at-present of x,' or 'the degree of confirmation of x' takes place somewhere between 1 and 0. One may note that in Whitehead's propositional interpretation of Boole's algebra, 'x1' or 'x $= 1$' is treated in the spirit of x being true and prompting "motives of assent"; 'x $= 0$' is taken as affirming that x is "self-condemned."[6]

Lest the introduction of the notions of 'belief in' or 'state-of-knowledge of x' seem too subjective as a representation of Peirce, we can switch to talking about *kinds of arguments*, a switch to talking about "experiential inference" and "genus of argument" which are Peircean locutions.[7] Propositions, says Peirce, "are either absolutely true or absolutely false."[8] But a genus of argument, by which propositions are inferred, will yield a certain proportion of true conclusions from true premisses.

A genus of argument is valid when from true premises it will yield a true conclusion—invariably if demonstrative, generally if probable.[9]

A "demonstrative" or analytic genus of argument will hence be placed in a class 1, akin by virtue of truth to the class 1 of true propositions. But other types of argument, yielding varying proportions of true conclusions from true premises, may be regarded as ranging between 1 and 0.

In any event, in thus philosophizing over Boole's elements x, y, z, etc., and taking '1' now to represent finished scientific truth, one may speak of continuous inquiry bringing our knowledge—or the affirmed and believed-in surrogate propositions or types of argument—in an approximation to 1. This, we saw (especially in §§ 22–24), is how Peirce sometimes speaks. The same idea is advanced in the speculative and metaphysical discussions of Boole's concluding chapter. Thus

[5] See Lewis and Langford, p. 17.
[6] *Universal Algebra*, p. 108. See also Quine, "Whitehead and the Rise of Modern Logic," p. 135.
[7] See § 22 above for instances.
[8] From Peirce's review of Venn, *CP* 8.2.
[9] *CP* 8.2.

Boole theorizes about the laws of thought—such as (1) above—and *being* becoming concomitants. This we also find in Peirce, and evidently he derived it from Schelling. But Boole also discusses the "ideal conditions" and limiting states by which our thinking continuously approaches truth. Referring to our ability to conceive accurately the "scientific elements of form, direction, magnitude," he adds in what was to become a theme characteristic of Peirce:

> an incurable imperfection attaches to all our attempts to realize with precision these elements . . . we can only affirm, that the more external objects do approach in reality, or the conceptions of fancy by abstraction, to certain *limiting* states, never, it may be, actually attained, the more do the general propositions of science concerning those things or conceptions approach to absolute truth, the actual deviation therefrom tending to disappear.[10]

[10] *The Laws of Thought*, p. 406.

Berkeley and Some Anticipations

of Pragmatism

Berkeley on the whole has more right to be
considered the introducer of pragmatism
into philosophy than any other one man, though
I was more explicit in enunciating it.

PEIRCE to JAMES[1]

On several occasions previously, references have been made to Berkeley as anticipating and influencing certain important developments in the history of
pragmatism. There are respects in which Berkeley is not at all a pragmatist, but
these do not concern us here. The several distinctive ideas well recognized by
Peirce, James, and Lewis as relevant to the historical formation of pragmatism,
do. This Appendix will serve to illustrate and substantiate the comments made in
earlier pages.

Berkeley's important creative contributions to philosophy and science have
been less noticed in modern times than has his effectiveness as a critic in behalf
of what he called "common sense," of the philosophies of Descartes, and of Locke
and Newton. His criticisms were primarily directed against the skepticism (thus
the lurking atheism) inherent in the Locke-Newton interpretation of the human
mind and its relation to the natural world. That world had been impressively
articulated in Newton's *Philosophiae Naturalis Principia Mathematica*, of 1686.

[1] From a letter of 1903, Perry, II, 425. In a description of the Metaphysical Club and of
the origin of his first papers, "the earliest attempt to formulate pragmatism," Peirce wrote
that "pragmatism . . . as a *practice,* had been, I think, best illustrated by Berkeley, especially
in his two works on vision." This important MS of 1909 is published by Fisch as an appendix to "Was There a Metaphysical Club?" pp. 24–29. For this passage, see p. 28. Peirce had
planned a volume in which "The Fixation of Belief" and "How to Make Our Ideas Clear"
were to be two chapters of an essay entitled "My Pragmatism." The document in question
was one of several drafts of a preface for the essay.

This recognition of the philosophic importance of Berkeley in the history of pragmatism,
it is worth remarking, was also felt by Calderoni and Vailati (§ 76), who regarded Berkeley's writings on vision as the source of their pragmatic theory of *prevision* (see above, Part
III, ch. 4, esp. note 90. In *Pragmatism*, pp. 89–90, James discusses Berkeley's "criticism of
'matter' " which he finds "was consequently absolutely pragmatistic."

The problem (referred to as "Locke's problem" in § 6) was that there seemed to be no equally impressive or even plausible explanation of how the human mind could ever have acquired knowledge of this world. The authoritative description of the world as a system of bodies composed of mass-particles, whose motions were given mathematical expression, simply excluded the presence of minds and the functions of sentient organisms. Newton and Locke attempted to provide explanations, guided by the mechanical model, of how the mind was able to know the world.[2] For knowledge it did have, as the great book of 1686 amply demonstrated. But these efforts, while roundly purporting to be empirical, invoking sense, experiment, and experience,[3] were subject to fatal logical difficulties, as Berkeley and Hume so forcibly pointed out.

Though prompted by moral and religious interests, Berkeley's criticisms are all concerned with the theory of knowledge. He argues for a new and more adequate conception of *mind, experience,* and *knowing*; at the same time he is acutely sensitive to the uses and abuses of language in philosophy. His critical investigations into the philosophizing of his predecessors, of Locke in particular, gave him an appreciation of how treacherous the professional language of philosophy could be if incautiously employed. It is this sensitivity to the role of language in achieving or defeating the purposes of philosophy[4] that guided Berkeley in what he called his own "common sense" outlook in contrast to the professional and "scientific" philosophizing of his day. Berkeley felt the contrast keenly, and expressed this in a comment penned in his notebook: "I side in all things with the mob." On the whole, the *ordinary* view and way of talking about knowledge and things known was to be preferred to the recondite and paradoxical doctrines of the philosophers. The same critical consciousness concerning the use of language led Berkeley to work out his own analytical test of the adequacy and function of terms and concepts. The method of testing became a criterion of meaning, as we shall see below. It is for this work, especially, that Berkeley received the attention and admiration of Peirce and James.

The object of Berkeley's critical attack was scientific materialism. For Berkeley, the Cartesian, Newtonian view of the world had become the foundation of an agnostic, morally impotent and conceptually confused philosophy of knowledge. The critical rejection of this philosophy was not unlike that conducted later by

---

[2] Locke's *Essay* is the classic attempt. For Newton's discussions of the subject see *Optics,* Book III, Query 31; the account of perception, *Optics,* p. 12, and Definition, pp. 108–109. These and related passages can be found in my *Newton's Philosophy of Nature,* pp. 99–105, 158–179.

[3] For Locke's famous appeal to *experience,* see the *Essay,* Book II, ch. 1, sec. 2. This turn to experience is discussed above, Part I, ch. 1 and again, in connection with pragmatism, §§ 27 and 106. Newton's argument that science is based on *experiments* ("the qualities of bodies are only known to us by experiments"), *experience* ("That the abundance of bodies are hard we learn by experience"), and *sensation* ("That all bodies are inpenetrable, we gather not from reason, but from sensation"), is found in *Principia,* Book III, the third of the Rules of Reasoning in Philosophy. The argument is discussed above in §§ 7 and 82.

[4] Or more strictly, one criterion for gauging the successful "communicating of ideas marked by words." For Berkeley recognized other uses and ends of language, see *Principles,* sec. 20.

the pragmatists against positivism, materialism, and empiricism of the nineteenth century—outlooks in which were found the same spectator theory of knowledge and separation of knowledge and value[5] characteristic of the philosophy that Berkeley had sought to destroy.

Kant (see § 10 above) is usually credited with introducing into modern philosophy the concept of the mind as an active agent in the acquisition of knowledge. The understanding prescribes, it does not merely receive, the order of experience. The Kantian theory of mind is then regarded as very different from the one developed by the British empiricists, who had argued for a spectator-like version of mind, that is, of the mind as wholly passive and acted upon by external objects and powers. The conception of mind as an active condition in the organization and interpretation of experience is important in the history of pragmatism. But that history derives from Berkeley as well as from Kant.

Berkeley describes mind as an active power, a "spirit." "By the word *spirit* we mean only that which thinks, wills, and perceives; this, and this alone constitutes the signification of that term."[6] Mind is then an activity of perceiving, not a Cartesian container of ideas nor a Newtonian mechanism. What the mind immediately perceives *is*, and what *is*, is a sensible quality, a thing or "immediate object of sense." Of these things, says Berkeley, "their *esse* is *percipi*."[7] To be, is to be perceived. Descartes and Locke had both argued that, in perceiving anything, the mind is most immediately aware of its own ideas; thus ideas are the primary objects and materials of knowledge. Much to the confusion of his readers, Berkeley proceeded to warp this traditional usage to suit his own novel theory. Since ideas are what the mind immediately perceives, since nothing but ideas can be immediately perceived, the objects of knowing, the *things* known are *ideas*. Moreover, since to *be* is to be perceived, and since what is perceived is an idea, or collection of ideas, existing things are ideas. Berkeley was aware of how strange this might seem: "it sounds very harsh to say we eat and drink ideas, and are clothed with ideas. I acknowledge it does so."[8] But he gave his reasons for this departure from the ordinary way of speaking about existing objects,[9] and he was willing to concede that 'thing' and, with caution, even 'matter' might be more acceptable than his use of 'idea.'[10]

What, we may ask, is the essential feature of *mind*, since it is not a thing or object and hence cannot itself be perceived? Berkeley answers: perceiving and inferring (i.e., thinking)—generally, with the aid of language created for this

[5] Thus, see above, §§ 27–28 and 99–101.
[6] *Principles,* sec. 138.
[7] *Ibid.,* sec. 3.
[8] *Ibid.,* sec. 38.
[9] *Ibid.,* secs. 38–39.
[10] E.g., the Third Dialogue: "In common talk, the objects of our senses are not termed *ideas* but *things*. Call them so still, provided you do not attribute to them any absolute external existence, and I shall never quarrel with you for a name. . . ." ". . . Retain the word *matter,* and apply it to the objects of sense, if you please, provided you do not attribute to them any subsistence distinct from their being perceived. I shall never quarrel with you for an expression."

purpose, to infer from given experience other attended experiences. Experience so interpreted and codified serves as marks or signs forewarning of other future experiences. In this emphasis upon acts of understanding as the apprehension of signs, and of the relation of "ideas" to the "things" they are about as signs to things signified, Berkeley is a descendant of the Ockhamite tradition.[11] Experience interpreted intelligently is sign-ificant of further experience.

> The connexion of ideas [i.e., things] does not imply the relation of *cause* and *effect*, but only of a mark or *sign* with the thing *signified*. The fire that I see is not . the cause of the pain I suffer upon my approaching it, but the mark that forewarns me of it.[12]

The "mark that forewarns" is a sign that has become interpreted and the material for predictions based upon past experience and observed "connexions of ideas." The fire I see is a sign that, under certain other conditions, I will suffer pain. To be thus forewarned of how the fire as *seen* might (under specified conditions) be *felt*, is an aid in avoiding that possible experience.

While this last point does not receive special notice in Berkeley's writings, it is frequently encountered. For, clearly, Berkeley was setting forth a theory of empirical knowledge in which the act of knowing finds expression in a conditional form (often, as in the above case of the fire, as counterfactual conditionals[13]) and in which the significance of an idea (e.g., fire) *is* the class of empirical consequences ("connexions") that *would* follow from the fulfillment of certain antecedent conditions. In this theory, the outlines of Peirce's pragmatism of § 21 are evident.

A simple schematic way of representing some of these last reflections may make what has been said somewhat clearer and will prove useful for elucidating some matters to come.

Let us adopt the following conventions: Let $I_1, I_2, I_3, \ldots$ etc. represent single *ideas* (or sensations); let $Ca, Cb, \ldots$ etc. represent the "regular" *conditions* under which, as Berkeley says, "such and such ideas are attended with such and such other ideas, in the ordinary course of things."[14] These "trains" or attendances of ideas make up the "laws of Nature," according to Berkeley.[15] Finally, let us use the symbol of the arrow '$\rightarrow$' to represent the *sign* function, the *signification* of ideas. The arrow represents that capacity of an idea I_1 to serve as a "mark" or "signify," as Berkeley puts it. Thus I_1 becomes: $I_1 \rightarrow. \ldots$ The arrow represents the all-important field of *relations*, of "connexions" among ideas. Con-

---

[11] For a further explanation of this remark, see my "Historical Patterns," from which the next several paragraphs have been borrowed with minor revisions.

[12] *Principles,* sec. 65.

[13] I.e., the fire I see warns me of pain I *would* suffer *if* I move in such and such a direction. I thus decide *not* to fulfill this conditional. For Berkeley's recognition of the role of counterfactual conditions see the next to the last sentence of the passage quoted below, identified in note 18. In § 21 we took note of Peirce's awareness of the function of counterfactual statements in his theory of empirical knowledge. See also Appendix 7.

[14] *Principles,* sec. 30.

[15] *Ibid.,* sec. 30.

nections, Berkeley insisted, and here he was followed by Hume, are not necessary relations, nor are they forces or powers. Ideas (i.e., things) are related
to other ideas (or things) as *signs* to things *signified*, "by an habitual connexion
that experience has made us to observe between them."[16]

Now, reverting to the passage quoted above, to see the *fire* (i.e., the visible
idea, I_1) as a sign of *pain* (i.e., the feeling, I_2) under certain conditions (i.e., my
moving in such and such a way, conditions Ca) is to reason:

$$i) \quad I_1 \text{ and } Ca \to I_2.$$

To avoid the unpleasant consequent in (i), the sensation of pain, I_2, we will act
to avoid conditions Ca, thus seeking to avoid the experience I_2, and leaving the
conditional (i) unfulfilled. A child, learning that the fire he sees can be painful,
gradually establishes "an habitual connexion" among the components I_1, Ca, and
I_2 of (i).

Knowledge, then, consists of conditionals like (i).

> . . . We learn by experience, which teaches us that such and such ideas are attended
> with such and such other ideas, in the ordinary course of things.
>   This gives us a sort of foresight, which enables us to regulate our actions for
> the benefit of life. . . . That food nourishes, sleep refreshes . . . all this we know
> not by discovering any necessary connexion between our ideas, but only by the
> observation of the settled laws of Nature. . . .[17]

Since man acts to fulfill, or to avoid fulfilling various possible experiential conditionals, this theory suggests a thoroughly active conception of knowledge as an
ordering of experience according to the satisfaction of interests lying in the
future. That the primary function of thought is the control of future experience
is, as we have seen (in §§ 99–101, 106) one of the basic ideas in the philosophy
of pragmatism.

Berkeley also emphasizes the practical character of natural knowledge.

> We may, from the experience we have had of the train and succession of ideas in
> our minds, often make, I will not say uncertain conjectures, but sure and well-
> grounded predictions concerning the ideas we shall be affected with pursuant to
> a great train of actions, and be enabled to pass a right judgment of what would
> have appeared to us in case we were placed in circumstances very different from
> those we are in at present. Herein consists the knowledge of nature. . . .[18]

Several conclusions can be drawn from the observations we have been making.

1) For something to be a *sign*, as distinct from sheer sensation (or idea), the
mind must make its contribution. Mind invests the raw data of sense with "significance." The once naked datum, for all of its engaging simplicity and aborigi-
nal vivacity, gets reformed by that bustling missionary, thought. The datum's

---

[16] *New Theory of Vision,* sec. 147.
[17] *Principles,* secs. 30–31.
[18] *Ibid.,* sec. 59.

unique presence is turned into something transitional and referential: the palpable *thing* becomes a *sign of* other things. Such is the conversion of native sentience to the civilized mores of knowledge.

One grants, of course, that for Berkeley, Divine mind also infuses the empirical world with significance. But in the absence of knowers, of minds (and God), if fire could be supposed to exist at all, it would *be* as a flame perhaps, but void of all significance. As a *sign* of other experiential conditions (as endowed with the arrow function lately discussed), *that* fire would not be at all. This is to say that the intelligible character of fire, or any other thing, consists in its interpretative content. But it is minds that do the interpreting. So Berkeley says:

> We know a thing when we understand it; and we understand it when we can interpret or tell what it signifies. Strictly, the sense knows nothing. We perceive indeed sounds by hearing, and characters by sight. But we are not therefore said to understand them.[19]

Understanding, Berkeley adds, is of "the connexion of natural things."

In other words, a single entertainment of sensation, unrelated to past experience, custom or habit, would not constitute knowledge, for Berkeley. For the sensation would not be "understood" as a sign.[20]

2) In saying, as he does above, that "the sense knows nothing," Berkeley is not repudiating his earlier radical empiricism. He is simply making explicit a logical condition of the position he had maintained from the start. The single sensation, the idea as such, is not knowledge, as we have been noticing above. This feature of Berkeley's theory of knowledge is interesting, among other reasons, for its anticipation of the analyses of the role of sensation in knowledge of Peirce, Dewey, Mead, and Lewis.

3) The scheme we have adopted in (i) also applies to Berkeley's analysis of objects. Objects are collections or "a congeries" of ideas or predictably associated sensible qualities.

> I see this cherry, I feel it, I taste it; and I am sure *nothing* cannot be seen or felt or tasted; it is therefore *real*. Take away the sensations of softness, moisture, redness, tartness, and you take away the cherry. . . . a cherry, I say, is nothing but a congeries of sensible impressions, or ideas perceived by various senses, which ideas are united into one thing (or have one name given them) by the mind because they are observed to attend each other. Thus when the palate is affected with such a particular taste, the sight is affected with a red color, the touch with roundness, softness, etc. Hence, when I see and feel and taste in sundry certain manners, I am sure the cherry exists, or is real; its reality being in my opinion nothing abstracted from those sensations.[21]

[19] *Siris,* sec. 253.
[20] As early as the *New Theory of Vision* he points this out. See the argument about a first experience of sight, sec. 41 (or a blind man suddenly made to see, the famous problem Molyneux sent to Locke, for which, see Locke's *Essay,* 2nd edn. [1694], Book II, ch. 9, sec. 8). See also secs. 147, 153.
[21] The Third Dialogue.

The name 'cherry' is thus not the name of an idea, but of a collection. Here I_1 (red color) $\rightarrow I_2$ (tart taste) $\rightarrow I_3$ (odor) ... etc. Also, any one idea, or member of a congeries, may signify the rest, thus: $I_3 \rightarrow I_1$, $I_2 \rightarrow I_1$, etc. As Berkeley argues in the *Theory of Vision*, visible ideas become associated with ideas of touch: the sensation of what we see is a sign of what, under Ca, we would touch. But in the dark, ideas (or sensations) of touch serve as signs of what we would see, if it were light.

A substance, such as a cherry, is nothing more than a class of sensible qualities whose members are (under certain conditions C) significant of one another. A substance is, therefore, not an independently existing thing; indeed, it is not a thing at all, but a *name* for what, traditionally, would be called the accidents or predicates of a thing. The thing may be a cherry or a die.

> ... To me a die seems to be nothing distinct from those things which are termed its modes or accidents. And to say a die is hard, extended, and square is not to attribute these qualities to a subject distinct from and supporting them, but only an explication of the meaning of the word *die*.[22]

Berkeley was fond of a venerable analogy according to which the system of nature is likened to a language.[23] The "connexions" of things, $I_1 \rightarrow I_2 \rightarrow I_3$ ... etc., as in (i), is compared to the order of words, or signs, in a system of language. Knowledge is then described as an apprehension of the grammar of nature. This is brought out most clearly in *Siris*, although the theme, and the analogy, are found in earlier writings.[24]

> There is a certain analogy, constancy, and uniformity, in the phenomena or appearance of nature, which are a foundation for general rules: and these are a grammar for the understanding of nature, or that series of effects in the visible world whereby we are enabled to foresee what will come to pass, in the natural course of things. ...[25]

And again:

> As the natural connexion of signs with the things signified is regular and constant, it forms a sort of rational discourse. ...[26]

4) Berkeley's analysis of knowledge, and of the objects of knowledge, suggested to Mach and William James a reductive radical empiricism and a thoroughly instrumentalistic conception of science (see Part Four, Chapter Two above). To Peirce it suggested the leading principles of pragmatism; and these received expression in Peirce's review, in 1871, of Frazer's edition of the works of Berkeley.[27]

---

[22] *Principles*, sec. 49.
[23] The comparison goes back at least to Plato's *Cratylus* and *Theaetetus*. It often appears in works by Renaissance and seventeenth-century writers.
[24] *New Theory of Vision*, sec. 147; *Principles*, sec. 44.
[25] *Siris*, sec. 252.
[26] *Ibid.*, sec. 254.
[27] *CP* 8.7–38. See above, § 23.

Berkeley's critical counsel that meaningful language be explicitly correlated with sense experience, that the meaning of an expression, or sign, is its specifiable empirical consequences (for Berkeley is the originator of the "verifiability theory of meaning" and "operationalism"); that all predication and all assertions about the objects of experience are predictive; that given data are inferentially significant of other data, in the manner indicated above in (i)—these insights are expanded and made central to the pragmatism of Dewey and Lewis. Both men agree with Berkeley that meanings have a futurative reference, to use Peirce's expression, and that immediate experience is not knowledge but material *for* knowledge as a condition for probability judgments about future experience. And, as remarked earlier (as well as in § 100), to anticipate the future is to evaluate and partially control events passing and those to come.

5) As we have seen illustrated by (i), Berkeley maintains that we understand an idea or sense-impression I_1, when we recognize the regular ways in which I_1 is a sign of certain other ideas signified by I_1. A parallel argument is to be found in Berkeley's method of determining the "significance" or "meaning" of words and alleged ideas. Names or descriptive terms are understood in a manner closely analogous to the arrow function for ideas. In nearly the same way that, in (i), the fire seen is a sign of something that may be felt (i.e., that $I_1 \rightarrow I_2$), so words—that is, those words purporting to have some empirical reference—are signs of ideas (i.e., of sensible qualities, or classes of qualities). The construction of (i), illustrative of the "significance" of *ideas*, is extendable to the significance of *words*. And in general, Berkeley's analysis of the significance of objects (such as the cherry or the die above) is one with his analysis of the meaning of words.[28]

Berkeley's critical criterion governing the meaning of descriptive terms then comes to this: A term T, purported to have some empirical reference, is significant to just the extent that a definite class K of ideas or sensible qualities I_1, I_2, I_3, ... I_n is signified by T. Thus, $T \rightarrow K$. Where no such class K is specifiable for some T, that T is meaningless. But also, if two seemingly different terms, T_1 and T_2, on analysis turn out to signify just the same class K, then the difference between T_1 and T_2 is merely verbal. This last consideration is an important feature of Berkeley's reductive analysis of terms and of objects alike. Thus, as we observed above, the *object* cherry, or die, is, on analysis, a collection of ideas or sensible qualities, $I_1 \rightarrow I_2 \rightarrow I_3$ ... etc. But Berkeley also argues that a single *term* T_1 (say, 'die') is the equivalent of, or replaceable by some group of terms $T_2, T_3,$ T_4 (e.g., 'hard,' 'extended,' 'square'), which as a class K of *terms* serves to explicate the one term T_1. Briefly, since $T_2, T_3, T_4 = K$, then $T_1 \rightarrow K$; because $T_1 = T_2, T_3, T_4$. For we found Berkeley urging that in describing a die as "hard, extended, and square," we are not attributing these qualities to a subject, but rather we are giving

an explication of the meaning of the word *die*.[29]

Berkeley's well-known application of the criterion of meaning just discussed

28 With the qualification mentioned above in note 4.
29 *Principles,* sec. 49.

was to the philosophic concepts of 'substance' and 'matter.' Essentially, he sought to show that no specification of a discernible class K of empirical conditions could be given for these terms. It was in this vein that he conducted his examination of the assertion, "matter supports extension." What, he asks, is the meaning (in effect, the pragmatic clarification of concepts, as in § 21) of 'support' in this claim?

> But let us examine a little the received opinion.—It is said extension is a mode or accident of matter, and that matter is the *substratum* that supports it. Now I desire that you would explain what is meant by matter's *supporting* extension. Say you, I have no idea of matter and, therefore, cannot explain it. I answer, though you have no positive, yet, if you have any meaning at all, you must at least have a relative idea of matter; though you know not what it is, yet you must be supposed to know what relation it bears to accidents, and what is meant by supporting them. It is evident "support" cannot here be taken in its usual or literal sense—as when we say that pillars support a building; in what sense therefore must it be taken?[30]

Berkeley's own conclusion is that 'support' has no empirical or pragmatic significance nor, for that reason, has the received theory of material substance in which 'support' and 'substratum' are fundamental notions. Or, in the light of the distinctions made in the previous paragraph, Berkeley argues in effect that no class K of specifiable empirical conditions can be assigned for the term 'support' or, in this case, 'material substance.'

In the same methodological fashion Berkeley argued against the thesis that bodies might exist "external" to (i.e., unperceived by all) minds. For since the connection between supposed external bodies and ideas produced in the mind remained unexplained, the very same evidence (namely, sensations) available to support the belief in externally existing bodies could be used to deny that belief. Pragmatically, then, this evidence does not substantiate the belief.

> In short, if there were external bodies, it is impossible we should ever come to know it; and if there were not, we might have the very same reasons to think there were that we have now.

The "pragmatic" test case is then adduced:

> Suppose—what no one can deny possible—an intelligence without the help of external bodies, to be affected with the same train of sensations or ideas that you are, imprinted in the same order and with like vividness in his mind. I ask whether that intelligence has not all the reason to believe the existence of corporeal substances, represented by his ideas and exciting them in his mind, that you can possibly have for believing the same thing?[31]

I conclude, then, that Peirce was right: in Berkeley's method of critical analysis and in his conception of knowledge as the way of discerning how, for given human purposes, certain kinds of experience are, or can be made significant (as signs) of other kinds of experience, he was "the introducer of pragmatism into philosophy."

[30] *Ibid.*, sec. 16.
[31] *Ibid.*, sec. 20.

Analytic and Synthetic

Unpremeditated, in the process of writing this book, discussion has several times happened upon the notions of *analytic* and *synthetic*. The distinction of analytic and synthetic statements or propositions is familiar to the philosophically trained; but for other readers, unaware of this currently much discussed topic, some explanatory comments follow.

From an initial consideration of analyticity we are led to take a closer look at Dewey's theory of propositions and Lewis' analysis of meaning than earlier pages afforded. In each of these constructions, the idea of analyticity is of considerable relevance in helping to elucidate some features of critical importance.

A. Analyticity

In a tradition stemming from Kant, but anticipated in Descartes, Leibniz, and Hume, 'analytic' and 'synthetic' have been defined as follows. An *analytic judgment* is one in which the idea (or concept) of the predicate is contained in the idea (or concept) of the subject. The idea of the predicate thus adds no new information to that of the subject. In the example "all bodies are extended in space," the idea of *body* includes in it that of *extension*. The judgments "some bodies are hard" or "all bodies possess weight" are taken as synthetic judgments since the idea of *body* does not include that of *hardness* or *weight*.

A more recent tradition has preferred to talk of propositions or statements rather than judgments, when using this distinction. However, the sense in which the idea of a predicate is *contained in* the subject has remained obscure and an obstacle to a clear definition of 'analytic proposition.' Frequently recourse is had to definition: an analytic proposition is one whose predicate is contained in the definition of the subject; or, simply, analytic propositions are true by definition. But truth by definition depends in turn upon the idea of a *definiendum* being *synonymous* with a *definiens*, and the notion of 'synonymous' in this case is no less obscure than that of 'analytic.' A further objection to thus characterizing analytic propositions (as those whose predicates are somehow included in their subjects) is that this confines analyticity to subject-predicate propositions only, ignoring a large and important class of propositions that do not happen to take form.

However, the notions of *truth by definition* and *logical truth*, are prominent in customary ways of defining 'analyticity.' Thus, generally, analytic propositions or statements are described as those "true by definition" or those whose truth depends upon the meanings of their terms. Synthetic propositions, in contrast, are thought to have their truth determined not by the meanings of their terms, but by their relation to matters of fact. Roughly, they are true if what they assert about matters of fact is the case (as explained, e.g., by Tarski, see § 42 above); otherwise they are false.

Finally, one further way of describing analytic propositions is that they are such that their denials are self-contradictory; if S is an analytic statement, to affirm 'not-S' is to embrace a contradiction. But the idea of contradiction here seems to rest on that of meaning, or have at its root that of sameness of meaning (i.e., "you *mean* by 'brother,' 'male sibling,' so that you cannot *meaningfully*, that is *consistently*, deny the proposition 'if x is a brother, x is a male sibling'"). But 'synonymy,' we noticed, is no more clear than 'analyticity.'[1]

B.   The Import of the Distinction

The distinction of analytic and synthetic propositions has long been thought basic to a sound philosophic grasp of the nature of logic, mathematics, and empirical science.

The most influential critical empiricist of modern times is Hume. For Hume, all reasoning is of two kinds: (1) concerning *relations among ideas* (wherein demonstrative or logical *certainty* are found, e.g., '1 + 2 = 3'; the denials of these instances of reasoning are contradictory or "inconceivable"); (2) concerning matters of fact (here arguments attain *probability*, e.g., 'Brutus stabbed Caesar,' 'the sun will rise tomorrow,' based on accumulations of evidence; but denials of this reasoning are not *necessarily* false or inconceivable). Hume is led to argue from this distinction that no reasoning about facts is capable of demonstration or logical necessity. The distinction here between (1) and (2) has its parallel—with suitable modifications—in the doctrine of analytic and synthetic propositions. Thus Hume argues, in effect, that propositions about matters of fact are never analytic.

Hume's attack upon rationalism, in which he has been followed by many contemporary empiricists, draws its strength from the same distinction: rationalism

---

[1] For further difficulties on this and other attempts to define 'analytic,' see Quine, *From A Logical Point of View*, ch. 2.

either falls into unintelligibility by confusing (1) and (2), or claims but cannot prove that some knowledge of facts as in (2) possesses the certainty or necessity of the sort found in (1). Most empiricists since Hume have held to this distinction of kinds of reasoning, and most have agreed with Hume that while the truths of logic and mathematics exhibit necessity, i.e., are of kind (1) or analytic, they tell us nothing about matters of fact.[2] Most empiricists have also followed Hume in holding that empirical science depends upon both kinds of reasoning; empirical knowledge is "mixed": synthetic propositions are linked via analytic propositions, functioning as definitions and means of logical implication, into the network of organized knowledge.

Whereas synthetic propositions (Hume's second type of reasoning) depend for their truth upon matters of fact—hence, are sometimes described as *contingently* true or false—it was regarded as a major discovery in our time that all logic and mathematics consisted of analytic statements.[3] This was not always the prevailing view. In 1900 Russell thought that the propositions of pure mathematics were synthetic.[4] However, the contemporary opinion, one which Russell has done more than any other philosopher to establish, and seemingly demonstrated in *Principia Mathematica*, has been that the truths of logic from which mathematics was derivable are analytic.

We are not concerned here with the detailed attempts to establish the purely analytic character of logic and mathematics (nor are we concerned with the other thesis—not to be confused with the one under consideration—that all mathematics is derivable from logic, a thesis which by one sense of "all mathematics" and "derivable" was doomed by Gödel's proof of the incompletability of number theory). The concern at the moment is solely that of indicating how the analytic-synthetic distinction seemed central to a widespread agreement as to the interpretation of logic and mathematical statements in contrast to those of empirical science.

In recent years the entire foundation and rationale of the analytic-synthetic dichotomy, apparently so basic to logic and secure in philosophic renditions of mathematical statements, has been seriously challenged. When we are told that mathematical and logical statements are analytic, that empirical science consists of both analytic and synthetic statements, that analytic statements derive their analyticity from rules or definitions, etc.—in each case our grasp of what is said is as precise as is our understanding of what 'analytic' means. In failing to be very sure about the meaning of the latter term we can hardly be confident about the

---

[2] Mill is an exception. He suggests—not always clearly— that the truths of mathematics were highly confirmed synthetic propositions, thus *conceivably* or *possibly* falsified. See *Logic*, Book II, ch. 6, secs. 2–3 on his discussion of the propositions of arithmetic as "generalizations from experience" and how (sec. 3) "1 + 1 = 2" could be falsified in application.

[3] This thesis had been stated earlier but seemed to have its clarification and substantiation in our day. Leibniz had described the truths of reason (foreshadowing Hume's point 1 above) as true for all possible worlds. This endows them with the analytic character. But he also viewed the truths of fact as taking an analytic form.

[4] See his *Critical Exposition of the Philosophy of Leibniz,* p. viii.

informative value of these contexts in which the notion of analyticity predominates. Such is the claim put forth by those who find that analyticity does not admit of precise formula or definition.[5]

C. The Analytic, Pragmatism, Dewey on Propositions, Lewis on Meaning

I have discussed some aspects of the question of analyticity in § 80 and will not repeat them here. There are, however, several issues to be noted in which the controversy over the analytic-synthetic distinction is relevant to the present study.

1) A pragmatic rendition of the idea of analyticity (one to be enlarged upon differently in the discussion of Dewey below) might first suggest itself sketchily as follows:

In the actual practice of empirical inquiries some statements, judgments, and kinds of information are operative as, in effect, analytic truths. That is, in practice, some statements are treated as privileged, as not only true but immune to questioning and revision. These tend to be focal and basic to the organization and direction of inquiry, functioning as presuppositions and leading principles for the further articulation of inquiry. To challenge these would thus be to commence an inquiry of a radical and unusual kind into the fundamental theoretical system of some part (or even the whole) of a science. Inquiries into the conceptual foundations of a science, presenting the possibility of revolutionary changes or a major overhauling of scientific theory, are obviously of a different order from inquiries that are facilitated and controlled by presumably well established theories. Every student in a laboratory course has had the experience of not coming out with the "right" results of an "experiment"; but the deviant and sometimes bizarre result is not hailed as a refutation of the old, a heralding of a new chapter in scientific theory. The student is told to do the work over again until he gets it "right." The conditions that determine what is "right" in such cases function as a guide of experimental procedures. As such these are privileged. They are not questioned; they are themselves necessary to the asking of questions, and are the standards for the correct answers.

Fundamental statements of the kind thus suggested do partake of *some* of the characteristics of analyticity as usually characterized to this extent: they are taken as true, and treated, moreover, as statements that will never be factually falsified. They are thus true "come what may," as Lewis says. Still, statements of this kind are not all that have been claimed or wanted as *analytic*. For we can conceive of alternatives to the statements of science—fundamental and procedurally necessary though they be. Such statements will never be falsified perhaps; but they could

---

[5] The main criticism is to be found in Quine's *From A Logical Point of View*, ch. 2. For further discussion and more of the literature, see his *Word and Object* and references therein. A careful investigation of this subject, leading to a "reconsideration of empiricism" from a pragmatic point of view, is to be found in Pasch.

conceivably be falsified, and analytic statements are such as cannot (i.e., not possibly) be falsified. Analytic statements, then, are necessarily true—true by virtue of meaning. But the problem remains: Is the appeal to 'necessary truth' or 'meaning' in this description any clearer than the term 'analytic' thus being clarified?

Perhaps in the end one must resort to defending the legitimacy of 'analytic' as in general a sensible notion for representing certain uses of natural language, but, like most natural language uses, not susceptible to precise formulation or inflexible application to specific cases.

The point of view suggested above, viz., to find a procedural partial equivalent of analytic statements in those that occupy a privileged status in scientific inquiries, is also vague. To define and specify precisely what a privileged status for statements really consists of may be difficult, perhaps impossible. For one thing, 'privileged,' like 'stipulation' or 'assumption,' refers to contexts and distinctions therein. Thus a statement S_1 is privileged and immune to revision or rejection relative to certain other statements S_2, S_3 . . . , in some context of statements or under some given circumstances. 'Analytic' is conceivably in this same boat. A statement S_1 is *analytic* relative to——what? For Carnap, S_1 is analytic in a certain language L_1. But there are difficulties with this procedure.[6]

What I have suggested above, however, is less a matter of semantical theory and more a rudimentary matter of practice when scientific investigations are launched. Thus we can observe something like the following distinction in use. In the organization and progress of a given inquiry I, certain statements Sa are analytic relative to other statements, Ss, meaning: (a) any Ss statement that would falsify an Sa statement is false; (b) Sa statements function as logical conditions of truth and relevance for Ss statements, thus Sa statements are regulative and directive of I; (c) in some inquiry I, if any Sa statements were to be challenged or opened for revision, *that* decision and the reasoning for it would constitute another and different inquiry—an inquiry into fundamental portions of scientific theory.

I do not pretend that this explains or defines 'analytic in I,' but do suggest that (a), (b), and (c) reflect something of the practices of scientists engaged in their investigations. It will be evident, however, that this way of construing analyticity leaves the notion scarcely recognizable by the traditional earmarks discussed earlier.

There are some suspected shortcomings in the above idea. Those philosophers who want to accept or reject *analyticity* as a property of statements, or language rules, will not be impressed with this tack toward a relativity of statements and strategic decisions—attitudes of inquirers to statements in inquiry—as the way of construing 'analytic' or its equivalent. For the analytic then becomes descriptive of attitudes and resolutions adopted concerning classes of statements, not a dis-

---

[6] Noted in passing in § 80 and discussed by Quine in *From A Logical Point of View*, ch. 2. Among other matters, Quine points out some problems in how *a* language L is determined.

tinctive property of statements or meanings. Further, in considering mathematical statements or those of logic, there is a problem of whether any conceivable circumstances would occasion their revision. This was queried earlier (and in a note in § 80).

2) Of the pragmatists, Lewis has given the most detailed account of how a priori and analytic propositions, while possessing necessary truth and immune to empirical falsification, can nonetheless be subject to revision or abandonment (see § 45). Dewey also has set forth a theory of universal propositions which recognizes them as formulating necessary relations among kinds of characteristics and possible modes of acting. Accordingly, Dewey maintains, certain propositions may have a definitory, or logically true status in specific inquiries, and yet be dependent for their acceptance upon standards of relevance and usefulness in integrating inquiry and assisting it to a conclusion. Some remarks on these matters follow.

3) In this theory of logic, Dewey is so devoted to describing and explaining the course and operations of inquiry in transforming problematic situations and existential conditions of such situations, that issues concerning logic and the formalization of discourse simply lie outside his concern. If, indeed, Dewey would accept the legitimacy of logical issues separable from the context of the theory of inquiry, it is speculative as to what his own attitude to them would be. As to the question of the analytic and synthetic, Dewey does seem to recognize the need of distinctions. But the distinctions do not repeat traditional doctrine (as surveyed in 1 above). The distinctions he is led to make are "operational" as he sees them, or "functional" as means in the development and successful termination of inquiry. The institution of formal distinctions among propositions, like everything else for Dewey, is relevant and acceptable only in contributing to the clarification of inquiry, in this case, "the structure of inquiry."[7] The entire discussion of formal properties of propositions, relations, language, thus has this orientation: "formal relations state conditions to be materially satisfied."[8] The vision always is directed to the *application* of formal techniques and idioms in the *directing* of inquiry. Dewey is thus not concerned with "pure forms"[9] in any possible (or plausibly suggested) separation from existential conditions and operations in inquiry. But just such a separate status has usually been supposed to characterize the analytic, the a priori, logical truth, and logical necessity.

The closest that Dewey comes to arguing for logically necessary truths or analytic propositions traditionally conceived, is in his identification of what he calls

[7] This is the title of Part II of the *Logic*.
[8] *Logic*, p. 382.
[9] *Logic*, p. 382; and cf. pp. 376–379; and p. 372, where Dewey states that his "logical theory holds that forms are forms of matter." Also, p. 386: "forms regularly accrue to matter in virtue of the adaptation of materials and operations to one another in the service of specified ends. . . . in all cases of formed-materials, form and matter are instituted, to develop and function in strict correspondence with each other. Every tool (using the word broadly to include every appliance and device instituted and used to effect consequences) is strictly *relational*, the relational form being that of means-to-consequences, while anything that serves as effective means has physical existence of some sort."

"universal propositions."[10] Dewey distinguishes two kinds of general propositions: the *generic* and the *universal*. The distinction corresponds roughly to the demarcation of perceptual and conceptual materials and conditions in the ordering of inquiry and the institution of judgment.[11] It also reflects Peirce's differentiation of *material* and *formal* leading principles as observed above in § 85.

Generic propositions are about "kinds and classes in the sense of kinds."[12] These have existential reference to traits of existing things and of kinds of things. Universal propositions, on the other hand, "are formulations of possible ways or modes of acting and operating."[13] Dewey does insist in a way not altogether clear that universal propositions are existential:

> Entertained and developed as *possibilities* of ways of acting which are *existentially* general (because they are *ways* and not singular acts or deeds) they acquire *logical* form.[14]

But he also says of the hypothetical 'if . . . then . . .' form of these propositions that: "the relation is purely logical, and the terms 'antecedent' and 'consequent' are to be understood in a logical, not an existential sense."[15] Moreover, he adds that "a universal hypothetical proposition has the form of a definition in the logical sense."[16] In preparing the reader to see the distinction between generic and universal propositions, Dewey cites "all men are mortal" as interpretable: "All men have died or will die." This is to assert a *generic proposition* about spatio-temporal matters of fact, an inductive proposition "of a certain order of probability."[17] Taken as a *universal proposition*, however, "all men are mortal"

> means that "If any thing is human *then* it is mortal": a necessary interrelation of the characters of *being* human and *being* mortal. Such a proposition does not imply nor postulate that either men or creatures who die actually exist. It would be valid, if valid at all, even if no men existed, since it expresses a *necessary* relation of abstract characters.[18]

The universal proposition thus described comes as close as anything can (in Dewey's theory) to passing for an *analytic* proposition. But there are difficulties in this identification. Dewey discusses in some detail two kinds of universal propositions. One kind is exemplified by the laws of mathematical physics (and, presumably, the mathematical laws of natural sciences generally). A physical law

[10] On universal propositions, see *Logic*, pp. 254–255, 264, 271 ff. There is a general sense in which no proposition can be analytic for Dewey, for since propositions are instruments in inquiry, they are not true or false (see § 40 above, with notes 102 and 122). But analytic propositions are usually said to be necessarily true or true by virtue of their meaning. This general restriction is waived in the present discussion.
[11] Cf. *Logic*, p. 274: "Universals and generics bear the same relation to each other in inquiry that material and procedural means sustain to each other in the institution of judgment."
[12] *Ibid.*, pp. 254–255. See, too, p. 268.
[13] *Ibid.*, p. 264. See, too, p. 271.
[14] *Ibid.*, p. 271.
[15] *Ibid.*, p. 271.
[16] *Ibid.*, p. 272.
[17] *Ibid.*, p. 256.
[18] *Ibid.*, p. 256.

"such as is expressed as a relation of abstract characters, is a universal hypothetical proposition."[19] Dewey cites as an illustration the Newtonian formulation of the principle of gravitation. The "law of gravitation is a formulation of the interrelation of the abstract characters mass, distance and 'attraction.' "[20] But, Dewey argues, since the proposition thus formulated represents "possible existential affairs" to which it may be applied, hypothetical universals of this kind are still subject to procedures of verification or to requirements of acceptability in the promotion and supporting of inquiry, i.e., requirements of relevance and effectiveness. Thus, Dewey frequently refers to a *testing* of these universal hypotheticals. Since they formulate possible operations and take a conditional form, their force and relevancy is tested by "execution of the operation that is prescribed and directed by the universal proposition." The proposition prescribes: *if* certain operations *then* certain consequences. If the prescribed operation is executed and the existential consequences indeed agree with content of the *then* clause (and if further evidence is adduced to show "that *only* if the antecedent is affirmed does the consequent follow"[21]), the proposition is "tested." Still *other* different universal hypotheticals might also prescribe operations whose formulated consequences also agree with these existential conditions. Thus the testing of one universal proposition requires considering it as a member of a system of related propositions more or less tested: the delimiting of possible universal propositions is effected through requirements of agreement with existential conditions *and* other propositions already established.[22] It is in this way that Dewey seeks to explain a *test* of a proposition that otherwise might be supposed to be untestable because logically true, or "a definition in its logical sense." Thus:

> a universal hypothetical proposition has the form of a definition in its logical sense. Thus the proposition "If anything is a material body, it attracts other material bodies directly as its mass and indirectly as the square of the distance" may read equally well in the linguistic form "*All* material bodies, etc." It is a (partial) definition of *being* a material body. It expresses a condition which any observed thing must satisfy if the property "*material*" is groundedly applicable to it. On the other hand, if things are found that on grounds provided by *other* universal propositions are determined to be material which yet fail to answer the requirements prescribed by the proposition quoted, then one or the other of the involved universal propositions must be revised and reformulated.[23]

---

19 *Ibid.*, p. 398.
20 *Ibid.*, p. 398.
21 *Ibid.*, p. 264. See, too, pp. 272–273.
22 This, I take it, is Dewey's point in *ibid.*, pp. 272–273: "Simple agreement of these actual conditions with the content of the apodosis clause of the hypothetical universal is not, however . . . a complete test of the hypothesis. The actual consequences must be shown, as nearly as possible, to be the only ones which would satisfy the requirements of the hypothesis. In order that the determination of this mode of satisfaction can be approximately attained, the universal in question must be one of a system of interrelated universal propositions. A universal proposition which is not a member of a system could, at the most, only produce consequences that agree with the conditions it prescribes, without excluding the possibility of their also agreeing with conditions prescribed by other conceptions."
23 *Ibid.*, p. 272.

The logic of the argument is very much the same as Lewis' pragmatic criterion for the a priori element in empirical knowledge (see § 45 above). But what distinguishes Dewey's universal hypothetical propositions from analytic propositions of old is not only the conditions of their testability thus described. Analytic propositions are said to be true (or necessarily true) by virtue of the meanings of the terms composing them. Dewey does not ascribe logical necessity to the relation of the contents of the clauses of the universal propositions we have been considering[24]—that is, one clause does not imply or entail another. For Dewey, implication holds between propositions, not among their contents. The clauses rather represent an analysis of a single conception into its logical constituents[25]—thus the definitional character of the proposition. But its "truth" is tied to the existential reference of the contents of its clauses in the manner indicated in above paragraphs. It is worth adding that on Dewey's theory, it seems that universal propositions (at least the first kind of universals thus far considered) become converted into generic ones in the process of testing them or in their application to existential conditions.[26]

So far we have considered but one kind of universal proposition, exemplified by propositions of mathematical physics. The other kind is found in the propositions of mathematics. These, unlike the former kind, are exempt from any existential or material limitations. In the case of a proposition such as '$2 + 2 = 4$,' says Dewey, "the interpretation to be put upon the contents is irrelevant to any material considerations whatever."[27] The former kind of universal propositions, say, physical laws, were limited in interpretation to *possible* existential applications, to what Dewey calls a "preferred or privileged interpretation, which is restrictive."[28] In the parallelogram law, which provides for calculations "ultimately applicable in existential determination," the content of 'forces' in that propositional formulation "affects the meaning of 'parallelogram.'"[29] But

> The contents of a mathematical proposition, *qua* mathematical, are free from the conditions that require any limited interpretation. They have no meaning or interpretation save that which is formally imposed by the need of satisfying the condition of transformability within the system, with no extra-systematic reference whatever. In the sense which "meaning" bears in any conception having even indirect existential reference, the terms have no meaning.[30]

[24] This, despite his saying that the relation of the *if* clause to the *then* clause is "necessary" and "purely logical," *ibid.*, p. 271. For see the explicit denial, commencing with "In neither of the two cases cited does one clause *follow* from the other," p. 272.
[25] *Ibid.*, p. 272.
[26] For the universal, in prescribing possible operations and existential conditions, then becomes *actualized* as a generic proposition in the process of testing. This "conversion," I suggest, is implied in Dewey's account of the "conjugate relation "of universals and generics and their cooperation.' Cf. *ibid.*, p. 275: "No grounded generic propositions can be formed save as they are products of the performance of operations indicated as possible by universal propositions."
[27] *Ibid.*, p. 398.
[28] *Ibid.*, p. 398.
[29] *Ibid.*, p. 398.
[30] *Ibid.*, pp. 398–399.

Here, in propositions illustrated by those in mathematics, we find Dewey's equivalent of the analytic proposition traditionally conceived. These, he says, "are certifiable by formal relations."[31] And this seems to mean that rules (of a syntactical kind) "determine" or fix the "terms or contents," the "material" of these propositions. "The type of relation which subsists between *propositions* in mathematical physics becomes here the determinant of the contents."[32] We are left with a sense, albeit vague, of certain propositions whose contents are defined by rules for using and relating terms in certain explicit ways.

It may be thought unfortunate that Dewey did not forthrightly characterize this last class of propositions as *analytic*. For then, to continue the thought, Dewey's philosophy of mathematics in his *Logic* (i.e., Chapter Twenty) might have gained in clarity of fundamental distinctions. But the notion of analyticity, we have seen earlier in section (1), is not so unquestionably clear as to be the touchstone of fundamental analyses of the propositions of logic and mathematics. At any rate, Dewey's interest was in an interpretation of mathematical discourse that accounted for two *distinguishable* yet not always separable features:

> The interpretation of the logical conditions of mathematical conceptions and relations must be such as to account for the form of discourse which is intrinsically free from the *necessity* of existential reference while at the same time it provides the *possibility* of indefinitely extensive existential reference—such as is exemplified in mathematical physics.[33]

One might have asked for a sharper and more basic distinction between propositions of mathematical physics and those of "pure" mathematics.[34] Or one might maintain that the distinction is a matter of degree, not of kinds of meaning or essential differences in content.[35] In either case one's preferences here will have been guided by a prior acceptance or repudiation of the notion of *analyticity* and its uses.

The stand taken on analyticity has significance for metaphysics. For if all statements are either analytic or synthetic and never both, and if the statements of logic and mathematics are analytic, no ontological or metaphysical consequences can be derived from them alone. If on the other hand the distinction is rejected, then presumably the laws and sentences of logical theory do entail some ontological consequences. Dewey saw the ontological issue and sided with those who, since Hume, have argued that mathematics and logic have no ontological ground. Speaking of mathematics, Dewey says:

> the system of interrelated meanings is *so* defined as to make possible a set of operations of transformations in which, on formal grounds—those determined by the

---

31 *Ibid.,* p. 399.
32 *Ibid.,* p. 399.
33 *Ibid.,* p. 394.
34 Such is the point of Nagel's critical comment in "Some Leading Principles of Professor Dewey's Logical Theory," pp. 579–581.
35 See the argument of White, "The Analytic and the Synthetic," who prefaces his discussion as being in accord with Dewey's attack upon dualisms.

postulates of the system—any given transformation is logically necessary. . . . While it is not claimed that this operational-functional interpretation of isomorphic patterns of relationships *disproves* the interpretation of mathematics that refers it to an ontological ground, it is claimed that it renders that interpretation unnecessary for *logical* theory leaving it in the position of any metaphysical theory that must be argued for or against on *metaphysical* grounds.[36]

The most salient feature of Dewey's theory of formal logic and logical necessity is his attempt to explicate the distinctive operational or functional characteristics of propositions rather than syntactical or semantical properties. His aim is to explain how the a priori and the logically necessary *function* in prescribing conditions to be satisfied in inquiry and judgment. Such is the spirit of the simple sketch of analyticity above in section (1).

4) Lewis' theory of the a priori has been discussed in § 45 and will not be restated here. On the subject of analyticity, Lewis took a more formalistic and traditional view than Dewey. He says in Leibnizian fashion: "an analytic proposition is one which would apply to or be true of every possible world."[37] But what, we might ask, is meant by a "possible world"? One answer comes easily: a *possible* world is one for which the falsification of analytic propositions is impossible. But if their falsification is impossible, then analytic propositions are necessarily true. The Leibnizian notion of "possible world" seems to be constructed with the help of ideas of necessary truth and analyticity—the very ideas it purports to illuminate.

But there are other more serious difficulties in Lewis' attempt to construct a technical version of analyticity as part of a more elaborate analysis of meaning.[38] There are difficulties, into which we need not go, in 'sameness of intension'[39] (corresponding to problems in defining 'synonymity') necessary to Lewis' definition of *analytic meaning*. There are difficulties in Lewis' concept of *sense meaning* basic to the analysis of "meaningfulness in general." Thus:

> Those who would demand theoretical verifiability or confirmability for significance in a statement, have in mind sense meaning as the prime requisite for meaningfulness in general. And those who would emphasize the operational significance of concepts are emphasizing sense meaning.[40]

Sense meaning Lewis describes as:

> intension in the mode of a criterion in mind by which one is able to apply or refuse to apply the expression in question in the case of presented things or situations.[41]

[36] *Logic,* p. 404.
[37] "The Modes of Meaning," p. 243, in Linsky, p. 63.
[38] See "The Modes of Meaning" and *An Analysis of Knowledge and Valuation,* Book I. For the difficulties here, see Pasch, pp. 23–33.
[39] "Modes of Meaning," p. 246, in Linsky, p. 60.
[40] *Ibid.,* p. 247, in Linsky, p. 61.
[41] *Ibid.,* p. 247, in Linsky, p. 61. But see also *An Analysis of Knowledge and Valuation,* p. 133.

Now much is to be said for an analysis of meaning behavioristically conceived as the application of a criterion for using or refusing to use expressions in certain kinds of situations and with respect to certain objects. But when Lewis comes to explain how this criterion is acquired and used (therefore, how it governs the constituent expressions and terms in analytic statements among others), he introduces notions of the "consistently thinkable"[42] and "experiment in imagination"[43] which are, in effect, somewhat dubious appeals to intuition and psychological capacities.[44] There are, in short, problems in specifying what a *thinkable* application of an expression is, and problems in the 'able' of a "criterion in mind by which one is able to apply or refuse to apply" an expression.

D. *Pragmatism and Formalism*

I come now to a final and general reflection of a historical nature upon pragmatism and the analytic.

The analytic, if there be such, is usually felt to be the province of statements possessing logical or necessary truth, truth by virtue of the meanings of their terms, and logical certainty. The analytic and logical truth accordingly have been most readily exhibited in systems of formal logic and mathematics. With the exceptions of Peirce and Lewis, a carefully developed interpretation of formal systems and logical truth (i.e., of analyticity) in the analysis of empirical knowledge is not found in the writings of the major pragmatists. One reason for this, the historical matter hinted of above, is that in the development of pragmatism there has been a certain antipathy to formal logic. Insofar as the analytic statement is the paradigm of logical and mathematical discourse, it represents an obstacle to a psychological interpretation of logic, and such an interpretation has been taken by many pragmatists.

Thus there has been a prolonged critical exchange between pragmatists defending a theory of "logic" as descriptive of thoughtful behavior, of how inferences and hypotheses function, and logicians viewing "logic" as concerned with implications among statements and the properties of formal systems. The critical exchange has mostly run at cross-purposes, a confusion engendered by assuming that the single word 'logic' represented a single common interest, whereas in fact one party was concerned with a generalized empirical theory of behavior, the other with certain abstract features of systems of statements. Both parties concealed this disparity of aims under the same word "logic," and were led therefore to suppose that competing logics—or logical theories—were at trial.

---

[42] For more on this, see sec. B of Appendix 7.

[43] Thus, e.g., *An Analysis of Knowledge and Valuation,* p. 151. For some suggested doubts about this, see White, "The Analytic and the Synthetic," p. 323, in Linsky, p. 279. Also see Pasch, pp. 27–33.

[44] Thus, in *An Analysis of Knowledge and Valuation,* p. 152: "The experiment of trying to put together in imagination the sense meanings of 'round' and 'square' [in order to satisfy the referential conditions of 'round square'] in the manner prescribed by the syntax of the phrase is sufficient to assure this universal non-applicability *a priori.*"

The obstacle that *analyticity* thus poses in the history of pragmatism is but a partial symbol of a whole philosophic point of view called "Intellectualism, Formalism, Absolutism." This is a main reason why, Peirce and Lewis excepted, an adequate analysis and interpretation of formal logic has not been forthcoming from pragmatism. Pragmatists of more recent standing (and of a more general and methodological subscription to "pragmatism," see § 101), such as Ramsey or Carnap or Quine, have inherited none of the uneasiness about formal reasoning felt by James, Dewey, and Schiller. For the latter thinkers, an anti-formalistic outlook was taken as an integral part of a general philosophical view of the nature of mind, knowing, and experience.

The philosophical motivation for the anti-formalistic point of view in pragmatism (a point of view well consigned to the past) is clear in James. In a letter to Peirce in 1909, he says: "I am *a*-logical, if not illogical, and glad to be so when I find Bertie Russell trying to excogitate what true knowledge means, in the absence of any concrete universe surrounding the knower and the known. . . ."[45] James, as we observed in the latter pages of § 34, was critical, if not of analytical thought itself, of the claims that philosophers had often made that the proper method of philosophy and the way to Truth was rational, conceptual, "logical." His chief objection was to what he called the "intellectualist logic," a broad categorical rug under which he rather hastily swept the dust of rationalism, Hegel, Bradley, Royce, and Russell, in keeping the philosophic house freshly empirical. James's objection to this "logic" had a twofold source. There was a temperamental dislike for abstract, logical, and conceptual modes of thought. The austere, abstract and, especially, the permanently fixed had a doomsday pall for James. Remove novelty and you take away life. But there was also in James a philosophic conviction that "real," immediately felt and lived experience could not be articulated or faithfully represented by the conceptual architecture, the abstract techniques and symbols of philosophic analysis. Thus James writes:

> In *principle*, then, the real units of our immediately-felt life are unlike the units that intellectualistic logic holds to and makes its calculations with.[46]
> In principle, then, as I said, intellectualism's edge is broken; it can only approximate to reality, and its logic is inapplicable to our inner life, which spurns its vetoes and mocks at its impossibilities.[47]

In this latter conviction James found more sympathy in Bergson than in Dewey and Peirce. Bergson and James, two masters of prose writing, both argued for the severely limited capacity of language to communicate the full character and inner import of experience. James sympathized with Bergson's critique of intellectual abstractions. He would also have agreed with Whitehead's similarly prompted comment that the exactness of science is a fake.

---

[45] Perry, II, 680.
[46] "The Continuity of Experience," in *Radical Empiricism and A Pluralistic Universe*, p. 287.
[47] *Ibid.*, p. 289.

James once wrote: "The prince of darkness may be a gentleman, as we are told he is, but whatever the God of earth and heaven is, he can surely be no gentleman."[48] But neither, we may add, for James, is He a mathematician.

Peirce, who was a practicing logician and who saw in logic and mathematics the exemplars of intellectual clarity, was not impressed with this trait of James. When James once confessed rather too easily his inability to understand mathematics, Peirce responded with the complaint that James was "blocking the road" to clarification and enlightenment of thought by this insistence "that he can't understand mathematics, that is to say, can't understand the *evident*."[49]

James's distrust of "intellectualist logic" was shared by Dewey, in spite of the appeal that the abstract Hegelian logic had for Dewey as a young man. Dewey viewed with strong reservations the flowering of modern formal logic and the discoveries of new and powerful deductive techniques. Logic, for Dewey, as we noticed in section (3) above, is the substance of inquiry. Divorced from the context of inquiry and the process of transforming problem situations into resolved outcomes, logical techniques and formal procedures are otiose for Dewey. He saw, as he once said, contemporary symbolic logic "separating form and matter" and operating with questionable "ideas of the conceptions and relations that are symbolized."[50] For Dewey, and even more so for Schiller, what passed for "logic" in most texts on the subject was, at best, only an isolated and preciously studied phase of the process of thought. The forms and structures of logical theory cut off from their instrumental functions and purposeful workings appeared empty of significance and intellectual value. However, since this conception of logic has been discussed (in connection with Dewey in § 36, and both Dewey and Schiller in the earlier pages of § 64 and in §§ 66, 69), it is unnecessary to pursue the subject any further here.

[48] *Pragmatism*, p. 57.
[49] Perry, II, 439.
[50] Dewey's Preface to *Logic: The Theory of Inquiry*, p. iv.

Pragmatism and the Category
of Possibility

So basic to pragmatism is the notion of a future that is "open" or can be affected or modified (as we saw in § 101) that the following pages are intended to supplement earlier remarks and afford us a closer look at the idea and some difficulties surrounding it.

A. The Importance of the Notion
of Physical Possibility

We may begin by considering the counterfactual statement S_1: "If when Smith smelled gas he had *thought* about what he was doing he would not have lit a match and the building would still be standing." This counterfactual affirms in a modest way the pragmatic thesis: the future would (or will) be different if thought occurs. Here one must try to disentangle a significant affirmation from the threat of triviality. And triviality threatens in two ways. First, if it is true that an occurrence of thought would modify the future in some distinct way, it is also true, relative to *that* distinct modification of the future, that no occurrence of thought could also be said to modify the future. S_1 argues that if Smith had done some thinking, the building would now be standing. But relative to that possible future—in which the building stands—Smith's failure to think modified the future, viz., as a factor in the building's vanishing. I do not mean to suggest that nonexistent events be endowed with causal efficacy. But I do say that, given two possible events e_1 and e_2, only one of which can be actualized at a given time, and two sets of causal conditions, C_1 as causative of e_1 and C_2 as causative of e_2; that C_1 should lead to the actualization of e_1 makes it no more privileged as a "modifier of the future" than the alternative C_2 which would lead to the establishment of e_2. A second threat of triviality lies in the fact that any number of kinds of occurrences at one time can be described as "modifying" the future. A sneeze or a giggle can have future consequences. The fact that intelligence (or rational behavior) does produce consequences that otherwise would not have occurred is not in itself explanatory of the distinctive nature of thought.

It is a curious shortcoming of pragmatist philosophy that this cardinal thesis of an "open future" resting upon some conception of *possible* events should have received little more than casual attention. Two of the fundamental concepts supporting the pragmatic theory of knowing and the nature of the empirical world are these of *physical possibility* and *potentiality*. It is, of course, always easy to call for explications and usually hard to undertake them.[1] Without some clarification, however, we remain in doubt, among other things, as to whether possibility (of the actualization of future events) characterizes the empirical world, or some of our beliefs and uncertain knowledge of the world, or both. There is, or seems to be, a difference between attributing possibility to events directly, and confining possibility to propositions about events as couched in some theory.[2]

One might say that relative to a theory θ an event e is possible if a statement of the occurrence of e does not contradict any statement in θ.[3] Thus, in the case of S_1, on some theory θ_1 it might be held that the alternate outcomes (the house exploding or not exploding) were each physically possible at a certain time; on some other theory θ_2, *one* of these outcomes might have been predicted as physically necessary. This vaguely suggests a doctrine of relative possibility, i.e., events as *possible* relative to some theory. But in the literature of pragmatism (in Peirce, James, Dewey, Mead, and Lewis), one finds a uniform tendency to treat possibility as an absolute character of experience and nature.[4] But what this sense of 'possibility' is, while of undoubted philosophic importance, is far from clear.

[1] Alternatively, of course, one is calling for explications of *physical impossibility* or *physical necessity*. Given these, the modality of *physical possibilty* (and, perhaps, *potentiality*) is rendered luminous in straightforward ways. For an attempt to provide a definition of *physical necessity*, see Popper, p. 433, and his discussion on pp. 420–441.

[2] The question of whether the category of possibility is to include events, or only statements, propositions, and theoretical judgments about events is reminiscent of disputes over interpretations of 'probability' as a relation among events or as a property of belief or a relation among propositions. Cf. Peirce's remarks on "materialistic and conceptualistic views of probability," *CP* 2.673.

[3] To give this a rigorous formulation, many supplementary conditions would have to be provided. E.g., the event e, and statements about it, would have to be statable in the language of θ via some descriptive or subject-matter terms. We want to avoid having to call some e_1 *possible* relative to some theory θ_1 since e_1 does not contradict any statement in θ_1 by virtue of being inexpressible in or wholly irrelevant to θ_1. Otherwise, e.g., that stones think, even that somebody is a female brother would be *possible* relative to theories of mechanics and economics.

[4] One can scarcely avoid being impressed with how significantly the notion of *possibility* (identified also as *potentiality*) is employed by Lewis in *An Analysis of Knowledge and Valuation*. Thus, e.g., pp. 17–18: "Only a creature that acts is capable of knowing because only an active being could assign to a content of his experience any meaning . . . only for an active being could anything be *possible* except what is actual and actually given. . . . Epistemologically the possible is, thus, antecedent to the real."

B.   The Problem of Clarifying the Concept
of Possibility

Granting the importance of the modality of *possibility* in the pragmatists' philosophy, since it is a modality, one naturally looks to its role and clarification in
Lewis' writings. In Lewis' modal logic the notion of *impossibility* is taken as
primitive and serves to introduce the other modalities.[5] Thus, let '(I)' symbolize
impossibility, then '(I)p' or 'p is impossible' means "it is impossible that p is
true," and possibility is defined as: 'not (I)p' or "it is false that p is impossible."
Necessity of p, in turn, is defined as '(I)not-p' or the impossibility that p is false.[6]
Here, in sum, a proposition is *possible* when its negation is not necessary.

Strict possibility as characterizing propositions is one thing, however, and
possibility as characterizing states or degrees of knowledge and *things* is another.
Yet that other and further extension is found in Lewis, too. When in his proposed
analysis of meaning he distinguishes the *denotation* and *comprehension* of terms,
he says of the latter: "the *comprehension* of a term is the classification of all consistently thinkable things to which the term would apply." The comprehension of
'square' "includes all imaginable as well as all actual squares, but does not include
round squares."[7] Here, as Carnap has noted, Lewis commits himself to (1) im-
possibles (e.g., round squares) and possibles, and (2) the two subclasses of possibles, actualized possibles (e.g., this book) and unactualized possibles (e.g.,
Apollo, unicorns).

That Lewis takes class (2), actualized and unactualized possibles, seriously
and literally we have already seen.[8] In so doing, we have been contending, he is
only affirming a general metaphysical thesis of pragmatism.

Philosophers with a nominalistic preference and scraped, too, by Ockham's
Razor, have registered reactions ranging from mild discontent to alarm at this
manner of extending an ontology, or bloating the notion of reality, to include
unactualized possibles, even impossible objects. There is Russell's criticism of
Meinong's impossible entities,[9] and Carnap's doubts about Lewis' category of
possible non-actual things.[10] Carnap's proposal is to eliminate the references to
objects having an actual, non-actual but possible, and impossible status, respectively, and supplant these instead with certain forms of expressions and intentions.[11] Quine, too, has expressed hopes of keeping 'possibility' attached to whole
statements rather than indulging in possible entities.[12] But Quine's hopes of

[5] *A Survey of Symbolic Logic*, ch. 5, esp. p. 292.
[6] *Ibid.*, p. 292. Lewis does not use the symbol '(I),' employed here for convenience.
[7] "The Modes of Meaning," p. 238, in Linsky, p. 52.
[8] See the quotation in note 4 above.
[9] Russell in "Denoting."
[10] Carnap, *Meaning and Necessity*, pp. 65–66.
[11] *Ibid.*, p. 66.
[12] E.g., *From A Logical Point of View*, p. 4.

carrying this out, that is, providing a semantical analysis of 'possibly' under the prescribed usage, are less sanguine than Carnap's and have not led him to take steps to this end, primarily because of certain doubts over 'analyticity.' For Quine, Carnap's technical procedure does not successfully avoid or render otiose the problems that are generated as to the meanings of analyticity and synonymy.[13]

A clarification of what is meant by 'is analytic' (see Appendix 6) would give us a start in clarifying the meaning of 'possibly.' We recognize that 'possible' (along with the other modal concepts, impossibility and necessity) attaches to propositions or statements to form a further statement, while 'is analytic' attaches to the name of a statement to form a statement about the named statement.[14] But we can explain 'possibility' by means of analyticity as follows: symbolizing *possibility* as 'P' and necessity as 'N' (recognizing, as we noticed some paragraphs earlier, that these are interdefinable: '$\sim P \sim$' = 'N' and '$\sim N \sim$' = 'P'), we are advised that the result of prefixing 'N' (or '$\sim P \sim$') to any statement is true if and only if the statement is analytic.[15]

But *physical* possibility, and indeed physical necessity, are notions that remain to be made sense of apart from any illumination that might come from modal logic.

This philosophical picture is not black but grey, and in it one point is clear. Statements about possible events regularly contain disposition terms and often take the form of counterfactual assertions. Thus in commencing to discuss the notion of physical possibility at the outset of A above, it seemed natural to introduce a counterfactual statement as an illustration of talk about possible events. But we have seen a number of times in this book, especially in studying some critical points in Peirce's pragmatism (in § 21), that the employment of disposition terms is linked to the use of counterfactuals, and analysis is therefore easily headed (at least for Peirce) toward some doctrine of "Real Possibility."

Disposition terms (notions of powers, potentialities, etc.), counterfactual statements, and assertions about possible events are not related accidentally in Peirce's writings. Nor are they in the discussions of and occasional allusions to these matters in earlier pages. Goodman has shown with great skill that the interrelatedness leads to a "cluster" of problems[16] (but also provides a focal point for analytical attack).[17] The disposition terms, e.g., 'hard,' 'soluble in water,' etc., if explicated by counterfactuals (e.g., 'x is hard' means—under such and such conditions—'x would not be scratched' or 'y is soluble in water' means 'y would dissolve in water') make the interrelations evident. So also do the predictive assertions from disposition terms, e.g., "since x is hard it will not be scratched" or "y will

[13] *Ibid.*, pp. 23–24, 32–37.
[14] We came upon this distinction earlier, see above, Appendix 6, but esp. § 44, notes 19 and 20.
[15] This is to quote Quine, "The Problem of Interpreting Modal Logic," p. 45.
[16] *Fact, Fiction, and Forecast*, esp. ch. 2.
[17] *Ibid.*, see esp. the latter pages of ch. 3 and all of ch. 4 for a working out of the view that "a whole cluster of troublesome problems concerning dispositions and possibility can be reduced to this problem of projection," p. 83.

dissolve if immersed in water." So finally does the ease with which *possibility* accommodates these modes of discourse. Thus: the hardness of *x* seems to be one of the possible characteristics of *x*, its would-not-be-scratchedness; "*y* is soluble" treats *y* as a possible dissolver, or dissolving is a possible career for *y*. While *y* may in fact never dissolve, the possible career remains a possibility. Thus the possibles and actuals become separated; and Lewis' classes (above) of actualized and unactualized possibles are also urged upon us.

To conclude with the observation already made in earlier pages, considering the importance of physical possibility in the philosophizing of pragmatism, it is surprising that the concept has not received a thorough analysis. And yet, while it was incumbent upon pragmatism to clarify the idea of a "plastic" world and future—and not to leave us guessing over how to assign meaning to *physical possibility*, the core of the doctrine in question—this happens not to be the responsibility of pragmatists only.

A more scrupuolus charity would have us notice that some sense of 'physical necessity' with a centrality of relevance and utility occupies many other philosophies. Thus any ethical theory that includes in the assessment of acts the provision that actions *might* (or might not) have been performed, or any historical theory allowing for the *possibility* of alternative events, events that *might* (or might not) have happened, enjoys the benefits that even unacknowledged uses of the notion of physical possibility amply supply. Furthermore, as Goodman has pointed out, "the interrelated problems of dispositions, counterfactuals, and possibles are among the most urgent and most pervasive that confront us today in the theory of knowledge and the philosophy of science."[18]

There has recently been considerable interest in the idea of future contingency,[19] a close relative of the concept of physical possibility. But so far the wanted remedial clarification of either idea has not come easily or at all. Thus the notion of physical possibility is in a first characteristic stage of growing philosophic thought: the stage of a prevailing agreement over the existence of initial disagreements and perplexities.

[18] *Ibid.*, p. 33.
[19] A large literature has grown on this subject in recent years. A historical text upon which the nature of future contingency has been focused is Aristotle's *De interpretatione* 9, 18a–19b. For an early and subsequently much discussed study of this passage and the reality of past and future, see Williams' "The Sea Fight Tomorrow."

William James's Theory of Truth *

The following discussion is intended to amplify and clarify some of the points in the account of James's theory of truth in §§ 31, 32 above.*

It was in *The Meaning of Truth* that James attempted to provide a rounded explanation of his theory and indicate its relevance as a criterion of truth in thought and conduct. It is with this book, consequently, that we will be almost exclusively concerned in these pages. We will first consider some of the historical factors affecting the development and formulation of James's theory. The second part of the discussion is devoted to a reconstruction of the theory in order to make its tenets as explicit and coherent as possible. While this way of representing James's theory takes a somewhat novel form it is, I should contend, fully in accord with his intentions and argument in *The Meaning of Truth.***

The Meaning of Truth was published in 1909, one year before William James died. The book was intended, the subtitle informs us, as sequel to *Pragmatism* (1907). But it differs from the earlier work in several fundamental ways. James makes clear in the Preface that this volume is a continuation and clarification of just one theme: the "pivotal part" of *Pragmatism,* namely, its account of truth. The subject matter to be treated is consequently narrower in scope and a less ambitious endeavor than the earlier volume of lectures, whose deceptive simplicity and popular style caused many readers to underestimate the value and depth of often novel analyses and suggestive insights into philosophic issues of science, epistemology, metaphysics, and religion.

* With minor changes and some additions most of this essay is drawn from my Introduction to *The Meaning of Truth,* The Works of William James (Cambridge, Mass.: Harvard University Press, 1975) designated in these pages as 'MT'. Unless otherwise specified all references to other books by James are to volumes in The Works of Williams James. Two of the three concluding Notes are from pages 10–13, 15–19 of an article on James's theory of truth in the *Transactions of the Charles S. Peirce Society,* 13 (1977), 3–19. I am grateful to the Harvard University Press and to the editors of the *Transactions* for permission to use these materials.
** For a statement of and substantiating evidence for this interpretation see the paper in the *Transactions of the Charles S. Peirce Society* cited in the previous footnote.

In *Pragmatism* James attempted to present a new and comprehensive philosophy, developing it in "broad strokes, and avoiding minute controversy." He conceived it nonetheless as a major effort. It was, he remarked in a letter, "The most important thing I've written yet, and bound, I am sure, to stir up a lot of attention."[1] The lectures that formed the book were delivered to large audiences, and much of the sparkle of sagacious humor is there to entertain as well as instruct. *The Meaning of Truth*, on the other hand, consists almost entirely of articles James had published in various journals. Although his style is characteristically vigorous, colloquial, and unpretentious, he is addressing not the public but professional philosophers. *Pragmatism* expresses a sense of urgency and mission in its deliverance of doctrines. *The Meaning of Truth* exhibits confidence in a movement that has established itself, positions won or requiring only further explanation in order to be accepted. Much of the discussion is polemical, and there are signs of James's impatience with some of his critics who continued to misunderstand the ideas in question or failed to take them seriously. Here he was prepared to enter into some of that minute controversy that he had avoided earlier.

The Meaning of Truth, then, is the most complete statement of his theory of truth James has left. This is a highly original and by no means simple theory. It well deserves study as a cardinal doctrine in James's philosophic outlook and an important contribution to our understanding of the meaning and value of the concept of truth.

Pragmatism was a popular and successful book. During James's lifetime it rapidly went through many printings, and served to focus the controversy over truth that had been occupying the journals since 1904. Just before it appeared, James had published his chapter on truth (Lecture VI of *Pragmatism*) in *The Journal of Philosophy, Psychology, and Scientific Methods*.[2] He wrote to F. C. S. Schiller about this "I find that my own chapter on Truth printed in the J. of P. already, convinces no one as yet, not even my most *gleichgesinnten* cronies. It will have to be worked in by much future labor . . . I think that the theory of truth is the key to all the rest of our positions" (*Letters*, II, 271). It must be acknowledged—and *The Meaning of Truth* bears it out—that the idea of truth is the key to James's position.

By the time *Pragmatism* was published James had begun to tire of the proliferation of critical discussions concerning pragmatic truth. In that year of 1907 he dutifully published seven articles explaining and defending his views; in these the topic of truth predominated. The following year he published four more pieces in the same vein. In the four years between 1904, when the controversy started, and 1908, James wrote and published twenty articles and one book (*Pragmatism*) expounding and defending his tenets.[3] It is not surprising,

---

[1] *The Letters of William James*, II, 276.
[2] "Pragmatism's Conception of Truth," *The Journal of Philosophy, Psychology, and Scientific Methods*, 4 (1907), 141–155.
[3] The reader may verify this by consulting Ralph Barton Perry's *Annotated Bibliography*

particularly for one who did not thrive on critical disputes, that by 1908 he was ready to leave further defense of pragmatic truth to Dewey and Schiller and turn his attention to other matters.

Some of the 1907 articles were reprinted in *The Meaning of Truth.* James intended this work as a final statement of his doctrine of truth. Explaining why he has set forth his views once more and reprinted his share of "so much verbal wrangling," he offers two interesting reasons. First, he says he is convinced that an understanding and "definitive settlement" of the pragmatic account of truth "will mark a turning-point in the history of epistemology, and consequently in that of general philosophy" (*MT*, p. 4). Second, he states his belief that the pragmatic theory of truth "is a step of first-rate importance in making radical empiricism prevail" (*MT*, p. 6). Radical empiricism was the epistemological and metaphysical theory of experience that James had worked on concurrently with pragmatism. These were cognate philosophic interests; each developed early in James's intellectual history and matured slowly. In 1904, while occupied with pragmatism, he also published two major essays on radical empiricism.[4] *Essays in Radical Empiricism* appeared in 1912, two years after his death; ten of its twelve chapters are reprintings of articles published in 1904–05.

The exact relation between his pragmatism and radical empiricism seems never to have been entirely distinct in James's mind. He several times asserted the logical separation and independence of these doctrines, saying that one could be accepted without the other. On the other hand, he also conceived some intimate connection between the doctrines of pragmatic truth and radical empiricism.

These and other matters might have become clearer had James lived to write one or more of the technical works, the "system," or the *Weltanschauung* he often longed to complete. In the last ten years of his life he frequency announced his intention to write a "serious, systematic, and syllogistic"[5] book, "a general system of metaphysics," or a "general treatise on philosophy," or a "system of tychistic and pluralistic philosophy of pure experience," a "magnum opus." But distractions of fame and of popular lecturing and writing, and periods of ill health and depression intervened to prevent him from accomplishing his hoped-for "immortal work."[6] With his unfinished *Some Problems of Philosophy* James left a memorandum in which he wrote: "Say it is fragmentary and unrevised . . .

---

of the Writings of William James (New York: Longmans, Green, 1920), revised with additions in John J. McDermott, ed., *The Writings of William James* (New York: Random House, 1967), pp. 812–858.

[4] "Does 'Consciousness' Exist?" *The Journal of Philosophy, Psychology, and Scientific Methods,* 1 (1904), 477–491. "A World of Pure Experience," *ibid.,* 1 (1904), 533–543, 561–570.

[5] Ralph Barton Perry, *The Thought and Character of William James,* II, 338.

[6] For these severally announced intentions see *Letters,* I, 179, 203, 127, and 203 respectively. For the reference to the "immortal work" see Perry, *Thought and Character of William James,* II, 468. Another expressed hope of writing a book "more original and groundbreaking than anything I have yet put forth (!)" is in a letter of Oct. 6, 1907, to his brother Henry; *Letters,* II, 299.

Say that I hoped by it to round out my system, which now is too much like an arch built only on one side."[7]

A.   Philosophic Background of the Controversy

In order to understand James's theory of truth and the motivating argument of his book, it is necessary to consider the specific critical and philosophical setting in which these ideas were formed and stated. The critical discussion over truth occurred in and as a part of a more general tension and clash of philosophies. James's pragmatism and notion of truth, his radical empiricism and pluralism were to a considerable extent developed in criticism of and as alternatives to absolute idealism, the dominant philosophic school in England and America at the turn of the century.

In a famous passage in *Pragmatism* James describes the history of philosophy as consisting "of a certain clash of human temperaments," namely, the "tender-minded" and "tough-minded" (WORKS, p. 13). The former is Rationalistic (going by principles), Intellectualistic, Idealistic, Religious, Free-willist, Monistic, Dogmatical. The tough-minded is Empiricist (going by facts), Sensationalistic, Materialistic, Irreligious, Fatalistic, Pluralistic, Skeptical. In James's day the most skillful and influential spokesman for a form of tender-minded idealism was F. H. Bradley. The tough-minded school of empiricists was led by T. H. Huxley, W. K. Clifford, and K. Pearson. The intellectual roots of British idealism were nurtured primarily in Kantian and Hegelian German idealism. German idealism had its initial transmission through Coleridge, Whewell, Hamilton, Ferrier, and J. H. Stirling, all critical of the older empiricism of Locke, Berkeley, and Hume. The most powerful critical proponent of this school was T. H. Green. His attack on the atomistic sensationalism and the associational psychology of Locke and Hume was devastating and considered by many to apply with equal effect to more recent empirical thinkers such as Mill, Bain, and Spencer. Green's critical focus was on the inability of sensationalism to account for relations, and thus, ultimately, its failure to explain how knowledge was possible at all (*see MT*, p. 79). The relating activity is essential over otherwise discrete sensations and ideas in order that we become aware of unified objects, of the world, or of ourselves. Since that unifying activity is not given in sense experience, Green argued for the presence of an ordering, intellectual consciousness, a living spirit in the world and acting through individual thinkers. Thus, as James remarked, we have "a monism of a devout kind."[8]

Led by Green and John and Edward Caird, and thereafter by Bradley, A. E. Taylor, Bosanquet, Joachim, McTaggart in Britain, and James's Harvard colleague Josiah Royce, idealism established itself as the prevailing system of Anglo-American thought. The philosophic preoccupations here were not only epis-

[7] *Some Problems of Philosophy*, p. 5.
[8] *A Pluralistic Universe*, p. 9. Green's views have been discussed earlier in Appendix I. sec. C above.

temological and metaphysical; there were also social and moral considerations. Thus, Green and the Cairds were critics of the utilitarianism of Mill and H. Sidgwick. Against individualistic utilitarianism, idealism advanced theories of the social, collectivistic, or unified nature of political and ethical life; the good and the moral law were embodied in social relationships, in the state, or in a higher spiritual community.

An important impetus to tough-minded philosophy came in the latter part of the nineteenth century after the publication of Darwin's *Origin of Species* (1859). The impact of and interest in Darwin's work was enormous. Darwin and Spencer were forces to be reckoned with. Idealists on the whole took one of two positions; some, like Bradley, tended to eschew or discount this form of empirical science, to remain philosophically unconcerned and aloof from what was, finally, a phenomenon of an unintelligible realm of appearance anyway. Others, like the young John Dewey (or Peirce and Royce) attempted to adopt the theory of evolution as evidence for and integral to a more comprehensive evolutionary idealism.

James regarded pragmatism as a way of mediating between the tender- and the tough-minded philosophies. The idea, as he put it to his audience early in the first lecture of *Pragmatism,* is to derive something of significant value between "an empirical philosophy that is not religious enough, and a religious philosophy that is not empirical enough for your purpose" (p. 15). And in the last words of the final lecture he says: "between the two extremes of crude naturalism on the one hand and transcendental absolutism on the other, you may find that . . . the pragmatistic or melioristic type of theism is exactly what you require" (p. 144).

James's characterization of the two kinds of temperament whose mutual antagonism marks the history of philosophy might, of course, be questioned. But this is of no moment to us since we are interested rather in how James conceived the problems and what he took to be the direction of philosophy in his own time. His description is revealing of what he understood to be the difficulties, the excesses and shortcomings in the intellectual traditions he had inherited and in which he was situated. By proposing pragmatism as a mediator he did not intend a synthesis of tender and tough outlooks. He was searching for a genuine alternative, a way of critically assimilating some while rejecting other parts of the philosophic legacy. In 1906 he found most persons to be of "a decidedly empiricist proclivity" but desiring, in addition to facts and science, moral and religious values (*Pragmatism,* p. 14). To clarify and resolve these human wants a method of critical analysis and procedure was needed; and James thought he had found this in the theory of pragmatic meaning and truth.

It is of curious interest that William James himself cannot be placed in his own classification of philosophic temperaments. He was a man of extraordinary complexity, of deep internal emotional divisions and conflicting intellectual tendencies. Outwardly (at times) an "adorable genius," as Whitehead said, but inwardly (at times) driven to despair of any worth or hope of accomplishment,

James could charm the world but could also entertain possibilities of madness or suicide. We can say, however, that, with important exceptions made for free-will, religious belief, and optimism, he generally inclined to the tough-minded outlook. And with religious idealism the dominant academic philosophy at the time, and because some of James's early work received most criticism from that quarter, the burden of his critical writing was directed against monistic idealism.

We are thus brought back to Bradley, for in opposition to the skillful and effective expression of philosophic idealism James advanced his pluralism, radical empiricism, and pragmatism. According to Bradley, reality is a single whole or unity in, but forever distinct from appearance. Reality "must be single, because plurality, taken as real, contradicts itself." And he adds that since any plurality implies relations, "through its relations, it unwillingly asserts always a superior unity."[9] Indeed all relations and predications lead to contradiction and so are unreal. In all judgments, Bradley argues, there is a difference between subject and predicate, "a difference which, while it persists, shows a failure in thought, but which, if removed, would wholly destroy the special essence of thinking" (AR, p. 361). The "main nature" of thinking is that "Thought essen-tially consists in the separation of the 'what' from the 'that.' It may be said to accept this dissolution as its effective principle" (AR, p. 360; for a critical notice by James, MT, p. 43): Predication and relations cannot represent reality, and they have meaning only in the world of appearance. Bradley is led accord-ingly to hold that all categorical judgments are to some extent false: "The subject and the predicate, in the end, cannot either be the other. If however we stop short of this goal, our judgment has failed to reach truth; while if we at-tained it, the terms and their relations would have ceased" (AR, p. 361). There is always "something else" supporting the predication, a reality which goes beyond the predicate. This something cannot be stated and lies outside of judgment or any progressive series of judgments. Ultimately this "something else" is the wholly real, coherent, self-identical Absolute, "a single and all-inclusive experi-ence, which embraces every partial diversity in concord" (AR, p. 147), the object of self-transcendence.

Bradley is classified as a Hegelian, and he constantly cites Hegel as the source of his doctrines; but the critical dialectical structure of his thought is very much like that of Parmenides. One main motif in this dialectic is that, although thought is imperfect and incapable of adequately representing the Absolute, the Ab-solute Reality is nonetheless the criterion of truth and falsehood, the better and worse, beauty and ugliness (AR, p. 552). This is the aim of thought; yet to attain it, thought would have to transcend its inherent 'that'-'what' subject-predi-cate distinction, and this, says Bradley, is the suicide of thinking (AR, p. 168). But since truth is the whole, as Hegel also taught, finiteness of thoughts and judg-ments is a condition of unreality and thus error (AR, p. 541). Each finite thing

---

[9] F. H. Bradley, *Appearance and Reality* (London: Swan Sonnenschein; New York: Macmillan, 1893), p. 519. Further references in the Introduction are to this edition, desig-nated 'AR'.

and each partial truth thus "contradicts" itself in pointing to its opposite, to something more as adding to and completing itself; and in so doing each thing passes beyond itself into its opposite and in turn makes for a wider unity. Since, however, even absolute truth and complete truth must consist of a subject, which would be the whole, and a predicate, Bradley concludes:

> Even absolute truth in the end seems thus to turn out erroneous—
> And it must be admitted that, in the end, no possible truth is quite true. It is a partial and inadequate translation of that which it professes to give bodily. And this internal discrepancy belongs irremoveably to truth's proper character (*AR*, p. 544).

All of this must be admitted "in the end," a phrase which, along with "finally" and "in itself" is ubiquitous in the writings of monistic idealists. Here "in the end" means: if you have reasoned carefully the idealistic conclusion will be inevitable. In the end, what can be known is severely limited. And truth, for Bradley, is defined, vaguely, as an ideal of satisfaction, our wanting a coherent whole. "Truth is an ideal expression of the Universe at once coherent and comprehensive": this sentence appeared in a valuable summary account of Bradley's outlook.[10] But for James, such a definition of truth really says very little. In any case, historically it was not only the pragmatists whose doctrine of truth courted unclarity.[11]

Thought and discourse proceed by means of distinctions and relations. For Bradley, however, reality is a differentiated yet seamless whole. Thus, the world of our intellectual efforts, and the world of final satisfaction and truth are severed realms. We can appreciate how difficult it was on this view to understand James's account of truth as the "workings" of ideas in particular cases; of his saying "Our account of truth is an account of truths in the plural, of processes of leading, realized *in rebus*, and having only this quality in common, that they *pay*" (*Pragmatism*, p. 104); of his conception of reality as "plastic," incomplete and in the making, awaiting part of its complexion from the future (*Pragmatism*, p. 123); he cites this as the important difference between pragmatism and rationalism); and of the possibility of different kinds of particular satisfaction (*Pragmatism*, p. 35). In this use of the concepts of 'truth,' 'reality,' and 'satisfaction,' James appeared to the rationalist mind to be speaking an alien and strange language and inviting intellectual anarchy. Moreover, his refusal to be pedantic and his vividness of expression led more solemn fellow philosophers to wonder whether he

---

[10] "Coherence and Contradiction," *Mind*, n.s. 18 (1909), 492. The article is reprinted in *Essays on Truth and Reality* (Oxford: The Clarendon Press, 1914), pp. 219–244. For James's reaction see "Bradley or Bergson?" *Collected Essays and Reviews* (New York and London: Longmans, Green, 1920), pp. 491–499.

[11] So, for example, this discussion of 'truth' in *Essays on Truth and Reality*, pp. 343–344: "Reality for me . . . is one individual Experience. It is a higher unity above our immediate experience. . . . But, though transcending these modes of experience, it includes them all fully. Such a whole is Reality, and, as against this whole, truth is merely ideal. It is indeed never a mere idea, for certainly there are no mere ideas. It is Reality appearing and expressing itself in that one-sided way which we call ideal. Hence truth is identical with Reality in the sense that, in order to perfect itself, it would have to become Reality. On the other side truth, while it is truth, differs from Reality, and, if it ceased to be different, would cease to be true. But how in detail all this is possible, cannot be understood."

was theorizing in earnest or having fun at their expense. James's alliance with F. C. S. Schiller deepened this suspicion in Oxford, where Schiller was regarded as something of an upstart and philosophic prankster in his irreverent attacks on Bradley and absolutism.

Even James's close friend Royce found the new language and doctrines difficult to comprehend fully. For Royce, a fundamental obstacle to developing a theory of truth was explaining the nature of error—a standing problem for monistic idealism. He constructed an ingenious and abstruse argument contending that to err, a judgment would have to disagree with its intended object. But a judging mind would not err about its own immediate ideas: either it knows its own ideas, and its judgments about them cannot err, or it does not know them in which case judgment would be meaningless. To know, however, that a judgment about an external object does or does not agree with that object—and especially to know that a thought is incomplete or inadequately represents its object—would require a more inclusive judgment, one that incorporates both the idea of the object and the object itself. This Royce calls the more "inclusive thought," a thought that includes particular thoughts and their intended objects. Since a judgment about an object cannot of itself "insure agreement with it," what is needed is the containing thought. Error, accordingly, "is an incomplete thought, that to a higher thought, which includes it and its intended object, is known as having failed in the purpose that it more or less clearly had, and that is fully realized in this higher thought." Without this "higher inclusive thought," Royce concludes, "an assertion has no external object, and is no error."[12] In order to realize and understand truth, we then require an "infinite unity of conscious thought" enveloping all finite thought. This is the "all-including Thought," or "the infinite content of the all-including mind" within which all finite minds, their ideas, and all objects represented by thought are contained. Royce elaborated on this notion of universal consciousness as an "infinite unity" in which was found all possible truth. It was the Absolute experience which related to all individual experiences as an organic whole to its fragmentary parts.

James did not wish to accept this theory of an omnipresent, overruling and, as he viewed it, fatalistic Absolute. But the argument impressed him. He expounded it to Renouvier and in his review of Royce's *The Religious Aspects of Philosophy*.[13] For many years he sought to discover some decisive logical weakness in the argument to justify his initial moral objections. In 1887 he remarked (*Letters*, I, 265): "I have vainly tried to escape from it. I still suspect it of inconclusiveness, but I frankly confess that I am *unable* to overthrow it." Finally, about 1893 he began to see, as he says in a note added to "The Function

---

[12] *The Religious Aspect of Philosophy* (Boston: Houghton Mifflin, 1885), p. 425. On the "infinite unity of conscious thought to which is present all possible truth," see p. 424; other passages quoted are from pp. 428–432.

[13] *Atlantic Monthly*, 55 (1885), 840–843; reprinted in *Collected Essays and Reviews*, pp. 276–284. For his letter to Renouvier see Perry, *Thought and Character of William James*, II, 702–705. In a letter to Bradley of July 9, 1805, he comments on Royce's argument, J. C. Kenna, "Ten Unpublished Letters from William James, 1842–1910, to Francis Herbert Bradley," *Mind*, n.s. 35 (1966), 312–313.

of Cognition," (*MT*, p. 23) that "any definitely experienceable workings would serve as intermediaries quite as well as the absolute mind's intentions would." The entire recondite apparatus of absolute mind was unnecessary. Knowing, objective reference, and truth and error could be explained perfectly well by an analysis of the activity of finite minds and ideas related to objects within experience, the relations being that of pointing, or leading cognition, through intermediate experience, to the reality or object. With some justice James later remarked about this paper and its argument that it is "the fons et origo of all *my* pragmatism";[14] and he reprinted it as the opening chapter of *The Meaning of Truth*.

The criticism of idealism deepened when it occurred to James that not only could knowledge and truth be explained without having to invoke the Absolute, and without having to depart from or transcend experience, but that the difficult notion of the absolute mind failed to explain any particular feature or event. In *Pragmatism* (p. 17) he offers the methodological pragmatic observation that the notion of "absolute mind" has no determinate empirical consequences: "You can deduce no single actual particular from the notion of it. It is compatible with any state of things whatever being true here below."

James's eventual resolution and reasoned rejection of Royce's doctrine is a central development in the historical formation of his pragmatism and theory of truth. Royce's argument for absolute mind provided the initial challenge to and testing of James's pragmatic conception of thought and action; these theories were further clarified and advanced in the exchanges with Bradley and the idealist school and his criticisms generally of intellectualism.

Bradley was something of an eccentric, and his metaphysical philosophy was far from being dogmatic or orthodox; it is carefully reasoned, often highly original, and deeply skeptical. But other monistic idealists, including Royce, very easily developed the more respectable theological implications of the Whole and the Absolute. Monistic idealism thus provided for religious affiliations and could be viewed as a bulwark against scientific materialism and agnosticism. It was a philosophy which, perhaps because individual selves and "mere" partial and particular experience count for so little in comparison to the all-inclusive Absolute, appealed to genteel sentiments.[15] It proved that the world was good and that present evils are necessary in serving a higher good, and was, therefore, favorably cultivated in the more exclusive academies of higher learning in America and expounded by professors whose training had usually been in theology (see *Pragmatism*, p. 16).

To James, the entire system of monistic idealism appeared labored, highly professional but somewhat insincere in motive and thin in consequences. Indeed, he found it suffocating. He mistrusted its respectability—for reality is anything

---

[14] From a letter to C. A. Strong, Sept. 17, 1907; James papers in Houghton Library, Harvard (bMS Am. 1092).

[15] In later writings Royce was to make of his idealism a thoroughly social theory. The very suggestive theory of meaning as a social activity within a community of interpretation (which was close to ideas of Peirce) seems to have had little interest for James.

but refined or respectable—its "disdain for the particular, the personal, and the unwholesome,"[16] its discomfort with variety, "its infallible, impeccable, all-pervasiveness,"[17] and its "block universe." He had a democratic abhorrence for the notion of evil as unreal, or as necessary to the realization of good. On more technical grounds James argued that by making truth a property or possession of reality, or the Absolute, idealists had rendered the concept of 'truth' unknowable and useless. Truth conceived as "an ideal expression of the universe," in Bradley's words, is of little aid in explaining just what conditions define a belief or a statement to be true, and how truths can occur or be known. Against the arguments that had been advanced by Green,[18] concerning the dumbness of sensations and how relations are therefore instituted by thought, or against Bradley's view of relations as unreal, James set forth a central thesis of radical empiricism: "relations between things . . . are just as much matters of direct particular experience, neither more so nor less so, than the things themselves." This, he adds (MT, p. 7), makes relations both real and experienced; the parts of experience are held together by relations that are parts of experience. There is no need to appeal to an absolute, or "higher unifying agency" to account for order in experience or a unified world. And this position also affords a genuine and knowable place for pluralities and individuals. Instead of a mysterious Infinite Mind, whose containment and coordinating of a knower and object known defines 'truth' (i.e., Royce's theory), the pragmatic theory, says James, can give a definite account of the truth-relation and in experiential terms.

Finally, although it may be held that the idealists had overindulged the role of mind and thought in their theory of reality, the tough-minded empiricist and agnostic philosophers, such as Spencer, Huxley, Clifford, and Pearson had taken the other extreme to view the world as complete and describable independently of knowing organisms. Against this "naturalism" James stressed the importance of the knower and the presence of human feelings, purposes, and intervening actions to any complete description of the world. "*The* world is surely the *total* world, including our mental reaction. The world *minus* that is an abstraction, useful for certain purposes, but always envelopable. Pure naturalism is surely envelopable in wider teleological or appreciative determinations."[19]

In addition to advancing the doctrines of pluralism, radical empiricism, and pragmatism, James argued that growth and novelty are ultimate traits of reality. Although it was in the last years of his lifetime that he hoped to set forth in detail the metaphysical significance of these ideas, they recur throughout his philosophical thought and writings. A year before his death he commented: "I think the center of my whole *Anschauung*, since years ago I read Renouvier, has been the belief that something is doing in the universe, and that *novelty* is real."[20] This mention of Renouvier is significant: it is a reflection at the end of

16 *A Pluralistic Universe*, p. 140.
17 *Essays in Radical Empiricism*, p. 142.
18 For James on Green's argument see *Principles of Psychology*, II, 9–13.
19 Perry, *Thought and Character of William James*, II, 476.
20 From a letter to James Ward, June 27, 1909; see Perry, II, 656.

a life upon its philosophical beginning. For it was in 1869–70, while suffering a severe psychological crisis, that James found in Renouvier's theory of free will a resolution of his despair and the restoration of health (see *Letters*, I, 147). In *Some Problems of Philosophy* James acknowledged this debt in his intended statement of dedication, saying of Renouvier: "he was one of the greatest of philosophic *characters*, and but for the decisive impression made on me in the 'seventies by his masterly advocacy of pluralism, I might never have got free from the monistic superstition under which I had grown up" (p. 85).

In order to develop the metaphysical implications of the notions of growth and novelty James had to reckon with the criticisms of the reality and intelligibility of possibility and change advanced by monistic idealists. He had also to work out an alternative to the reductive analysis of change by materialistic empiricists and to defend the idea of novelty against scientific determinists. On this issue James regarded the idealists and the scientific empiricists as alike in taking an Intellectualist or Abstractionist position; in each case change, growth, novelty, and genuine variety are either denied outright or given "sterile" and schematic representations untrue to the thick, deep, moving character of reality.

These critical reflections led James also to believe that logico-mathematical analyses of time, motion, and infinity were inadequate for expressing the fully continuous character of conscious experience and of reality. Although he had no objection to the construction and analysis of formal and mathematical systems, he mistrusted the philosophical claims often made for these disciplines as providing complete and final explanations of reality or revealing the ultimate metaphysical categories of the world. Peirce, among others, accused him of refusing to acknowledge the value of exact thinking. It must be said that what James was refusing to accept was not exact thought for its own sake or as an ideal but rather the view that exact systems mirror a corresponding exactness in reality or that such systems yield the final truth concerning the nature of things. In any event, in accord with his opposition to this form of Intellectualism, James enthusiastically greeted the work of Bergson. And while he had anticipated some of those ideas in his own earlier philosophizing, he addressed Bergson as a "magician" whose work constituted a turning-point of thought. He wrote him: "I feel that at bottom we are fighting the same fight. . . . The position we are rescuing is 'Tychism' and a really growing world" (*Letters*, II, 292). He felt that Bergson had killed Intellectualism. But for the less enthusiastic response of Peirce and Dewey, James might have been tempted further to pursue the more mystical and irrational tendencies in Bergson's outlook. As to this later development of his thought, however, no more need be said here. It remains in what follows to examine more carefully James's theory of truth.

B. *The Meaning of Truth*

I pass now from the more historical concerns that affected the growth and formation of James's theory of truth, to that theory itself. It was an unusually controversial theory, and the controversy stemmed from fundamental differences of entire philosophical positions and orientation to an extent not fully realized by any of the parties to it; but the conspicuous point of conflict was in the concept of truth.

On this matter James is open to criticism for devoting so much attention to the polemical aspects of the discussion of truth that he was deterred from setting forth a careful and rounded statement of his theory. The fifteen chapters of *The Meaning of Truth* contain treatments, and divers essays on the notion of truth. Because it is central to an understanding of James's philosophy and influence, it is worth attempting to exhibit the essential interconnections of these sundry treatments and separate analyses and arguments, in the hope of providing a unified formulation of James's theory. This attempt requires a reconstruction and piecing together of the leading ideas and intentions in his several expositions into a schematic and coherent whole. We can then consider briefly some of the standing critical difficulties that have been addressed to and associated with the theory.

At the outset it is important to be clear upon one point that should have received some attention by James and his critics, for much misunderstanding and irrelevant argumentation would have been avoided. I refer to the fact that when James argues for his conception of truth it should not be thought that he is arguing against or rejecting all other theories of truth. The reason this caused misunderstanding is that it is natural to assume that when a philosopher sets forth his theory on some subject he is denying other theories on that subject and, implicitly at least, treating them as erroneous. So it was assumed that in offering his theory of pragmatic truth James meant to deny and exclude any other version of truth from what he took to be the right view of the meaning of that concept. But this was not the case. On the contrary, James was attempting a remolding rather than a renunciation of older ideas. He was concerned with clarifying, deepening, and extending the application of the more familiarly received conception, and with accounting for the function of the concept of truth in contexts which remained ignored or inexplicable by traditional theories. Thus, occasionally he will claim that his doctrine includes, absorbs, and supports others; that "Pragmatic truth contains the whole of intellectualist truth and a hundred other things in addition" (*MT*, p. 111).

The generally accepted "dictionary" definition of 'truth' in James's day was: the agreement of ideas with reality (falsehood being the disagreement of an idea with reality). He acknowledges this definition (for example, *Pragmatism*, p. 96, and *MT*, p. 117). For Bradley, since truth is Reality, agreement would be conceived as the harmony and unity of Reality with (or in) itself. For Royce the agreement lies between fragmentary judgments and the whole of Absolute Truth, within an Absolute Mind. But James first asks, what specifically is *meant* by 'agreement'? And he finds the idealists and intellectualists producing no very clear answer. It is not that what they say is wrong, he contends, but that their use of 'agreement' is uninformative. Accordingly, he develops the pragmatic meaning of the concept. He took a similar critical view of the notion of truth as correspondence. He does not reject the thesis that truth is the correspondence of ideas or statements with reality, but again he finds the formulation vague (*MT*, pp. 44–45, 105). In each case we need and do not have an explanation of what the complete conditions are that constitute an 'agreement' or 'correspondence.' Overstating it somewhat, James concludes that these definitions of 'truth' tell us no more than that what is true *is* true (*MT*, p. 128).

In order to understand James's theory of truth we must recognize, then, not one exclusive theory, but two stages and two fundamental ways through which claims and ascriptions of truth proceed. There is first what we may for convenience call *cognitive truth* (drawing on the discussion of "cognitio," *MT*, p. 50, although by "cognitive truth" here we do not mean a "copy" theory of thoughts and things). This is the conception of truth that James accepts but judges of little philosophical value. This is dictionary truth in its simplest abstract form, namely, as the agreement (or correspondence) between beliefs and statements and what these may be said to be about. 'Truth' characterizes the circumstances that pertain when what is believed or stated to be the case *is* the case. Such circumstances might pertain, for example, between the belief or statement that it is raining, and the occurrence of raining. This is a doctrine of truth according to which what is believed or stated "agrees" or "corresponds" with the subject matter it "describes" or is "about." This is not to be confused with a more recent theory in which to say "true" is to express *agreement* with a statement made in an appropriately related context.[21] For our present purposes it is not necessary to attempt a more accurate definition of 'cognitive truth' (and to do so is not an easy task). There is secondly *pragmatic truth,* the doctrine James advocated and the subject of his book.

There are important conditions holding in common for cognitive truth and pragmatic truth as well as important differences. However, if the distinction is sound, and is, as I believe, in accord with James's own views, it has the merit of reducing and clearing up a mass of confused opinions and misapprehensions that grew between James and his critics.

Keeping now to this distinction, we can say that an idea (judgment, statement), to be true or false, must at least be cognitively true or false—it will or will not "agree" or "correspond" with reality. James does not deny this, as some critics mistakenly charged; nor is he rightly accused of rejecting the law of excluded middle, or the existence of a reality external to thought and belief (in *MT* see p. 8, and the Third and Fourth misunderstandings of pragmatism in Ch. VII) On the other hand, an idea could be cognitively true and yet *pragmatically* neither true nor false. The appearance of paradox here is easily dispelled when

---

[21] For this analysis developed by P. F. Strawson and its assimilation to Dewey's theory of truth see Gertrude Ezorsky, "Truth in Context," *The Journal of Philosophy,* 60 (1963), 113–135. For a survey of James and Dewey on truth and their theories discussed in the light of other contemporary views see Ezorsky's article, "Pragmatic Theory of Truth," in Paul Edwards, ed., *The Encyclopedia of Philosophy,* 6 (New York: Macmillan & Free Press; London: Collier-Macmillan, 1967), 427–430.

we consider that the class of cognitive truths (and falsehoods) is wider than that of pragmatic truth; some cognitive truths have no pragmatic significance or "cash value," but they are no less true (cognitively) for that. Thus, cognitive truth is a necessary but not sufficient condition of pragmatic truth.

Among the cognitive truths whose pragmatic truth or falsehood might in this way be indeterminate (or whose truth value, like cash value, might even fluctuate, as will be explained later), are those James characterizes as our accumulated "stock of *extra* truths, of ideas . . . true of merely possible situations" (*Pragmatism*, p. 98). When an extra truth is needed to meet some emergency in conduct or solve some problem, "it passes from cold-storage to do work in the world." But in so passing into the world it becomes more than cognitive truth; for with its needed function and practical use it has issued in pragmatic truth. If we incorporate this distinction in a paraphrase of one of James's well known pronouncements we can say of such occasions of an activated truth: it is useful because it is true (cognitively) or it is true (pragmatically) because it is useful. This accords with his further comment that: "True is the name for whatever idea starts the verification-process, useful is the name for its completed function in experience." For these reasons, considering James's primary interest in that smaller class of truths that come out of cold-storage and acquire distinctively pragmatic value, his doctrine might be more accurately described as a theory of pragmatic truth rather than a pragmatic theory of truth.

The foregoing distinction meets one of the most frequent and serious charges of irrationalism and subjectivity directed against James's theory. As a consequence of his account of truth, he was accused of maintaining that a belief or statement could be true for some persons and false for others (hence the claim that he had abandoned the law of excluded middle). This is largely a misunderstanding. What James did in effect hold was: a cognitively true statement might be neither true nor false pragmatically for some persons (that is, roughly, not pragmatically significant), while pragmatically true for others (that is, pragmatically significant). Moreover, on his theory the "same" statement, or linguistic form, might differ in pragmatic truth and meaning in different contexts, because the pragmatic meaning and truth of beliefs and statements are alike determined to some extent by factors in the occasion and particular circumstances in which they are entertained or asserted.

It can be seen that pragmatic truth requires further additional conditions for its realization than is the case for cognitive truth. If we ask what these further conditions may be we are led to the main idea of James's theory.

In *Pragmatism* James says:

the question 'what is *the* truth?' is no real question (being irrelative to all conditions) and . . . the whole notion of *the* truth is an abstraction from the fact of truths in the plural, a mere useful summarizing phrase like *the* Latin Language or *the* Law (pp. 115–116).

He is not claiming, it is to be noticed, that an abstract definition of *the* truth is impossible or wrong.[22] The dictionary definition has its summarizing uses, and in this he may be understood to be referring to what we have been calling *cognitive* truth. But such truth, he says, is "irrelative to all conditions." The determination of pragmatic truth, however, requires a specification of certain kinds of conditions. James often remarked that the conditions in question are not those of merely believing what is pleasant or believing that the consequences of an idea will be useful or wishing whatever one wants to be true. One basic condition of the theory and definition of pragmatic truth is found in the concept of *working*. A true idea is one that works. The notion of the working of a belief or statement is explained, in turn, as entailing a certain kind of satisfaction, one in which there is a resolution of initially uncertain or discordant circumstances or an adaptation to an environment or the location of some needed or intended object (a practical or theoretical object-ive). The concept of 'working' supplies the pragmatic meaning of the doctrine of truth as "agreement." Pragmatism, James says, in *Meaning of Truth*:

> defines 'agreeing' to mean certain ways of 'working,' be they actual or potential. Thus, for my statement "the desk exists" to be true of a desk recognized as real by you, it must be able to lead me to shake your desk, to explain myself by words that suggest that desk to your mind. . . . Reference then to something determinate, and some sort of adaptation to it worthy of the name of agreement, are thus constituent elements in the definition of any statement of mine as 'true' (pp. 117–118).

Again quoting *Pragmatism* in his Preface, James says:

> To 'agree' in the widest sense with a reality, *can only mean to be guided either straight up to it or into its surroundings*. . . . Any idea that helps us to *deal*, whether practically or intellectually, with either the reality or its belongings, that doesn't entangle our progress in frustrations, that *fits*, in fact, and adapts our life to the reality's whole setting, will agree sufficiently to meet the requirement. It will hold true of that reality (p. 102).

The concept of 'working' is essential in the explanation of pragmatic truth. If we recall James's interpretation of the purposive nature of thought and the instrumental character of concepts, we can appreciate even more clearly the argument here concerning the working and adaptational function of true ideas.

Let us consider James's theory more closely. The theory, as I shall try to show, formulates three fundamental conditions that must be fulfilled if a belief

[22] As will be argued below, the notion of *cognitive truth* as a necessary but not sufficient condition of pragmatic truth is important. It resolves a multitude of objections raised against James's theory. It is unfortunate that James did not make his point clearer, but he was absorbed in developing the distinctively *pragmatic* aspect of truth in the "working" and "satisfactory" functions. Still, that he did recognize what I have here called "cognitive truth" can be seen, in addition to the passages cited in the text, in *MT* when, (e.g., p. 118) he refers to just such true statements and beliefs as "inertly and statically true only by courtesy: they practically pass for true; but you *cannot define what you mean* by calling them true without referring to their functional possibilities." In *Pragmatism*, he says: "Truth with a big T, and in the singular, claims abstractly to be recognized, of course" (p. 111). And he speaks of rationalist definitions of truth as trivial, but adds: "They are absolutely true, of course, but absolutely insignificant until you handle them pragmatically" (p. 109). This truth, with the big T, is what we are here pointing to as cognitive truth.

(or statement, or judgment) is to be pragmatically true. A survey of these three conditions will then enable us to construct a general definition of William James's doctrine of truth.

(1) The first condition is that of cognitive truth. To be true, the objective reference of a belief or statement must be the case. James says "The truth of the idea is one relation of it to the reality." He often mentions the role of "objective reference" and comments: "My mind was so filled with the notion of objective reference that I never dreamed that my hearers would let go of it" (*MT*, p. 128). Falsehood then would be an erroneously intended or purported objective reference; affirming something to be the case when in fact it is not. This is the main feature of what James regards as the *realism* of pragmatic truth (*see MT*, Ch. IX and pp. 104 ff.). The pragmatist "posits . . . a reality and a mind with ideas. What, now, he asks, can make those ideas true of that reality?" (*MT*, p. 104) The complete answer remains to be developed below, but one part of it is before us: to be true, the idea must agree or correspond with reality.

(2) The second condition of pragmatic truth has to do with the idea of the assimilating of new forms of experience into the existing system of our beliefs or, as James puts it, the marrying of old opinions with new facts.

In criticizing the idealists' identification of truth with reality, James argues that the order of sensible experience and facts is neither true nor false. Changes and additions to the content of this order "simply *come* and *are*. Truth is *what we say about* them" (*Pragmatism*, p. 36). And among the important things we say is how certain occurrences of experience are signs of other experiences, how "One bit of it can warn us to get ready for another bit, can 'intend' or be 'significant of that remoter object. The object's advent is the significance's verification" (*ibid.*, p. 99). This organization of beliefs about facts and relations among the items of experience is one part of our system of truth and knowledge. The other part consists of what James calls "relations among purely mental ideas" (*ibid.*, p. 100). He refers to such "absolute, or unconditional" beliefs as that "1 and 1 make 2" or that "white differs less from gray than it does from black." These definitional truths or "principles" are necessary for organizing systems of logical and mathematical ideas and relations and ordering the sensible facts of experience. They provide possible ways in which to arrange and interpret the facts of experience so as to reliably anticipate future experience. "This marriage of fact and theory is endlessly fertile." Of these two orders, James continues,

> Between the coercions of the sensible order and those of the ideal order, our mind is thus wedged tightly. Our ideas must agree with realities, be such realities concrete or abstract, be they facts or be they principles, under penalty of endless inconsistency and frustration (*ibid.*, p. 101).

Thus, we find ourselves endowed with a stock of beliefs, our system of knowledge, acquired partly through experience and partly as an inheritance from our ancestors and our culture. It may happen, James points out, that certain experiences may strain some of our old beliefs: we may be contradicted by somebody or may contradict ourselves, or we may discover facts that are incompatible with a belief. "The result is an inward trouble" from which we seek to escape. Some modification of our beliefs or a reinterpretation of the facts, or both, is demanded. The critical process of and readjustment in the mass of one's opinions continues,

> until at last some new idea comes up which he can graft upon the ancient stock with a minimum of disturbance of the latter, some idea that mediates between the stock and the new experience and runs them into one another most felicitously and expediently.
>
> This new idea is then adopted as the true one. It preserves the older stock of truths with a minimum of modification . . . New truth is always a go-between, a smoother-over of transitions (*Pragmatism*, p. 35).

This is how new truth "marries old opinion to new fact," James adds, and different ideas and theories accomplish this integrative function with varying degrees of success from different points of view, so that to some degree "everything here is plastic."

James emphasizes the controlling importance of the old truths. We seek to preserve them and we depend on them even when making revisions among them. Conservatism is the strategy. If an experience so novel as to threaten most of our fundamental beliefs occurred, we would incline, if possible, to ignore it or classify it as illusory. As to the skeptical possibility that all our beliefs are mistaken or illusory, we might retort that it is only within the accepted stock of our beliefs —or some part of it—that we are given criteria for distinguishing the real from the illusory; it makes little sense to question the veracity of the system as a whole. James does, however, remark that some of our most firmly established old beliefs could be subject to revision with the advent of new experience. He alludes to the transformation, at the time of his writing in 1907, "of logical and mathematical ideas, a transformation which seems even to be invading physics" (*Pragmatism*, p. 37).

Since alternative theories and organization of beliefs for interpreting experience are available, there is no one absolute "right" way of viewing reality, no one true theory. Reality is what it is known *as*, James is fond of saying. And what an object is known *as* depends on a certain prior focusing of interests and needs that guide conceptualization, and partly upon similarly conditioned terminations in sense experience (thus *MT*, p. 76).

Since we live in a common world, we learn to conceptualize in common, or because we conceptualize in common, we posit a common world. In either case, James argues, we eschew solipsism and we share in and use alike the stock of old truths. Our confidence in this system of beliefs is increased through "face to face" verification of beliefs with experience, or by more elaborate and extended indirect verifications. But although we share a common system of knowledge, we are each to some extent differently situated in it and the uses we make of it. These individuating differences of perspective and interest, of needs and purposes, allow for James some variations among persons as to how the world is viewed, relativism in decisions about how it is to be "carved" and categorized, and what things are known *as*.

The third condition of pragmatic truth is the most novel and controversial part of James's theory.

(3) For an idea to be true of reality, it "must point to or lead towards *that* reality and no other, and . . . the pointings and leadings must yield satisfaction as their result" (*MT*, p. 104). Here, I believe, we find the most distinctive characteristic of William James's theory of truth. Pragmatic truth is not a property of ideas or statements but of the circumstances and events in which an idea or statement contributes to an action with a beneficial and satisfactory outcome. The mere occurrence of a feeling of satisfaction does not suffice for truth; it is indispensable for (pragmatic) truth but insufficient "unless reality be also incidentally led to" (*MT*, p. 106). James does not argue that satisfaction *is* truth or alone determines truth. Beliefs about events and objects supposed real but which do not exist would be false "in spite of all their satisfactoriness" (*MT*, pp. 8, 106). He recognizes the "notorious" fact that "the temporarily satisfactory is often false" (*MT*, p. 54). And he protests against associating this idea of satisfaction with his "Will to Believe" argument (*MT*, pp. 86–87).

In "The Function of Cognition" (Ch. I of *MT*) James argued that the test of the truth and meaning of ideas was their termination in "definite percepts," that is, the sensations to which they lead or which can be derived from them. In later parts of *The Meaning of Truth* a less subjective and philosophically more realistic position is taken; the truth of beliefs will be how they terminate in reality: "there can be no truth if there is nothing to be true about. . . . This is why as a pragmatist I have so carefully posited 'reality' *ab initio,* and why, throughout my whole discussion, I remain an epistemological realist" (*MT*, p. 106).

The process of *working* or *leading* is thus described by James as a continuous order of psychological and physical events linking the entertainment of an idea "as a *terminus a quo* in someone's mind and some particular reality as a *terminus ad quem*" (*MT*, pp. 129–130). The idea has an instrumental function; it is "an instrument for enabling us the better to *have to do* with the object and to act about it" (*MT*, p. 80). Successive ideas can then be regarded as increasingly more true of an object when subjected to the corrective process of critical inquiry and testing. In this case the pragmatic meaning of "Absolute truth" would be "an ideal limit to the series of successive termini . . . the ideal notion of an ultimate completely satisfactory terminus" (*MT*, pp. 88–89) or "an ideal opinion in which all men might agree" (*MT*, pp. 142, 143; also p. 76, and *Pragmatism*, pp. 106–107). It is the entire process of events mediating between an idea and its object and issuing in satisfactory terminations of sensation and action that determine truth. "Such mediating events *make* the idea 'true'" (*MT*, p. 109). These are or make possible the "functional workings" of ideas or statements (*MT*, p. 122). Concerning this notion of 'workings' two observations are necessary.

(a) James occasionally ascribes to ideas, beliefs, and statements certain inhering tendencies or properties which, under appropriate conditions, are causative factors in the mediating process through which verification and truth occur. So far as I know, he never completely developed this notion; but it has a role in his analyses of thinking, and the concept of 'tendencies' is prominent in the famous discussion of the "stream of thought" in *The Principles of Psychology* (I, ch. IX). He can be seen to ascribe dispositional properties to ideas (beliefs and statements, the latter construed as occasions of stating something) when he argues: "The trueness of an idea must mean *something definite in it that determines its tendency to work.*" He goes on to maintain that just as a man's mortality—which is the possibility of his death—is to be understood as "something in man that accounts for his tendency towards death," so there "is something of this sort in the idea" that accounts for its tendency to "work." There is also "something" in "bread that accounts for its tendency to nourish." In one of his clearest statements he then describes the complexity of causal and dispositional conditions that constitute the 'working' of an idea:

> What that something is in the case of truth psychology tells us: the idea has associates peculiar to itself, motor as well as ideational; it tends by its place and nature to call these into being, one after another; and the appearance of them in succession is what we mean by the 'workings' of the idea. According to what they are, does the trueness or falseness which the idea harbored come to light. These tendencies have still earlier conditions which, in a general way, biology, psychology and biography can trace. This whole chain of natural causal conditions produces a resultant state of things in which new relations, not simply causal, can now be found, or into which they can now be introduced—the relations namely which we epistemologists study, relations of adaptation, of substitutability, of instrumentality, of reference and of truth (*MT*, p. 96).

(b) The other observation concerning the 'working' of ideas and statements is the importance James attaches to the presence of an interest or need. The causal working tendencies just discussed are relative to specific interests and needs; the working that issues in pragmatic truth, issues accordingly in satisfactions. Truth, James says, is an "adaptive relation," and he asks: "What meaning, indeed, can an idea's truth have save its power of adapting us either mentally or physically to a reality?" (*MT*, p. 130). This recognition of human purposes guiding our thinking led him to regard truth as one species of good: "The true is the name of whatever proves itself to be good in the way of belief, and good, too, for definite, assignable reasons" (*Pragmatism*, p. 42). And it is this aspect of the 'working' of thought that James referred to as its "expediency," saying " 'The true' . . . is only the expedient in the way of our thinking . . . expedient in the long run and on the whole" (*MT*, p. 4, or *Pragmatism*, p. 106). It should be evident, then, that the satisfaction of "some vital human need" (*MT*, p. 5) is one further necessary condition of pragmatic truth (although not of cognitive truth).

These last tenets prompted the most controversy and misunderstanding in critical discussions of James's theory. But before turning to these difficulties, we may sum up this part of our discussion: for an idea (belief, judgment, statement) to be pragmatically true three conditions are to be fulfilled. The idea must:

*1. Be cognitively true.
*2. Be compatible with the older body of truths.
*3. Work. It must provide some satisfaction of a need or purpose (recalling the two aspects of 'working' just discussed). In short, "thoughts are true which guide us to *beneficial interaction* with sensible particulars" (*MT*, p. 51).

In this schematic form we are given a general definition of James's conception of 'truth.'

We can even cast this general definition in the distinctively pragmatic form that Peirce recommended for explicating the meaning of abstract concepts. Put very roughly, his counsel was: to determine the meaning of terms like 'force,' or 'hard,' one should formulate a description of the use of the term in contexts of experiment and testing; how the term is applied and the consequences of that application will yield a description of its meaning.[23] Thus, as an example, Peirce says we mean by 'hard'—or that something x is hard—if you perform the experimental operation, O, of scratch-testing on x, it would result as a consequence that x will not be scratched. The explication proceeds by specifying a certain experimental situation, E (the presence of x and conditions for scratch-testing), an operation, O (scratch-testing), and general result, R (would not be scratched by many substances in repeated cases of testing). So, to say "x is hard" means: if E, and O, then R (x would not be scratched). Now we can fit our definition of James's concept of truth into this explicative scheme as follows. We want to consider the meaning of "P is true" where 'P' is a belief or statement which, as a necessary first step, we take to be cognitively true (so fulfilling condition *1). We take P as part of a situation E, which includes personal needs and interests to be satisfied, as discussed (in 3.(b)) above. "P is true" then means: If E, and O (that is, acting on P, the "leading" of P) then R (that is, P would fulfill conditions *2 and *3). Briefly, the truth of P on James's theory comes to mean: if P fulfills *1, and is acted upon, P would fulfill *2 and *3. In this way P would become pragmatically true and verified in the manner and under the conditions that particularly interested James.

To avoid misunderstanding, it should be added that the above sequence of three conditions in which I have represented James's theory of truth is not proposed as a temporal order—or order of discovery—according to which truth will

---

[23] A more complete account of the matter is to be found in § 21 above.

occur first in a cognitive sense and thence, in successive stages, fulfill conditions *2 and *3. The three conditions are to be construed solely as logical conditions and hence as components of the *definition* of pragmatic truth, not as phases of the process of *verification*.

It remains finally to consider some of the major difficulties directed to James's theory. We need not reopen all of the original controversy—much of which is now of limited historical curiosity—but some of the criticisms, notably those advanced by Moore, Russell, Pratt, and Lovejoy, are of interest and relevance. The most important of these can be briefly sketched and commented on in the light of the above definition. Let us, for convenience, use the expression 'Belief-assertion' so as to capture the objective of truth ascriptions for James. He mentions ideas, beliefs, judgments, and statements as alike capable of truth or falsehoods; but—especially in his express doubts about construing propositions as abstract capsules containing truth or falsehood as properties (*MT*, p. 151)—it is clear that he is interested in contexts in which acts of believing and asserting occur as constituents and are the occasions of pragmatic truth or falsehood.[24]

Of the various objections to James's theory, three have generally been regarded as the most serious.

First: James maintains a Belief-assertion is true if it works or is expedient. But, it will be objected, a false Belief-assertion under certain circumstances can be expedient. It may be useful for us to have someone believe a lie. It might be useful to believe other persons exist even if they did not (Russell's argument, *MT*, p. 149). The Belief-assertion "God exists" may be useful, or work, for some persons, even if God does not exist (*MT*, Preface, p. 6, and notice James's reference to this "slander," p. 147). Finally, some true Belief-assertion might not be expedient. As to this kind of objection we are now in a position to see how it turns on a confusing of senses of 'truth' (senses *1, *2, and *3). The critical force of the instances adduced against James here derives from the supposition that he meant to equate 'truth' and 'working' or 'useful.' But he did not argue that 'true' = 'useful' (thus *MT*, pp. 148–150). The useful is a sign (not infallibly so) of truth; but as we have seen, for a Belief-assertion to be pragmatically true, conditions other than *3 are required. Lastly, while a (cognitively) false Belief-assertion might be useful or expedient in some particular case, in "the long run" a false Belief-assertion will conflict with our old stock of truths (that is, *2) and so will eventually prove not to "work." Hence, although every pragmatically true Belief-assertion is useful, not every useful Belief-assertion is pragmatically true.

Second: James errs in failing to recognize the difference between the truth of a Belief-assertion and the useful effects of believing that Belief-assertion, for

---

[24] In these pages I have followed James's language in assigning truth or falsity severally to ideas, beliefs, judgments, and statements. As to statements, I think it is clear that James was construing these as events of utterance (or inscription) in linguistic occasions, as true or false. These would be token instances of types of linguistic forms and expressions. The use here of 'Belief-assertion' is intended to represent these several kinds of token instance of truth or falsehood for James.

he equates 'x is true' with 'it is useful to believe x' (see *MT*, p. 149). But this is a misrepresentation. James says: "The social proposition 'other men exist' and the pragmatist proposition 'it is expedient to believe that other men exist' come from different universes of discourse. . . . The first expresses the object of a belief, the second tells of one condition of the belief's power to maintain itself" (*MT*, p. 150). Misunderstanding on this point has led to some ridicule of pragmatism: A company of philosophers staying the night at an Inn are informed by the host that the establishment is on fire. Concerned to determine the truth of this report, all but one of the philosophers look about the rooms; the one, the pragmatist, asks himself instead what will be expedient for him to believe. If he is a pessimist, and heavily insured, he will conclude the announcement is false and go to bed; but if he reflects on the value of life he will decide the host is telling the truth and will join his colleagues in rushing outside. The parable depends on ignoring the role of conditions *1 and *2 in establishing pragmatic truth: it also overlooks such pronouncements as: "Truth . . . is manifestly incompatible with waywardness on our part. Woe to him whose beliefs play fast and loose with the order which realities follow in his experience: they will lead him nowhere or else make false connexions" (*Pragmatism*, p. 99).

Third: James confuses *truth* and *verification*. This has been a persistent criticism (see his discussion, *MT*, p. 108, of the sixth misunderstanding of pragmatism, his reply to Pratt, pp. 94 ff., and the note to 93.1, p. 181 below). Clearly, the verification of some Belief-assertion, or corroborating our belief in it, is distinct from the truth of that Belief-assertion. In order to be verifiable at all— or be subject to verification—a Belief-assertion would have to be either true or false; the truth value is logically prior to and distinct from the verification. So too, an unverified Belief-assertion remains either true or false, verification neither creating nor being truth. Furthermore, knowing what we mean by a belief being true, and knowing whether the belief *is* true are distinct (for we can know what the truth of "the earth is flat" would mean, although in fact the statement is false). All of this is to say that cognitive truth and verification cannot be equated. James, however, was interested in verification as a process under conditions *2 and *3, rather than *1 (which latter he may have taken for granted). It is the workings of a Belief-assertion as constituting its pragmatic truth that he also called verification, thus seeming to treat truth and verification as synonymous. He says that an idea "is *made* true by events. Its verity *is* . . . a process: the process namely of its verifying itself, its veri-*fication*. Its validity is the process of its valid-*ation*" (*MT*, pp. 3–4). But the process he speaks of here, in which verity is verification, is the fulfilling of conditions *2 and *3. The process, as we might rephrase it, *makes* out of otherwise mere cognitive truth (of *1), pragmatic truth; and verities (of *1) become veri-*fications* (of *2 and *3). Still, cognitive truth and verification remain distinctly different in meaning.

It would be more judicious to decide that James was vague rather than glaringly mistaken about verification. And he would have helped to advance understanding and reduce futile controversy if he had clearly developed and distinguished his doctrine of pragmatic verification from more generally accepted notions of testing and confirmation.

In conclusion, it might be asked why, considering its importance, James was not more explicit in acknowledging the notion of cognitive truth which can be found alternately suggested, employed, and alluded to in his writings. One reason, we have seen, is that the general idea of "absolute" truth, made so much of by many of his contemporaries, held little interest for James. It was truths in the plural and the particular verification procedures and their specific contributions to the control and clarification of experience that he regarded as of primary philosophic importance. He does, however, recognize "absolute" truth as a regulative ideal; it means "what no farther experience will ever alter" (*Pragmatism*, p. 106). This serves as an ideal of "potential better truth," a stimulus to continued investigation. Accordingly, although certain past systems of thought, such as Ptolemaic astronomy or Euclidean space "were expedient for centuries," we now consider them as "only relatively true, or true within those borders of ex-experience." But James concludes, " 'Absolutely' they are false" (*Pragmatism*, p. 107). The absolute condition here is our cognitive truth. And of this absolute sense of truth 'functioning as a regulative ideal he says: "the proposition 'There *is* absolute truth' is the only absolute truth of which we can be sure" (*MT*, p. 143). On the other hand, he was wary of the danger of hypostatizing concepts as the names of essences. Now the concept of "absolute truth" can readily be made to eventuate in a theory of *the* Truth as an integral part of absolute Reality. James had witnessed philosophers in his day thus affirming a "non-utilitarian, haughty, refined, remote, exalted" conception of "objective truth" as an "absolute correspondence of our thoughts with an equally absolute reality" (*Pragmatism*, p. 38). In short, he saw the idea of absolute truth leading all too easily to monistic idealism. He was to focus on this form of hypostatization calling it "vicious abstractionism" (*MT*, Ch. XII, and p. 135), namely, when what is selectively referred to by a concept is taken as the only real feature in an otherwise "originally rich phenomenon," and all other features are denied and expunged. In wanting to keep clear of such abstractionism James was uneasy about the notion of a single "absolute" definition of truth. The one dictionary definition, he feared, if made too much of, could encourage discounting the importance of truths in the plural and verification processes on the grounds that these are "nothing but" instances of the one absolute truth and thus, merely the partial aspects of one ideal reality.

On this I think we must observe that, though his critical reservations concerning abstractionism are on the whole cogent, James underestimated the value of general definitions and the legitimate use of very general and abstract concepts in philosophy. In the present instance, because of his interest in the role of particular truths and verifications of belief, he was occasionally misled into supposing that knowledge of the "absolute" meaning of 'truth' would entail possession of absolute knowledge. He thus confused the quite distinct ideas of one fixed "absolute" meaning of 'truth' and the probabilistic character of knowledge. He thought that to understand the meaning of truth in some absolute sense might constitute a denial of the relative, mutable, and fallible nature of the confirmation of hypotheses and beliefs. Apparently he failed to see that an absolute definition of 'truth' is not incompatible with the idea that knowledge never attains absolute certainty or that confirmation of belief is of degrees and, in the light of new knowledge, is subject to change and even disconfirmation.[25] On these points James was frequently inconsistent and mistaken. But these same points form part of the reason why the notion of cognitive truth, while present in James's theorizing, receives little emphasis.

C. Conclusion

The object of the above interpretation and reformulation of James's argument has been both to clarify and suggest some of the very real philosophical merits of his theory of truth. In bringing this discussion to a close I do not wish to leave the impression that I think no serious difficulties remain to be encountered in his writings on truth. There are merits, but there are also shortcomings; and some of each have been formative in diverse ways in the critical and speculative currents of later philosophic thought.

I hope, however, that contrary to the familiar imputation that James had indulged in hasty and indefensible pronouncements on truth, the preceding has made it evident that this theory was an unusually ambitious undertaking. For what he was attempting was to show how complex interrelated, psychological, moral, epistemological and metaphysical considerations converge in the idea of *truth,* if the philosophic implications and significance of that idea are to be clarified, and if its function as a ruling condition of successful conduct in a malleable and changing world is to be understood. The concept of truth, for James, was accordingly envisaged and developed as integral to a more inclusive philosophic system and as an essential linking of two principle parts: a critical (rather than descriptive) theory of behavior and a metaphysics of experience. The vision was never entirely fixed and the system never fully articulated.

I suggest that this was the dominant motivation of the theme of *The Meaning of Truth,* namely, the quest for a coherent and comprehensive philosophic expression of the varied forms and ends of human action and experience, and of how it is possible for thought to be a source of alteration, novelty, and value in the world of which it is also an objective condition and part. This aim, however, was almost destined to be conceived imperfectly by a man of James's mercurial intellectual temperament and deep distrust of system-building and certainty and finality in philosophy.

This is not how James has usually been interpreted. His theory of truth is usually explained as resulting from an interest in justifying religious and metaphysical convictions, the contention then being that if a religious belief "works," it is true. This is an elliptical way of characterizing James's view of truth. No

[25] This critical problem in James is discussed by Israel Scheffler, *Four Pragmatists* (New York: Humanities Press, 1974), pp. 112–116.

doubt the great importance of his father's Swedenborgian religious investigations and the early influence of his father's friend Emerson had a deep emotional effect on his thinking. And this was reinforced by encountering Renouvier's writings in a later period of crisis, which contributed to James's lifelong appreciation of the subtle psychological value and 'working' functions of religious belief. Furthermore, as a psychologist, James took an almost clinical interest in the pathology of belief, and how, under specific circumstances, differing kinds of beliefs could lead to beneficial adaptations to the world. Thus, he attempted to show how religious and metaphysical beliefs as well as ordinary moral and esthetic aspirations could be pragmatically meaningful and, in special cases, self-fulfilling and perhaps true. But there is another way of viewing this pragmatic defense of moral and emotional interests and of taking the conduct they inspire seriously. It may appear on one side as an apologia for religious yearnings; it can even have been partly that. But the sword cuts two ways. By arguing that religious and metaphysical assertions can be pragmatically meaningful claims to truth, James was also showing these to be serious hypotheses rather than closed dogmas. He was thus encouraging the extended application of critical inquiry, of pragmatic analysis and justification to the spheres of religion and metaphysics. So viewed, James's pragmatism was not a retreat from reason or defense of unreason; it was an enlarging of the subject matter of reason where dogma had hitherto often prevailed.

The ultimate value of thought, for William James, is its power of directing and transforming sensory experience, its terminations in specific forms of illumination and action. How and in what measure is ordinary experience clarified and made serviceable to human needs and to our individual and socially shared wants and satisfactions? Such is James's pragmatic critique of the uses of intelligence. The critique is central to his conception of philosophy. Philosophy is not an isolated, esoteric, and autonomous discipline. Its full significance emerges with wider terminations in the traffic of human affairs and individual conduct. Truth is essential here both as a controlling end and a clarification of procedures for successful and creative action. For James truth is not constitutive of a realm of being or of essence, but a regulative ideal for the effective organization of human energies in conscientious interaction with environing reality and prospective goods.

THREE NOTES

(1)

There is another way of regarding the relation of cognitive and pragmatic senses of truth not touched on above. James makes an interesting methodological distinction between what he calls "saltatory" and "ambulatory" designations and descriptions of subject matters (*MT*, p. 79 ff.). The saltatory formulates the "abstract" and "essential skeletons or outlines" of facts or processes; the ambulatory is directed to the "concrete" particularities and unique but vitally significant features of a subject. James discusses these two ways of analysis and investigation in the case of *knowing* as a process. His own view he makes clear is ambulatory: knowing is "functionally . . . an instrument for enabling us the better to *have to do* with the object and to act about it" (*MT*, p. 80). But he also points out that any process can be considered "abstractly" as saltatory; for "a concrete matter of fact always remains identical under any form of description." And any one description may be "more expedient to use at one time, one at another" (*MT*, p. 85). And he says: "There is no ambulatory process whatsoever, the results of which we may not describe, if we prefer to, in saltatory terms" (*MT*, p. 84). He instances *prudence*. We can call a person prudent and mean "a permanent tone of character." This would be a saltatory reference "in abstraction from any one of his acts." Or we can mean in an ambulatory way, "concretely," that he "takes out insurance, hedges in betting, looks before he leaps" (*MT*, p. 84).

There is no question that James advocates the ambulatory approach for attaining the full meaning of experienced facts, processes and relations. But he also recognizes the convenience and legitimate use of the saltatory. Now the above exposition of James's theory of truth, is comprising both cognitive and pragmatic components, is quite in accord with this distinction: cognitive truth is the saltatory "abstract" concept and pragmatic truth is the ambulatory process, the "concrete" development of the same notion.

(2)

Something should be said, if only briefly, concerning two points of somewhat more technical philosophic interest in James's discussions of truth; his criticism of *propositions* as objects of truth attributions; his perception of difficulties of reference in the notion of truth as agreement.

1. Propositions. James observed that a considerable confusion in discussions of truth was due to a shifting between a "subjective" referent of truth as a "property of opinions," and an "objective" referent as "the facts which the opinions assert." (*MT*, p. 151). We might say the opinion, 'Caesar was killed' is true; or we might say that the fact asserted—viz., that Caesar was killed—is true. (We would not these days be so confident about the latter assertion, for there is a large critical literature on the appropriate and the misleading uses of 'fact' and of 'that' in expressions commencing with 'it is a fact that . . .'). Many writers, including Russell and Moore, revert to the notion of truth as a property of propositions. But this, says James, only fosters the confusion. For the proposition 'Caesar is dead' can be construed as referring to the fact, or complex, *that*-Caesar-is-dead. Or it might express the belief, 'Caesar is no longer living' (*MT*, p. 283). The word 'that' makes for ambiguity; for "in

naming propositions it is almost impossible not to use the word 'that.' *That* Caesar is dead, *that* virtue is its own reward, are propositions" (*MT*, p. 151). Among other difficulties, he draws attention to the often unnoticed difference between the proposition as (a supposed) *meaning* with a reference to the "facts" (Caesar is dead) and an expression of *belief* (that "Caesar is dead"). He writes in a letter (of 1908) critical of Russell and Moore:

> "Propositions" are expressly devised for quibbling between realities and beliefs. They seem to have the objectivity of one and the subjectivity of the other, and he who uses them can straddle as he likes, owing to the ambiguity of the word *that* which is essential to them. "*That* Caesar existed" is "true," sometimes means the *fact that* he existed is real, sometimes the *belief that* he existed is true.[25]

This was in 1908. Russell was much later (in 1940) to discuss some of these same difficulties concerning 'that' as attached to propositions and sentences.[26]

2. Truth and Reference. We say:

> 'Jones is smoking' is true if and only if Jones is smoking.

This seems clear (and for Quine's remark on the example see (3) below). But there is a difficulty which, while artificial, serves to bring out one of James's reservations concerning "formal" or "abstract" formulations of cognitive truths. In the above, the part in quotation marks is the name of a sentence which contains therein the name 'Jones.' And 'Jones' names Jones. But how do we know this: suppose there are two Joneses, Jones 1 and Jones 2, each of whom may or may not smoke? We could not regard the above as correct since it would allow:

> 'Jones 1 is smoking' is true if and only if Jones 2 is smoking.

It will be replied that this is merely a gross confusion. For 'Jones 1' *names* Jones 1, and nothing else. In any careful development of the explication of the truth predicate (such as in Tarski's theory) the unambiguous assignment of names and sentences, and hierarchies of the same within increasing enclosures of quotation marks, is fixed at the start. This is surely reasonable and we have thus obviated the question of reference and interpretation in the beginning and it need never have occurred. Various stipulated conventions, such as that sentences with $n + 1$ quotation marks will refer to the same sentence or sequence of words in n quotation marks, establish the unambiguous direction and objects of reference.[27] They thus resolve the question that had troubled James, a question originating not in semantics but in Royce's argument for the necessity of an enveloping or "Infinite Thought" as supplying the reference of an individual thought to its object. For while a thought might represent some object, the representative function and conditions of accuracy and truth are not produced in the thought

---

[25] Letter to Horace M. Kallen, January 26, 1908. See MT, Appendix IV, p. 305.
[26] *An Inquiry Into Meaning and Truth* (New York: W. W. Norton & Company, 1940), p. 226, 357, 192 "there are no facts 'that so-and-so'."
[27] An alternative to quotation marks is Tarski's device of spelling by which the names of the letters and concatenation supply a unique structural description of a sentence named.

itself or in its object; some more inclusive thought is required within which the finite thought *and* its object can be compared and judged. Thus if the truth of an idea is said to be its "agreement" with an object, James raises this question: "But then you are met by Royce's old argument: How do you know it *means* to be true of *that* object? It might 'agree' perfectly in the sense of copying, yet not be true, unless it *meant* to copy . . . that particular original. An egg isn't true of another egg, because it is not supposed to aim at the other egg at all, or intend it. Neither is my toothache true of your toothache. Royce makes the absolute do the aiming and intending. I make the chain of empirical intermediaries do it."[28]

Royce had offered his idealistic response to the impossible contention of empirical realism that ideas in the mind were (somehow) known to resemble (and be true of) external objects. In rejecting Royce's complex and recondite theory, James was led to emphasize the notion of 'workings' and 'empirical inter-mediaries' as the referential mechanism by which (say) the truth of 'Jones is smoking' has reference to Jones and his smoking. His distrust of some abstract notion of truth as *agreement* came of its failure to specify the conditions of agreement (and of reference). He may be criticized for not appreciating how the formal (and cognitive) concept can function informatively and can be far from trivial. But it is to his credit that he had perceived such inadequacies in the earlier versions of the definition of truth as agreement—especially as articulated by idealist philosophers—which were to stimulate the development of a sufficient and explicitly formulated concept in our time.

It must be acknowledged, finally, that James was not always clear or consistent concerning this distinction of cognitive and pragmatic truth. There is sufficient evidence, I think, to allow us to conclude that he did indeed intend the distinction we have been discussing. But there are some troublesome cases. There is the passage which exercised Russell in which James began by observing that "in any concrete account of what is denoted by 'truth' in human life, the word can only be used relatively to some particular trower." He then goes on to say that "it may be true for me" that Shakespeare wrote the plays that bear his name, while a critic, as a Baconian, "believes that Shakespeare never wrote the plays in question" (*MT*, p. 147). Does James mean (for he does not fully say) *both* views can be true? Russell so interpreted him to mean this and was rightly indignant.[29] We must decide either that James was seriously inconsistent or that he is not clear.[30] As to the latter possibility, James might have meant only that each party to the dispute believes his view to be true. Or, where the cognitive truth is unknown (in this case whether it was Shakespeare or Bacon who wrote the plays) then the "workings of the opinion" for the Shakespearian and for the Baconian, in each case provide some *evidence,* and some reason, for each thinking

[28] *Collected Essays and Reviews* (New York: Longmans, Green and Co., 1926), p. 481; *Essays in Radical Empiricism,* p. 152.

[29] See *My Philosophical Development* (New York: Simon and Schuster, 1959), p. 180.

[30] The manuscript of this chapter (i.e., ch. 14, MT) shows that James had difficulties and made many changes. A valuable record of the controversy between James and Russell over truth is to be found in MT, Appendix IV.

his opinion is true. One further condition James states in this connection is that "the opinion must not be contradicted by anything else I am aware of" (*MT*, p. 148). We can witness a similarity with the argument in *The Will to Believe* here. But whatever the "workings of opinion" will be, the cognitive truth of the belief is theoretically and in principle decisive. And James also adds: "When I call a belief true, and define its truth to mean its workings, I certainly do not mean that the belief is a belief *about* the workings. It is a belief about the object" (*MT*, p. 149).

(3)

After contending (against idealism) that truth is not reality itself, but something "known, thought or said about the reality, and consequently numerically additional to it," James agrees that there are facts which—although never stated—could only be truly stated in certain "predetermined" ways: "There have been innumerable events in the history of our planet of which nobody ever has been or ever will be able to give an account, yet of which it can already be said abstractly [as cognitively] that only one sort of possible account can ever be true. The truth about any such event is thus already generically predetermined by the event's nature." See also *MT*, p. 157. In this discussion ("A Dialogue") James appears clearly aware of the notion of cognitive truth even to also sensing the curious feature of redundancy in its role when exhibited as a predicate having a references to sentences. Indeed, sensing the feature of redundancy may have been one mistaken reason for James's mistrust of and distain for the notion of cognitive truth. To the assertion that "it *is true* that the facts are so-and-so, and false that they are otherwise," James comments (*MT*, p. 156):

> '*It*' is true that the facts are so-and-so—I won't yield to the temptation of asking you *what* is true; but I do ask you whether your phrase that 'it is true that' the facts are so-and-so really means anything really additional to the bare *being* so-and-so of the facts themselves.

This is just the feature that Ramsey was to point out later (in 1927, "Facts and Propositions," *The Foundations of Mathematics*, New York and London, 1931, pp. 142–43); the expression 'p is true' is (he says) the same as 'p.' Thus to say "It is true that Caesar was murdered" means no more than Caesar was murdered. It is worth notice that G. E. Moore had stated and questioned this view earlier (in 1911). "We may assert: 'To say that the belief that I have gone away is *true*, is *the same thing* as to say that I have gone away; this is the very definition of what we *mean* by saying that the belief is true'" (*Some Main Problems of Philosophy*, London, 1953, p. 275). The idea leads to Tarski's celebrated elaboration about which W. V. Quine comments informally: "The circumstances under which the statement 'Jones smokes' would be said to be true, e.g., are precisely the circumstances under which Jones himself would be said to smoke. Truth *of the statement* is no more mysterious than the notions of Jones and smoking." (*Mathematical Logic,* Cambridge, Mass., 1940, p. 4). James goes on to argue that this form of (cognitive) truth must constitute a "potential" kind of knowledge: what would be known to be true in case the knower existed (*MT*, p. 157): he would know what *would* be the truth about the facts.

This last point becomes clearer when we recall his earlier discussion (*MT*, p. 56) concerning the Dipper constellation: "We call it by that name, we count the stars and call them seven, we say they were seven before they were counted." But he adds that they were not "explicitly" Dipper-like or seven before the human act of comparing and counting them occurred. He means that the seven stars in their Dipper-like arrangement existed before they were first counted and compared, but the "explicit" (cognitive) *truth* 'The Dipper is seven stars' is the human contribution resulting from an act of naming ('Those stars are the Dipper') and counting ('Those stars are seven'). For he continues: "They were only implicitly or virtually what we call them, and we human witnesses first explicated them and made them 'real.' A fact virtually pre-exists when every condition of its realization save one is already there. In this case the condition lacking is the act of the counting and comparing mind. But the stars (once the mind considers them) themselves dictate the result." The result is the *cognitive truth*, 'The Dipper is seven stars' and this is "dictated" by the Dipper being seven stars.

James regards this as a "quasi-paradox" namely, "something comes by the counting that was not there before. And yet that something was *always true.* In one sense you create it, and in another sense you find it" (*MT*, p. 56). But it is not paradoxical, we may conclude, for what is created or contributed is our counting and assertion of the cognitive truth 'these are seven stars' (or even 'these were always or for a long time seven before being counted'). What is created is summed up graphically in the statement that "'there are seven stars' is true." But this is due to it being found that what was there before was seven stars.

Epilogue

I

1968: A Reflection on the Philosophic Scene

When *Meaning and Action* appeared in 1968, the time was not auspicious for a book on pragmatism. The heyday of pragmatism had long since waned—some forty years earlier. Its major philosophers, Peirce, James, and Dewey, were studied and respected in some quarters. But, with the exception of Dewey, the doctrines of these thinkers had never been appropriated and made the nucleus and creed of a school or won disciples and partisan loyalties. And in the case of Dewey, whose liberalism, philosophic naturalism, and faith in education and democracy had gained him a following in professional and intellectual circles and in departments of philosophy and education, there was a noticeable weakening of the influence he had commanded in the first quarter of the present century.

In 1968 (and indeed for some twenty years previously) it was "Analytic philosophy" or "Analysis," the Oxford philosophy of ordinary language, that dominated American academic philosophy and the major journals.[1] Other critical and speculative movements such as existentialism and phenomenology and the thought of Kierkegaard, Nietzsche, Husserl and Heidegger, Camus, Sartre, and Merleau–Ponty were making effective incursions in the prospering and expanding universities of the post-World War II period. But these various currents never succeeded in forming the main stream of contemporary philosophic opinion or practice. The central and prevailing conviction as to how the discipline of philosophy is to be exercised, how philosophers are to understand and perform their office, came from the vigorous school of analytic philosophy. The scene was of course far more complicated; both too diversified and diffuse to be easily sketched. There remained, throughout the changes at the center, inveterate if peripheral remnants of traditional orthodoxies. After the war, and again in the turbulent sixties, there appeared a medley of dissident ideologies and doctrines some of them having migrated from Indian and oriental sources. Each of these more or less tangential lines of thought promised enlightenment and a saving wisdom not found in the texts or meetings of the university professors. And in

---

[1] On the history see J. O. Urmson, *Philosophical Analysis: Its Development Between the two World Wars* (Oxford: Oxford University Press, 1956).

still another more circumscribed area there was a rapidly growing and increasingly technical study of logic, linguistics, and the philosophy of science—a development which was at points quite antithetical to analytic philosophy.

In this same post-war era naturalism under Dewey tended to take a defensive position.[2] It viewed the promiscuous intellectual interests and enthusiasms in those years of confusion and anxiety as markedly a "retreat from reason" and responsibility. But what precisely was the responsibility of philosophy, and how was it to be articulated for a new generation recovering from a great war and confronted by greatly altered social conditions and national and international tensions? The answer was far from evident. Nor was it very clear what were the intellectual and social problems of the age that philosophers were peculiarly well qualified to illuminate and suggest the needed remedies. Here enjoining the employment of liberal reason, the appeal to inquiry and scientific reason—bulwarks of naturalism—appeared facile and inconclusive. For this was in effect a reaffirmation of method; but method will instruct us as to how to go about solving a problem; it does not tell us what the problems are or where we ought to be going and what the aim. I am not at present concerned with the soundness of this objection; I am simply reporting what I think was the reaction at the time.[3] The feeling was that the naturalists' recommendation of a scientific approach to human problems, while not mere cant, remained so broad in its prescriptive bearing as to provide no specific insights into the problems philosophers were agitating or the acute perplexities of life in the atomic age.[4]

But the conclusion of the war produced a deeper question particularly disturbing to those who had inherited the confident liberal assumption that reason was always a force for good and that, consequently, the workings and effects of scientific intelligence were invariably beneficial cultural gains. This optimistic conviction was severely shaken. For a marvel of scientific theorizing had been harnessed by brilliant feats of technological ingenuity and industry to produce a military weapon of unprecedented violence. If the nineteenth-century belief in progress was killed by World War I, the twentieth-century faith in the inherently ameliorative activity of science was badly wounded by World War II.

The response of naturalism to these critical doubts about the social value, even the threat, of science and its prized prerogative of autonomy of research and discovery was, if again defensive, again eminently reasonable. There was, in the first place, a distinction of importance to be made between the logic and methods of science—whose intrinsic and instrumental value the naturalist continued to affirm—and programs of scientific technology shaped by politicians, industrialists, and the military, about which naturalists and many scientists expressed concern. The naturalists also argued that any responsible assessment of the social

[2] This is the travail of much of the spirit in *Naturalism and the Human Spirit* (New York: Columbia University Press, 1944). We should not overlook the fact, however, that it was the naturalists who most effectively opposed a powerful movement in the 1940s to introduce religious instruction in the public schools and to establish a supernaturalistically inspired moral and metaphysical reform of higher education. For some of the issues see V. T. Thayer, *American Education Under Fire* (New York: Harper & Brothers, 1944).

[3] For a consideration of the criticisms and a response, see Ernest Nagel, "Naturalism Reconsidered." In *Logic Without Metaphysics* (Glencoe: The Free Press, 1956), pp. 3–18.

[4] We noticed a similar kind of problem occurring earlier in the history of pragmatism, §106.

nature and implications of contemporary science must be based on a thoroughly informed understanding of the structure and methods of scientific knowledge. And such understanding was to be gained only through an examination of the history and practice of science itself, rather than proceeding from pre-scientific philosophical principles or metaphysical presuppositions.

In all this the pragmatism and naturalism of Dewey, or the naturalistic systems of Santayana or Whitehead, had not been refuted. Philosophies do not take root, or wither, or undergo revivals by proofs or disproofs. The fortunes of philosophy derive from far more subterranean tensions and disequilibriums of a culture, not all of them rational or always explicable. It was rather that these systems were isolated and by-passed by the new analytic philosophy intent upon a quite different quarry according to a quite different conception of the aims of philosophy. Here was a lesson in history repeating itself. The new philosophy was as intolerant of what had preceded it and which it was replacing, as the old had been in its ascendancy. The leaders of the new movement saw themselves as inaugurating a revolution in philosophy,[5] or so they proclaimed and with some inconsistency since this philosophy—unlike any revolution—was supposed to have no antecedents. Theirs was a conception of philosophy immaculately conceived as unstained by the sins of the past—indeed as having no past. Philosophy, some of the enthusiasts were to declare, began in 1921, or thereabouts.

What had occurred, it would now appear in retrospect, was not a revolution but a long overdue reformation of slack and uncritical uses of certain philosophical concepts, and mismatches among concepts, for the manufacture and trade in some of the "perennial problems" of philosophy. The puzzlements, cramps, and diagnostic treatment of concern to analytic philosophy were not so much problems of philosophy as problems of some professional philosophers. So the analyses of the analysts were conducted in insular fashion; they were deliberately not addressed to problems troubling ordinary persons or specialists in other fields of learning. Analytic philosophy was not a revolution but an episode; and within limits a healthy one. It has shown us that for some special kinds of problems an exposure of certain errant twists and violations of the grammatical anatomy of the problem is required and that analysis is the indispensable technique to be employed.

There is a curious development in the later history of pragmatism concerning which only a few allusions occur in *Meaning and Action*. In the period following World War I, pragmatism had become broadly entrenched in the universities and established effectively, even stridently, in American intellectual life. Many of the leading pragmatists were well-known public figures and their works widely read. Dewey was world-famous. How, then, did it happen that in the nineteen-forties pragmatism was so quickly eclipsed by the movements of logical positivism and analytic philosophy? The change was so complete that a decade later pragmatism was not even a respectable subject of interest in most departments of philosophy. It is only comparatively recently that its philosophers are beginning to be studied again.

---

[5] So the volume, *The Revolution in Philosophy* (London: Macmillan Company, 1956). A. J. Ayer *et al.*

I do not pretend to know the complete answer to this question. I suggested some difficulties in Dewey's pragmatic view of the role of philosophy as a form of cultural reconstruction and "social engineering" (in the latter pages of §§ 105 and 106). While Dewey's associates and disciples—Max Otto, Boyd Bode, Horace Kallen, and Sidney Hook—inspired generations of students to take the social responsibility and ongoing critical task of philosophy seriously, using "intelligence" in specifying and resolving human problems, the students of those students were to be less clear about how this function philosophy was to be performed. To some extent the influence of pragmatism as, so to speak, a public philosophy and critique of culture in expressing and also directing the thinking of many persons on practical social issues was due to its ties with the parties of progressivism and liberalism in American politics. And fate has not been kind to liberalism which has become increasingly diffident and uncertain of its prospects and aims and under assault from the right and left. In 1943, in a reflection on his earlier study, *Sociology and Pragmatism,* C. Wright Mills wrote of "the present situation of pragmatism in America":

> Perhaps never before in its eighty years' existence has this style of thinking been so under attack as it has since the world crises which came to fruition in the late thirties. The attack has been in "spiritual" or "religious" terms and also on "political" grounds . . . The personal and political reasons for such a course of events must be examined from a standpoint as removed from these reasons as possible. To so examine it would offer the possibility of a fundamental understanding of the conditions for the future development of philosophy in the United States.[6]

Under such critical pressures from outside and within the universities, a pragmatist mindful of his professional career had few choices to make. One could, of course, change allegiances and find a new life in another philosophy—even in the opportune and expedient spirit of an unscrupulous pragmatism become an anti-pragmatist. Or one could unpragmatically turn from the world, either to find deliverence in some reaches of a more commodious reality, or to find solace in the pursuit of technical accomplishment in a specialized area of philosophic study. Or, beyond merely repeating the words of Dewey and explaining them, one could attempt to find some vital new forms which might be given to the doctrines of pragmatism.

Now this last option, I think, helps partly to account for what happened to pragmatism. It explains a certain attraction and amiable receptivity among many of the younger pragmatists to logical positivism and analytic philosophy as these movements began to gain ground in this country. The motivating insight was that despite some accidental differences of historical lineage and style of expression, these philosophies were fundamentally in accord and reconcilable with pragmatic convictions. Here, it was supposed, were the new forms and directions for a rejuvenation of pragmatism. And there were certain affinities in underlying ideas and general aims among these outlooks (as noted in the conclusion of § 80).[7]

---

[6] *Sociology and Pragmatism,* Irving L. Horowitz, ed. (New York: Oxford University Press, 1964), p. 467.

[7] For a critical and constructive view of some of the philosophic harmonies and discords within the analytic, positivistic, and pragmatic movements and the development of a point of deriving from but going beyond them, see Morton White, *Toward Reunion in Philosophy* (Cambridge, Mass.: Harvard University Press, 1956).

I will not name names, but it would be possible to cite a number of able young American philosophers who were reared in the naturalism and pragmatism of Dewey and who became increasingly concerned with one or both of the newer movements. When Gilbert Ryle's influential book *The Concept of Mind* appeared in 1949, it was not difficult for those who had read Dewey to find a number of very pertinent similarities between Ryle's critical objectives and analyses and ideas Dewey had advanced and developed in considerable detail some thirty years earlier.

But there were differences. Dewey himself preserved a sceptical attitude toward this course of events and preferences. He took a critical view of the growing preoccupation with purely professional problems, of the cultivation of formal techniques or analytic procedures for dealing with newly resurrected problems of epistemology which he thought had long been decisively resolved.

There was also a relatively brief alliance of pragmatists and naturalists with logical positivists in the coalition of "logical empiricism."[8] The common cause was in recognizing the importance of the scientific attitude as a powerful antidote to authoritarian doctrines; of the role of the sciences in improving the conditions of modern civilization; and the needed pursuit of greater understanding of the unity and interrelations of the sciences. But the two parties to the alliance were at bottom inimical in their respective conceptions of empirical knowledge and moral experience. C. I. Lewis took note of the underlying disparities in an illuminating essay on the subject.[9] Indeed while Dewey's *Theory of Valuation* (1939) was ostensibly a contribution to this cooperative venture, its sharpest criticisms are directed to epistemological assumptions and the emotive theory of ethical statements held by most of the logical positivists and analytic philosophers associated with the logical empiricist movement.

These observations, however, do not explain why pragmatism soon ceased to be taken seriously as a philosophy. In conducting his survey of the pragmatic movement, Charles Morris comments on the "termination of the Chicago School."[10] The leaders of the school at the University of Chicago were Addison Moore, James Tufts, Edward Ames, and George Mead. When this generation had passed away, Morris says, the "termination was a voluntary decision." "There was a common feeling that the group had done its work, and that the department henceforth should manifest a diversity of viewpoints." This decision was taken presumably in the nineteen-thirties. Morris went on to become a prominent exponent of logical empiricism. But one wonders, and Morris does not say, how this voluntary coroner's verdict was reached and what in the work of this school of thinkers was judged to have become moribund. It can be arued, of course, that all philosophies, like all men, are mortal and pragmatism had simply had its day. But I have tried to indicate in this book, and to suggest below, that some of the leading ideas of pragmatism remain unfinished business for philosophy and will reward consideration.

[8] Herbert Feigl was an effective exponent of the alliance. See his "Logical Empiricism." In *Twentieth Century Philosophy* (New York: Philosophical Library, 1943), esp. pp. 382, 408.
[9] "Logical Positivism and Pragmatism." In *Collected Papers,* pp. 92–112. Complete reference in II below.
[10] *The Pragmatic Movement in American Philosophy,* p. 190. Complete reference in II below.

The answer to our query about pragmatism is, I think, as follows. The initial and temporary association of pragmatists, positivists, and analytic philosophers induced an infectious persuasion that something really new was happening in philosophy: new methods with new prospects of employment; new or vastly improved techniques of using logic and language for detecting fallacies and correcting or rejecting erroneous theories and promising finally to dispose of the old problems of philosophy and old philosophies altogether. In the case of pragmatism, the broader and more fundamental philosophic outlook of which it was a related part, the organized expression of thought and vision elaborated by Peirce, James, and Dewey began to be either forgotten or completely ignored. Pragmatism came to be identified as a suggestive methodological principle of semantics. To ask what an idea, or better, a sentence "means" is to ask for its testable consequences or how it would be verified. But this is a truncated version of pragmatism. It was taken as a crude anticipation of the verifiability theory of meaning so carefully expounded by the logical positivists (§ 21). And if this was all pragmatism had to teach, it was little wonder that it should soon cease to be of interest. The more basic sense in which James held that truth is a species of good (§ 21) or that Peirce and Dewey conceived the developmental, purposive, and social character of inquiry and intelligent conduct were passed over as irrelevant to the pursuit of new technical analyses of scientific and philosophic ideas. And inspiring many of the new endeavors was the traditional conception of philosophy as the quest for certainty, a search for the grounding of knowledge in antecedent sensory data, or basic propositions, or analytical principles, which had been extensively criticized earlier by most of the pragmatists. The pragmatic view of philosophy as a continuous effort to develop methods of understanding and effective control of specific human and cultural problems was alien to the spirit of the time in which it was increasingly fashionable to regard philosophy as a highly specialized academic discipline. James was dismissed as a proponent of irrationalism in moral and religious matters; Peirce and Dewey as too recondite and obscure.

In due course the logical positivists and empiricists were confronted by two insuperable difficulties. This group of philosophers had succeeded in remaining impervious to the criticisms that other philosophers, including Dewey and Lewis, had made of its epistemological theories and interpretation of ethical statements. But the two difficulties could not be avoided since they threatened disaster for the entire program and main doctrines of positivism and logical empiricism. The first difficulty was that the verifiability theory of meaning admitted of no formulation sufficiently precise to include just what these philosophers wanted to include as "meaningful" (or "cognitively significant") discourse and to exclude all else. (Thus see the last three paragraphs of § 21 for a brief discussion and references.) The second difficulty was that the notion of analyticity and the dichotomy of analytic and synthetic meaning, which was central to the theory and analysis of scientific knowledge, logic, and mathematics, could not be successfully maintained (on which see Appendix 6). The first difficulty, while serious, might have been partially circumvented; but the second was a fatal blow to logical positivism and logical empiricism and to some tenets of analytic philosophy as well.

By the nineteen-forties, however, it was with some irony that pragmatism was to find itself dislodged and driven from the academic premises by the very movements to which it had initially been so hospitable.

It would be interesting and instructive to inquire into the reasons for these changes in philosophic opinion and doctrines, why they assumed just the particular form and direction they have taken, and what in the experience of World War II and the vicissitudes of political and social affairs subsequently might have affected them. And such an inquiry, if brought up to date, would be obliged to consider why some of the most able proponents of analytic philosophy have turned lately either to historical studies, or to engage in currently contested theses in legal and ethical subjects of an urgently practical nature—a turn quite contrary to the spirit originally animating this movement; a development rather "pragmatic," it happens; and one that Dewey would have welcomed. All this would constitute a chapter on the history of contemporary philosophy in America. But to pursue the matter here would lead too far from the present purpose.

My purpose, to return to the starting point of this limited preambulation, is to report the philosophic atmosphere in which this book came to be. The prevailing opinion, as I have indicated, was not favorable to a work on pragmatism. I was not, of course, attempting to revive or reassert pragmatism; I was surveying a historical development and assessing the central doctrines and insights and still valuable lessons to be learned from a study of the work of the major pragmatists. If I was urging anything, it was that the problems to which the pragmatists addressed their attention, and their manner of conceiving the problems and solutions, would well repay further examination in the light of contemporary philosophic concerns.

In any case, there has been a change in the weather. The article on "Naturalism" in *The Encyclopedia of Philosophy* recorded the demise of that philosophy. That was in 1967. But one year later, in the John Dewey Lectures at Columbia University, W. V. Quine was espousing a very much alive and influential version of naturalism.[11] Prophesying intellectual trends is a risky business. In the last decade there has been an increasing diversity of interests and subjects of study in philosophy, and a corresponding absence of any one dominant orthodoxy zealously proscribing how philosophy is to be performed and what its province must be.[12] One of several changes has been that philosophers are again taking the history of philosophy seriously. The earlier belief that history and philosophy are entirely separate domains, that philosophy "proper" has no history, seems now to have become history. This is a promising advance (or return); for it is only by some understanding of the philosophical past that present problems are to be gauged and any future progress is to be measured. I am not suggesting that philosophers should become slaves of history or that they follow Marlowe's Dr. Faustus:

[11] *Ontological Relativity and Other Essays* (New York: Columbia University Press, 1969).

[12] Twenty years ago it would have been hardly conceivable that philosophers would engage in serious analyses of such subjects as abortion, rights of future generations, rights of animals, fair taxation, sex, and death. These are now issues under discussion.

And live and die in Aristotle's works.

On the contrary, some sense of the past is essential if we are not to become its victims. Or, as Peirce said: "One of the main purposes of studying history ought to be so free us from the tyranny of preconceived notions" (*CP* 7.227).

A singular instance of this growing recognition of how philosophy is affected by and utilizes its past, has been a new concern with the history of American philosophy. While important scholarly work on American philosophic thought has been carried on for many years, I think it is fair to say that very little attention has been given to the subject, especially by philosophers.[13] Perhaps (as suggested in §§ 102–103) because Americans have been schooled in the great traditions of English and European philosophy, they have been prone to regard their own philosophical past as a foreigner might view it: as a manifestation of native eccentricity and naivete, and the lineal ties, therefore, to be acknowledged, if at all, with some embarrassment, as one might a dissolute uncle. But in recent years the perspective and the sentiments have changed considerably. Mark Twain tells a story of the man who confessed that in his youth he could scarcely bear his father's ignorance, but some years later was amazed to discover how much the old gentleman had learned in the meantime. As we begin to acquire a more substantial knowledge of the efforts and outlook of our philosophical ancestors, it is astonishing how they seem to have suddenly gained in acuity and wisdom.

As for pragmatism, the revival of interest is clearly evident in a rapidly expanding literature on the philosophers as well as on central tenets and themes that have been suggestive and pertinent in current discussions in the philosophy of science, the analysis of knowledge, and in legal, ethical, and social philosophy.

There are at least three reasons for this revival which may be noted briefly.

(1) The pragmatic theory of the relation of knowledge to action. This theory has evident philosophical connections (although not, so far as I know, of a historical kind) with some versions of contemporary Marxism and certain influential European views of a philosophy of praxis.[14] It is also germane to the methodology of the newly developing disciplines of bio-medical ethics, ecology and environmental decision making, and more generally as to how the role of the social sciences in forming social policies and programs is to be conceived.

(2) The pragmatic theory of inquiry. The endeavor of the pragmatists to formulate a logical theory of intelligent conduct, communication, and problem-solving, and the conditions under which beliefs and statements are warranted, is of pertinence to current investigations of scientific explanation and to the study of concept formation and methodological procedures in psychiatry, sociology, and history. And in this connection there is the important argument, advanced especially by Peirce and Dewey, that the foundations of knowledge and

---

[13] This is noted, for example, by Blau in his Preface. Complete reference in the Bibliography.

[14] Thus see the books by Bernstein and Habermas cited in II below. The contemporary developments mentioned here are remarked on by John Smith in *Purpose and Thought*, p. 9, also cited in II below.

standards of credence are located not outside but within the evolving operations of inquiry. Scientific knowledge itself is to be likened to a growing organism—a changing network of developing strategies and adjustments for anticipating and explaining events—a process, rather than the traditionally imagined conceptual system derived from first principles and antecedent certainties. Principles are reinterpreted as policies. The justification of belief is no longer regarded as a search for prior causes or reasons as guarantees of truth, but turns rather on the consequences which belief, as a rule of inference and action, contributes to the stability and efficacy of the overall organization of knowledge.

For the pragmatist, then, the cognitive strength and warrant of a system of beliefs is not dependent on, or measured by, certain indubitable constituents, but by considerations of utility and success in accounting for and foreseeing experience and by the practices made possible by the system as a whole. The structure of knowledge has usually been pictured as an elaborate edifice resting on a foundation of unshakable truths. Peirce suggested that we think of the system not as a "chain which is no stronger than its weakest link, but a cable whose fibers may be ever so slender, provided they are sufficiently numerous and intimately connected." And we are to trust, he says, "rather to the multitude and variety of its arguments than to the conclusiveness of any one" (*CP* 5.265).[15]

(3) The pragmatic theory of the relation of scientific knowledge and human values. A main theme of the present book is that developments in modern natural science and technology have transformed traditional moral beliefs and ideals. There is thus an acute and persistent problem of critically reinterpreting ethical and religious ideals, and in forming moral doctrines as effective guides for conduct, in accordance with—rather than directed against or away from—such advances of our knowledge of human nature and the world. These problems are surely philosophical but are not of concern only to philosophers.

I will not recapitulate what has already been discussed in earlier chapters except to remark that the generally accepted and long favored assumption of a difference in kind between judgments of fact and of value is rejected by pragmatism. As an alternative to that assumption, the pragmatists developed an interpretation of scientific inquiry and the attainment of truth as profoundly moral activities; truth, as James stated the argument, is a species of good. This was a radical conclusion drawn from the theory of the adaptive and purposive nature of the thinking process as mediated by general habits in the realization of certain goals. It leads to no less than a major revision of traditional conceptions of knowledge and valuation and what has hitherto been regarded as the separate provinces of "natural" and "moral" philosophy. The view of experimental inquiry as a paradigm of moral activity was novel in its own time and its significance still remains to be fully appreciated; it has been neglected even in most expositions of the philosophy of pragmatism. C. I. Lewis aptly summarized the main idea:

---

[15] This and part of the preceding paragraph is drawn from my paper "The Revolution in Empiricism: Peirce on Scientific Knowledge and Truth," *The Southern Journal of Philosophy*, 17 (1979), 531–545.

pragmatism might almost be defined as the contention that all judgments of truth are judgments of value: that verification is value-determination, and the criterion of truth is the realization of some kind of value.[16]

This conception of the ethical character of inquiry and truth is, I believe, one reason for the renewal of interest in pragmatism in America and Europe. A more complete development of the argument in the light of our present understanding of natural science and of ethical theory is to be recommended.

II

Some Recent Literature[17]

Many books and many more articles on American philosophy, its philosophers, and pragmatism have appeared since *Meaning and Action* was first published. Of very great value, and indispensable to future scholarship, are the publications of scrupulously edited and reliable texts of primary sources: the works of James and Dewey. And there is soon to appear a comprehensive edition of Peirce's writings which will include a large amount of still unpublished material.

On Dewey: *The Early Works* and *Middle Works*—1882–1924. Jo Ann Boydston, Editor. Carbondale, Illinois: Southern Illinois University Press, 1969 —. Thirteen volumes to date.

On James: *The Works of William James*. Frederick Burkhardt, General Editor. Cambridge, Mass.: Harvard University Press, 1975 —. Seven volumes to date.

On Peirce: The Peirce Edition Propect, under the direction of Max H. Fisch, plans a selection of Peirce's writings in chronological order to begin appearing in 1980, published by Indiana University Press. Twenty volumes are planned.

As to the secondary literature cited below, with apologies to many authors, I have had to be selective. My principle of selection is to include works of varying points of view and which are especially helpful in providing further references and stimulating further study. With a few exceptions, I have confined the list to books; even a representative list of the periodical literature would be too lengthy to be useful here. Certain convenient collections of source materials are noted as well as helpful reference guides to the works of the philosophers considered.

---

[16] *Collected Papers*, p. 112. Complete reference in II below. Lewis also writes, p. 112:

> For the pragmatist, there can be no final division between 'normative' and 'descriptive.' The validity of any standard of correctness has reference to some order of 'descriptive facts'; and every determination of fact reflects some judgment of values and constitutes an imperative for conduct. The validity of cognition itself is inseparable from that final test of it which consists in some valuable result of the action which it serves to guide. Knowledge—so the pragmatist conceives—is for the sake of action; and action is directed to realization of what is valuable.

[17] I am indebted to Professors Max H. Fisch and John J. McDermott for helpful advice concerning some features of the bibliography that follows. They are not to be held responsible, however, for the selections or omissions.

AMERICAN PHILOSOPHY. For a valuable survey and discussion of the literature, see John J. McDermott, "The Renascence of Classical American Philosophy," *American Studies International* 16 (1978), 5–17.

Caws, Peter, ed., *Two Centuries of Philosophy: American Philosophy Since the Revolution.* Oxford: Basil Blackwell, 1980.

Flower, Elizabeth, and Murray G. Murphey, *A History of Philosophy in America.* 2 vols. New York: G. P. Putnam's Sons, 1977.

Kuklick, Bruce, *The Rise of American Philosophy—Cambridge, Massachusetts, 1860–1930.* New Haven: Yale University Press, 1977.

Novak, Michael, ed., *American Philosophy and the Future.* New York: Charles Scribner's Sons, 1968.

Reck, Andrew. *The New American Philosophers.* Baton Rouge: Louisiana State University Press, 1968.

Shahan, Robert W., and Kenneth R. Merrill, eds. *American Philosophy from Edwards to Quine.* Norman, Oklahoma: University of Oklahoma Press, 1977.

Smith, John. *Themes in American Philosophy.* New York: Harper and Row, Harper Torchbooks, 1970.

White, Morton. *Science and Sentiment in America.* New York: Oxford University Press, 1968.

PRAGMATISM. An excellent, thoughtful guide is Sandra B. Rosenthal's "Recent Perspectives in American Pragmatism," *Transactions of the Charles S. Peirce Society* 10 (1974), 76–93, 166–184.

Ayer, A. J. *The Origins of Pragmatism.* San Francisco, California: Freeman, Cooper & Company, 1968.

Eames, S. Morris. *Pragmatic Naturalism.* Carbondale: Southern Illinois University Press, 1977.

Fisch, Max H., "American Pragmatism Before and After 1898." In *American Philosophy from Edwards to Quine,* pp. 78–110.

Hook, Sidney. *Pragmatism and the Tragic Sense of Life.* New York: Basic Books, Inc., 1974.

Morris, Charles. *The Pragmatic Movement in American Philosophy.* New York: George Braziller, 1970.

Rorty, Richard M., "Pragmatism, Relativism, and Irrationalism." Presidential Address, Seventy-sixth Annual Meeting of the American Philosophical Association, Eastern Division. Forthcoming in the *Proceedings and Addresses of the American Philosophical Association* 54 (1980).

Rucker, Darnell. *The Chicago Pragmatists.* Minneapolis: University of Minnesota Press, 1969.

Scheffler, Israel. *Four Pragmatists: A Critical Introduction to Peirce, James, Mead, and Dewey.* New Jersey: Humanities Press, 1974.

Smith, John. *Purpose and Thought: The Meaning of Pragmatism.* London: Hutchinson and Co.; New Haven: Yale University Press, 1978.

Thayer, H. S., ed. *Pragmatism: The Classic Writings.* New York: A Mentor Book, New American Library, 1970.

——————. "Pragmatism." In the *Encyclopaedia Britannica.* Fifteenth Edition. vol. 14. Chicago: Encyclopaedia Britannica, Inc., 1974, 725–744.

White, Morton. *Pragmatism and the American Mind.* New York: Oxford University Press, 1973.

PEIRCE.
Ketner, Kenneth L., Christian J. W. Kloesel, Joseph M. Ransdell, eds. *A Comprehensive Bibliography and Index of the Published Works of Charles S. Peirce with a Bibliography of Secondary Studies.* Microfiche Edition. Lubbock, Texas: Texas Tech Press, 1977.

Eisele, Carolyn, ed. *New Elements of Mathematics by Charles S. Peirce.* 4 vols. The Hague: Mouton & Co.; New Jersey, Humanities Press, 1976.

Fisch, Max H. "Peirce's Place in American Thought," *Ars semeiotica* 1 (1977), 21–37.

——————, "Peirce's General Theory of Signs." In Thomas A. Sebeok, ed. *Sight, Sound, and Sense.* Bloomington, Indiana: University of Indiana Press, 1978.

——————, "Peirce as Scientist, Mathematician, Historian, Logician, and Philosopher." Presidential Address, C. S. Peirce Bicentennial International Congress, Amsterdam, 1976. Forthcoming in *Proceedings* of the Congress. Lubbock, Texas: Texas Tech Press, 1980.

Hardwick, Charles S., ed. *Semantics and Significance: The Correspondence between Charles S. Peirce and Victoria Lady Welby.* Bloomington, Indiana University Press, 1977.

Ketner, Kenneth L., and James E. Cook, eds. *Charles Sanders Peirce: Contributions to* THE NATION. 3 vols. Lubbock, Texas: Texas Tech Press, 1975–1979.

Rescher, Nicholas. *Peirce's Philosophy of Science.* Notre Dame, Indiana: University of Notre Dame Press, 1978.

Reilly, Francis E. *Charles Peirce's Theory of Scientific Method.* New York: Fordham University Press, 1970.

Roberts, Don D. *The Existential Graphs of Charles S. Peirce.* The Hague: Mouton & Co., 1973.

Skagestad, Peter. *The Road to Inquiry: Charles Peirce's Pragmatic Realism.* New York: Columbia University Press, forthcoming.

JAMES.
There is a helpful annotated bibliography in John McDermott's volume of the writings of William James cited below. Also useful is Ignas Scrupskelis's *William James: A Reference Guide* (Boston: G. K. Hall and Co., 1977). A new Biography using the important James family papers in the Harvard University collection, but a study marred by serious philosophical misunderstandings, is Gay Wilson Allen, *William James* (New York: The Viking Press, 1967).

Corti, Walter Robert, ed. *The Philosophy of William James.* Hamburg: Felix Meiner Verlag, 1976.

Edie, James M. "William James and Phenomenology," *The Review of Metaphysics* 23 (1970), 481–526.

Levinson, H. S. *Science, Metaphysics, and the Chance of Salvation: An Interpretation of the Thought of William James.* Missoula, Montana: Scholars Press, 1978.

McDermott, John J., ed. *The Writings of William James.* Chicago: University of Chicago Press, 1977.

Roggerone, G. *James e la crisi della conscienza contemporanea.* Milano: Marzorati, 1967.

Roth, John K. *Freedom and the Moral Life: The Ethics of William James.* Philadelphia: Westminster Press, 1969.

Seigfried, Charlene Haddock. *Chaos and Context: A Study of William James.* Athens, Ohio: Ohio University Press, 1978.

Wild, John. *The Radical Empiricism of William James.* New York: Doubleday & Company, Inc., 1969.

Wilshire, Bruce. *William James and Phenomenology: A Study of the Principles of Psychology.* Bloomington, Indiana: Indiana University Press, 1968.

DEWEY.

Jo Ann Boydston has edited a valuable guide to the central themes of Dewey's thought with bibliographical references in *Guide to the Works of John Dewey* (Carbondale and Edwardsville: Southern Illinois University Press, 1970). See also, Jo Ann Boydston and Kathleen Poulos, eds. *Checklist of Writings About John Dewey* (Carbondale and Edwardsville: Southern Illinois University.Press, 1978). For a comprehensive biography, see George Dykhuizen, *The Life and Mind of John Dewey* (Carbondale and Edwardsville: Southern Illinois University Press, 1973). Also of interest is Neil Couglan, *Young John Dewey* (Chicago: University of Chicago Press, 1975).

Cahn, Steven M., ed. *New Studies in the Philosophy of John Dewey.* Hanover, New Hampshire: The University Press of New England, 1977.

Clopton, Robert W. and Tsuni-chen Ou, eds. and trans. *John Dewey, Lectures in China, 1919–1920.* Honoloulu: University of Hawaii Press, 1973.

Deledalle, G. *L'Idee D'Experience Dans la Philosophie De John Dewey.* Paris: University Presses of France, 1967. (A work that should have been mentioned in the first edition of *Meaning and Action.*)

Dicker, George. *Dewey's Theory of Knowledge.* Philadelphia: Philosophical Monographs, 1976.

Gouinlock, James. *John Dewey's Philosophy of Value.* New York: Humanities Press, 1972.

McDermott, John J., ed. *The Philosophy of John Dewey,* 2 vols. New York: G. P. Putnam's Sons, 1973.

Milanesi, Vincenzo. *Logica della valutazione ed etica naturalistica in Dewey.* Padova: Liviana Editrice, 1977.

Morgenbesser, Sidney. *Dewey and His Critics: Essays from the Journal of Philosophy.* The Journal of Philosophy, Inc., 1977.

Peters, R. S., ed. *John Dewey Reconsidered.* London: Routledge & Kegan Paul, 1977.

MEAD.

Corti, Watler R., ed. *The Philosophy of George Herbert Mead*. Hamburg: Felix Meiner Verlag, 1973. (Essays by European and American scholars and a bibliography of Mead's writings.)

Miller, David L. *George Herbert Mead: Self, Language, and the World*. Austin: University of Texas Press, 1973.

LEWIS. Important for the study and understanding of Lewis's thought is Paul A. Schillp, ed. *The Philosophy of C. I. Lewis* (La Salle, Illinois: The Open Court Publishing Co., 1968).

Goheen, John D., and John L. Mothershed, Jr., eds. *Collected Papers of Clarence Irving Lewis*. Stanford: Stanford University Press, 1970.

Lange, John F., ed. *Clarence Irving Lewis, Values and Imperatives, Studies in Ethics*. Stanford: Stanford University Press, 1969.

Rosenthal, Sandra B. *The Pragmatic A Priori: A Study in the Epistemology of C. I. Lewis*. St. Louis, Missouri: Warren H. Green, Inc., 1976.

SOME FURTHER RECENT WORKS. A number of important recent studies cannot be placed in the above categories, for they are not primarily addressed to pragmatism or to one or more of the above philosophers. But in each case—although in very different ways and in different degrees—the orientation or background of reference to the tradition, or the philosophers, is evident in these independent ventures in critical and constructive philosophizing.

Bernstein, Richard. *Praxis and Action*. Philadelphia, Pennsylvania:, University of Pennsylvania Press, 1971.

Habermas, Jurgen. *Knowledge and Human Interests*. Jeremy Shapiro, trans. Boston: Beacon Press, 1972.

Lee, H. N., *Percepts, Concepts, and Theoretic Knowledge*. Memphis, Tenn.: Memphis State University Press, 1973.

McDermott, John J. *The Culture of Experience: Philosophical Essays in the American Grain*. New York: New York University Press, 1976.

Nagel, Ernest. *Teleology Revisited: and Other Essays in the History and Philosophy of Science*. New York: Columbia University Press, 1979.

Quine, W. V. "The Pragmatists' Place in Empiricism." In a *Symposium on Pragmatism: Its Sources and Prospects*. Columbia, South Carolina: University of South Carolina Press, forthcoming. (Other essays by Ernest Gellner, James Gouinlock, John J. McDermott, and H. S. Thayer.)

Rescher, Nicholas. *The Primacy of Practice: Essays Towards a Pragmatically Kantian Theory of Empirical Knowledge*. Oxford: Basil Blackwell, 1973.

_____. *Methodological Pragmatism: A Systems-Theoretic Approach to the Theory of Knowledge*. New York: New York University Press, 1977.

REVIEWS OF *Meaning and Action*. The two most comprehensive and detailed (and by no means uncritical) studies are: Gary M. Brodsky, "The Pragmatic Movement," *The Review of Metaphysics* 15 (1971), 262–291 (devoted also to Ayer's *The Origins of Pragmatism*); "Perspectives on the History of Pragmatism: A Symposium on H. S. Thayer's *Meaning and Action: A Critical History of Pragmatism*," *Transactions of the Charles S. Peirce Society* 11 (1975), 229–288.

Bibliographical References

This bibliography contains only those works to which references have been made by author or by title in the foregoing pages. In a number of instances reprintings of works are also listed as an aid to the interested reader. Where pagination of the original text and its reprinting differ, the one used is indicated by an asterisk.

Abel, Reuben. *The Pragmatic Humanism of F. C. S. Schiller.* New York: King's Crown Press, 1955.

Adams, G. P., and W. P. Montague, eds. *Contemporary American Philosophy.* 2 vols. New York: The Macmillan Company, 1930.

Anderson, P. R., and Max H. Fisch, eds. *Philosophy in America.* New York: D. Appleton-Century Company, 1939.

Angell, J. R. "The Relations of Structural and Functional Psychology to Philosophy." *The Decennial Publications of the University of Chicago,* First Series, Vol. III, pp. 55–73. Chicago: University of Chicago Press, 1903.

————. *Psychology.* New York: Henry Holt and Company, 1904.

Aquinas, St. Thomas. *Summa Theologiae.* Vols. IV–XII in *St. Thomae Aquinatis Opera Omnia, issue Leonis XIII edita.* 16 vols. Rome: Ex Typographia Polyglotta, S. C. Dé Propaganda Fide, 1882–1948.

Aristotle. *Aristotelis Opera edidit Academia Regia Borussica.* I. Bekker, ed. Berlin, 1831–1870.

————. *Nicomachean Ethics.* M. Ostwald, trans. The Library of Liberal Arts, No. 73. New York: Bobbs-Merrill Company, 1962.

Auden, W. H. *The Dyer's Hand.* New York: Random House, 1962.

Austin, J. L. *Sense and Sensibilia.* New York: Oxford University Press, 1964.

Ayer, A. J. *The Problem of Knowledge.* Baltimore: Penguin Books, 1956.

————. "Chance," *Scientific American,* 213, No. 4 (Oct. 1965), 44–54.

Ayers, M. R. "Counterfactuals and Subjunctive Conditionals," *Mind,* LXXIV (1965), 347–364.

Baldwin, James Mark, ed. *Dictionary of Philosophy and Psychology.* 2 vols. New York: The Macmillan Company, 1901–1902.

Barnes, Winston H. F. "Peirce on 'How to Make Our Ideas Clear.' " In Wiener and Young, pp. 53–60.

Baylis, C. A. "C. I. Lewis's Theory of Value and Ethics." In *C. I. Lewis Commemorative Symposium*, pp. 559–567.

Bergson, Henri L. *Essai sur les données immédiates de la conscience.* Paris: Felix Alcan, 1889.

Berkeley, George. *An Essay Towards A New Theory of Vision.* Dublin, 1709.

———. *A Treatise Concerning the Principles of Human Knowledge.* Dublin, 1710.

———. *Three Dialogues between Hylas and Philonous.* London, 1713.

———. *Siris.* Dublin, 1744.

Bernays, Paul. "Zur Rolle der Sprache in erkenntnistheoretischer Hinsicht," *Synthese,* 13. (1961), 185–200.

Bernheim, Ernst. *Lehrbuch der historischen Methode.* Leipzig: Dunker & Humbolt, 1889.

Bernoulli, Jacob. *Ars conjectandi, opus posthumum.* Basileae, 1713.

Bernstein, Richard J. "Peirce's Theory of Perception." In Moore and Robin, pp. 165–189.

Berthelot, René. *Un romantisme utilitaire.* 3 vols. Paris: Felix Alcan, 1911.

Blau, Joseph L. *Men and Movements in American Philosophy.* Englewood Cliffs, New Jersey: Prentice-Hall, 1952.

Blondel, Maurice. *L'Action.* Paris: Felix Alcan, 1893.

———. "Le point de départ de la recherche philosophique," *Annales de philosophie chrétienne,* 151, Oct. 1905—Mars 1906, pp. 337–360; 152, Oct. 1905—Mars 1906, pp. 225–249.

Bode, Boyd. "Consciousness and Psychology." In Dewey, *et al., Creative Intelligence,* pp. 228–281.

Boole, George. *The Laws of Thought.* London, 1854. Reprinted, New York: Dover Publications, 1950.

Boutroux, Emile. *Science et religion dans la philosophie contemporaine.* Paris: E. Flammarion, 1908.

Bradley, F. H. *The Principles of Logic.* 2 vols. Oxford: Clarendon Press, 1883. 2nd edn., 1922.

———. "On Truth and Practice," *Mind,* XIII (1904), 309–335. Reprinted with changes as ch. 7 in *Essays on Truth and Reality.*

———. *Essays on Truth and Reality.* Oxford: Clarendon Press, 1914.

Braithwaite, R. B. *Scientific Explanation.* Cambridge, Eng.: Cambridge University Press, 1953.

Bridgman, P. W. *The Logic of Modern Physics.* New York: The Macmillan Company, 1927.

Bronstein, D. J. "Inquiry and Meaning." In Wiener and Young, pp. 33–52.

Buchler, Justus. *Charles Peirce's Empiricism.* New York: Harcourt, Brace and Company, 1939.

Büchner, L. F. *Kraft und Stoff.* Leipzig: Verlag von Th. Thomas, 1855.

Burks, Arthur W. "Peirce's Two Theories of Probability." In Moore and Robin, pp. 141–150.

Caird, Edward. Preface in *Essays in Philosophical Criticism,* pp. 1–7. Andrew Seth, and R. B. Haldane, eds. London: Longmans, Green and Co., 1883.

Calderoni, Mario. "La prévision dans la théorie de la connaissance," *Revue de metaphysique et de morale,* XV (1907), 559–576.

———. "L'arbitrario nel funzionamento della vita psichica," *Rivista Psicologia Applicata,* VI (1910), 166–183, 234–248, 385–416.

————, and G. Vailati. *Il Pragmatismo.* G. Papini, ed. Lanciano: R. Carubba, 1918.

————. *Scritti.* O. Campa, ed. Preface by G. Papini. 2 vols. Florence: Societa anon, editrice "La Voce," 1924.

————, and Vailati. *See* Vailati.

Campbell, N. *What Is Science?* London: Methuen & Co., 1921. Reprinted, New York: Dover Publications, 1952.

Carnap, Rudolf. *Der logische Aufbau der Welt.* Berlin-Schlactensee: Weltkreis-Verlag, 1928.

————. "Testability and Meaning," *Philosophy of Science*, III (Oct. 1936), 419–471; V (Jan. 1937), 1–40. Reprinted, New Haven, Conn.: Graduate Philosophy Club, Yale University, 1950.

————. *The Logical Syntax of Language.* London: Kegan Paul, Trench, Trubner & Co., 1937.

————. "Logical Foundations of the Unity of Science." *International Encyclopedia of Unified Science*, Vol. I, No. 1, pp. 42–62. Chicago: University of Chicago Press, 1938.

————. *Meaning and Necessity.* Chicago: University of Chicago Press, 1947. Enlarged ed., 1956.

————. "The Methodological Character of Theoretical Concepts." *Minnesota Studies in the Philosophy of Science*, Vol. I, pp. 38–76. Minneapolis: University of Minnesota Press, 1956.

Cassirer, Ernst. *The Philosophy of the Enlightenment.* Fritz C. A. Koelln, and James P. Pettegrove, trans. Boston: Beacon Press, 1955.

Catlin, George. *The Story of the Political Philosophers.* New York: Tudor Publishing Company, 1947.

Childs, John. *American Pragmatism and Education.* New York: Henry Holt and Company, 1956.

Chiocchetti, E. *Il Pragmatismo.* Milan: Edizione Athena, 1926.

Chisholm, R. M. "The Contrary-to-Fact Conditional," *Mind*, LV (1946), 289–307. Reprinted in Feigl and Sellars, pp. 482–497.

Church, A. *Introduction to Mathematical Logic.* Vol. I. Princeton, New Jersey: Princeton University Press, 1956.

Cohen, Morris, ed. *Chance, Love, and Logic.* New York: Harcourt Brace and Company, 1923.

————. "Charles S. Peirce and a Tentative Bibliography of His Published Works," Peirce commemorative issue of *The Journal of Philosophy, Psychology and Scientific Methods*, pp. 726–737.

Coleridge, S. T. *Letters.* E. H. Coleridge, ed. 2 vols. London: Heinemann, 1895.

Courant, Richard, and Herbert Robbins. *What is Mathematics?* New York: Oxford University Press, 1941.

Couturat, Louis. *La logique de Leibniz.* Paris: Felix Alcan, 1901.

————. "The Principles of Logic." *Encyclopedia of The Philosophical Sciences*, Vol. I, pp. 136–198. London: Macmillan and Co., 1913.

Cudworth, Ralph. *The True Intellectual System of the Universe.* London, 1678. Reprinted, 3 vols., London: T. Tegg, 1845.*

Curry, H. B. *A Theory of Formal Deducibility.* Notre Dame Mathematical Lectures, No. 6, Notre Dame, Ind.: University of Notre Dame Press, 1950.

Darwin, Charles. *On The Origin of Species by Means of Natural Selection, or, the Preservation of Favoured Races in the Struggle for Life.* London: John Murray, 1859.

————. *Expression of the Emotions in Man and Animals.* London: John Murray, 1872.

Descartes, René. *Meditations on First Philosophy.* L. J. Lafleur, trans. The Library of Liberal Arts, No. 29. New York: Bobbs-Merrill Company, 1960.

————. *Regulae ad directionem ingenii. Opuscula Posthuma.* Amsterdam, 1701.

Dewey, John. "The Metaphysical Assumptions of Materialism," *Journal of Speculative Philosophy,* XVIII (1884), 162–174.

————. "The Psychological Standpoint," *Mind,* XI (1886), 1–19.

————. "Psychology as Philosophic Method," *Mind,* XI (1886), 153–173.

————. "Soul and Body," *The Bibliotheca Sacra,* XLIII (1886), 239–263.

————. *Psychology.* New York: Harper & Brothers, 1887. 3d. edn. revised, 1891.

————. "Knowledge as Idealization," *Mind,* XII (1887), 382–396.

————, and J. A. McLellan. *Applied Psychology.* Boston: Educational Publishing Company, n.d. (1889).

————. "The Late Professor Morris." *The Palladium. An Annual Edited by College Fraternities at the University of Michigan,* Vol. XXXI (1889), pp. 110–118.

————. "The Philosophy of Thomas Hill Green," *Andover Review,* XI (1889), 337–355.

————. "On Some Current Conceptions of the Term 'Self,'" *Mind,* XV (1890), 58–74.

————. Review of Edward Caird's *The Critical Philosophy of Immanuel Kant,* in *Andover Review,* XIII (1890), 325–327.

————. *Outlines of a Critical Theory of Ethics.* Ann Arbor: Register Publishing Company, 1891.

————. "The Present Position of Logical Theory," *The Monist,* XI (1891), 1–17.

————. "Green's Theory of the Moral Motive," *Philosophical Review,* I (1892), 593–612.

————. "Self-Realization as the Moral Ideal," *Philosophical Review,* II (1893), 652–664.

————. "The Ego as Cause," *Philosophical Review,* III (1894), 337–341.

————. "The Theory of Emotion," *Psychological Review,* I–II (1894–1895). "I. Emotional Attitudes," I (1894), 553–569. "II. The Significance of Emotions," II (1895), 13–32.

————. "The Reflex Arc Concept in Psychology," *The Psychological Review,* III (1896), 357–370. Reprinted as "The Unit of Behavior" in *Philosophy and Civilization,* pp. 233–248.

————. "Evolution and Ethics," *The Monist,* VIII (1898), 321–341.

————. "Interpretation of Savage Mind," *The Psychological Review,* IX (1902), 217–230. Reprinted in *Philosophy and Civilization,* pp. 166–187.

————, with the cooperation of Members and Fellows of the Department of Philosophy. *Studies in Logical Theory.* Chicago: University of Chicago Press, 1903.

————. *Logical Conditions of a Scientific Treatment of Morality.* Chicago: University of Chicago Press, 1903. Reprinted in *Problems of Men,* pp. 211–249.

————. Review of Ferdinand Canning Scott Schiller's *Humanism,* in *Psychological Bulletin,* II (1904), 335–340.

————. "The Control of Ideas by Facts," *Journal of Philosophy,* IV (1907). Part I, April 11, pp. 197–203; Part II, May 9, pp. 253–259; Part III, June 6, pp. 309–319. Reprinted in *Essays in Experimental Logic,* pp. 230–249.

————. "Does Reality Possess Practical Character?" In *Essays, Philosophical and Psychological, in Honor of William James,* pp. 53–80. New York: Longmans, Green and Co., 1908. Reprinted as "The Practical Character of Reality" in *Philosophy and Civilization,* pp. 36–55.

——. "What Does Pragmatism Mean by Practical?" *Journal of Philosophy,* V (1908), 85–99. Reprinted in *Essays in Experimental Logic,* pp. 303–329.

——. *How We Think.* Boston: D. C. Heath & Company, 1910. Revised edn., New York: D. C. Heath & Company, 1933.

——. *The Influence of Darwin on Philosophy and Other Essays in Contemporary Thought.* New York: Henry Holt and Company, 1910.

——. *Interest and Effort in Education.* Boston: Houghton Mifflin Company, 1913.

——. *The School and Society.* Revised edn., Chicago: University of Chicago Press, 1915.

——. "The Existence of the World as a Problem," *Philosophical Review,* XXIV (1915), 357–370. Reprinted in *Essays in Experimental Logic,* pp. 281–302.

——. "The Logic of Judgments of Practice," *Journal of Philosophy,* XII (Sept. 16, 1915), 505–523; XII (Sept. 30, 1915), 533–543. Reprinted in *Essays in Experimental Logic,* pp. 335–342.

——. *Democracy and Education.* New York: The Macmillan Company, 1916.

——. *Essays in Experimental Logic.* Chicago: University of Chicago Press, 1916. Reprinted, New York: Dover Publications, 1953.

——. "The Pragmatism of Peirce," Peirce commemorative issue of the *Journal of Philosophy, Psychology and Scientific Methods,* pp. 709–715. Reprinted in Cohen, *Chance,* pp. 301–308.

——, George Herbert Mead, Boyd H. Bode, Horace M. Kallen, *et al. Creative Intelligence, Essays in The Pragmatic Attitude.* New York: Henry Holt and Company, 1917.

——. *Reconstruction in Philosophy.* New York: Henry Holt and Company, 1920.* Reprinted with new Introduction, "Reconstruction As Seen Twenty-Five Years Later," Boston: The Beacon Press, 1948; New York: Mentor Books, 1950.

——. *Human Nature and Conduct.* New York: Henry Holt and Company, 1922.

——. "The Development of American Pragmatism." *Studies in the History of Ideas,* Vol. II, pp. 353–377. New York: Columbia University Press, 1925. Reprinted in *Philosophy and Civilization,* pp. 13–35.*

——. *Experience and Nature.* Chicago and London: Open Court Publishing Company, 1925. Revised edn., New York: W. W. Norton & Co., 1929.*

——. "Substance, Power, and Quality in Locke," *Philosophical Review,* XXXV (1926), pp. 22–38.

——. "The Construction of Good." In *The Quest for Certainty,* pp. 254–286. Reprinted in Sellars and Hospers, pp. 272–291.

——. *The Quest for Certainty.* New York: Minton, Balch & Company, 1929.

——. *Individualism, Old and New.* New York: Minton, Balch & Company, 1930.

——. "Conduct and Experience." In Carl Murchison, ed., *Psychologies of 1930,* pp. 409–422. Worcester, Mass.: Clark University Press, 1930. Reprinted in *Philosophy and Civilization,* pp. 249–270.

——. "From Absolutism to Experimentalism." In Adams and Montague, Vol. II, pp. 13–27.

——. *Philosophy and Civilization.* New York: Minton, Balch & Company, 1931.

——. "George Herbert Mead," *Journal of Philosophy,* XXVIII (1931), 309–314.

——. *Art as Experience.* New York: Minton, Balch & Company, 1934.

——. "An Empirical Survey of Empiricisms." *Studies in the History of Ideas,* Vol. III, pp. 3–22. New York: Columbia University Press, 1935.

——. Chairman. *Not Guilty: Report of the Commission of Inquiry into the Charges Made Against Leon Trotsky in the Moscow Trials.* New York: Harpers, 1937.

——. *Logic: The Theory of Inquiry.* New York: Henry Holt and Company, 1938.

————. *Theory of Valuation. International Encyclopedia of Unified Science*, Vol. II, No. 4. Chicago: University of Chicago Press, 1939.

————. "The Vanishing Subject in the Psychology of James," *Journal of Philosophy*, XL (1940), 589–599. Reprinted in *Problems of Men*, pp. 396–409.

————. "Ethical Subject-Matter and Language," *Journal of Philosophy*, XCII (1945), 701–712.

————. "Propositions, Warranted Assertibility and Truth," *Journal of Philosophy*, XXXVIII (1946), 169–186. Reprinted in *Problems of Men*, pp. 331–353.

————. *Problems of Men*. New York: Philosophical Library, 1946.

Diogenes Laertius. *Lives of Eminent Philosophers*. R. D. Hicks, trans. 2 vols. Loeb Classical Library. London: William Heinemann, 1925.

Duhem, Pierre. *La theorie physique*. Paris: Marcel Riviere & Co., 1906. 2nd edn., 1914.

Eddington, A. S. *The Nature of the Physical World*. New York: The Macmillan Company, 1928.

Einstein, Albert. *Relativity. The Special and General Theory*. New York: Crown Publishers, 1961.

Ellis, Leslie. "On The Foundations of the Theory of Probabilities," *Transactions of the Cambridge Philosophy Society*, VIII (1849), 1–6. (Read on Feb. 14, 1842.)

Ezorsky, Gertrude. "Truth in Context," *Journal of Philosophy*, LX (1963), 113–135.

Feigl, H., and W. Sellars, eds. *Readings in Philosophical Analysis*. New York: Appleton-Century-Crofts, 1949.

Fichte, J. G. *The Vocation of Man*. R. M. Chisholm, ed. Library of Liberal Arts, No. 50. New York: Bobbs-Merrill Company, 1956.

Fisch, Max H. "Justice Holmes, The Prediction Theory of the Law, and Pragmatism," *Journal of Philosophy*, XXXIX (1942), 85–97.

————. "Alexander Bain and the Genealogy of Pragmatism," *Journal of the History of Ideas*, XV (1954), 413–444.

————. "Was There a Metaphysical Club in Cambridge?" In Moore and Robin, pp. 3–32.

————. "A Chronicle of Pragmaticism, 1865–1879," *The Monist*, XLVIII (1964), 441–466.

Frankena, W. K. "The Naturalistic Fallacy," *Mind*, XLVIII (1939), 464–477. Reprinted in Sellars and Hospers, pp. 103–114.

————. "C. I. Lewis on the Ground and Nature of the Right," *Journal of Philosophy*, LXI (1964), 489–496.

Galileo, G. *Il Saggiatore*. 1623. In Vol. IV of *Le Opera di Galileo Galilei*. E. Alberi, ed. 16 vols. Florence: Societa editrice fiorentina, 1842–1856.

Gallie, W. D. *Peirce and Pragmatism*. London: Penguin Books, 1952.

Geiger, George R. *John Dewey in Perspective*. New York: Oxford University Press, 1958.

Gerhardt, C. I. *Der Briefwechsel von Gottfried Wilhelm Liebniz mit Mathematikern*. Hildesheim: Georg Olms Verlagsbuchhandlung, 1962.

Goethe, Johann Wolfgang von. *Faust. Erster Teil*. In Vol. VIII of *Goethes Werke*. Tübingen: J. C. Cotta, 1808. *Zweiter Teil*. Vol. I in *Goethe's nachgelassene Werke*. Eckermann and Reiner, eds. Stuttgart and Tübingen: J. C. Cotta, 1832.

Goodman, Nelson. "The Problem of Counterfactual Conditionals," *Journal of Philosophy*, XLIV (1947), 113–128. Reprinted in Linsky, pp. 231–246. Reprinted in *Fact, Fiction, and Forecast*, pp. 3–27.

————. "On Likeness of Meaning," *Analysis*, X (1949), 1–7. Reprinted with revisions in Linsky, pp. 67–74.

————. *The Structure of Appearance*. Cambridge, Mass.: Harvard University Press, 1951. 2nd edn., New York: Bobbs-Merrill Company, 1966.

————. *Fact, Fiction, and Forecast*. Cambridge, Mass.: Harvard University Press, 1955. 2nd edn., New York: Bobbs-Merrill Company, 1965.*

Goudge, Thomas A. *The Thought of Charles Sanders Peirce*. Toronto: University of Toronto Press, 1950.

Green, Thomas Hill. "The Philosophy of Aristotle," *North British Review*, XLV (1866), 105–144. Reprinted in *Works*, Vol. III, pp. 46–91.

————. "Mr. Herbert Spencer and Mr. G. H. Lewes: Their Application of the Doctrines of Evolution to Thought," *Contemporary Review*, Vols. XXXI–XXXII. Part I, "Mr. Spencer on the Relation of Subject to Object," XXXI (1878), 24–53. Part II, "Mr. Spencer on the Independence of Matter," XXXI (1878), 745–769. Part III, "Mr. Lewes' Account of Experience," XXXII (1878), 751–772. Reprinted in *Works*, Vol. I, pp. 373–470.

————. Introduction to Hume, *A Treatise of Human Nature and Dialogues Concerning Natural Religion*. Vol. I, pp. 1–299; Vol. II, pp. 1–71. T. H. Green, and T. H. Grose, eds. 4 vols. London: Longmans, Green and Co., 1878. Reprinted in *Works*, Vol. I, pp. 1–371.

————. *Prolegomena to Ethics*. A. C. Bradley, ed. Oxford: Clarendon Press, 1883. 5th edn., with Preface by E. Caird, 1906.

————. "Lectures on Mill." *Works*, Vol. II, pp. 195–306.

————. *Works of Thomas Hill Green*. R. L. Nettleship, ed. 3 vols. London: Longmans, Green and Co., 1885–1888.

Gullace, Giovanni. "The Pragmatist Movement in Italy," *Journal of the History of Ideas*, XXIII (1962), 91–105.

Hare, R. M. *The Language of Morals*. Oxford: Clarendon Press, 1952.

Hébert, Marcel. *Le pragmatisme. Etude de ses diverses formes anglo-américaines*. Paris: Emil Nourry, 1908.

Hegel, G. W. F. *Reason in History. A General Introduction to the Philosophy of History*. R. Hartman, trans. Library of Liberal Arts, No. 35. New York: Bobbs-Merrill Company, 1953.

Hempel, C. G. "Problems and Changes in the Empiricist Criterion of Meaning," *Revue internationale de philosophie*, XI (1950), 41–63. Reprinted in Linsky, pp. 163–185.

————. *Fundamentals of Concept Formation in Empirical Science. International Encyclopedia of Unified Science*, Vol. II, No. 7. Chicago: University of Chicago Press, 1952.

Hermann, Conrad. *Geschichte der Philosophie in pragmatischer Behandlung*. Leipzig: Fleischer, 1867.

Hesiod. *The Homeric Hymns and Homerica*. H. G. Evelyn-White, trans. Loeb Classical Library. London: William Heinemann, 1914.

Hobbes, Thomas. *Leviathan, or the Matter, Forme, & Power of a Common-Wealth Ecclesiasticall and Civill*. London, 1651.

Holmes, Oliver Wendell. *The Common Law*. Boston: Little, Brown and Company, 1881. Reissued, Mark DeWolf Howe, ed. Boston: Little, Brown and Company, 1963.*

Hook, Sidney. *John Dewey: An Intellectual Portrait*. New York: The John Day Co., 1939.

————. "The Desirable and Emotive in Dewey's Ethics." In S. Hook, ed. *John Dewey*.

Philosopher of Science and Freedom, pp. 194–216. New York: Dial Press, 1950.

Horton, Walter Marshall. *The Philosophy of Abbe Boutain*. New York: New York University Press, 1926.

Hume, David. *A Treatise of Human Nature*. L. A. Selby-Bigge, ed. Oxford: Oxford University Press, 1888.

Husserl, E. C. A. *Logische Untersuchungen*. 2 vols. Halle a.d. S.: M. Niemeyer, 1900–1901.

Huxley, Thomas H. *Evolution and Ethics and Other Essays*. New York and London: D. Appleton and Company, 1914.

James, William. "The Sentiment of Rationality," *Mind*, IV (1874), 317–364. Reprinted in *Collected Essays and Reviews*, pp. 83–136.

————. "Remarks on Spencer's Definition of Mind as Correspondence," *Journal of Speculative Philosophy*, XII (1878), 1–18. Reprinted in *Collected Essays and Reviews*, pp. 43–68.

————. "Are We Automata?" *Mind*, IV (1879), 1–22.

————. "The Spatial Quale," *Journal of Speculative Philosophy*, XIII (1879), 64–87.

————. "The Feeling of Effort." *Anniversary Memoirs of the Boston Society of Natural History*. 32 pgs. Boston, 1880. Reprinted in *Collected Essays and Reviews*, pp. 151–219.

————. "Reflex Action and Theism," *Unitarian Review*, XVI (1881), 389–416. Reprinted in *The Will to Believe*, pp. 111–144.

————. "What is an Emotion?" *Mind*, IX (1884), 188–205. Reprinted in *Collected Essays and Reviews*, pp. 244–275.

————. "On the Function of Cognition," *Mind*, X (1885), 27–44. Reprinted in *The Meaning of Truth*, pp. 1–42.

————. *The Principles of Psychology*. 2 vols. New York: Henry Holt and Company, 1890. Reprinted, New York: Dover Publications, 1950.

————. *The Will to Believe and other Essays in Popular Philosophy*. New York: Longmans, Green and Co., 1897.

————. "Philosophical Conceptions and Practical Results." *The University of California Chronicle*, Berkeley, Sept. 1898. 24 pgs. Reprinted with some changes as "The Pragmatic Method," *Journal of Philosophy, Psychology and Scientific Methods*, I (1904), 673–687. The original paper reprinted in *Collected Essays and Reviews*, pp. 406–437.

————. *Talks to Teachers on Psychology: And to Students on some of Life's Ideals*. New York: Henry Holt and Company, 1899.

————. *The Varieties of Religious Experience: A Study in Human Nature*. New York and London: Longmans, Green and Co., 1902.

————. "Does 'Consciousness' Exist?" *Journal of Philosophy, Psychology and Scientific Methods*, I (1904), 477–491. Reprinted in *Essays in Radical Empiricism*, pp. 1–38, and in *Radical Empiricism and A Pluralistic Universe*, pp. 1–38.

————. "Humanism and Truth," *Mind*, XIII (1904), 457–475. Reprinted "with slight verbal revision" as ch. 3 in *The Meaning of Truth*.

————. "G. Papini and The Pragmatist Movement in Italy," *Journal of Philosophy, Psychology and Scientific Methods*, III (1906), 337–341. Reprinted in *Collected Essays and Reviews*,* pp. 459–466.

————. *Pragmatism: A New Name for Some Old Ways of Thinking*. New York and London: Longmans, Green and Co., 1907.* Enlarged edn. (including the Preface and three essays from *The Meaning of Truth*), New York: Longmans, Green and Co., 1943. Reprinted, New York: Meridian Books, 1955.

———. Review of M. Hébert, *Le Pragmatisme*, in *Journal of Philosophy, Psychology and Scientific Methods*, V (1908), 689–694. Reprinted as ch. 12 in *The Meaning of Truth*.

———. *The Meaning of Truth, A Sequel to "Pragmatism."* New York and London: Longmans, Green and Co., 1909.

———. "Bradley or Bergson?" *Journal of Philosophy, Psychology and Scientific Methods*, VII (1910), 29–33. Reprinted in *Collected Essays and Reviews*, pp. 491–499.

———. *Essays in Radical Empiricism.* New York and London: Longmans, Green and Co., 1912.

———. *Collected Essays and Reviews.* Ralph Barton Perry, ed. New York and London: Longmans, Green and Co., 1920.

———. *Letters of William James.* Henry James, ed. 2 vols. Boston: The Atlantic Monthly Press, 1920.

———. *Radical Empiricism and A Pluralistic Universe.* New York: Longmans, Green and Co., 1943.

Jerusalem, W. (trans.). William James, *Der Pragmatismus.* Leipzig: Verlag von Dr. Werner Klinkhardt, 1908.

Joergensen, Joergen. *A Treatise of Formal Logic.* 3 vols. London: Humphrey Milford, Oxford University Press, and Copenhagen: Levin & Munksgaard, 1931.

———. *The Development of Logical Empiricism. International Encyclopedia of Unified Science*, Vol. II, No. 6. Chicago: University of Chicago Press, 1951.

Johnson, Samuel. *A Dictionary of the English Language.* London, 1755.

Jones, Marc E. *George Sylvester Morris.* Philadelphia: David McKay Company, 1948.

Kallen, Horace M. "Pragmatism and its 'Principles,'" *Journal of Philosophy, Psychology and Scientific Methods*, VIII (1911), 617–636.

———, ed. *The Philosophy of William James.* New York: Modern Library, n.d.

Kant, Immanuel. *Immanuel Kant's Critique of Pure Reason.* Norman K. Smith, trans. London: Macmillan and Co., 1933.

———. *Prolegomena to Any Future Metaphysics.* Mahaffy-Larus, trans. Revised, Lewis White Beck. Library of Liberal Arts, No. 27. New York: Bobbs-Merrill Company, 1951.

———. *Beantwortung der Frage: Was heist Aufklärung?* 1784.

———. *Fundamental Principles of the Metaphysic of Morals.* In T. K. Abbot, trans., *Kant's Theory of Ethics*, pp. 1–84. London and New York: Longmans, Green and Co., 1909. Reprinted, Library of Liberal Arts, No. 16. New York: Bobbs-Merrill Company, 1949.*

Kaplan, Abraham. *The Conduct of Inquiry.* San Francisco: Chandler Publishing Company, 1964.

Kenna, J. C. "Ten Unpublished Letters from William James, 1842–1910 to Francis Herbert Bradley, 1846–1924," *Mind*, LXXV (1966), 309–331.

Kennedy, Gail. "The Pragmatic Naturalism of Chauncey Wright." *Studies in the History of Ideas*, Vol. III, pp. 477–503. New York: Columbia University Press, 1935.

Keynes, J. M. *A Treatise on Probability.* London: Macmillan and Co., 1931.

Kneale, William. *Probability and Induction.* Oxford: Oxford University Press, 1949.

Kraushaar, Otto F. "Lotze's Influence on the Pragmatism and Practical Philosophy of William James," *Journal of the History of Ideas*, I (1940), 439–458.

Krikorian, Y. H., ed. *Naturalism and the Human Spirit.* New York: Columbia University Press, 1944.

Ladd-Franklin, Christine. "Charles S. Peirce at the Johns Hopkins," Peirce commemorative issue of the *Journal of Philosophy, Psychology and Scientific Methods,* pp. 715–722.

Lalande, Andre. "Pragmatisme et pragmaticisme," *Revue philosophique,* LXI (1906), 121–146.

Lamont, Corliss. "New Light on Dewey's Common Faith," *Journal of Philosophy,* LVIII (1961), 21–28.

Langford, C. H., and C. I. Lewis, see Lewis, 1932.

Lenz, John. "Induction as Self-Corrective." In Moore and Robin, pp. 151–162.

Lenzen, V. F. "Charles S. Peirce as Astronomer." In Moore and Robin, pp. 33–50.

Leroux, E. *Le Pragmatisme americain et anglais.* Paris: Felix Alcan, 1923.

Le Roy, E. "Science et philosophie," *Revue de metaphysique et de morale,* VII (1899), 375–425, 503–562, 708–731; VIII (1900), 37–72.

———. *Dogme et critique.* Paris: Blaud, 1907.

Lewis, C. I. "Types of Order and the System Sigma," *Philosophical Review,* XXV (1916), 407–419. Reprinted in J. E. Creighton, ed., *Papers in Honor of Josiah Royce on His Sixtieth Birthday,* pp. 179–191. New York: Longmans, Green and Co., 1916.

———. "The Issues Concerning Material Implication," *Journal of Philosophy, Psychology and Scientific Methods,* XIV (1917), 350–356.

———. *A Survey of Symbolic Logic.* Berkeley: University of California Press, 1918.

———. "A Pragmatic Conception of the *a Priori,*" *Journal of Philosophy,* XX (1923), 169–177. Reprinted in Feigl and Sellars, pp. 286–294.

———. "The Pragmatic Element in Knowledge." *University of California Publications in Philosophy,* Vol. VI, No. 3, pp. 205–227. Berkeley: University of California Press, 1926.

———. *Mind and the World Order.* New York: Charles Scribner's Sons, 1929. Reprinted, New York: Dover Publications, 1956.

———, and C. H. Langford. *Symbolic Logic.* New York and London: The Century Co., 1932.

———. "Experience and Meaning," *Philosophical Review,* XLIII (1934), 125–146. Reprinted in Feigl and Sellars, pp. 128–145.

———. "Meaning and Action," in A Symposium of Reviews of John Dewey's *Logic: The Theory of Inquiry,* in *Journal of Philosophy,* XXXVI (1939), 572–576.

———. "The Modes of Meaning," *Philosophy and Phenomenological Research,* IV (1944), 236–249. Reprinted in Linsky, pp. 50–63.

———. *An Analysis of Knowledge and Valuation.* La Salle, Ill.: Open Court Publishing Company, 1946.

———. *The Ground and Nature of Right.* New York: Columbia University Press, 1955.

———. *Our Social Inheritance.* Bloomington: Indiana University Press, 1957.

———. *C. I. Lewis Commemorative Symposium, Journal of Philosophy,* LXI (1964).

Lieb, Irwin C. *Charles S. Peirce's Letters to Lady Welby.* New Haven: Whitlock's Inc. 1953.

Linsky, Leonard, ed. *Semantics and the Philosophy of Language.* Urbana, Ill.: University of Illinois Press, 1952.

Lloyd, Alfred. *Dynamic Idealism.* Chicago: A. C. McClurg and Company, 1898.

Locke, John. *An Essay Concerning Human Understanding.* London, 1690.

———. *Two Treatises of Government.* 1690. 6th edn., 1764.

Lotze, Rudolph Hermann. *Logik.* Leipzig, 1843. English trans. and ed. by B. Bosanquet, *Logic.* Oxford: Clarendon Press, 1884.

———. *Mikrokosmos: Ideen zur Naturgeschichte und Geschichte der Menschen.* Leipzig, 1856–1858.

Lovejoy, A. O. "The Thirteen Pragmatisms," *Journal of Philosophy*, V, (Jan. 2, 1908), 1–12; (Jan. 16, 1908), 29–39.
———. *Essays in the History of Ideas*. Baltimore: Johns Hopkins Press, 1948.
Lusky, Louis. "Nine Men: How They Do What They Do." *New York Times Book Review*, Vol. LXIX, No. 27 (July 5, 1964), pp. 3, 16–17.

Mach, E. *Popular Scientific Lectures*. Chicago: Open Court Publishing Company, 1910.
———. *The Analysis of Sensations*. Chicago: Open Court Publishing Company, 1914.
Madden, Edward H., ed. *The Philosophical Writings of Chauncey Wright*. American Heritage Series, No. 23. New York: Bobbs-Merrill Company, 1958.
———. *Chauncey Wright and the Foundations of Pragmatism*. Seattle: University of Washington Press, 1963.
———. "Peirce on Probability." In Moore and Robin, pp. 122–140.
Malcolm, Norman. *Ludwig Wittgenstein. A Memoir*. London: Oxford University Press, 1958.
Marx, Karl. *Über Feuerbach*. In Friedrich Engels, *Ludwig Feuerbach und der Ausgang der klassischen deutschen Philosophie*, Appendix, "Karl Marx über Feuerbach vom Jahre 1845," pp. 69–72. Stuttgart: Verlag von J. H. W. Dietz, 1888.
McKeon, Charles K. "Peirce's Scotistic Realism." In Wiener and Young, pp. 238–250.
Mead, George Herbert. "The Definition of the Psychical." *The Decennial Publications of the University of Chicago*, First Series, Vol. III, pp. 77–112. Chicago: University of Chicago Press, 1903. Reprinted with some deletions in *Selected Writings*, pp. 25–59.
———. "The Social Self," *Journal of Philosophy, Psychology and Scientific Methods*, X (1913), 374–380. Reprinted in *Selected Writings*, pp. 142–149.
———. "A Behavioristic Account of the Significant Symbol," *Journal of Philosophy*, XIX (1922), 157–163. Reprinted in *Selected Writings*, pp. 240–266.
———. "The Genesis of the Self and Social Control," *International Journal of Ethics*, XXXV (1924–1925), 251–277. Reprinted in *Selected Writings*, pp. 267–293.
———. "A Pragmatic Theory of Truth." *Studies in the Nature of Truth*. University of California Publications in Philosophy, Vol. XI, pp. 65–88. Berkeley: University of California Press, 1929. Reprinted in *Selected Writings*, pp. 320–344.
———. *The Philosophy of the Present*. Introduction by Arthur E. Murphy, ed. Prefatory remarks by John Dewey. La Salle, Ill.: Open Court Publishing Company, 1932.
———. *Mind, Self and Society*. Introduction by Charles W. Morris, ed. Chicago: University of Chicago Press, 1934.
———. *Movements of Thought in the Nineteenth Century*. Introduction by Merritt H. Moore, ed. Chicago: University of Chicago Press, 1936.
———. *The Philosophy of the Act*. Introduction by Charles W. Morris, ed., with John M. Brewster, Albert M. Dunham, David L. Miller. Chicago: University of Chicago Press, 1938.
———. *The Social Psychology of George Herbert Mead*. Introduction by Anselm Strauss, ed. Phoenix Books. Chicago: University of Chicago Press, 1956.
———. *Selected Writings*. Introduction by Andrew J. Reck, ed. Library of Liberal Arts, No. 177. New York: Bobbs-Merrill Company, 1964.
Mill, John Stuart. *A System of Logic*. 2 vols. London: 1843. 8th edn., New York: Henry Holt and Company, 1881.

————. "Coleridge." *Dissertations and Discussions,* Vol. II, pp. 5–78. 2 vols. London, 1859. Vol. II reprinted, Boston: William V. Spencer, 1865.* In *On Bentham and Coleridge,* pp. 99–168. Introduction by F. R. Leavis. Harper Torchbooks. New York: Harper & Brothers, 1962.

————. *An Examination of Sir William Hamilton's Philosophy.* London, 1865. New York: Henry Holt and Company, 1884.*

————. *Autobiography.* Helen Taylor, ed. London, 1873. Reprinted, Library of Liberal Arts, No. 91. New York: Bobbs-Merrill Company, 1957.*

————. "Berkeley's Life and Writings." *Three Essays on Religion.* London, 1874. Reprinted, New York: Henry Holt and Company, n.d.*

Mises, R. von. *Positivism, an Essay in Human Universtanding.* Cambridge, Mass.: Harvard University Press, 1951.

Moore, Edward C., and Richard S. Robin, eds. *Studies in the Philosophy of Charles Sanders Peirce.* Second Series. Amherst: University of Massachusetts Press, 1964.

Moore, G. E. *Principia Ethica.* Cambridge, Eng.: Cambridge University Press, 1903.

————. "The Refutation of Idealism," *Mind,* XII (1903), 433–453. Reprinted in *Philosophical Studies,* pp. 1–30.

————. *Philosophical Studies.* London: Routledge & Kegan Paul, 1922.

————. "Wittgenstein's Lectures in 1930–33," *Mind,* LXIII (1954), 1–15, 289–316; LXIV (1955), 1–27. Reprinted in *Philosophical Papers,* pp. 252–324.*

————. *Philosophical Papers.* London: George Allen & Unwin, and New York: The Macmillan Company, 1959.

Morley, John Viscount. *Rousseau and His Era.* 2 vols. London: Macmillan and Co., 1923.

Morris, Charles. *Logical Positivism, Pragmatism, and Scientific Empiricism.* Paris: Hermann, 1937.

Morris, George Sylvester. "Friedrich Adolf Trendelenburg," *The New Englander,* XXXIII (1874), 287–336.

————. *British Thought and Thinkers.* Chicago: S. C. Griggs and Company, 1880.

————. "Philosophy and Its Specific Problems," *The Princeton Review,* IX (1882), 208–232.

————. *Philosophy and Christianity.* New York: Robert Carter and Brothers, 1883.

Murphey, Murray G. *The Development of Peirce's Philosophy.* Cambridge, Mass.: Harvard University Press, 1961.

Myers, Francis M. *The Warfare of Democratic Ideals.* Yellow Springs, Ohio: Antioch Press, 1956.

Myrdal, G. *The American Dilemma.* 2 vols. New York: Harper & Brothers, 1944.

Nagel, Ernest. *Principles of the Theory of Probability. International Encyclopedia of Unified Science,* Vol. I, No. 6. Chicago: University of Chicago Press, 1939.

————. "Some Leading Principles of Professor Dewey's Logical Theory," in A Symposium of Reviews of John Dewey's *Logic: The Theory of Inquiry,* in *Journal of Philosophy,* XXXVI (1939), 576–581.

————. "Naturalism Reconsidered." *Proceedings and Addresses of the American Philosophical Association,* Vol. XXVIII (1954–1955). Reprinted in *Logic Without Metaphysics,* pp. 3–18.

————. Review of Toulmin's *Philosophy of Science,* in *Mind,* LXIII (1954), 403–412. Reprinted as "A Perspective on Theoretical Physics" in *Logic Without Metaphysics,* pp. 303–315.

————. *Logic Without Metaphysics.* Glencoe, Ill.: The Free Press, 1956.

————. *The Structure of Science.* New York: Harcourt, Brace & World, 1961.

Newton, Isaac. *Philosophiae Naturalis Principia Mathematica.* London, 1686.

————. *Opticks: or, a Treatise of the Reflections, Refractions, Inflections and Colours of Light.* London, 1704. 4th edn., corrected, 1730.

O'Connor, Daniel D. "Peirce's Debt to F. E. Abbot," *Journal of the History of Ideas,* XXV (1964), 543-564.

O'Connor, D. J., ed. *A Critical History of Western Philosophy.* Glencoe, Ill.: The Free Press, and London: Collier-Macmillan Limited, 1964.

Ogden, C. K., and I. A. Richards. *The Meaning of Meaning.* London: Kegan Paul, Trench, Trubner & Co., and New York: Harcourt, Brace and Company, 1923. 3d edn., revised, 1930.*

Papini, Giovanni. *Il Crepuscolo dei Filosofi.* Milan: Societa Editrice Lombarda, 1906.

————. "Introduzione al pragmatismo," *Leonardo,* V (1907), 26-37.

————. "What Pragmatism is Like." Katherine Royce, trans. *Popular Science Monthly,* LXXI (1907), 351-358.

————. *L'altra meta.* Ancona: Puccini, 1912. 3d edn., Florence: Vallecchi, 1919. 4th edn., 1923.

————. *24 Cervelli.* Ancona: Puccini, 1912. 6th edn., revised, Florence: Vallecchi, 1924.*

————. *Pragmatismo.* Milan: Libreria Editrice Milanese, 1913.

————. *Stroncature.* Florence: Liberia della Voce, 1916.

————. *Storia di Cristo.* 1st, 2nd, 3d edns., Florence: Vallecchi, 1921.

Parry, W. T. "Modalities in the Survey System of Strict Implication," *The Journal of Symbolic Logic,* IV (1939), 137-154.

Pasch, Alan. *Experience and the Analytic.* Chicago: University of Chicago Press, 1958.

Passmore, John. *A Hundred Years of Philosophy.* London: Gerald Duckworth & Co., 1957. Reprinted, 1959, 1962.

Peirce, Charles Sanders. "On an Improvement in Boole's Calculus of Logic," *Proceedings of the American Academy of Arts and Sciences,* VII (1867), 261-287. In *CP* 3.1-19.

————. Review of John Venn's *The Logic of Chance,* in *North American Review,* CV (1867), 317-321. In *CP* 8.1-6.

————. Review of *The Works of GEORGE BERKELEY, D.D., formerly Bishop of Cloyne,* A. C. Fraser, ed., in *North American Review,* CXII (1871), 449-472. In *CP* 8.7-38.

————. "On the Theory of Errors of Observation." *Report of the Superintendent of the United States Coast Survey Showing the Progress of the Work for the Fiscal Year Ending With June 1870,* Appendix 21, pp. 200-224. Washington, D.C.: Government Printing Office, 1873.

————. "Illustrations of the Logic of Science," *Popular Science Monthly,* XII-XIII (1877-1878). (1) "The Fixation of Belief," XII (1877), 1-15. In *CP* 5.358-387. (2) "How to Make Our Ideas Clear," XII (1878), 286-302. In *CP* 5.388-410. (3) "The Doctrine of Chances," XII (1878), 604-615. In *CP* 2.645-660. (4) "The Probability of Induction," XII (1878), 705-718. In *CP* 2.669-693. (5) "The Order of Nature," XIII (1878), 203-217. In *CP* 6.395-427. (6) "Deduction, Induction, and Hypothesis," XIII (1878), 470-482. In *CP* 2.619-644.

————. *Photometric Researches.* Annals of the Astronomical Observatory of Harvard College, Vol. IX. Leipzig, 1878.

————. "On the Algebra of Logic," *American Journal of Mathematics,* III (1880), 15-57. In *CP* 3.154-251.

————. "A Theory of Probable Inference." *Studies in Logic, By Members of the*

Johns Hopkins University, pp. 126–181. C. S. Peirce, ed. Boston: Little, Brown and Company, 1883. In *CP* 2.694–754.

———. "Leading Principle." In Baldwin, Vol. 2, pp. 1–2.

———. Review of Herbert Nichols's *A Treatise on Cosmology.* Cambridge, Mass.: Harvard University Press, 1904. In *CP* 8.191–193, entitled "On Pragmatism, From a Review of a Book on Cosmology."

———. "What Pragmatism Is," *The Monist*, XV (1905), 161–181. In *CP* 5.411–437.

———. *Collected Papers.* 8 vols. Vols. I–VI, C. Hartshorn and P. Weiss, eds. Vols. VII–VIII, A. W. Burks, ed. Cambridge, Mass.: Harvard University Press, 1931–1958.

Peirce commemorative issue of the *Journal of Philosophy, Psychology and Scientific Methods*, XII (1916).

Perry, R. B. *The Thought and Character of William James.* 2 vols. Boston: Little, Brown and Company, 1936.

———. "William James." *Dictionary of American Biography*, Vol. IX, pp. 590–600. New York: Charles Scribner's Sons, 1943.

Plato. *Platonis Opera.* Ioannes Burnet, ed. 5 vols. Scriptorum Bibliotheca Oxoniensis. Oxonii: E Typographeo Clarendoniano, 1899–1906.

Pledge, H. T. *Science Since 1500.* Harper Torchbooks. New York: Harper & Brothers, 1959.

Poincaré, H. *The Foundations of Science.* G. B. Halstead, trans. New York: The Science Press, 1921.

Popper, Karl R. *The Logic of Scientific Discovery.* New York: Basic Books, 1959.

Pradines, Maurice. *Critique des Conditions de l'Action. L'Erreur Morale etablie par l'histoire et l'evolution des Systemes.* Paris: Felix Alcan, 1909.

———. *Critique des Conditions de l'Action, Principes de toute Philosophie de l'Action.* Paris: Felix Alcan, 1909.

Presley, C. F. "Laws and Theories in the Physical Sciences," *The Australasian Journal of Philosophy*, XXXII (1954), 79–103.

Prezzolini, Giuseppe. *L'arte di persuadere.* Florence: Lumachi, 1907.

Pringle-Pattison, A. S., ed. *Locke's Essay Concerning Human Understanding.* Oxford: Clarendon Press, 1924.

Quine, W. V. O. *Mathematical Logic.* Cambridge, Mass.: Harvard University Press, 1940. Revised edn., 1951.

———. "Whitehead and the Rise of Modern Logic." In Schilpp, *The Philosophy of Alfred North Whitehead*, pp. 127–163.

———. "The Problem of Interpreting Modal Logic," *The Journal of Symbolic Logic*, XII (1947), 43–48.

———. *From a Logical Point of View.* Cambridge, Mass.: Harvard University Press, 1953.

———. *Methods of Logic.* Revised edn., New York: Henry Holt and Company, 1959.

———. *Word and Object.* Cambridge, Mass.: The Technology Press of the Massachusetts Institute of Technology, and New York: John Wiley & Sons, 1960.

Quinton, A. M. "Contemporary British Philosophy." In D. J. O'Connor, pp. 532–566.

Ramsey, Frank Plumpton. Review of L. Wittgenstein's *Tractatus Logico-Philosophicus*, in *Mind*, XXXII (1923), 465–478. Reprinted in *The Foundations of Mathematics*, pp. 270–286.

———. Review of Ogden and Richards' *The Meaning of Meaning*, in *Mind*, XXXIII (1924), 108–109.

————. "Truth and Probability." In *The Foundations of Mathematics and Other Logical Essays*, pp. 156–198.

————. *The Foundations of Mathematics and Other Logical Essays*. New York: Harcourt, Brace and Company, 1931. Reprinted, New York: Humanities Press, 1950.

Randall, John Herman, Jr. "Dewey's Interpretation of the History of Philosophy." In Schilpp, *The Philosophy of John Dewey*, pp. 77–102.

————. *The Career of Philosophy*. Vol. I. New York: Columbia University Press, 1962.

————. "John Stuart Mill and the Working-Out of Empiricism," *Journal of the History of Ideas*, XXVI (1965), 59–88.

————. "T. H. Green and English Thought," *Journal of the History of Ideas*, XXVII (1966), 217–244.

Renauld, J. F. "L'Oeuvre Inachevée de Mario Calderoni," *Revue de metaphysique et de morale*, XXV (1918), 208–231.

Renouvier, Charles. "Traité de Psychologie rationnelle d'apres les principes du criticisme." In *Essais de critique générale*, Vol. II, Essay 2, as "L'homme: la raison, la passion, la liberte, la certitude, la probabilite morale."

————. *Essais de critique générale*. 2 vols. Paris: Librairie philosophique de Ladrange, 1854–1859. Vols. III and IV, 1864.

Robinson, Daniel S., ed. *Royce's Logical Essays*. Dubuque, Iowa: Wm. C. Brown Company, 1951.

Rossi-Landi, F. "Materiale per lo studio di Vailati," *Rivista Critica di Storia filosofia*, XII (1957), 468–485; XIII (1958), 82–108.

Rousseau, Jean-Jacques. *Contrat Social*. 1762.

Royce, Josiah. "The World of Postulates." In *The Religious Aspect of Philosophy*, ch. 9, pp. 291–332.

————. *The Religious Aspect of Philosophy*. Boston and New York: Houghton Mifflin Company, 1885. Reprinted, Harper Torchbooks, New York: Harper & Brothers, 1958.

————. *The World and the Individual*. New York: The Macmillan Company, 1899. Second Series, 1901. Reprinted, New York: Dover Publications, 1959.

————. "The Relation of the Principles of Logic to the Foundations of Geometry," *Transactions of the American Mathematical Society*, XXIV (1905), 353–415. Reprinted in Robinson, pp. 379–441.

————. "The Problem of Truth in the Light of Recent Discussion." *Proceedings of the International Congress of Philosophy at Heidelberg*, Sept. 1908. Reprinted in *William James and Other Essays on the Philosophy of Life*, pp. 187–254. New York: The Macmillan Company, 1911.* Reprinted in Robinson, pp. 63–97.

————. *The Problem of Christianity*. New York: The Macmillan Company, 1913.

————. "The Principles of Logic." *Encyclopaedia of the Philosophical Sciences*, Vol. I, *Logic*, pp. 67–135. Vol. I. Arnold Ruge, Wilhelm Windelband, Josiah Royce, Louis Couturat, Benedetto Croce, Frederige Enriques, and Nicolaj Losskij. London: Macmillan and Co., 1913. Reprinted in Robinson, pp. 310–378.

Russell, Bertrand. *A Critical Exposition of The Philosophy of Leibniz*. Cambridge, Eng.: Cambridge University Press, 1900. 2nd edn. London: George Allen & Unwin, 1937.

————. *The Principles of Mathematics*. Cambridge, Eng.: Cambridge University Press, 1903.

————. "On Denoting," *Mind*, XIV (1905), 479–493. Reprinted in *Logic and Knowledge*, pp. 41–56.

————. "Mathematical Logic as Based on the Theory of Types," *American Journal* of *Mathematics*, XXX (1908), 222–262. Reprinted in *Logic and Knowledge*, pp. 59–102.*

————, and Alfred North Whitehead. *Principia Mathematica*. Vol. I. Cambridge, Eng.: Cambridge University Press, 1910. 2nd edn., 1925.

————. *Philosophical Essays*. London and New York: Longmans, Green and Co., 1910.

————. *Our Knowledge of the External World as a Field for Scientific Method in Philosophy*. Chicago and London: Open Court Publishing Company, 1914.

————. *Introduction to Mathematical Philosophy*. London: George Allen & Unwin, and New York: The Macmillan Company, 1919. 2nd edn., 1920. Reprinted, 1924.

————. *The ABC of Relativity*. New York: Harper & Brothers, 1925.

————. *Philosophy*. New York: W. W. Norton & Company, 1927.

————. *Freedom versus Organization, 1814–1914*. New York: W. W. Norton & Company, 1934.

————. "Science and Ethics." In *Religion and Science*, ch. 9, pp. 223–243.

————. *Religion and Science*. London: Thornton Butterworth, 1935.

————. *Power: A New Social Analysis*. New York: W. W. Norton & Company, 1938.

————. "Dewey's New Logic." In Schilpp, *The Philosophy of John Dewey*, pp. 135–156.

————. *An Inquiry into Meaning and Truth*. New York: W. W. Norton & Company, 1940.

————. *A History of Western Philosophy*. New York: Simon and Schuster, 1943.

————. *Unpopular Essays*. London: George Allen & Unwin, 1950.

————. *Logic and Knowledge*. R. C. Marsh, ed. New York: The Macmillan Company, 1956.

————. *My Philosophical Development*. New York: Simon and Schuster, 1959.

Ryle, Gilbert. *The Concept of Mind*. Hutchinson's University Library. London: Hutchinson House, 1949.

Sailly, B. de. "Les éléments de la philosophie de l'action," *Annales de philosophie chrétienne*, 151. Oct. 1905—Mars 1906, 180–195.

Santayana, George. "Dewey's Naturalistic Metaphysics," *Journal of Philosophy*, XXII (1925), 673–688. Reprinted in *Obiter Scripta*, pp. 213–240. New York: Charles Scribner's Sons, 1936.*

————. *My Host the World*. Vol. III of *Persons and Places*. New York: Charles Scribner's Sons, 1953.

Santucci, A. *Il Pragmatismo in Italia*. Bologna: Il Mulino, 1963.

Schiller, F. C. S. *Riddles of the Sphinx: A Study of the Philosophy of Evolution*. London: Swan Sonnenschein & Co., and New York: The Macmillan Company, 1891. New and revised edn., with subtitle, *A Study in the Philosophy of Humanism*, 1910.*

————. "Axioms as Postulates." In Henry Sturt, ed., *Personal Idealism*, pp. 47–133. London and New York: The Macmillan Company, 1902.

————. *Humanism*. London and New York: The Macmillan Company, 1903.

————. "The Relations of Logic and Psychology." Ch. 3 in *Studies in Humanism*, pp. 71–113.

————. "The Making of Reality." Ch. 19 in *Studies in Humanism*, pp. 421–451.

————. *Studies in Humanism*. London and New York: The Macmillan Company, 1907. 2nd edn., 1912.

————. Review of Pradines' *Critique des Conditions de l'Action*, in *Mind*, XX (1911), 422–425.

———. "Scientific Discovery and Logical Proof." In Charles J. Singer, ed., *Studies in the History and Methods of Science,* Vol. I., 235–281. Oxford: Clarendon Press, 1917.

———. "William James and the Making of Pragmatism," *The Personalist,* VIII (1927), 81–93.

———. *Logic For Use.* London: G. Bell, 1929.

———. *Must Philosophers Disagree?* London: Macmillan and Co., 1934.

Schilpp, Paul Arthur, ed. *The Philosophy of John Dewey.* The Library of Living Philosophers, Vol. I. Evanston and Chicago: Northwestern University Press, 1939.

———, ed. *The Philosophy of Bertrand Russell.* Library of Living Philosophers, Vol. V. Evanston and Chicago: Northwestern University Press, 1944.

———, ed. *The Philosophy of Alfred North Whitehead.* The Library of Living Philosophers, Vol. III. 2nd edn., New York: Tudor Publishing Company, 1951.

Schneider, Herbert W. *A History of American Philosophy.* New York: Columbia University Press, 1946.* 2nd edn., 1963.

Schröder, E. *Vorlesungen über die Algebra der Logik.* 3 vols. Leipzig: Teubner, 1890–1895.

Scotus, John Duns. *Quaestiones subtilissmae super libros Metaphysicorum Aristotelis. Opera Omnia,* Vol. VII. Apud Ludovicum Vives, Bibliopolam Editorem. Paris, 1891–1895.

Sellars, Wilfrid, and John Hospers, eds. *Readings in Ethical Theory.* New York: Appleton-Century-Crofts, 1952.

Sheffer, H. M. "A Set of Five Independent Postulates for Boolean Algebras," *Transactions of the American Mathematical Society,* XIV (1913), 481–488.

Shirk, Evelyn U. *Adventurous Idealism.* Ann Arbor: University of Michigan Press, 1952.

Sorel, Georges. *Reflections on Violence.* T. E. Hulme, trans. London: George Allen & Unwin, 1925.

———. *De l'utilité du pragmatisme.* Paris: Marcel Riviere, 1921.

Spinoza, B. *Ethica.* 1677.

Stebbing, L. Susan. *Pragmatism and French Voluntarism.* Cambridge, Eng.: Cambridge University Press, 1914.

Stevenson, Charles L. *Ethics and Language.* New Haven: Yale University Press, 1945.

Sullivan, Harry Stack. *The Interpersonal Theory of Psychiatry.* New York: W. W. Norton & Company, 1953.

Tarski, Alfred. "The Semantic Conception of Truth," *Philosophy and Phenomenological Research,* IV (1944), 341–375. Reprinted in Feigl and Sellars, pp. 52–84, and in Linsky, pp. 13–47.

Thayer, H. S. "Two Theories of Truth: The Relation Between the Theories of John Dewey and Bertrand Russell," *Journal of Philosophy,* XLIV (1947), 516–527.

———. "Critical Notes on Dewey's Theory of Propositions," *Journal of Philosophy,* XLVIII (1951), 607–613.

———. *The Logic of Pragmatism.* New York: Humanities Press, 1952.

———, ed. *Newton's Philosophy of Nature.* New York: Hafner Classics, 1953.

———. "Pragmatism." In D. J. O'Connor, pp. 438–462.

———. "Historical Patterns, Empiricism, and Some Reflections on Ockham and Berkeley." In John P. Anton, ed., *Naturalism and Historical Understanding: Essays on the Philosophy of John Herman Randall, Jr.,* pp. 69–82. New York: State University of New York Press, 1967.

Thayer, V. T. *Formative Ideas in American Education.* New York: Dodd, Mead & Company, 1965.

Thompson, Manley. *The Pragmatic Philosophy of Charles S. Peirce.* Chicago: University of Chicago Press, 1953.

Toulmin, Stephan E. *The Philosophy of Science.* London: Hutchinson's University Library, 1953.

Tyrrell, G. *The Program of Modernism.* New York: G. P. Putnam's Sons, 1908.

Urmson, J. O., ed. *The Concise Encyclopedia of Western Philosophy and Philosophers.* New York: Hawthorn Books, 1960.

Vailati, Giovanni. Review of Peirce's "What Pragmatism Is," in *Leonardo*, III (1905). Reprinted in *Scritti*, pp. 639–640.

————. "A Study of Platonic Terminology," *Mind*, XV (1906), 473–485.

————. "Uno Zoologo Pragmatista," *Leonardo*, IV (1906). English trans., "A Pragmatic Zoologist," *The Monist*, XVIII (1908), 142–151. Original article reprinted in *Scritti*, pp. 728–735.

————. "Pragmatismo e Logica Matematica," *Leonardo*, IV (1906). Reprinted in *Scritti*, pp. 689–694. English trans. by H. D. Austin, "Pragmatism and Mathematical Logic," *The Monist*, XVI (1906), 481–491.

————. "De quelques caractères du mouvement philosophique contemporain en Italie," *La Revue du Mois*, III (1907), 162–185. Reprinted in *Scritti*, pp. 753–769.

————. "The Attack on Distinctions," *Journal of Philosophy, Psychology and Scientific Methods*, IV (1907), 701–709.

————. "On Material Representations of Deductive Processes," *Journal of Philosophy, Psychology and Scientific Methods*, V (1908), 309–316.

————, and M. Calderoni. "Le origini e l'idea fondamentale del Pragmatismo," *Revista di Psicologia Applicata*, V (1909), 10–29.

————. *Scritti.* M. Calderoni, U. Ricci, and G. Vacca, eds. Florence: Successori B. Seeber, and Leipzig: Johann Ambrosius Barth, 1911.

Veblen, Thorstein. *The Theory of the Leisure Class.* New York: The Macmillan Company, 1899.

————. "The Place of Science in Modern Civilization," *American Journal of Sociology*, XI (1906), 585–609. Reprinted in Wesley C. Mitchell, ed., *What Veblen Taught*, pp. 3–38. New York: The Viking Press, 1936.

Venn, John. *The Logic of Chance, An Essay on the Foundations and Province of the Theory of Probability, with especial Reference to its Application to Moral and Social Science.* London and Cambridge, 1866.

Waiblel, E. P. B. *Der Pragmatismus in der Geschichte der Philosophie.* Bonn: Heinrich Ludwig Spezial-Druckerie für Dissertationen, 1915.

Walsh, W. H. "F. H. Bradley." In D. J. O'Connor, pp. 426–436.

Watson, John B. *Behavior: An Introduction to Comparative Psychology.* New York: Henry Holt and Company, 1914.

Watson, W. H. *On Understanding Physics.* Cambridge, Eng.: Cambridge University Press, 1938.

Weiss, Paul. "Charles Sanders Peirce." *Dictionary of American Biography*, Vol. XIV, pp. 398–403. New York: Charles Scribner's Sons, 1943.

Welby, Lady V. *What is Meaning?* London and New York: The Macmillan Company, 1903.

————. *Echoes of Larger Life: A Selection from the Early Correspondence of Victoria Lady Welby.* Mrs. Henry Cust, ed. London: Jonathan Cape, 1929.

————. *Other Dimensions: A Selection from the Later Correspondence of Victoria Lady Welby*. Mrs. Henry Cust, ed. London: Jonathan Cape, 1931.

Wenley, R. M. *The Life and Work of G. S. Morris*. New York: The Macmillan Company, 1917.

White, Morton G. *The Origin of Dewey's Instrumentalism*. New York: Columbia University Press, 1943.

————. *Social Thought in America*. New York: Viking Press, 1949. Reprinted with new Preface and an Epilogue, Boston: Beacon Press, 1957.*

————. "Value and Obligation in Dewey and Lewis," *Philosophical Review*, LVIII (1949), 321–329. Reprinted in Sellars and Hospers, pp. 332–339.

————. "The Analytic and the Synthetic: An Untenable Dualism." In Sidney Hook, ed., *John Dewey: Philosopher of Science and Freedom*, pp. 316–330. New York: Dial Press, 1950.

Whitehead, A. N. *A Treatise on Universal Algebra, with Applications*. Cambridge, Eng.: Cambridge University Press, 1898.

————. "The Axioms of Geometry." Part VII of "Geometry," *Encyclopaedia Britannica*, Vol. XI, pp. 730–736. 11th edn. Cambridge, Eng.: Cambridge University Press, 1910.

————, and Bertrand Russell, see Russell, 1910.

Wiener, Philip P. *Evolution and the Founders of Pragmatism*. Cambridge, Mass.: Harvard University Press, 1949.

————, and F. H. Young, eds. *Studies in the Philosophy of Charles Sanders Peirce*. Cambridge, Mass.: Harvard University Press, 1952.

Willey, Basil. *Nineteenth Century Studies*. New York: Columbia University Press, 1949.

Williams, Donald C. "The Sea Fight Tomorrow." In Paul Henle, Horace M. Kallen, Susanne K. Langer, eds., *Structure, Method and Meaning. Essays in Honor of Henry M. Sheffer*, pp. 282–306. New York: The Liberal Arts Press, 1951.

Wittgenstein, Ludwig. *Tractatus Logico-Philosophicus*. New York: Harcourt, Brace and Company, 1922.

————. *Philosophical Investigations*. New York: The Macmillan Company, 1953.

————. *The Blue and Brown Books*. New York: Harper & Brothers, 1958.

Wollheim, Richard. *F. H. Bradley*. Baltimore: Penguin Books, 1959.

Woodworth, Robert S. *Contemporary Schools of Psychology*. New York: Ronald Press, 1931.

Wright, Chauncey. "The Philosophy of Herbert Spencer," *North American Review*, C (1865), 423–476. Reprinted in *Philosophical Discussions*, pp. 43–96.

————. "Evolution of Self-Consciousness," *North American Review*, CXVI (1873), 245–310. Reprinted in *Philosophical Discussions*, pp. 199–266.

————. *Philosophical Discussions*. Charles E. Norton, ed. New York: Henry Holt and Company, 1877.

————. *The Philosophical Writings of Chauncey Wright*. See Madden.

Wright, G. H. von. "Biographical Sketch" (of Ludwig Wittgenstein). In Malcolm, pp. 1–22.

Index

Abel, Reuben, 284*n.*, 289*n.*, 527
Abbot, F. E., 69, 492*n.*
Absolute
   action as revelation of, 316–319
   as all-inclusive experience, 275*n.*
   God as, 156–159
   growth and, 176
   James on, 441
   realization of the state as, 280
   Schiller opposed to, 281–282
   Spirit, 469–470
Absolutism, 292
   English, 279–280
Abstract ideas, Berkeley's criticism of, 369*n.*,
   506–507
Action, 8
   belief as basis for, 84–85, 120–121
   determination of, by occupations, 238–
   239
   future, 403–404
   general theory of, ix, 184, 189
      analysis of, 65
      Descartes, 18
      James, 133–135
   ideal aim of, 120
      habits, 121
   ideas as plans of, 147
   individual, 442
   instrumentalism and, 443–444
   intelligent, 422, 443
   knowledge and, 55–56
      as guide, 423
   leading principles in, 376–377
      ends-in-view as guides, 399–402
   Lewis on, 423
   logic and, 208
   man-god and, 332

Action—*cont.*
   Mead on, 177*n.*, 184
   meaning and, ix
   moral good and, 199–200
   new organon in, 454–458
   philosophy of, 314–319
      definition, 316
      pragmatism and, 317
      truth, 318–319
   pragmatism and, 139–140, 317
      as intellectual content, vii, 4
   as process, 410–411
   results as content of, 407*n.*
   romanticism and, 48–49, 51
   social
      the act, 264–266
      defined, 261
      myths and, 320–321
      social objects, 261–264
      unconscious considerations, 321–322
   systems of order and modes of, 209–210
   teleological, 178–179
   thought as, 494
      as conceived action, 88
      unifying action, 484–485
   transformation of reality by, 328–331
      creativity, 329–330
   usefulness in, 6
   see also Behaviorism; Psychology
Acts, Dewey's theory of stimulus and response as constituents of, 185–190
Actual possibles, James on, 142; Lewis on,
   542; *see also* Possibility
Adams, G. P., 527
Adaptation
   to environment, 177–178
   to reality, 147

Addams, Jane, 75
Agassiz, Louis, 72
Agathon, 409
Agreement
  with reality
    of thought, 151–152, 206
    of truth, 149–151
Ähnlich, 209n.
Aitia, 398, 399
Algebra
  Boole's logical, 69n., 105n.
  of relations, 496–498
Amendola, Giovanni, 324, 325
Analytic and synthetic, 465–466, 508–521
  classification of truth and, 226, 361
  as a priori, 40–42, 226–227
    Peirce's rejection of, 138
  defined, 508–509
  distinction between, 361, 509–511
Analyticity, 525
  a priori in knowledge and, 225–228
  defined, 508–509
  in logic, 509–510
    logical truths, 291
  mathematical physcis and, 514–515
  in meaning, 518
  in natural language, 512
  truth and, 291, 511–512, 519–520
  see also Analytic and synthetic
Anamnesis, 29
Anderson, P. R., 7n.,,527
Angell, James R., 75, 175–177, 184, 527
Anschauungen, 39, 134
Anstösse, 47
Antinomies, Kant and, 41
Appleton, W. H., 69
A priori
  analyticity and, 518
  belief and, 115
  conditions, morals and, 43
  contexts and, 358–363
  experience and
    a priori principles, 38
    before experience, 467
  the given and, 216–217
  knowledge, 28
    analyticity, 225–228
    logic and, 358–363
  Mill on, 279
  pragmatic, 207, 210
    analytic, 226
    as definitive, 215, 220, 231
    determination of values, 225
    experience in, 213–214, 216, 220–221
    knowing the world, 227–228
    truth, 212
  probability, 112

A priori—*cont.*
  pure forms and, 513
  Schiller's rejection of, 291
  subjective interests as, 142–143
  synthetic, 40–42
    Peirce's rejection of, 138
  see also Axioms; Given; Postulates
Approximation of truth, 127
Aquinas, St. Thomas, ix, 15, 16, 21, 36,
    82n., 85n., 449, 527
Archai, 367
Archē, 287, 367
Architecture, analogy of theory of knowl-
    edge with, 102, 376n.
Aretē, 412
Aristotle, 5, 7, 15, 16, 50, 65, 70, 74, 82,
    85, 89, 97n., 102, 108, 136n., 195,
    196, 228, 229n., 232, 286–287, 333,
    366–368, 370, 386, 387n., 398–
    399, 430, 435n., 445, 449, 467, 473,
    479, 484, 485n., 526n., 527
Arrow-sign, function of, 249–252, 478n.,
    502–503, 505
Ashley, M. L., 440 n.
Asquith, Herbert, 475
Assertability, warranted, 42, 125, 193–195
Assertion, meaning of, 335, 343
Atom, 47–48
  as theoretical term, 372, 374
  discovery of, 13
  sodium, 381
Atom bomb, 65, 127
Atomic age, 65
Augustine, St., 6, 174, 387
  Augustinian philosophy of knowledge,
    13, 19, 28–29
Auden, W. H., 436n., 527
Austin, J. L., 428n., 527
Avenarius, 56
Averroism, 21
Ayer, A. J., 109n., 527
Ayers, M. R., 93n., 527
Axioms
  pragmatic function of, 335, 343
  postulates and, 292–293
  see also A priori; Given; Postulates

Bacon, Francis, 5, 6n., 115n., 294, 454
Bacon, Roger, 6n., 28
Bain, Alexander, 80, 81, 108n., 134, 139n.,
    455, 467
Baldwin, James M., 5n., 71, 527
Barnes, Albert, 75
Barnes, Winston H. F., 97n., 528
Baylis, C. A., 22n., 528
Beard, Charles, 443, 444
Beautiful, romantic idealism and, 51

Behaviorism
causality in, 398
laws and, 399
social, 185–90, 232, 236–237, 443
discovery of self, 252–261
in experience, 187–190
language, 234
language as gesture, 246–247
social act, 237
social gesture, 241–244
social objects, 261–264
symbol, 244–246, 248–252
see also Desire
thought and, 396*n.*
Belief
action and, 84–85, 120–121
right to believe, 322
Bain's definition of, 81
in causal laws, 369–371, 379
in continuity of reality, 446
error in, 349
explanation of, 455
instrumentalism and beliefs about the world, 373
justification of, 153–159
truthfulness and, 154–155
Kant on, 139*n.*
methods of maintaining, 115–116, 123
propensity to, 342
science and, 166
thought and, 83–86
truth and, 124–125, 128–132
usefulness of belief, 148, 344
validation of religious, 318
Venn on, 108*n.*
see also Faith
Bentham, Jeremy, 81
Bentley, A. E., 201*n.*
Berengarius of Tours, 86
Bergson, Henri L., 50, 57, 146, 270, 271, 315, 317*n.*–321, 332, 427*n.*, 520, 528
Bergsonianism, 320
Berkeley, George, 5, 10, 24–26, 37, 56, 122*n.*, 138, 187, 206, 207, 217, 220, 250, 263*n.*, 329*n.*, 344*n.*, 360, 369, 371, 381*n.*, 384, 456, 468, 478*n.*, 480*n.*, 483, 484, 489, 499–507, 528
Bernays, Paul, 365*n.*, 528
Bernheim, Ernst, 8*n.*, 528
Bernoulli, Daniel, 107
Bernoulli, Jacob, 107, 108, 528
Bernstein, Edward, 321
Bernstein, Richard J., 92*n.*, 140*n.*, 528
Berthelot, René, 314*n.*, 319*n.*, 528
Bigness, James on, 441–442

Blake, William, 44
Blau, Joseph L., viii*n.*, 528
Blondel, Maurice, 8, 314–317, 528
Bode, Boyd, 266*n.*, 528
Bonaventure, St., 28
Boole, George, 69*n.*, 70, 105*n.*, 128, 496–498, 528
Bosanquet, Bernard, 62*n.*, 63, 277, 282, 294, 295*n.*, 468
Boutroux, Emile, 317*n.*, 320, 528
Bowen, Francis, 69
Boyle, Robert, 23
Bradley, F. H., 10, 63, 148*n.*, 149, 275–282, 288, 293–294, 295*n.*, 299*n.*, 330, 391*n.*, 455, 463*n.*, 474, 477*n.*, 485, 487, 520, 528
Braithwaite, R. B., 111*n.*, 528
Bridgman, P. W., 92*n.*, 528
Bronstein, Daniel J., 90*n.*, 95*n.*, 528
Brouwer, L. E. J., 309
Burks, Arthur W., 111*n.*, 113*n.*, 528
Butler, Bishop, 112
Byron, Lord (George Gordon), 45, 46*n.*, 51
Buchler, Justus, 3*n.*, 85, 88*n.*, 528
Büchner, L. F., 277, 528
Business, pragmatism and, 6
Business ethic, 438–439

Caird, Edward, 276*n.*, 277, 278*n.*, 468, 474, 475*n.*, 528
Calderoni, Mario, 95*n.*, 272, 307*n.*, 324–325, 499*n.*, 528, 529, 544
Calvin, John, 433
Campbell, N., 5, 365*n.*, 529
Campbell-Bannerman, Henry, 475
Capitalism
growth of, 444
Protestant ethic and, 7
Carlyle, Thomas, 50, 278, 478*n.*
Carnap, Rudolf, 92, 100*n.*, 136, 211*n.*, 227, 356*n.*, 431, 512, 520, 524, 525, 529
Cassirer, Ernst, 5, 529
Categories
empirical judgments as, 41
Fichte on, 55
inclusive, 174–183
Lewis and Royce on, 209–210, 212, 214, 215*n.*
Catholicism, 334
Catlin, George, 322*n.*, 529
Cattel, James McKeen, 74
Causa, 398
Causality
in behavior, 398
in ideas
causal relations, 38

Causality—*cont.*
  derivation of ideas, 137
  generation of ideas, 451
  principle of, 69–71, 379
    facts and, 340
Change
  experience and, 65, 424–425
  problem of knowledge and, 64–65, 198
Charles VI (Holy Roman emperor), 7
Chemistry, Peirce and, 105*n*., 494
Childs, John, 3, 174*n*., 529
Chiocchetti, E., 330*n*., 529
Chisholm, R. M., 93*n*., 529
Church, A., 209*n*., 529
Cicero, 29*n*.
Classification of philosophers, 454
Clausius, 104, 107
Clifford, W. K., 70
Coeur, le, 31
Cogito, 27
Cognition
  nature of
    purposive, 138–139
    reconstructive, 427*n*.
  subjective interests and, 142–143
Cohen, Morris, 80*n*., 490, 529
Cole, G. D. H., 475
Coleridge, Samuel T., 45, 50, 74, 278, 529
Commercialism, 438–439
Common sense
  Berkeley and, 499, 500
  critique of, 315, 316
  fallibilism and, 123
  Hume and, 25
  importance of, 15
  as inherited prejudice, 355
  Locke's emphasis on, 22
  Moore and, 308
  Pierce and, 138
  of pragmatism, 352–353, 495
  vagueness in, 373–374
Communication
  of experience, 359–360
  games as, 255–258
  generalized other in system of, 260
  logic and, 260–261
  pragmatism and clarification of, 416
  preparation for, 250–252
  purposeful, 429, 430
  schematization of, 248–250
  self and, 240–241
    discovery of self, 252–254
    as language, 241–244
  theory of
    Dewey's ethical theory, 412
    suggested theory, 362–363
  vagueness in, 373–374

Communication—*cont.*
  see also Language
Community of interpreters, truth and, 126–127, 205–206
Comte, Auguste, 10
Conceivable, *see* Possibility
Conception
  of experience, 345–350
    dualism in, 469
  of knowing, ix
  of knowledge, 5
  mind and, 144
  of morals, 454–455
  of objects, 96*n*.–97*n*.
  Peirce's definition of, 88, 115–118, 123–124
  possibility as, 97–99
  the real as, 124, 130
  of reality, Peirce's, 115–118, 123–124
  of truth, 22
  vagueness in, 374
Concepts
  consequences as, 430*n*.
  of continuity, 486–487
  as criteria of reality, 219–220
  definitions and, 339
  of identity, 486–487
  in knowledge, 37
  meaning of, 86–87, 89
    conditional statements, 92–93
    contextual procedure, 103
    moral, 342
    Peirce on, 86, 88
      analysis of, 493–494
      percepts and, 39
    of possibility, 486–487
      clarification, 524–526
    pragmatic methodology and, 79–80
    pure, 216
    sense experience and, 139–140
    situation, 170–171
    of substance, 25
  see also Signs
Concipere, 87
Concretus, 430
Conditional
  contrary-to-fact
    Ayers and, 93*n*.
    Berkeley and, 502-503
    Chisholm and Goodman and, 93*n*.
    Lewis and, 219, 223–224
    Peirce and, 92–93, 113–114
    possibility and, 522, 525
  external world as, 142
  form for explicating meanings
    Berkeley and, 99*n*., 505–507
    Peirce and, 86, 91–92, 95, 118–120

Conditional definitions, 339
Conditional statement, forms of laws and, 373
see also Probability; *Would-be*
Consciousness
  critique of, 315
  definition of, 262
  elimination of, 350
  evolution of, 235
  as instrument, 266
  of meaning, 243–247
  self, 53–55, 321, 466*n*., 469–470, 478–483
  stream of, 465, 477–478
  theory of morals and, 480–483
  as thought, 485
  universal, 473
Consequences
  of actions, 423
  basic truths and, 103
  concepts and, 430*n*., 494
  definitions and purposive, 339, 341
  generality and, 140
  of ideas
    in empiricism, 137
    as meaning of ideas, 96–97, 99
    predictive consequences, 333
  meaning and
    meaning of ideas, 410
    purposive consequences, 315–336
    theoretical terms, 376
  truth and
    satisfactory truth, 203–204
    as test of truth, 156
  verification of, 491
Context, *see* Situations
Contextualism, 352–358
  of Dewey, 172–173
  in knowledge of external world, 352–354
  experience, 354–357
  of Mead, 262
  of meaning, 296–297
  pluralism in, 362–363
Continuity, 443, 460–487
  background of, 461–466
  concept of, 460–487
  as core of philosophy, 59
  defined, 460–461
  Hegelian, 440*n*.
  as inclusive category, 174–183
  morals and, 460–461
  19th-century philosophizing and, 486–487
  as primary postulate, 173
  reality of, 446
  in situations, 358

Contradiction
  analyticity and, 509
  principle of, 496–497
Conventionalism
  knowledge and, 349
  laws and, 369–370
  theoretical structure of science and, 369–371
Copernicus, 13
Correspondence
  theory of knowledge, 453
  realism and, 124
  theory of truth, Dewey and, 193–197
Costello, 173*n*.
Courant, Richard, 107*n*., 529
Cournot, Antoine A., 108
Cousin, Victor, 320
Couturat, Louis, 128*n*., 529
Criticism
  of common sense, 315, 316
  of consciousness, 315
  defined, vii
  of empiricism, 468–471, 473–474, 476, 483–484
  Enlightenment as age of, 30, 44
  of epistemology, 315
  of implication, 210–212
  of logic, 294–297
  of rationalism, 317*n*., 319
  as role of philosophy, 460
Croce, Benedetto, 324
Cudworth, Ralph, 28*n*., 529
Culture
  origin of American, ix, 433–435
  U.S. as two-part, 436–447
Curry, H. B., 207*n*., 529
Cusanus, Nicholas, 49

D'Alembert, Jean le Rond, 30
Dante (Alighieri), 457
Darwin, Charles, 59–62, 104, 105, 107, 134, 165, 236, 241, 268, 450, 460–466, 529–530
Darwinism, 371, 444, 446, 449, 450, 454, 455, 486
  Dewey influenced by, 167, 177, 185, 463–466
  in England, 277
  impact of, 59–62
Dedekind, Richard, 208, 209
Deductions
  ought and, 386
  in science, 366–367
Definiendum, 508
Definiens, 509
Definitions, 336–342
  propositions in, 339–341

Definitions—*cont.*
 Valiati's view of, 336
  instrumental theories, 341–342
  meaning of words, 337–338
  purposive consequences, 339
De Morgan, Augustus, 69*n*., 304*n*.
Democritus, 16, 20, 235*n*.
Derivation, of ideas, 136
Desire
 biological basis for, 393–395
 the desirable and, 402–409
 intelligent, 398–400
 rational element in, 395–398
 reality molded by, 424
Descartes, René, ix, *13–23*, 27, 28, 30, 37,
  38, 82, 97, 98, 102, 124, 206, 214*n*.,
  228, 370, 384, 397, 399*n*., 450, 499,
  501, 508, 530
Dewey, John, 11, 64, 68, 127*n*., 137, 145,
  149, 155*n*., *165–204*, 207, 234*n*.,
  259*n*., 268, 271, 289*n*., 313, 314,
  335, 345, 380*n*., 381, 422, 430*n*.,
  431, 441, 457–458, 460–487, 506,
  530–532
 background of, 73–76
 behavior and
  psychophysical behavior, 241
  reflective behavior, 261
 concepts and, 343
 consequences and, 139
  test of truth, 156
 continuity and, 174–183, 460–487
  Hegel's influence, 461–466
  Morris and Green's influence, 172*n*.,
   173–174*n*., 200*n*., 466–486
 correlatives and, 143
 dualism and, 109, 172–174, 185–186,
  194*n*., 385
 experience and, 173*n*., 353*n*.
  consequent phenomena, 451
  possibility, 523
  reconstruction of experience, 265
 French thought and, 318
  instrumentalism, 319
 the given and, 216
 inaccuracy and, 128, 190–192
 instrumentalism of, 53, 169–174
  logic and, 362
 James and
  differences, 442
  Jamesian belief, 148*n*.
  Jamesian theory, 159
  support for, 440
 knowledge and, 16
  measure of knowledge, 377–378
  sensation, 504

Dewey, John—*cont.*
 logic and, 294
  influence of idealism, 295
  symbolization, 302*n*.
 Lotze and, 63
  Dewey's indebtedness, 278
 methodology and, 449
  practical consequences, 452
 organisms and, 262
  adaptation, 428
 Peirce and, 70, 165, 171, 174*n*.
  Peirce's hotel, 80
  Peirce's view of concepts, 121
 pragmatism and, vii, viii, x, 3–5, 8, 58,
   165–169, 275
  English thought, 432
  morals and, 456
  possibility, 426
  problems, 200–204
  prophetic beginnings, 454
  Schiller's view, 276*n*.
  use of term, 348
 propositions and, 192, 193*n*., 196, 198,
   359, 395–398, 411–414
 purposive conceptualization and, 429
 reality and, 425*n*.
 Schiller and, 276*n*., 284, 297
  theory of method, 303
 science and, 65
  liberalized conception, 365
  logical character of, 376
  morality and, 444
 sensation and response and, 183–190
 social views of, 443
  war, 446
 subjectivity and, 141, 342*n*.
 theory of inquiry and
  continuity, 358
  evolution of theory, 61, 199–200
  judgment, 351*n*.
 theory of mind of, 236
  circuit coordination, 252
  function of mind, 238
  gesture, 241–242
  psychophysical behavior, 241
  social occupations, 239, 240
  stimulus and response, 237, 243, 249*n*.
 thought and, 206, 266
 truth and, 42, 125, 160, 192–199
 unique wholes of, 275*n*.
 warranted assertibility of, 42, 125, 193–
   195
 wit and, 445
 world in making and, 427
 writing of, 326
Dikē, 399*n*.

Ding-an-sich (thing-in-itself), 39, 55, 138, 470
Diogenes Laërtius, 29*n*.
Disposition terms, *see* Terms–disposition
Distinction, Vailati and, 336
Doubt
action and, 120
definition of, 84
Humean causal laws and, 369–371
truth and, 115–116, 128
Dualism
in conception of experience, 469
Dewey and, 109, 172–174, 185–186, 194*n*., 385
of heart and head, 30
self and, 478–479, 484
Duhem, Pierre, 271, 315, 318*n*., 532
Durkheim, Emile, 321
Dynameis, 357
Dynamis, 175, 287

Eckermann, Johann Peter, 49*n*.
Economy
activity in, 438
deterministic, 443, 444
thought and
changes in economy, 64
principle of economy, 343, 344
traditional ideals and expansion of, 445
see also Capitalism
Eddington, A. S., 20, 355, 532
Education
continuity and, 174–183
Dewey and, 167–168
Edwards, Jonathan, 7
Ego, *see* Self
Egotism, Fichte and, 53
Einstein, Albert, 60, 100*n*., 532
Electrons, interpretation of, 372–375, 380–381
Eliot, Charles W., 71, 72
Ellis, Leslie, 108, 532
Emerson, Ralph Waldo, 45, 69, 74, 278
Emotions, James-Lange theory of, 73
Empiricism, 137, 455, 501
criticism of, 468–471, 473–474, 476, 483–484
in England, 277, 278
evaluation and, 221–225
experience and, 149
historical, 449–451
ideas and, 22, 24
instrumentalist, 490–491
judgments in, 41
logical, 271*n*.
Mead and, 233–234
meaning in, 99

Empiricism—*cont.*
of Mill, 63
of Peirce, 101–120
pragmatism and, 133, 136–141, 426
radical, 440, 441
Berkeley's, 504, 505
James's, 3, 422
science and, 261
senses in, 37
17th-century, 22, 24
Ends and means
action and, 399–402
growth and, 200
mathematical postulates and, 335–336
will and, 342
Engels, F., 63, 537
Enlightenment, 10, 24–26, 43–45
defined as heart and head, 11
18th-century, 29–35, 437
in Germany, 32–34
Environment
action and, ix
adaptation to, 177–178
control over, 239, 265–266
habit and, 179–180
meaning of and adaptation to, 177–178
organism and, 394–395
reflection as response to, 428*n*.
social act and, 261–262
Epistēmē, 82
Epistomology
critique of, 315
Dewey's interest in, 165
difficulties of, 20
in modern philosophy, 230–231
pragmatic humanism and, 289–290
of Protestant theology, 34
received stimuli and, 213*n*.
self and, 283
Erasmus, 49
Erdmann, J. E., 467
Esprit de système, 29, 30
Esse, 501
Essence
Aristotle and, 89
context and, 297
definition of, 340
James and, 12, 139*n*.
of moral activity, 423
of scientific knowledge, 478
Ethics
capitalism and Protestant, 7
construction of good and, 383–414
criterion of valuation, 400–402
end-means, 398–400
ethical judgment, 384–385
naturalistic ethic, 389–390

Ethics—*cont.*
 ought and *is*, 385–389
 situations, 390–393
 valuation, 390–398
 value, 390–393
  see also Good
 judgments by, ix, 384–385
  value judgments, 221–222
 language in, 408*n.*, 409
 pragmatic theory of, 167–169, 383
 science and, 65, 166
 of success, 438–439
  see also Valuation
Eucharist, 86
Eucken, Rudolph C., 331*n.*
Euclid, 131, 338*n.*
Euler, Leonhard, 35
Evaluation, procedure of, 351–352
Evolution
 of consciousness, 235
 discovery of, 13
 idealism and, 277
 inquiry theory and, 61, 199–200
 pragmatism and, 10
 of science, 239–240, 358
 theory of, 59–62, 454–455
Existence
 Berkeley on, 99*n.*
 Descartes' argument on, 18
 of external world, 471–473; *see also*
  External world
 Peirce on, 118
 real, 22–23, 82
 struggle for, 60, 61
Existentialism, 13, 356–357
 Fichte's influence on, 57
Ex nihilo, 13
Experience
 absolute, 275*n.*
 a priori and, 38, 467
  pragmatic a priori, 213–214, 216, 220–
   221
 behaviorism and, 187–190
 Berkeley and, 500
 change and, 424–425
 conceptualization of, 345–350
  conceptual schemes, 359–363
 conscious, 480–481
 consciousness as reconstruction of, 266
 control of, 410, 422
 Darwinism and, 61
 Dewey and, 173*n.*, 353*n.*
  consequent phenomena, 451
  possibility, 523
  reconstruction of experience, 265
 dualistic conception of, 469
 Enlightenment's theory of, 25

Experience—*cont.*
 of experience, 352*n.*–353*n.*
 experimental, 288–291
 exploration of, 379–380
 faith and, 34
 future, 423–424
 immediate
  knowledge and, 369–370
  thought and, 275
 interpretation of, 53
 James and, 291–292
  reworking conceptual schemes, 349
 Kant and, 36–37
 knowledge and, 52, 201
  external world, 354–357
  as original of knowledge, 449–452
  single sensations, 476–477
 language and, 520
  meaningful language, 506
  observational language, 375
 learning by, 503
 meaning of signs and, 119
 mind and, 228–231
 moral and scientific, 43–45
 nature of, 470–472
  theories of truth, 196*n.*–197*n.*
 necessary conditions of, 39
 ordering of, 213–217
  qualia, 217–219
 perception and, 501–502
 philosophy as reconstruction of, 168–169
 practice as control of, 330
 predictability in, 368–369
 probability in, 112
 Protestant reformers and, 34
 psychology and, 292
 reality and, 147
 reliance upon, 163–164
 science and conditions of, 491
 self and, 54–56
 self-realization and, 47, 48
 sense, 21
  functional psychology, 140–141
  ideas as derived from, 37, 41, 136–140
  knowledge and probability in, 360
  sight, 186–187
  see also Sense perception
 social change and, 65
 symbols in, 245–246
 systems of order and, 210, 212
 thought and, 427
  unifying action of, 484–485
 transcendentalism and, 57
 truth and
  basic truths, 367–369
  empirical experience, 149
  understanding of, 377

Experience—*cont.*
  valuation and, 221–225, 383, 391
External world
  conditional, 142
  existence of, 471–473; *see also* Existence
  general types in, 495
  knowledge of, 288–289, 354–357, 403
    denial, 352–354
    experimental construction, 283–287, 299–300
  mind, 499–500
  meaning and, 507
  organism and, 261–262
  postulated, 285–292
  should-be and, 142, 143*n*., 144
  will and, 206
  see also Environment; Objects; Organisms; Social context
Ezorski, Gertrude, 196*n*., 532

Faith (*Glaube*)
  apologetic for religious, 328, 342
    Christian faith, 315, 317
  Fichte and, 56
  intuitive truth as, 50
  Kant's defense of, 40, 43, 44
  as original of experience, 34
  reason and, ix
  science and, 15, 384
    19th-century, 62–63
Fallibilism, 349–352
  justification and, 350–351
  of Peirce, truth and, 122–123, 127–128
  pluralities of construction and, 349–350
Fay, Harriet M., 69
Feigl, H., 210*n*., 214*n*., 217*n*., 220*n*., 532
Fichte, Johann G., 10, 47, 48, 52–58, 61, 206, 270, 284, 328, 433, 456, 467, 468, 472, 478, 532
Fideism, 328
Fisch, Max H., viii*n*., 70, 80*n*., 81*n*., 105*n*., 108*n*., 455*n*., 488*n*., 527, 532
Fiske, John, 69, 277
Ford, Franklin, 413*n*.
Formalism, pragmatism and, 519–521
Frankena, W. K., 222*n*., 532
Franklin, Benjamin, 7
Frazer, Sir James, 450
Frege, Gottlob, 89, 309, 331*n*.
Froebel, Friedrich, 176
Froissy, Juliette (Mme. Pourtalai), 70
Future
  action, 403–404
  contingency, 526
  control of, 444–445
  experience and

Future—*cont.*
  planning of, 423–424
  predictive experience, 506
God and, 159
  knowledge and, 344*n*.
  meaning and, 122
    future referred to, 506
  open, 522–523
  possibility, 426
  probability, 113, 119*n*.
  valuation-propositions and, 407–408
  variable hypotheticals and, 311
  see also Possibility; Probability
Futurism, 332

Galileo Galilei, 16, 19–20, 22, 23, 355, 384, 450, 532
Gallie, W. D., 3*n*., 71*n*., 97*n*., 532
Games
  communication through, 255–258
  language, 312–313
  social objects and, 263
Gauss, Karl F., 106, 107
Geiger, George R., 3*n*., 532
Gentile, Giovanni, 324
Geometry
  basic truths and, 367–368
    geometry as model for, 102
  ideal conditions in, 131
  Kant and, 42
  logic and, 208*n*.
  as science of space, 367
  of souls, 27
Gerhardt, C. I., 21*n*., 532
Gestalt, 262
Given, the
  a priori and, 216–217; *see also* A priori
    as object-*ified*, 217
  external world as, 472; *see also* External world
  as independent, 230
  logic and, 358–363
  self and, 55, 56
  see also Axioms; Posits; Postulates
Glaube, see Faith
God
  in Cartesian philosophy, 18–19, 21, 27
  evolution as, 62
  Fichte and, 47, 56
  as gentleman, 521
  German Protestantism and, 34
  as immutable being, 387
  justification for, 154–159
  Kantian Idea of, 41, 43
  as maker, 213
  man as, 332
  personality and, 483

God—*cont.*
  philosophy of action and, 317
  scientific world-view and, 31–32
  as sympathizer, 300*n.*
Gödel, Kurt, 510
Goethe, Johann Wolfgang von, 45, 46*n.*,
    48, 49, 60, 328, 468, 532
Good
  construction of, 383–414
  criterion of valuation, 400–402
  ends-means, 398–400
  ethical judgment in, 384–385
  naturalistic ethic, 389–390
  ought and *is*, 385–389
  situations, 390–393
  valuation, 390–395
  valuation-propositions, 395–398
  value, 390–393
  evolution of, 61
  ideal self as, 482
  life as, 134
  romantic idealism and, 51
  statistically grounded version of, 59
  truth and, 147–148
  ultimate, 199–200, 399–400, 409–410,
    481–483
  as useful, 150
Goodman, Nelson, 93*n.*, 218, 302*n.*, 525,
    526, 532
Gore, W. C., 440*n.*
Goudge, Thomas A., 3*n.*, 533
Green, Nicholas St. John, 81
Green, T. H., 10, 63, 74, 172*n.*, 174*n.*,
    200*n.*, 232*n.*, 275*n.*, 276, 278*n.*,
    279, 282, 391*n.*, 410*n.*, 455, 461*n.*,
    465–488, 533
Grose, T. H., 533
Grosseteste, Robert, 28
Growth
  derivation of, 450
  idea of, 487
  morals and, 200, 460–461
  as process, 462
  of science, 14–16, 59, 444
  theory of education and, 174–183
  of things, 61*n.*
  wise, 446
Gullace, Giovanni, 332*n.*, 333*n.*, 533
Gurney, Edmund, 73

Habits, 110
  environment and, 179–180
  induction as, 310
  meaning and action by, 120, 121
  occupations and, 238–239
  Peirce on, 85
  reasoning by, 376, 377

Haeckel, Ernst, 277
Haldane, Viscount, 475
Hall, G. Stanley, 72, 74, 185, 284*n.*
Hamilton, Sir William, 278, 279, 371*n.*
Hare, R. M., 389*n.*, 533
Harris, W. T., 74
Heart and head
  defined, 11
  duality expressed in, 30
  God and, 32
Hébert, Marcel, 316*n.*, 319*n.*, 533
Hegel, Georg, 8*n.*, 10, 34, 46*n.*, 48, 50, 59,
    61, 63, 74, 176, 275*n.*, 276*n.*, 277,
    278, 280, 331, 333, 434, 441, 455,
    456, 460–467, 469*n.*, 470, 472–
    474, 486–487, 496, 520, 533
Hegelianism, 58, 371, 434, 440, 444, 446
  Darwinism and, 61
  Dewey and, 165, 167, 173, 174, 184,
    185, 422, 442, 461, 463, 464,
    521
  in England, 276, 277, 281, 469, 473, 474
  waning of, 308
  knowing and, 53
  Mead and, 234
  reaction against, 320
Heidel, W. H., 440*n.*
Heine, Heinrich, 40, 468
Helmholtz, Hermann Ludwig von, 72
Hempel, C. G., 100*n.*, 356*n.*, 533
Herapath, John, 107
Herbart, J. F., 56, 276*n.*, 278
Herder, Johann von, 52
Herodotus, 148
Hermann, Conrad, 8*n.*, 533
Hesiod, 399*n.*, 533
Hobbes, Thomas, 16, 19, 20, 30, 233, 370,
    533
Hodgson, Shadworth, 73
Hölderlin, Friedrich, 33
Holmes, Oliver Wendell, Jr., viii, 50, 50*n.*,
    81, 333, 443, 444, 533
Hook, Sidney, 3*n.*, 409*n.*, 533–534
Horton, Walter Marshall, 314*n.*, 315*n.*,
    317*n.*, 318*n.*, 319, 534
Hospers, John, 403*n.*–407*n.*, 543
Humanism
  pragmatic, 270, 273–276, 323
    critique of logic, 295
    individuals, 286
    knowledge in, 289–291
    limitations of, 301–303
    of Schiller, 283–285
Hume, David, 5, 10, 19, 21, 24–26, 31, 35–
    39, 43, 44, 136–138, 149, 206, 214,
    215, 293, 322, 342, 349, 360, 361,
    369–370, 379, 384, 385*n.*, 386, 389,

Hume, David—*cont.*
433, 455, 466*n.*, 468, 473, 476, 483,
500, 508, 509, 517, 534
Husserl, E. C. A., 63, 271, 534
Huxley, Thomas H., 277, 463*n.*, 464*n.*, 534
Hylē (matter), 286–290, 297, 299, 300,
329

Ideal conditions, 131–132
Idealism, 46–65, 455, 466
common sense and, 15
in England, 276–279, 473–475
criticized, 279–280
waning of, 308
experimental, 173*n.*–174*n.*
Hegelian, 58
in Italy, 324, 325
of Lotze, 278
of Mead, 233–234
modern types of, 46–65
of Morris, 467–468
objective, 3
of philosophy of action, 319
pragmatism and, 7, 10
romantic, 26, 46–52
self and, 478–479
transcendental, 40–43
Ideas, 427*n.*
analytic proposition and, 508
Berkeley and, 56, 506–507
causality and
derivation of ideas, 137
generation of ideas, 451
relations of, 38
consequences of, 452
in empiricism, 137
consequences as meaning of, 18, 87*n.*,
96–97, 99, 410
predictive consequences, 333
Darwinism and, 61
Descartes and, 20–21, 27
dualism of sensation and, 185–186
empirical, 22, 24, 450
Enlightenment and, 25
functional test of, 448
inquiry and, 191–192
as instruments, 169
Locke and, 28
logic and, 18, 207–208
meaning of, 18, 87*n.*, 96–97, 99
in consequences, 410
derivation of ideas, 137–138
objects and, 23
as plans of action, 147
pragmatic methodology and, 80
of primary and secondary qualities, 23, 24
as reality, 47

Ideas—*cont.*
agreement, 149
reason and, 41–42, 51
regulative
function of, 40–44, 132
of knowledge, 52
of reason, 51
transformation of propositions, 359
sense experience and, 37, 136–140
functional psychology, 140–141
as signs, 501–504
subjective realm of, 20
unicity of, 371–372
Identity, in plastic world, 291*n.*
Identity of indiscernibles, 85
Imagination, conception and, 97
Imperatives, in *should,* 408
Implication
material and Lewis' criticism of, 210–212
notion of, 207
Individualism, 422, 438
Dewey and, 442–443
of James, 232, 441–442
see also Subjectivism
Induction
basic truths and, 367
habit as, 310
by knowledge, 454
premises and, 372, 379*n.*–380*n.*
probability and, 110–112, 115
science and, 350
by will to believe, 331
Inferences
leading principles in, 376–377, 381–382
logic of, 294
probability and, 110, 111*n.*, 113*n.*, 118
science and, 350
terminology and, 374–375
Infinite series
defined, 208–209
innumerable series, 223
Information, interpretive activity and, 56
Inquiry, vii
basic truths and, 102–103
Dewey's theory of, 166, 167, 443
ethics, 388, 389
inquiry as evaluation, 199–200
pattern of inquiry, 190–192
pattern of inquiry and truth, 192–199
knowledge and, 358, 497
logic of, 294, 295
Peirce's theory of, 83–86, 132, 350
pure forms in, 513
scientific, 15
truth and
ideal limit, 496
inquiry into need, 156

Institutionalism, 444
Instrumentalism, 8, 53, 319, 349, 362, 441,
    446, 474, 485–486
action and, 443–444
consciousness in, 266
emergence of, 166–168
empiricism and, 490–491
interpretation of scientific knowledge in,
    4, 364–382
    historical factors in, 366–369
    instrumentalist point of view, 371–375
    leading principles, 376–382
    logic and science, 364–366
    structure of science, 369–371
of laws, 310–311
as logic, 169–174, 183–190
Lotze's influence on, 278
pragmatism and, 421
source of, 74
truth and, 192–199
as wit, 445
see also Inquiry; Situations
Intension, Lewis and, 226, 227*n.*, 518
Interests, subjective, thought and, 141–144
In the long run, of occurrences, 112–113,
    115, 117, 153; *see also* Probability

Jacobi, Friedrich H., 48, 50
James, Henry, 71, 434
James, William, 51, 56, 64, 68, 81, 88, *133–
    164,* 170, 171*n.,* 184, 206, 207,
    235*n.,* 268, 282, 304, 306, 308,
    360*n.,* 369, 407*n.,* 413*n.,* 416, 419,
    431, 437*n.,* 474, 484, 499, 505,
    534–535
background of, 71–73
Berkeley and, 484, 505
Dewey and
    differences, 442
    influence of James, 177
    Jamesian belief, 148*n.*
    Jamesian theory, 159
    support from, 440
disposition terms and, 176
empiricism and, 136–140
European precedents of, 270, 271
experience and, 291-292
    reworking conceptual schemes, 349
facts and, 350
faith and, 43
Fichte and, 57
function of thought, 58
Green and, 479–480, 483
    as humanist, 167, 475
ideas and
    as instruments, 169

James, William—*cont.*
    meaning of ideas for, 87*n.,* 96
individualism of, 232, 441–442
Lange theory, 242*n.*
language and, 145–146
legacy of, 159–164
logic and, 294, 302*n.,* 520, 521
Lotze and, 278
Mead and, 76, 236
    teleological mind, 237
meaning and, 135, 146–147
    of ideas, 87 *n.,* 96
Mill and, 279
mind and
    as teleological, 141–145, 185, 237
order and, 477
Peirce and, 69, 71, 74, 170, 302*n.*
    Peirce's legacy, 132
    pragmatic maxim, 420
pluralism and, 299, 443
possibility and, 523
pragmatism and, vii, viii, 3–5, 7, 8, 133–
    140, 420, 439
    as dominant spirit, 421
    English thought, 432
    in France, 314–322
    in Italy, 324–331*n.,* 333*n.,* 341, 342,
        344*n.*–346
    as meaning and truth, 348
    method, 79–80, 439, 452, 487
    origins, 456
    purposive conceptualization, 429
    science and ethics, 65
    sensations, 493
    unstiffening of laws of nature, 53
reality and, 430
    pre-human reality, 291
religion and, 194
Schiller and, 273, 283
    bad taste of Schiller, 281
    differences, 275, 284, 285, 289
    humanism, 276*n.*
    hylē, 288
    James's anticipation, 274
    plural truths, 299
    will to believe, 295
science and
    conservatism, 221 *n.*
    Kantian science, 221 *n.*
social views of, 422, 441
transcendental self and, 465–466
theory of belief of, 153–159
thought and
    continuity of, 466
    function of, 58, 61
    logic and, 520, 521

James, William—*cont.*
transcendental self and, 465–466
truth and, 125, 147–151, 193
as good, 199
Wittgenstein and, 313
world in making and, 427
Wright and, 491, 492
Jastrow, Joseph, 70
Jerusalem, W., 330*n.*, 535
Joachim, H. H., 277*n.*
Joergensen, Joergen, 209*n.*, 271*n.*, 339*n.*, 340*n.*, 535
John, St., 49, 246, 470*n.*
Johnson, Samuel, 89, 535
Jones, Marc E., 466, 535
Jowett, Benjamin, 276 *n.*

Kallen, Horace M., 163 *n.*, 284*n.*, 535
Kant, Immanuel, ix, 5, 8, 10, 15, 25, 26, 30, 33–53, 56–58, 63, 65, 68, 77, 81, 82, 132, 138, 139, 167, 206, 207, 210, 229, 258*n.*, 263, 276*n.*–278, 333, 349, 359, 361, 371, 373, 376, 384, 451, 455, 456, 466*n.*, 467, 469*n.*, 470, 472, 479, 484, 501, 508, 535
Kaplan, Abraham, 430*n.*, 535
Keats, John, 33
Kempe, A. B., 209*n.*
Kenna, J. C., 282*n.*, 535
Kennedy, Gail, 80*n.*, 491*n.*, 535
Kepler, Johannes, 13
Keynes, John Maynard, 107*n.*, 305, 427*n.*, 535
Kneale, William, 108*n.*, 535
Knowing
conception of, ix
Hegel and, 53
mind and, 37
sense perception and, 27
transcendental, defined, 29
valuation and, 383
Knowledge, vii
action and, 55–56
analytical, 17
antinomies and, 41
a priori, 28
change and problem of, 64–65, 198
concepts in, 37
construction of, 349–350
continuity of, 183
conventionalism and, 349
defined as power, 6, 16, 17, 206
Descartes and
content of, 27
primacy of knowledge, 21–22, 37

Knowledge—*cont.*
as description, 20–21, 342
as discovery, 479
evolution of, 358
experience and, 52
as original of knowledge, 449–452
single sensations, 467–477
of external world, 288–289, 354–357, 403, 471–472
denial, 352–354
experiential construction, 286–287, 299–300
mind, 21, 499–500
future and, 344*n.*
inductive, 454
inquiry and, 358, 497; *see also* Inquiry
instrumentalist interpretation of, 364–382; *see also* Instrumentalism
justification of, 350–351
language and, 102
Lewis' theory of, 207, 210–231
mind and meaning, 225–231
mind and world order, 212–221
valuation, 221–225
morals and, 419–420
natural, 503
organism of, 467, 472–473
pragmatic theory of, 45, 422–423, 428
definition, 431
experience, 424
practical character of, 425–426
pragmatic humanism, 289–291
problem of, 11, 81–82
psychology and, 292–293
of real, 22–24
reality as, 284
romanticism and, 48, 49
scientific, ix, 490
ethics and, 412–414
fallibilism, 123
instrumental interpretation, 4
moral conceptions, 454–456
nature, 16, 19
problems of synthesis, 14
spiritual essence, 478
transformation of man's social existence, 17
self and, 54–56
sense experience in, 360, 504
sense perception and, 39–42
social conditions and, 168
static view of, 469
synthesis of values with, ix, x, 11, 16, 19
theory of
Berkeley's, 499–507
correspondence, 453

Knowledge—*cont.*
  Enlightenment, 25
  Hume's 36
  instrumental, 183–190
  Locke's, 22–24
  Peirce's, 101–120
  spectator theory of, 500–501
  transcendental, 28
  useful, 6, 7
  valuation and, 383–384, 423–424
  virtue as, 412
  warranted assertibility and, 195
  see also Epistemology
Kraushaar, Otto F., 278*n.*, 535
Krikorian, Y. H., 173*n.*, 535
Kritik, 30
Krönig, 107

Ladd-Franklin, Christine, 70, 140*n.*, 275*n.*,
    488, 489*n.*, 490*n.*, 492, 536
Lalande, André, 8*n.*, 316*n.*, 317, 345*n.*, 536
Lamont, Corliss, 301*n.*, 348*n.*, 536
Lange, C. L., 73, 242*n.*
Langford, C. H., 77, 207*n.*, 497*n.*; *see also*
    Lewis and, 536
Language
  analytic statements in, 227
  analyticity in natural, 512
  Berkeley and, 26, 500
  class-attributes in, 372
  continuity in, 440*n.*
  conceptual clarity and, 88
  disposition terms in, 426
  ethical
    as expressive, 408*n.*
    hortatory use, 409
  experience and, 520
    meaningful language, 506
  generalized other and, 260–261
  as gesture, 246–247
  implication and, 212
  as instrument, 357, 427
  James's use of, 145–146
  Johnson on, 89*n.*
  logic and, 312–313
    beauty of language, 332
  meaning and, 296–297, 308
    words, 79–80, 337–338; *see also* Words
  observational, 375
  ordinary, 429–430
  origin of, 212–213
  of philosophic phraseology, 229–232
  psychic processes and, 296
    meaning, 297
  real and, 93–95
  reality and, 355–356, 375

Language—*cont.*
  reductionism and, 136–137
  religious, function of, 158–159
  sentence defined in, 310
  as social art, 232
  in social behaviorism, 234, 236
    social gestures, 241–244
  universal, theories and, 337
  use of, 440
    analyzed, 363
    utterance in, 430
  valuation and, 390
    desire, 396–397
  see also Terms
Laplace, Simon de, 31, 108
Laski, Harold J., 475
Laws
  behavior and, 399
  of bodies, 25
  causal, 369–371, 379
  conventionalism and, 369–370
  focus of, on antecedent phenomena, 452
  formalization of, 364–365
  instrumentalist treatment of, 310–311,
    372–373
  logical, 361–362
  of motion, 385*n.*, 367–369
  of nature, 53
    causal relationships in, 38
    God and, 19
  observational language and, 375
  scientific
    function of, 365–366
    logical character of, 376–380
    truth of, 366
  of thought, 496–497
  universal mathematical, 16
Leading principles, knowledge and, 376–
    382; *see also* Knowledge
Leibniz, Gottfried von, 15, 16, 21, 30, 33,
    35, 37, 52, 61, 85, 128, 176, 361,
    370, 496, 508, 510*n.*
Lenz, John, 111*n.*, 118*n.*, 536
Lenzen, V. F., 69*n.*, 105*n.*, 106*n.*, 536
Le Roy, Edouard, 271, 314, 315, 317, 318,
    536
Leroux, E., 345*n.*, 536
Lessing, Gotthold Ephraim, 33, 52
Lewis, C. I., 205–231, 305, 406*n.*, 416,
    476, 497*n.*, 499, 508, 526, 536
  on action, 423
  background of, 77
  on categories, 210–216, 220–221
  ethical theory and, 383
  on experience, 349, 427*n.*, 506
  on future, 424

Lewis, C. I.—*cont.*
  predictive experience, 506
  instrumentalism and, 421
  James and, 422
  logic and, 207–212
    conditions of organization, 260
    impossibility in, 524
    techniques of, 334 *n.*
  moral judgments and, 352
  order and, 207–212
    mind and world order, 212–221
  pragmatism and, vii, viii, 3, 4, 8, 58, 68,
      205–207, 268, 523
    use of term, 348
  probability and, 360*n.*
  rational power and, 359
  sensation and, 504
  theories of
    of meaning, 225–231, 511–520
    of objects, 263
  valuation and, 221–225
Liberalism, reaction against, 322
Lieb, Irwin C., 68*n.*, 128*n.*, 536
Lincoln, Abraham, 433
Linksy, Leonard, 100*n.*, 518*n.*, 519*n.*, 536
Lloyd, Alfred, 74, 167, 440*n.*, 471*n.*, 536
Locke, John, 5, 10, 15, 20, 22–25, 27–28,
    30, 37, 45, 50, 81, 82, 89, 110, 136,
    149, 184, 206, 230*n.*, 287*n.*, 293,
    334, 353*n.*, 384, 434, 449, 451,
    466*n.*, 468, 469, 473, 476, 499–
    501, 504*n.*, 536
Logic, 8, 302*n.*
  analyticity in, 509–510, 513, 517–521
  a priori and, 358–363
  in algebra, 69*n.*, 105*n.*
  Cartesian philosophy and, 17, 97
  communication and, 260–261
  consequences and, 99
  critique of, 294–297
  the given and, 358–363
  Green and, 484
  inductive, 310
  of inquiry, 294, 295
  instrumentalism as, 169–173, 183–190
    truth in, 192–199
  justification of belief and, 153
  Kant and, 42
  language and, 312–313, 332
  Lewis and, 207–212
    conditions of organization, 260
    impossibility, 524
    techniques of logic, 334*n.*
  Locke and, 22
  Lotze and, 278
  mathematical pragmatism and, 334–343
    definitions, 337–341

Logic—*cont.*
  maxim of, 421
  in meaning, purposive bearing of, 121
  modern, context and, 354
  naturalistic theory of, 460–461
  opposition to, 301–302
  order and, 207–212
  ought and *is* in, 386
  of Parmenides, 18
  Peirce and, 69, 70, 167*n.*, 170, 302*n.*,
      421, 520, 521
    influence of Peirce, 305–307
    infinite class, 209*n.*
    innumerable series, 223
  positivism and, 343
  pragmatism and, 167–168, 494
  psychology of, 292–294
  Schiller and, 170*n.*, 291, 301
  of science, 491
    natural science, 35
    scientific laws, 368–380
    structure of science, 364–366
  of situations, 409–412
  synthetic a priori and, 40–41
  in thought, 520, 521
  for use, 303
  Vailati and, 334–335
  see also Deduction; Induction; Inferences
Logos, 21, 338*n*
  mind and, 29
  romanticism and, 49
Lotze, Rudolph Hermann, 63, 277–278, 536
Lovejoy, A. O., 5, 46*n.*, 537
Lucretius, 450
Lusky, Louis, 452*n.*, 537
Luther, Martin, 34

McCosh, James, 278*n.*
Mach, Ernst, 56, 57, 73, 271, 343, 369, 505,
    537
Mackenzie, J. S., 277
McKeon, Charles K., 90*n.*, 537
McLennan, S. F., 440*n.*
McTaggart, 277, 280
Madden, Edward H., 80*n.*, 111*n.*, 491*n.*,
    537
Malcom, Norman, 309*n.*, 311*n.*, 313*n.*, 537
Malebranche, Nicholas, 19
Malthus, Thomas, 60
Maria Theresa (empress of Austria), 8
Martinetti, 332
Marx, Karl, 63, 198, 321, 537
Marxism, 323
Materialism
  in England, 277, 278, 280
  scientific, 500, 501

Mead, George Herbert, 74, 75, 185*n.*, 231,
    289*n.*, 295, 313, 383, 416, 421, 452,
    456, 523, 531, 537
  action and, 177*n.*, 184
  background of, 76–77
  Dewey and, 167, 170*n.*
  games and, 255–258
  language and, 241–244
    language as gesture, 246–247
  pragmatism and, vii, viii, x, 3, 4, 8, 58, 68
    moral role, 422
    social pragmatism, 264–268
    use of term, 348
  psychology and, 237–241
  realism of, 477
  science and, 11*n.*, 234
  social behaviorism and, 236–237
    social gesture, 241–244
    social objects, 261–264
  social viewpoint and, 232–234
  symbols and, 244–246
    schematization of, 248–250
  theory of mind of, 232–268
    behavioral analysis, 428*n.*
  theory of self of, 181, 252–254
    generalized other, 255–258
    the "I," 258–261
    influence, 267–268
  writing of, 326
Mead, Hiram, 76
Meaning
  of action, ix, 429–430
  analysis of
    Hume's, 25
    importance of, 65
  analyticity in, 518
  of assertion, 335, 343
  Berkeley and, 26, 500
  of concepts, 86–87, 89, 92–93, 103
  consciousness of, 243–247
  as consequences, 96–97, 99, 410
    theoretical terms, 376
  of ethical expressions, 389
  external world and, 472
    externally existing bodies, 507
  futurative reference of, 506
  of ideas, 18, 87*n.*, 96
    in consequences, 410
    derivation of ideas, 137–138
  interpretation of, vii, 4
  in language, 79–80, 241, 308
  Lewis' theory of, 225–231, 511–520
  Locke and, 23–24
  of mathematical propositions, 516
  maxim of, 420–421
  in meaninglessness, 356–357
  mind and, 225–231

Meaning—*cont.*
  of objects, 23–24
  organon in, 454–458
  Peirce's theory of, 120–125
    background to, 488–492
    definition, 494–495
    meaning and action, 429–430
  in pragmatism, 5, 419–431
    pragmatic methodology, 79
  psychic processes and, 295–296
  purpose and, 335–336
  of science, 16
  signs and, 79–80, 82–83, 85, 87–91, 95,
    96, 103–104, 138
    Peirce's influence, 305–308
    probability and, 114–115, 118–120
  of social action, 263–264
  social wholes and, 233
  subjective feelings and, 87–88
  theory of, ix, 5, 327*n.*
    James, 135, 146–147
    picture theory, 312–313
  of thought, 5
  transformation in, 359
  truth and, 120–132
  valuation and, 383
  variable hypotheticals in, 310–311
  verification of, 343
    behavior as, 151
    theory of, 99–101
  of words, 126*n.*, 337–338, 506
Meaninglessness, 86, 96
  of experience, 356–357
  of reality, 126
Meinong, Alexius, 63, 524
Mendelssohn, Moses, 40
Metafisiche, 328
Methodology
  experimental, 452
  pragmatic, 79–80, 349–363, 449
    contextualism in, 352–357
    defined, 79
    fallibilism in, 349–352
    James's view compared to Peirce's, 135
    Papini's view, 327–328
  of pragmatic humanism, 289–291, 302–
    303
  of Vailati, 342
Mill, John Stuart, 5, 10, 63, 138, 277, 278–
    280, 293, 310, 334, 351*n.*, 370–
    373, 377*n.*, 382, 409*n.*, 449, 455,
    456, 467–469, 473, 483, 490–492*n.*,
    510*n.*, 537–538
Miller, Dickinson, 274*n.*
Mind
  American, 432–433

Mind—*cont.*
  behaviorism and, 182
    behavioral analysis of, 428*n.*
  circuit coordination of, 252
  concept of, 25
  as conscious intelligence, 469
  Descartes and, 27
  Dewey's theory of, 236
    function of mind, 238
    psychophysical behavior, 241
    social occupations, 239, 240
    stimulus and response, 237, 243, 249*n.*
  experience and, 228–231, 291
  external world and, 21, 499–500
  as gesture, 241–242
  God and, 21
  knowing and, 37
  knowledge and, mind as active agent, 501
  language and, 313
  meaning and, 225–231
  modern, 14
  passive, 425
  physical location of, 384
  senses and
    perception, 27-29
    sense data, 40
  subjectivity and, 20, 203–204
  as teleological, 141–145, 187, 237
  theories of
    Dewey's, 236–241, 243
    Lewis', 225–231
    Mead's, 231–268
    psychological theory, 409
  universal nature of, 284
  world order and, 212–221
  see also Cognition; Conception; Thought
Mirandola, Pico della, 496
Mises, R. von, 108*n.*, 538
Mitchell, Oscar, 70.
Modality, 524–525
  Peirce on, 98
  see Necessity; Possibility
Modernism, 314–316
Molyneux, William, 504*n.*
Montague, W. P., 75, 527
Montaigne, 49
Moore, Addison, 75, 440*n.*
Moore, Edward C., 111*n.*, 538
Moore, G. E., 62*n.*, 63, 211*n.*, 282, 308, 309, 311*n.*, 538
Morals
  action and, 199–200
  a priori conditions and, 43
  concepts and, 342
  consciousness and theory of, 480–483
  continuity and growth of, 460–461
  knowledge and

Morals—*cont.*
  moral conceptions, 454–456
  moral values, 419–420
  practical reason and, 40
  pragmatism and, 416, 419–423
  truth and, 147–148
  validation of judgment and, 350–352
  values in
    knowledge and, 419–420
    mediation, 440
    science and, 35, 166, 419–423
  see also Ethics
More, Henry, 37
Morley, John, 26*n.*, 538
Morris, Charles, 271*n.*, 538
Morris, G. S., 74, 172*n.*, 174*n.*, 278*n.*, 466–488, 538
Murphey, Murray G., 3*n.*, 68*n.*, 70*n.*, 71*n.*, 538
Mussolini, Benito, 321–323, 346
Myers, Francis M., 445*n.*, 538
Myrdal, Gunnar, 437, 538

Nagel, Ernest, xi, 109*n.*, 111*n.*, 356*n.*, 358*n.*, 365*n.*, 380*n.*, 382*n.*, 431, 465, 517*n.*, 538
Napoleon, 51
Nationalism
  idealism and, 48
  self and, 54
Naturalism, 287, 486
  of Dewey, 3
  in ethics, 389–390
  theory of logic and, 460–461
Necessity
  analyticity and, 509–510
  conception and, 98
  Kant and, 38
  possibility and, 212
  psychic processes in, 295
Need
  disturbed equilibration as, 179
  ends-in-view and, 400–401
  inquiry into, 156
Nettleship, Richard L., 474, 475*n.*, 478*n.*
Neurath, Otto, 367*n.*
Newton, Isaac, 17, 19, 20, 23, 24, 30, 31, 38, 60, 62, 367–370, 372, 384, 499, 500, 538–539
Nietzsche, Friedrich, 46*n.*, 57, 206, 270, 319*n.*, 322
Nominalism, 495
  of Hobbes, 233
  of James, 139
    vs. realism of Peirce, 140
  Peirce and, 95*n.*, 372
    opposition by, 139, 140

Nominalism—*cont.*
  realism and, 371–372
  words and, 327
Nomos, 20
Nonsense, *see* Meaninglessness
Nous, 21, 228, 367
Novalis (Friedrich von Hardenberg), 46*n.*

Objects
  cognition of, 38
  conception of, 96*n.*–97*n.*
  as congeries of ideas, 504
  definition of, 217
  ideas and, 23
    as congeries, 96*n.*–97*n.*
    Kantian Ideas, 40, 41
  logic and, 208
  meaning of, 23–24
  objectivity of, 353–354
  phenomenal, 470*n.*
  possibility and, 524
  properties of, 343*n.*
  self and external, 484
  as signs, 381
  social, 261–264
  truth as conformity to, 127, 130–132
  of value, 403
Occupations
  organization of activity by, 238–240
  self, 240
O'Connor, Daniel D., 492*n.*, 539
O'Connor, D. J., x, 539
Ogden, C. K., 305–308, 539
Operationalism, 506
  defined, 91-92
Organisms
  adaptations of, 428
  desire and, 406–407
  environment and, 177–178, 179, 261–262, 394–395
  external world and, 261–262
  of knowledge, 467, 472–473
  self as distinct from, 240
Ostwald, Wilhelm, 271
Ought
  consciousness and, 481
  desire and, 402–403
  evolution and, 62
  Hume on, 385
  is and, 385–389
  morals and, 43
Ousia, 29, 287

Papini, Giovanni, 73, 272, 273*n.*, 275, 319, 322, 323, 324–346, 529, 539
Parmenides, 18, 118, 276*n.*
Parry, W. T., 207, 539

Pascal, Blaise, 31, 43
Pasch, Alan, 511*n.*, 518*n.*, 519*n.*, 539
Passmore, John, 276*n.*, 313*n.*, 539
Peano, Guiseppe, 334, 335, 337, 339–340
Pearson, Karl, 57, 271
Peirce, Benjamin, 68
Peirce, Charles Sanders, 60*n.*, 64, 79–132, 145, 149, 150, 153*n.*, 166*n.*, 212, 215*n.*, 261*n.*, 268, 271, 275, 416, 443, 449*n.*, 451*n.*, 455, 474, 502*n.*, 504, 539–540
  abductive reasoning and, 303*n.*
  analyticity and, 519
  background of, 68–71
  belief and, 205
  Berkeley and, 484, 505, 507
  on cognition, 429
  on concepts, 86–88
    analysis of, 493–494
  consequences and, 137, 452
    test of truth, 156, 159
  Dewey and, 70, 86, 121, 165, 174*n.*
    influence of Peirce, 171
  disposition terms and, 176, 426, 525
  empiricism of, 101–120
  experience and, 56
  error and, 349
  the given and, 216
  on growth, 61*n.*, 487
  ideas and
    cases equally frequent, 427*n*
    as consequences, 452
  induction and, 279*n.*–280*n.*
  on inquiry, 350
  James and, 71, 74, 170
    encounter, 69
    logic, 302*n.*
    Peirce's legacy, 132
    pragmatic maxim, 420
  Lewis and, 206
  on leading principles, 376
  logic and, 69, 70, 167*n.*, 169, 302*n.*, 305–307, 421, 520, 521
    induction, 279*n.*–280*n.*
    infinite class, 209*n.*
    innumerable series, 223
  Mead and
    Peirce's influence, 235, 250, 262
    self, 267*n.*
    use of symbols, 236
  nominalism and, 95*n.*, 372
    opposition to, 139, 140
  possibility and, 523
  pragmatism and, vii, viii, 3–5, 8, 42, 273, 420
    background of, 488–499
    development of pragmatism, 79–83, 86–101

Peirce, Charles Sanders—*cont.*
  in England, 304–310
  in France, 317*n.*–319
  function of thought, 58
  in Italy, 325, 326, 330*n.*, 332–335,
    342, 344*n.*, 345
  as method, 348, 357–358
  origin of term, 138
  as originator, 432
  origins of, 456
  science and ethics, 65
  systematic reasoning, 163
  premisses and, 382
  realism of, 90*n.*, 140, 285, 477
    scholastic, 94, 95, 117–119, 122
  reality and, 115–118, 123–124
  reasoning and, 163, 377
  Schiller and, 276*n.*
    differences, 297
  science and, 101–120
    communal inquiry, 53
  sense data for, 360
  Sheffer's stroke function and, 373*n.*
  theory of inquiry of, 83–86, 132, 350
  theory of meaning and, 120–125
    action, 429–430
    background, 488–492
    definition, 494–495
  thought and, purposive nature of, 144*n.*,
    179
  truth and, 120–125, 496–498
    definition, 125–132
    methods of arriving at, 115–118
Perception, *see* Sense perception
Percipi, 501
Perry, R. B., 3*n.*, 71*n.*, 72*n.*, 148*n.*, 155*n.*,
    170*n.*, 171*n.*, 270*n.*, 274*n.*, 284*n.*,
    289*n.*, 291*n.*, 295*n.*, 320*n.*, 322*n.*,
    323*n.*, 325*n.*, 326*n.*, 404*n.*, 407*n.*,
    413*n.*, 427*n.*, 437*n.*, 440*n.*, 441*n.*,
    442*n.*, 473*n.*, 487*n.*, 499*n.*, 520*n.*,
    521*n.*, 540
Personalism, 283, 295
Petitio principii, 371
Petrarch, 49
Phenomena, 59
Phenomenalism, 355–356
Philosophes
  critical radicalism of, 44
  of 18th century Enlightenment, 30
Philosophy
  of action, 314–319
  critical function of, 147, 166, 168–169,
    460
  as instrument for appropriation, 328
  modern
    epistemology of, 230–231

Philosophy—*cont.*
  knowledge, 454
  problem of, 10–45
  19th-century English, 277
  physics and, 16, 18, 42
  pragmatism as method for, 348
  as reconstruction of experience, 168–169
  of salvations, 6
  of science of 17th century, 19–24
  as study of a priori, 216, 227–228
  U.S. contribution to, viii, 3
  *see also specific aspects of philosophy; for
    example:* Experience; Knowledge;
    Ideas; *and specific philosophies;
    for example:* Empiricism; Instru-
    mentalism
Physicalism, 356
Physics
  analyticity and mathematical, 514–515
  function of, 19
  laws in modern, 378
  operationalism in, 92
  philosophy and
    Descartes, 18
    influence in 17th century, 16
    Kant, 42
    verification theory of meaning in, 100*n.*
Physis, 20, 387*n.*
Pius X, Pope, 314
Plastic world, 426–427
  hylē in, 286–290, 297, 299, 300, 329
  identity in, 291*n.*
  individual action in, 442
  see also Possibility
Plato, 7, 15, 16, 29, 89, 97*n.*, 151, 175, 195,
    196, 233*n.*, 276*n.*, 322, 333, 349,
    366, 386, 398–399, 454, 470*n.*,
    505*n.*, 540
Platonism, 13, 16, 29*n.*
  in England, 277
Pleasure, cognition and pain and, 143
Pledge, H. T., 59, 540
Plenum, 18
Pluralism, 3, 5
  in contextualism, 362–363
  Dewey's, 3
  of James, 422, 440, 443
  of Lewis, 215, 216
  of Papini, 328
  romanticism as, 47
Poe, Edgar Allan, 433
Poiēsis, 287*n.*
Poincaré, Henri, 129, 271, 315, 317*n.*,
    318*n.*, 540
Poisson, Siméon Denis, 107, 108
Polis, 232
Pollock, Frederick, 73
Polybius, 8

Pope, Alexander, 31, 62
Popper, Karl R., 523*n.*, 540
Positivism, 271*n.*, 328, 501
   logical, 343
   self and, 54–55
Possibility
   actual, 142, 542
   concept of, 486–487
      ambiguity in, 214–215
      importance of, 427
   conception as, 97–99
   control of, 424
   in definitions, 339
   ends and mathematical, 335–336
   of error, truth and, 124
   future and, 426
   necessity and, 212
   pragmatism and
      category of possibility, 522–526
      clarification of concept, 524–526
      physical possibility, 522–523
   propositions as, 514
   reality and, 426
   of valuation-propositions, 396*n.*
Postulates
   axioms and, 292–293
   continuity as primary, 173
   definition by, 340–341
   external world and, 285–292
   in religion, 300
Power
   knowledge defined as, 6, 16, 17, 206
   rational, 359
   will to, 344
Pradines, Maurice, 317*n.*–318*n.*, 540
Pragma, 7
Pragmatisch, 138
Pragmatism, defined, 431
Pragmatisme, 314–323
Pragmatismo, 323
Praktisch, 138
Presley, C. F., 382*n.*, 540
Prezzolini, Giuseppe, 324–346, 540
Pringle-Pattison, A. S., 82, 540
Probability
   of arguments, 509
   future and, 113, 119*n.*
   inferences and, 110, 111*n.*, 113*n.*, 118
   knowledge and, 360
   in modern physics, 378
   Peirce's theory of, 69*n.*, 104–120
      induction, 110–112
      the long run of occurrences, 112–113,
         115, 117, 153
      meaning of signs, 114–115
      relative frequency interpretation, 109,
         112, 118

Probability—*cont.*
   statistical version, 105–107
   truth, 115–118
   of satisfaction, 224–225
Prolepsis, 28*n.*, 29*n.*
Property, Locke's theory of, 50
Propositions, Dewey's theory of in inquiry,
   192, 193*n.*, 196, 198, 513–518; as
   valuations, 395–398, 400–402, 411–
   414; *see also* Analytic and Synthetic;
   Truth; Warranted assertability
Protestantism
   ethics of, and capitalism, 7
   German
      Enlightenment and, 34
      God in, 34
Protestant Reformation, 32, 34
Proton hypokeimenon, 287*n.*
Proudhon, Pierre, 321
Psychoanalysis, 356–357
Psychologism, 293, 295, 296, 297
Psychology, 3
   functional, 184
   James's pragmatism and, 140
      function of ideas, 140–141
      subjective interest, 143
   logic and
      critique of logic, 294–297
      dependence on, 292–294
   Mill and, 455
   psychoanalysis as, 356–357
   as science of reality, 183–184
   social, 180; *see also* Behaviorism
   social theory and genetic, 237–241
   transcendental self and Jamesian, 465–
      466
Pyramus and Thysbe, 48

Quetelet, Lambert A., 105, 107
Quine, W. V. O., 89, 129*n.*, 211*n.*, 212*n.*,
   227, 356*n.*, 361, 362*n.*, 431, 497*n.*,
   509*n.*, 511*n.*, 512*n.*, 520, 524,
   525*n.*, 540
Quinton, A. M., 312*n.*, 540

Ramsey, Frank Plumpton, 271, 304, 305,
   308–313, 360*n.*, 364*n.*, 379*n.*–
   380*n.*, 431, 520, 540–541
Randall, John Herman, Jr., x, 11*n.*, 137,
   455*n.*, 475, 479*n.*, 541
Random sample, Peirce's definition of, 111*n.*
Rationalism
   criticism of, 317*n.*, 319
   Hume and, 509–510
   knowledge in, 37
   of Leibniz, 35
   reaction against, 322

Rationalism—*cont.*
  reason in, 37
  rejection of, 334
  scientific, 32
Ratios, 21
Real, 39
  as conception, 124, 130
  as experience, 216; *see also* Experience
  the general as, 122*n.*
  independence of, 285
  knowledge and, 22–23
  language and, 93–95
  life as, 134
  Locke and, 23–24
  Peirce's definition of, 123–124, 205–206
  subatomic particles as, 47–48
  truth and, 123–125
  as what is, 495
  would-be and, 114
Realism
  commercial, 438
  common sense in, 352–353
  legal, 444
  of Lotze, 278
  of Mead, 477
  medieval, 82
  nominalism and, 371–372
  of Peirce, 90*n.*, 140, 285, 477
    scholastic, 94, 95, 117–119, 122
  of Schiller, 284, 289
  truth and, 124
Reality
  action and discovery of, 316
  community of interpretors and, 126–127
  concepts as criteria of, 219–220
  construction of, 286–287, 297–301
  continuity of, 446
  desire molding, 424
  for Fichte, 55
  ideas as, 47
  as knowledge, 284
  language and, 355–356
  of objects as congeries, 504
  observational language and, 375
  Peirce's conception of, 115–118, 123–124
  possibility and, 524
  practical character of, 425–430
  as process, 280
  psychology as science of, 183–184, 292
  social wholes and falsified, 233
  thought and
    coerciveness of reality, 144
    thought as adaptation to, 147
  transformation of, 328–331
    by creativity, 329–330
  truth as agreement with, 149–151
  will to power and, 344

Reality—*cont.*
  see also Environment; External world;
    Objects; Plastic world; Real
Reason (*Vernunft*)
  Cartesian, 19
  Enlightenment as age of, 32
  faith and, ix
  Fichte and, 52
  function of, 39
  German Enlightenment and, 34
  ideas as reflection of, 41–44
  Kantian, 47, 48, 50–51, 57
  Lewis' departure from traditional, 228
  limitations of, 24, 31, 35
  Pascal and, 31
  practical, moral impulses in, 40
  in rationalism, 37
  science and, 18, 50–52
  spirit of systems and, 30
  universality of, 22
Reck, Andrew J., 235*n.*, 537
Reductionism, sense experience and, 136–137
Reichenbach, Hans, 431
Reid, Thomas, 278*n.*
Religion, 6, 194
  Cartesian philosophy and, 18, 31
  Dewey and, 200
  first postulate in, 300
  Hume on, 26
  justification of, 154
  language and, 158–159, 246
  pragmatism and concern for, 419
  science and, 15, 31, 277–278
    harmony, 476, 483
  truth and belief in, 318
  see also Belief; Faith; God
Renauld, J. F., 344*n.*, 541
Renouvier, Charles, 56, 57, 73, 134, 270, 274*n.*, 317*n.*, 318, 320, 541
Response and stimulus, *see* Behaviorism
Richards, I. A., 305–306, 308, 539
Robbins, Herbert, 107*n.*, 529
Robertson, George Croom, 73
Robin, Richard S., 111*n.*, 538
Robinson, Daniel S., 208*n.*, 209*n.*, 541
Robinson, James Harvey, 443
Romanticism, 46–52, 479
  Darwinism and, 60–61
  in 18th-century Enlightenment, 32
  in England, 277
  thought and, 329
    post-Kantian, 43–45
Rossi-Landi, F., 333*n.*, 541
Rousseau, Jean-Jacques, 10, 26, 43–45, 233*n.*, 285*n.*, 541
Royce, Josiah, 63, 70, 76, 77, 144, 148*n.*, 149, 177, 207–210, 212, 232*n.*, 236,

Royce, Josiah—*cont.*
  262*n.*, 274*n.*, 275, 277, 280, 443,
    520, 541
Russell, Bertrand, 20, 54, 62*n.*, 63, 89, 127,
    151, 154, 158*n.*, 193, 196*n.*, 198*n.*,
    202*n.*, 203*n.*, 207, 208, 210–212,
    217*n.*, 282, 293, 305–309, 311,
    333*n.*, 334, 355, 374*n.*, 396–397,
    408, 428*n.*, 472*n.*, 483, 510, 520,
    524, 541–542
Ryle, Gilbert, 173, 203*n.*, 357*n.*, 364*n.*,
    428*n.*, 542

Sailly, B. de, 314, 315, 319, 542
Santayana, George, 3*n.*, 63, 137, 173, 217,
    259*n.*, 282, 324*n.*, 542
Santucci, A., 333*n.*, 334*n.*, 342*n.*, 343*n.*, 542
Schelling, Friedrich Wilhelm von, 46*n.*,
    50, 270, 275*n.*, 277, 278, 284, 456,
    472, 498
Schiller, F. C. S., 270, 271, 273–303, 307,
    310, 542–543
  Dewey and, 276*n.*, 284, 297, 303
  identity and, 487
  James's hotel and, 80
  logic and, 170*n.*, 291, 301
  meaning and, 308
  on possibility, 426*n.*
  on Pradines' work, 317*n.*–318*n.*
  pragmatism and, 5, 144*n.*, 145, 149
    butt-end-foremost of, 283–285
    critical orientation of, 276–283
    in France, 319, 322–323
    importance of, 305
    in Italy, 325–327*n.*, 329, 330, 332,
      341, 345
    logic, 292–297, 521
    making truth, 297–301
    psychology, 292–294
    subjectivism, 285–292, 301
  reasoning and, 520
  subjectivism of, 232, 285–292, 301
Schiller, Friedrich von, 33, 45, 46*n.*, 68
Schilpp, Paul Arthur, 127, 173*n.*, 196*n.*,
    198*n.*, 203*n.*, 278*n.*, 284*n.*, 463*n.*,
    464*n.*, 466*n.*, 543
Schlegel, August Wilhelm von, 46*n.*
Schneider, Herbert W., viii, 149*n.*, 466*n.*,
    543
Schopenhauer, Arthur, 57, 206, 333, 468
Schröder, E., 304–305, 543
Schubert, G. H., 46*n.*
Science
  analyticity in, 509–510
  communication and empirical, 261
  defined, 11
    as conceptual shorthand, 57
  Descartes and, 14, 21

Science—*cont.*
  Cartesian meaning of, 16
  organization of, 19
  Dewey and, 165–166
  18th-century
    critical reaction in Germany, 35
    preponderance, 31–32
  ethics and, 284–285, 412–414
    knowledge as, 412–414
  evaluation in, 351–352
  evolution of, 239–240
    knowledge, 258
  exactness of, 520
  faith and, 15, 62–63
  growth in, 59, 444
  inductive method of, 454
  inductive inference, 350
  is and, 16
  James and
    conservatism in science, 221*n.*
    Kantian science, 53
  Kant's explanation of, 36–37, 40, 43–45,
    53
  Mead on, 11*n.*, 234
  method of inquiry of
    truth, 115–117, 122–126, 128–132
  modernism and, 314–316
  moral values and, 35, 166, 419–423
  nature controlled by, 17
  19th-century, 59–60
    Darwinism, 62
    faith in, 62–63
    English philosophy and, 277
  Peirce and, 101–120
    communal inquiry, 53
  philosophy affected by, 14–15
  primary quality idea and, 23, 24
  problem of modern, 64–65
  reality and, 183–184, 355
  reason and, 50–52
  religion and, 15, 31, 166, 277–278
    harmony, 376, 483
  romanticism and, 48, 49
  17th-century philosophy of, 19–22
  Sorel's opposition to outlook of, 321
  structure of
    historical factors, 366–369
    instrumentalist viewpoint, 371–376
    leading principles, 376–382
    logic, 364–366
    theoretical structure interpreted, 369–
      371
  truth in, 298
    principle of science, 490–491
  as universal institution, 239–240
  see also specific sciences; for example:
    Algebra; Geometry; Physics; Psy-
      chology

Scientism, 455
Scotus, John Duns, 36*n.*, 82, 543
Self
  centralness of, 283–284
  consciousness, 53–55, 321, 466*n.*, 469–470, 487–483; *see also* Consciousness
  discovery of, 252–261
    generalized other, 254–258
    as "I," 258–261
  dualism and, 478–479, 484; *see also* Dualism
  emergence of, 238–243
    occupations and, 239
    significant symbols, 244–246
  epistemology and, 283
  external objects and, 484
  Fichte and, 53–56
  ideal, as Good, 482
  ideas and, 137
  James and, 134
  Mead's theory of, 181, 252–254
    generalized other, 254–258
    the "I," 258–261
    influence of Mead's theory, 267–268
  as object, 250*n.*, 253, 254, 259
  realization, 47, 48
  as soul, 41
  transcendental, 465–466
  world as property of, 50
  see also Subjectivity
Sellars, Wilfred, 210*n.*, 214*n.*, 217*n.*, 220*n.*, 403*n.*–407*n.*, 532, 543
Sense perception, 367
  Berkeley and, 26
  Descartes and, 27–28
  Galileo on, 19–20
  Locke and, 23
  mind and, 27–29
  nature and, 37
  Newton on, 24–25
  organization of, 39–42
Seth, Andrew, 277, 468
Shakespeare, William, 267*n.*, 387*n.*, 453
Shall's, 142
Sheffer, H. M., 373*n.*, 543
Shelley, Percy B., 45
Shirk, Evelyn U., 440*n.*, 543
Should-be, 142, 408
  external conditions and, 142, 143*n.*, 144
Sidgwick, Henry, 73
Signs
  defined, 83
  as ideas, 501–504
  man as, 235–236
  meaning of, 79–80, 82–83, 85, 87–91, 95, 96, 103–104, 138, 305–308
  objects as, 381

Signs—*cont.*
  probability and, 114–115, 118–120
  sensations as, 478*n.*
  thought as, 494–495
Sigwart, 278
Simmel, Georg, 271
Situations
  continuity in, 358
  ethics and, 388–393
    ethical judgment in, 413
  as key concept, 170
  defined, 171
  logic of, 409–412
  thought as clarifier of, 191
  truth and, 160–162
  unicity of, 442, 462
Small, Albion, 237*n.*
Social context
  functional psychology and, 184
  in Mead's theory of mind, 232–234
  of pragmatism
    in England, 304–308
    Europe, 345
    in Italy, 324–327
    in U.S., 7
  scientific knowledge and, 17
  of thought
    Dewey's thought, 422
    19th-century thought, 58–64
    20th-century thought, 64–65
    post-Kantian, 43–45
Socialism, 446
  Sorel and, 321
Social wholes
  Mead on, 233, 234, 237
  unique, 275*n.*
Sociology, 238
Socrates, 5, 51, 196
Solgar, 46*n.*
Solipcism of Fichte, 53–54
Sorel, Georges, 320–323, 332, 543
Soul
  body and, 228–229
  Dewey on, 185–186
  geometry of, 27
  morals and immortality of, 43
  self as, 41; *see also* Self
  as thing, 350
  universals and, 367
Speech, *see* Language
Spencer, Herbert, 10, 70, 72, 142, 144, 277, 279, 467, 469, 472*n.*, 476, 477*n.*, 478*n.*, 479*n.*, 491
Speusippos, 235*n.*
Spinoza, Baruch, ix, 5, 16, 17, 30, 36, 37, 150*n.*, 318, 450, 543
Sraffa, Piero, 311
State, self and, 48

Stebbing, L. Susan, 316*n.*, 543
Stephen, Leslie, 73
Sterēsis, 177
Stevenson, Charles L., 388*n.*, 498*n.*, 409*n.*, 543
Stimulus and response, *see* Behaviorism
Strauss, David F., 235*n.*
Structuralism, 184
Stuart, N. W., 440*n.*
Stumpf, Carl, 73
Sturm und Drang, 33
Subjectivism
    of Fichte, 55
    of Schiller, 232, 285–292, 301
    of thought, 141–144
Subjectivity
    arbitrariness of, 342–343
    Darwin and, 241
    Dewey and, 141, 342*n.*
    Locke and, 23–24
    meaning of feelings in, 87–88
    mind and, 203–204
    truth and, 297–298
    pragmatic truth, 141–153
Sub specie aeternitatis, 425
Substance
    Locke and, 23
    as objective unknown, 25
Success, ethics of, 438–439
Sullivan, Harry Stack, 367, 543
Summum bonum, 409
Survival
    of the fittest, 60, 61
    subjective interests and, 143*n.*, 144
    thought as instrument for, 141
Syllogism
    Mill's interpretation of, 371–372
    in scientific demonstration, 366
Syllogismo, 29
Syndicalism, 323
    revolutionary, 320
Synthetic and analytic, *see* Analytic and synthetic

Tarski, Alfred, 196, 309, 509, 543
Taylor, A. E., 277*n.*
Technē, 287*n.*
Telos, 177, 387*n.*, 398
Terms
    disposition
        Chisholm on, 93*n.*
        Dewey and, 405, 406*n.*
        Goodman on, 93*n.*, 218*n.*, 525
        James and, 176
        Lewis and, 224–245
        Peirce and, 176, 426, 525
    translation of, in analysis, 91, 99

Thayer, H. S., 25*n.*, 191*n.*, 196*n.*, 376*n.*, 500*n.*, 502*n.*, 543
Thayer, V. T., 174, 543
Theatre, 425
Theoria, 425
Theories
    as instruments, 341–342
    language and, 337
    nature of pragmatic, 53
Thing-in-itself (Ding-an-sich), 39, 55, 138, 470
Thompson, H. B., 440*n.*
Thompson, Manley, 3*n.*, 544
Thomas, W. I., 237*n.*
Thoreau, Henry David, 45, 433
Thought
    action and, 88
    relations, 316, 317
    as agreement, 206
    criticized, 151–152
    behavior and, 396*n.*
    belief and, 83–86
    continuity of, 466
    Darwinism and, 61
    dehumanization of, 293–294
    economic changes and, 64
    experience and
        consequences, 427
        immediate experience, 275
        unifying action of thought, 484–485
    function of, 5, 58, 61, 83, 85–86, 206
    natural, 425
    synthesizing function, 479–480
    instrumentalism and, 169, 170
    as instruments, 147
    laws of, 496–498
    logic in, 520, 521
    Lotze's view of, 278
    meaning of, 5
    mediating way of, 439–440
    practical character of, 425–429
    pragmatic, 448–453
    principle of economy of, 343, 344
    problem of American, 433–435
    purposive nature of, 125, 140–141, 144*n.*, 199
    real and, 123–124
    revision of traditional, 349–350
    romantic interpretation of, 329
    as signs, 494–495
    situations and, 191
    social, 443–447
    social context and
        Dewey's thought, 422
        19th-century thought, 58–64
        post-Kantian thought, 43–45
        20th-century thought, 64–65

Thought—*cont.*
subjective interests and, 141–144
usefulness in, 6
see also Beliefs; Cognition; Habits; Ideas;
Inquiry
Torrey, H. A. P., 73, 278*n.*
Toulmin, Stephan E., 364*n.,* 544
Thrasymachus, 151
Tichner, E. B., 334*n.*
Transcendentalism
experience and, 57
idealism and, 40–43
theory of knowledge in, 28
Transubstantiation, doctrine of, 86
Trendelenburg, Friedrich, 467
Trotsky, Leon, 75
True, romantic idealism and, 51
Truth
analytic, 511–512, 519–520
analyticity of logical, 291
a priori and, 212, 226
basic
doubts and, 370
experience and, 367–369
knowledge and, 102–103
Cartesian formulation of, 16–17
as common consent, 126–127
conception of, 22
by definition, 509
desire and, 397
evolution of, 61
of experience, conceptual schemes and,
361–362
fated opinions and, 128–130
Fichte's view of, 55–56
habit and premises, 376, 377; *see also*
Habits
ideas and, 137
instrumentalism and
scientific truth, 371–375
workableness of truth, 378–379
intuitive, 50
justification of belief and workable, 154–
159
making of, 297–301
Mead's conception of, 266
meaning and, 120–132
fallibilism, 122–123, 127–128
Peirce's definitions, 125–132
warranted assertibility, 42, 125, 193–
194
pattern of inquiry and, 192–199
Peirce on, 120–125, 496–498
definitions, 125–132
methods of arriving at truth, 115–118
philosophy of action and, 315, 318, 319
pragmatic interpretation of, 4, 5

Truth—*cont.*
probability and, 110
psychic processes and, 295
science and, 490–491
scientific laws, 366
statistical approximation of, 106–107
subjectivity and, 297–298
pragmatic truth, 151–153
theory of
James's pragmatism as, 135–136, 149–
150, 159–165
Tarski's, 309
thought and, 83
as usefulness, 147–148
as agreement with reality, 149–151
criticized, 201–224
uncertainty, 148–149
vagueness and, 153–154
verification of, 93–94, 343–344
as workableness, 298–299
Tufts, James H., 74, 75, 237*n.*
Tychism, 427
Tyrrell, G., 314*n.,* 544

Ulrici, Herman, 467
Ultimate good, 199–200, 399–400, 409–
410, 481–483; *see also* Good
Understanding (*Verstand*)
of experience, 377
Kant's conclusion on, 39
Locke and, 23–24
necessity and, 38
perception and, 21
for romantic idealists, 48, 50
universality of, for Descartes, 27
Urmson, J. O., 389*n.,* 544
Usefulness
of belief, 344
the good and, 150
of knowledge, 6, 7
of logic, 303
practical, 5
of Protestant ethic, 7
standard of, for thought and action, 6
truth as, 147–148, 298–299
as agreement with reality, 149–151
criticized, 201–204
uncertainty, 148–149
Utilitarianism, 6, 63, 409
the good and British, 59
pragmatism and, 327–328
Utterance, 430

Vacuum, nature abhors, 461–463
Vaihinger, Hans, 56, 271
Vailati, Giovanni, 102*n.,* 272, 307*n.,* 324–
346, 499*n.,* 529, 544

Valuation
  as empirical judgment, 221–225
  knowledge as, 423–424
  theory of, 383, 388, 390–414
    criterion of valuation, 400–402
    desire, 393–409
    ends-means, 398–400
    origins of valuation, 393–395
    valuation-propositions, 395–398
    truth as, 298
Value, vii, 147–148
  commodity exchange and, 339
  determination of, 225
  of ends, 400
  ethics and, 390–393
    value judgments, 221–222
  knowledge and, ix, x, 4, 11, 16, 19
  mediation by, 440
  objects of, 403
  science and, 35, 166, 419–423
Veblen, Thorstein, 70, 237*n.*, 439, 443, 444, 544
Venn, John, 80*n.*, 108, 109, 115*n.*, 455, 497*n.*, 544
Verification
  meaning, theory of, 99–101, 104
    behavior as, 151
    single predicates, 122
  of quale, 218–219
  subjective arbitrariness and, 343
  of theoretical constructions, 491
  of truth, 93–94, 343–344
    as process, 162–163
Vernunft, see Reason
Verstand, see Understanding
Via moderna, via antiqua, 14
Voltaire, 44
Voluntarism, 283, 318, 328
Vorstellung, 39

Wager, Pascal's, 31
Waiblel, E. P. B., 8, 544
Walsh, W. H., 276*n.*, 544
Ward, Mrs. Humphry, 476
Ward, Lester, 70
Warranted assertibility, 42, 125, 193–195;
    see also Truth
Watson, John B., 364*n.*, 428*n.*, 544
Watson, W. H., 311*n.*, 382*n.*, 544
Weiss, Paul, 68*n.*, 69*n.*, 71*n.*, 544
Welby, Lady Victoria, 128*n.*, 305–308, 333, 334, 338, 463*n.*, 544–545
Wenley, R. M., 466*n.*, 467*n.*, 468*n.*, 469*n.*, 470*n.*, 471, 472*n.*, 474*n.*, 475*n.*, 545
Weyl, Hermann, 309
White, Morton G., 406*n.*, 407*n.*, 409*n.*, 413*n.*, 443–444, 445*n.*, 464*n.*, 472*n.*, 517*n.*, 519*n.*, 545

Whitehead, Alfred N., 261*n.*, 207, 210–212, 309, 334, 397, 520, 545
Whitman, Walt, 433, 435–436, 442
Wiener, Norbert, 211*n.*
Wiener, Philip, viii, 104*n.*, 166, 455*n.*, 545
Wilbois, 271
Will
  to believe, 32, 144, 295
    induction by, 331
    Peirce on, 155*n.*
    undesirable consequences of, 345–346
  divine, 34
  ends and, 342
  external world and, 206
  Faustian, 49–50
  James and free, 134
  objects of, 40
  to power, 331, 344
  self and, 56
Wille zur Macht (will to power), 331, 344;
    see also Will
Willey, Basil, 38*n.*, 545
Williams, Donald C., 526*n.*, 545
Winkelmann, Johann J., 33
Wit, 435–436, 445
Wittgenstein, Ludwig, 79*n.*–80*n.*, 146*n.*, 271, 304, 305, 308–310*n.*, 311–313, 333, 382*n.*, 545
Wolff, Christian, 35
Wollheim, Richard, 293*n.*, 487*n.*, 545
Woodbridge, F. J. E., 75, 173*n.*
Woods, Frederick Adams, 91*n.*
Woodworth, Robert S., 184, 545
Words
  Berkeley and meaning of, 506
  defining, 337–338
  Dewey's use of, 173*n.*, 175
    adverbs, 182, 194, 410
  meaning of, 126*n.*, 337–338
  nominalism and, 327
  use of, 145–146
    external world and, 353
Wordsworth, William, 33, 37, 45, 478*n.*
Would-be, 91*n.*–93*n.*, 94, 98*n.*, 495
  probability and, 113–114, 117–120; *see also* Probability
    see also Possibility
Wright, Chauncey, 80, 81, 235, 455, 488, 490–492, 545
Wright, G. H. von, 309*n.*, 311*n.*, 545
Wundt, Wilhelm Max, 72, 236–237, 242

Young, Ella Flagg, 75
Young, F. H., 166, 545

Zeno, 276*n.*
Zōon politikos anthropōs, 232